S
BAHRAIN
HONG KONG
TOKYO AND SYDNEY

TOKYO

BAHRAIN

HONG KONG

SINGAPORE

SYDNEY

| 1000 | 0900 | 0800 | 0700 | 0600 | 0500 | 0400 | 0300 | 0200 | 0100 | 2400 | 2300 |
|------|------|------|------|------|------|------|------|------|------|------|------|

Greenwich Mean Time

+2    +3    +4    +5    +6    +7    +8    +9    +10   +11   +12

Hours different from GMT

# FUNDAMENTALS OF
# MULTINATIONAL FINANCE

## SECOND EDITION

# The Addison-Wesley Series in Finance

# FUNDAMENTALS OF
# MULTINATIONAL FINANCE

### SECOND EDITION

**MICHAEL H. MOFFETT**
*Thunderbird – The Garvin School of International Management*

**ARTHUR I. STONEHILL**
*University of Hawaii at Manoa*

**DAVID K. EITEMAN**
*University of California, Los Angeles*

PEARSON

Addison
Wesley

Boston  San Francisco  New York
London  Toronto  Sydney  Tokyo  Singapore  Madrid
Mexico City  Munich  Paris  Cape Town  Hong Kong  Montreal

Editor-in-Chief: *Denise Clinton*
Senior Acquisitions Editor: *Donna Battista*
Assistant Development Editor: *Amy Fleischer*
Executive Marketing Manager: *Stephen Frail*
Managing Editor: *James Rigney*
Project Management, Composition, and Art: *Argosy Publishing*
Text and Cover Design: *Leslie Haimes*
Senior Manufacturing Buyer: *Hugh Crawford*
Media Producer: *Bethany Tidd*
Supplements Coordinator: *Kirsten Dickerson*
Rights and Permissions Advisor: *Dana Weightman*

The World of Foreign Exchange Dealing, copyrighted by Richard Olsen & Associates Data from Euromoney, April 1979, p. 14, is reprinted with permission.

Portions of FASB Statement No. 52, Foreign Currency Translation, copyrighted by the Financial Accounting Standards Board, 401 Merritt 7, P.O. Box 5116, Norwalk, Connecticut 06856-5116, U.S.A., are reprinted with permission. Complete copies of this document are available from the FASB.

Exchange rate charts are provided courtesy of the Pacific Exchange Rate Service (http://fx.sauder.ubc.ca), a service for academic research and teaching provided by Prof. Werner Antweiler at the Sauder School of Business, University of British Columbia, Vancouver, BC, Canada. (See Exhibits 2.2, 2.5, 2.7, 5.3, 5.4, 5.7, and charts on pp. 142, 144, 146, 147, 281, 282.)

**Library of Congress Cataloging-in-Publication Data**
Moffett, Michael H.
   Fundamentals of multinational finance / Michael H. Moffett, Arthur I.
Stonehill, David K. Eiteman.— 2nd ed.
      p. cm. — (The Addison-Wesley series in finance)
   Includes bibliographical references and index.
   ISBN 0-321-28031-8
   1.  International business enterprises—Finance. 2.  International finance.
   3.  Foreign exchange.  I. Stonehill, Arthur I. II. Eiteman, David K. III. Title. IV. Series.

   HG4027.5.M64 2005
   332'.042—dc22                                    2004023647
                                                        CIP

For information on obtaining permission for the use of material from this work, please submit a written request to Pearson Education, Inc., Rights and Contracts Department, 75 Arlington St., Suite 300, Boston, MA 02116.

ISBN 0-321-28031-8
345678910—QWT—0908070605

# PREFACE

*Fundamentals of Multinational Finance,* Second Edition, views the multinational enterprise (MNE) as an organization that poses unique demands on the *business leaders* of tomorrow. Those leaders — possibly some of the readers of this text — will be confronted with a multitude of challenges that will test their ability not only to *comprehend* global markets, but more importantly, to *lead* their organizations through the constantly shifting currents and tides of global change. Competent leadership may indeed be the scarcest global commodity.

This book is about multinational management, and more specifically, the financial management dimensions of leading a multinational enterprise. The MNE itself acts as a *catalyst* and a *facilitator* of international trade, and as an important producer and distributor in the host countries where it operates. The MNE's potential success, however, rests in the hands of the truly competent *global leader.* The success of any MNE is dependent on its leadership's ability to lead and manage the global organization.

Our vision in writing this book is to aid in the development of tomorrow's MNE leaders. It is their ability to recognize and benefit from business opportunities such as imperfections in national markets, unequal costs, and efficiencies of the factors of production, to tap the well-springs of intellectual property, and to access sources of global funding to facilitate growth, that will add value.

The financial managers of MNEs face numerous foreign exchange and political risks. These risks can be daunting, but they also present opportunities for creating value if properly understood. These opportunities and risks are most effectively understood in the context of the global business itself, and the ability of management to integrate the strategic and financial challenges that business faces.

## Audience

*Fundamentals of Multinational Finance,* Second Edition, is aimed at university-level courses in international financial management, international business finance, international finance, and similar titles. It can be used at either the undergraduate or the graduate level, as well as in executive education courses.

A prerequisite course or experience in corporate finance or financial management would be ideal. However, we review the basic finance concepts before we extend them to the multinational case. We also review the basic concepts of international economics and international business.

We recognize that a sigificant portion of our audience lives outside of the United States and Canada. Therefore, we have included a significant number of non–U.S. examples, mini-cases, and *Real World Examples* (anecdotes and illustrations).

## Organization

*Fundamentals of Multinational Finance,* Second Edition, is organized into six parts. The six parts are unified by the common thread of the globalization process by which a firm moves from a domestic to a multinational business orientation. Part 1 introduces the global financial environment. Part 2 explains foreign exchange theory and markets.

Part 3 analyzes foreign exchange exposure, both measurement and management. Part 4 covers the financing of the global firm. Part 5 analyzes international investment decisions. Part 6 examines the management of multinational operations.

## What Is New in the Second Edition?

- We have added 12 new mini-cases and retained 10 of the most popular ones in response to user feedback.
- We have expanded the number of *Real World Examples* (formerly titled *Global Finance Perspectives*), spread throughout the text, to 37.
- We have updated and expanded the number and use of Internet exercises, end-of-chapter questions, and end-of-chapter problems. There are now at least 10 quantitative problems in each chapter — more than 210 problems throughout the text.
- Chapter 1, Financial Goals and Corporate Governance, includes an expanded treatment of corporate governance, including failures, reform, family ownership, ethics, and a comparison with a number of countries.
- Chapter 2, The International Monetary System, now covers eurocurrencies, LIBOR, and the expansion of the euro zone by 10 new countries.
- Chapter 3, The Balance of Payments, features expanded coverage on the interaction of balance of payments with other macroeconomic variables, including GDP, exchange rates, interest rates, and inflation.
- Chapter 5, Foreign Exchange Rate Determination, replaces the Brazilian crisis with the Argentine crisis of 2002.
- Chapter 11, *Global Cost and Availability of Capital*, now covers the relationship between corporate governance and the cost of capital. The mini-case for the chapter describes how Nestlé could use the international capital asset pricing model (ICAPM) to calculate its cost of capital.
- Chapter 17, Political Risk Assessment and Management, has been revised to focus only on political risk, with an expanded section on global-specific risks such as terrorism.
- Chapter 21, Repositioning Funds, and Chapter 22, Working Capital Management, from the first edition have been revised and combined to create a new Chapter 21. We have also moved leads and lags and reinvoicing centers to Chapter 9, Operating Exposure, and transfer pricing to Chapter 20, Tax Management.
- The second edition has moved the following mini-cases from the text to the book's Web site for selective instructor and student use: Tsar Alexander III's Russian Gold Loan, Russian Purchasing Power and Western Automakers, Ford Range Rover Asia Pacific, Telecom Italia, Romanian Communications and Cyprus Offshore, Private Equity in Latin America (Soto Group), Corporate Governance at Brasil Telecom, Motorola and TelSim of Turkey, and Cemex of Mexico Bids for Semen Gresik of Indonesia.

## PEDAGOGICAL TOOLS

In order to make *Fundamentals of Multinational Finance*, Second Edition, as comprehensible as possible we utilize a large number of proven pedagogical tools. Our efforts have been informed by the detailed reviews and suggestions of a panel of professors who have earned recognition individually for teaching excellence in the field of international finance, particularly at the undergraduate level. Among these pedagogical tools are:

- A student-friendly writing style combined with a tightly structured presentation, beginning with *learning objectives* for each chapter, and ending with a summary of how those learning objectives have been realized.
- A wealth of *illustrations and exhibits* that provide a visual parallel to the concepts and content presented. The entire book utilizes a multicolor presentation, which provides a visual attractiveness that contributes significantly to reader attention and retention.
- A running case on a hypothetical U.S.–based firm, *Trident Corporation,* which provides a cohesive framework for the multifaceted globalization process and is reinforced in several end-of-chapter problems.
- *Spreadsheet analyses,* prepared by our colleague Francis Clauss, that illustrate the quantitative dimensions of the analysis. These spreadsheet analyses provide not only the computational support to improve reader understanding, but also the detailed formulas behind their construction.
- A *mini-case* at the end of each chapter (22 in all) that illustrates the chapter content and extends it to the multinational financial business environment.
- *Real World Examples* in nearly every chapter to illuminate the theory with accounts of actual business practices. These applications extend the concepts without adding to the length of the text itself.
- The power and resources of the *Internet,* which are leveraged throughout the text in a variety of applications. Most chapters have a number of end-of-chapter exercises requiring the use of the Internet, while a variety of Internet references are dispersed throughout the chapters in text and exhibits.
-  An increased number of end-of-chapter *Questions* and *Problems,* which assess the students' understanding of the course material. End-of-chapter problems that use spreadsheets available online at www.aw-bc.com/moffett are flagged with a spreadsheet icon.

## A Rich Array of Support Materials

A robust package of materials for students and instructors accompanies the text to facilitate learning and to support teaching and testing.

- **Instructor's Manual.** The Instructor's Manual, prepared by the authors, contains complete answers to all end-of-chapter questions, problems, and chapter mini-cases. All quantitative end-of-chapter problems are solved using spreadsheets, which are accessible from the online catalog page for this textbook (found at www.aw-bc.com/finance) and the Instructor's Resource Disk.
- **Test Bank.** The Test Bank, prepared by Curtis J. Bacon of Southern Oregon University, contains over 1,200 multiple-choice and short-essay questions. The multiple-choice questions are labeled by topic and by category — recognition, conceptual, and analytical types.
- **Computerized Test Bank.** The Test Bank is also available in Pearson Education's TestGen Software. Fully networkable, it is available for Windows and Macintosh.

TestGen's graphical interface enables instructors to view, edit, and add questions; transfer questions to tests; and print different forms of tests. Search-and-sort features enable the instructor to locate questions quickly and arrange them in a preferred order. The TestGen plug-in allows the instructor to administer TestGen tests in CourseCompass. QuizMaster, working with TestGen and the school's computer network, automatically grades exams, stores the results on a disk, and allows the instructor to view and print a variety of reports. More information on TestGen software is available at www.aw-bc.com/testgen.

- **PowerPoint Presentation Slides.** Prepared by Shafiq Jadallah and Mark J. Bradt, the extensive set of PowerPoint slides available on the Instructor's Resource Disk and on the online catalog page for this textbook provides lecture outlines and selected graphics from the text for each chapter.

- **Study Guide.** Written by Timo Korkeamaki of Gonzaga University, the Study Guide enhances students' understanding and retention of concepts by providing detailed study outlines and helps students prepare for tests through a series of self-test questions, including true/false, multiple-choice, and short essay. The answers to the self-test questions also appear in the Study Guide.

- **Instructor's Resource Disk.** This CD-ROM contains the Computerized Test Bank files (TestGen), the Instructor's Manual files (PDFs), Test Bank files (Word), spreadsheet solutions (Excel), and PowerPoint files.

- **Web Site.** A companion Web site at www.aw-bc.com/moffett contains the Internet exercises from the book with wired links, electronic flash cards of glossary terms, self-assessment quizzes, a Web chapter, and selected solutions and spreadsheets for end-of-chapter problems.

- **Web Chapter: Cross-Border Mergers & Acquisitions.** Available as a PDF on the Companion Web site (www.aw-bc.com/moffett), the *Cross-Border Mergers & Acquisitions* chapter has been updated for the second edition and includes a mini-case and expanded questions and problems sections. This Web chapter introduces students to the increasingly important field of cross-border mergers and acquisitions, a viable alternative to a greenfield foreign direct investment.

## INTERNATIONAL EDITIONS

*Fundamentals of Multinational Finance* and *Multinational Business Finance* have been used throughout the world to teach students of international finance. Our books are published in several foreign languages, including Chinese, French, Indonesian, Portuguese, Spanish, and Ukrainian.

## Acknowledgments

The authors are very thankful for the many detailed reviews and suggestions from a number of colleagues. These reviews included 15 detailed chapter-by-chapter reviews, and answers to a comprehensive questionnaire by 104 adopters and nonadopters. The final version of this second edition reflects most of the suggestions provided by these reviewers. The survey reviewers were anonymous, but the 15 reviewers who submitted detailed comments are as follows:

Morten Balling
Aarhus School of Business (Denmark)

W. Brian Barrett
University of Miami

Cetin Ciner
Northeastern University

Joseph F. Greco
California State University, Fullerton

Ken Hunsader
University of South Alabama

Charmen Loh
Rider University

Beverly B. Marshall
Auburn University

Daniel L. McCounaughy
California State University, Northridge

Simona Mola
Pennsylvania State University

Ali M. Parhizgari
Florida International University

Jimmy Senteza
Drake University

Olgun Fuat Shahin
Minnesota State University, Moorhead

Miland M. Shrikhande
Georgia State University

James G. Tompkins
Kennesaw State University

Phil Uhlmann
Bentley College

We would also like to recognize the reviewers of the first edition:

Curtis J. Bacon
Southern Oregon University

Cetin Ciner
Northeastern University

Kam C. (Johnny) Chan
University of Dayton

J. Jay Choi
Temple University

Maria E. de Boyrie
New Mexico State University

Larry Fauver
University of Miami, Coral Gables

Joel Harper
Florida Atlantic University

Ghassem Homaifar
Middle Tennessee State University

Timo Korkeamaki
Gonzaga University

James S. Linck
University of Georgia

Ali Parhizgari
Florida International University

Sidney B. Rosenberg
University of North Florida

Min Shi
University of Wisconsin, Madison

Paul J. Swanson, Jr.
University of Cincinnati

Benjamin Uzoaru
Southeast Missouri State University

We would also like to thank the staff at Addison-Wesley who have worked so diligently on this edition, notably Donna Battista, Acquisitions Editor for Finance, and Amy Fleischer, Assistant Development Editor.

Finally, we would like to dedicate this book to our parents, Bennie Ruth and Hoy Moffett, the late Harold and Norma Stonehill, and the late Wilford and Sylvia Eiteman, who gave us the motivation to become academicians and authors. We thank our wives, Megan, Kari, and Keng-Fong, for their patience while we were preparing *Fundamentals of Multinational Finance*, Second Edition.

| | | | |
|---|---|---|---|
| Glendale, Arizona | M.H.M. | Pacific Palisades, California | D.K.E. |
| Honolulu, Hawaii | A.I.S. | | |

**MICHAEL H. MOFFETT**   Michael H. Moffett is Associate Professor of Finance at Thunderbird, The Garvin Graduate School of International Management. He was formerly Associate Professor of Finance at Oregon State University (1985–1993). He has also held teaching or research appointments at the University of Michigan, Ann Arbor (1991–1993), the Brookings Institution, Washington, D.C., the University of Hawaii at Manoa, the Aarhus School of Business (Denmark), the Helsinki School of Economics and Business Administration (Finland), the International Centre for Public Enterprises (Yugoslavia), and the University of Colorado, Boulder.

Professor Moffett received a B.A. (economics) from the University of Texas at Austin (1977), an M.S. (resource economics) from Colorado State University (1979), an M.A. (economics) from the University of Colorado, Boulder (1983), and a Ph.D. (economics) from the University of Colorado, Boulder (1985).

He has authored, co-authored, or contributed to six books and 15 other publications. His articles have appeared in the *Journal of Financial and Quantitative Analysis, Journal of Applied Corporate Finance, Journal of International Money and Finance, Journal of International Financial Management and Accounting, Contemporary Policy Issues, Brookings Discussion Papers in International Economics,* and others. He has contributed to a number of collected works, including the *Handbook of Modern Finance,* the *International Accounting and Finance Handbook,* and the *Encyclopedia of International Business.* He is also co-author of two books in multinational business with Michael Czinkota and Ilkka Ronkainen, *International Business* (6th edition) and *Global Business* (4th edition).

**ARTHUR I. STONEHILL**   Arthur I. Stonehill is a Professor of Finance and International Business, Emeritus, at Oregon State University, where he taught for 24 years (1966–1990). From 1991 to 1997 he held a split appointment at the University of Hawaii at Manoa and Copenhagen Business School. From 1997 to 2001 he continued as a visiting professor at the University of Hawaii at Manoa. He has also held teaching or research appointments at the University of California, Berkeley, Cranfield School of Management (U.K.), and the North European Management Institute (Norway). He was a president of the Academy of International Business and a western director of the Financial Management Association.

Professor Stonehill received a B.A. (history) from Yale University (1953), an M.B.A. from Harvard Business School (1957), and a Ph.D. in business administration from the University of California, Berkeley (1965). He has been awarded honorary doctorates from the Aarhus School of Business (Denmark, 1989), the Copenhagen Business School (Denmark, 1992), and Lund University (Sweden, 1998).

He has authored or co-authored nine books and 25 other publications. His articles have appeared in *Financial Management, Journal of International Business Studies, California Management Review, Journal of Financial and Quantitative Analysis, Journal of International Financial Management and Accounting, International Business Review, European Management Journal, The Investment Analyst (U.K.), Nationaløkonomisk Tidskrift (Denmark), Sosialøkonomen (Norway), Journal of Financial Education,* and others.

**DAVID K. EITEMAN**     David K. Eiteman is Professor Emeritus of Finance at the John E. Anderson Graduate School of Management at UCLA. He has also held teaching or research appointments at the Hong Kong University of Science & Technology, Showa Academy of Music (Japan), the National University of Singapore, Dalian University (China), the Helsinki School of Economics and Business Administration (Finland), the University of Hawaii at Manoa, the University of Bradford (U.K.), Cranfield School of Management (U.K.), and IDEA (Argentina). He is a former president of the International Trade and Finance Association, Society for Economics and Management in China, and Western Finance Association.

Professor Eiteman received a B.B.A. (business administration) from the University of Michigan, Ann Arbor (1952), an M.A. (economics) from the University of California, Berkeley (1956), and a Ph.D. (finance) from Northwestern University (1959).

He has authored or co-authored four books and 29 other publications. His articles have appeared in *The Journal of Finance, The International Trade Journal, Financial Analysts Journal, Journal of World Business, Management International, Business Horizons, MSU Business Topics, Public Utilities Fortnightly,* and others.

## BRIEF CONTENTS

# CONTENTS

# Global Financial Environment

Part 1 is an introduction to the global financial environment in which the multinational enterprise (MNE) exists.

**CHAPTER 1** describes the globalization process experienced by Trident, a hypothetical MNE that is used as an example throughout the book. It starts as a domestic firm, enters the international trade phase, and then expands its operations to an overseas location, thereby becoming an MNE. During this globalization process, Trident's management must understand the theories and activities introduced in Chapter 1 and explained in the rest of this book. Thus, we eventually examine foreign exchange theory and markets, foreign exchange exposure and management, financing the global firm, the foreign investment decision, and management of working capital, taxes, and international trade finance. Chapter 1 continues with an analysis of management goals. This involves a description of the shareholder versus corporate wealth maximization behavior, corporate operational goals, corporate governance, failures in corporate governance, and reform.

**CHAPTER 2** defines currency terminology. It describes the history of the international monetary system from 1876 to the present. It introduces the Eurocurrency market and LIBOR. It then compares contemporary currency regimes (systems) and the special case of emerging market currency regimes, including currency boards and dollarization. Chapter 2 concludes with a detailed examination of European monetary unification resulting in the launch of the new currency — the euro.

**CHAPTER 3** examines the balance of payments. We analyze each account and the most important summary accounts. It explains why the balance of payments always "balances." It then presents the detailed U.S. balance of payments accounts for the 1998–2002 period. It concludes with an analysis about how the balance of payments interacts with such key macroeconomic variables as gross domestic product, the exchange rate, interest rates, and inflation rates.

# Financial Goals and Corporate Governance

## LEARNING OBJECTIVES

Consider how the globalization process moves a business from a purely domestic focus in its financial relationships and composition to one truly global in scope

Learn what the implications of phase one of globalization — the international trade phase — means for the risks and returns of a business

Discover what three major corporate currency exposures arise from multinational business

Examine how the continuing globalization process extends from international trade to multinational operations to global activities

Examine how financial and operational goals are perceived in a global context

See how globalization affects corporate governance of the organization and how it creates value for its stakeholders

Investigate failures in global corporate governance

This book is about international financial management with special emphasis on the *multinational enterprise* (MNE). The MNE is defined as one that has operating subsidiaries, branches, or affiliates located in foreign countries. It also includes firms in service activities such as consulting, accounting, construction, legal, advertising, entertainment, banking, telecommunications, and lodging.

MNEs are headquartered all over the world. Many of them are owned by a mixture of domestic and foreign shareholders. The ownership of some firms is so dispersed internationally that they are known as transnational corporations. The transnationals are usually managed from a global perspective rather than from the perspective of any single country.

Although *Fundamentals of Multinational Finance* emphasizes MNEs, purely domestic firms also often have significant international activities. These include the import and export of products, components, and services. Domestic firms can also license foreign firms to conduct their foreign business. They have exposure to foreign competition in their domestic market. They also have indirect exposure to international risks through their relationships with customers and suppliers. Therefore, domestic firm managers need to understand international financial risk, especially those related to foreign exchange rates and the credit risks related to trade payments.

*Fundamentals of Multinational Finance* is written in English and usually uses the U.S. dollar in its exposition. However, the authors have tried to make it relevant for all multinational enterprises by using numerous non-U.S.-based MNEs. We use the term *multinational enterprise* throughout this text for two very important reasons. First, the term *multinational* is used rather than *international* because we focus on the third phase of the globalization process, in which firms operate businesses in many different countries. Secondly, we use the term *enterprise* instead of *corporation* because as businesses move into many emerging markets, they enter into joint ventures, strategic alliances, or simply operating agreements with enterprises which may not be publicly traded or even privately owned (and therefore not corporations), but actually extensions of government.

## What Is Different About Global Financial Management?

Exhibit 1.1 details some of the main differences between international and domestic financial management. These component differences include institutions, foreign exchange and political risks, and the modifications required of financial theory and financial instruments.

International financial management requires an understanding of cultural, historical, and institutional differences such as those affecting corporate governance. Although both domestic firms and MNEs are exposed to foreign exchange risks, MNEs alone face certain risks that are not normally a threat to domestic operations such as political risks.

MNEs also face other risks that can be classified as extensions of domestic finance theory. For example, the normal domestic approach to the cost of capital, sourcing debt and equity, capital budgeting, working capital management, taxation, and credit analysis needs to be modified to accommodate foreign complexities. Moreover, a number of financial instruments that are used in domestic financial management have been modified for use in international financial management. Examples are foreign currency options and futures, interest rate and currency swaps, and letters of credit.

**EXHIBIT 1.1**

What Is Different About International Financial Management?

| Concept | International | Domestic |
|---|---|---|
| Culture, history, and institutions | Each foreign country is unique and not always understood by MNE management. | Each country has a known environment. Base case. |
| Corporate governance | Foreign countries' regulations and institutional practices are all uniquely different. | Regulations and institutions are well known. |
| Foreign exchange risk | MNEs face foreign exchange risks due to their subsidiaries, as well as import/export and foreign competitors. | Foreign exchange risks arise from import/export and foreign competition, but not from subsidiaries. |
| Political risk | MNEs face political risks because of their foreign subsidiaries and high profile. | Political risks are negligible. |
| Modification of domestic finance theories | MNEs must modify finance theories like capital budgeting and cost of capital because of foreign complexities. | Base case. |
| Modification of domestic financial instruments | MNEs utilize modified financial instruments such as options, futures, swaps, and letters of credit. | Base case. |

The main purpose of this book is to describe and analyze how a firm's financial management tasks evolve as it pursues global strategic opportunities and new constraints emerge. In this opening chapter, we take a brief look at the challenges and risks associated with a company evolving from domestic in scope to being truly multinational. This will include the constraints that a company will face in terms of managerial goals and governance as it becomes increasingly involved in multinational operations. In the rest of this chapter we examine how cultural, historical, and institutional differences affect a firm's choice of financial goals and corporate governance.

## The Globalization Process

Trident Corporation (Trident) is a hypothetical U.S.–based firm that will be used as an illustrative example throughout the book to demonstrate the *globalization process*. The *globalization process* is the structural and managerial changes and challenges experienced by a firm as it moves from domestic to global in operations.

## Global Transition I: Trident Moves from the Domestic Phase to the International Trade Phase

Trident is a young firm that manufactures and distributes an array of telecommunication devices. Its initial strategy is to develop a sustainable competitive advantage in the U.S. market. Like many other young firms it is constrained by its small size, other competitors, and lack of access to cheap and plentiful sources of capital. The top half of Exhibit 1.2 shows Trident in its early *domestic phase*. Trident sells its products in U.S. dollars to U.S. customers and buys its manufacturing and service inputs from U.S. suppliers, paying U.S. dollars. The creditworth of all suppliers and buyers is established under domestic U.S.

**EXHIBIT 1.2**

Trident Corp:
Initiation of the
Globalization
Process

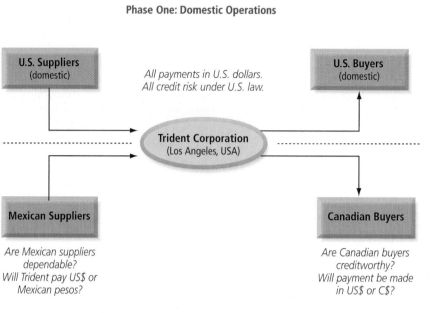

practices and procedures. A potential issue for Trident at this time is that although Trident itself is not international or global in its operations, some of its competitors or suppliers or buyers may be. This is often one of the key drivers to push a firm like Trident into the first transition of the globalization process, the international trade phase.

Trident was founded by James and Edgar Winston in Los Angeles in 1948 to make telecommunications equipment. The family-owned business expanded slowly but steadily over the following 40 years. The demands of continual technological investment in the 1980s, however, required that the firm raise additional equity capital in order to compete. This need led to its initial public offering (IPO) in 1988. As a U.S.–based publicly traded company on NASDAQ, Trident's management sought to *create value for its shareholders*. Issues related to the goals and control of multinational enterprises are discussed in more detail later in this chapter.

As Trident became a visible and viable competitor in the U.S. market, strategic opportunities arose to expand the firm's market reach by exporting products and services to one or more foreign markets. The North American Free Trade Agreement (NAFTA) made trade with Mexico and Canada attractive. This second phase of the globalization process is depicted in the lower half of Exhibit 1.2. Trident responded to these globalization forces by importing inputs from Mexican suppliers and making export sales to Canadian buyers. We define this stage of the globalization process as the *international trade phase*.

Exporting and importing products and services increases the demands of financial management over and above the traditional requirements of the domestic-only business. First, direct *foreign exchange risks* are now borne by the firm. Trident may now need to quote prices in foreign currencies, accept payment in foreign currencies, or pay suppliers in foreign currencies. As the value of currencies change from minute to minute in the global marketplace, Trident will now experience significant risks from the changing values associated with these foreign currency payments and receipts.

Second, the evaluation of the credit quality of foreign buyers and sellers is now more important than ever. Reducing the possibility of non-payment for exports and non-delivery of imports becomes one of two main financial management tasks during this international trade phase. This *credit risk management* task is much more difficult in international business, as buyers and suppliers are new, subject to differing business practices and legal systems, and generally more challenging for Trident to assess.

## Global Transition II: The International Trade Phase to the Multinational Phase

If Trident is successful in its international trade activities, the time will come when the globalization process will progress to the next phase. Trident will soon need to establish foreign sales and service affiliates. This step is often followed by establishing manufacturing operations abroad or by licensing foreign firms to produce and service Trident's products. The multitudes of issues and activities associated with this second larger global transition is the true purpose of this book.

Trident's continued globalization will now require it to identify the sources of its competitive advantage, and with that knowledge in-hand, expand its intellectual capital and physical presence globally. A variety of strategic alternatives are available to Trident — the *foreign direct investment sequence* — as illustrated in Exhibit 1.3. These alternatives include the creation of foreign sales offices or the licensing of everything from its name to the manufacturing and distribution of its products to other firms in foreign markets. As Trident moves further down and to the right in Exhibit 1.3, the degree of its physical presence in foreign markets increases. It may now own its own

**EXHIBIT 1.3**

Trident's Foreign Direct Investment Sequence

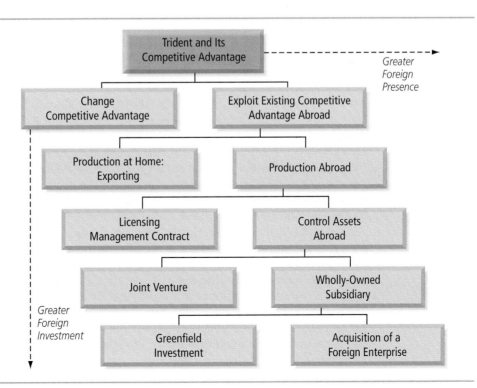

distribution and production facilities, and ultimately, may find it wishes to own other companies which they acquire. Once Trident owns assets and enterprises in foreign countries it has entered the *multinational phase* of its globalization.

## PART I: THE GLOBAL FINANCIAL ENVIRONMENT

But as Trident moves further down and to the right in this multinational phase, it bears greater risks, which arise from multinational activities. The foreign exchange risks and credit management risks suffered by Trident now only grow. In order to identify and manage its foreign currency risks, Trident must first develop a background knowledge of the *global financial environment* that influences the value of currencies. The international monetary system and the balance of payments are discussed in Chapters 2 and 3 of this book.

## PART II: FOREIGN EXCHANGE THEORY AND MARKETS

Trident's financial managers must now understand how foreign exchange rates are determined so they can develop some feel for forecasting exchange rates. This is the subject of Chapters 4 and 5. Trident's management must also understand the institutional processes of how currencies are traded on world markets in order to undertake the currency trading activities needed to manage its growing global operations. This is covered in Chapter 6.

The task of forecasting foreign exchange rates is a subjective one and often yields unsatisfactory results. Therefore, Trident's financial management must know what instruments exist that can reduce foreign exchange risks, regardless of whether or not exchange rates can be correctly forecast in practice. Trident's financial managers will need to become adept in the use of various financial instruments and derivatives used to manage many of these foreign exchange rate and interest rate risks. This is the subject of Chapter 7.

## PART III: FOREIGN EXCHANGE EXPOSURE MEASUREMENT AND MANAGEMENT

Part III of the text reaches directly into the core of multinational business and its financial management, as Trident is now faced with three major sources of *foreign exchange exposure*. The fact that more and more of Trident's cash flows are denominated in foreign currency presents a significant risk that must be managed. This foreign exchange risk is called *transaction exposure* and is the subject of Chapter 8.

As the globalization process continues, Trident's financial management tasks become considerably more complex. Foreign currency transaction exposures (Chapter 8) now include foreign exchange risks generated by Trident's ownership of foreign sales, manufacturing, and service subsidiaries. Because Trident's value as a firm will now vary with future unexpected changes in exchange rates, its *operating exposure* — its long-term competitiveness and ability to generate cash flows — becomes a major concern for management. The topic of operating exposure is the subject of Chapter 9.

The final major currency exposure that Trident faces is *translation exposure*. Translation exposure, sometimes referred to as *accounting exposure*, arises from the process of restating the foreign currency-denominated financial statements of Trident's foreign subsidiaries into the home currency (the U.S. dollar) for reporting purposes. In order for Trident's global operations to be reported to stockholders and creditors, it must be able to measure global financial results in a single currency. The consolidation process and the exchange rate risks associated with it are analyzed in Chapter 10.

## PART IV: FINANCING THE GLOBAL FIRM

As Trident prospers and grows larger at home and abroad, it begins to confront a significant constraint to further growth — access to cheap and plentiful capital. This capital constraint prevents it from competing with its global competitors, as they have access to larger quantities of capital at lower cost. Trident can overcome this constraint by gaining access to global equity and debt markets while maintaining an *optimal financial structure* (the ratio of debt to equity in the company as a whole). The strategy of *globalizing the cost and availability of capital* is a critical one for firms wishing to reach true global competitiveness. The issues and opportunities in implementing this strategy are covered in Chapters 11–14. This analysis will include the current debate as to whether multinational enterprises have a lower or higher cost of capital than their domestic counterparts.

## PART V: FOREIGN INVESTMENT DECISIONS

Trident Corporation's *foreign investment decisions* combine strategy and finance. Trident's global expansion is creating a portfolio of international assets. The management of Trident, as well as its current and potential shareholders, need to understand the risks and rewards of global portfolio diversification. This is analyzed in Chapter 15.

As Trident Corporation seeks to implement foreign direct investment, as shown in Exhibit 1.3, fundamental strategic questions need to be answered. What is Trident's competitive advantage and is it transferable abroad? Does a foreign investment truly build value for shareholders? If it wishes to produce abroad should it attempt to control the assets or does it prefer to license another firm? If it wishes to control the assets should that control be through a wholly owned subsidiary or through a joint venture? These strategic questions are analyzed in Chapter 16.

Foreign direct investment will subject Trident to additional political and country risks. Trident may face risks that are firm-specific and controllable. However, it may also face risks that are country-specific and global-specific and uncontrollable. These risks are the subject of Chapter 17.

As is the case for domestic capital projects, Trident must analyze and evaluate all proposed new foreign-located projects using a *capital budgeting framework*. This financial management task becomes extremely complex since foreign projects involve analysis of foreign inflation, foreign exchange risks, blocked funds and other political risks, method of financing, expected cash flows to both the project and the parent (Trident Corporation), guesstimates of the project's terminal value in both local currency and parent currency terms, and other complications. Capital budgeting is analyzed in Chapter 18.

We will follow Trident as it invests in a variety of forms around the world (see Exhibit 1.4). Trident's first step in the implementation of its strategic plan is to build a new manufacturing and distribution center in Germany. This is typically termed a *greenfield investment* because prior to construction there was nothing there but a green field. It is most likely a long-term investment in business services or productive capabilities. The company follows this foreign expansion with the acquisition of an existing company in Brazil. *Cross-border acquisitions* are typically preferred when the acquisition target has capabilities which a firm like Trident cannot duplicate (for example through greenfield investing). The Brazilian investment was followed by the creation of a *joint venture* in China, in which Trident agreed to share investments and earnings with a partner. In many of the world's emerging markets, like China, a foreign multinational firm like Trident is not allowed to hold sole ownership of enterprises without a local partner.

**EXHIBIT 1.4**

Trident's
Potential Risks
and Returns
Multiply with
Global
Operations

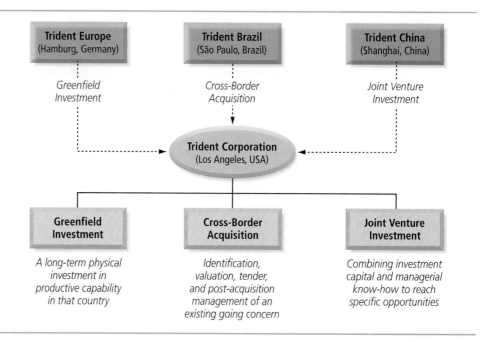

The financial management tasks associated with these international investment activities are again different than those conducted domestically. Trident would now need to conduct a *cross-border valuation* for any prospective acquisition target. After acquisition, Trident would need to assure a successful integration of any acquisition into Trident's global operations. This is often constrained by different corporate cultures and styles of *corporate governance*, and may confront Trident with a complex set of post-acquisition management challenges. Exhibit 1.5 presents some of these issues

**EXHIBIT 1.5**

Trident's
Evaluation of
Global
Investments

*What is the company's global expansion strategy?*

**Trident Corporation**
(Los Angeles, USA)

*Does the foreign investment truly build value for shareholders?*

*What is the company willing to pay to pursue its strategy?*

*Will the new business unit stand on its own or be integrated with global operations?*

**Valuation Issues**

*Analysis of Foreign Investment or Acquisition*

**Governance Issues**

| What are the expected local currency cash flows to occur over time? | Who currently owns it? Is it a privatization, a divestiture, a greenfield investment? |

| What are these expected cash flows worth in U.S. dollars? | Will the project be wholly-owned or a joint venture? |

related to global investment valuation and governance. The international acquisition and valuation process is the subject of the chapter available on this book's web-site.

## PART VI: MANAGING MULTINATIONAL OPERATIONS

The globalization process for Trident has to this point focused on how it has expanded its global scope and depth of operations. Financial management associated with the daily management of global operations, however, is not trivial; this is the subject of the final section of this book. Chapter 19 describes the processes involved in conducting international transactions in foreign trade, including contracts, documents, and procedures. It also analyzes how trade can be financed by using *bankers' acceptances* and other specialized instruments.

Managerial strategies and tactics employed by Trident for the reduction of its global tax liabilities include, among other techniques, the use of *transfer pricing* (the prices charged on sales of goods and services between units of Trident itself globally), assessment of charges for intellectual capital used by foreign subsidiaries owned by the parent company — *royalties and license fees*, and differing financing structures. Trident must also consider the impact on taxation and the potential for *blocked funds* (governmental regulations that hinder the movement of capital out of a country) when choosing strategies that reposition earnings and cash flows. This is the subject of Chapter 20, tax management. Trident's currency and tax environments are shown in Exhibit 1.6.

The financial management of *working capital* is a very important yet complex task faced by Trident's management as the scope of its global business expands. Working capital management combines the cash, accounts receivable, inventories, accounts payable, short-term loans and access to banks, and other ongoing revenues and expenses associated with the day-to-day operations of each and every business unit around the globe. Working capital practices are integrally associated with the cultural

## EXHIBIT 1.6

The Currency and Tax Environments of Trident Corporation and Its Foreign Subsidiaries

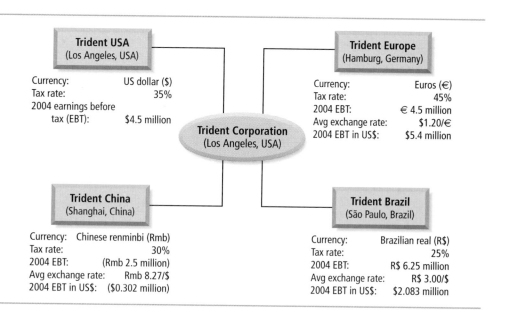

and traditional business practices within each host country as well as the level of economic development and sophistication of the social and industrial infrastructure. The complexity of Trident's global supply chain will require astute financial management and an integration of finance with procurement, logistics, global supplier management, and marketing. These issues and the associated management strategies that Trident might employ across global operations are the subject of Chapter 21.

## What Is the Goal of Management?

As Trident becomes more deeply committed to multinational operations, a new constraint develops, one that springs from divergent worldwide opinions and practices as to just what the firms' overall goal should be from the perspective of top management:

> *What do investors want? First, of course, investors want performance: strong predictable earnings and sustainable growth. Second, they want transparency, accountability, open communications and effective corporate governance. Companies that fail to move toward international standards in each of these areas will fail to attract and retain international capital.*
>
> "The Brave New World of Corporate Governance,"
> *Latinfinance,* May 2001.

An introductory course in finance is usually taught within the framework of maximizing shareholders' wealth as *the goal of management.* In fact, every business student memorizes the concept of *maximizing shareholder value* somewhere in his or her collegiate education. This rather rote memorization, however, has at least two major challenges: (1) it is not necessarily the accepted goal of management across countries to maximize the wealth of shareholders — other stakeholders may carry substantial weight, and (2) it is extremely difficult to carry out. *Creating value* is — like so many lofty goals — much easier said than done. One must realize that the so-called *universal truths* taught in basic finance courses are actually *culturally determined norms.*

### SHAREHOLDER WEALTH MAXIMIZATION

The Anglo-American markets are characterized by a philosophy that a firm's objective should be to *maximize shareholder wealth.* Anglo-American is defined to mean the United States, United Kingdom, Canada, Australia, and New Zealand. This theory assumes that the firm should strive to maximize the return to shareholders — those individuals owning equity shares in the firm, as measured by the sum of capital gains and dividends, for a given level of risk. This in turn implies that management should always attempt to minimize the risk to shareholders for a given rate of return.

This shareholder focus has a tendency to assume that stock markets — the markets in which the individual shares of ownership of these firms are listed and traded between investors — are *efficient.* Efficiency in the field of finance has a very strict set of meanings, including the assumption that the market share price is typically "correct" because it captures all or most of the expectations of return and risk as seen by investors. The theory also assumes that the market moves quickly to incorporate all new information in the share price. And, in the end, it assumes that share prices are the best allocators of capital in the macro economy.

The shareholder wealth theory also defines *risk* in a very strict financial sense. Risk is defined as the added risk that the firm's shares bring to a diversified portfolio, *systematic risk*. The total operational risk of the firm can be eliminated through portfolio diversification by the investors. Thus, *unsystematic risk*, the risk of the individual security, should not be a prime concern for management unless it increases the prospect of bankruptcy. Systematic risk, the risk of the market in general, cannot be eliminated. This reflects risk that the share price will be a function of the stock market.

## CORPORATE WEALTH MAXIMIZATION

> *Horoshi Suzuki's first day on the job as president of Hoya Corporation differed from most senior management appointments. The company's board of directors asked him to sit down and write down the name of his successor. "What they were telling me is if I screw up, I'll be out," says Suzuki with a smile.*
> "Day of the Shareholder," *Far Eastern Economic Review*, September 13, 2001.

The above definitions of *return* and *risk* are not universally accepted, and the experience of Horoshi Suzuki is not always the norm. In contrast to the shareholder focus, Continental European and Japanese markets are characterized by a philosophy that all of a corporation's stakeholders should be considered, and the objective should be to *maximize corporate wealth*. Thus a firm should treat shareholders on a par with other corporate stakeholders, such as management, labor, the local community, suppliers, creditors, and even the government. The goal is to earn as much as possible in the long run, but to retain enough to increase the corporate wealth for the benefit of all. This model has also been labeled the *stakeholder capitalism model*.

The definition of *corporate wealth* is much broader than just "financial wealth." It includes the firm's technical, market, and human resources. This means that an MNE that believes it must close a manufacturing facility in Stuttgart, Germany, and shift its operations to Penang, Malaysia, may not do so without considering the employment and other social impacts on the Stuttgart community. As one study put it, "[Corporate wealth] goes beyond the wealth measured by conventional financial reports to include the firm's market position as well as the knowledge and skill of its employees in technology, manufacturing processes, marketing and administration of the enterprise."[1]

The corporate wealth philosophy does not assume that equity markets are either efficient or inefficient. It does not really matter because the firm's financial goals are not exclusively shareholder-oriented. In any case, the model assumes that long-term "loyal" shareholders should influence corporate strategy, not the transient portfolio investor. The stakeholder capitalism theory assumes that *total risk* — that is, operating and financial risk — does count. It is a specific corporate objective to generate growing earnings and dividends over the long run with as much certainty as possible, given the firm's mission statement and goals. Risk is measured more by product market variability than by short-term variation in earnings and share price. Exhibit 1.7 provides a simplified comparison of the stakeholder and shareholder wealth maximization theories. Note that "the firm" is defined in a physical sense as its management.

There are, however, *primary stakeholders* in both the shareholder wealth and corporate wealth maximization models. These primary stakeholders are those individuals or entities that directly influence the development and implementation of the corporate strategy. In the Anglo-American markets, the primary stakeholders are clearly the shareholders. Management, those employed to act on behalf of shareholders (their *agents*), is positioned between shareholders and those providing debt capital to the

---

[1]Gordon Donaldson and Jay Lorsch, *Decision Making at the Top: The Shaping of Strategic Direction*, New York: Basic Books, 1983, pp. 162–163.

## EXHIBIT 1.7

The Corporate
Wealth and
Shareholder
Wealth
Maximization
Models as
Practiced in
Anglo-American
and Non–Anglo-
American
Markets

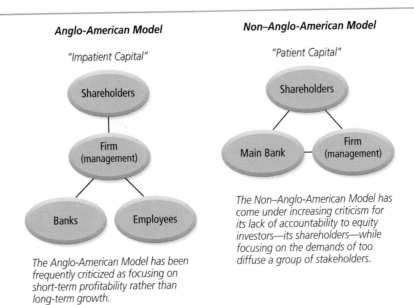

**Anglo-American Model**

"Impatient Capital"

Shareholders

Firm
(management)

Banks     Employees

*The Anglo-American Model has been
frequently criticized as focusing on
short-term profitability rather than
long-term growth.*

**Non–Anglo-American Model**

"Patient Capital"

Shareholders

Main Bank     Firm
(management)

*The Non–Anglo-American Model has
come under increasing criticism for
its lack of accountability to equity
investors—its shareholders—while
focusing on the demands of too
diffuse a group of stakeholders.*

firm, and the markets in which the firm offers its goods and services. Management is expected to make decisions that build value (generate earnings and hopefully capital appreciation) for shareholders. Although creditors and employees and other stakeholders must be considered, they are clearly of secondary importance. Financial profit is the goal and is often termed *impatient capital*.

Corporate wealth maximization as practiced in the European and Japanese markets combines the interests and inputs of shareholders with creditors, management, employees, and society. This is obviously a much more complex process and typically results in an organization which moves more slowly and carefully. In the simplified form illustrated in Exhibit 1.7, the firm is a combination of these groups. The deliberateness of the process demonstrated in the European and Japanese governance system has sometimes been termed *patient capital*.

Although both forms of wealth maximization have their strengths and weaknesses, two trends in recent years have led to an increasing focus on the shareholder wealth form. First, as more of the non–Anglo-American markets have increasingly privatized their industries, the shareholder wealth focus is seemingly needed to attract international capital from outside investors, many of whom are from other countries. Second, and still quite controversial, many analysts believe that shareholder-based MNEs are increasingly dominating their global industry segments. Nothing attracts followers like success.

## OPERATIONAL GOALS FOR MNEs

Whether an MNE is trying to maximize shareholder or corporate wealth, it must be guided by operational goals suitable for various levels of the firm. Even if the firm's goal is to maximize shareholder value, the manner in which investors value the firm is not always obvious to the firm's top management. Many top executives believe that the stock market moves in mysterious ways and is not always consistent in its conclusions.

Therefore, most firms hope to receive a favorable investor response to the achievement of operational goals that can be controlled by the way in which the firm performs.

Because the MNE is a collection of many business units operating in a multitude of economic environments, each MNE must determine for itself the proper balance between two common operational financial objectives:

1. Maximization of consolidated after-tax income and, subsequently, the minimization of the firm's effective global tax burden
2. Correct positioning of the firm's income, cash flows, and available funds as to country and currency

These goals are frequently incompatible, in that the pursuit of one may result in a less desirable outcome in regard to another. Management must make decisions about the proper tradeoffs between goals about the future — which is why people rather than computers are employed as managers.

The primary operational goal of the MNE is to *maximize consolidated profits, after-tax. Consolidated profits* are the profits of all the individual units of the firm originating in many different currencies expressed in the currency of the parent company. This is not to say that management is not striving to maximize the present value of all future cash flows. It is simply the case that most of the day-to-day decision-making in global management is about current earnings. The leaders of the MNE, the senior management team who are developing and implementing the firm's strategy, must think far beyond current earnings.

For example, Trident's foreign subsidiaries have their own set of traditional financial statements: (1) a statement of income, summarizing the revenues and expenses experienced by the firm over the year; (2) a balance sheet, summarizing the assets employed in generating the unit's revenues and the financing of those assets; and (3) a statement of cash flows, summarizing those activities of the firm that generate and then use cash flows over the year. These financial statements are expressed initially in the local currency of the unit for tax and reporting purposes to the local government, but must be consolidated with the parent company's financial statements for reporting to shareholders.

## Corporate Governance

The relationship among stakeholders used to determine and control the strategic direction and performance of an organization is termed *corporate governance*. The corporate governance of the organization is therefore the way in which order and process is established to ensure that decisions are made and interests are represented — for all stakeholders — properly.

Although the governance structure of any company, domestic, international, or multinational, is fundamental to its very existence, this subject has become the lightning rod of political and business debate in the past few years as failures in governance in a variety of forms have led to corporate fraud and failure. Abuses and failures in corporate governance have dominated global business news in recent years. Beginning with the accounting fraud and questionable ethics of business conduct at Enron culminating in its bankruptcy in the fall of 2001, to the retirement pay package of Richard Grasso, the Chairman of the New York Stock Exchange, in September 2003, failures in corporate governance have raised issues about the very ethics and culture of the conduct of business.

## THE GOAL OF CORPORATE GOVERNANCE

The single overriding objective of corporate governance in the shareholder wealth model is the optimization over time of the returns to shareholders. In order to achieve this, good governance practices should focus the attention of the board of directors of the corporation on this objective by developing and implementing a strategy for the corporation which ensures corporate growth and improvement in the value of the corporation's equity. At the same time, it should assure an effective relationship with stakeholders.[2]

The most widely accepted statement of good corporate governance practices are those established by the Organisation for Economic Cooperation and Development (OECD) in 1999:[3]

- **The rights of shareholders.** The corporate governance framework should protect shareholders' rights.
- **The equitable treatment of shareholders.** The corporate governance framework should ensure the equitable treatment of all shareholders, including minority and foreign shareholders. All shareholders should have the opportunity to obtain effective redress for violation of their rights.
- **The role of stakeholders in corporate governance.** The corporate governance framework should recognize the rights of stakeholders as established by law and encourage active cooperation between corporations and stakeholders in creating wealth, jobs, and the sustainability of financially sound enterprises.
- **Disclosure and transparency.** The corporate governance framework should ensure that timely and accurate disclosure is made on all material matters regarding the corporation, including the financial situation, performance, ownership, and governance of the company.
- **The responsibilities of the board.** The corporate governance framework should ensure the strategic guidance of the company, the effective monitoring of management by the board, and the board's accountability to the company and the shareholders.

These principles obviously focus on several key areas — shareholder rights and roles, disclosure and transparency, and the responsibilities of boards — which we will discuss in more detail below.

## THE STRUCTURE OF CORPORATE GOVERNANCE

Our first challenge is to try and capture what people mean when they use the expression "corporate governance." Exhibit 1.8 provides an overview of the various parties and their associated responsibilities associated with the governance of the modern corporation. The modern corporation is a complex organism living in a complex environment. Its actions and behaviors are directed and controlled by both *internal forces* and *external forces*.

---

[2]This definition of the corporate objective is based on that supported by the International Corporate Governance Network (ICGN), a nonprofit organization committed to improving corporate governance practices globally.

[3]"Principles of Corporate Governance," OECD, 1999. Used with permission.

**EXHIBIT 1.8**

The Structure of
Corporate
Governance

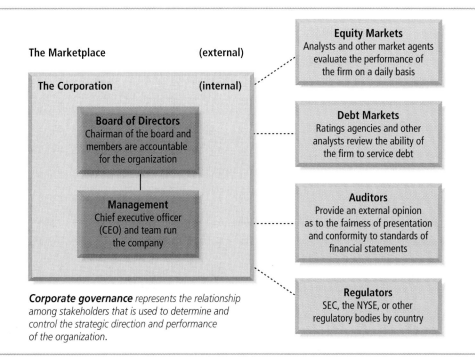

**The Marketplace**                    (external)

**The Corporation**                    (internal)

**Board of Directors**
Chairman of the board and
members are accountable
for the organization

**Management**
Chief executive officer
(CEO) and team run
the company

**Equity Markets**
Analysts and other market agents
evaluate the performance of
the firm on a daily basis

**Debt Markets**
Ratings agencies and other
analysts review the ability of
the firm to service debt

**Auditors**
Provide an external opinion
as to the fairness of presentation
and conformity to standards of
financial statements

**Regulators**
SEC, the NYSE, or other
regulatory bodies by country

*Corporate governance* represents the relationship
among stakeholders that is used to determine and
control the strategic direction and performance
of the organization.

The *internal forces*, the officers of the corporation (such as the chief executive officer or CEO) and the board of directors of the corporation (including the chairman of the board), are those directly responsible for determining both the strategic direction and the execution of the company's future. But they are not acting within a vacuum; they are subject to the constant prying eyes of the *external forces* in the marketplace who question the validity and soundness of their decisions and performance. These include the equity markets in which the shares are traded, the analysts who critique their investment prospects, the creditors and credit agencies who lend them money, the auditors who testify to the fairness of their reporting, and the multitude of regulators who oversee their actions in order to protect the investment public.

**THE BOARD OF DIRECTORS.**   The legal body which is accountable for the governance of the corporation is its board of directors. The board is composed of both employees of the organization (inside members) and senior and influential nonemployees (outside members). Areas of debate surrounding boards include the following: (1) the proper balance between inside and outside members; (2) the means by which board members are compensated for their service; and (3) the actual ability of a board to adequately monitor and manage a corporation when board members are spending sometimes less than five days a year on board activities. Outside members, very often the current or retired chief executives of other major companies, may bring with them a healthy sense of distance and impartiality, which although refreshing, may also result in limited understanding of the true issues and events within the company.

**OFFICERS AND MANAGEMENT.**   The senior officers of the corporation — the chief executive officer (CEO), the chief financial officer (CFO), and the chief operating officer (COO) — are not only the most knowledgeable of the business, but the creators and directors of its strategic and operational direction. The management of the firm is, according to theory, acting as a contractor — as an *agent* — of shareholders to pursue value creation. They are motivated by salary, bonuses, and stock options (positively) or the risk of losing their jobs (negatively). They may, however, have biases of self-enrichment or personal agendas which the board and other corporate stakeholders are responsible for overseeing and policing. Interestingly enough, in more than 80% of the companies in the *Fortune* 500, the CEO is also the chairman of the board. This is, in the opinion of many, a conflict of interest and not in the best interests of the company and its shareholders.

**EQUITY MARKETS.**    The publicly traded company, regardless of country of residence, is highly susceptible to the changing opinion of the marketplace. The equity markets themselves, whether they be the New York Stock Exchange, London Stock Exchange, or Mexico City Bolsa, should reflect the market's constant reflections on the promise and performance of the individual company. The analysts are those self-described experts employed by the many investment banking firms who also trade in the client company shares. They are expected (sometimes naively) to evaluate the strategies, plans for execution of the strategies, and financial performance of the firms on a real-time basis. Analysts depend on the financial statements and other public disclosures of the firm for their information.

**DEBT MARKETS.**    Although the debt markets (banks and other financial institutions providing loans and various forms of securitized debt like corporate bonds), are not specifically interested in building shareholder value, they are indeed interested in the financial health of the company. Their interest, specifically, is in the company's ability to repay its debt in a timely and efficient manner. These markets, like the equity markets, must rely on the financial statements and other disclosures (public and private in this case) of the companies with which they work.

**AUDITORS.**    Auditors are responsible for providing an external professional opinion as to the fairness and accuracy of corporate financial statements. In this process, they attempt to determine whether the firm's financial records and practices follow what in the United States is termed *generally accepted accounting principles* (GAAP) in regard to accounting procedures. But auditors are hired by the firms they are auditing, leading to a rather unique practice of policing their employers. The additional difficulty which has arisen in recent years is that the major accounting firms pursued the development of large consulting practices, often leading to a conflict of interest. An auditor not giving a clean bill of health to a client could not expect to gain many lucrative consulting contracts from that same firm in the near future.

**REGULATORS.**    Publicly traded firms in the United States and elsewhere are subject to the regulatory oversight of both governmental organizations and nongovernmental organizations. In the United States the Securities and Exchange Commission (SEC) is a careful watchdog of the publicly traded equity markets, both in the behavior of the companies themselves in those markets and of the various investors participating in those markets. The SEC and other authorities like it outside of the United States require a regular and orderly disclosure process of corporate performance in order that all investors may evaluate the company's investment value with adequate, accurate, and fairly distributed information. This regulatory oversight is often focused on when and what information is released by the company, and to whom.

A publicly traded firm in the United States is also subject to the rules and regulations of the exchange on which they are traded (New York Stock Exchange, American Stock Exchange, and NASDAQ being the largest). These organizations, typically categorized as "self-regulatory" in nature, construct and enforce standards of conduct for both their member companies and themselves in share trading. Unfortunately, as the recent case of Richard Grasso and his retirement package of $148 million pointed out, it often appears that the "fox is in charge of the hen house."

## COMPARATIVE CORPORATE GOVERNANCE

The origins of the need for a corporate governance process arise from the separation of ownership from management, and from the varying views by culture of who the stakeholders are and of what significance. This assures that corporate governance practices will differ across countries, economies, and cultures. As described in Exhibit 1.9, though, the various corporate governance regimes may be classified by regime. The regimes in turn reflect the evolution of business ownership and direction within the countries over time.

*Market-based regimes*, like those of the United States and the United Kingdom, are characterized by relatively efficient capital markets in which the ownership of publicly traded companies is widely dispersed. *Family-based systems*, like those characterized in many of the emerging markets, Asian markets, and Latin American markets, not only started with strong concentrations of family ownership (as opposed to partnerships or small investment groups which are not family based), but have continued to be largely controlled by families even after going public. *Bank-based* and *government-based regimes* are those reflecting markets in which government ownership of property and industry has been the constant force over time, resulting in only marginal "public ownership" of enterprise, and even then, subject to significant restrictions on business practices.

These regimes are therefore a function of at least three major factors in the evolution of corporate governance principles and practices globally: (1) financial market development, (2) the degree of separation between management and ownership, and (3) the concept of disclosure and transparency.

## EXHIBIT 1.9

Comparative Corporate Governance Regimes

| Regime Basis | Characteristics | Examples |
| --- | --- | --- |
| Market based | Efficient equity markets; dispersed ownership | United States, United Kingdom, Canada, Australia |
| Family based | Management and ownership is combined; family/ majority and minority shareholders | Hong Kong, Indonesia, Malaysia, Singapore, Taiwan, France |
| Bank based | Government influence in bank lending; lack of transparency; family control | Korea, Germany |
| Government affiliated | State ownership of enterprise; lack of transparency; no minority influence | China, Russia |

Source: Based on "Corporate Governance in Emerging Markets: An Asian Perspective," by J. Tsui and T. Shieh, in *International Finance and Accounting Handbook*, Third Edition, Frederick D. S. Choi, editor, Wiley, 2004, pp. 24.4–24.6.

**FINANCIAL MARKET DEVELOPMENT.**    The depth and breadth of capital markets is critical to the evolution of corporate governance practices. Country markets which have had relatively slow growth, as in the emerging markets, or have industrialized rapidly utilizing neighboring capital markets (as is the case of Western Europe), may not form large public equity market systems. Without significant public trading of ownership shares, high concentrations of ownership are preserved and few disciplined processes of governance developed.

**SEPARATION OF MANAGEMENT AND OWNERSHIP.**    In countries and cultures in which the ownership of the firm has continued to be an integral part of management, agency issues and failures have been less a problem. In countries like the United States, in which ownership has become largely separated from management (and widely dispersed), aligning the goals of management and ownership is much more difficult.

**DISCLOSURE AND TRANSPARENCY.**    The extent of disclosure regarding the operations and financial results of a company vary dramatically across countries. Disclosure practices reflect a wide range of cultural and social forces, including the degree of ownership which is public, the degree to which government feels the need to protect investor's rights versus ownership rights, and the extent to which family-based and government-based business remains central to the culture. Transparency, a parallel concept to disclosure, reflects the visibility of decision-making processes within the business organization.

Note that the word *ethics* has not been used. All of the principles and practices described so far have assumed that the individuals in roles of responsibility and leadership pursue them truly and fairly. That, however, has not always been the case.

## FAMILY OWNERSHIP AND CORPORATE GOVERNANCE

Although much of the discussion about corporate governance concentrates on the market-based regimes (Exhibit 1.9), family-based regimes are arguably more common and more important worldwide, including in the United States and Western Europe. For example, in a study of 5,232 corporations in 13 Western European countries, family-controlled firms represented 44.29% of the sample, compared to 36.93% that were widely held.[4]

Recent research indicates that, as opposed to popular belief, family-owned firms in some highly developed economies typically outperform publicly owned firms. This is true not only in Western Europe but also in the United States. A recent study of firms included in the S&P500 found that families are present in fully one third of the S&P500 and account for 18% of their outstanding equity. And, as opposed to popular opinion, family firms outperform nonfamily firms. (An added insight is that firms possessing a CEO from the family also perform better than those with outside CEOs.) Interestingly, it seems that minority shareholders are actually better off according to this study when part of a family-influenced firm.[5]

Another study based on 120 Norwegian, founding-family controlled and non-founding family controlled firms, concluded that founding-family control was associated with higher firm value. Furthermore, the impact of founding-family directors on

[4]Mara Faccio and Larry H. P. Lang, "The Ultimate Ownership of Western European Corporations," *Journal of Financial Economics*, 65 (2002), p. 365. See also: Torben Pedersen and Steen Thomsen, "European Patterns of Corporate Ownership," *Journal of International Business Studies*, Vol. 28, No. 4, Fourth Quarter, 1997, pp. 759–778.

[5]Ronald C. Anderson and David M. Reeb, "Founding Family Ownership and Firm Performance from the S&P500," *The Journal of Finance*, June 2003, p. 1301.

firm value is not affected by corporate governance conditions such as firm age, board independence, and number of share classes. The authors also found that the relationship between founding-family ownership and firm value is greater among older firms, firms with larger boards, and particularly when these firms have multiple classes of stock.[6] It is common for Norwegian firms and firms based in several other European countries to have dual classes of stock with differential voting rights.

## FAILURES IN CORPORATE GOVERNANCE

Failures in corporate governance have become increasingly visible in recent years. The Enron scandal in the United States is described in the mini-case at the end of this chapter. In addition to Enron, other U.S. firms that have revealed major accounting and disclosure failures, as well as executives looting the firm, are WorldCom, Global Crossing, Tyco, Adelphia, and HealthSouth.

In each case, prestigious auditing firms, such as Arthur Andersen, missed the violations or minimized them presumably because of lucrative consulting relationships or other conflicts of interest. Moreover, security analysts urged investors to buy the shares of these and other firms that they knew to be highly risky or even close to bankruptcy. Even more egregious, most of the top executives that were responsible for the mismanagement that destroyed their firms, walked away with huge gains on shares sold before the downfall, and even overly generous severance payments.

It appears that the day of reckoning has come. The first to fall was Arthur Andersen, for its involvement with Enron. However, many more legal actions against former executives are underway. Some of these are described in *Real World Example 1.1*.

## Real World Example 1.1
### CORPORATE CRIME: THE RECKONING

The federal indictment of Bernard J. Ebbers, the former CEO and chairman of WorldCom, is but the latest in a long list of actions taken in reaction to the wave of corporate fraud and financial finagling that accompanied America's great boom and bust. To those cynics who predicted that nothing much would be done to reform Big Business and Wall Street, just look at the record.

New York Attorney General Eliot Spitzer negotiated settlements that reduce conflicts of interest among stock analysts, clean up the initial public offering market, provide independent research to investors, and punish investment banks for past sins. He is now taking the mutual-fund industry to task for late trading. Congress passed Sarbanes-Oxley legislation that reforms both accounting and corporate governance while the Financial Accounting Standards Board is about to implement new rules requiring companies to expense stock options.

Meanwhile, the list of corporate chieftains charged with illegal acts grows. WorldCom's Scott D. Sullivan pleaded guilty, Enron Corp. Ex-Chief Financial Officer Andrew S. Fastow pleaded guilty, and former CEO Jeffrey K. Skilling is under indictment. Only former Chairman Kenneth L. Lay remains untouched. Tyco International Ltd.'s Mark Schwartz and L. Dennis Kozlowski are on trial. HealthSouth Corp.'s Richard M. Scrushy is about to go on trial. Adelphia Communications Corp. founder John Rigas and his two sons are on trial.

America has many strengths, but none is as important as its ability to quickly repair itself. After a series of business and financial scandals unprecedented in modern times, the system is now fairer and more transparent. The quality of earnings is higher, boards are more independent, and investors have renewed confidence. Thanks to reform, the foundation for a strong rebound in the economy in the months ahead has been laid.

Source: "Corporate Crime: The Reckoning," *Business Week*, March 15, 2004, p. 128. © 2004 The McGraw-Hill Companies. All Rights Reserved.

[6]Chandra S. Mishra, Trond Randøy, and Jan Inge Jenssen, "The Effect of Founding Family Influence on Firm Value and Corporate Governance," *Journal of International Financial Management and Accounting*, Vol. 12, No. 3, Autumn 2001, pp. 235–259.

## Real World Example 1.2
### WHEN SCANDALS GO GLOBAL

The cockroach theory of financial scandals says that, for every one you see, hundreds more are hiding in the woodwork. So it was in the U.S., when the scandal at Enron was followed by blowups at WorldCom, HealthSouth, and elsewhere. And so it is now abroad; first Dutch grocer Ahold, then Italian dairy-products company Parmalat, and now Hollinger International Inc., the newspaper company controlled by Conrad M. Black, a Canadian-born British lord.

Scandals break out in bunches because they have common causes. They occur when insiders take advantage of weak corporate governance, feeble government oversight, and a financial system that too often looks the other way.

Indeed, Parmalat's failure reflects badly on what were some of the biggest names in international finance in the '90's. Bank of America, Chase Manhattan, Bank of Boston, Deutsche Bank, Barclays, and Merrill Lynch sold billions of dollars in Parmalat debt over the years. While there's no evidence that the financial giants broke rules, a little skeptical probing would have revealed the rot at the heart of Parmalat years ago.

The slow-motion fall of Conrad Black appears to be a case of high-handedness and questionable governance. The press baron is denying allegations in a lawsuit that he arranged payments to himself and others that weren't properly authorized by the board of directors. If the board let Black run Hollinger for his own benefit, it reflects badly on luminary directors such as Henry A. Kissinger and Richard N. Perle.

There is obvious harm to these companies' shareholders and creditors, such as Parmalat bondholder AFLAC Inc. Less visible but more serious is the destruction of trust, which makes it harder for honest companies to raise the money they need to grow. Overseas, as in the U.S., the solutions are clear: Transparency. Accountability. Tough audits. And criminal penalties for those who cheat. Halfway measures are an invitation to more cheating.

Source: "When Scandals Go Global," *Business Week*, February 2, 2004, p. 96.

Although the corruption scandals were first revealed in the United States, they have spread to Canada and the European Union countries. These scandals are described in *Real World Example 1.2*.

## GOOD GOVERNANCE AND REPUTATION

Does good governance matter? This is actually a difficult question, and the realistic answer has been largely dependent on outcomes historically. For example, as long as Enron's share price continued to rise dramatically throughout the 1990s, questions over transparency, accounting propriety, and even financial facts were largely overlooked by all of the stakeholders of the corporation. Yet, eventually, the fraud and deceit and failure of the multitude of corporate governance practices resulted in the bankruptcy of the firm, destroying not only the wealth of investors, but the careers, incomes, and savings of so many of its basic stakeholders — its own employees. Ultimately, yes, good governance does matter. A lot.

A second way of valuing good governance is by measuring the attitudes and tendencies of the large global institutional investors who make the largest decisions about where capital may go. A recent McKinsey study surveyed over 200 institutional investors as to the value they placed on good governance. The survey results, presented in Exhibit 1.10, quantify good governance as the premium that institutional investors would be willing to pay for companies with good governance within specific country markets. Although this is not exactly equivalent to saying who has "good" or "bad" corporate governance globally, it does provide some insight as to in which countries institutional investors see good governance as scarce. It is again important to note that

**EXHIBIT 1.10**

The Value of Good
Governance

How much more (what premium) would you be willing to pay for a share in a 'good governance' company in the following countries?

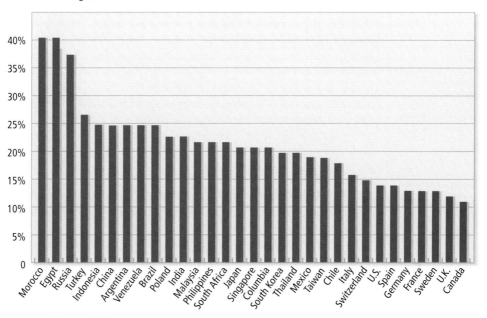

Source: "McKinsey Global Investor Opinion Survey on Corporate Governance, 2002," McKinsey & Company, July 2002.

most of the emerging market nations have relatively few publicly traded companies even today.

This is not a surprise to the "sell-side" — the companies themselves. Corporate leadership globally is increasingly concerned with the nature of its reputation, and corporate governance failures are high on the list of issues that impact corporate reputation.

## CORPORATE GOVERNANCE REFORM

The debate regarding what needs to be done about corporate governance reform depends on which systems and regimes are deemed superior. To date, reform in the United States has been largely regulatory.

**SARBANES-OXLEY ACT.**    The U.S. Congress passed the Sarbanes-Oxley Act in July 2002. It had three major requirements: (1) CEOs of publicly traded firms must vouch for the veracity of the firm's published financial statements; (2) corporate boards must have audit committees drawn from independent (outside) directors; and (3) companies are prohibited from making loans to corporate officers and directors. The first provision — the so-called signature clause — has already had significant impacts on the way in which companies prepare their financial statements. Although the provision was intended to instill a sense of responsibility and accountability in senior management (and therefore fewer explanations of "the auditors signed off on it"), the companies themselves have pushed the same procedure downward in their organizations, often requiring business unit managers and directors at lower levels to sign their financial statements.

Sarbanes-Oxley has been quite controversial internationally, as it is in conflict with a number of the existing corporate governance practices already in place in markets that view themselves as having better governance records than the United States. A foreign firm wishing to list or continue listing their shares on a U.S. exchange must comply with the law. Some companies, such as Porsche, withdrew plans for a U.S. listing specifically in opposition to Sarbanes-Oxley. Other companies, however, including many of the largest foreign companies traded on U.S. exchanges such as Unilever, Siemens, and ST Microelectronics, have stated their willingness to comply — if they can find acceptable compromises between U.S. law and the governance requirements and principles in their own countries. For example, in Germany, supervisory board audit committees must include employee representatives, but according to U.S. law, employees are not independent.

**BOARD STRUCTURE AND COMPENSATION.**   Many critics have argued for the United States to move toward structural reforms more consistent with European standards, such as prohibiting CEOs from also being chairmen. Although this is increasingly common, there is no regulatory or other legal requirement to force the issue. Second, and more radically, would be to move toward the two-tiered structure of countries like Germany, in which there is a supervisory board (largely outsiders, and typically large — Siemens' board has 18 members) and a management board (predominantly insiders, and smaller — Siemens' has eight members). As illustrated by Exhibit 1.11, it is not clear that the director composition of boards is truly the problem.

Also under considerable debate is the amount and form of board compensation. In the past, the United States was characterized by boards in which compensation was a combination of an annual stipend and the award of significant stock options. The stock option incentive, although intended to align the goals and objectives of boards and executive directors with the interests of shareholders, seemingly resulted in a mind-set more akin to the gift of lotto tickets — encouraging aggressive growth and accounting in the interest of earnings growth and share price appreciation.

**TRANSPARENCY, ACCOUNTING, AND AUDITING.**   The concept of transparency has been raised in a variety of markets and contexts. *Transparency* is a rather common term used to describe the degree to which an investor — either existing or potential —

**EXHIBIT 1.11**

Board Composition and Compensation, *Fortune* 100

| Size of Company (sales) | Total Directors | Outside Directors | Avg. Annual Retainer |
|---|---|---|---|
| Less than $3 billion | 9 | 7 | $33,792 |
| $3–$4.9 billion | 10 | 8 | $37,567 |
| $5–$9.9 billion | 12 | 10 | $42,264 |
| $10–$19.9 billion | 12 | 10 | $47,589 |
| $20 billion and over | 13 | 11 | $6,587 |

Source: Korn/Ferry International, as quoted in "The Way We Govern Now," *The Economist*, January 9, 2003 (print edition).

can discern the true activities and value drivers of a company from the disclosures and financial results reported. For example, Enron was often considered a "black box" when it came to what the actual operational and financial results and risks were for its multitude of business lines. The consensus of corporate governance experts is that all firms, globally, should work toward increasing the transparency of the firm's risk-return profile.

The accounting process itself has now come under debate. The U.S. system is characterized as strictly rule-based, rather than conceptually based, as is common in Western Europe. Many critics of U.S. corporate governance practices point to this as a fundamental flaw, in which constantly more clever accountants find ways to follow the rules, yet not meet the underlying purpose for which the rules were intended. An extension of the accounting process debate is that of the role and remuneration associated with auditing, the process of using third parties, paid by the firm, to vet their reporting practices as being consistent with generally accepted accounting principles. As illustrated by the collapse of Arthur Andersen following the Enron debacle, there are serious questions as to how much faith investors can place in the results of this current practice.

**MINORITY SHAREHOLDER RIGHTS.**   Finally, the issue of minority shareholder rights continues to rage in many of the world's largest markets. Many of the emerging markets are still characterized by the family-based corporate governance regime, where the family remains in control even after the firm has gone public. But what of the interests and voices of the other shareholders? How are their interests preserved in organizations where families or private investors control all true decisions, including the boards? As *Real World Example 1.3* on Conrad Black of Hollinger International points out, minority shareholder rights are threatened in all markets, industrialized or emerging.

Poor performance of management usually requires changes to management, ownership, or both. Exhibit 1.12 illustrates some of the alternative paths available to shareholders when dissatisfied with firm performance.

## Real World Example 1.3
### CONRAD BLACK AND MINORITY SHAREHOLDER RIGHTS

Conrad Black was CEO of Hollinger International, a Canadian corporation listed on the New York Stock Exchange. Black controlled the company via a complex management agreement and through a holding company which held a majority of Hollinger's voting shares. He was known to have little patience for shareholder questions, particularly when they were about how he was managing the firm. In a 2003 stockholder meeting he responded to continued questions with the following: "You have a right to say whatever it is that is on your mind, all of you," he informed his investors. "You don't know what you are talking about, but you are still welcome as shareholders." He resigned as chairman and CEO in November 2003, under pressure.

Source: Adapted from "Hollinger Black & Blue," David Leonard, *Fortune*, September 29, 2003.

**EXHIBIT 1.12**

Potential Responses to Shareholder Dissatisfaction

*What counts is that the management of a publicly quoted company, and its board of directors, know that the company can become the subject of a hostile takeover bid if they fail to perform.*

## MINI-CASE

# The Failure of Corporate Governance at Enron

*"The tragic consequences of the related-party transactions and accounting errors were the result of failures at many levels and by many people: a flawed idea, self-enrichment by employees, inadequately-designed controls, poor implementation, inattentive oversight, simple (and not-so-simple) accounting mistakes, and overreaching in a culture that appears to have encouraged pushing the limits. Our review indicates that many of those consequences could and should have been avoided."*

"Report of Investigation by the Special Investigative Committee of the Board of Directors of Enron Corporation," Board of Directors, Enron, February 1, 2002, pp. 27–28.

On December 2, 2001, Enron Corporation filed for bankruptcy protection under Chapter 11. Enron failed as a result of a complex combination of business and governance failures. As noted in the quotation from the board report reprinted above, the failures involved organizations and individuals both inside and outside of Enron. But outside of the courts and sensational press, the question remains as to how the system allowed it to happen. Why did the many structures and safeguards within the U.S. corporate governance system not catch, stop, or prevent the failure of Enron?

### Enron's Collapse

According to former Enron CEO Jeffrey Skilling, Enron failed because of a "run on the bank." This in fact, is probably technically correct. When Enron's credit rating was downgraded to below investment grade in November 2001 by the credit rating agencies, its business was effectively stopped. This was because as a trading company it needed to maintain an investment-grade rating in order for other companies to trade with it. No grade, no trade.

But that answer largely begs the question of *why* the company was downgraded — because Enron's total indebtedness was now determined to be $38 billion, not $13 billion. Why was the debt now, suddenly, so high? Because much of the debt that had been classified as *off-balance sheet* was now reclassified to *on-balance sheet*. Why the reclassification? Because many of the *special-purpose entities* (SPEs) and off-balance sheet partnerships carrying this debt were either found to have been misclassified to begin with or were reconsolidated with the company as a result of their equity falling in value (Enron shares). Which leads us back to the beginning — why did Enron's share price tumble in 2001? Was it simply a natural result of a failing business, or had Enron's reported and prospective earnings, in combination with its general financial health, not been honestly reported and evaluated?

## Failure of Corporate Governance at Enron

Enron's senior management team, primarily the CEO Kenneth Lay and COO Jeffrey Skilling (later CEO) were responsible for the formulation and implementation of the company's strategy, including its operating and financial results. Like most companies of its size, Enron had literally hundreds of accountants and lawyers on its permanent staff. It was the concerns of one accountant, Sherron Watkins, which became public in August and September 2001 and contributed to the rapidly escalating examination of Enron and its operations in the fall of 2001.

In the case of Enron, the external corporate governance bodies have been the focus of much criticism.

- **Auditor.** Arthur Andersen (one of the so-called *Big Five*) was Enron's auditor. Andersen's job was to determine and annually testify as to whether Enron had followed generally accepted accounting practices in the statements of its financial results. Andersen, like all auditors, was hired and paid by the company it was auditing: Enron. Andersen also provided a large variety of consulting activities for Enron, the sum of which was a much larger line of business than the basic audit practice.

- **Legal counsel.** Enron's legal counsel, primarily the firm of Vinson & Elkins of Houston, was responsible for providing legal opinions on the many strategies, structures, and general legality of much of what Enron did. As was the case with Arthur Andersen, when questioned later as to why it did not oppose certain ideas or practices, Vinson & Elkins explained that it had not been fully informed of all of the details and complexities of the management and ownership of the SPEs.

- **Regulators.** Enron actually fell between the cracks of most U.S. regulatory bodies by industry. Because Enron was a trader in the energy markets, the Federal Energy Regulatory Commission (FERC) had some distant oversight responsibilities in regard to some of the markets and trading which the company participated in, but were largely separate issues from Enron's overall activities.

- **Equity markets.** As a publicly traded company, Enron was subject to the rules and regulations of the Securities and Exchange Commission (SEC). The SEC, however, does little firsthand investigation or confirmation of reporting diligence itself, relying instead on the testimonials of other bodies like the company's auditor.

  Because its shares were traded on the New York Stock Exchange (NYSE), Enron was governed by the rules and regulations of that exchange. At this time, however, the reporting requirements of the NYSE differed little if at all from those of the SEC. The NYSE did no firsthand verification of compliance on its own.

  Analysts for a multitude of investment banking firms were responsible for following, analyzing, and evaluating Enron's results on a constant basis. Enron's relation-ships with its investment bankers frequently involved quid pro quo behavior, in which firms that cooperated with Enron and supported its performance stories were rewarded with new business and new mandates for other investment banking activities that were profitable to the firms.

- **Debt markets.** Enron, like all companies who desired and needed a credit rating, paid companies like Standard & Poor's and Moody's to provide it with a credit rating. These ratings are needed for the company's debt securities to be issued and traded in the marketplace. Again, one of the problems which the credit ratings agencies had with Enron was that they could only provide analysis on what was known to them of Enron's operational and financial activities and results. And, in the case of debt knowingly held by off-balance sheet special-purposes entities, there is considerable debate as to whether the credit rating agencies had full detail and knowingly chose to overlook them in the company's total indebtedness or not.

And finally let's not forget the banks and bankers themselves, who provided the access to the debt capital. Most of these banks made millions in interest and fees as a result of leading and managing debt issuances for Enron.

## Feeding the Beast

A particularly troublesome feature of Enron's emerging business model in the late 1990s was that revenues grew much faster than earnings. The cost of undertaking large international power projects (such as in India), electrical power trading, and even new trading ventures such as the trading in water rights and broadband, were, in the words of one former executive, "hideous." The salaries, bonuses, startup costs, and general lack of control over all operating costs drowned whatever profits arose from the new ventures. Even the more successful trading lines, including electricity, did not generate the margins the marketplace had come to expect from Enron and its older portfolio of businesses (primarily natural gas trading). As illustrated in Exhibit 1, the actual operating income (income before interest and taxes or IBIT) by business line was not growing at the same pace as revenues.

The growing deficit in corporate cash flows also led to a more fundamental financial management problem for Enron, the growing need for external capital, or as it was described in-house, "feeding the beast." Rapidly escalating investments in new businesses, whether they be the Portland General Electric (PGE) acquisition of 1997 or the power projects pursued by Rebecca Mark (the director of Enron's international development group) globally, were absorbing more capital than current business could self-finance. Enron's cash flows fell increasingly behind its investments and sales.

**EXHIBIT 1**

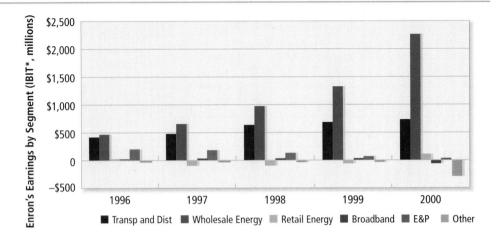

* IBIT is income before interest and taxes

Enron needed additional external capital — new debt and new equity. Ken Lay and Jeff Skilling, however, were both reluctant to issue large amounts of new equity because it would dilute earnings and the holdings of existing shareholders. The debt option was also limited, given the already high debt levels Enron was carrying (and which it had carried since its inception) which left it in the continuously precarious position of being rated BBB, just barely *investment grade*, by credit agency standards.

Although Jeff Skilling had first employed the concept of a fund of capital to be created to support business development within Enron with the creation of the *Cactus Fund* in 1991, it was Andrew Fastow who took the concept to a whole new level. Fastow's experience in banking, specifically in the use of special-purpose entities (SPEs), a common tool in financial services, was his ticket up the corporate ladder at Enron. He eventually rose to the CFO position.

*Many of the transactions involve an accounting structure known as a "special purpose entity" or "special purpose vehicle" (referred to as an "SPE" in this Summary and in the Report). A company that does business with an SPE may treat that SPE as if it were an independent, outside entity for accounting purposes if two conditions are met: (1) an owner independent of the company must make a substantive equity investment of at least 3% of the SPE's assets, and that 3% must remain at risk throughout the transaction; and (2) the independent owner must exercise control of the SPE. In those circumstances, the company may record*

*gains and losses on transactions with the SPE, and the assets and liabilities of the SPE are not included in the company's balance sheet, even though the company and the SPE are closely related. It was the technical failure of some of the structures with which Enron did business to satisfy these requirements that led to Enron's restatement.[7]*

The SPEs created by Andy Fastow and his assistant Michael Kopper served two very important purposes. First, by selling troubled assets to the partnerships, Enron removed them from its balance sheet, taking pressure off the firm's total indebtedness and simultaneously hiding underperforming investments. This also freed up additional room on the balance sheet to fund new investment opportunities. Secondly, the sale of the troubled investments to the partnerships generated income which Enron could then use to make its quarterly earnings commitments to Wall Street.

The problem with this solution was that it was only temporary. The SPEs were largely funded from three sources: (1) equity in the form of Enron shares by Enron; (2) equity in the form of a minimum 3% of assets by an unrelated third party (in principle, although this was later found to not be true in a number of cases); and (3) large quantities of debt from major banks. This capital base made up the right-hand side of the

[7]"Report of Investigation: Special Investigative Committee of the Board of Directors of Enron Corporation," Board of Directors, Enron, February 1, 2002 (often called *The Powers Report*), p. 5.

SPE's balance sheet. On the left-hand side, the capital was used to purchase a variety of assets from Enron. Fastow sold these partnership deals to the banks on the premise that because he was uniquely positioned as both the CFO of Enron and the managing partner in the SPE, he could essentially *cherry-pick* the assets to be purchased by the SPE. Fastow did indeed cherry-pick, but they were the rotten cherries. Most of the assets purchased by the SPEs were troubled or underperforming.

A final detail of the SPEs proved in the end devastating to the financial future of Enron. Since the primary equity in the SPEs was Enron stock, as the share price rose throughout 1999 and 2000, the SPEs could periodically be marked-to-market, resulting in an appreciation in the value of the SPE and contributing significant earnings to Enron. These same shares, once their price began sliding in 2001, resulted in partnerships which should have been marked-to-market for substantial losses, but were not. As Enron's share price plummeted in the early fall of 2001, the equity in the SPEs would no longer meet accounting guidelines for remaining off-balance sheet. The SPEs were becoming something of a synthetic business for Enron.

> *"The trouble was, the Raptors, like the rest of LJM2, had become something of a dumping ground for bad properties. In an effort to make quarterly earnings (and, of course, annual bonuses), Enron originators were hooked on making deals with Fastow instead of outside third parties — who would have asked a lot of questions, slowed down the process, and, in many cases, killed deals. Again, none of this mattered to most people at Enron, as long as the stock kept rising."*[8]

## The Failure of People

As it turns out, much of what Enron reported as *earnings* were not. Much of the debt raised by the company via the partnerships which was not disclosed in corporate financial statements should have been. Simultaneously to the over-reporting of profits and the underreporting of debt, were the massive compensation packages and bonuses earned by corporate officers. So how could this happen?

- It appears that the executive officers of the firm were successful in manipulating the board of directors. Management had moved the company into a number of new markets in which the firm suffered substantial losses, resulting in redoubled attempts on their part to somehow generate the earnings needed to meet Wall Street's unquenchable thirst for profitable growth.

- The board failed in its duties to protect shareholder interests through lack of due diligence and most likely a faith in the competence and integrity of the company's senior officers. It is also notable that Enron's legal advisors, some of whom reported to the board directly, also failed to provide leadership on a number of instances of malfeasance.

- Enron's auditors, Arthur Andersen, committed serious errors in its judgments regarding accounting treatment for many Enron activities, including the SPE partnerships. Andersen was reported to have had serious conflicts of interest, earning $5 million in auditing fees from Enron in 2001, but more than $50 million in consulting fees in the same year.

- Enron's analysts were, in a few cases, blinded by the sheer euphoria over Enron's successes in the mid to late 1990s, or were working within investment banks that were earning substantial investment banking fees related to the complex partnerships. Although a few analysts continued to note that the company's earnings seemed strangely large relative to the falling cash flows reported, Enron's management was generally successful in arguing their point.

The rise and fall of Enron is a story that is far from complete. It may be in the end, however, that the true moral of the story is not in the failure of any specific process in place within the American system of corporate governance, nor in the mistaken focus on fair value accounting, nor in the lack of diligence of the board's own audit committee, but simply the failure of people in a wide variety of positions in a great many different organizations to act reputably and responsibly.

## Case Questions

1. Which parts of the corporate governance system, *internal* and *external*, do you believe failed Enron the most?

2. Describe how you think each of the individual stakeholders and components of the corporate governance system should have either prevented the problems at Enron or acted to resolve the problems before they reached crisis proportions.

3. If all publicly traded firms in the United States are operating within the same basic corporate governance system as Enron, why would some people believe this was an isolated incident and not an example of many failures to come?

[8]*Power Failure*, by Sherron Watkins, p. 232. "Raptors" and "LJM2" refer to special-purpose entities.

## Summary of Learning Objectives

*Consider how the globalization process moves a business from a purely domestic focus in its financial relationships and composition to one truly global in scope*

- Financial management is an integral part of a firm's strategy. The main purpose of this book is to analyze how a firm's financial management tasks evolve as it pursues global strategic opportunities and new constraints unfold.

*Learn what the implications of phase one of globalization — the international trade phase — are for the risks and returns of a business*

- The evolution of firms from purely domestic to multinational is called the *globalization process*. A firm may first enter into international trade transactions, then international contractual arrangements such as sales offices and franchising, and ultimately the acquisition of foreign subsidiaries. It is at this final stage that it truly becomes a multinational enterprise (MNE).

- This globalization process results in a firm becoming increasingly influenced by exchange rate movements and other global political and economic forces in general.

*Examine how the continuing globalization process extends from international trade to multinational operations to global activities*

- The decision whether or not to invest abroad is driven by strategic motives, and may require the MNE to enter into global licensing agreements, joint ventures, cross-border acquisitions, or greenfield investments.

*Discover what three major corporate currency exposures arise from multinational business*

- The three major currency exposures arising from the conduct of multinational business that impact all firms are transaction exposure, operating exposure, and translation exposure.

*See how globalization affects governance of the organization and how it creates value for its stakeholders*

- The definitions of *return* and *risk* are not universally accepted. Indeed, they may be culturally determined norms that vary by country.

- In the Anglo-American markets, the shareholder wealth maximization model is the culturally-determined norm. In many non–Anglo-American markets, the corporate wealth maximization model is the culturally determined norm. Distinct differences exist as to how these models treat return and risk. Additionally, these culturally determined norms are in process of evolution within many countries.

- As MNEs become more dependent on global capital markets for financing they may need to modify their policies of corporate governance. A trend exists for firms resident in non–Anglo-American markets to move toward being more "stockholder friendly." Simultaneously, firms from the Anglo-American markets may be moving toward being more "stakeholder friendly."

*Investigate failures in global corporate governance*

- The relationship among stakeholders used to determine and control the strategic direction and performance of an organization is termed corporate governance.

- Dimensions of corporate governance include agency theory; composition and control of boards of directors; and cultural, historical, and institutional variables.

- Failures in corporate governance, especially in the United States, have recently been in the spotlight and have been given partial blame for the decline in value of the U.S. stock markets.

- Shareholders who are dissatisfied with their firm's performance typically have four choices: remain quietly disgruntled; sell their shares; change management; or initiate a takeover.

- The recent failures in corporate governance in the Untied States have spawned a flurry of government and private initiatives to prevent the same kind of failures in the future.

- The United States has already reacted to the recent failures in corporate governance by passing the Sarbanes-Oxley Act of 2002. The Act specifically asks the CEOs of firms to vouch for their financial statements and to create audit committees from independent directors. The Act, however, is inconsistent with the policies and practices employed in many other countries, and has been a point of contention for firms considering listing (or continued listings) in the United States.

- The coming decade may see a growing consensus of corporate leaders who see the objectives of the firm to include the environmental and social soundness of the firm's activities in addition to the pursuit of profit.

## QUESTIONS

1. **Trident's globalization.** After reading the chapter's description of Trident's globalization process, how would you explain the distinctions between *international, multinational,* and *global* companies?

2. **Trident, the MNE.** At what point in the globalization process did Trident become a multinational enterprise (MNE)?

3. **Trident's advantages.** What are the main advantages that Trident gains by developing a multinational presence?

4. **Trident's phases.** What are the main phases that Trident passed through as it evolved into a truly global firm? What are the advantages and disadvantages of each?

5. **Corporate goals: shareholder wealth maximization.** Explain the assumptions and objectives of the shareholder wealth maximization model.

6. **Corporate goals: corporate wealth maximization.** Explain the assumptions and objectives of the corporate wealth maximization model.

7. **Corporate governance.** Define the following terms
   a. Corporate governance
   b. The market for corporate control
   c. Agency theory
   d. Stakeholder capitalism

8. **Operational goals.** What should be the primary operational goal of an MNE?

9. **Knowledge assets.** Knowledge assets are a firm's intangible assets, the sources and uses of its intellectual talent — its competitive advantage. What are some of the most important knowledge assets that create shareholder value?

10. **Labor unions.** In Germany and Scandinavia, among others, labor unions have representation on boards of directors or supervisory boards. How might such union representation be viewed under the shareholder wealth maximization model compared to the corporate wealth maximization model?

11. **Interlocking directorates.** In an interlocking directorate, members of the board of directors of one firm also sit on the board of directors of other firms. How would interlocking directorates be viewed by the shareholder wealth maximization model compared to the corporate wealth maximization model?

12. **Leveraged buyouts.** A leveraged buyout is a financial strategy in which a group of investors gain voting control of a firm and then liquidate its assets in order to repay the loans used to purchase the firm's shares. How would leveraged buyouts be viewed by the shareholder wealth maximization model compared to the corporate wealth maximization model?

13. **High leverage.** How would a high degree of leverage (debt/assets) be viewed by the shareholder wealth maximization model compared to the corporate wealth maximization model?

14. **Conglomerates.** Conglomerates are firms that have diversified into unrelated fields. How would a policy of conglomeration be viewed by the shareholder wealth maximization model compared to the corporate wealth maximization model?

15. **Risk.** How is risk defined in the shareholder wealth maximization model compared to the corporate wealth maximization model?

16. **Stock options.** How would stock options granted to a firm's management and employees be viewed by the shareholder wealth maximization model compared to the corporate wealth maximization model?

17. **Shareholder dissatisfaction.** If shareholders are dissatisfied with their company, what alternative actions can they take?

18. **Dual classes of common stock.** In many countries it is common for a firm to have two or more classes of common stock with different voting rights. In the United States the norm is for a firm to have one class of common stock with one-share-one-vote. What are the advantages and disadvantages of each system?

**19. Emerging markets corporate governance failures.** It has been claimed that failures in corporate governance have hampered the growth and profitability of some prominent firms located in emerging markets. What are some typical causes of these failures in corporate governance?

**20. Emerging markets corporate governance improvements.** In recent years emerging market MNEs have improved their corporate governance policies and become more shareholder-friendly. What do you think is driving this phenomenon?

## PROBLEMS

*Use the following formula for shareholder returns to answer questions 1 through 3, where $P_t$ is the share price at time t, and $D_t$ is the dividend paid at time t.*

$$\text{Shareholder return} = \frac{P_2 - P_1 + D_2}{P_1}$$

**1. Shareholder returns.** If a share price rises from $16.00 to $18.00 over a one-year period, what was the rate of return to the shareholder if

   **a.** The company paid no dividends?

   **b.** The company paid a dividend of $1.00 per share?

**2. Shareholder choices.** Wilford Fong, a prominent investor, is evaluating investment alternatives. If he believes an individual equity will rise in price from $62 to $74 in the coming one-year period, and the share is expected to pay a dividend of $2.25 per share, and he expects at least a 12% rate of return on an investment of this type, should he invest in this particular equity?

**3. Microsoft's dividend.** In January 2003 Microsoft announced that it would begin paying a dividend of $0.16 per share. Given the following share prices for Microsoft stock in the recent past, how would a constant dividend of $0.16 per share per year have changed the company's return to its shareholders over this period?

| First Trading Day | Closing Share Price | First Trading Day | Closing Share Price |
|---|---|---|---|
| 1998 (Jan 2) | $131.13 | 2001 (Jan 2) | $43.38 |
| 1999 (Jan 4) | $141.00 | 2002 (Jan 2) | $67.04 |
| 2000 (Jan 3) | $116.56 | 2003 (Jan 2) | $53.72 |

**4. Dual classes of common stock (A).** Dual classes of common stock are popular in a number of countries. Assume that Powlitz Manufacturing has the following capital structure at book value:

| Powlitz Manufacturing | Local Currency (millions) |
|---|---|
| Long-term debt | 200 |
| Retained earnings | 300 |
| Paid-in common stock: 1 million A-shares | 100 |
| Paid-in common stock: 4 million B-shares | 400 |
| Total long-term capital | 1,000 |

The A-shares each have 10 votes; the B-shares each have 1 vote per share.

   **a.** What proportion of the total long-term capital has been raised by A-shares?

   **b.** What proportion of voting rights is represented by A-shares?

   **c.** What proportion of the dividends should the A-shares receive?

**5. Dual classes of common stock (B).** Assuming all of the same debt and equity values for Powlitz Manufacturing as in problem 4, with the sole exception that both A-shares and B-shares have the same voting rights, 1 vote per share:

   **a.** What proportion of the total long-term capital has been raised by A-shares?

   **b.** What proportion of voting rights is represented by A-shares?

   **c.** What proportion of the dividends should the A-shares receive?

**6. Price/earnings ratios and acquisitions.** During the 1960s many conglomerates were created by a firm enjoying a high price/earnings ratio (P/E). They then used their highly valued stock to acquire other firms that had lower P/E ratios, usually in unrelated domestic industries. These conglomerates went out of fashion during the 1980s when they lost their high P/E ratios, thus making it more difficult to find other firms with lower P/E ratios to acquire.

During the 1990s, the same acquisition strategy was possible for firms located in countries where high P/E ratios were common compared to firms in other countries where low P/E ratios were common. Assume the following hypothetical firms in the pharmaceutical industry.

*End-of-chapter problems that utilize spreadsheets are available online at www.aw-bc.com/moffett and are accompanied by this icon.

| | P/E Ratio | Number of Shares | Market Value per Share | Earnings | EPS | Total Market Value |
|---|---|---|---|---|---|---|
| Pharm-Italy | 20 | 10,000,000 | $20 | $10,000,000 | $1.00 | $200,000,000 |
| Pharm-USA | 40 | 10,000,000 | $40 | $10,000,000 | $1.00 | $400,000,000 |

Pharm-USA wants to acquire Pharm-Italy. It offers 5,500,000 shares of Pharm-USA, with a current market value of $220,000,000 and a 10% premium on Pharm-Italy's shares, for all of Pharm-Italy's shares.

a. How many shares would Pharm-USA have outstanding after the acquisition of Pharm-Italy?

b. What would be the consolidated earnings of the combined Pharm-USA and Pharm-Italy?

c. Assuming the market continues to capitalize Pharm-USA's earnings at a P/E ratio of 40, what would be the new market value for Pharm-USA?

d. What is the new earnings per share of Pharm-USA?

e. What is the new market value of a share of Pharm-USA?

f. How much did Pharm-USA's stock price increase?

g. Assume that the market takes a negative view of the merger and lowers Pharm-USA's P/E ratio to 30. What would be the new market price per share of stock? What would be its percentage loss?

7. **Corporate governance: Overstating earnings.** A number of firms, especially in the United States, have had to lower their previously reported earnings due to accounting errors or fraud. Assume that Pharm-USA (problem 6) had to lower its earnings to $5,000,000 from the previously reported $10,000,000. What might be its new market value prior to the acquisition? Could it still do the acquisition?

**Trident Corporation**

Problems 8 through 10 are based on the hypothetical MNE Trident Corporation. Trident is a U.S.–based multinational manufacturing firm, with wholly-owned subsidiaries in Brazil, Germany, and China, in addition to domestic operations in the United States. Trident is traded on the NASDAQ. Trident currently has 650,000 shares outstanding. The basic operating characteristics of the various business units is as follows:

| (000s, local currency) | USA (dollars, $) | Brazil (real, R$) | Germany (euros, €) | China (renminbi, Rmb) |
|---|---|---|---|---|
| Earnings before tax (EBT) | $4,500 | R$6,250 | €4,500 | Rmb2,500 |
| Corporate income tax rate | 35% | 25% | 40% | 30% |
| Average exchange rate for period | — | R$3.50/$ | €0.9260/$ | Rmb8.50/$ |

8. **Trident Corporation's consolidated earnings.** Trident must pay corporate income tax in each country in which it currently has operations.

a. After deducting taxes in each country, what are Trident's consolidated earnings and consolidated earnings per share in U.S. dollars?

b. What proportion of Trident's consolidated earnings arise from each individual country?

c. What proportion of Trident's consolidated earnings arise from outside the United States?

9. **Trident's EPS sensitivity to exchange rates.** Assume a major political crisis wracks Brazil, first affecting the value of the Brazilian real and, subsequently, inducing an economic recession within the country.

a. What would be the impact on Trident's consolidated EPS if the Brazilian real were to fall to R$4.50/$, with all other earnings and exchange rates remaining the same?

b. What would be the impact on Trident's consolidated EPS if, in addition to the fall in the value of the real to R$4.50/$, but earnings before taxes in Brazil fell as a result of the recession to R$5,800,000?

10. **Trident's earnings and global taxation.** All MNEs attempt to minimize their global tax liabilities. Return to the original set of baseline assumptions and answer the following questions regarding Trident's global tax liabilities.

a. What is the total amount — in U.S. dollars — which Trident is paying across its global business in corporate income taxes?

b. What is Trident's effective tax rate on a global basis (total taxes paid as a percentage of pretax profits)?

c. What would be the impact on Trident's EPS and global effective tax rate if Germany instituted a corporate tax reduction to 28%, and Trident's earnings before tax in Germany rose to €5,000,000?

## Internet Exercises

1. **Multinational firms and global assets/income.** The differences across MNEs is striking. Using a sample of firms such as those listed here, pull from their individual Web pages the proportions of their incomes that are earned outside their country of incorporation. (Note how Nestlé calls itself a "transnational company.")

   Walt Disney
      http://disney.go.com/
   Nestlé S. A.
      http://www.nestle.com/
   Intel
      http://www.intel.com/
   DaimlerChrysler
      http://www.daimlerchrysler.com/dccom
   Mitsubishi Motors
      http://www.mitsubishi.com/
   Nokia
      http://www.nokia.com/
   Royal Dutch/Shell
      http://www.shell.com/

   Also note the way in which international business is now conducted via the Internet. Several of the above home pages allow the user to choose the language of the presentation viewed.

2. **Corporate governance.** There is no hotter topic in business today than corporate governance. Use the following sites to view recent research, current events and news items, and other information related to the relationships between a business and its stakeholders.

   Corporate Governance Net
      http://www.corpgov.net/

3. ***Fortune* Global 500.** *Fortune* magazine is famous for its listing of the *Fortune* 500 firms in the global marketplace. Use *Fortune's* Web site to find the most recent list of which firms from which countries are in this distinguished club.

   Fortune
      http://www.fortune.com/fortune/

4. ***Financial Times.*** The *Financial Times*, based in London — the global center of international finance — has a Web site that possesses a wealth of information. After going to the home page, go to the Markets & Funds Data page, and examine the recent stock market activity around the globe. Note the similarity in movement on a daily basis among the world's major equity markets.

   *Financial Times*
      http://www.ft.com/

# The International Monetary System

## LEARNING OBJECTIVES

Define terms that are used in reference to exchange rates and currency regimes

Define the difference between "devaluation" and "depreciation"

Learn how the international monetary system has evolved from the days of the gold standard to today's eclectic currency arrangement

Discover the origin and development of the Eurocurrency market

Analyze the characteristics of an ideal currency

Explain the currency regime choices faced by emerging market countries

Describe how the euro, a single currency for the European Union, was created and what its effects are

The increased volatility of exchange rates is one of the main economic developments of the past 42 years. Under the current system of partly floating and partly fixed exchange rates, earnings of multinational firms, banks, and individual investors undergo real and paper fluctuations as a result of changes in exchange rates. Policies to forecast and react to exchange rate fluctuations are still evolving as we understand better the international monetary system, accounting and tax rules for foreign exchange gains and losses, and the economic effect of exchange rate changes on future cash flows and market values.

Although volatile exchange rates increase risk, they also create profit opportunities for firms and investors, given a proper understanding of exchange risk management. In order to manage foreign exchange risk, however, management must first understand how the international monetary system functions. The *international monetary system* is the structure within which foreign exchange rates are determined, international trade and capital flows are accommodated, and balance of payments adjustments made. All of the instruments, institutions, and agreements that link together the world's currency, money markets, securities, and real estate and commodity markets are also encompassed within that term.

## Currency Terminology

Let us begin with some basic terms in order to prevent confusion in reading this chapter.

- A *foreign currency exchange rate,* or simply *exchange rate,* is the price of one country's currency in units of another currency or commodity (typically gold or silver). If the government of a country — for example, China — regulates the rate at which its currency — the renminbi (yuan) — is exchanged for other currencies, the system or *regime* is classified as a *fixed* or *managed exchange rate regime.* The rate at which the currency is fixed, or pegged, is frequently referred to as its *par value.* If the government does not interfere in the valuation of its currency in any way, we classify the currency as *floating* or *flexible.*
- *Spot exchange rate* is the quoted price for foreign exchange to be delivered at once, or in two days for interbank transactions. For example, ¥114/$ is a quote for the exchange rate between the Japanese yen and the U.S. dollar. We would need 114 yen to buy one U.S. dollar for immediate delivery.
- *Forward rate* is the quoted price for foreign exchange to be delivered at a specified date in the future. For example, assume the 90-day forward rate for the Japanese yen is quoted as ¥112/$. No currency is exchanged today, but in 90 days it will take 112 yen to buy one U.S. dollar. This can be guaranteed by a *forward exchange contract.*
- *Forward premium* or *discount* is the percentage difference between the spot and forward exchange rate. To calculate this, using the quotes from above, one formula is

$$\frac{S-F}{F} \times \frac{360}{n} \times 100 = \frac{¥114/\$ - ¥112/\$}{¥112/\$} \times \frac{360}{90} \times 100 = 7.14\%$$

where S is the spot exchange rate, F is the forward rate, and *n* is the number of days until the forward contract becomes due.

- *Devaluation of a currency* refers to a drop in foreign exchange value of a currency that is pegged to gold or to another currency. In other words, the par value is reduced. The opposite of devaluation is revaluation.
- *Weakening, deterioration,* or *depreciation* of a currency refers to a drop in the foreign exchange value of a floating currency. The opposite of weakening is *strengthening* or *appreciating*, which refers to a gain in the exchange value of a floating currency.
- *Soft* or *weak* describes a currency that we expect to devalue or depreciate relative to major currencies. It also refers to currencies whose values are being artificially sustained by their governments. A currency is considered *hard* or *strong* if it is expected to revalue or appreciate relative to major trading currencies.

This chapter begins with a brief history of the international monetary system from the days of the classical gold standard to the present time. This is followed by an analysis of contemporary currency regimes and the relative advantages of fixed versus floating rate systems. The most recent currency regime began with the launching of the *euro,* a common currency for 12 of the 25 countries that are members of the European Union. The number of countries expanded on May 1, 2004 from 15 to 25, but only 12 countries currently participate in the euro.

## History of the International Monetary System

Over the ages, currencies have been defined in terms of gold and other items of value, and the international monetary system has been subject to a variety of international agreements. A review of these systems provides useful perspective against which to understand today's system and to evaluate weaknesses and proposed changes in the present system.

### THE GOLD STANDARD, 1876–1913

Since the days of the pharaohs (about 3000 B.C.) gold has served as a medium of exchange and a store of value. The Greeks and Romans used gold coins and passed on this tradition through the mercantile era to the nineteenth century. The great increase in trade during the free-trade period of the late nineteenth century led to a need for a more formalized system for settling international trade balances. One country after another set a par value for its currency in terms of gold and then tried to adhere to the so-called rules of the game. This later came to be known as the classical gold standard. The gold standard as an international monetary system gained acceptance in Western Europe in the 1870s. The United States was something of a latecomer to the system, not officially adopting the standard until 1879.

The "rules of the game" under the gold standard were clear and simple. Each country set the rate at which its currency unit (paper or coin) could be converted to a weight of gold. The United States, for example, declared the dollar to be convertible to gold at a rate of $20.67 per ounce of gold (a rate in effect until the beginning of World War I). The British pound was pegged at £4.2474 per ounce of gold. As long as both currencies were freely convertible into gold, the dollar/pound exchange rate was:

$$\frac{\$20.67 \text{ / ounces of gold}}{\pounds 4.2474 \text{ / ounces of gold}} = \$4.8665 \text{ / } \pounds$$

Because the government of each country on the gold standard agreed to buy or sell gold on demand with anyone at its own fixed parity rate, the value of each individual currency in terms of gold, and therefore fixed exchange rates between currencies, was fixed. Maintaining adequate reserves of gold to back its currency's value was very important for a country under this system. The system also had the effect of implicitly limiting the rate at which any individual country could expand its money supply. Any growth in the amount of money was limited to the rate at which official authorities could acquire additional gold.

The gold standard worked adequately until the outbreak of World War I interrupted trade flows and the free movement of gold. This caused the main trading nations to suspend operation of the gold standard.

## THE INTER-WAR YEARS AND WORLD WAR II, 1914–1944

During World War I and the early 1920s, currencies were allowed to fluctuate over fairly wide ranges in terms of gold and each other. Theoretically supply and demand for a country's exports and imports caused moderate changes in an exchange rate about a central equilibrium value. This was the same function that gold had performed under the previous gold standard. Unfortunately, such flexible exchange rates did not work in an equilibrating manner. On the contrary, international speculators sold the weak currencies short, causing them to fall further in value than warranted by real economic factors. *Selling short* is a speculation technique in which an individual speculator sells an asset such as a currency to another party for delivery at a future date. The speculator, however, does not yet own the asset, expecting the price of the asset to fall by the date when the asset must be purchased in the open market by the speculator for delivery.

The reverse happened with strong currencies. Fluctuations in currency values could not be offset by the relatively illiquid forward exchange market except at exorbitant cost. The net result was that the volume of world trade did not grow in the 1920s in proportion to world gross national product but instead declined to a very low level with the advent of the Great Depression in the 1930s.

The United States adopted a modified gold standard in 1934 when the U.S. dollar was devalued to $35 per ounce of gold from the $20.67 per ounce price in effect prior to World War I. Contrary to previous practice, the U.S. treasury traded gold only with foreign central banks, not private citizens. From 1934 to the end of World War II, exchange rates were theoretically determined by each currency's value in terms of gold. During World War II and its chaotic aftermath, however, many of the main trading currencies lost their convertibility into other currencies. The dollar was the only major trading currency that continued to be convertible.

## BRETTON WOODS AND THE INTERNATIONAL MONETARY FUND, 1944

As World War II drew to a close in 1944, the Allied Powers met at Bretton Woods, New Hampshire, in order to create a new postwar international monetary system. The Bretton Woods Agreement established a U.S. dollar-based international monetary system and provided for two new institutions, the International Monetary Fund and the World Bank. The International Monetary Fund (IMF) aids countries with balance of payments and exchange rate problems. The International Bank for Reconstruction and Development (World Bank) helped fund postwar reconstruction and since then has supported general economic development.

The IMF was the key institution in the new international monetary system, and it has remained so to the present. The IMF was established to render temporary assistance to member countries trying to defend their currencies against cyclical, seasonal, or random occurrences. It also assists countries having structural trade problems if they promise to take adequate steps to correct their problems. If persistent deficits occur, however, the IMF cannot save a country from eventual devaluation. In recent years it has attempted to help countries facing financial crises. It has provided massive loans as well as advice to Russia and other former Russian republics, Brazil, Indonesia, and South Korea to name but a few.

Under the original provisions of the Bretton Woods Agreement, all countries fixed the value of their currencies in terms of gold but were not required to exchange their currencies for gold. Only the dollar remained convertible into gold (at $35 per ounce). Therefore each country established its exchange rate vis-à-vis the dollar, and then calculated the gold par value of its currency to create the desired dollar exchange rate. Participating countries agreed to try to maintain the value of their currencies within 1% (later expanded to $2^1/4$%) of par by buying or selling foreign exchange or gold as needed. Devaluation was not to be used as a competitive trade policy, but if a currency became too weak to defend, a devaluation of up to 10% was allowed without formal approval by the IMF. Larger devaluations required IMF approval.

The *Special Drawing Right* (SDR) is an international reserve asset created by the IMF to supplement existing foreign exchange reserves. It serves as a unit of account for the IMF and other international and regional organizations, and is also the base against which some countries peg the exchange rate for their currencies.

Defined initially in terms of a fixed quantity of gold, the SDR has been redefined several times. It is currently the weighted value of currencies of the five IMF members having the largest exports of goods and services. Individual countries hold SDRs in the form of deposits in the IMF. These holdings are part of each country's international monetary reserves, along with official holdings of gold, foreign exchange, and its reserve position at the IMF. Members may settle transactions among themselves by transferring SDRs.

**EUROCURRENCIES.** *Eurocurrencies* are domestic currencies of one country on deposit in a second country. Eurodollar time deposit maturities range from call money and overnight funds to longer periods. Certificates of deposit are usually for three months or more and in million-dollar increments. A Eurodollar deposit is not a demand deposit; it is not created on the bank's books by writing loans against required fractional reserves, and it cannot be transferred by a check drawn on the bank having the deposit. Eurodollar deposits are transferred by wire or cable transfer of an underlying balance held in a correspondent bank located within the United States. A domestic analogy in most countries would be the transfer of deposits held in non-bank savings associations. These are transferred by having the association write its own check on a commercial bank.

Any convertible currency can exist in "Euro-" form. (Note that this use of the expression "Euro-" should not be confused with the new common European currency called the *euro*.) The Eurocurrency market includes Eurosterling (British pounds deposited outside the United Kingdom), Euroeuros (euros on deposit outside the euro zone), and Euroyen (Japanese yen deposited outside Japan), as well as Eurodollars. The exact size of the Eurocurrency market is difficult to measure because it varies with daily decisions by depositors on where to hold readily transferable liquid funds, and particularly on whether to deposit dollars within or outside the United States.

Eurocurrency markets serve two valuable purposes: (1) Eurocurrency deposits are an efficient and convenient money market device for holding excess corporate liquidity; and (2) the Eurocurrency market is a major source of short-term bank loans to finance corporate working capital needs, including the financing of imports and exports.

Banks in which Eurocurrencies are deposited are called *Eurobanks*. A Eurobank is a financial intermediary that simultaneously bids for time deposits and makes loans in a currency other than that of the currency in which it is located. Eurobanks are major world banks that conduct a Eurocurrency business in addition to all other banking functions. Thus the Eurocurrency operation that qualifies a bank for the name *Eurobank* is in fact a department of a large commercial bank, and the name springs from the performance of this function.

The modern Eurocurrency market was born shortly after World War II. Eastern European holders of dollars, including the various state trading banks of the Soviet Union, were afraid to deposit their dollar holdings in the United States because these deposits might be attached by U.S. residents with claims against communist governments. Therefore Eastern European holders deposited their dollars in Western Europe, particularly with two Soviet banks: the Moscow Narodny Bank in London, and the Banque Commerciale pour l'Europe du Nord in Paris. These banks redeposited the funds in other Western banks, especially in London. Additional dollar deposits were received from various central banks in Western Europe, which elected to hold part of their dollar reserves in this form to obtain a higher yield. Commercial banks also placed their dollar balances in the market for the same reason as well as because specific maturities could be negotiated in the Eurodollar market. Additional dollars came to the market from European insurance companies with a large volume of U.S. business. Such companies found it financially advantageous to keep their dollar reserves in the higher-yielding Eurodollar market. Various holders of international refugee funds also supplied funds.

Although the basic causes of the growth of the Eurocurrency market are economic efficiencies, a number of unique institutional events during the 1950s and 1960s helped its growth.

- In 1957, British monetary authorities responded to a weakening of the pound by imposing tight controls on U.K. bank lending in sterling to nonresidents of the United Kingdom. Encouraged by the Bank of England, U.K. banks turned to dollar lending as the only alternative that would allow them to maintain their leading position in world finance. For this they needed dollar deposits.

- Although New York was home base for the dollar and had a large domestic money and capital market, London became the center for international trading in the dollar because of that city's expertise in international monetary matters and its proximity in time and distance to major customers.

- Additional support for a European-based dollar market came from the balance of payments difficulties the United States experienced during the 1960s, which temporarily separated the U.S. domestic capital market from that of the rest of the world.

Ultimately, however, the Eurocurrency market continues to thrive because it is a large international money market relatively free from governmental regulation and interference.

**EUROCURRENCY INTEREST RATES: LIBOR.**    In the Eurocurrency market the reference rate of interest is the *London Interbank Offered Rate* (LIBOR). LIBOR is now the most widely accepted rate of interest used in standardized quotations, loan agreements, and financial derivatives valuations. LIBOR is officially defined by the *British Bankers Association* (BBA). For example, U.S. dollar LIBOR is the mean of 16 multinational banks interbank offered rates as sampled by the BAA at 11 A.M. *London time in London.* Similarly, the BBA calculates the Japanese yen LIBOR, euro LIBOR, and other currency LIBOR rates at the same time in London from samples of banks.

The interbank interest rate is not, however, confined to London. Most major domestic financial centers construct their own interbank offered rates for local loan agreements. These rates include PIBOR (Paris Interbank Offered Rate), MIBOR (Madrid Interbank Offered Rate), SIBOR (Singapore Interbank Offered Rate), and FIBOR (Frankfurt Interbank Offered Rate), to name but a few.

The key factor attracting both depositors and borrowers to the Eurocurrency loan market is the narrow interest rate spread within that market. The difference between deposit and loan rates is often less than 1%. Interest spreads in the Eurocurrency market are small for a number of reasons. Low lending rates exist because the Eurocurrency markets is a *wholesale market*, where deposits and loans are made in amounts of $500,000 or more on an unsecured basis. Borrowers are usually large corporations or government entities that qualify for low rates because of their credit standing and because the transaction size is large. In addition, overhead assigned to the Eurocurrency operation by participating banks is small.

Deposit rates are higher in the Eurocurrency markets than in most domestic currency markets because the financial institutions offering Eurocurrency activities are not subject to many of the regulations and reserve requirements imposed on traditional domestic banks and banking activities. With these costs removed, rates are subject to more competitive pressures, deposit rates are higher, and loan rates are lower. A second major area of cost avoided in the Eurocurrency markets is the payment of deposit insurance fees (such as the Federal Deposit Insurance Corporation, FDIC, assessments paid on deposits in the United States). Exhibit 2.1 provides an illustration of how Eurodollar deposit and loan rates, including dollar LIBOR and LIBID rates, compared with traditional domestic interest rates in February 2004.

## FIXED EXCHANGE RATES, 1945–1973

The currency arrangement negotiated at Bretton Woods and monitored by the IMF worked fairly well during the post-World War II period of reconstruction and rapid growth in world trade. However, widely diverging national monetary and fiscal policies, differential rates of inflation, and various unexpected external shocks eventually resulted in the system's demise. The U.S. dollar was the main reserve currency held by central banks and was the key to the web of exchange rate values. Unfortunately the United States ran persistent and growing deficits in its balance of payments. A heavy capital outflow of dollars was required to finance these deficits and to meet the growing demand for dollars from investors and businesses. Eventually the heavy overhang of dollars held by foreigners resulted in a lack of confidence in the ability of the United States to meet its commitment to convert dollars to gold.

This lack of confidence forced President Richard Nixon to suspend official purchases or sales of gold by the U.S. Treasury on August 15, 1971, after the United States suffered outflows of roughly one third of its official gold reserves in the first seven

**EXHIBIT 2.1**

U.S. Dollar–
Denominated
Interest Rates,
February 2004

*3-Month Maturities*

— 4.00 %   U.S. Prime Rate

**LIBOR**
London Interbank Offer Rate
1.1300 % —— $1\frac{1}{8}$ = 1.12500 %   Eurodollar Deposit Offer Rate

} *Eurodollar Spread*

1.0300 % —— $1\frac{1}{32}$ = 1.03125 %   Eurodollar Deposit Bid Rate
**LIBID**
London Interbank Bid Rate

— 1.02 % Certificate of Deposit Rate (domestic)

— 1.00 %   U.S. Federal Funds Rate (domestic)

London interbank rates apply to the buying and selling of Eurodollar deposits between banks in the international markets.

Eurodollar deposits are dollar-denominated accounts in financial institutions outside of the United States.

Source: *The Financial Times*, February 10, 2004, p. 27. © 2004 The Financial Times. Reprinted with permission.

months of the year. Exchange rates of most of the leading trading countries were allowed to float in relation to the dollar and thus indirectly in relation to gold. By the end of 1971 most of the major trading currencies had appreciated vis-a-vis the dollar. This change was — in effect — a devaluation of the dollar.

A year and a half later the U.S. dollar once again came under attack, thereby forcing a second devaluation on February 12, 1973, this time by 10% to $42.22 per ounce of gold. By late February 1973, a fixed-rate system no longer appeared feasible given the speculative flows of currencies. The major foreign exchange markets were actually closed for several weeks in March 1973. When they reopened, most currencies were allowed to float to levels determined by market forces. Par values were left unchanged. The dollar floated downward an average of 10% by June 1973.

## AN ECLECTIC CURRENCY ARRANGEMENT, 1973–PRESENT

Since March 1973, exchange rates have become much more volatile and less predictable than they were during the "fixed" exchange rate period, when changes occurred infrequently. Exhibit 2.2 illustrates the wide swings exhibited by one of the oldest and fundamental currency rates, the U.S. dollar to British pound exchange rate. The dollar/pound rate has historically been called "cable" as a result of its early trading via the transatlantic cable which first connected London and New York over a century ago. The U.S. dollar to British pound exchange rate fluctuations mirror similar volatility between other exchange rate pairs.

Exhibit 2.3 summarizes the key events and external shocks that have affected currency values since March 1973. The most important shocks in recent years have been

## EXHIBIT 2.2

The U.S. Dollar–
British Pound
Exchange Rate,
1971–2004

Source: ©2004 by
Prof. Werner
Antweiler, University
of British Columbia,
Vancouver BC,
Canada. Time period
shown in diagram:
1/Jan/1971–
19/May/2004

**Monthly Avg. Exchange Rates: U.S. Dollars per British Pound**

## EXHIBIT 2.3

World Currency Events, 1971–2004

| Date | Event | Impact |
|------|-------|--------|
| August 1971 | Dollar floated | Nixon closes the U.S. gold window, suspending purchases or sales of gold by U.S. Treasury; temporary imposition of 10% import surcharge |
| December 1971 | Smithsonian Agreement | Group of Ten reaches compromise whereby the US$ is devalued to $38/oz of gold; most other major currencies are appreciated versus US$ |
| February 1973 | U.S. dollar devalued | Devaluation pressure increases on US$ forcing further devaluation to $42.22/oz of gold |
| February–March 1973 | Currency markets in crisis | Fixed exchange rates no longer considered defensible; speculative pressures force closure of international foreign exchange markets for nearly two weeks; markets reopen on floating rates for major industrial currencies |
| June 1973 | U.S. dollar depreciation | Floating rates continue to drive the now freely floating US$ down by about 10% by June |
| Fall 1973–1974 | OPEC oil embargo | Organization of Petroleum Exporting Countries (OPEC) impose oil embargo eventually quadrupling the world price of oil; because world oil prices are stated in US$, value of US$ recovers some former strength |
| January 1976 | Jamaica Agreement | IMF meeting in Jamaica results in the "legalization" of the floating exchange rate system already in effect; gold is demonetized as a reserve asset |
| 1977–1978 | U.S. inflation rate rises | Carter administration reduces unemployment at the expense of inflation increases; rising U.S. inflation causes continued depreciation of the US$ |
| March 1979 | EMS created | European Monetary System (EMS) is created, establishing a cooperative exchange rate system for participating members of the European Economic Community (EEC) |

*(continues)*

**EXHIBIT 2.3 (CONTINUED)**

World Currency Events, 1971–2004

| Date | Event | Impact |
|------|-------|--------|
| Summer 1979 | OPEC raises prices | OPEC nations raise price of oil again |
| Spring 1980 | U.S. dollar begins rise | Worldwide inflation and early signs of recession coupled with real interest differential advantages for dollar-denominated assets contribute to increased demand for dollars |
| August 1982 | Latin American debt crisis | Mexico informs U.S. Treasury on Friday 13, 1982, that it will be unable to make debt service payments; Brazil and Argentina follow in months |
| February 1985 | U.S. dollar peaks | The U.S. dollar peaks against most major industrial currencies, hitting record highs against the deutsche mark and other European currencies |
| September 1985 | Plaza Agreement | Group of Ten members meet at the Plaza Hotel in New York City to sign an international cooperative agreement to control the volatility of world currency markets and to establish target zones |
| February 1987 | Louvre Accords | Group of Six members state they will "intensify" economic policy coordination to promote growth and reduce external imbalances |
| December 1991 | Maastricht Treaty | European Union concludes a treaty to replace all individual currencies with a single currency — the euro |
| September 1992 | EMS crisis | High German interest rates induce massive capital flows into deutsche mark-denominated assets causing the withdrawal of the Italian lira and British pound from the EMS's common float |
| July 31, 1993 | EMS realignment | EMS adjusts allowable deviation band to ±15% for all member countries (except the Dutch guilder); U.S. dollar continues to weaken; Japanese yen reaches ¥100.25/$ |
| 1994 | EMI founded | European Monetary Institute (EMI), the predecessor to the European Central Bank, is founded in Frankfurt, Germany |
| December 1994 | Peso collapse | Mexican peso suffers major devaluation as a result of increasing pressure on the managed devaluation policy; peso falls from Ps3.46/$ to Ps5.50/$ within days. The peso's collapse results in a fall in most major Latin American exchanges in a contagion process — the "tequila effect" |
| August 1995 | Yen peaks | Japanese yen reaches an all-time high versus the U.S. dollar of ¥79/$; yen slowly depreciates over the following two-year period, rising to over ¥130/$ |
| June 1997 | Asian crisis | The Thai baht is devalued in July, followed soon after by the Indonesian rupiah, Korean won, Malaysian ringgit, and Philippine peso. Following the initial exchange rate devaluations, the Asian economy plummets into recession |
| August 1998 | Russian crisis | On Monday August 17 the Russian Central Bank devalues the rouble by 34%. The rouble continues to deteriorate in the following days sending the already weak Russian economy into recession |
| January 1, 1999 | Euro launched | Official launch date for the single European currency, the euro. Eleven European Union member states elect to participate in the system, which irrevocably locks their individual currencies rates between them |
| January 1999 | Brazilian real crisis | The real, initially devalued 8.3% by the Brazilian government on January 12, is allowed to float against the world's currencies |

**EXHIBIT 2.3 (*CONTINUED*)**

World Currency Events, 1971–2004

| Date | Event | Impact |
|------|-------|--------|
| January 1, 2002 | Euro coinage | Euro coins and notes are introduced in parallel with home currencies. National currencies are phased out during the six-month period beginning January 1 |
| January 8, 2002 | Argentine peso crisis | The Argentine peso, its value fixed to the U.S. dollar at 1:1 since 1991 through a currency board, is devalued to Ps1.4/$, then floated |
| February 13, 2002 | Venezuelan bolivar floated | The bolivar, fixed to the dollar since 1996, is floated as a result of increasing economic crisis |
| February 14, 2004 | Venezuelan bolivar devalued | Venezuela devalues the bolivar by 17% versus the U.S. dollar, in an attempt to deal with its growing fiscal deficit |

the European Monetary System (EMS) restructuring in 1992 and 1993; the emerging market currency crises, including that of Mexico in 1994, Thailand (and a number of other Asian currencies) in 1997, Russia in 1998, Brazil in 1999; the introduction of the euro in 1999; Turkey in 2001; and Argentina and Venezuela in 2002.

## Contemporary Currency Regimes

The international monetary system today is composed of national currencies, artificial currencies (such as the SDR), and one entirely new currency (euro) that replaced the 11 national European Union currencies on January 1, 1999. All of these currencies are linked to one another via a "smorgasbord" of currency regimes.

### IMF'S EXCHANGE RATE REGIME CLASSIFICATIONS

The International Monetary Fund classifies all exchange rate regimes into eight specific categories. The eight categories span the spectrum of exchange rate regimes from rigidly fixed to independently floating.

1. **Exchange arrangements with no separate legal tender.** The currency of another country circulates as the sole legal tender or the member belongs to a monetary or currency union in which the same legal tender is shared by the members of the union.

2. **Currency board arrangements.** A monetary regime based on an implicit legislative commitment to exchange domestic currency for a specified foreign currency at a fixed exchange rate, combined with restrictions on the issuing authority to ensure the fulfillment of its legal obligation.

3. **Other conventional fixed peg arrangements.** The country pegs its currency (formally or *de facto*) at a fixed rate to a major currency or a basket of currencies (a *composite*), where the exchange rate fluctuates within a narrow margin or at most ±1% around a central rate.

4. **Pegged exchange rates within horizontal bands.** The value of the currency is maintained within margins of fluctuation around a formal or *de facto* fixed peg that are wider than ±1% around a central rate.

5. **Crawling pegs.** The currency is adjusted periodically in small amounts at a fixed, preannounced rate or in response to changes in selective quantitative indicators.

6. **Exchange rates within crawling pegs.** The currency is maintained within certain fluctuation margins around a central rate that is adjusted periodically at a fixed preannounced rate or in response to change in selective quantitative indicators.

7. **Managed floating with no preannounced path for the exchange rate.** The monetary authority influences the movements of the exchange rate through active intervention in the foreign exchange market without specifying, or precommitting to, a preannounced path for the exchange rate.

8. **Independent floating.** The exchange rate is market determined, with any foreign exchange intervention aimed at moderating the rate of change and preventing undue fluctuations in the exchange rate, rather than at establishing a level for it.

The most prominent example of a rigidly fixed system is the euro area, in which the euro is the single currency for its member countries. However, the euro itself is an independently floating currency against all other currencies. Other examples of rigidly fixed exchange regimes include Ecuador and Panama, which use the U.S. dollar as their official currency, the Central African Franc (CFA) zone, in which countries such as Mali, Niger, Senegal, Cameroon, and Chad among others use a single common currency (the franc, tied to the euro), and the Eastern Caribbean Currency Union (ECCU) whose members use a single common currency (the Eastern Caribbean dollar).

At the other extreme are countries with independently floating currencies. These include many of the most developed countries such as Japan, the United States, the United Kingdom, Canada, Australia, New Zealand, Sweden, and Switzerland. However, this category also includes a number of unwilling participants — emerging market countries that tried to maintain fixed rates but were forced by the marketplace to let them float. Among these are Korea, the Philippines, Brazil, Indonesia, Mexico, and Thailand.

It is important to note that only the last two categories, approximately 80 of the 186 countries covered, are actually "floating" in any real degree. Although the contemporary international monetary system is typically referred to as a "floating regime," it is clearly not the case for the majority of the world's nations.

## FIXED VERSUS FLEXIBLE EXCHANGE RATES

A nation's choice as to which currency regime to follow reflects national priorities about all facets of the economy, including inflation, unemployment, interest rate levels, trade balances, and economic growth. The choice between fixed and flexible rates may change over time as priorities change.

At the risk of overgeneralizing, the following points partly explain why countries pursue certain exchange rate regimes. They are based on the premise that, other things being equal, countries would prefer fixed exchange rates.

- Fixed rates provide stability in international prices for the conduct of trade. Stable prices aid in the growth of international trade and lessen risks for all businesses.

- Fixed exchange rates are inherently anti-inflationary, requiring the country to follow restrictive monetary and fiscal policies. This restrictiveness, however, can often be a burden to a country wishing to pursue policies that alleviate continuing internal economic problems, such as high unemployment or slow economic growth.
- Fixed exchange rate regimes necessitate that central banks maintain large quantities of international reserves (hard currencies and gold) for use in the occasional defense of the fixed rate. As international currency markets have grown rapidly in size and volume, increasing reserve holdings has become a significant burden to many nations.
- Fixed rates, once in place, may be maintained at levels inconsistent with economic fundamentals. As the structure of a nation's economy changes, and as its trade relationships and balances evolve, the exchange rate itself should change. Flexible exchange rates allow this to happen gradually and efficiently, but fixed rates must be changed administratively — usually too late, too highly publicized, and at too large a one-time cost to the nation's economic health.

## ATTRIBUTES OF THE "IDEAL" CURRENCY

If the ideal currency existed in today's world, it would possess three attributes (illustrated in Exhibit 2.4), often referred to as *the impossible trinity*:

1. **Exchange rate stability.** The value of the currency would be fixed in relationship to other major currencies so traders and investors could be relatively certain of the foreign exchange value of each currency in the present and into the near future.

2. **Full financial integration.** Complete freedom of monetary flows would be allowed, so traders and investors could willingly and easily move funds from one country and currency to another in response to perceived economic opportunities or risks.

3. **Monetary independence.** Domestic monetary and interest rate policies would be set by each individual country to pursue desired national economic policies, especially as they might relate to limiting inflation, combating recessions, and fostering prosperity and full employment.

The reason these qualities are termed *the impossible trinity* is that a country must give up one of the three goals described by the sides of the triangle, monetary independence, exchange rate stability, or full financial integration. The forces of economics do not allow the simultaneous achievement of all three. For example, a country with a pure float exchange rate regime can have monetary independence and a high degree of financial integration with the outside capital markets, but the result must be a loss of exchange rate stability (the case of the United States). Similarly, a country which maintains very tight controls over the inflow and outflow of capital will retain its monetary independence and a stable exchange rate, but at the loss of being integrated with global financial and capital markets (the case of Malaysia in the 1998–2002 period).

As illustrated in Exhibit 2.4, the consensus of many experts is that the force of increased capital mobility has been pushing more and more countries toward full financial integration in an attempt to stimulate their domestic economies and feed the capital appetites of their own MNEs. As a result, their currency regimes are being

**EXHIBIT 2.4**

The Impossible Trinity

Source: Adapted from "The International Financial Architecture," Jeffrey A. Frankel, *Brookings Policy Brief #51*, June 1999.

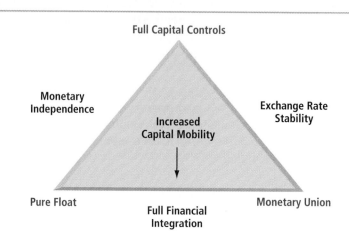

Economic and financial theory clearly states that a country cannot be on all three sides of the triangle at once. It must give up one of the three "attributes" if it is to achieve one of the states described by the corners of the triangle.

"cornered" into being either purely floating (like the United States) or integrated with other countries in monetary unions (like the European Union).

## Emerging Markets and Regime Choices

The 1997–2004 period saw increasing pressures on emerging market countries to choose among more extreme types of exchange rate regimes. The increased capital mobility pressures noted in the previous section have driven a number of countries to choose between either a free-floating exchange rate (such as Turkey in February 2002) or the opposite extreme, a fixed-rate regime — a *currency board* (Argentina, which proved unsuccessful) or even *dollarization* (as in the case of Ecuador in 2000).

### CURRENCY BOARDS

A *currency board* exists when a country's central bank commits to back its monetary base — its money supply — entirely with foreign reserves at all times. This means that a unit of domestic currency cannot be introduced into the economy without an additional unit of foreign exchange reserves being obtained first. Eight countries, including Hong Kong, utilize currency boards as a means of fixing their exchange rates.

**ARGENTINA.**   In 1991, Argentina moved from its previous managed exchange rate of the Argentine peso to a currency board. The currency board structure fixed the Argentine peso's value to the U.S. dollar on a one-to-one basis. The Argentine government preserved the fixed rate of exchange by requiring that every peso issued through the Argentine banking system be backed by either gold or U.S. dollars held on account in banks in Argentina. This 100% reserve system made the monetary policy of Argentina depend on the country's ability to obtain U.S. dollars through trade or investment. Only after Argentina had earned these dollars through trade could its money supply be expanded. This eliminated the possibility of the nation's money supply growing too rapidly and causing inflation.

An additional feature of the Argentine currency board system was the ability of all Argentines or foreigners to hold dollar-denominated accounts in Argentine banks. These accounts were in actuality *Eurodollar accounts* — dollar-denominated deposits in non-U.S. banks. These accounts provided savers or investors the ability to choose whether or not to hold pesos.

From the very beginning, however, there was substantial doubt in the market that the Argentine government could maintain the fixed exchange rate. Argentine banks regularly paid slightly higher interest rates on peso-dominated accounts than on dollar-dominated accounts. This interest differential represented a market-determined *risk premium* of the system itself. Depositors were rewarded for accepting risk — for keeping their money in peso-dominated accounts. This was an explicit signal by the marketplace that there was a perceived possibility that what was then "fixed" would not always be so.

The market proved to be correct. In January 2002, after months of economic and political turmoil and nearly three years of economic recession, the Argentine currency board was ended. The peso was first devalued from Peso 1.00/$ to Peso 1.40/$, then floated completely. It fell in value dramatically within days. The Argentine decade-long experiment with a rigidly fixed exchange rate was over. The devaluation followed months of turmoil, including continuing bank holidays and riots in the streets of Buenos Aires.

## DOLLARIZATION

Several countries have suffered currency devaluation for many years, primarily as a result of inflation, and have taken steps toward dollarization. *Dollarization* is the use of the U.S. dollar as the official currency of the country. Panama has used the dollar as its official currency since 1907. Ecuador, after suffering a severe banking and inflationary crisis in 1998 and 1999, adopted the U.S. dollar as its official currency in January 2000. One of the primary attributes of dollarization was summarized well by *Business Week* in a December 11, 2000, article entitled "The Dollar Club":

> *One attraction of dollarization is that sound monetary and exchange-rate policies no longer depend on the intelligence and discipline of domestic policymakers. Their monetary policy becomes essentially the one followed by the U.S., and the exchange rate is fixed forever.*

The arguments for dollarization follow logically from the previous discussion of the impossible trinity. A country which dollarizes removes any currency volatility (against the dollar) and would theoretically eliminate the possibility of future currency crises. Additional benefits are expectations of greater economic integration with the United States and other dollar-based markets, both product and financial markets. This last point has led many to argue in favor of regional dollarization, in which several countries which are highly economically integrated may benefit significantly from dollarizing together.

Three major arguments exist against dollarization. The first is the loss of sovereignty over monetary policy. This was, however, the point of dollarization. Secondly, the country loses the power of seignorage, the ability to profit from its ability to print its own money. Third, the central bank of the country, because it no longer has the ability to create money within its economic and financial system, can no longer serve the role of lender of last resort. This role carries with it the ability to provide liquidity to save financial institutions which may be on the brink of failure during times of financial crisis.

**ECUADOR.**    Ecuador officially completed the replacement of the Ecuadorian sucre with the U.S. dollar as legal tender on September 9, 2000. This made Ecuador the largest national adopter of the U.S. dollar, and in many ways set it up as a test case of dollarization for other emerging market countries to watch closely. As illustrated by Exhibit 2.5, this was the last stage of a massive depreciation of the sucre in a brief two-year period.

During 1999, Ecuador suffered a rising rate of inflation and a falling level of economic output. In March of 1999 the Ecuadorian banking sector was hit with a series of devastating "bank runs," financial panics in which all depositors attempted to withdraw all of their funds simultaneously. Although there were severe problems in the Ecuadorian banking system, the truth was that even the healthiest financial institution would fail under the strain of this financial drain. Ecuador's president at that time, Mr. Jamil Mahuad, immediately froze all deposits (what was termed a *bank holiday* in the United States in the 1930s in which banks closed their doors). The Ecuadorian sucre, which in January 1999 was trading at roughly Sucre 7,400/dollar, plummeted in early March to Sucre 12,500/dollar. Ecuador defaulted on more than $13.6 billion in foreign debt in 1999 alone. President Mahuad moved quickly to propose dollarization to save the failing Ecuadorian economy.

By January 2000, when the next president took office (after a rather complicated military coup and subsequent withdrawal), the sucre had fallen in value to Sucre 20,000/dollar. The new president, Gustavo Naboa, continued the dollarization initiative. Although not supported by either the U.S. government or the International

**EXHIBIT 2.5**

The Ecuadorian Sucre Exchange Rate, November 1998–March 2000

Source: Pacific Currency Exchange, http://pacific. commerce.ubc.ca/xr

©2001 by Prof. Werner Antweiler, University of British Columbia, Vancouver, BC, Canada.

**Daily Exchange Rates: Ecuadorian Sucre per U.S. Dollar**

**EXHIBIT 2.6**

The Currency
Regime Choices
for Emerging
Markets

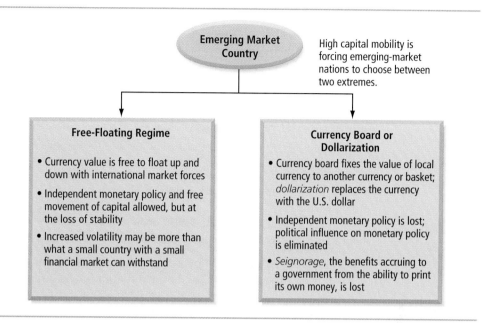

Monetary Fund, Ecuador completed its replacement of its own currency with the dollar over the next nine months.

The results of dollarization in Ecuador are still unknown. Ecuadorian residents did immediately return over $600 million into the banking system, money which they had withheld from the banks in fear of bank failure. This added capital infusion along with new IMF loans and economic restructurings allowed the country to actually close 2000 with a small 1.0% economic gain. Inflation, however, remained high, closing the year at over 91% (up from 66% in 1999). Clearly, dollarization alone did not eliminate inflationary forces. Ecuador continues to struggle to find the balance both economically and politically with its new currency regime.

There is no doubt that for many emerging markets a currency board, dollarization, and freely floating exchange rate regimes are all extremes. In fact, many experts feel that the global financial marketplace will drive more and more emerging market nations toward one of these extremes. As illustrated by Exhibit 2.6, there is a distinct lack of middle ground left between rigidly fixed and freely floating. In anecdotal support of this argument, a poll of the general population in Mexico in 1999 indicated that 9 out of 10 people would prefer dollarization over a floating-rate peso. Clearly, there are many in the emerging markets of the world who have little faith in their leadership and institutions to implement an effective exchange rate policy.

## The Birth of a Currency: The Euro

The original 15 members of the European Union are also members of the European Monetary System (EMS). This group has tried to form an island of fixed exchange rates among themselves in a sea of major floating currencies. Members of the EMS rely heavily on trade with each other, so they perceive that the day-to-day benefits of fixed exchange rates between them are great. Nevertheless the EMS has undergone a number of major changes since its inception in 1979, including major crises and reorganizations in 1992 and 1993, and conversion of 11 members to the euro on January 1, 1999 (Greece joined in 2001). In December 1991, the members of the European Union met at Maastricht, the Netherlands, and concluded a treaty which changed Europe's currency future.

**TIMETABLE.**    The Maastricht Treaty specified a timetable and a plan to replace all individual ECU currencies with a single currency, called the *euro*. Other steps were adopted that would lead to a full European Economic and Monetary Union (EMU).

**CONVERGENCE CRITERIA.**    To prepare for the EMU, the Maastricht Treaty called for the integration and coordination of the member countries' monetary and fiscal policies. The EMU would be implemented by a process called *convergence*. Before becoming a full member of the EMU, each member country was originally expected to meet the following convergence criteria:

1. Nominal inflation should be no more than 1.5% above the average for the three members of the EU with the lowest inflation rates during the previous year.
2. Long-term interest rates should be no more than 2% above the average for the three members with the lowest interest rates.
3. The fiscal deficit should be no more than 3% of gross domestic product.
4. Government debt should be no more than 60% of gross domestic product.

The convergence criteria were so tough that few, if any, of the members could satisfy them at that time, but 11 countries managed to do so just prior to 1999.

**STRONG CENTRAL BANK.**    A strong central bank, called the European Central Bank (ECB), has been established in Frankfurt, Germany, in accordance with the Treaty. The bank is modeled after the U.S. Federal Reserve System. This independent central bank dominates the country central banks, which continue to regulate banks resident within their borders; all financial market intervention and the issuance of euros will remain the sole responsibility of the ECB. The single most important mandate of the ECB is to promote price stability within the European Union.

## WHY MONETARY UNIFICATION?

According to the EU, EMU is a single-currency area, now known informally as *euro zone*, within the EU single market in which people, goods, services, and capital are supposed to move without restrictions. Beginning with the Treaty of Rome in 1957 and continuing with the Single European Act of 1987, the Maastricht Treaty of 1991–1992, and the Treaty of Amsterdam of 1997, a core set of European countries worked steadily toward integrating their individual countries into one larger, more efficient, domestic market. Even after the launch of the 1992 Single Europe program, however, a number of barriers to true openness remained. The use of different currencies required both consumers and companies to treat the individual markets separately. Currency risk of cross-border commerce still persisted. The creation of a single currency is designed to move beyond these vestiges of separated markets.

The official abbreviation of the euro, EUR, has been registered with the International Standards Organization (letter abbreviations are needed for computer-based worldwide trading). This is similar to the three-letter computer symbols used for the U.S. dollar, USD, and the British pound sterling, GBP. The official symbol of the euro is €. According to the EU, the symbol was inspired by the Greek letter *epsilon* (ε), simultaneously referring to Greece's ancient role as the source of European civilization and recalling the first letters of the word *Europe*.

## THE LAUNCH OF THE EURO

On January 4, 1999, 11 member states of the EU initiated the EMU. They established a single currency, the *euro*, which replaced the individual currencies of the participating member states. The 11 countries were Austria, Belgium, Finland, France, Germany, Ireland, Italy, Luxembourg, the Netherlands, Portugal, and Spain. The United Kingdom, Sweden, and Denmark chose to maintain their individual currencies. Greece did not qualify for EMU but joined the euro group in 2001. On December 31, 1998, the final fixed rates between the 11 participating currencies and the euro were put into place. On January 4, 1999, the euro was officially launched. Although the result of a long-term and methodical program for the alignment of all political and economic forces in the EU, the launch of the euro was only the first of many steps to come. The impacts of the euro on the economic environment and on society in general within the participating countries have been and will continue to be dramatic. It is only now becoming apparent what some of the impacts might be.

The euro affects markets in three ways: (1) countries within the euro zone enjoy cheaper transaction costs; (2) currency risks and costs related to exchange rate uncertainty are reduced; and (3) all consumers and businesses both inside and outside the euro zone enjoy price transparency and increased price-based competition.

## ACHIEVING MONETARY UNIFICATION

If the euro is to be a successful replacement for the currencies of the participating EU states, it must have an economic foundation that is solid. The primary driver of a currency's value is its ability to maintain its purchasing power (money is worth what money can buy). The single largest threat to maintaining purchasing power is inflation. So, job one for the EU since the beginning has been to construct an economic system which would work to prevent inflationary forces from undermining the euro.

**FISCAL POLICY AND MONETARY POLICY.**   Monetary policy for the EMU is conducted by the European Central Bank (ECB), which has one responsibility: to safeguard the stability of the euro. Following the basic structures which were used in the establishment of the Federal Reserve System in the United States and the Bundesbank in Germany, the ECB is free of political pressures that have historically caused monetary authorities to yield to employment pressures by inflating economies. The ECB's independence allows it to focus simply on the stability of the currency without falling victim to history's trap.

**FIXING THE VALUE OF THE EURO.**   The December 31, 1998, fixing of the rates of exchange between national currencies and the euro were permanent fixes for these currencies. The United Kingdom has been skeptical of increasing EU infringement on its sovereignty, and has opted not to participate. Sweden, which has failed to see significant benefits from EU membership (although it is one of the newest members), has also been skeptical of EMU participation. Denmark, like the United Kingdom and Sweden, has a strong political element which is highly nationalistic, and so far has opted not to participate.

On January 4, 1999, the euro began trading on world currency markets. Its introduction was a smooth one. The euro's value slid steadily following its introduction, however, primarily as a result of the robustness of the U.S. economy and U.S. dollar, and continuing sluggish economic sectors in the EMU countries. Exhibit 2.7 illustrates the euro's value since its introduction in January 1999. After declining in value against the U.S. dollar over 1999 and 2000, the euro traded in a relatively narrow band throughout 2001. Beginning in early 2002, however, the euro started a strong and steady rise in value versus the dollar, peaking $1.36/€ in late 2004.

**CAUSES OF THE DOLLAR DECLINE.**    During the whole period since the introduction of the euro to the present time, the United States has experienced severe balance of payments deficits on current account (explained in Chapter 3). The biggest deficits were with China and Japan. However, in order to protect their export competitiveness, both China and Japan followed macroeconomic policies that would maintain fixed exchanges rates between their currencies and the U.S. dollar. In order to accomplish this result, both China and Japan had to intervene in the foreign exchange market by buying up massive amounts of U.S. dollars while selling corresponding amounts of their own currencies, the Chinese renminbi (Rmb) and the Japanese yen (¥). These purchases showed up as capital inflows into the United States. However, as the United

**EXHIBIT 2.7**

The U.S. Dollar/Euro Spot Exchange Rate, 1999–2004 (Monthly Average)

Source: ©2004 by Prof. Werner Antweiler, University of British Columbia, Vancouver BC, Canada. Time period shown in diagram: 1/Jan/1999– 31/Dec/2004.

Monthly Avg. Exchange Rates: U.S. Dollars per European Euro

States continued to maintain historically low interest rates to stimulate its domestic economy, some critics wondered if China and Japan would continue to hold so many U.S. dollars. *Real World Example 2.1* illustrates this dilemma for China.

**EXPANSION OF THE EUROPEAN UNION AND THE EURO.**   On May 1, 2004 the European Union added 10 more countries to its ranks. Although none of the new countries is qualified at the moment to adopt the euro as its currency, expansion of the euro is expected over the next six years. *Real World Example 2.2* lists these 10 countries, their currency regimes, and their likely transition to the euro.

## Real World Example 2.1
### THE CHINESE YUAN (OR RENMINBI)

For years, China has effectively exported deflation to the U.S. by flooding the market with cheap goods. The U.S. and other industrialized nations have long argued that China is able to do so largely because its currency, the yuan, is grossly undervalued at its current peg of 8.28 to the dollar. That may be about to change. Under global pressure, Chinese authorities have been making noises about allowing the yuan to drift higher soon. That would raise the price of Chinese exports to the U.S. and elsewhere. Here is a guide to the major issues.

**Are the Whispers That China Is Weighing a Revaluation True?**

What has the markets whipped up are media reports out of Beijing suggesting that China will let its currency appreciate 5% perhaps as early as March, and another 5% in 2005. Yet Beijing has signaled that it is in no great hurry to free the yuan. China needs a cheap yuan to fuel its high-speed growth and keep employment expanding. Also, clobbering the profits of exporters could be doubly damaging, since many of them are indebted to the country's already ailing Big Four state-owned banks.

\* \* \*

**How Will China's Financial Mandarins Manage Revaluation, However Modest?**

The government could simply change the peg. Or it could widen the trading band — now a constricted .03% — so that the yuan will naturally rise. Another approach is to create a basket of currencies consisting of the dollar, yen, and euro, along with regional currencies such as the Korean won, all of which are important to Chinese trade. Each component of the basket would trade — or, in market jargon, "crawl" — vs. the yuan. The yuan might appreciate against the dollar, but depreciate against other currencies, so that Chinese products remain price-competitive in other markets.

**If the Dollar Weakens Against the Yuan, Will China Lose Its Healthy Appetite for U.S. Treasury Bonds?**

It's true that to maintain the currency's peg to the dollar, the Chinese have recycled their massive export earnings and capital inflows into U.S. Treasuries. Some 70% of Beijing's $400 billion in foreign currency reserves are in dollars. If China opts for a basket, it may rebalance its reserves by investing in more yen and euro bonds. But scare stories about a Chinese exodus that triggers a U.S. bond crash are nonsense. "At the margin, the Chinese might purchase less U.S. debt," says Michael D. Kurtz, a currency strategist with Bear Stearns Asia Ltd. in Hong Kong. But it won't be enough to roil the markets: The U.S. still boasts the most liquid and safest bond market in the world.

\* \* \*

**But Hasn't China Committed Itself to Serious Financial Reform?**

Yes, Beijing understands that it needs to recapitalize its banks, clean up its equity markets, and somehow keep the economy firing on all cylinders to absorb a massive army of jobseekers. And Chinese officials see the benefits of a more flexible currency regime if China is going to become a full-fledged member of the international community. Whether they carry through on those reforms is still an open question. But the answer could have big implications for U.S. and global inflation.

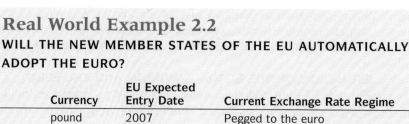

## Real World Example 2.2
### WILL THE NEW MEMBER STATES OF THE EU AUTOMATICALLY ADOPT THE EURO?

| Country | Currency | EU Expected Entry Date | Current Exchange Rate Regime |
|---|---|---|---|
| Cyprus | pound | 2007 | Pegged to the euro |
| Czech Republic | koruna | 2009/10 | Free floating, references the euro |
| Estonia | kroon | 2007 | Pegged to the euro in early 1999 |
| Hungary | forint | 2009/10 | ERM-II type band since May 2001 |
| Latvia | lat | 2008 | Pegged to the IMF's SDR since 1994 |
| Lithuania | litas | 2007 | Pegged to the euro since February 2002 |
| Malta | lira | 2007/08 | Pegged to a basket (70% euro, 20% sterling, 10% dollar) |
| Poland | zloty | 2008/09 | Free floating since April 2000 |
| Slovakia | koruna | 2009 | Free floating since October 1998 |
| Slovenia | tolar | 2008 | Managed float, euro reference rate |

The 10 new member states acceding to the EU on May 1, 2004 (Czech Republic, Estonia, Cyprus, Latvia, Lithuania, Hungary, Malta, Poland, Slovenia and Slovakia) will not automatically adopt the euro by joining the EU. They will only do so once they have achieved the high degree of sustainable economic convergence with the euro area required for membership of the single currency.

They will thus need to fulfill the same Maastricht convergence criteria that were applied to the existing euro area members, namely a high degree of price stability, sustainable government finances (in terms of both public deficit and public debt levels), a stable exchange rate, and conver-

gence in long-term interest rates. There is no pre-defined timetable for adoption of the euro by the new member states, but the levels of convergence required for membership will be assessed by the Council of the EU on a proposal from the European Commission and on the basis of convergence reports by the Commission and the European Central Bank. These reports are produced at least every two years or at the request of a member state wishing to adopt the euro.

Sources: "EU Enlargement and the Adoption of the Euro," *AIG Global Treasury*, Economic Research Unit; The euro homepage, http://europa.eu.int/comm/economy_finance/euro/faqs/faqs_19_en.htm. Accessed May 19, 2004.

## Exchange Rate Regimes: What Lies Ahead?

All exchange rate regimes must deal with the tradeoff between *rules* and *discretion*, as well as between *cooperation* and *independence*. Exhibit 2.8 illustrates the tradeoffs between exchange rate regimes based on rules, discretion, cooperation, and independence.

- Horizontally, the tradeoff for countries participating in a specific system is between consulting and acting in unison with other countries — *cooperation* — or operating as a member of the system, but acting on their own — *independence*.

- Vertically, different exchange rate arrangements may dictate whether the country's government has strict intervention requirements — *rules* — or whether it may choose whether, when, and to what degree to intervene in the foreign exchange markets — *discretion*.

Regime structures like the gold standard required no cooperative policies among countries, only the assurance that all would abide by the "rules of the game." In the gold standard in effect prior to World War II, this translated into the willingness of governments to buy or sell gold at parity rates on demand. The Bretton Woods

## EXHIBIT 2.8

The Tradeoffs
Between
Exchange Rate
Regimes

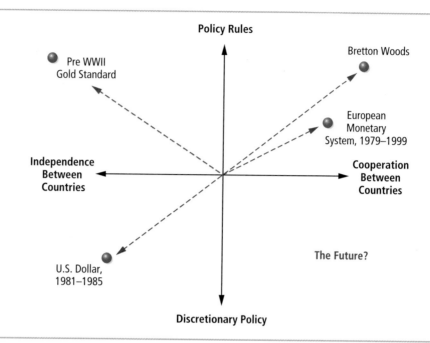

Agreement, the system in place between 1944 and 1973, required more in the way of cooperation in that gold was no longer the "rule," and countries were required to cooperate to a higher degree to maintain the dollar-based system. Exchange rate systems, like the European Monetary System's fixed exchange rate band system used from 1979 to 1999, were hybrids of these cooperative and rule regimes.

The present international monetary system is characterized by no rules, with varying degrees of cooperation. Although there is no present solution to the continuing debate over what form a new international monetary system should take, many believe that it could succeed only if it combined cooperation among nations with individual discretion to pursue domestic social, economic, and financial goals.

## MINI-CASE

# The Creation of Eurodollars

Eurodollar creation can be explained with a simple example. Assume a French firm (FF) has $10 million in a soon-maturing certificate of deposit (CD) in a New York bank (NYB) on which it is earning 5%. The $10,00,000 shows on the books of the two entities as follows (000 omitted):

### New York Bank (NYB)

| | | |
|---|---|---|
| | I CD $_{FF @ 5.00\%}$ | 10,000 |

### French Firm (FF)

| | | |
|---|---|---|
| CD $_{NYB @ 5.00\%}$   10,000 I | | |

FF wants to continue holding U.S. dollars but would like a higher rate of interest. A London bank (LB) offers to pay 5.25% on dollar-denominated deposits with a three-month

maturity. When the New York bank CD matures, FF instructs its NYB to transfer funds to the London bank, where the sum is placed in a three-month Eurodollar deposit account paying 5.25%. Because the London bank maintains a correspondent account with the New York bank, the actual transfer is effected by the New York bank debiting the account of the French firm and crediting the demand deposit (DD) correspondent account of the London Bank. The books now look like this:

### New York Bank (NYB)

| | | |
|---|---|---|
| | I ~~CD~~ ~~FF @ 5.00%~~ | ~~10,000~~ |
| | I DD $_{LB}$ | 10,000 |

**London Bank (LB)**

| | | |
|---|---|---|
| DD $_{NYB}$  10,000 | CD $_{FF\ @\ 5.25\%}$ | 10,000 |

**French Firm (FF)**

| | |
|---|---|
| CD $_{LB\ @\ 5.25\%}$  10,000 | |

Transfer of the dollar deposit from the New York bank to the London bank creates a Eurodollar deposit: A bank outside of the United States (the London bank) now has a deposit liability denominated in dollars rather than in British pounds. Behind this dollar liability lies a dollar asset in the form of a demand deposit held by the London bank with the New York bank. Hence total deposits in the United States have not diminished, but a NYB liability to a foreign firm has become a liability to a foreign bank. In three months the London bank must return $10,000,000 (plus interest) to FF, which it will do by giving FF a demand deposit on a New York bank or by transferring a New York deposit to any party specified by FF.

At this point, the London bank is temporarily holding a dollar demand deposit in New York, on which it is earning nothing, while simultaneously owing dollars to the FF on which it has promised to pay 5.25%. If the London bank is not to lose on the transaction, it must loan its dollar asset (the New York demand deposit) to an entity at a rate higher than the 5.25% it is paying. Suppose the London bank loans $10,000,000 to an Italian bank (IB) at 5.50%. The books would then look like this:

**New York Bank (NYB)**

| | | |
|---|---|---|
| | ~~CD $_{FF\ @\ 5.00\%}$~~ | ~~10,000~~ |
| | ~~DD $_{LB}$~~ | ~~10,000~~ |
| | DD $_{IB}$ | 10,000 |

**London Bank (LB)**

| | | |
|---|---|---|
| ~~DD $_{NYB}$~~   ~~10,000~~ | CD $_{FF\ @\ 5.25\%}$ | 10,000 |
| Loan $_{IB\ @\ 5.50\%}$   10,000 | | |

**French Firm (FF)**

| | |
|---|---|
| CD $_{LB\ @\ 5.25\%}$   10,000 | |

**Italian Bank (IB)**

| | | |
|---|---|---|
| DD $_{NYB}$   10,000 | Loan $_{LB\ @\ 5.50\%}$ | 10,000 |

The New York bank's deposit liability has now shifted to the Italian bank, and the London bank owns a dollar asset in the form of a dollar loan to the Italian bank on which it is earning one quarter of a percent more than it is paying the FF for the funds. The Italian bank is paying 5.50% for the dollars and (for the moment) is earning nothing.

This chain of lending and relending at slightly higher interest rates can continue for some time. To end the sequence, assume the Italian bank loans dollars to an Italian manufacturer (IM) at 5.75%. The dollars in New York are transferred to the account of the Italian manufacturer, and the books look like this:

**New York Bank (NYB)**

| | | |
|---|---|---|
| | ~~CD $_{FF\ @\ 5.00\%}$~~ | ~~10,000~~ |
| | ~~DD $_{LB}$~~ | ~~10,000~~ |
| | ~~DD $_{IB}$~~ | ~~10,000~~ |
| | DD $_{IM}$ | 10,000 |

**London Bank (LB)**

| | | |
|---|---|---|
| ~~DD $_{NYB}$~~   ~~10,000~~ | CD $_{FF\ @\ 5.25\%}$ | 10,000 |
| Loan $_{IB\ @\ 5.50\%}$   10,000 | | |

**French Firm (FF)**

| | |
|---|---|
| CD $_{LB\ @\ 5.25\%}$   10,000 | |

**Italian Bank (IB)**

| | | |
|---|---|---|
| ~~DD $_{NYB}$~~   ~~10,000~~ | Loan $_{LB\ @\ 5.50\%}$ | 10,000 |
| Loan $_{IM\ @\ 5.75\%}$   10,000 | | |

**Italian Manufacturer (IM)**

| | | |
|---|---|---|
| DD $_{NY}$   10,000 | Loan $_{IB\ @\ 5.75\%}$ | 10,000 |

The Italian manufacturer (IM) borrowed the funds for a business purpose, perhaps to pay for the purchase of new machine tools from the United States. If so, the Italian manufacturer transfers the money to the machine tool manufacturer and the deposit in New York becomes a bank liability to that domestic firm. The residual value of the Eurodollar deposit is that any U.S. person or firm will accept it as payment for goods or services.

Each bank in the chain between the New York bank and the Italian manufacturer has a dollar asset as well as a dollar liability and is earning a profit on the spread between the interest rates. The underlying dollar deposit remains in the New York bank (or in some other U.S. bank), but ownership of it shifts from one depositor to another and eventually back to an American entity.

To repay the loan in six months, the Italian manufacturer must either buy or accumulate (perhaps from exports to the United States) dollars and transfer them to the Italian bank, which will transfer the dollars to the London bank, which will transfer the dollars back to the French firm in the form of a deposit in New York.

The sequence of events just described could have evolved in other directions. Any holder of Eurodollar balances could have invested them in the New York money market, in shares of common stock traded in the United States, in the U.S. real estate market, or directly in a U.S. subsidiary. In all these cases, as in the original, a demand deposit in a U.S. bank is behind each Eurodollar transaction. Foreign banks accepting time deposits in Eurodollars do not "create" funds or expand the dollar money supply in the fashion described in textbooks on domestic money and banking. That is, they do not create new demand deposits in return for loans, as do domestic banks, but simply transfer deposits held in New York at a markup in interest rates.

One might ask why the French firm did not deposit its dollars directly in the Italian bank to earn a higher rate, or why the Italian manufacturer did not borrow directly from the London bank at the lower rate being charged there? Part of the answer lies in the imperfections of international capital markets and part in participants' different perceptions of risk. The French firm may not have known of the Italian bank or have had any easy way to find out that a bank in Italy was paying a higher rate for Eurodollar deposits. In addition the French firm may simply have had more confidence in British banks — a confidence born of geographic proximity and a long history of association, or it

may have wanted to be a good bank client so the London bank would provide other services in the future.

The Italian bank may or may not have aggressively pursued the dollar deposit of the French firm. The Italian manufacturer might be unknown in London and so unable to borrow there without first going through a long process of establishing a credit rating. If the Italian manufacturer were unknown in London, it might have to pay the London bank a rate higher than the rate paid to the Italian bank.

## Summary of Learning Objectives

*Define terms used in reference to exchange rates and currency regimes*

- A *foreign currency exchange rate,* or simply *exchange rate,* is the price of one country's currency in units of another currency or commodity (typically gold or silver).

- *Spot exchange rate* is the quoted price for foreign exchange to be delivered at once, or in two days for interbank transactions. For example, ¥114/$ is a quote for the exchange rate between the Japanese yen and the U.S. dollar.

- *Forward rate* is the quoted price for foreign exchange to be delivered at a specified date in the future. For example, assume the 90-day forward rate for the Japanese yen is quoted as ¥112/$. No currency is exchanged today, but in 90 days it will take 112 yen to buy one U.S. dollar. This can be guaranteed by a *forward exchange contract.*

*Define the difference between devaluation and depreciation*

- *Devaluation* of a currency refers to a drop in foreign exchange value of a currency that is pegged to gold or to another currency. In other words, the par value is reduced. The opposite of devaluation is *revaluation.*

- *Weakening, deterioration,* or *depreciation* of a currency refers to a drop in the foreign exchange value of a floating currency. The opposite of weakening is *strengthening* or *appreciating,* which refers to a gain in the exchange value of a floating currency.

*Learn how the international monetary system has evolved from the days of the gold standard to today's eclectic currency arrangement*

- Under the gold standard (1876–1913), the rules were that each country set the rate at which its currency unit could be converted to a weight of gold.

- During the inter-war years (1914–1944) currencies were allowed to fluctuate over fairly wide ranges in terms of gold and each other. Supply and demand forces determined exchange rate values.

- The Bretton Woods Agreement (1944) established a U.S. dollar-based international monetary system. Under the original provisions of the Bretton Woods Agreement, all countries fixed the value of their currencies in terms of gold but were not required to exchange their currencies for gold. Only the dollar remained convertible into gold ($35 per ounce).

- A variety of economic forces led to the suspension of the convertibility of the dollar into gold in August 1971. Exchange rates of most of the leading trading countries were then allowed to float in relation to the dollar and thus indirectly in relation to gold. After a series of continuing crises in 1972 and 1973, the U.S. dollar and the other leading currencies of the world have floated in value since that time.

*Discover the origin and development of the eurocurrency market*

- Eurocurrencies are domestic currencies of one country on deposit in a second country.

- Although the basic causes of the growth of the Eurocurrency market are economic efficiencies, a number of unique institutional events during the 1950s and 1960s helped its growth. In 1957, British monetary authorities responded to a weakening of the pound by imposing tight controls on U.K.

bank lending in sterling to nonresidents of the United Kingdom. Encouraged by the Bank of England, U.K. banks turned to dollar lending as the only alternative that would allow them to maintain their leading position in world finance. For this they needed dollar deposits. Although New York was home base for the dollar and had a large domestic money and capital market, London became the center for international trading in the dollar because of that city's expertise in international monetary matters and its proximity in time and distance to major customers.

- Additional support for a European-based dollar market came from the balance of payments difficulties the United States experienced during the 1960s, which temporarily separated the U.S. domestic capital market from that of the rest of the world.

*Analyze the characteristics of an ideal currency*

- If the ideal currency existed in today's world, it would possess three attributes: a fixed value, convertibility, and independent monetary policy.

*Explain the currency regime choices faced by emerging market countries*

- Emerging market countries must often choose between two extreme exchange rate regimes, either a free-floating regime or an extremely fixed regime such as a *currency board* or *dollarization.*

*Describe how the euro, a single currency for the European Union, was created and what its effects are*

- The original 15 members of the European Union are also members of the European Monetary System (EMS). This group has tried to form an island of fixed exchange rates among themselves in a sea of major floating currencies. Members of the EMS rely heavily on trade with each other, so the day-to-day benefits of fixed exchange rates between them are perceived to be great.

- On May 1, 2004 the European Union admitted an additional 10 countries, reaching a total of 25 countries as members. The 10 new members are expected to work toward adoption of the euro gradually over the next six to seven years.

- The euro affects markets in three ways: (1) countries within the euro zone enjoy cheaper transaction costs; (2) currency risks and costs related to

exchange rate uncertainty are reduced; and (3) all consumers and businesses both inside and outside the euro zone enjoy price transparency and increased price-based competition.

## QUESTIONS

1. **The gold standard and the money supply.** Under the gold standard all national governments promised to follow the "rules of the game." This meant defending a fixed exchange rate. What did this promise imply about a country's money supply?

2. **Causes of devaluation.** If a country follows a fixed exchange rate regime, what macroeconomic variables could cause the fixed exchange rate to be devalued?

3. **Fixed versus flexible exchange rates.** What are the advantages and disadvantages of fixed exchange rates?

4. **The impossible trinity.** Explain what is meant by the term *impossible trinity* and what it implies.

5. **Currency board or dollarization.** Fixed exchange rate regimes are sometimes implemented through a *currency board* (Hong Kong) or *dollarization* (Ecuador). What is the difference between the two approaches?

6. **Emerging market exchange rate regimes.** High capital mobility is forcing emerging-market nations to choose between free-floating regimes and currency board or dollarization regimes. What are the main outcomes of each of these regimes from the perspective of emerging market nations?

7. **Argentine currency board.** How did the Argentine currency board function from 1991 to January 2002 and why did it collapse?

8. **The euro.** On January 4, 1999, 11 member states of the European Union initiated the European Monetary Union (EMU) and established a single currency, the euro, which replaced the individual currencies of participating member states. Describe three of the main ways that the euro affects the members of the EMU.

9. **Mavericks.** The United Kingdom, Denmark, and Sweden have chosen not to adopt the euro but rather to maintain their individual currencies. What are the motivations of each of these three countries, which are also members of the European Union?

10. **International Monetary Fund (IMF).** The IMF was established by the Bretton Woods Agreement (1944). What were its original objectives?

11. **Special Drawing Rights.** What are the Special Drawing Rights?

12. **Definitions.** Define the following currency terms:

    a. devaluation

    b. revaluation

    c. depreciation

    d. appreciation

    e. soft or weak

    f. hard or strong

    g. Eurodollar

    h. Euroyen

13. **Exchange rate regime classifications.** The IMF classifies all exchange rate regimes into eight specific categories, which are summarized in this chapter. Under which exchange rate regime would you classify the following countries?

    a. France

    b. United States

    c. Japan

    d. Thailand

14. **The ideal currency.** What are the attributes of the ideal currency?

15. **Bretton Woods failure.** Why did the fixed exchange rate regime of 1945–1973 eventually fail?

16. **EU and euro expansion.** With so many new countries joining the European Union in 2004, when will they officially move to the euro — if ever?

## PROBLEMS

1. **Frankfurt and New York.** In Frankfurt, one can buy a U.S. dollar for €0.9200. In New York, one can buy a euro for $1.0870. What is the foreign exchange rate between the dollar and the euro?

2. **Peso exchange rate changes.** In December 1994 the government of Mexico officially changed the value of the Mexican peso from 3.2 pesos per dollar to 5.5 pesos per dollar. Was this a *devaluation, revaluation, depreciation,* or *appreciation*? Explain.

3. **Good as gold.** Under the gold standard, the price of an ounce of gold in U.S. dollars was $20.67, while the price of that same ounce in British pounds was £4.2474. What would the exchange rate between the dollar and the pound be if the U.S. dollar price had been $38.00 per ounce?

4. **Gold standard.** Before World War I, $20.67 was needed to buy one ounce of gold. If, at the same time one ounce of gold could be purchased in France for FF310.00, what was the exchange rate between French francs and U.S. dollars?

5. **Spot rate — customer.** The spot rate for Mexican pesos is Ps9.5200/$. If your company buys Ps100,000 spot from your bank on Monday, how much must your company pay and on what date?

6. **Forward rate.** The 180-day forward rate for the euro is quoted at €0.9210/$. If your company bought €100,000 forward 180 days on September 6, 2003, how much did your company pay and on what date to settle the forward agreement?

7. **Forward discount on the dollar.** What is the forward discount on the dollar if the spot rate is $1.0200/€ and the 180-day forward rate is $1.0858/€?

8. **Forward premium on the euro.** What is the forward premium on the euro if the spot rate on September 3, 2003 was €0.9804/$ and the 180-day forward rate was €0.9210/$?

9. **Saudi import.** A European-based manufacturer ships a machine tool to a buyer in Jordan. The purchase price is €375,000. Jordan imposes a 12% import duty on all products purchased from the European Union. The Jordanian importer then re-exports the product to a Saudi Arabian importer, but only after imposing their own resale fee of 22%. Given the following spot exchange rates on May 25, 2004, what is the total cost to the Saudi Arabian importer in Saudi Arabian riyal, and what is the U.S. dollar equivalent of that price?

| | |
|---|---|
| Spot rate, Jordanian dinar (JD) per euro (€) | JD 0.8700/€ |
| Spot rate, Jordanian dinar (JD) per U.S. dollar ($) | JD 0.7080/$ |
| Spot rate, Saudi Arabian riyal (SRI) per U.S. dollar | SRI3.750/$ |

10. **Chinese yuan (renminbi) revaluation**. As discussed in *Real World Example 2.1,* many experts believe that the Chinese currency should be floated, or at least revalued, against the U.S. dollar. Assuming that revaluations are for the same rough percentage change as most devaluations, say 20%, what would be the new exchange rate value be if it is currently Rmb8.27/$?

 ## Internet Exercises

1. **International Monetary Fund's Special Drawing Rights.** The Special Drawing Right (SDR) is a composite index of six key participant currencies. Use the IMF's Web site to find the current weights and valuation of the SDR.

    International Monetary Fund
    http://www.imf.org/external/np/exr/facts/sdr.htm

2. **Capital controls.** One of the key sides of the impossible trinity discussed in this chapter is the degree of capital mobility into and out of a country. Use the International Finance subsection of Yahoo! to determine the current state of capital movement freedom for the following countries: Chile, China, Malaysia, Taiwan, and Russia.

    Yahoo!
    http://biz.yahoo.com/ifc/

3. **Dollarization and currency boards.** Use the following Web sites, and any others you may find, to track the on going debate of the relative success of dollarization and currency boards.

    International Monetary Fund
    http://www.imf.org/external/pubind.htm
    National Bureau of Economic Research
    http://papers.nber.org/papers/
    Cato Institute
    http://www.cato.org/pubs/pubs.html
    European Central Bank
    http://www.ecb.inf

4. **Malaysian currency controls.** The institution of currency controls by the Malaysian government in the aftermath of the Asian currency crisis is a classic response by government to unstable currency conditions. Use the following Web site to increase your knowledge of how currency controls work.

    EconEdLink
    http://www.econedlink.org/lessons/index.cfm?lesson=EM25

5. **Personal transfers.** As anyone who has traveled internationally learns, the exchange rates available to private retail customers are not always as attractive as those available to companies. The OzForex Web site possesses a section on "customer rates" which illustrates the difference. Use the site to calculate what the percentage difference between Australian dollar/U.S. dollar spot exchange rates are for retail customers versus interbank rates.

    OzForex
    http://www.ozforex.com.au/cgi-bin/sellQuotes.asp

# The Balance of Payments

## LEARNING OBJECTIVES

Explain how nations measure their own levels of international economic activity and how that is measured by the balance of payments

Examine the economic relationships underlying the two basic subcomponents of the balance of payments — the current account and the financial/capital account balances

Identify the financial dimensions of international economic activity and how they differ between merchandise and services trade

Identify balance of payment activities by nations in the pursuit of macroeconomic policies

Evaluate the history of capital mobility and the conditions that lead to capital flight in times of crisis

International business transactions occur in many different forms over the course of a year. The measurement of all international economic transactions between the residents of a country and foreign residents is called the *balance of payments (BOP)*. The official terminology used throughout this chapter is that of the International Monetary Fund (IMF). Because the IMF is the primary source of similar statistics for balance of payments and economic performance by nations worldwide, its language is more general than other terminology such as that employed by the United States Department of Commerce. Government policymakers need such measures of economic activity in order to evaluate the general competitiveness of domestic industry, to set exchange rate or interest rate policies or goals, and for many other purposes. Multinational businesses use various BOP measures to gauge the growth and health of specific types of trade or financial transactions by country and regions of the world against the home country.

Home-country and host-country BOP data are important to business managers, investors, consumers, and government officials because the data influences and is influenced by other key macroeconomic variables such as gross domestic product, employment, price levels, exchange rates, and interest rates. Monetary and fiscal policy must take the BOP into account at the national level. Business managers and investors need BOP data to anticipate changes in host country economic policies that might be driven by BOP events. BOP data may be important for any of the following reasons:

- The BOP is an important indicator of pressure on a country's foreign exchange rate, and thus on the potential for a firm trading with or investing in that country to experience foreign exchange gains or losses. Changes in the BOP may predict the imposition or removal of foreign exchange controls.
- Changes in a country's BOP may signal the imposition or removal of controls over payment of dividends and interest, license fees, royalty fees, or other cash disbursements to foreign firms or investors.
- The BOP helps to forecast a country's market potential, especially in the short run. A country experiencing a serious trade deficit is not likely to expand imports as it would if running a surplus. It may, however, welcome investments that increase its exports.

## Typical Balance of Payments Transactions

International transactions take many forms. Each of the following examples is an international economic transaction which is counted and captured in the U.S. balance of payments.

- Honda U.S. is the U.S. distributor of automobiles manufactured in Japan by its parent company, Honda of Japan.
- A U.S.–based firm, Fluor Corporation, manages the construction of a major water treatment facility in Bangkok, Thailand.
- The U.S. subsidiary of a French firm, Saint Gobain, pays profits (dividends) back to its parent firm in Paris.
- DaimlerChrysler, the well-known German/American automobile manufacturer, purchases a small automotive parts manufacturer outside Chicago, Illinois.
- An American tourist purchases a small Lapponia necklace in Finland.

**EXHIBIT 3.1**

Generic Balance
of Payments

**A. Current Account**
1. Net export/imports of goods (balance of trade)
2. Net exports/imports of services
3. Net income (investment income from direct and portfolio investment plus employee compensation)
4. Net transfers (sums sent home by migrants and permanent workers abroad, gifts, grants, and pensions)

*A (1–4) = Current Account Balance*

**B. Capital Account**
Capital transfers related to the purchase and sale of fixed assets such as real estate

**C. Financial Account**
1. Net foreign direct investment
2. Net portfolio investment
3. Other financial items

*A + B + C = Basic Balance*

**D. Net Errors and Omissions**
Missing data such as illegal transfers

*A + B + C + D = Overall Balance*

**E. Reserves and Related Items**
Changes in official monetary reserves including gold, foreign exchange, and IMF position

- The U.S. government finances the purchase of military equipment for its NATO (North Atlantic Treaty Organization) military ally, Norway.
- A Mexican lawyer purchases a U.S. corporate bond through an investment broker in Cleveland.

This is a small sample of the hundreds of thousands of international transactions that occur each year. The balance of payments provides a systematic method for classifying these transactions. One rule of thumb always aids the understanding of BOP accounting: "Follow the cash flow."

The BOP is composed of a number of subaccounts that are watched quite closely by groups as diverse as investment bankers, farmers, politicians, and corporate executives. These groups track and analyze the two major subaccounts, the *current account* and the *financial/capital account*, on a continuing basis. Exhibit 3.1 provides an overview of these major subaccounts of the BOP.

## Fundamentals of Balance of Payments Accounting

The BOP must balance. If it does not, something has not been counted or has been counted improperly. It is therefore incorrect to state that the BOP is in disequilibrium. It cannot be. The supply and demand for a country's currency may be imbalanced, but supply and demand are not the same thing as the BOP. A subaccount of the BOP, such as the merchandise trade balance, may be imbalanced, but the entire BOP of a single country is always balanced.

There are three main elements of the actual process of measuring international economic activity: (1) identifying what is and is not an international economic transaction; (2) understanding how the flow of goods, services, assets, and money create debits and credits to the overall BOP; and (3) understanding the bookkeeping procedures for BOP accounting.

## DEFINING INTERNATIONAL ECONOMIC TRANSACTIONS

Identifying international transactions is ordinarily not difficult. The export of merchandise, goods such as trucks, machinery, computers, telecommunications equipment, and so forth, is obviously an international transaction. Imports such as French wine, Japanese cameras, and German automobiles are also clearly international transactions. But this merchandise trade is only a portion of the thousands of different international transactions that occur in the United States or any other country each year.

Many other international transactions are not so obvious. The purchase of a glass figure in Venice, Italy, by a U.S. tourist is classified as a U.S. merchandise import. In fact, all expenditures made by U.S. tourists around the globe for services (meals, hotel accommodations), but not for goods, are recorded in the U.S. balance of payments as imports of travel services in the current account. The purchase of a U.S. Treasury bill by a foreign resident is an international financial transaction and is duly recorded in the financial/capital account of the U.S. balance of payments.

## THE BOP AS A FLOW STATEMENT

The BOP is often misunderstood because many people infer from its name that it is a balance sheet, whereas in fact it is a *cash flow statement*. By recording all international transactions over a period of time such as a year, the BOP tracks the continuing flows of purchases and payments between a country and all other countries. It does not add up the value of all assets and liabilities of a country on a specific date like a balance sheet does for an individual firm.

Two types of business transactions dominate the balance of payments:

1. **Exchange of real assets.** The exchange of goods (for example, automobiles, computers, watches, textiles) and services (for example, banking services, consulting services, travel services, etc.) for other goods and services (barter) or for money.

2. **Exchange of financial assets.** The exchange of financial claims (for example stocks, bonds, loans, purchases or sales of companies, etc.) for other financial claims or money.

Although assets can be identified as real or financial, it is often easier simply to think of all assets as goods that can be bought and sold. The purchase of a hand-woven area rug in a shop in Bangkok by a U.S. tourist is not all that different from a Wall Street banker buying a British government bond for investment purposes.

## BOP ACCOUNTING

The measurement of all international transactions in and out of a country over a year is a daunting task. Mistakes, errors, and statistical discrepancies will occur. The primary problem is that double-entry bookkeeping is employed in theory, but not in practice. Individual purchase and sale transactions should — in theory — result in financing entries in the balance of payments that match. In reality, the entries are recorded independently. Current and financial/capital account entries are recorded independently of one another, not together as double-entry bookkeeping would prescribe. Thus there will be serious discrepancies (to use a nice term for it) between debits and credits.

# The Accounts of the Balance of Payments

The balance of payments is composed of two primary subaccounts, the current account and the financial/capital account. In addition, the *official reserves account* tracks government currency transactions, and a fourth statistical subaccount, the *net errors and omissions account*, is produced to preserve the balance in the BOP. The international economic relationships between countries do, however, continue to evolve, as the recent revision of the major accounts within the BOP discussed below indicates.

## THE CURRENT ACCOUNT

The *current account* includes all international economic transactions with income or payment flows occurring within the year, the *current* period. The current account consists of four subcategories:

1. **Goods trade:** the export and import of goods. Merchandise trade is the oldest and most traditional form of international economic activity. Although many countries depend on imports of goods (as they should according to the theory of comparative advantage), they also normally work to preserve either a balance of goods trade or even a surplus.

2. **Services trade:** the export and import of services. Common international services are financial services provided by banks to foreign importers and exporters, travel services of airlines, and construction services of domestic firms in other countries. For the major industrial countries, this subaccount has shown the fastest growth in the past decade.

3. **Income:** predominantly *current income* associated with investments that were made in previous periods. If a U.S. firm created a subsidiary in South Korea to produce metal parts in a previous year, the proportion of net income that is paid back to the parent company in the current year (the dividend) constitutes current investment income. Additionally, wages and salaries paid to nonresident workers are also included in this category.

4. **Current transfers:** the financial settlements associated with the change in ownership of real resources or financial items. Any transfer between countries that is one-way — a gift or grant — is termed a *current transfer*. For example, funds provided by the U.S. government to aid in the development of a less-developed nation would be a current transfer. Transfers associated with the transfer of fixed assets are included in a separate account, the *financial/capital account*.

All countries possess some amount of trade, most of which is merchandise. Many smaller and less-developed countries have little in the way of service trade, or items that fall under the income or transfers subaccounts.

The *current account* is typically dominated by the first component described, the export and import of merchandise. For this reason, the *balance of trade* (BOT) which is so widely quoted in the business press in most countries refers to the balance of

**EXHIBIT 3.2**

The United States
Current Account,
1998–2002
(billions of US$)

|  | 1998 | 1999 | 2000 | 2001 | 2002 |
|---|---|---|---|---|---|
| Goods exports | 672 | 687 | 775 | 722 | 685 |
| Goods imports | −917 | −1030 | −1224 | −1146 | −1165 |
| Goods trade balance (BOT) | −245 | −343 | −450 | −424 | −479 |
| Services trade credits | 260 | 271 | 291 | 286 | 289 |
| Services trade debits | −182 | −189 | −217 | −219 | −227 |
| Services trade balance | 78 | 81 | 74 | 66 | 61 |
| Income receipts | 259 | 285 | 353 | 277 | 256 |
| Income payments | −265 | −299 | −368 | −267 | −260 |
| Income balance | −6 | −14 | −15 | 11 | −4 |
| Current transfers, credits | 9 | 9 | 10 | 9 | 12 |
| Current transfers, debits | −54 | −58 | −64 | −55 | −70 |
| Net transfers | −44 | −49 | −54 | −47 | −59 |
| Current account balance | −217 | −324 | −445 | −394 | −481 |

Source: Derived from International Monetary Fund's *Balance of Payments Statistics Yearbook, 2003.*

exports and imports of goods trade only. If the country is a larger industrialized country, however, the BOT is somewhat misleading in that service trade is not included.

Exhibit 3.2 summarizes the current account and its components for the United States for the 1998–2002 period. As illustrated, the U.S. goods trade balance has been consistently negative but has been partially offset by the continuing surplus in services trade balance.

## GOODS TRADE

Exhibit 3.3 places the current account values of Exhibit 3.2 in perspective over time by dividing the current account into its two major components: (1) *goods trade* and (2) *services trade and investment income.* The first and most striking message is the magnitude of the goods trade deficit in the period shown (a continuation of a position created in the early 1980s). The balance on services and income, although not large in comparison to net goods trade, has with few exceptions run a surplus over the past two decades.

The deficits in the BOT of the past decade have been an area of considerable concern for the United States, in both the public and private sectors. Merchandise trade is the original core of international trade. The manufacturing of goods was the basis of the industrial revolution, and the focus of the theory of comparative advantage in international trade to be reviewed in Chapter 15. Manufacturing is traditionally a sector of the economy that employs most of a country's workers. The goods trade deficit of the 1980s saw the decline of traditional heavy industries in the United States, industries that through history employed many U.S. workers. Declines in the BOT in areas such as steel, automobiles, automotive parts, textiles, and shoe manufacturing caused massive economic and social disruption.

Understanding merchandise import and export performance is much like understanding the market for any single product. The demand factors that drive both are income, the economic growth rate of the buyer, and price of the product in the eyes of

**EXHIBIT 3.3**

U.S. Trade Balance and Balance on Services and Income, 1985–2002 (billions of US$)

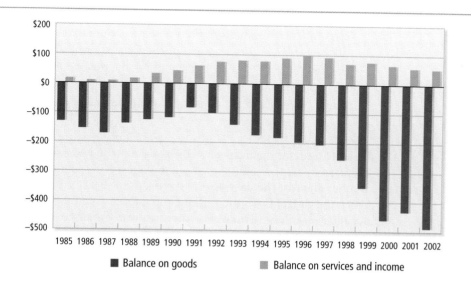

■ Balance on goods ■ Balance on services and income

Source: International Monetary Fund, *Balance of Payments Statistics Yearbook, 2003.*

the consumer after passing through an exchange rate. For example, U.S. merchandise imports reflect the income level of U.S. consumers and growth of industry. As income rises, so does the demand for imports.

Exports follow the same principles but in the reversed position. U.S. manufacturing exports depend not on the incomes of U.S. residents, but on the incomes of buyers of U.S. products in all other countries around the world. When these economies are growing, the demand for U.S. products will also rise.

The service component of the U.S. current account is a mystery to many. As illustrated in both Exhibit 3.2 and Exhibit 3.3, the United States has consistently achieved a surplus in services trade income. The major categories of services include travel and passenger fares, transportation services, expenditures by U.S. students abroad and foreign students pursuing studies in the United States, telecommunications services, and financial services.

## The Capital/Financial Account

The capital/financial account of the balance of payments measures all international economic transactions of financial assets. It is divided into two major components, the capital account and the financial account.

- **The capital account.** The capital account is made up of transfers of financial assets and the acquisition and disposal of nonproduced/nonfinancial assets. This account has been introduced as a separate component in the International Monetary Fund's balance of payments only recently. The magnitude of capital transactions covered is relatively minor, and we will include it in principle in all the following discussion of the financial account.

- **The financial account.** The financial account consists of three components, *direct investment, portfolio investment,* and *other asset investment.* Financial assets can be classified in a number of different ways including the length of the life of the asset (its maturity) and the nature of the ownership (public or private). The financial account, however, uses a third method, the degree of control over assets or operations: *portfolio investment,* where the investor has no control, or *direct investment,* where the investor exerts some explicit degree of control over the assets.

**DIRECT INVESTMENT.**    This is the net balance of capital dispersed from and into the United States for the purpose of exerting control over assets. If a U.S. firm builds a new automotive parts facility in another country or actually purchases a company in another country, this is a *direct investment* in the U.S. balance of payments accounts. When the capital flows out of the United States, it enters the balance of payments as a negative cash flow. If, however, a foreign firm purchases a firm in the United States, it is a capital inflow and enters the balance of payments positively. Whenever 10% or more of the voting shares in a U.S. company are held by foreign investors, the company is classified as the U.S. affiliate of a foreign company, and a *foreign direct investment.* Similarly, if U.S. investors hold 10% or more of the control in a company outside the United States, that company is considered the foreign affiliate of a U.S. company.

The 1980s boom in foreign investment into the United States, or foreign resident purchases of assets in the United States, was extremely controversial. The source of concern over foreign investment in any country, including the United States, focuses on two topics, control and profit. Some countries possess restrictions on what foreigners may own in their country. This rule is based on the premise that domestic land, assets, and industry in general should be owned by residents of the country. On the other hand, the United States has traditionally had few restrictions on what foreign residents or firms can own or control; most restrictions remaining today relate to national security concerns. Unlike the case in the traditional debates over whether international trade should be free, there is no consensus that international investment should necessarily be free. This question is still very much a domestic political concern first, and an international economic issue second.

The second major source of concern over foreign direct investment is who receives the profits from the enterprise. Foreign companies owning firms in the United States will ultimately profit from the activities of the firms, or put another way, from the efforts of U.S. workers. In spite of evidence that indicates foreign firms in the United States reinvest most of their profits in their U.S. businesses (in fact at a higher rate than domestic firms), the debate on possible profit drains has continued. Regardless of the actual choices made, workers of any nation feel the profits of their work should remain in their own hands. Once again, this is in many ways a political and emotional concern more than an economic one.

The choice of words used to describe foreign investment can also influence public opinion. If these massive capital inflows are described as "capital investments from all over the world showing their faith in the future of U.S. industry," the net capital surplus is represented as decidedly positive. If, however, the net capital surplus is described as resulting in "the United States being the world's largest debtor nation," the negative connotation is obvious. Both are essentially spins on the economic principles at work.

Capital, whether short-term or long-term, flows to where the investor believes it can earn the greatest return for the level of risk. And although in an accounting sense this is "international debt," when the majority of the capital inflow is in the form of direct investment, a long-term commitment to jobs, production, services, technological, and other competitive investments, the impact on the competitiveness of industry located within the U.S. is increased. When the "net debtor" label is applied to equity investment, it is misleading in that it invites comparison with large debt crisis conditions suffered by many countries in the past.

**PORTFOLIO INVESTMENT.**    This is net balance of capital that flows in and out of the United States but does not reach the 10% ownership threshold of direct investment. If a U.S. resident purchases shares in a Japanese firm but does not attain the 10% threshold, we define the purchase as a *portfolio investment* (and in this case an outflow of capital). The purchase or sale of debt securities (like U.S. Treasury bills) across borders is also classified as *portfolio investment* because debt securities by definition do not provide the buyer with ownership or control.

*Portfolio investment* is capital invested in activities that are purely profit-motivated (return), rather than ones made to control or manage the investment. Purchases of debt securities, bonds, interest-bearing bank accounts, and the like are intended only to earn a return. They provide no vote or control over the party issuing the debt. Purchases of debt issued by the U.S. government (U.S. Treasury bills, notes, and bonds) by foreign investors constitutes *net portfolio investment* in the United States. It is worth noting that most U.S. debt purchased by foreigners is U.S. dollar-denominated—denominated in the currency of the issuing country. Most foreign debt issued by countries such as Russia, Mexico, Brazil, and Southeast Asian countries is also U.S. dollar-denominated — in this case the currency of a foreign country. The foreign country must earn dollars to repay its foreign-held debt. The United States need not earn any foreign currency to repay its foreign debt.

As illustrated in Exhibit 3.5, portfolio investment has shown much more volatile behavior than net foreign direct investment over the past decade. Many U.S. debt securities such as U.S. Treasury securities and corporate bonds were in high demand in the late 1980s, while surging emerging markets in both debt and equities caused a reversal in direction in the 1990s. The motivating forces for portfolio investment flows are always the same, *return* and *risk*. This fact, however, does not make the flows any more predictable.

**OTHER INVESTMENT ASSETS/LIABILITIES.**    This final category consists of various short-term and long-term trade credits, cross-border loans from all types of financial institutions, currency deposits and bank deposits, and other accounts receivable and payable related to cross-border trade.

Exhibit 3.4 shows the major subcategories of the U.S. financial account balance from 1998 to 2002: *direct investment, portfolio investment,* and *other long-term and short-term capital investment.*

Exhibit 3.5 shows how the major subaccounts of the U.S. financial account — *net direct investment, portfolio investment,* and *other investment* — have changed since 1985.

**EXHIBIT 3.4**

| The U.S. Financial Account and Components, 1998–2002 (billions of US$) | 1998 | 1999 | 2000 | 2001 | 2002 |
|---|---|---|---|---|---|
| Direct investment | | | | | |
| Direct investment abroad | −143 | −155 | −152 | −120 | −138 |
| Direct investment in the U.S. | 178 | 301 | 288 | 152 | 40 |
| Net direct investment | 36 | 146 | 135 | 32 | −98 |
| Portfolio investment | | | | | |
| Assets, net | −136 | −131 | −125 | −85 | 16 |
| Liabilities, net | 269 | 355 | 475 | 425 | 421 |
| Net portfolio investment | 133 | 224 | 350 | 340 | 437 |
| Other investment | | | | | |
| Other investment assets | −74 | −159 | −303 | −140 | −53 |
| Other investment liabilities | 57 | 158 | 262 | 189 | 246 |
| Net other investment | −17 | −1 | −41 | 48 | 193 |
| Net financial account balance | 152 | 368 | 444 | 421 | 532 |

Source: Derived from International Monetary Fund's *Balance of Payments Statistics Yearbook 2003*.

**EXHIBIT 3.5**

The U.S. Financial Account, 1985–2002 (billions of US$)

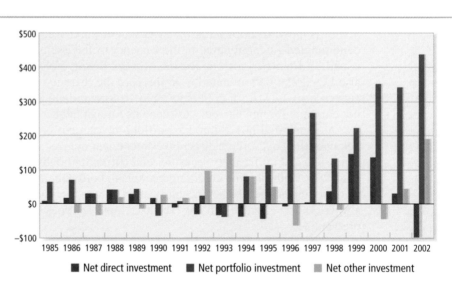

Source: International Monetary Fund, *Balance of Payments Statistics Yearbook, 2003*.

## CURRENT AND FINANCIAL ACCOUNT BALANCE RELATIONSHIPS

Exhibit 3.6 illustrates the current and financial account balances for the United States over recent years. What the exhibit shows is one of the basic economic and accounting relationships of the balance of payments: *the inverse relation between the current and financial accounts*. This inverse relationship is not accidental. The methodology of the balance of payments, double-entry bookkeeping in theory, requires that the current and financial accounts be offsetting. Countries experiencing large current account deficits "finance" these purchases through equally large surpluses in the financial account, and vice versa.

**NET ERRORS AND OMISSIONS.** As noted before, because current and financial account entries are collected and recorded separately, errors or statistical discrepancies will occur. The *net errors and omissions account* ensures that the BOP actually balances.

**OFFICIAL RESERVES ACCOUNT.** The *official reserves account* is the total reserves held by official monetary authorities within the country. These reserves are normally composed of the major currencies used in international trade and financial transactions (so-called hard currencies like the U.S. dollar, European euro, British pound, and the Japanese yen; gold; and Special Drawing Rights, SDRs).

The significance of official reserves depends generally on whether the country is operating under a *fixed exchange rate* regime or a *floating exchange rate* system. If a country's currency is fixed, the government of the country officially declares that the currency is convertible into a fixed amount of some other currency. For example, the South Korean won was fixed to the U.S. dollar for many years. It was the Korean government's responsibility to maintain this fixed rate, also called *parity rate*. If for some reason there was an excess supply of Korean won on the currency market, to prevent the value of the won from falling, the South Korean government had to support the won's value by purchasing won on the open market (by spending its hard currency reserves, its *official reserves*) until the excess supply was eliminated. Under a floating rate system, the Korean government possesses no such responsibility and the role of official reserves is diminished.

**EXHIBIT 3.6**

Current and Financial/Capital Account Balances for the United States, 1992–2002 (billions of US$)

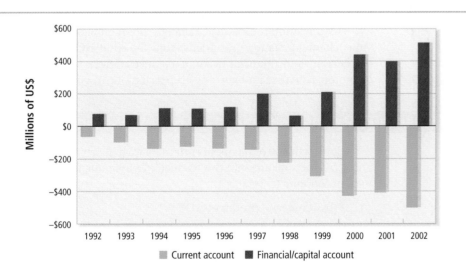

Source: International Monetary Fund, *Balance of Payments Statistics Yearbook, 2003*.

## The Balance of Payments in Total

Exhibit 3.7 provides the official balance of payments for the United States as presented by the International Monetary Fund (IMF), the multinational organization that collects these statistics for over 160 different countries around the globe. Now that the individual accounts and the relationships among the accounts have been discussed, Exhibit 3.7 allows us a comprehensive overview of how the individual accounts are combined to create some of the most useful summary measures for multinational business managers.

The current account (line A in Exhibit 3.7), the capital account (line B), and the financial account (line C) combine to form the *basic balance (Total, Groups A through C).* This balance is one of the most frequently used summary measures of the BOP. It describes the international economic activity of the nation, which is determined by market forces, not by government decisions (such as currency market intervention). The U.S. *basic balance* totaled a deficit of $50 billion in 2002. A second frequently used measure, the *overall balance*, also called the *official settlements balance (Total, Groups A through D* in Exhibit 3.7), was at a surplus of $4 billion in 2002.

The meaning of the BOP has changed over the past 30 years. As long as most of the major industrial countries were still operating under fixed exchange rates, the interpretation of the BOP was relatively straightforward:

- A surplus in the BOP implied that the demand for the country's currency exceeded the supply and that the government should allow the currency value to increase — in value — or intervene and accumulate additional foreign currency reserves in the official reserves account. This intervention would occur as the government sold its own currency in exchange for other currencies, thus building up its stores of hard currencies.
- A deficit in the BOP implied an excess supply of the country's currency on world markets, and the government would then either *devalue* the currency or expend its official reserves to support its value.

The transition to floating exchange rate regimes in the 1970s (described in the previous chapter) changed the focus from the total BOP to its various subaccounts like the current and financial account balances. These subaccounts are the indicators of economic activities and currency repercussions to come.

## The Balance of Payments Interaction with Key Macroeconomic Variables

A nation's balance of payments interacts with nearly all of its key macroeconomic variables. *Interacts* means that the balance of payments affects and is affected by such key macroeconomic factors as

1. Gross domestic product (GDP)
2. The exchange rate
3. Interest rates
4. Inflation rates

## EXHIBIT 3.7

The U.S. Balance of Payments, Analytic Presentation, 1993–2002 (billions of US$)

| | 1993 | 1994 | 1995 | 1996 | 1997 | 1998 | 1999 | 2000 | 2001 | 2002 |
|---|---|---|---|---|---|---|---|---|---|---|
| **A. Current Account** | −82 | −118 | −110 | −121 | −140 | −217 | −324 | −445 | −394 | −481 |
| Goods: exports FOB | 459 | 505 | 577 | 614 | 680 | 672 | 687 | 775 | 722 | 685 |
| Goods: imports FOB | −589 | −669 | −749 | −803 | −877 | −917 | −1030 | −1224 | −1146 | −1165 |
| *Balance on Goods* | −131 | −164 | −172 | −189 | −196 | −245 | −343 | −450 | −424 | −479 |
| Services: credit | 184 | 199 | 217 | 238 | 255 | 260 | 271 | 291 | 286 | 289 |
| Services: debit | −122 | −132 | −142 | −151 | −166 | −182 | −189 | −217 | −219 | −227 |
| *Balance on Goods and Services* | −69 | −97 | −96 | −102 | −108 | −167 | −262 | −376 | −358 | −418 |
| Income: credit | 134 | 165 | 212 | 226 | 261 | 259 | 285 | 353 | 277 | 256 |
| Income: debit | −110 | −149 | −191 | −205 | −252 | −265 | −299 | −368 | −267 | −260 |
| *Balance on Goods, Services, and Income* | −45 | −80 | −76 | −81 | −99 | −173 | −275 | −391 | −347 | −422 |
| Current transfers: credit | 6 | 6 | 8 | 9 | 8 | 9 | 9 | 10 | 9 | 12 |
| Current transfers: debit | −44 | −45 | −42 | −49 | −49 | −54 | −58 | −64 | −55 | −70 |
| **B. Capital Account** | 0 | 0 | 0 | 1 | 0 | 1 | −4 | 1 | −1 | −1 |
| Capital account: credit | 0 | 0 | 1 | 1 | 0 | 1 | 0 | 1 | 1 | 1 |
| Capital account: debit | 0 | −1 | 0 | 0 | 0 | 0 | −4 | 0 | −2 | −2 |
| ***Total, Groups A Plus B*** | −83 | −119 | −110 | −120 | −139 | −217 | −328 | −444 | −395 | −482 |
| **C. Financial Account** | 83 | 125 | 123 | 165 | 273 | 152 | 368 | 444 | 421 | 532 |
| Direct investment | −33 | −34 | −41 | −5 | 1 | 36 | 146 | 135 | 32 | −98 |
| Direct investment abroad | −84 | −80 | −99 | −92 | −105 | −143 | −155 | −152 | −120 | −138 |
| Direct investment in United States | 51 | 46 | 58 | 87 | 106 | 178 | 301 | 288 | 152 | 40 |
| Portfolio investment assets | −146 | −60 | −123 | −150 | −119 | −136 | −131 | −125 | −85 | 16 |
| Equity securities | −63 | −48 | −65 | −83 | −58 | −101 | −114 | −100 | −109 | −18 |
| Debt securities | −83 | −12 | −57 | −67 | −61 | −35 | −17 | −25 | 24 | 33 |
| Portfolio investment liabilities | 111 | 139 | 237 | 368 | 386 | 269 | 355 | 475 | 425 | 421 |
| Equity securities | 21 | 1 | 17 | 11 | 68 | 42 | 112 | 194 | 121 | 53 |
| Debt securities | 90 | 139 | 221 | 357 | 318 | 227 | 242 | 281 | 304 | 368 |
| Other investment assets | 31 | −41 | −121 | −179 | −263 | −74 | −159 | −303 | −140 | −53 |
| Monetary authorities | 0 | 0 | 0 | 0 | 0 | 0 | 0 | 0 | 0 | 0 |
| General government | 0 | 0 | −1 | −1 | 0 | 0 | 3 | −1 | 0 | 0 |
| Banks | 31 | −4 | −75 | −92 | −141 | −36 | −76 | −138 | −135 | −21 |
| Other sectors | 1 | −36 | −45 | −86 | −122 | −38 | −86 | −164 | −5 | −32 |
| Other investment liabilities | 120 | 120 | 170 | 132 | 268 | 57 | 158 | 262 | 189 | 246 |
| Monetary authorities | 68 | 10 | 47 | 57 | −19 | 7 | 25 | −7 | 35 | 65 |
| General government | 1 | 3 | 1 | 1 | −3 | −3 | −1 | −1 | −5 | 3 |
| Banks | 40 | 108 | 64 | 22 | 171 | 30 | 67 | 94 | 88 | 109 |
| Other sectors | 11 | 0 | 59 | 52 | 118 | 23 | 67 | 176 | 70 | 70 |
| ***Total, Groups A Through C*** | 0 | 6 | 14 | 45 | 133 | −65 | 40 | 0 | 26 | 50 |
| **D. Net Errors and Omissions** | 1 | −11 | −4 | −52 | −132 | 72 | −49 | 1 | −21 | −46 |
| ***Total, Groups A Through D*** | 1 | −5 | 10 | −7 | 1 | 7 | −9 | 0 | 5 | 4 |
| **E. Reserves and Related Items** | −1 | 5 | −10 | 7 | −1 | −7 | 9 | 0 | −5 | −4 |

Source: International Monetary Fund, *Balance of Payments Statistics Yearbook 2003*, p. 957. Copyright 2003 by International Monetary Fund. Reproduced with permission via Copyright Clearance Center.

Note: Totals may not match original source due to rounding.

## THE BOP AND GDP

In a static (accounting) sense, a nation's GDP can be represented by the following equation:

$$GDP = C + 1 + G + X - M$$

where:

C      = *consumption spending*
I      = *capital investment spending*
G      = *government spending*
X      = *exports of goods and services*
M      = *imports of goods and services*
X − M = *the balance on current account (when including current income and transfers)*

Thus, a positive current account balance (surplus) contributes directly to increasing the measure of GDP, but a negative current account balance (deficit) decreases GDP.

In a dynamic (cash flow) sense, an increase or decrease in GDP contributes to the current account deficit or surplus. As GDP grows, so does disposable income and capital investment. Increased disposable income leads to more consumption, a portion of which is supplied by more imports. Increased consumption eventually leads to more capital investment.

Growth in GDP also should eventually lead to higher rates of employment. However, some of that theoretical increase in employment may be blunted by foreign sourcing (i.e., the purchase of goods and services from other enterprises located in other countries).

*Supply chain management* has increasingly focused on cost reduction through imports from less costly (lower wages) foreign locations. These imports can be from foreign-owned firms or from foreign subsidiaries of the parent firm. In the latter case, foreign subsidiaries tend to buy components and intellectual property from their parent firms, thus increasing exports. Although outsourcing has always been a factor in determining where to locate or procure manufactured goods and commodities, during the past decade an increasing amount of high-tech goods and services have been sourced from abroad. Foreign sourcing from the United States and Western Europe has been to countries such as India (software and call centers), China, Eastern Europe, Mexico, and the Phillippines. This has caused a loss of some white collar jobs in the United States and Western Europe and a corresponding increase elsewhere.

## THE BOP AND EXCHANGE RATES

A country's BOP can have a significant impact on the level of its exchange rate and vice versa, depending on that country's exchange rate regime. The relationship between the BOP and exchange rates can be illustrated by use of a simplified equation that summarizes BOP data:

| *Current Account Balance* | | *Capital Account Balance* | | *Financial Account Balance* | | *Reserve Balance* | | *Balance of Payments* |
|---|---|---|---|---|---|---|---|---|
| (X − M) | + | (CI − CO) | + | (FI − FO) | + | FXB | = | BOP |

where:

| | |
|---|---|
| X | = exports of goods and services |
| M | = imports of goods and services |
| CI | = capital inflows |
| CO | = capital outflows |
| FI | = financial inflows |
| FO | = financial outflows |
| FXB | = official monetary reserves such as foreign exchange and gold |

The effect of an imbalance in the BOP of a country works somewhat differently depending on whether that country has fixed exchange rates, floating exchange rates, or a managed exchange rate system.

**FIXED EXCHANGE RATE COUNTRIES.**   Under a fixed exchange rate system the government bears the responsibility to assure a BOP near zero. If the sum of the current and capital accounts do not approximate zero, the government is expected to intervene in the foreign exchange market by buying or selling official foreign exchange reserves. If the sum of the first two accounts is greater than zero, a surplus demand for the domestic currency exists in the world. To preserve the fixed exchange rate, the government must then intervene in the foreign exchange market and sell domestic currency for foreign currencies or gold so as to bring the BOP back near zero.

If the sum of the current and capital accounts is negative, an excess supply of the domestic currency exists in world markets. Then the government must intervene by buying the domestic currency with its reserves of foreign currencies and gold. It is obviously important for a government to maintain significant foreign exchange reserve balances to allow it to intervene effectively. If the country runs out of foreign exchange reserves, it will be unable to buy back its domestic currency and will be forced to devalue.

**FLOATING EXCHANGE RATE COUNTRIES.**   Under a floating exchange rate system, the government of a country has no responsibility to peg its foreign exchange rate. The fact that the current and capital account balances do not sum to zero will automatically (in theory) alter the exchange rate in the direction necessary to obtain a BOP near zero. For example, a country running a sizable current account deficit, with a capital and financial accounts balance of zero will have a net BOP deficit. An excess supply of the domestic currency will appear on world markets. Like all goods in excess supply, the market will rid itself of the imbalance by lowering the price. Thus the domestic currency will fall in value, and the BOP will move back toward zero. Exchange rate markets do not always follow this theory, particularly in the short to intermediate term. This delay is known as the *J-curve effect*. The deficit gets worse in the short run but moves back toward equilibrium in the long term.

**MANAGED FLOATS.**   Although still relying on market conditions for day-to-day exchange rate determination, countries operating with managed floats often find it necessary to take action to maintain their desired exchange rate values. They therefore seek to alter the market's valuation of a specific exchange rate by influencing the motivations of market activity, rather than through direct intervention in the foreign exchange markets.

The primary action taken by such governments is to change relative interest rates, thus influencing the economic fundamentals of exchange rate determination. In the context of the equation on the previous page, a change in domestic interest rates is an attempt to alter the term (CI − CO), especially the short-term portfolio component of these capital flows, in order to restore an imbalance caused by the deficit in the current account. The power of interest rate changes on international capital and exchange rate movements can be substantial. A country with a managed float that wishes to defend its currency may choose to raise domestic interest rates to attract additional capital from abroad. This will alter market forces and create additional market demand for the domestic currency. In this process, the government signals exchange market participants that it intends to take measures to preserve the currency's value within certain ranges. The process also raises the cost of local borrowing for businesses, however, so the policy is seldom without domestic critics.

## THE BOP AND INTEREST RATES

Apart from the use of interest rates to intervene in the foreign exchange market, the overall level of a country's interest rates compared to other countries does have an impact on the financial account of the balance of payments. Relatively low real interest rates should normally stimulate an outflow of capital seeking higher interest rates in other country currencies. However, in the case of the United States, the opposite effect has occurred. Despite relatively low real interest rates and large BOP deficits on current account, the U.S. BOP financial account has experienced offsetting financial inflows due to relatively attractive U.S. growth rate prospects, high levels of productive innovation, and perceived political safety. Thus the financial account inflows have helped the United States to maintain its lower interest rates and to finance its exceptionally large fiscal deficit.

However, it is beginning to appear that the favorable inflow on the financial account is diminishing while the U.S. balance on current account is worsening. *Real World Example 3.1* shows that the United States is becoming a bigger debtor nation vis-à-vis the rest of the world.

## THE BOP AND INFLATION RATES

Imports have the potential to lower a country's inflation rate. In particular, imports of lower-priced goods and services places a limit on what domestic competitors charge for comparable goods and services. Thus, foreign competition substitutes for domestic competition to maintain a lower rate of inflation than might have been the case without imports.

On the other hand, to the extent that lower-priced imports substitute for domestic production and employment, gross domestic product will be lower and the balance on current account will be more negative.

## Capital Mobility

The degree to which capital moves freely cross-border is critically important to a country's balance of payments. We have already seen how the United States, while experiencing a deficit in its current account balance over the past 20 years, has simultaneously enjoyed a financial account surplus. This financial account surplus has probably been one of the major reasons the U.S. dollar has been able to maintain its value over this period. Other countries however, for example Brazil in 1998–1999 and

## Real World Example 3.1
### THE UNITED STATES AS THE WORLD'S LARGEST DEBTOR NATION

The United States has become the world's largest debtor nation rather than the world's largest creditor, the position it held in earlier years. Net foreign purchases of U.S. securities have retreated from their peak in 2001, while the U.S. balance on Current Account has worsened, as shown in Exhibit A. Exhibit B shows that the U.S. net international investment position at market value, as a percentage of GDP, is also sinking — to a negative 25%.

**Losing Their Lustre**

Source: Deutsche Bank; US Bureau of Economic Analysis

**Sinking into Debt**

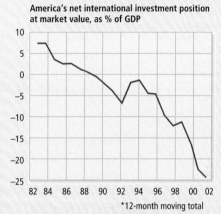

Source: US Bureau of Economic Analysis

Argentina in 2001–2002, have experienced massive financial account outflows, which were major components of their economic and financial crises. Before leaving our discussion of the balance of payments we need to gain additional insights into the history of capital mobility and the contribution of capital outflows — *capital flight* — to balance of payments crises.

## HISTORICAL PATTERNS OF CAPITAL MOBILITY

Has capital always been free to move in and out of a country? Definitely not. The ability of foreign investors to own property, buy businesses, or purchase stocks and bonds in other countries has been controversial. Obstfeld and Taylor (2001) studied the globalization of capital markets and concluded that the pattern illustrated in Exhibit 3.8 is a fair representation of the conventional wisdom on the openness of global capital markets in recent history. Since 1860, the gold standard in use prior to the World War I and the post-1971 period of floating exchange rates have seen the greatest ability of capital to flow cross-border. Note that Obstfeld and Taylor use no specific quantitative measure of mobility. The diagram uses only a stylized distinction between "low" and "high," combining two primary factors; the exchange rate regimes and the state of international political and economic relations.

The authors argue that the post-1860 era can be subdivided into four distinct periods.

1. The first, 1860–1914, is a period characterized by continuously increasing capital openness as more and more countries adopted the gold standard and expanded international trade relations.

**EXHIBIT 3.8**

A Stylized View of
Capital Mobility
in Modern History

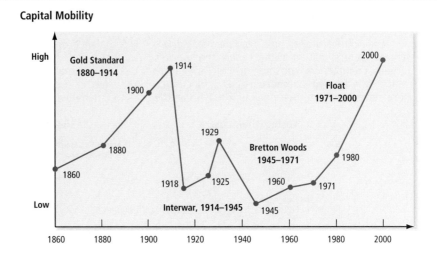

2. The second, 1914–1945, is a period of global economic destruction. The combined destructive forces of two world wars and a worldwide depression led most nations to move toward highly nationalistic and isolationist political and economic policies, effectively eliminating any significant movement of capital between countries.

3. The third period, 1945–1971, the Bretton Woods era, saw a great expansion of international trade in goods and services. This time also saw the slow but steady recovery of capital markets. The fixed exchange rate regime of Bretton Woods may have failed because the sheer forces of global capital could no longer be held in check.

4. The fourth, 1971–2000 [2004], is a period characterized by floating exchange rates and economic volatility, but rapidly expanding cross-border capital flows. The major industrial countries either no longer try to, no longer need to, or no longer can control the movement of capital. Because currency markets are free to reflect underlying economic fundamentals and investor sentiments about the future, capital movements increased in response to this openness.

The currency crises of the latter half of the 1990s and of the early twenty-first century may result in the reversal of this freedom of cross-border capital movement; it is still too early to tell. It is clear, however, that the ability of capital to move instantaneously and massively cross-border has been one of the major factors in the severity of recent currency crises.

## CAPITAL FLIGHT

A final issue is *capital flight*. Although no single accepted definition of capital flight exists, Ingo Walter's discussion has been one of the more useful:

> *International flows of direct and portfolio investments under ordinary circumstances are rarely associated with the capital flight phenomenon. Rather, it is when capital transfers by residents conflict with political objectives that the term "flight" comes into general usage.*
> Ingo Walter, "The Mechanisms of Capital Flight,"
> in *Capital Flight and Third World Debt*, edited by Donald R. Lessard and John Williamson, Institute for International Economics, Washington, D.C., 1987, p. 104.

Although it is not limited to heavily indebted countries, the rapid and sometimes illegal transfer of convertible currencies out of a country poses significant economic and political problems. Many heavily indebted countries have suffered significant capital flight, which has compounded their problems of debt service.

Five primary mechanisms exist by which capital may be moved from one country to another.

1. Transfers via the usual international payments mechanisms, regular bank transfers, are obviously the easiest and lowest cost, and are legal. Most economically healthy countries allow free exchange of their currencies, but of course for such countries "capital flight" is not a problem.

2. Transfer of physical currency by bearer (the proverbial smuggling out of cash in the false bottom of a suitcase) is more costly and, for transfers out of many countries, illegal. Such transfers may be deemed illegal for balance of payments reasons or to make difficult the movement of money from the drug trade or other illegal activities.

3. Cash is transferred into collectibles or precious metals, which are then transferred across borders.

4. Money laundering is the cross-border purchase of assets that are then managed in a way that hides the movement of money and its ownership.

5. False invoicing of international trade transactions occurs when capital is moved through the underinvoicing of exports or the overinvoicing of imports, where the difference between the invoiced amount and the actual agreed-upon payment is deposited in banking institutions in a country of choice.

## MINI-CASE

# Turkey's Kriz (A): Deteriorating Balance of Payments

It was only when optimistic Turks started snapping up imports that investors began to doubt that foreign capital inflows would be sufficient to fund both spendthrift consumers and the perennially penurious government.

"On the Brink Again,"
*The Economist*, February 24, 2001.

In February 2001 Turkey's rapidly escalating economic *kriz*, or crisis, forced the devaluation of the Turkish lira. The Turkish government had successfully waged war on the inflationary forces embedded in the country's economy in 1999 and early 2000. But just as the economy began to boom in the second half of 2000, pressures on the country's balance of payments and currency rose. The question asked by many analysts in the months following the crisis was whether the crisis had been predictable, and what early signs of deterioration should have been noted by the outside world.

### The Accounts

Exhibit 1 presents the Turkish balance on current account and financial account between 1993 and 2000 (ending less than two months prior to the devaluation). Several issues are immediately evident.

- First, Turkey seemingly suffered significant volatility in the balances on key international accounts. The financial account swung between surplus (1993) and deficit (1994), and back to surplus again (1995–1997). After plummeting in 1998, the financial surplus returned in 1999 and 2000.

- Secondly, as is typically the case, the current account behaved in a relatively inverse manner to the financial account, running deficits in most of the years shown. But significantly, the deficit on current account grew

## EXHIBIT 1

Turkey's Balance
of Payments,
1993–2000

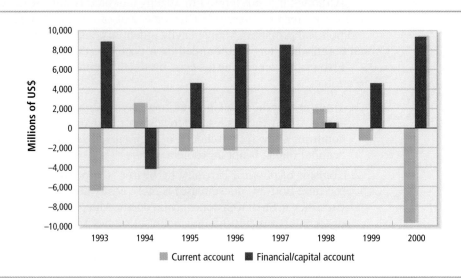

Current account    Financial/capital account

---

dramatically in 2000, to over $9.8 billion, from a deficit in 1999 of only $1.4 billion.

Many analysts are quick to point out that the sizeable increase in the current account deficit should have been seen as a danger signal of imminent collapse. Others, however, point out quite correctly that most national economies experience rapid increases in trade and current account deficits during rapid periods of economic growth. And to add weight to the argument, the net surplus on the financial account seemed to indicate a growing confidence in the Turkish economy's outlook by foreign investors.

An examination of the subcomponents of these major account balances is helpful. As illustrated in Exhibit 2, the rapid deterioration of the current account in 2000 was largely the result of a rapid jump in imported goods and merchandise. The goods import bill rose from $39.8 billion in 1999 to over $54.0 billion in 2000, an increase of 36% in one year. At the same time, services trade and current income accounts, both credits and debits subcomponents, showed little change. Unfortunately, the statistics reported to the IMF provide little in additional detail as to the composition of these rapid imports, their industry or nature, and their financing.

A similar decomposition of the surplus on the financial account also allows us to identify where in the various inflows and outflows of capital in Turkey there was a significant change. Exhibit 3 provides this financial account decomposition. According to Exhibit 3, the doubling of the Turkish financial account surplus in 2000 was largely the result of a massive increase—over $7 billion—in "net other investment."

One very important determinant of these account balances was the telecommunications sector. Throughout 2000 TelSim, the national telecommunications provider in Turkey, imported billions of dollars worth of equipment from Nokia (Finland) and Motorola (United States). The equipment was purchased on trade credit, meaning that TelSim would repay Nokia and Motorola at a future date for the equipment, primarily from the proceeds of activating the equipment for telecommunications services. TelSim, however, defaulted on its payments, and Nokia and Motorola were left with billions of dollars in losses.

## Case Questions

1. Where in the current account would the imported telecommunications equipment be listed? Would this correspond to the increase in magnitude and timing of the financial account?

2. Why do you think that net direct investment declined from $571 million in 1998 to $112 million in 2000?

3. Why do you think that TelSim defaulted on its payments for equipment imports from Nokia and Motorola?

## EXHIBIT 2

**Subaccounts of the Turkish Current Account, 1998–2000 (millions of US$)**

| | 1998 | 1999 | 2000 |
|---|---|---|---|
| Goods: exports | 31,220 | 29,325 | 31,664 |
| Goods: imports | −45,440 | −39,768 | −54,041 |
| Balance on goods | −14,220 | −10,443 | −22,377 |
| Services: credit | 23,321 | 16,398 | 19,484 |
| Services: debit | −9,859 | −8,953 | −8,149 |
| Balance on services | 13,462 | 7,445 | 11,335 |
| Income: credit | 2,481 | 2,350 | 2,836 |
| Income: debit | −5,466 | −5,887 | −6,838 |
| Balance on income | −2,985 | −3,537 | −4,002 |
| Current transfers: credit | 5,860 | 5,294 | 5,317 |
| Current transfers: debit | −133 | −119 | −92 |
| Balance on transfers | 5,727 | 5,175 | 5,225 |
| Balance on current account | 1,984 | −1,360 | −9,819 |

Source: International Monetary Fund, *Balance of Payments Statistics Yearbook, 2001*, p. 913.

## EXHIBIT 3

**Subaccounts of the Turkish Financial Account, 1998–2000 (millions of US$)**

| | 1998 | 1999 | 2000 |
|---|---|---|---|
| Net direct investment | 573 | 138 | 112 |
| Net portfolio investment | −6,711 | 3,429 | 1,022 |
| Net other investment | 6,586 | 1,103 | 8,311 |
| Balance on financial account | 448 | 4,670 | 9,445 |

Source: International Monetary Fund, *Balance of Payments Statistics Yearbook, 2001*, p. 915.

## Summary of Learning Objectives

*Explain how nations measure their own levels of international economic activity, and how that creates the balance of payments*

- The balance of payments (BOP) is the summary statement of all international transactions between one country and all other countries.

- The BOP is a flow statement, summarizing all the international transactions that occur across the geographic boundaries of the nation over a period of time, typically a year.

- Although in theory the BOP must always balance, in practice there are substantial imbalances as a result of statistical errors and misreporting of current account and financial/capital account flows.

*Examine the economic relationships underlying the two basic subcomponents of the balance of payments — the current account and financial/capital account balances*

- The two major subaccounts of the balance of payments, the current account and the financial/capital account, summarize the current trade and international capital flows of the country, respectively.

- The current account and financial/capital account are typically inverse on balance, one in surplus while the other experiences deficit.

- Although most nations strive for current surpluses, it is not clear that a balance on current or capital account, or a surplus on current account, is either sustainable or desirable.

*Identify the financial dimensions of international economic activity, and how they differ between merchandise and services trade*

- Although merchandise trade is more easily observed (e.g., goods flowing through ports of entry), the growth of services trade is more significant to the balance of payments for many of the world's largest industrialized countries today.

*Identify balance of payment activities by nations in the pursuit of macroeconomic policies*

- Monitoring of the various subaccounts of a country's balance of payment activity is helpful to decision-makers and policy-makers on all levels of government and industry in detecting the underlying trends and movements of fundamental economic forces driving a country's international economic activity.
- The balance of payments interacts with nearly all of a nation's key macroeconomic variables, such as gross domestic product, the exchange rate, interest rates, and inflation rates.

*Evaluate the history of capital mobility, and the conditions that lead in times of crisis to capital flight*

- The ability of capital to move instantaneously and massively cross-border has been one of the major factors in the severity of recent currency crises. In a number of cases, such as Malaysia in 1997 and Argentina in 2001, the national governments concluded that they had no choice but to impose drastic restrictions on the ability of capital to flow.
- Although not limited to heavily indebted countries, the rapid and sometimes illegal transfer of convertible currencies out of a country poses significant economic and political problems. Many heavily indebted countries have suffered significant capital flight, which has compounded their problems of debt service.

## QUESTIONS

1. **Balance of payments defined.** The measurement of all international economic transactions between the residents of a country and foreign residents is called the balance of payments (BOP). What institution provides the primary source of similar statistics for balance of payments and economic performance worldwide?

2. **Importance of BOP.** Business managers and investors need BOP data to anticipate changes in host country economic policies that might be driven by BOP events. List three specific signals that a country's BOP data can provide to business managers and investors.

3. **Economic activity.** What are the two main types of economic activity measured by a country's BOP?

4. **Balance.** Why does the BOP always "balance"?

5. **BOP accounting.** If the BOP were viewed as an accounting statement, would it be a balance sheet of the country's wealth, an income statement of the country's earnings, or a funds flow statement of money into and out of the country?

6. **Current account.** What are the main component accounts of the current account? Give one debit and one credit example for each component account for the United States.

7. **Real versus financial assets.** What is the difference between a real asset and a financial asset?

8. **Direct versus portfolio investments.** What is the difference between a direct foreign investment and a portfolio foreign investment? Give an example of each. Which type of investment is a multinational industrial company more likely to make?

9. **Capital and financial accounts.** What are the main components of the financial accounts? Give one debit and one credit example for each component account for the United States.

10. **Classifying transactions.** Classify the following as a transaction reported in a subcomponent of the current account or the capital and financial accounts of the two countries involved:

    **a.** A U.S. food chain imports wine from Chile.

    **b.** A U.S. resident purchases a euro-denominated bond from a German company.

    **c.** Singaporean parents pay for their daughter to study at a U.S. university.

    **d.** A U.S. university gives a tuition grant to a foreign student from Singapore.

**e.** A British company imports Spanish oranges, paying with Eurodollars on deposit in London.

**f.** The Spanish orchard deposits half the proceeds of its sale in a New York bank.

**g.** The Spanish orchard deposits half the proceeds in a Eurodollar account in London.

**h.** A London-based insurance company buys U.S. corporate bonds for its investment portfolio.

**i.** An American multinational enterprise buys insurance from a London insurance broker.

**j.** A London insurance firm pays for losses incurred in the United States because of an international terrorist attack.

**k.** Cathay Pacific Airlines buys jet fuel at Los Angeles International Airport so it can return to Hong Kong.

**l.** A California-based mutual fund buys shares of stock on the Tokyo and London stock exchanges.

**m.** The U.S. army buys food for its troops in South Asia from local vendors.

**n.** A Yale graduate gets a job with the International Committee of the Red Cross in Bosnia and is paid in Swiss francs.

**o.** The Russian government hires a Norwegian salvage firm to raise a sunken submarine.

**p.** A Colombian drug cartel smuggles cocaine into the United States, receives a suitcase of cash, and flies back to Colombia with that cash.

**q.** The U.S. government pays the salary of a foreign service officer working in the U.S. embassy in Beirut.

**r.** A Norwegian shipping firm pays U.S. dollars to the Egyptian government for passage of a ship through the Suez canal.

**s.** A German automobile firm pays the salary of its executive working for a subsidiary in Detroit.

**t.** An American tourist pays for a hotel in Paris with her American Express card.

**u.** A French tourist from the provinces pays for a hotel in Paris with her American Express card.

**v.** A U.S. professor goes abroad for a year on a Fullbright grant.

**11. The balance.** What are the main summary statements of the balance of payments accounts and what do they measure?

**12. Drugs and terrorists.** Where in the balance of payments accounts do the flows of laundered money by drug dealers and international terrorist organizations flow?

**13. Capital mobility — United States.** The U.S. dollar has maintained or increased its value over the past 20 years despite running a gradually increasing current account deficit. Why?

**14. Capital mobility — Brazil.** Brazil has experienced periodic depreciation of its currency over the past 20 years despite occasionally running a current account surplus. Why?

**15. BOP transactions.** Identify the correct BOP account for each of the following transactions:

**a.** A German pension fund buys U.S. government 30-year bonds for its investment portfolio.

**b.** Scandinavian Airlines System (SAS) buys jet fuel at Newark Airport for its flight to Copenhagen.

**c.** Hong Kong students pay tuition to the University of California, Berkeley.

**d.** The U.S. Air Force buys food in South Korea to supply its air crews.

**e.** A Japanese auto company pays the salaries of its executives working for its U.S. subsidiaries.

**f.** A U.S. tourist pays for a restaurant meal in Bangkok.

**g.** A Colombian citizen smuggles cocaine into the United States, receives cash, and smuggles the dollars back into Colombia.

**h.** A U.K. corporation purchases a euro-denominated bond from an Italian MNE.

## PROBLEMS

***Australia's current account.*** *Use the following data from the International Monetary Fund to answer questions 1 through 4.*

1.  What is Australia's balance on goods trade?
2.  What is Australia's balance on services?
3.  What is Australia's balance on goods and services?
4.  What is Australia's current account balance?

| *Australia's Current Account* (Millions of US$) | *1998* | *1999* | *2000* | *2001* | *2002* | *2003* |
|---|---|---|---|---|---|---|
| Goods: exports | 55,884 | 56,096 | 64,052 | 63,676 | 65,099 | 70,577 |
| Goods: imports | 61,215 | 65,857 | 68,865 | 61,890 | 70,530 | 85,946 |
| Services: credit | 16,181 | 17,399 | 18,677 | 16,689 | 17,906 | 21,205 |
| Services: debit | 17,272 | 18,330 | 18,388 | 16,948 | 18,107 | 21,638 |
| Income: credit | 6,532 | 7,394 | 8,984 | 8,063 | 8,194 | 9,457 |
| Income: debit | 17,842 | 18,968 | 19,516 | 18,332 | 19,884 | 24,245 |
| Current transfers: credit | 2,651 | 3,003 | 2,622 | 2,242 | 2,310 | 2,767 |
| Current transfers: debit | 2,933 | 3,032 | 2,669 | 2,221 | 2,373 | 2,851 |

***Uruguay's current account.*** *Use the following Uruguayan current account data from the IMF to answer questions 5 through 9.*

5.  What is Uruguay's balance on goods?
6.  What is Uruguay's balance on services?
7.  What is Uruguay's balance on goods and services?
8.  What is Uruguay's balance on goods, services, and income?
9.  What is Uruguay's current account balance?

| *Uruguay's Current Account* (Millions of US$) | *1998* | *1999* | *2000* | *2001* | *2002* |
|---|---|---|---|---|---|
| Goods: exports | 2,829.3 | 2,290.6 | 2,383.8 | 2,139.4 | 1,933.1 |
| Goods: imports | 3,601.4 | 3,187.2 | 3,311.1 | 2,914.7 | 1,872.9 |
| Services: credit | 1,319.1 | 1,261.6 | 1,275.7 | 1,122.5 | 774.7 |
| Services: debit | 883.6 | 802.3 | 881.8 | 801.4 | 652.2 |
| Income: credit | 608.0 | 735.5 | 781.5 | 832.0 | 455.9 |
| Income: debit | 805.9 | 879.3 | 841.8 | 895.2 | 446.3 |
| Current transfers: credit | 75.0 | 78.4 | 48.0 | 48.0 | 83.7 |
| Current transfers: debit | 16.0 | 4.9 | 20.5 | 18.3 | 14.3 |

***Myanmar's balance of payments.*** *Use the following Myanmar balance of payments data to answer questions 10 through 13.*

10.  Is Myanmar experiencing a net capital inflow or outflow?
11.  What is Myanmar's total for groups A and B?
12.  What is Myanmar's total for groups A through C?
13.  What is Myanmar's total for groups A through D?

| Myanmar's Balance of Payments (Millions of US$) | 1998 | 1999 | 2000 | 2001 |
|---|---|---|---|---|
| A. Current account balance | −499.1 | −284.7 | −211.7 | −308.5 |
| B. Capital account balance | 0.0 | 0.0 | 0.0 | 0.0 |
| C. Financial account balance | 540.9 | 251.2 | 212.8 | 399.1 |
| D. Net errors and omissions | 18.7 | −12.4 | −24.5 | 89.3 |
| E. Reserves and related items | −60.4 | 45.9 | 23.4 | −179.8 |

**Argentina's balance of payments**. *Argentina used a currency board to maintain its peso on a par with the U.S. dollar. In January 2002 the peso collapsed. Argentina's BOP could have signaled this event. Listed below is Argentina's BOP for the period 1998–2000. Use this data to answer questions 14 through 20.*

**14.** What is Argentina's balance on services?

**15.** What is Argentina's current account balance?

**16.** What seems to have been the primary driver of Argentina's current account balance between 1998 and 2000?

**17.** What is Argentina's financial account balance?

**18.** What is Argentina's total for groups A through C?

**19.** What is Argentina's total for groups A through D?

**20.** Argentina's balance of payments was clearly deteriorating during this period. What would the BOP forecast to happen to the country's currency board regime?

| Argentina's Balance of Payments (Millions of US$) | 1998 | 1999 | 2000 | 2001 | 2002 |
|---|---|---|---|---|---|
| **A. Current Account** | | | | | |
| Goods: exports | 26,434 | 23,309 | 26,341 | 26,543 | 25,709 |
| Goods: imports | 29,531 | 24,103 | 23,889 | 19,158 | 8,473 |
| Services: credit | 4,704 | 4,554 | 4,765 | 4,398 | 2,966 |
| Services: debit | 9,136 | 8,660 | 9,039 | 8,298 | 4,577 |
| Income: credit | 6,125 | 6,095 | 7,489 | 5,370 | 3,176 |
| Income: debit | 13,531 | 13,558 | 14,959 | 13,117 | 9,645 |
| Current transfers: credit | 720 | 704 | 724 | 681 | 570 |
| Current transfers: debit | 314 | 307 | 369 | 399 | 167 |
| **B. Capital Account** | 73 | 86 | 106 | 101 | 39 |
| **C. Financial Account** | | | | | |
| Direct investment abroad | 2,325 | 1,730 | 901 | 161 | −627 |
| Direct investment in Argentina | 7,291 | 23,988 | 10,418 | 2,166 | 785 |
| Portfolio investment assets, net | −1,906 | −2,005 | −1,252 | 1,797 | 477 |
| Portfolio investment liabilities, net | 10,693 | −4,780 | −1,331 | −9,574 | −6,596 |
| Balance on other investment, net | 5,183 | −1,065 | 784 | −7,596 | −18,738 |
| **D. Net Errors and Omissions** | −389 | −515 | −63 | −4,155 | −1,422 |
| **E. Reserves and Related Items** | −4,090 | −2,013 | 1,176 | 21,405 | 15,269 |

**Internet Exercises**

1. **World organizations and the economic outlook.** The IMF, World Bank, and United Nations are only a few of the major world organizations that track, report, and aid international economic and financial development. Using these Web sites and others that may be linked, briefly summarize the economic outlook for the developed and emerging nations of the world. For example, the full text of Chapter 1 of the *World Economic Outlook* published annually by the World Bank is available through the IMF's Web page.

   International Monetary Fund
      http://www.imf.org/
   United Nations
      http://www.unsystem.org/
   The World Bank Group
      http://www.worldbank.org/
   Europa (EU) Homepage
      http://europa.eu.int/
   Bank for International Settlements
      http://www.bis.org/

2. **Federal Reserve Bank of St. Louis.** The Federal Reserve Bank of St. Louis provides a large amount of recent open-economy macroeconomic data online. Use the following addresses to track down recent BOP and GDP data for the major industrial countries.

   Recent international economic data
      http://research.stlouisfed.org/publications/iet/
   Balance of payments statistics
      http://research.stlouisfed.org/fred2/categories/14/41

3. **Capital controls.** All countries regulate, in some form, the flow of capital in and out of their country. Use the following Web site to determine the current openness of the following countries to capital movements: Argentina, Colombia, Malaysia, Nepal, and Taiwan.

   Yahoo International Finance Center
      http://biz.yahoo.com/ifc/

4. **The latest BOP numbers for the United States and Japan.** Use the following Bureau of Economic Analysis (U.S. government) and the Ministry of Finance (Japanese government) Web sites to find the most recent balance of payments statistics for both countries.

   Bureau of Economic Analysis
      http://www.bea.gov/
   Ministry of Finance
      http://www.mof.go.jp/

5. **World Trade Organization and Doha.** The World Trade Organization (WTO) is in a multiple-year round of negotiations on international trade. The current round is taking place in Doha, Qatar, and is scheduled to conclude most of its tasks by January 1, 2005. Visit the WTO Web site and find the most recent evidence presented by the WTO on the progress of talks on issues including international trade in services and international recognition of intellectual property.

   World Trade Organization
      http://www.wto.org/

# Foreign Exchange Theory and Markets

Part 2 examines how foreign exchange theories and markets operate as background knowledge that must be understood by management of MNEs in order to measure and manage their firms' foreign exchange risks.

**CHAPTER 4** examines international parity conditions that are the underlying determinants of foreign exchange rates. It explores the relationship between prices and exchange rates, defined as *purchasing power parity*. It then explains the relationship between interest and exchange rates through the *Fisher effect* and the *international Fisher effect*. It shows how covered interest arbitrage ensures that *interest rate parity* will hold. This means that the difference between short-term interest rates in two countries should be equal to the forward premium or discount on their currencies. It also shows how speculators can use uncovered interest arbitrage to gamble on their expectations about future spot exchange rates. Chapter 4 then discusses whether the forward exchange rate is a good predictor of the future spot rate. It concludes with a model showing how prices, interest rates, and exchange rates should trend toward equilibrium.

**CHAPTER 5** examines how to forecast foreign exchange rates. It describes the *asset market approach* and the *technical analysis approach*. It then describes how disequilibrium has characterized exchange rates in a number of emerging country markets. Chapter 5 presents detailed analyses of currency and economic crises in Asia starting in 1997, Russia in 1998, and Argentina in 2002.

**CHAPTER 6** describes the foreign exchange markets with respect to their geographical extent, functions performed, market participants, and size. The chapter ends with a detailed description of how foreign exchange rates are quoted, cross rates are determined, and international arbitrage occurs.

**CHAPTER 7** explains the world of foreign currency derivatives. It starts with a description of foreign currency futures and how they compare to forward contracts. It then describes foreign currency put and call options and the markets on which they are traded. It then shows how options are quoted and how they can be used for speculation. The chapter concludes with an analysis of how we can price and value options. A mini-case illustrates the potential dangers if foreign currency futures and options are abused.

# International Parity Conditions

## LEARNING OBJECTIVES

Demonstrate how price levels and price-level changes (inflation) in a country determine the exchange rate at which its currencies is traded

Show how interest rates reflect inflationary forces within each country and currency

Explain how interest rates for currencies reflect expectations held by market participants about the future spot exchange rate

Analyze how, in equilibrium, the spot and forward currency markets are aligned with interest differentials

What are the determinants of exchange rates? Are changes in exchange rates predictable? These are fundamental questions that managers of multinational enterprises (MNEs), international portfolio investors, importers and exporters, and government officials must deal with every day. This chapter will describe the core financial theories surrounding the determination of exchange rates. Chapter 5 will introduce two other major theoretical schools of thought regarding currency valuation, and combine the three different theories in a variety of real-world applications.

The economic theories that link exchange rates, price levels, and interest rates together are called *international parity conditions*. In the eyes of many, these international parity conditions form the core of the financial theory that is considered unique to the field of international finance. These theories do not always work out to be "true" when compared to what students and practitioners observe in the real world, but they are central to any understanding of how multinational business is conducted and funded in the world today. And, as is often the case, the mistake is not always in the theory itself, but in the way it is interpreted or applied in practice.

## Prices and Exchange Rates

If the identical product or service can be sold in two different markets, and no restrictions exist on the sale or transportation costs of moving the product between markets, the product's price should be the same in both markets. This is called the *law of one price*.

A primary principle of competitive markets is that prices will equalize across markets if frictions or costs of moving the products or services between markets do not exist. If the two markets are in two different countries, the product's price may be stated in different currency terms, but the price of the product should still be the same. Comparing prices would require only a conversion from one currency to the other. For example,

$$P^\$ \times S = P^¥$$

where the price of the product in U.S. dollars ($P^\$$), multiplied by the spot exchange rate (S, yen per U.S. dollar), equals the price of the product in Japanese yen ($P^¥$). Conversely, if the prices of the two products were stated in local currencies, and markets were efficient at competing away a higher price in one market relative to the other, the exchange rate could be deduced from the relative local product prices:

$$S = \frac{P^¥}{P^\$}$$

### PURCHASING POWER PARITY AND THE LAW OF ONE PRICE

If the law of one price were true for all goods and services, the *purchasing power parity* (PPP) exchange rate could be found from any individual set of prices. By comparing the prices of identical products denominated in different currencies, we could determine the "real" or PPP exchange rate that should exist if markets were efficient. This is the absolute version of the *theory of purchasing power parity*. Absolute PPP states that the spot exchange rate is determined by the relative prices of similar baskets of goods.

The "hamburger standard," as it has been christened by *The Economist* (Exhibit 4.1), is a prime example of this law of one price. Assuming that the Big Mac is indeed

**EXHIBIT 4.1**

The Hamburger
Standard

| | Big Mac price in dollars[*] | Implied PPP[†] of the dollar | Under (−)/ over (+) valuation against the dollar, % | | Big Mac price in dollars[*] | Implied PPP[†] of the dollar | Under (−)/ over (+) valuation against the dollar, % |
|---|---|---|---|---|---|---|---|
| United States[‡] | 2.90 | – | – | Aruba | 2.29 | 1.41 | −21 |
| Argentina | 1.48 | 1.50 | −49 | Belarus | 1.37 | 1021 | −53 |
| Australia | 2.27 | 1.12 | −22 | Bulgaria | 1.85 | 1.03 | −36 |
| Brazil | 1.70 | 1.86 | −41 | Colombia | 2.35 | 2241 | −19 |
| Britain | 3.37 | 1.54[§] | +16 | Costa Rica | 2.61 | 390 | −10 |
| Canada | 2.33 | 1.10 | −20 | Croatia | 2.42 | 5.14 | −17 |
| Chile | 2.18 | 483 | −25 | Dom.Rep. | 1.32 | 20.7 | −54 |
| China | 1.26 | 3.59 | −57 | Estonia | 2.27 | 10.2 | −22 |
| Czech Rep. | 2.13 | 19.5 | −27 | Fiji | 2.35 | 1.47 | −19 |
| Denmark | 4.46 | 9.57 | +54 | Georgia | 1.90 | 1.26 | −34 |
| Egypt | 1.62 | 3.45 | −44 | Guatemala | 2.01 | 5.52 | −31 |
| Euro area | 3.28** | 1.06[††] | +13 | Honduras | 1.08 | 12.4 | −32 |
| Hong Kong | 1.54 | 4.14 | −47 | Iceland | 6.01 | 151 | 107 |
| Hungary | 2.52 | 183 | −13 | Jamaica | 1.88 | 39.0 | −35 |
| Indonesia | 1.77 | 5,552 | −39 | Jordan | 3.65 | 0.89 | 26 |
| Japan | 2.33 | 90.3 | −20 | Kuwait | 7.33 | 0.74 | 153 |
| Malaysia | 1.33 | 1.74 | −54 | Latvia | 2.00 | 0.38 | −31 |
| Mexico | 2.08 | 8.28 | −28 | Lebanon | 2.84 | 1483 | −2 |
| New Zealand | 2.65 | 1.50 | −8 | Lithuania | 2.26 | 2.24 | −22 |
| Peru | 2.57 | 3.10 | −11 | Macau | 1.40 | 3.86 | −52 |
| Philippines | 1.23 | 23.8 | −57 | Macedonia | 1.84 | 32.8 | −36 |
| Poland | 1.63 | 2.17 | −44 | Moldova | 1.93 | 7.93 | −33 |
| Russia | 1.45 | 14.5 | −50 | Morocco | 0.26 | 0.82 | −91 |
| Singapore | 1.92 | 1.14 | −34 | Nicaragua | 2.19 | 11.9 | −25 |
| South Africa | 1.86 | 4.28 | −36 | Norway | 5.18 | 12.2 | 79 |
| South Korea | 2.72 | 1,103 | −6 | Pakistan | 1.90 | 37.9 | −34 |
| Sweden | 3.94 | 10.3 | +36 | Qatar | 0.68 | 0.85 | −77 |
| Switzerland | 4.90 | 2.17 | +69 | Saudi Arabia | 0.64 | 0.83 | −78 |
| Taiwan | 2.24 | 25.9 | −23 | Slovakia | 1.98 | 22.8 | −32 |
| Thailand | 1.45 | 20.3 | −50 | Slovenia | 2.42 | 166 | −17 |
| Turkey | 2.58 | 1,362,069 | −11 | Sri Lanka | 1.41 | 48.3 | −51 |
| Venezuela | 1.48 | 1,517 | −49 | Ukraine | 1.36 | 2.50 | −53 |
| | | | | UAE | 0.67 | 0.84 | −77 |
| | | | | Uruguay | 1.00 | 10.3 | −65 |

[*]At current exchange rates [†]Purchasing-power parity [‡]Average of New York, Chicago, San Francisco and Atlanta
[§]Dollars per pound **Weighted average of member countries [††]Dollars per euro

Source: "The Big Mac Index," *The Economist*, May 27, 2004, economist.com. Data not provided in printed editions of *The Economist* for the countries listed in the right-hand column. © 2004 The Economist Newspaper Ltd. All Rights Reserved. Reprinted with permission. Further reproduction prohibited. www.economist.com

identical in all countries listed, it serves as one form of comparison of whether currencies are currently trading at market rates that are close to the exchange rate implied by Big Macs in local currencies.

For example, using Exhibit 4.1, a Big Mac in Japan cost ¥262 (local currency and not shown in the table), while the same Big Mac in the United States cost $2.90. The actual exchange rate was ¥112.50/$ at this time. The price of a Big Mac in Japan in terms of the U.S. dollar was therefore

$$\frac{¥262}{¥112.50/\$} = ¥233$$

This is the value in column 1 of Exhibit 4.1 for Japan. *The Economist* then calculates the implied PPP rate of exchange using the actual price of the Big Mac in Japanese yen over U.S. dollars:

$$\frac{¥262}{\$2.90} = ¥90.34/\$$$

This is the value in column 2 for Japan in Exhibit 4.1. Now comparing the implied PPP rate of exchange, ¥90.34/$, with the actual market rate of exchange at that time, ¥112.50/$, the degree to which the Japanese yen is either undervalued or overvalued versus the U.S. dollar is calculated:

$$\frac{¥90.34/\$ - ¥112.50/\$}{¥112.50/\$} = -0.197 \text{ or } \approx -20\%$$

In this case, the Big Mac index indicates that the Japanese yen is undervalued by 20% versus the U.S. dollar, as indicated in the third column for Japan in Exhibit 4.1.

A less extreme form of this principle would be that in relatively efficient markets the price of a basket of goods would be the same in each market. Replacing the price of a single product with a price index allows the PPP exchange rate between two countries to be stated as

$$S = \frac{PI^{¥}}{PI^{\$}}$$

where $PI^{¥}$ and $PI^{\$}$ are price indices expressed in local currency for Japan and the United States, respectively. For example, if the identical basket of goods cost ¥1000 in Japan and $10 in the United States, the PPP exchange rate would be

$$\frac{¥1000}{\$10} = ¥100/\$$$

An alternative to the hamburger standard is the "Starbucks tall-latte index" introduced by *The Economist* in January 2004. *Real World Example 4.1* provides a comparison of these high-profile food and beverage staples.

## RELATIVE PURCHASING POWER PARITY

If the assumptions of the absolute version of PPP theory are relaxed a bit more, we observe what is termed *relative purchasing power parity*. Relative PPP holds that PPP is not particularly helpful in determining what the spot rate is today, but that the relative change in prices between two countries over a period of time determines the change in the exchange rate over that period. More specifically, *if the spot exchange rate between two countries starts in equilibrium, any change in the differential rate of inflation between them tends to be offset over the long run by an equal but opposite change in the spot exchange rate.*

Exhibit 4.2 shows a general case of relative PPP. The vertical axis shows the percentage appreciation or depreciation of the foreign currency relative to the home

## Real World Example 4.1
### PURCHASING POWER PARITY: BURGERS OR BEANS?

In the never-ending search for the perfect index of exchange rate purchasing power, *The Economist* introduced the Starbucks tall-latte index in January 2004 to compare the Big Mac index with an index of Starbucks' coffee in a multitude of countries.

By coincidence, the average price of a Starbucks tall latte in the United States is the same as the average price of a Big Mac in the United States — $2.80. The local currency price of the tall latte and Big Mac are then divided by the dollar price to calculate a theoretical purchasing power parity exchange rate. This in turn is compared against the actual exchange rate in the market at the time. The percentage difference is the percent under- or overvaluation.

True to the on-going debate of the time, the tall-latte index, like the Big Mac, indicated that the euro was significantly overvalued compared to the dollar (33% and 24%, respectively). Similarly, both indexes indicated that the Swiss franc was also dramatically overvalued versus the dollar.

The two indexes, however, seemed to have vastly different opinions on the value of a number of Asian currencies versus the dollar. For example, the Japanese yen was overvalued according to the tall-latte index (+13%), whereas the Big Mac index indicated that the yen was undervalued (−12%). The Chinese renminbi was also vastly different, being only slightly undervalued by the latte index (−1%), but dramatically undervalued according to the Big Mac index (−56%).

Which is better? Its hard to say. A good measure of purchasing power is one constructed by products that are produced locally, either through completely domestically sourced goods and services, or through the acquisition of traded goods. Both of these products have large local cost components in labor and material costs, but both suffer the deficiency of having large local real estate and rental rates which are nontraded costs. What both indexes do fulfill, however, is that which drives the brand value of both companies — the delivery of an identical good and service when purchased anywhere in the world.

### Our hot tips
Local currency under (−)/over (+) valuation against the dollar, %, using:

|  | Starbucks tall-latte index | McDonald's Big Mac index |
|---|---|---|
| Australia | −4 | −17 |
| Britain | +17 | +23 |
| Canada | −16 | −16 |
| China | −1 | −56 |
| Euro area | +33 | +24 |
| Hong Kong | +15 | −45 |
| Japan | +13 | −12 |
| Malaysia | −25 | −53 |
| Mexico | −15 | −21 |
| New Zealand | −12 | −4 |
| Singapore | +2 | −31 |
| South Korea | +6 | 0 |
| Switzerland | +62 | +82 |
| Taiwan | −5 | −21 |
| Thailand | −31 | −46 |
| Turkey | +6 | +5 |

Source: *The Economist*

currency, and the horizontal axis shows the percentage higher or lower rate of inflation in the foreign country relative to the home country. The diagonal parity line shows the equilibrium position between a change in the exchange rate and relative inflation rates. For instance, point P represents an equilibrium point where inflation in the foreign country, Japan, for example, is 4% lower than in the home country, the United States, for example. Therefore, relative PPP would predict that the yen would appreciate by 4% per annum with respect to the U.S. dollar.

The main justification for purchasing power parity is that if a country experiences inflation rates higher than those of its main trading partners, and its exchange rate does not change, its exports of goods and services become less competitive with comparable products produced elsewhere. Imports from abroad become more price competitive with higher-priced domestic products. These price changes lead to a deficit on *current account* in the balance of payments unless offset by capital and financial flows.

**EXHIBIT 4.2**

Relative
Purchasing
Power Parity
(PPP)

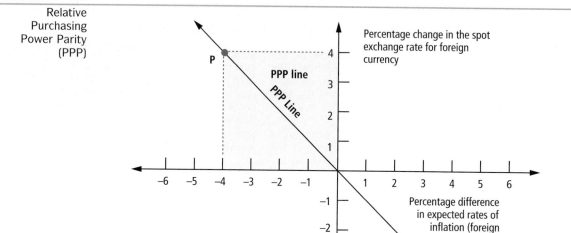

## EMPIRICAL TESTS OF PURCHASING POWER PARITY

Extensive testing of both the absolute and relative versions of purchasing power parity and the law of one price has been done.[1] These tests have, for the most part, not proved PPP to be accurate in predicting future exchange rates. Goods and services do not in reality move at zero cost between countries, and in fact many goods are not "tradeable" — for example, haircuts. Many goods and services are not of the same quality across countries, reflecting differences in the tastes and resources of the countries of their manufacture and consumption.

Two general conclusions can be made from these tests: (1) PPP holds up well over the very long run but poorly for shorter time periods, and (2) the theory holds better for countries with relatively high rates of inflation and underdeveloped capital markets.

## EXCHANGE RATE INDICES: REAL AND NOMINAL

Since any single country trades with numerous partners, we need to track and evaluate its individual currency value against all other currency values in order to determine relative purchasing power. The objective is to discover whether its exchange rate is "overvalued" or "undervalued" in terms of PPP. One of the primary methods of dealing with this problem is the calculation of *exchange rate indices*. These indices are

[1]See, for example, Kenneth Rogoff, "The Purchasing Power Parity Puzzle," *Journal of Economic Literature,* Volume 34, Number 2, June 1996, 647–668; and Barry K. Goodwin, Thomas Greenes, and Michael K. Wohlgenant, "Testing the Law of One Price When Trade Takes Time," *Journal of International Money and Finance,* March 1990, 21–40.

formed by trade-weighting the bilateral exchange rates between the home country and its trading partners.

The *nominal effective exchange rate index* uses actual exchange rates to create an index, on a weighted average basis, of the value of the subject currency over time. It does not really indicate anything about the "true value" of the currency, or anything related to PPP. The nominal index simply calculates how the currency value relates to some arbitrarily chosen base period, but it is used in the formation of the real effective exchange rate index. The *real effective exchange rate index* indicates how the weighted average purchasing power of the currency has changed relative to some arbitrarily selected base period. Exhibit 4.3 plots the real effective exchange rate indexes for the United States and Japan over the past 20 years.

The real effective exchange rate index for the U.S. dollar, $E_R^\$$, is found by multiplying the nominal effective exchange rate index, $E_N^\$$, by the ratio of U.S. dollar costs, $C^\$$, over foreign currency costs, $C^{FC}$, both in index form:

$$E_R^\$ = E_N^\$ \times \frac{C^\$}{C^{FC}}$$

If changes in exchange rates just offset differential inflation rates—if purchasing power parity holds—all the real effective exchange rate indices would stay at 100. If an exchange rate strengthened more than was justified by differential inflation, its index would rise above 100. If the real effective exchange rate index is above 100, the currency would be considered "overvalued" from a competitive perspective. An index value below 100 would suggest an "undervalued" currency.

Exhibit 4.3 shows that the real effective exchange rate has varied considerably from year to year for both the U.S. dollar and the Japanese yen, and the data lends some support to the concept that PPP may hold—even for the long run. For example,

**EXHIBIT 4.3**

IMF's Real Effective Exchange Rate Indexes for the United States and Japan (1995 = 100)

Source: *Balance of Payments Statistics Yearbook—International Financial Statistics*. © 2003 by International Monetary Fund. Reproduced with permission of International Monetary Fund via Copyright Clearance Center. May 2004, monthly, 1995 = 100.

the index of the real effective exchange rate for the U.S. dollar rose from a level of 135 in 1981 to a value level of 166 in 1985, only to fall to 100 (the index base year) in 1995. The dollar immediately rose again, to over 132 in 2000 before falling back in 2002 and 2003. The Japanese yen has been undervalued every year for which the dollar was over-valued. Beginning with a value of 63 in 1981, the yen rose relatively steadily toward parity in 1995. After 1995, however, the yen returned to its undervalued ways, falling to an index value of 85 in 1999.

Apart from measuring deviations from PPP, a country's real effective exchange rate is an important tool for management when predicting upward or downward pressure on a country's balance of payments and exchange rate, as well as being an indicator of the desirability to produce for export from that country. *Real World Example 4.2* shows deviations from PPP in the twentieth century.

## Real World Example 4.2
### DEVIATIONS FROM PURCHASING POWER PARITY IN THE 20<sup>TH</sup> CENTURY

The recent seminal work by Dimson, Marsh, and Staunton (2002) found that for the 1900–2000 period, relative purchasing power parity generally held. They did, however, note that significant short-run deviations from PPP did occur. "When deviations from PPP appear to be present it is likely that exchange rates are responding not only to relative inflation but also to other economic and political factors. Changes in productivity differentials, such as Japan's post-war productivity growth in the traded-goods sector, can bring similar wealth effects, with domestic inflation that does not endanger the country's exchange rate."

Real Exchange Rate Changes Against the U.S. Dollar, Annually 1900–2000

| Country | Geometric Mean (%) | Arithmetic Mean (%) | Standard Deviation (%) | Minimum Change (Year, %) | Maximum Change (Year, %) |
|---|---|---|---|---|---|
| Australia | −0.6 | −0.1 | 10.7 | 1931: −39.0 | 1933: 54.2 |
| Belgium | 0.2 | 1.0 | 13.3 | 1919: −32.1 | 1933: 54.2 |
| Canada | −0.5 | −0.4 | 4.6 | 1931: −18.1 | 1933: 12.9 |
| Denmark | 0.1 | 1.0 | 12.7 | 1946: −50.3 | 1933: 37.2 |
| France | −0.4 | 2.5 | 24.0 | 1946: −78.3 | 1943: 141.5 |
| Germany | −0.1 | 15.1 | 134.8 | 1945: −75.0 | 1948: 1302.0 |
| Ireland | −0.1 | 0.5 | 11.2 | 1946: −37.0 | 1933: 56.6 |
| Italy | −0.2 | 4.0 | 39.5 | 1946: −64.9 | 1944: 335.2 |
| Japan | 0.2 | 3.2 | 29.5 | 1945: −78.3 | 1946: 253.0 |
| The Netherlands | −0.1 | 0.8 | 12.6 | 1946: −61.6 | 1933: 55.7 |
| South Africa | −1.3 | −0.7 | 10.5 | 1946: −35.3 | 1986: 37.3 |
| Spain | −0.4 | 1.1 | 18.8 | 1946: −56.4 | 1939: 128.7 |
| Sweden | −0.4 | 0.2 | 10.7 | 1919: −38.0 | 1933: 43.5 |
| Switzerland | 0.2 | 0.8 | 11.2 | 1936: −29.0 | 1933: 53.3 |
| United Kingdom | −0.3 | 0.3 | 11.7 | 1946: −36.7 | 1933: 55.2 |

"While real exchange rates do not appear to exhibit a long-term upward or downward trend, they are clearly volatile, and on year-to-year basis, PPP explains little of the fluctuations in foreign exchange rates. Some of the extreme changes [in the table above] reflect exchange rates or inflation indexes that are not representa-tive, typically (as in Germany) because of wartime controls, and this may amplify the volatility of real exchange rate changes. Given the potential meas-urement error in inflation indexes, and the fact that real exchange rates involve a ratio of two dif-ferent price index series, it is all the more striking that, with the exception of South Africa, all real exchange rates appreciate or depreciate annually by no more than a fraction of one percentage point."

Source: Elroy Dimson, Paul Marsh, and Mike Staunton, *Triumph of the Optimists: 101 Years of Global Investment Returns*, Princeton University Press, 2002, pp. 97–98.

## EXCHANGE RATE PASS-THROUGH

Incomplete *exchange rate pass-through* is one reason that a country's real effective exchange rate index can deviate for lengthy periods from its PPP-equilibrium level of 100. The degree to which the prices of imported and exported goods change as a result of exchange rate changes is termed *pass-through*. Although PPP implies that all exchange rate changes are passed through by equivalent changes in prices to trading partners, empirical research in the 1980s questioned this long-held assumption. For example, sizeable current account deficits of the United States in the 1980s and 1990s did not respond to changes in the value of the dollar.

To illustrate exchange rate pass-through, assume BMW produces an automobile in Germany and pays all production expense in euros. When the firm exports the auto to the United States, the price of the BMW in the U.S. market should simply be the euro value converted to dollars at the spot exchange rate:

$$P_{BMW}^\$ = P_{BMW}^\euro \times S$$

where $P_{BMW}^\$$ is the BMW price in dollars, $P_{BMW}^\euro$ is the BMW price in euros, and S is the number of dollars per euro. If the euro appreciated 10% versus the U.S. dollar, the new spot exchange rate should result in the price of the BMW in the United States rising a proportional 10%. If the price in dollars increases by the same percentage change as the exchange rate, the pass-through of exchange rate changes is complete (or 100%).

However, if the price in dollars rises by less than the percentage change in exchange rates (as is often the case in international trade), the pass-through is *partial*, as illustrated in Exhibit 4.4. The 71% pass-through (U.S. dollar prices rose only 14.29% when the euro appreciated 20%) implies that BMW is absorbing a portion of the adverse exchange rate change. This absorption could result from smaller profit margins, cost reductions, or both. For example, components and raw materials imported to Germany cost less in euros when the euro appreciates. It is also likely that some time

### EXHIBIT 4.4

**Exchange Rate Pass-Through**

*Pass-through* is the measure of response of imported and exported product prices to exchange rate changes. Assume the price in dollars and euros of a BMW automobile produced in Germany and sold in the United States at the spot exchange rate is

$$P_{BMW}^\$ = P_{BMW}^\euro \times (\$/\euro) = \euro35,000 \times \$1.000/\euro = \euro35,000$$

If the euro were to appreciate 20% versus the U.S. dollar, from $1.0000/€, to $1.2000/€, the price of the BMW in the U.S. market should theoretically be $42,000. But if the price of the BMW in the U.S. does not rise by 20%—for example, it rises only to $40,000—then the degree of pass-through is partial:

$$\frac{P_{BMW,2}^\$}{P_{BMW,1}^\$} - \frac{\$40,000}{\$35,000} = 1.1429, \text{ or a 14.29\% increase}$$

The degree of pass-through is measured by the proportion of the exchange rate change reflected in dollar prices. In this example, the dollar price of the BMW rose only 14.29%, while the euro appreciated 20.0% against the U.S. dollar. The degree of pass-through is partial, 14.29% ÷ 20.00%, or approximately 0.71. Only 71% of the exchange rate change was passed through to the U.S. dollar price. The remaining 29% of the exchange rate change has been absorbed by BMW.

may pass before all exchange rate changes are finally reflected in the prices of traded goods, including the period over which previously signed contracts are delivered upon. It is obviously in the interest of BMW to keep the appreciation of the euro from raising the price of its automobiles in major export markets.

The concept of *price elasticity of demand* is useful when determining the desired level of pass-through. Recall that the own-price elasticity of demand for any good is the percentage change in quantity of the good demanded as a result of the percentage change in the good's own price:

$$\text{Price elasticity of demand} = e_p = \frac{\%\Delta Q_d}{\%\Delta P}$$

where $Q_d$ is quantity demanded and P is product price. If the absolute value of $e_p$ is less than 1.0, the good is relatively "inelastic," while greater than 1.0 indicates a relatively "elastic" good.

A German product that is relatively price inelastic, meaning that the quantity demanded is relatively unresponsive to price changes, may often demonstrate a high degree of pass-through. This is so because a higher dollar price in the United States market would have little noticeable effect on the quantity of the product demanded by consumers. Dollar revenue would increase, but euro revenue would remain the same. However, products that are relatively price elastic would respond in the opposite direction. If the 20% euro appreciation resulted in 20% higher dollar prices, U.S. consumers would decrease the number of BMWs purchased. If the price elasticity of demand for BMWs in the United States were greater than one, total dollar sales revenue of BMWs would decline.

## Interest Rates and Exchange Rates

We have already seen how prices of goods in different countries should be related through exchange rates. We now consider how interest rates are linked to exchange rates.

### THE FISHER EFFECT

The Fisher effect, named after economist Irving Fisher, states that nominal interest rates in each country are equal to the required real rate of return plus compensation for expected inflation. More formally this is derived from $(1 + r)(1 + \pi) - 1$:

$$i = r + \pi + r\pi$$

where i is the nominal rate of interest, r is the real rate of interest, and $\pi$ is the expected rate of inflation over the period of time for which funds are to be lent. The final compound term, $r\pi$, is frequently dropped from consideration due to its relatively minor value. The Fisher effect then reduces to (approximate form):

$$i = r + \pi$$

The Fisher effect applied to the United States and Japan would be:

$$i^{\$} = r^{\$} + \pi^{\$}; \quad i^{\yen} = r^{\yen} + \pi^{\yen}$$

where the superscripts $ and ¥ pertain to the respective nominal (i), real (r), and expected inflation ($\pi$) components of financial instruments denominated in dollars and yen, respectively. We need to forecast the future rate of inflation, not what inflation has been. Predicting the future can be difficult.

Empirical tests using ex-post national inflation rates have shown the Fisher effect usually exists for short-maturity government securities such as treasury bills and notes. Comparisons based on longer maturities suffer from the increased financial risk inherent in fluctuations of the market value of the bonds prior to maturity. Comparisons of private sector securities are influenced by unequal creditworthiness of the issuers. All the tests are inconclusive to the extent that recent past rates of inflation are not a correct measure of future expected inflation.

## THE INTERNATIONAL FISHER EFFECT

The relationship between the percentage change in the spot exchange rate over time and the differential between comparable interest rates in different national capital markets is known as the *international Fisher effect*. "Fisher-open," as it is often termed, states that the spot exchange rate should change in an equal amount but in the opposite direction to the difference in interest rates between two countries. More formally,

$$\frac{S_1 - S_2}{S_2} = i^\$ - i^\yen$$

where $i^\$$ and $I^\yen$ are the respective national interest rates, and S is the spot exchange rate using indirect quotes (an indirect quote on the dollar is, for example, ¥/$) at the beginning of the period ($S_1$) and the end of the period ($S_2$). This is the approximation form commonly used in industry. The precise formulation is

$$\frac{S_1 - S_2}{S_2} = \frac{i^\$ - i^\yen}{1 + i^\yen}$$

Justification for the international Fisher effect is that investors must be rewarded or penalized to offset the expected change in exchange rates. For example, if a dollar-based investor buys a 10-year yen bond earning 4% interest, instead of a 10-year dollar bond earning 6% interest, the investor must be expecting the yen to appreciate vis-à-vis the dollar by at least 2% per year during the 10 years. If not, the dollar-based investor would be better off remaining in dollars. If the yen appreciates 3% during the 10-year period, the dollar-based investor would earn a bonus of 1% higher return. However, the international Fisher effect predicts that with unrestricted capital flows, an investor should be indifferent to whether his bond is in dollars or yen, since investors worldwide would see the same opportunity and compete it away.

Empirical tests lend some support to the relationship postulated by the international Fisher effect, although considerable short-run deviations occur. A more serious criticism has been posed, however, by recent studies that suggest the existence of a foreign exchange risk premium for most major currencies. Also, speculation in uncovered interest arbitrage (described below) creates distortions in currency markets. Thus the expected change in exchange rates might consistently be more than the difference in interest rates.

## THE FORWARD RATE

A *forward rate* is an exchange rate quoted today for settlement at some future date. A forward exchange agreement between currencies states the rate of exchange at which a foreign currency will be *bought forward* or *sold forward* at a specific date in the future (typically 30, 60, 90, 180, 270, or 360 days).

The forward rate is calculated for any specific maturity by adjusting the current spot exchange rate by the ratio of euro currency interest rates of the same maturity for the two subject currencies. For example, the 90-day forward rate for the Swiss franc/U.S. dollar exchange rate ($F^{SF/\$}_{90}$) is found by multiplying the current spot rate ($S^{SF/\$}$) by the ratio of the 90-day euro-Swiss franc deposit rate ($i^{SF}$) over the 90-day Eurodollar deposit rate ($i^{\$}$):

$$F^{SF/\$}_{90} = S^{SF/\$} \times \frac{\left[1 + \left(i^{SF} \times \dfrac{90}{360}\right)\right]}{\left[1 + \left(i^{\$} \times \dfrac{90}{360}\right)\right]}$$

Assuming a spot rate of SF1.4800/$, a 90-day euro Swiss franc deposit rate of 4.00% per annum, and a 90-day eurodollar deposit rate of 8.00% per annum, the 90-day forward rate is SF1.4655/$:

$$F^{SF/\$}_{90} = SF1.4800/\$ \times \frac{\left[1 + \left(.0400 \times \dfrac{90}{360}\right)\right]}{\left[1 + \left(.0800 \times \dfrac{90}{360}\right)\right]} = SF1.4800/\$ \times \frac{1.01}{1.02} = SF1.4655/\$$$

The *forward premium* or *discount* is the percentage difference between the spot and forward exchange rate, stated in annual percentage terms. When the foreign currency price of the home currency is used as in this case of SF/$, the formula for the percent-per-annum premium or discount becomes

$$f^{SF} = \frac{\text{Spot} - \text{Forward}}{\text{Forward}} \times \frac{360}{\text{days}} \times 100$$

Substituting the SF/$ spot and forward rates, as well as the number of days forward (90),

$$f^{SF} = \frac{SF1.4800/\$ - SF1.4655/\$}{SF1.4655/\$} \times \frac{360}{90} \times 100 = +3.96\% \text{ per annum}$$

The sign is positive, indicating that the Swiss franc is *selling forward at a 3.96% per annum premium* over the dollar (it takes 3.96% more dollars to get a franc at the 90-day forward rate).

As illustrated in Exhibit 4.5, the forward premium on the eurodollar forward exchange rate series arises from the differential between eurodollar interest rates and Swiss franc interest rates. Because the forward rate for any particular maturity utilizes the specific interest rates for that term, the forward premium or discount on a currency is visually obvious—the currency with the higher interest rate (in this case the U.S. dollar) will sell forward at a discount, and the currency with the lower interest rate (in this case the Swiss franc) will sell forward at a premium.

The forward rate is calculated from three observable data items—the spot rate, the foreign currency deposit rate, the home currency deposit rate—and is not a forecast of the future spot exchange. It is, however, frequently used by managers within MNEs as a forecast, with mixed results as the section below describes.

## INTEREST RATE PARITY (IRP)

The theory of *interest rate parity* (IRP) provides the link between the foreign exchange markets and the international money markets. The theory states: *The difference in the national interest rates for securities of similar risk and maturity should be equal to, but*

**EXHIBIT 4.5**

Currency Yield
Curves and the
Forward
Premium

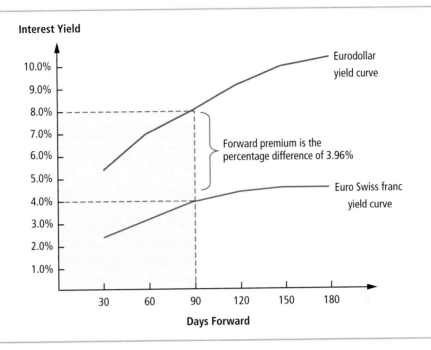

**EXHIBIT 4.6**

Interest Rate
Parity (IRP)

*Note that the Swiss
franc investment
yields $1,019,993,
$7 less on a
$1 million
investment.

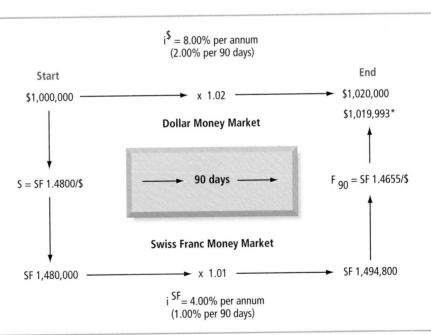

*opposite in sign to, the forward rate discount or premium for the foreign currency, except
for transaction costs.*

Exhibit 4.6 shows how the theory of interest rate parity works. Assume that an
investor has $1,000,000 and several alternative but comparable Swiss franc (SF) mone-
tary investments. If the investor chooses to invest in a dollar money market instrument,

the investor would earn the dollar rate of interest. This results in $(1 + i^\$)$ at the end of the period, where $i^\$$ is the dollar rate of interest in decimal form. The investor may, however, choose to invest in a Swiss franc money market instrument of identical risk and maturity for the same period. This would require that the investor exchange the dollars for francs at the spot rate of exchange, invest the francs in a money market instrument, sell the francs forward (in order to avoid any risk that the exchange rate would change), and at the end of the period convert the resulting proceeds back to dollars.

A dollar-based investor would evaluate the relative returns of starting in the top-left corner and investing in the dollar market (straight across the top of the box) compared to investing in the Swiss franc market (going down and then around the box to the top-right corner). The comparison of returns would be:

$$\left(1 + i^\$\right) = S^{SF/\$} \times \left(1 + i^{SF}\right) \times \frac{1}{F^{SF/\$}}$$

where $S$ = the spot rate of exchange and $F$ = the forward rate of exchange. Substituting in the spot rate (SF1.4800/\$) and forward rate (SF1.4655/\$) and respective interest rates ($i^\$ = 0.02$, $i^{SF} = 0.01$) from Exhibit 4.6, the interest rate parity condition is

$$(1 + .02) = 1.4800 \times (1 + .01) \times \frac{1}{1.4655}$$

The left-hand side of the equation is the gross return the investor would earn by investing in dollars. The right-hand side is the gross return the investor would earn by exchanging dollars for Swiss francs at the spot rate, investing the franc proceeds in the Swiss franc money market, and simultaneously selling the principal plus interest in Swiss francs forward for dollars at the current 90-day forward rate.

Ignoring transaction costs, if the returns in dollars are equal between the two alternative money market investments, the spot and forward rates are considered to be at IRP. The transaction is "covered" because the exchange rate back to dollars is guaranteed at the end of the 90-day period. Therefore, as in Exhibit 4.6, in order for the two alternatives to be equal, any differences in interest rates must be offset by the difference between the spot and forward exchange rates (in approximate form)

$$\frac{F}{S} = \frac{\left(1 + i^{SF}\right)}{\left(1 + I^\$\right)} \quad \text{or} \quad \frac{SF1.4655 / \$}{SF1.4800 / \$} = \frac{1.01}{1.02} = 0.9902 \approx 1\%$$

## COVERED INTEREST ARBITRAGE (CIA)

The spot and forward exchange markets are not, however, constantly in the state of equilibrium described by interest rate parity. When the market is not in equilibrium, the potential for "riskless" or arbitrage profit exists. The arbitrager who recognizes such an imbalance will move to take advantage of the disequilibrium by investing in whichever currency offers the higher return on a covered basis. This is called *covered interest arbitrage* (CIA).

Exhibit 4.7 describes the steps that a currency trader, most likely working in the arbitrage division of a large international bank, would implement to perform a CIA transaction. The currency trader, Fye Hong, may utilize any of a number of major eurocurrencies that his bank holds to conduct arbitrage investments. The morning conditions indicate to Fye Hong that a CIA transaction that exchanges 1 million U.S. dollars for Japanese yen, invested in a six-month euroyen account and sold forward

## EXHIBIT 4.7

Covered Interest
Arbitrage (CIA)

Eurodollar rate = 8.00 % per annum

**Start**

$1,000,000   →   x 1.04   →   $1,040,000

**End**

$1,044,638  } Arbitrage Potential

**Dollar Money Market**

S = ¥106.00/$

→ 180 days →

F₁₈₀ = ¥103.50/$

**Yen Money Market**

¥106,000,000   →   x 1.02   →   ¥108,120,000

Euroyen rate = 4.00% per annum

back to dollars, will yield a profit of $4,638 ($1,044,638 − $1,040,000) over and above that available from a eurodollar investment. Conditions in the exchange markets and euromarkets change rapidly, however, so if Fye Hong waits even a few minutes, the profit opportunity may disappear. Fye Hong executes the following transaction:

Step 1:  Convert $1,000,000 at the spot rate of ¥106.00/$ to ¥106,000,000 (see "Start").

Step 2:  Invest the proceeds, ¥106,000,000, in a euroyen account for six months, earning 4.00% per annum, or 2% for 180 days.

Step 3:  Simultaneously sell the future yen proceeds (¥108,120,000) forward for dollars at the 180-day forward rate of ¥103.50/$. This action "locks in" gross dollar revenues of $1,044,638 (see "End").

Step 4:  Calculate the cost (opportunity cost) of funds used at the eurodollar rate of 8.00% per annum, or 4% for 180 days, with principal and interest then totaling $1,040,000. Profit on CIA ("End") is $4,638 ($1,044,638–$1,040,000).

Note that all profits are stated in terms of the currency in which the transaction was initialized, but that a trader may conduct investments denominated in U.S. dollars, Japanese yen, or any other major currency.

This process of CIA drives the international currency and money markets toward the equilibrium described by interest rate parity. Slight deviations from equilibrium provide opportunities for arbitragers to make small riskless profits. Such deviations provide the supply and demand forces which will move the market back toward parity (equilibrium).

Covered interest arbitrage opportunities continue until interest rate parity is reestablished, because the arbitragers are able to earn risk-free profits by repeating the cycle as often as possible. Their actions, however, nudge the foreign exchange and money markets back toward equilibrium for the following reasons:

1. Purchase of yen in the spot market and sale of yen in the forward market narrows the premium on the forward yen. This is so because the spot yen strengthens from the extra demand and the forward yen weakens because of the extra sales. A narrower premium on the forward yen reduces the foreign exchange gain previously captured by investing in yen.

2. The demand for yen-denominated securities causes yen interest rates to fall, while the higher level of borrowing in the United States causes dollar interest rates to rise. The net result is a wider interest differential in favor of investing in the dollar.

## UNCOVERED INTEREST ARBITRAGE (UIA)

A deviation from covered interest arbitrage is *uncovered interest arbitrage* (UIA), wherein investors borrow in countries and currencies exhibiting relatively low interest rates and convert the proceeds into currencies that offer much higher interest rates. The transaction is "uncovered" because the investor does not sell the higher yielding currency proceeds forward, choosing to remain uncovered and accept the currency risk of exchanging the higher yield currency into the lower yielding currency at the end of the period. Exhibit 4.8 demonstrates the steps an uncovered interest arbitrager takes when undertaking what is termed the "yen carry trade."

The "yen carry trade" is an age-old application of UIA. Investors, from both inside and outside Japan, take advantage of extremely low interest rates in Japanese yen (0.40% per annum) to raise capital. Investors exchange the capital they raise for other currencies like U.S. dollars or euros. They then reinvest these dollar or euro proceeds in dollar or euro money markets where the funds earn substantially higher rates of return (5.00% per annum in Exhibit 4.8). At the end of the period, a year in this case, they convert the dollar proceeds back into Japanese yen in the spot market. The result is a tidy profit over what it costs to repay the initial loan.

## EXHIBIT 4.8

Uncovered Interest Arbitrage (UIA): The Yen Carry Trade

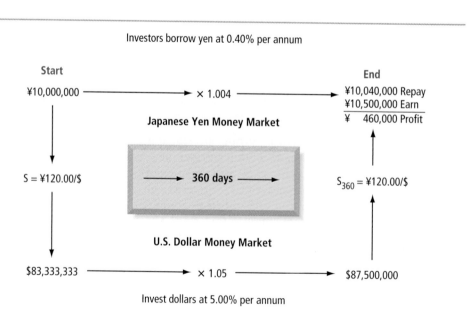

Investors borrow yen at 0.40% per annum

**Start**                                                      **End**

¥10,000,000 ——————→ × 1.004 ——————→ ¥10,040,000 Repay
                                                               ¥10,500,000 Earn
                                                               ¥    460,000 Profit

**Japanese Yen Money Market**

$S = ¥120.00/\$$        ——→ **360 days** ——→        $S_{360} = ¥120.00/\$$

**U.S. Dollar Money Market**

$83,333,333 ——————→ × 1.05 ——————→ $87,500,000

Invest dollars at 5.00% per annum

The trick, however, is that the spot exchange rate at the end of the year must not change significantly from what it was at the beginning of the year. If the yen were to appreciate significantly against the dollar, as it did in late 1999, moving from 120/$ to 105/$, these "uncovered" investors would suffer sizeable losses when they convert their dollars into yen to repay the yen they borrowed. The higher return does indeed come at higher risk!

## EQUILIBRIUM BETWEEN INTEREST RATES AND EXCHANGE RATES

Exhibit 4.9 illustrates the conditions necessary for equilibrium between interest rates and exchange rates. The vertical axis shows the difference in interest rates in favor of the foreign currency, and the horizontal axis shows the forward premium or discount on that currency. The interest rate parity line shows the equilibrium state, but transaction costs cause the line to be a band rather than a thin line. Transaction costs arise from foreign exchange and investment brokerage costs on buying and selling securities. Typical transaction costs in recent years have been in the range of 0.18% to 0.25% on an annual basis. For individual transactions like Fye Hong's arbitrage activity in the previous example, there is no explicit transaction cost per trade; rather the costs of the bank in supporting Fye Hong's activities are the transaction costs. Point X shows one possible equilibrium position, where a 4% lower rate of interest on yen securities would be offset by a 4% premium on the forward yen.

The disequilibrium situation, which encouraged the interest rate arbitrage in the previous CIA example, is illustrated by point U. It is located off the interest rate parity line because the lower interest on the yen is −4% (annual basis), whereas the

**EXHIBIT 4.9**

Interest Rate Parity (IRP) and Equilibrium

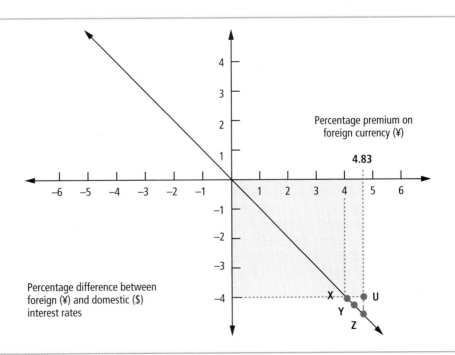

premium on the forward yen is slightly over 4.8% (annual basis). Using the formula for forward premium presented earlier, we find the premium on the yen thus:

$$\frac{\yen 106.00 / \$ - \yen 103.50 / \$}{\yen 103.50 / \$} \times \frac{360 \text{ days}}{180 \text{ days}} \times 100 = 4.83\%$$

The situation depicted by point U is unstable because all investors have an incentive to execute the same covered interest arbitrage. Except for a bank failure, the arbitrage gain is virtually risk free.

Some observers have suggested that political risk does exist, because one of the governments might apply capital controls that would prevent execution of the forward contract. This risk is fairly remote for covered interest arbitrage between major financial centers of the world, especially because a large portion of funds used for covered interest arbitrage is in eurodollars. The concern may be valid for pairings with countries not noted for political and fiscal stability.

The net result of the disequilibrium is that fund flows will narrow the gap in interest rates and/or decrease the premium on the forward yen. In other words, market pressures will cause point U in Exhibit 4.9 to move toward the interest rate parity band. Equilibrium might be reached at point Y, or at any other locus between X and Z, depending on whether forward market premiums are more or less easily shifted than interest rate differentials.

## Forward Rate as an Unbiased Predictor of the Future Spot Rate

Some forecasters believe that foreign exchange markets for the major floating currencies are "efficient" and forward exchange rates are *unbiased predictors* of future spot exchange rates.

Exhibit 4.10 demonstrates the meaning of "unbiased prediction" in terms of how the forward rate performs in estimating future spot exchange rates. If the forward rate is an unbiased predictor of the future spot rate, the expected value of the future spot rate at time 2 equals the present forward rate for time 2 delivery, available now, $E_1(S_2) = F_{1,2}$.

Intuitively this means that the distribution of possible actual spot rates in the future is centered on the forward rate. The fact that it is an unbiased predictor, however, does not mean that the future spot rate will actually be equal to what the forward rate predicts. Unbiased prediction simply means that the forward rate will, on average, overestimate and underestimate the actual future spot rate in equal frequency and degree. The forward rate may, in fact, never actually equal the future spot rate.

The rationale for this relationship is based on the hypothesis that the foreign exchange market is reasonably efficient. Market efficiency assumes that (a) all relevant information is quickly reflected in both the spot and forward exchange markets, (b) transaction costs are low, and (c) instruments denominated in different currencies are perfect substitutes for one another.

Empirical studies of the efficient foreign exchange market hypothesis have yielded conflicting results. Nevertheless, a consensus is developing that rejects the efficient market hypothesis. It appears that the forward rate is not an unbiased predictor of the future spot rate and that it does pay to use resources to attempt to forecast exchange rates.

If the efficient market hypothesis is correct, a financial executive cannot expect to profit in any consistent manner from forecasting future exchange rates, because current quotations in the forward market reflect all that is presently known about likely future rates. While future exchange rates may well differ from the expectation implicit

**EXHIBIT 4.10**

Forward Rate as
an Unbiased
Predictor for
Future Spot Rate

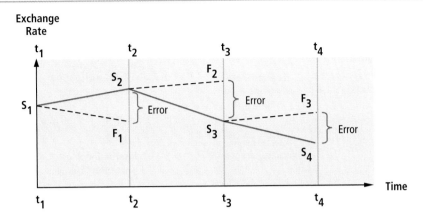

The forward rate available today ($F_{t,t+1}$), time t, for delivery at future time $_{t+1}$, is used as a "predictor" of the spot rate that will exist at that day in the future. Therefore, the forecast spot rate for time $S_{t2}$ is $F_1$; the actual spot rate turns out to be $S_2$. The vertical distance between the prediction and the actual spot rate is the forecast error.

When the forward rate is termed an "unbiased predictor of the future spot rate," it means that the forward rate over- or underestimates the future spot rate with relatively equal frequency and amount. It therefore "misses the mark" in a regular and orderly manner. The sum of the errors equals zero.

in the present forward market quotation, we cannot know today which way actual future quotations will differ from today's forward rate. The expected mean value of deviations is zero. The forward rate is therefore an "unbiased" estimator of the future spot rate.

Tests of foreign exchange market efficiency, using longer time periods of analysis, conclude that either exchange market efficiency is untestable or, if it is testable, the market is not efficient. Furthermore, the existence and success of foreign exchange forecasting services suggest that managers are willing to pay a price for forecast information even though they can use the forward rate as a forecast at no cost. The "cost" of buying this information is, in many circumstances, an "insurance premium" for financial managers who might get fired for using their own forecast, including forward rates, when that forecast proves incorrect. If they "bought" professional advice that turned out wrong, the fault was not in their forecast!

If the exchange market is not efficient, it would be sensible for a firm to spend resources on forecasting exchange rates. This is the opposite conclusion to the one in which exchange markets are deemed efficient.

## Prices, Interest Rates, and Exchange Rates in Equilibrium 84–85

Exhibit 4.11 illustrates all of the fundamental parity relations simultaneously, in equilibrium, using the U.S. dollar and the Japanese yen. The forecasted inflation rates for Japan and the United States are 1.0% and 5.0%, respectively, a 4% differential. The nominal interest rate in the U.S. dollar market (one-year government security) is 8%, a differential of 4% over the Japanese nominal interest rate of 4%. The spot rate, $S_1$, is ¥104/$, and the one-year forward rate is ¥100/$.

**EXHIBIT 4.11**

International
Parity Conditions
in Equilibrium
(Approximate
Form)

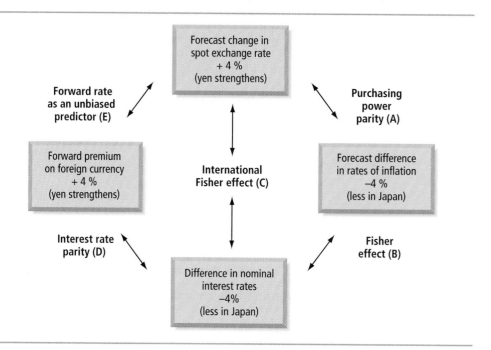

- **Relation A: Purchasing Power Parity (PPP).** According to the relative version of purchasing power parity, the spot exchange rate one year from now, $S_2$, is expected to be ¥100/$:

$$S_2 = S_1 \times \frac{1 + \pi^{¥}}{1 + \pi^{\$}} = ¥104 \: / \: \$ \times \frac{1.01}{1.05} = ¥100 \: / \: \$$$

This is a 4% change and equal, but opposite in sign, to the difference in expected rates of inflation (1% − 5% or 4%).

- **Relation B: The Fisher Effect.** The real rate of return is the nominal rate of interest less the expected rate of inflation. Assuming efficient and open markets, the real rates of return should be equal across currencies. Here, the real rate is 3% in U.S. dollar markets (r = i −π = 8%–5%), and in Japanese yen markets (4%–1%). Note that the 3% real rate of return is not in the box above, but rather the Fisher effect's relationship — that nominal interest rate differentials equal the difference in expected rates of inflation, −4%.

- **Relation C: International Fisher Effect.** The forecast change in the spot exchange rate, in this case 4%, is equal to but opposite in sign to the differential between nominal interest rates:

$$\frac{S_1 - S_2}{S_2} \times 100 = i^{¥} - i^{\$} = 4\% - 8\% = -4\%$$

- **Relation D: Interest Rate Parity (IRP).** According to the theory of interest rate parity, the difference in nominal interest rates is equal to, but opposite in sign to, the forward premium. For this numerical example, the nominal yen interest rate (4%) is 4% less than the nominal dollar interest rate (8%):

$$i^{¥} - i^{\$} = 4\% - 8\% = -4\%$$

and the forward premium is a positive 4%:

$$f^{¥} = \frac{S_1 - F}{F} \times 100 = \frac{¥104/\$ - ¥100/\$}{¥100/\$} \times 100 = 4\%$$

- **Relationship E: Forward Rate as an Unbiased Predictor.** Finally, the one-year forward rate on the Japanese yen, ¥100/$, if assumed to be an unbiased predictor of the future spot rate, also forecasts ¥100/$.

## MINI-CASE

# The Introduction of the Porsche 911 Carrera 4S Cabriolet

Based in Germany, and with manufacturing and assembly exclusively located in Germany, Slovakia, and Finland, Porsche's entire cost base is the euro or Slovakian koruna (which is managed by the Slovakian government to maintain stability against the euro). This means that all of the direct costs in its automobile manufacturing are incurred (for practical purposes) in euro-denominated operations (cost, markup, basic pricing). The three product lines (911, Boxster, Cayenne) are then exported and distributed in the major industrial country markets. Porsche therefore has little local sourcing or local currency costs in the non-European markets, where it sells more than half its total annual volumes.

If Porsche were not actively managing this exchange rate exposure, the company would see declining profitability — or at least declining rates of profitable growth — as a result of its euro-denominated products priced and sold in non-euro currency environments like the U.S. dollar. Assuming there is a limit to the price consumers in the U.S. dollar market are willing and able to pay for Porsche products, the U.S. price will hit a ceiling, and, if the euro continues to rise against the dollar, this will result in declining margins, or declining volumes, or both. A simple numerical example using the following equation can make the limitations of a dollar-price readily apparent.

$$\text{Price}^{\$} = \text{Price}^{m} \times \text{Spot rate}^{\$/m}$$

The following exhibit illustrates a possible scenario of the European costing and pricing for the planned North American launch of the new Porsche 911 4S Carbriolet (a 3.6-liter six-cylinder engine with a top track speed of 174 mph; 0 to 62 mph in 5.3 seconds). Assume that Porsche first established the price of the car in euros, and then — in April 2003 — set the U.S. dollar price at the then current exchange rate of $1.0862/€, approximately $93,200.

As illustrated in the exhibit on the next page, in the months following the price-setting, the company's margin would have been largely eliminated as a result of the continued appreciation of the euro versus the dollar. The analysis highlights the squeeze suffered by a European producer exporting to the U.S. dollar markets. Independent of what method, degree, or effectiveness of hedging was undertaken by Porsche, the company was faced with a continuing pricing dilemma for all of its North American sales.

## Case Questions

1. Clearly, at some point sooner or later, Porsche must raise the U.S. dollar price of this model and all product models (particularly if the euro continues to strengthen and maintains this strength compared to the dollar). But when would that be?
2. What would it take to convince Porsche's management that "now is the time" to pass-through more of the exchange rate change in the price?

**Pass-Through Analysis for the 911 Carrera 4S Cabriolet, 2003**

Assume that Porsche established what it considered the target price in April 2003, when the exchange rate was $1.0862/€. This allowed Porsche to price in a margin of approximately 15% on a full-cost basis, with a European price of €85,900 and a target North American price of $93,200, which preserved the 15% margin.

Actual North American launch of the 4S Cabriolet did not occur until July. By then, the spot exchange rate had effectively reduced the margin earned by Porsche on the new model. As 2003 continued, the margin continued to erode.

| Price Component | Pricing Apr | May | Jun | NA Launch Jul | Aug | Sep | Oct | Nov | Dec |
|---|---|---|---|---|---|---|---|---|---|
| Full cost | €74,696 | €74,696 | €74,696 | €74,696 | €74,696 | €74,696 | €74,696 | €74,696 | €74,696 |
| Margin (@ 15%) | €11,204 | €11,204 | €11,204 | €11,204 | €11,204 | €11,204 | €11,204 | €11,204 | €11,204 |
| European price | €85,900 | €85,900 | €85,900 | €85,900 | €85,900 | €85,900 | €85,900 | €85,900 | €85,900 |
| Spot rate ($/€) | 1.0862 | 1.1565 | 1.1676 | 1.1362 | 1.1286 | 1.1267 | 1.1714 | 1.1710 | 1.2298 |
| Base price in US$ if 100% pass-through | $93,305 | $99,343 | $100,297 | $97,600 | $96,947 | $96,784 | $100,623 | $100,589 | $105,640 |
| | | | | Effective Margin on 4S Cabriolet with Capped US$ Price | | | | | |
| Target price in US$ | $93,200 | $93,200 | $93,200 | $93,200 | $93,200 | $93,200 | $93,200 | $93,200 | $93,200 |
| Spot rate ($/€) | 1.0862 | 1.1565 | 1.1676 | 1.1362 | 1.1286 | 1.1267 | 1.1714 | 1.1710 | 1.2298 |
| Price received in euros | €85,804 | €80,588 | €79,822 | €82,028 | €82,580 | €82,719 | €79,563 | €79,590 | €75,785 |
| Less full cost | (€74,696) | (€74,696) | (€74,696) | (€74,696) | (€74,696) | (€74,696) | (€74,696) | (€74,696) | (€74,696) |
| Residual margin | €11,108 | €5,892 | €5,126 | €7,332 | €7,885 | €8,024 | €4,867 | €4,894 | €1,089 |
| Margin (%) | 14.9% | 7.9% | 6.9% | 9.8% | 10.6% | 10.7% | 6.5% | 6.6% | 1.5% |

## Summary of Learning Objectives

*Demonstrate how price levels and price level changes (inflation) in a country determine the exchange rate at which its currency is traded*

- Parity conditions have traditionally been used by economists to help explain the long-run trend in an exchange rate.

- Under conditions of freely floating rates, the expected rate of change in the spot exchange rate, differential rates of national inflation and interest, and the forward discount or premium are all directly proportional to each other and mutually determined. A change in one of these variables has a tendency to change all of them with a feedback on the variable that changes first.

- If the identical product or service can be sold in two different markets and there are no restrictions on its sale or the transportation costs of moving it between markets, its price should be the same in both markets. This is called the law of one price.

- The absolute version of the theory of purchasing power parity states that the spot exchange rate is determined by the relative prices of similar baskets of goods.

- The relative version of the theory of purchasing power parity states that if the spot exchange rate between two countries starts in equilibrium, any change in the differential rate of inflation between them tends to be offset over the long run by an equal but opposite change in the spot exchange rate.

*Show how interest rates reflect inflationary forces within each country and currency*

- The Fisher effect, named after economist Irving Fisher, states that nominal interest rates in each country are equal to the required real rate of return plus compensation for expected inflation.

*Explain how interest rates for currencies reflect expectations held by market participants about the future spot exchange rate*

- The international Fisher effect, "Fisher-open" as it is often termed, states that the spot exchange rate should change in an equal amount but in the opposite direction to the difference in interest rates between two countries.

*Analyze how, in equilibrium, the spot and forward currency markets are aligned with interest differentials*

- The theory of interest rate parity (IRP) states that the difference in the national interest rates for securities of similar risk and maturity should be equal to, but opposite in sign to, the forward rate discount or premium for the foreign currency, except for transaction costs.

- When the spot and forward exchange markets are not in equilibrium as described by interest rate parity, the potential for "riskless" or arbitrage profit exists. This is called covered interest arbitrage (CIA).

- Some forecasters believe that for the major floating currencies, foreign exchange markets are "efficient" and forward exchange rates are unbiased predictors of future spot exchange rates.

## QUESTIONS

1. **Purchasing power parity.** What is the law of one price? According to this "law," what should happen to the currency of a country experiencing hyper-inflation?

2. **Undervalued and overvalued.** What is an undervalued currency? What is an overvalued currency?

3. **Hamburger standard.** Using the data in Exhibit 4.1, separate the countries in which the actual exchange rate on May 27, 2004, was overvalued (above the hamburger parity rate), from those in which the actual exchange rate was undervalued (below the implied parity rate). What can you conclude?

4. **Relativity.** What is the difference between the absolute theory of purchasing power parity and the relative version of that theory?

5. **PPP and the BOP.** What is the connection between changes in purchasing power parity and changes in a country's balance of payments?

6. **Validating PPP.** What two general conclusions can be made about the actual working of purchasing power parity?

7. **Exchange rate indices.** What is a nominal effective exchange rate index and how does it differ from a real effective exchange rate index?

8. **Interest rates.** What is the difference between nominal interest rates and real interest rates?

9. **International Fisher effect.** What did Irving Fisher postulate about the relationship between nominal interest rates and foreign exchange rates?

10. **Fisher effect.** What did Irving Fisher state to be the relationship between nominal and real interest rates?

## PROBLEMS

1. **Passing through.** In Japan, Honda's export price per vehicle, FOB Yokohama, was ¥4,000,000 at a time when the exchange rate was ¥125/$. The expected rate of inflation in Japanese yen markets for the coming year was 1.0%; the expected rate of inflation in U.S. dollar markets 3.0%. Honda actively tried to limit pass through of exchange rate changes into prices to 60% of annual changes.

   a. What was the price of a Honda in U.S. dollars at the beginning of the year?

   b. Assuming purchasing power parity, what was the expected spot exchange rate at the end of the coming year?

   c. Assuming 100% pass through of exchange rate changes, what would the price of a Honda be at the end of the coming year in U.S. dollars?

   d. Assuming 60% pass through of exchange rate changes, what would the price of a Honda be at the end of the coming year in U.S. dollars?

2. **Chilean pesos.** One year ago the spot exchange rate between the Chilean peso and the U.S. dollar was Ps500.00/$. During the past year, the Chilean peso fell 25% in value against the dollar. During this same 12-month period, prices in the United States were stable but Chilean prices rose 22%.

**a.** What is the actual exchange rate today?

**b.** What should be the exchange rate today, based on purchasing power parity and assuming the initial year was "normal"?

**c.** By what percentage is the Chilean peso over-valued or undervalued today?

3. **International interest rates.** One-year interest rates are currently 1.5% in the United States and 4.8% in Great Britain. The current spot rate between the pound and the dollar is $1.85/£. What would you expect the spot rate for the pound to be one year hence if you believe in the international Fisher effect?

4. **Trident borrows euros.** Trident is able to borrow €4,000,000 from a European bank for one year at 5% per annum, a saving of 3 percentage points over what it would pay to borrow dollars in the United States. Trident plans to exchange the borrowed euros for dollars in order to finance a U.S. project. The current spot rate is $1.32/€. Maria Gonzalez, Trident's CFO, believes that U.S. inflation will continue at 3% per annum while European inflation will be only 2%. The spot rate one year hence, when Trident must buy euros spot to repay the euro loan, will follow purchasing power parity. What is Trident's real cost of financing its project with euros?

5. **Covering.** How does the risk of an uncovered interest arbitrage investment differ from the risk of a covered interest arbitrage investment?

6. **Mary Smyth—CIA.** Mary Smyth is a foreign exchange dealer for a bank in New York City. She has $1,000,000 for a short-term money market investment and wonders if she should invest in U.S. dollars for three months or make a covered interest arbitrage investment in the Swiss franc. She faces the following rates:

| | |
|---|---|
| Spot exchange rate: | SF1.1520/$ |
| 3-month forward rate: | SF1.1472/$ |
| 3-month U.S. interest rate: | 4.500% per annum |
| 3-month Swiss interest rate: | 3.200% per annum |

Where do you recommend Ms. Smyth invest, and why?

7. **Mary Smyth—UIA.** In the situation described in question 6 above, Mary Smyth decides to seek the full 3.200% return available in Switzerland by not covering her forward dollar receipts. Assess this decision.

8. **Mary Smyth—one month later.** One month after the events described in question 6, above, Mary Smyth again has $1,000,000 to invest for three months. She now faces the following rates. Should she enter into a covered interest arbitrage investment?

| | |
|---|---|
| Spot exchange rate: | SF1.1800/$ |
| 3-month forward rate: | SF1.1680/$ |
| 3-month U.S. interest rate: | 4.80% per annum |
| 3-month Swiss rate: | 3.00% per annum |

9. **Langkawi Island Resort.** You are planning a 30-day vacation on Langkawi Island, Malaysia, one year from now. The present charge for a luxury suite plus meals is RM760 per day, and the Malaysian ringgit presently is traded at RM3.8000/$. Hence, the dollar cost today for a 30-day stay would be $6,000.

The hotel has informed you that any increase in its room charges will be limited to any increase in the Malaysian cost of living. Malaysian inflation is expected to be 4% per annum, while U.S. inflation is only 1% per annum.

**a.** How many dollars might you expect to need one year hence to pay for your 30-day vacation?

**b.** By what percent has the dollar cost gone up? Why?

10. **Covered interest against the krone.** A foreign exchange trader sees the following prices on his screen:

| | |
|---|---|
| Spot rate: | NKr6.2280/$ |
| 3-month forward rate: | NKr6.2640/$ |
| U.S. 3-month treasury bill rate: | 4.400% per annum |
| Norwegian 3-month treasury bill rate: | 4.800% per annum |

Could the trader profit by placing $500,000 of principal in a covered interest arbitrage operation in Norway?

**11. Frankfurt and New York.** Money and foreign exchange markets in Frankfurt and New York are very efficient. The following information is available:

| | Frankfurt | New York |
|---|---|---|
| Spot exchange rate | $1.22/€ | $1.22/€ |
| One-year treasury bill rate | 2.1% | 1.50% |
| Expected inflation rate | unknown | 2.00% |

**a.** What do the financial markets suggest for inflation in Europe next year?

**b.** Estimate today's one-year forward exchange rate between the dollar and the euro.

**12. The Beer Standard.** In 1999 *The Economist* reported the creation of an index or standard for the evaluation of currency values in Africa. Beer, rather than the Big Mac hamburger, was chosen as the product for comparison because McDonald's had not penetrated the African continent beyond South Africa and beer met most of the same product and market characteristics required for the construction of a proper currency index.

Investec, a South African investment banking firm, has replicated the process of creating a measure of purchasing power parity like that of the Big Mac Index of *The Economist,* for Africa. The index compares the cost of a 375-milliliter bottle of clear lager beer across sub-Sahara Africa. As a measure of purchasing power parity, the beer needs to be relatively homogeneous in qualities across countries, and needs to possess substantial elements of local manufacturing, distribution, and service, in order to actually provide a measure of relative purchasing power.

The beers are first priced in local currency (purchased in the taverns of the local man, and not in the high-priced tourist centers and servers), then converted to South African rand. The prices of the beers in rand are then compared to form one measure of whether the local currencies are either undervalued (2%) or overvalued (+%) versus the South African rand.

Use the data in the exhibit and complete the calculation of whether the individual African currencies listed are overvalued or undervalued.

| The Beer Standard | | Beer Prices | | | Spot | Under or |
|---|---|---|---|---|---|---|
| Country | Beer | In local currency | In rand | Implied PPP rate | rate 3/15/99 | overvalued to rand% |
| South Africa | Castle | Rand 2.30 | 2.30 | — | — | — |
| Botswana | Castle | Pula 2.20 | 2.94 | 0.96 | 0.75 | _____ |
| Ghana | Star | Cedi 1,200 | 3.17 | 521.74 | 379.10 | _____ |
| Kenya | Tusker | Shilling 41.25 | 4.02 | 17.93 | 10.27 | _____ |
| Malawi | Carisberg | Kwacha 18.50 | 2.66 | 8.04 | 6.96 | _____ |
| Mauritius | Phoenix | Rupee 15.00 | 3.72 | 6.52 | 4.03 | _____ |
| Namibia | Windhoek | N$2.50 | 2.50 | 1.09 | 1.00 | _____ |
| Zambia | Castle | Kwacha 1,200 | 3.52 | 521.74 | 340.68 | _____ |
| Zimbabwe | Castle | Z$9.00 | 1.46 | 3.91 | 6.15 | _____ |

Beer price in rand = price in local currency/spot rate. Implied PPP rate = price in local currency/2.30.
Under/overvalued to rand = implied PPP rate/spot rate −1 × 100. © 1999 The Economist Newspaper Ltd.
All Rights Reserved. Reprinted with permission. Further reproduction prohibited. www.economist.com

**Internet Exercises**

1. **Currency volatility**. Although major currencies like the U.S. dollar and the euro are some of the most widely traded currencies that are frequently referred to as *hard currencies,* they are in fact quite volatile in their relative values. Use the following Web site of the Pacific Exchange Rate Service to study currency volatility. The analysis page quoted below is for currencies quoted against the U.S. dollar, but it is also available for quotes against the Canadian dollar and the euro.

   Pacific Exchange Rate Service
      http://fx.sauder.ubc.ca/USD/analysis.html

2. **Exchange rate indices**. JP Morgan Chase calculates and maintains indices of many of the world's major currencies' values relative to baskets of other major currencies. Like those published by the IMF, these indices serve as more fundamental and general indicators of relative currency value.

   JP Morgan Currency Indices
      http://www2.jpmorgan.com/cgi-bin/Indices

3. **Big Mac index updated**. Use *The Economist*'s Web site to find the latest edition of the Big Mac index of currency over- and undervaluation. (You will need to do a search for "Big Mac currencies.") Create a worksheet to compare how the British pound, the euro, the Swiss franc, and the Canadian dollar have changed from the version presented in this chapter.

   *The Economist*
      http://www.economist.com/

# Foreign Exchange Rate Determination

## LEARNING OBJECTIVES

Examine how the supply and demand for any currency can be viewed as an asset choice issue within the portfolio of investors

Explore how the three major approaches to exchange rate determination — parity conditions, the balance of payments, and the asset approach — combine to explain in part the recent currency crises experienced in Asia, Russia, and Argentina

Observe how forecasters combine technical analysis with the three major theoretical approaches to forecasting exchange rates

Exchange rate determination is complex. Chapter 3 explained how a country's balance of payments can have a significant impact on the level of its exchange rate and vice versa, depending on that country's exchange rate regime. Chapter 4 analyzed the international parity conditions that integrate exchange rates with inflation and interest rates, and provided a theoretical framework for the global financial markets and the management of international financial activities. This chapter extends the discussion of exchange rate determination to the other major school of thought on the determination of exchange rates, the *asset market approach*.

Exhibit 5.1 provides an overview of the many determinants of exchange rates. This road map is first organized by the three major schools of thought (parity conditions, balance of payments approach, asset market approach), and second by the individual drivers within those approaches. At first glance the idea that there are three sets of theories may appear daunting, but it is important to remember that these are not *competing theories*, but rather *complementary theories*. Without the depth and breadth of the various approaches combined, our ability to capture the complexity of the global market for currencies is lost.

In addition to gaining an understanding of the basic theories, it is equally important to gain a working knowledge of how the complexities of international political economy, societal and economic infrastructures, and random political, economic, or social events affect the exchange rate markets. Here are a few examples:

- *Infrastructure weaknesses* were among the major causes of the exchange rate collapses in emerging markets in the late 1990s. On the other hand, infrastructure

**EXHIBIT 5.1**

The Determinants of Foreign Exchange Rates

**Parity Conditions**

1. Relative inflation rates
2. Relative interest rates
3. Forward exchange rates
4. Interest rate parity

*Is there a well-developed and liquid money and capital market in that currency?*

**Spot Exchange Rate**

*Is there a sound and secure banking system in place to support currency trading activities?*

**Asset Approach**

1. Relative real interest rates
2. Prospects for economic growth
3. Supply and demand for assets
4. Outlook for political stability
5. Speculation and liquidity
6. Political risks and controls

**Balance of Payments**

1. Current account balances
2. Portfolio investment
3. Foreign direct investment
4. Exchange rate regimes
5. Official monetary reserves

strengths help explain why the U.S. dollar continued to be strong, at least until the September 11, 2001 terrorist attack on the United States, despite record balance of payments deficits on current account.

- *Speculation* contributed greatly to the emerging market crises that are described later in this chapter. Some characteristics of speculation are hot money flowing into and out of currencies, securities, real estate, and commodities. Uncovered interest arbitrage caused by exceptionally low borrowing interest rates in Japan coupled with high real interest rates in the United States was a problem in much of the 1990s. Borrowing yen to invest in safe U.S. government securities, hoping that the exchange rate did not change, was popular.
- *Cross-border foreign direct investment and international portfolio investment* into the emerging markets dried up during their crises.
- *Foreign political risks* have been much reduced in recent years as capital markets became less segmented from each other and more liquid. More countries adopted democratic forms of government. However, recent occurrences of terrorism may be changing perceptions of political risk.

Finally, note that most determinants of the spot exchange rate are also in turn affected by changes in the spot rate. In other words, they are not only linked but mutually determined.

## The Asset Market Approach to Forecasting

The *asset market approach* assumes that whether foreigners are willing to hold claims in monetary form depends on an extensive set of investment considerations or drivers. These drivers, as depicted in Exhibit 5.1, include the following:

1. Relative real interest rates are a major consideration for investors in foreign bonds and short-term money market instruments.
2. Prospects for economic growth and profitability are an important determinant of cross-border equity investment in both securities and foreign direct investment.
3. Capital market liquidity is particularly important to foreign institutional investors. Cross-border investors are not only interested in the ease of buying assets, but also in being able to sell those assets quickly for fair market value.
4. A country's economic and social infrastructure is an important indicator of that country's ability to survive unexpected external shocks and to prosper in a rapidly changing world economic environment.
5. Political safety is exceptionally important to both foreign portfolio and direct investors. The outlook for political safety is usually reflected in political risk premiums for a country's securities and for purposes of evaluating foreign direct investment in that country.
6. The credibility of corporate governance practices is important to cross-border portfolio investors. A firm's poor corporate governance practices can reduce foreign investors' influence and cause subsequent loss of the firm's focus on shareholder wealth objectives.
7. *Contagion* is defined as the spread of a crisis in one country to its neighboring countries and other countries that have similar characteristics, at least in the eyes

of cross-border investors. Contagion can cause an "innocent" country to experience capital flight and a resulting depreciation of its currency.

8. Speculation can both cause a foreign exchange crisis or make an existing crisis worse. We will observe this effect through the three illustrative cases that follow later in this chapter.

*Real World Example 5.1* shows a recent example of how contagion can wreck a seemingly solid economy and currency.

Foreign investors are willing to hold securities and undertake foreign direct investment in highly developed countries based primarily on relative real interest rates and the outlook for economic growth and profitability. All the other drivers described in Exhibit 5.1 and detailed above are assumed to be satisfied.

For example, during the 1981–1985 period the U.S. dollar strengthened despite growing current account deficits. This strength was due partly to relatively high real interest rates in the United States. Another factor, however, was the heavy inflow of foreign capital into the U.S. stock market and real estate, motivated by good long-run prospects for growth and profitability in the United States.

The same cycle was repeated in the United States in the period between 1990 and 2000. Despite continued worsening balances on current account, the U.S. dollar strengthened in both nominal and real terms due to foreign capital inflow motivated by rising stock and real estate prices, a low rate of inflation, high real interest returns, and a seemingly endless "irrational exuberance" about future economic prospects.

## Real World Example 5.1
### URUGUAY INFECTED

Uruguay has been called the Switzerland of Latin America: a stronghold of financial stability in an often chaotic region. Today, however, it is a case study in contagion — the victim of its reckless neighbor across the Rio de la Plata, Argentina.

The warm waters of Uruguay's beaches and its generous tax and banking secrecy laws have long been a magnet for rich Argentines in times of crisis. Foreign investors were attracted to the country's investment grade status — the only Latin country besides Mexico to enjoy that rank. So Uruguayan assets became an anchor for many Latin American portfolios.

But the impressive track record came to an end in January [2002], when Argentina devalued and defaulted. That country's strict capital controls forced Argentines to dip into their Uruguayan savings, reducing those deposits by 80% since then. In June, Uruguay floated its peso, which promptly fell by 45%. Panicky investors pushed the country's banks to the brink of collapse, and bouts of looting occurred. After the bank run, the central bank on June 29 ordered a four-day bank holiday, its first in 70 years. And the congress swiftly passed legislation to exchange $2.2 billion in fixed-term dollar deposits for government bonds.

Responding to the government's proactive stance, the U.S. made Uruguay a direct loan of $1.5 billion as a bridge until the International Monetary Fund approves its own aid package. Although IMF aid should stem the deposit outflow, nobody can guarantee for how long, and the country's benchmark bonds still trade at default levels.

Although international banks have small exposure in Uruguay — $7.7 billion in March, 2002, vs. $50 billion in Argentina — the country's rapid demise portends a grim future for the region. The two bright spots left in Latin America, Chile and Mexico, are still little affected by the crisis in the Southern Cone. But the near-collapse of one stalwart economy shows that no nation is safe from the turmoil.

Source: James C. Cooper, Kathleen Madigan, and Joshua Goodman, "Uruguay: A Bright Latin Beacon Is Snuffed Out," *Business Week*, August 26, 2002, p. 30. © 2002 The McGraw-Hill Companies. All Rights Reserved.

This time the bubble burst following the September 11, 2001 terrorist attack on the United States. The attack and its aftermath caused a negative reassessment of long-term growth and profitability prospects in the United States as well as a newly formed level of political risk for the United States itself. This negative outlook was reinforced by a very sharp drop in the U.S. stock markets based on lower expected earnings. Further damage to the economy was caused by a series of revelations about failures in corporate governance of several large corporations. These failures included accounting overstatement of earnings, insider trading, and self-serving loans by firms to their own executives, as described in Chapter 1.

Loss of confidence in the U.S. economy led to a large withdrawal of foreign capital from U.S. security markets. As would be predicted by both the balance of payments and asset market approaches, the U.S. dollar depreciated. Indeed, its nominal rate depreciated by 18% between mid-January and mid-July 2002 relative to the euro alone. Further depreciation occurred due to the war in Iraq and the terrorism and instability that followed.

The experience of the United States, as well as other highly developed countries, illustrates why some forecasters believe that exchange rates are more heavily influenced by economic prospects than by the current account. One scholar summarizes this belief using an interesting anecdote.

> *Many economists reject the view that the short-term behavior of exchange rates is determined in flow markets. Exchange rates are asset prices traded in an efficient financial market. Indeed, an exchange rate is the relative price of two currencies and therefore is determined by the willingness to hold each currency. Like other asset prices, the exchange rate is determined by expectations about the future, not current trade flows.*
>
> *A parallel with other asset prices may illustrate the approach. Let's consider the stock price of a winery traded on the Bordeaux stock exchange. A frost in late spring results in a poor harvest, in terms of both quantity and quality. After the harvest the wine is finally sold, and the income is much less than the previous year. On the day of the final sale there is no reason for the stock price to be influenced by this flow. First, the poor income has already been discounted for several months in the winery stock price. Second, the stock price is affected by future, in addition to current, prospects. The stock price is based on expectations of future earnings, and the major cause for a change in stock price is a revision of these expectations.*
>
> *A similar reasoning applies to exchange rates: Contemporaneous international flows should have little effect on exchange rates to the extent they have already been expected. Only news about future economic prospects will affect exchange rates. Since economic expectations are potentially volatile and influenced by many variables, especially variables of a political nature, the short-run behavior of exchange rates is volatile.*[1]

The asset market approach to forecasting is also applicable to emerging markets. In this case, however, a number of additional variables contribute to exchange rate determination. These variables, as described previously, are illiquid capital markets, weak economic and social infrastructure, political instability, corporate governance, contagion effects, and speculation. These variables will be illustrated in the sections on crises that follow.

[1]Bruno Solnik, *International Investments,* Addison Wesley, 1996, p. 58. Reprinted by permission of Pearson Education, Inc.

## Disequilibrium: Exchange Rates in Emerging Markets

Although the three schools of thought on exchange rate determination (parity conditions, balance of payments approach, asset approach) make understanding exchange rates appear to be straightforward, that is rarely the case. The large and liquid capital and currency markets follow many of the principles outlined so far relatively well in the medium to long term. The smaller and less liquid markets, however, frequently demonstrate behaviors that seemingly contradict theory. The problem lies not in the theory, but in the relevance of the assumptions underlying the theory. An analysis of the emerging market crises illustrates a number of these seeming contradictions.

After a number of years of relative global economic tranquility, the second half of the 1990s was racked by a series of currency crises that shook all emerging markets. The devaluation of the Mexican peso in December 1994 was a harbinger. The Asian crisis of July 1997, the Russian ruble's collapse in August 1998, and the fall of the Argentine peso in 2002 provide a spectrum of emerging market economic failures, each with its own complex causes and unknown outlooks. These crises also illustrated the growing problem of capital flight and short-run international speculation in currency and securities markets. We will use each of the individual crises to focus on a specific dimension of the causes and consequences:

- **The Asian crisis.** Although this was not the collapse of any one currency, economy, or system, the complex structures combining government, society, and business throughout the Far East provide a backdrop for understanding the tenuous link between business, government, and society.
- **The Russian crisis.** The loss of the relatively stable ruble, once considered the cornerstone and symbol of success of President Boris Yeltsin's regime, was a death blow to the Yeltsin-led Russian government and led to the rise of Vladimir Putin. Russian borrowers found themselves *persona non grata* in the immediate post-1998 period in the global capital markets.
- **The Argentine crisis.** In 1991, Argentina adopted a currency board structure. The Argentine peso was tied to the U.S. dollar on a 1-to-1 basis. The resulting austerity program caused by the need to defend its fixed exchange rate caused Argentina to plunge into recession. Starting in 1998 and continuing for the next four years, the austerity program and recession caused increasing political turmoil, capital flight, and eventually the demise of the currency board itself.

## Illustrative Case: The Asian Crisis

The roots of the Asian currency crisis extended from a fundamental change in the economics of the region, the transition of many Asian nations from being net exporters to net importers. Starting as early as 1990 in Thailand, the rapidly expanding economies of the Far East began importing more than they exported, requiring major net capital inflows to support their currencies. As long as the capital continued to flow in — capital for manufacturing plants, dam projects, infrastructure development, and even real estate speculation — the pegged exchange rates of the region could be maintained. When the investment capital inflows stopped, however, crisis was inevitable.

The most visible roots of the crisis were in the excesses of capital inflows into Thailand in 1996 and early 1997. With rapid economic growth and rising profits forming the backdrop, Thai firms, banks, and finance companies had ready access to capital on the international markets, finding U.S. dollar debt cheap offshore. Thai banks continued to raise capital internationally, extending credit to a variety of domestic investments and enterprises beyond what the Thai economy could support. As capital flows into the Thai market hit record rates, financial flows poured into investments of all kinds, including manufacturing, real estate, and even equity market margin-lending. As the investment bubble expanded, some participants raised questions about the economy's ability to repay the rising debt. The baht came under attack.

## CURRENCY COLLAPSE

The Thai government and central bank intervened in the foreign exchange markets directly (using up precious hard currency reserves) and indirectly (by raising interest rates to attempt to stop the continual outflow). The Thai investment markets ground to a halt. This caused massive currency losses and bank failures. On July 2, 1997, the Thai central bank finally allowed the baht to float (or sink in this case). The baht fell 17% against the U.S. dollar and more than 12% against the Japanese yen in a matter of hours. By November, the baht had fallen from Baht25/US$ to Baht40/US$, a fall of about 38%. In the aftermath, the international speculator and philanthropist George Soros was the object of much criticism, primarily by the Prime Minister of Malaysia, Dr. Mahathir Mohamad, for being the cause of the crisis because of massive speculation by his and other hedge funds. Soros, however, was likely only the messenger.

Within days, in Asia's own version of what is called the *tequila effect*, a number of neighboring Asian nations, some with and some without characteristics similar to Thailand's, came under speculative attack by currency traders and capital markets. ("Tequila effect" is the term used to describe how the Mexican peso crisis of December 1994 quickly spread to other Latin American currency and equity markets, a form of financial panic termed *contagion*.) The Philippine peso, the Malaysian ringgit, and the Indonesian rupiah all fell in the months following the July baht devaluation (see Exhibits 5.2 and 5.3).

**EXHIBIT 5.2**

The Economies and Currencies of Asia, July–November 1997

| | 1996 Current Acct (bil US$) | Liabilities to Foreign Banks (bil US$) | Exchange Rate July (per US$) | Exchange Rate November (per US$) | % Change |
|---|---|---|---|---|---|
| **Weaker Economies** | | | | | |
| Indonesia (rupiah) | −9.0 | 29.7 | 2400 | 3600 | −33.3% |
| Korea (won) | −23.1 | 36.5 | 900 | 1100 | −18.2% |
| Malaysia (ringgit) | −8.0 | 27.0 | 2.5 | 3.5 | −28.6% |
| Philippines (peso) | −3.0 | 2.8 | 27 | 34 | −20.6% |
| Thailand (baht) | −14.7 | 48.0 | 25 | 40 | −37.5% |
| **Stronger Economies** | | | | | |
| China (renminbi) | 47.2 | 56.0 | 8.4 | 8.4 | +0.0% |
| Hong Kong (dollar) | 0.0 | 28.8 | 7.75 | 7.73 | +0.0% |
| Singapore (dollar) | 14.3 | 55.3 | 1.43 | 1.60 | −10.6% |
| Taiwan (dollar) | 11.0 | 17.6 | 27.8 | 32.7 | −15.0% |

Source: International Monetary Fund, *International Financial Statistics*, October–November, 1997.

**EXHIBIT 5.3**

Comparative Daily
Exchange Rates:
Relative to U.S.
Dollar

Source: Pacific
Exchange Rate
Service,
http://fx.sauder.ubc.ca
©1999 by Prof.
Werner Antweiler,
Sauder School of
Business, University
of British Columbia,
Vancouver, BC,
Canada. Time period
shown in diagram:
1/Apr/1997–
30/Sep/1998.

In late October 1997, Taiwan caught the markets off balance with a surprise competitive devaluation of 15%. The Taiwanese devaluation seemed only to renew the momentum of the crisis. Although the Hong Kong dollar survived (at great expense to the central bank's foreign exchange reserves), the Korean won was not so lucky. In November 1997 the historically stable Korean won fell from Won900/US$ to more than Won1100/US$. The only currency that had not fallen besides the Hong Kong dollar was the Chinese renminbi (Rmb), which was not freely convertible. Although the renminbi was not devalued, there was rising speculation that the Chinese government would devalue soon for competitive reasons (it did not).

## CAUSAL COMPLEXITIES

The Asian economic crisis — for it was more than just a currency collapse — had many roots besides traditional balance of payments difficulties. The causes were different in each country, yet there are specific underlying similarities that allow comparison: corporate socialism; corporate governance; banking stability and management.

**CORPORATE SOCIALISM.**    Although Western markets have long known the volatility of the free market, the countries of post–World War II Asia have largely known only stability. Because of the influence of government and politics in the business arena, even in the event of failure, it was believed that government would not allow firms to fail, workers to lose their jobs, or banks to close. That was true until the problems reached the size seen in 1997 and business liabilities exceeded the capacities of governments to bail business out. Practices that had persisted for decades without challenge, such as lifetime employment, were no longer sustainable. The result was a painful lesson in the harshness of the marketplace.

**CORPORATE GOVERNANCE.**   Little doubt exists that many local firms operating within the Far Eastern business environments were controlled either by families or by groups related to the governing party or body of the country. This tendency has been labeled *cronyism*. Cronyism means that the interests of minority stockholders and creditors are often secondary, at best, to the primary motivations of corporate management. When management did not focus on "the bottom line," the bottom line deteriorated.

**BANKING LIQUIDITY AND MANAGEMENT.**   The banking sector has fallen out of favor in the past two decades. Bank regulatory structures and markets have been deregulated nearly without exception across the globe. The central role played by banks in the conduct of business, however, has largely been ignored and underestimated. As firms across Asia collapsed, government coffers were emptied and speculative investments made by the banks themselves failed. Without banks, the "plumbing" of business conduct was shut down. Firms could not obtain the necessary working capital financing to manufacture and sell their products or provide their services. This pivotal role of banking liquidity was the focus of the IMF's bailout efforts.

The Asian economic crisis had global impacts. What started as a currency crisis quickly became a region-wide recession. The magnitude of economic devastation in Asia is still largely unappreciated by Westerners. At a 1998 conference sponsored by the Milken Institute, a speaker noted that the world's preoccupation with the economic problems of Indonesia was incomprehensible because "the total gross domestic product of Indonesia is roughly the size of North Carolina." The following speaker observed, however, that the last time he had checked, "North Carolina did not have a population of 220 million people." The slowed economies of the region quickly caused major reductions in world demands for many products, especially commodities. World oil, metal, and agricultural products markets all saw severe price falls as demand fell. These price drops were immediately noticeable in declining earnings and growth prospects for other emerging economies. The problems of Russia in 1998 were reflections of those declines.

## Illustrative Case: The Russian Crisis of 1998

The crisis of August 1998 was the culmination of a continuing deterioration in general economic conditions in Russia. During the period from 1995 to 1998, Russian borrowers — both governmental and nongovernmental — had gone to the international capital markets for large quantities of capital. Servicing this debt soon became an increasing problem, as dollar debt requires earning dollars to service that debt. The Russian current account, a surprisingly healthy surplus ranging between $15 billion and $20 billion per year, was not, however, finding its way into internal investment and external debt service. Capital flight accelerated, as hard-currency earnings flowed out as fast as they found their way in. Finally, in the spring of 1998, even Russian export earnings began to decline. Russian exports were predominantly commodity based, and global commodity prices had been on the decline since the onset of the Asian economic crisis in the summer and fall of 1997.

The Russian currency, the ruble, operated under a managed float. This meant that the Central Bank of Russia allowed the ruble to trade within a band. The band, for example, was Rub5.750/$ to Rub6.350/$ in the weeks prior to August 17, 1998. The exchange rate band had been adjusted continually throughout 1996, 1997, and the first half of 1998. Theoretically, the Central Bank allowed the exchange rate and associated band to slide daily at a 1.5% per month rate. Automatically, the Central Bank announced an official exchange rate each day at which it was willing to buy and sell rubles, always within the official band. In the event that the ruble's exchange rate came under pressure at the limits of the band, the Central Bank intervened in the market by buying and selling rubles — usually buying — using the country's foreign exchange and gold reserves. The stability of the ruble in the 1990s was considered the single most observable success of President Boris Yeltsin. But in spite of a $4.3 billion loan from the IMF in July of 1998, the ruble came under intense pressure in August of that year.

## THE AUGUST COLLAPSE

On Friday, August 7, 1998, the Russian Central Bank announced that its hard currency reserves had fallen by $800 million in the last week of July to a level of $18.4 billion on July 31. Prime Minister Sergei Kiriyenko said that Russia would issue an additional $3 billion in foreign bonds to help pay its rising debt, a full $1 billion more than had been previously scheduled. The ruble, however, continued to trade within a very narrow range of Rub6.24/$ to Rub6.26/$.

On Monday, August 10, Russian stocks fell more than 5% as investors feared a Chinese currency (renminbi) devaluation. The Chinese currency was the only Asian currency of size not devalued in 1997 and 1998. Devaluation would aid Chinese exports in cutting into Russian export sales. Analysts worldwide speculated that international markets were waiting to see if the Russian government would increase its tax revenues as it had promised the IMF throughout the year. Russian oil companies were publicly warned by the Russian government to pay past due taxes. (Russian tax revenue collections averaged slightly over $1 billion per month in 1998, less than those of New York City.) By Wednesday of that week, Russian financing choices narrowed further as the government canceled the government debt auction for the third week in a row. On international markets, Russia's outstanding eurobonds due in 2001 sank in price for a sixth straight day, the yield (implicit cost of borrowing) rising 350 basis points to 23.6%. The ruble fell to Rub6.30/$.

Thursday, August 13, saw a series of press releases by senior governmental officials committing the government to stabilizing the markets and assuring the general population that all was in hand.

> If we thought that devaluation was unavoidable, we would not be taking the measures we are taking now.
>
> Mikhail Zadornov, Finance Minister

Mr. Zadornov went on to explain that Russia expected an additional $4.3 billion from the IMF in September. Analysts believed that Russia had $23.4 billion due in payments on domestic debt, and $4.5 billion due on foreign debt, throughout the remainder of the year. Despite the statements from Finance Minister Zadornov, the stock and bond markets in Moscow and St. Petersburg plummeted. Rumors regarding the likely collapse of the banking system spread.

On Friday, August 14, the press releases and statements of commitment from senior governmental officials continued. The government stated that the panic was psychological, not fiscal, and repeated, as it had in recent days, that it had money to meet its obligations through the fall of the year. "A stable ruble is the anchor of an inflation-free economy," according to Alexander Livshits, deputy head of President Boris Yeltsin's administration. He added that the loss of a stable ruble "will start rocking our ship again. The result is well known—nausea."

The Russian Central Bank continued to trade rubles throughout Friday at Rub6.30/$, but at many unofficial exchanges throughout Moscow the rate was Rub7.00/$ or more. President Yeltsin, in a speech in the ancient city of Novgorod, stated

> There will be no devaluation — that's firm and definite. That would signify that there was a disaster and that everything was collapsing. On the contrary, everything is going as it should.

"As it should" turned out to mean devaluation. On Monday, August 17, the floodgates were opened. Late in the day the Russian Central Bank announced that the ruble would be allowed to fall by 34%, from Rub6.30/$ to about Rub9.50/$. It also postponed the payment of $43 billion in short-term domestic debt to help it through the cash crisis. As a final blow to international markets, the government announced a 90-day moratorium on all repayment of foreign debt — debt owed by Russian banks and all private borrowers — in order to avert a banking collapse.

On Tuesday, August 18, the ruble continued to fall, quickly passing the Rub9.50/$ limit. Reports from Moscow to Vladivostok quoted trading at between Rub10.00 and Rub12.00 per dollar. International circles debated whether Russia's postponement of debt service was in fact a default.

The currency's fall continued into the following week (see Exhibit 5.4). On Thursday, August 27, Acting Prime Minister Viktor Chernomyrdin traveled to the Ukraine to meet with the visiting head of the IMF, Michael Camdessus. A sense of urgency was felt after the ruble fell from Rub10.0/$ to Rub13.0/$ the previous day

**EXHIBIT 5.4**

Daily Exchange Rates: Russian Rubles per U.S. Dollar

Source: Pacific Exchange Rate Service, http://fx.sauder.ubc.ca ©1999 by Prof. Werner Antweiler, Sauder School of Business, University of British Columbia, Vancouver, BC, Canada.

alone. In related matters, the Central Bank of Russia, in an attempt to defray criticism of its management of the ruble's devaluation, disclosed that it had expended $8.8 billion in the preceding eight weeks defending the ruble's value. On Friday, August 28, the Moscow currency exchange closed after 10 minutes of trading as the ruble continued to fall.

## THE AFTERMATH

It is hard to say when a crisis begins or ends, but for the Russian people and the Russian economy, the deterioration of the economic conditions continued. As illustrated in Exhibit 5.4, the ruble continued to fall throughout late 1998. In early December, rumors that the Russian state was printing money to make long-overdue payments to state workers and pensioners added insult to injury. The tumbling ruble finally stabilized in January and February of 1999, at a rate of approximately Rub25.0/$.

Spring and early summer of 1999 saw a Russian government battling within and without to find ways to service its outstanding sovereign and private debts without impoverishing the country further. Domestic bonds issued by the Russian government, ruble bonds, were now in default, with repayment uncertain. The primary task for survival was the servicing of the dollar debt, with Russia's outstanding eurobonds at the top of the list. No sovereign borrower has ever rescheduled or defaulted on outstanding eurobonds.

What is likely of more substantial concern is the toll the crisis has taken on Russian society. For many, the collapse of the ruble and the loss of Russia's access to the international capital markets has brought into question the benefits of a free-market economy, long championed by the advocates of Western-style democracy.

## Illustrative Case: The Argentine Crisis of 2002

*Now, most Argentines are blaming corrupt politicians and foreign devils for their ills. But few are looking inward, at mainstream societal concepts such as viveza criolla, an Argentine cultural quirk that applauds anyone sly enough to get away with a fast one. It is one reason behind massive tax evasion here: One of every three Argentines does so — and many like to brag about it.*

Anthony Faiola, "Once-Haughty Nation's Swagger Loses Its Currency,"
*The Washington Post*, March 13, 2002.

Argentina's economic ups and downs have historically been tied to the health of the Argentine peso. South America's southernmost country — which oftentimes considered itself more European than Latin American — had been wracked by hyperinflation, international indebtedness, and economic collapse in the 1980s. By early 1991 the people of Argentina had had enough. Economic reform in the early 1990s was a common goal of the Argentine people. They were not interested in quick fixes, but in lasting change and a stable future. They nearly got it.

## THE CURRENCY BOARD

In 1991 the Argentine peso had been fixed to the U.S. dollar at a one-to-one rate of exchange. The policy was a radical departure from traditional methods of fixing the rate of a currency's value. Argentina adopted a *currency board*, a structure for —

## EXHIBIT 5.5

Argentina's Economic Performance, 1991–2000

| | 1991 | 1992 | 1993 | 1994 | 1995 | 1996 | 1997 | 1998 | 1999 | 2000 |
|---|---|---|---|---|---|---|---|---|---|---|
| Real GDP growth rate (%) | 10.5 | 9.6 | 5.8 | 5.8 | −2.8 | 5.5 | 8.2 | 3.9 | −3.5 | −0.4 |
| Unemployment rate (%) | 6.3 | 7.2 | 9.1 | 11.7 | 15.9 | 16.3 | 14.2 | 14.1 | 15.5 | 15.0 |
| Inflation rate (%) | 172.0 | 24.6 | 10.6 | 4.3 | 3.3 | 0.2 | 0.5 | 0.9 | −1.2 | −0.9 |

Source: International Monetary Fund, Political Risk Services, Argentina Economic Development Agency.

rather than merely a commitment to — limiting the growth of money in the economy. Under a currency board, the central bank of a country may increase the money supply in the banking system only with increases in its holdings of hard currency reserves. These reserves were in this case U.S. dollars. By removing the ability of government to expand the rate of growth of the money supply, Argentina believed it was eliminating the source of inflation which had devastated its standard of living.

The idea was elegantly simple and in many ways simplistic: limit the rate of growth in the country's money supply to the rate at which the country receives net inflows of U.S. dollars as a result of trade growth and general surplus. It was both a recipe for conservative and prudent financial management, and a decision to eliminate the power of politicians, elected and unelected, to exercise judgment both good and bad. It was an automatic and unbendable rule. And from the beginning, it had shown the costs and benefits of its rigor.

Exhibit 5.5 illustrates the three traditional measures of a country's macroeconomic performance: real growth in gross domestic product (GDP), inflation, and unemployment.

But Exhibit 5.5 also illustrates the austerity dimension to the currency board structure. Although hyperinflation had indeed been the problem, the cure was a restrictive monetary policy which slowed economic growth in the coming years. The first and foremost cost of the slower economic growth had been in unemployment. Beginning with a decade low unemployment rate of 6.3% in 1991, unemployment rose to double-digit levels in 1994 and stayed there. The real GDP growth rate, which opened the decade with booming levels over 10%, settled into recession in late 1998. GDP growth shrank in 1999 (−3.5%) and 2000 (−0.4%). Preliminary estimates for 2001 indicated a further deterioration in GDP: −3% for the year.

As part of the continuing governmental commitment to the currency board's fixed exchange rate for the peso, Argentine banks allowed depositors to hold their money in either form — pesos or dollars. This was intended to provide a market-based discipline to the banking and political systems, and to demonstrate the government's unwavering commitment to maintaining the peso's value parity with the dollar. Although considered by many an excellent policy to build confidence, in the end it proved disastrous to the Argentine banking system.

## ECONOMIC CRISIS, 2001

The 1998 recession proved to be unending. Three and a half years later, Argentina was still in recession. By 2001 crisis conditions had revealed three very important underlying problems with Argentina's economy: (1) the Argentine peso was overvalued; (2) the currency board regime had eliminated monetary policy alternatives for macroeconomic policy; and (3) the Argentine government budget deficit — and deficit spending — was out of control.

**THE ARGENTINE PESO.** The peso had indeed been stabilized, but inflation had not been eliminated, and the other factors that are important in the global market's evaluation of a currency's value — economic growth, corporate profitability, and so on — had not necessarily always been positive. The inability of the peso's value to change with market forces led many to believe increasingly that it was overvalued, and that the overvaluation gap was rising as time passed.

Argentina's large neighbor to the north, Brazil, had also suffered many of the economic ills of hyperinflation and international indebtedness in the 1980s and early 1990s. Brazil's response, the *Real Plan*, was introduced in July 1994.[2] The Real Plan worked for a while, but eventually collapsed in January 1999 as a result of the rising gap between the real's official value and the market's assessment of its true value.

Brazil was by far Argentina's largest trading partner. With the fall of the Brazilian real, however, Brazilian consumers could no longer afford Argentine exports. It simply took too many real to purchase a peso. In fact, Argentine exports became some of the most expensive in all of South America as other countries saw their currencies slide marginally against the dollar over the decade. But not the Argentine peso.

**THE CURRENCY BOARD AND MONETARY POLICY.** The increasingly sluggish economic growth in Argentina warranted expansionary economic policies argued many policy makers in and out of the country. But the currency board's basic premise was that the money supply to the financial system could not be expanded any further or faster than the ability of the economy to capture dollar reserves. This eliminated monetary policy as an avenue for macroeconomic policy formulation, leaving only fiscal policy for economic stimulation.

**GOVERNMENT BUDGET DEFICITS.** Government spending was not slowing, however. As the unemployment rate grew higher, as poverty and social unrest grew, government in the civil center of Argentina, Buenos Aires, and in the outer provinces was faced with growing expansionary spending, needed to close the economic and social gaps. Government spending continued to increase, but tax receipts did not. Lower income led to lower taxes on income.

Argentina then turned to the international markets to aid in the financing of its government's deficit spending. As illustrated in Exhibit 5.6, the total foreign debt of the country began rising dramatically in 1997 and 1998. Only a number of International Monetary Fund capital injections in 2000 and 2001 prevented the total foreign debt of

## EXHIBIT 5.6

Argentina's Debt and Key Balances, 1991–2000

|  | 1991 | 1992 | 1993 | 1994 | 1995 | 1996 | 1997 | 1998 | 1999 | 2000 |
|---|---|---|---|---|---|---|---|---|---|---|
| Foreign debt (billion $) | 65.4 | 71.9 | 60.3 | 69.6 | 68.2 | 105.2 | 123.2 | 139.0 | 149.0 | 123.7 |
| Current account (billion $) | −0.65 | −5.49 | −8.03 | −11.22 | −5.30 | −6.94 | −12.43 | −14.55 | −11.95 | −8.90 |
| Budget balance (billion $) | −1.01 | −0.07 | −1.58 | −1.88 | −1.42 | −5.24 | −4.35 | −4.15 | −8.13 | −6.86 |

Source: International Monetary Fund, Political Risk Services, Argentina Economic Development Agency.

[2]Brazil introduced a new currency at that time, the *real* (*reais*). The real's value was not, however, fixed to the U.S. dollar but pegged to the dollar with a predictable and promised rate of daily devaluation. This allowed the real to weaken commensurate with Brazil's still higher rate of inflation and lower rate of growth, but control its value change over time.

the country from skyrocketing. When the decade was over, however, total foreign debt had effectively doubled and the economy's earning power had not.

Also seen in Exhibit 5.6 was Argentina's failure to turn the current account toward surplus. Although this is not surprising given the overvalued currency relative to its major South American neighbors, it was only through running a trade surplus that Argentina could earn additional dollar reserves and allow a loosening of monetary policy constraints.

In the end, the government budget deficit continued to grow. Continuing recession required large fiscal expenditures by federal and local governments. Government spending was increasingly financed by international capital. International investors were beginning to doubt Argentina's ability to repay them.

## SOCIAL REPERCUSSIONS

As economic conditions continued to deteriorate, banks suffered increasing runs. Depositors, fearing that the peso would be devalued, lined up to withdraw their money, both Argentine peso cash balances and U.S. dollar cash balances. Pesos were converted to dollars, once again adding fuel to the growing fire of currency collapse. The government, fearing that the increasing financial drain on banks would cause their collapse, closed the banks on December 1, 2001, in an effort to stop the flight of cash and capital out of Argentina. Consumers, unable to withdraw more than $250 per week, were instructed to use debit cards and credit cards to make purchases and conduct everyday transactions.

Riots in the streets of Buenos Aires in December 2001 intensified the need for rapid change. As the new year of 2002 arrived, the second president in two weeks, Fernando de la Rua, was driven from office. He was succeeded by a Peronist, President Adolfo Rodriguez Saa, who lasted all of one week as president before he too was driven from office. President Saa did, however, leave his legacy. In his one week as president of Argentina, Saa declared the largest sovereign debt default in history. Argentina announced it would not be able to make interest payments due on $155 billion in sovereign (government) debt.

Saa was succeeded by Eduardo Duhalde, Argentina's fifth president in a little more than two weeks. A presidential candidate in 1999 and a senator for Buenos Aires province, Duhalde faced a massive task. He was immediately granted emergency powers to try and save what was left of the Argentine economic system.

## DEVALUATION

On Sunday January 6, 2002, in the first act of his presidency, Duhalde devalued the peso from Ps1.00/$ to Ps1.40/$. It was hoped that once the peso was devalued, the country could calm the nerves of its people.

But the economic pain continued. Two weeks after the devaluation, the banks were still closed. Most of the state governments outside of Buenos Aires, basically broke and without access to financing resources, began printing their own money — *script* — promissory notes of the provincial governments. The provincial governments were left with little choice — the economy of Argentina was nearing complete collapse as people and businesses could not obtain money to conduct the day-to-day commercial transactions of life.

But the notes were only a partial answer. Because the notes were promissory notes of the provincial governments, not the federal government, people and businesses would not accept notes from other provinces. Store shelves stood empty because although consumers could buy what was already in the store, the store could not make acceptable payment to regional, national, or international suppliers. The population became trapped within its own province, because their money was not accepted in the outside world in exchange for goods, services, travel, or anything else.

On February 3, 2002, the Argentine government announced that the peso would be floated. The government would no longer attempt to fix or manage its value to any specific level, allowing the market to find or set the exchange rate. The value of the peso now began a gradual depreciation.[3]

As the year wore on the country was confronted with issue after issue of social, political, and economic collapse. The banks and bankers were increasingly the target of the ire of the population. As banks collapsed, business fell with them. In February and March a growing series of investigations into illegal trading and financial fraud covered the Buenos Aires headlines. In February and March 2002 continued negotiations between the IMF and Argentina went in fits and starts as the IMF demanded increasing fiscal reform over the growing government budget deficits and bank mismanagement. The IMF itself became an increasing target of the Argentine population's discontent.

On March 24 and 25 the peso was once again hit by massive sell-offs. In a country long considered the wealthiest and most sophisticated in all of South America, the people were increasingly opposed to all politicians, all banks and financial service providers, and in many cases each other. The path of the peso's collapse is illustrated in Exhibit 5.7. In the spring of 2002, Argentina was a country in considerable trouble.

**EXHIBIT 5.7**

The Collapse of the Argentine Peso

© 2002 by Prof. Werner Antweiler, University of British Columbia, Vancouver BC, Canada. Time period shown in diagram: 26/Dec/2001– 26/Mar/2002.

Daily Exchange Rates: Argentine Pesos per U.S. Dollar

[3]When a currency which is under a fixed exchange rate regime is officially altered in its value — downward — it is termed a *devaluation*. When a currency which is freely floated on exchange markets moves downward in value it is termed *depreciation*.

Former Harvard professor and member of the U.S. President's Council of Economic Advisors Martin Feldstein summed up the hard lessons of the Argentine story.

> In reality, the Argentines understood the risk that they were taking at least as well as the IMF staff did. Theirs was a calculated risk that might have produced good results. It is true, however, that the IMF staff did encourage Argentina to continue with the fixed exchange rate and currency board. Although the IMF and virtually all outside economists believe that a floating exchange rate is preferable to a "fixed but adjustable" system, in which the government recognizes that it will have to devalue occasionally, the IMF (as well as some outside economists) came to believe that the currency board system of a firmly fixed exchange rate (a "hard peg" in the jargon of international finance) is a viable long-term policy for an economy. Argentina's experience has proved that wrong.[4]

Exhibit 5.8 on the next page summarizes many of the political and economic events surrounding the Argentine collapse.

## Forecasting in Practice

In addition to the three approaches to forecasting depicted in Exhibit 5.1, forecasting practitioners use *technical analysis*. Numerous foreign exchange forecasting services exist that use technical analysis as well as the traditional theoretical approaches.

### TECHNICAL ANALYSIS

Technical analysts, traditionally referred to as *chartists*, focus on price and volume data to determine past trends that are expected to continue into the future. The single most important element of technical analysis is that future exchange rates are based on the current exchange rate. Exchange rate movements, similar to equity price movements, can be divided into three periods: (1) day-to-day movement, which is seemingly random; (2) short-term movements extending from several days to several months; (3) long-term movements, characterized by up-and-down long-term trends. Long-term technical analysis has gained popularity as a result of recent research into the possibility that long-term "waves" in currency movements exist under floating exchange rates.

The longer the time horizon of the forecast, the more inaccurate the forecast is likely to be. Whereas forecasting for the long run must depend on economic fundamentals of exchange rate determination, many of the forecast needs of the firm are short- to medium-term in their time horizon and can be addressed with less theoretical approaches. Time series techniques infer no theory or causality but simply predict future values from the recent past. Forecasters freely mix fundamental and technical analysis, presumably because forecasting is like horseshoes: Getting close counts!

### FORECASTING SERVICES

Numerous foreign exchange forecasting services exist, many of which are provided by banks and independent consultants. In addition, some multinational firms have their own in-house forecasting capabilities. Predictions can be based on elaborate econometric models, technical analysis of charts and trends, intuition, and a certain measure of gall.

---

[4] "Argentina's Fall," Martin Feldstein, *Foreign Affairs*, March/April 2002.

**EXHIBIT 5.8**

| A Timeline of Events in the Argentine Crisis | | |
|---|---|---|
| December 10, 1999 | President Fernando de la Rua is inaugurated, inheriting a continual recession and increasing financial crisis. The policies of the outgoing president, Carlos Menem, are blamed for the deterioration of the society and the growing culture of corruption. | |
| May 29, 2000 | Argentina's government unveils $938 million in government budget cuts in order to meet its fiscal targets of rebalancing the budget. | |
| December 18, 2000 | Argentina announces a package of financial borrowing totaling $40 billion, heading off growing concern in the international community that it will default on its international debt. | |
| March 20, 2001 | Domingo Cavallo, the architect of the original currency board implemented in 1991, returns to government to take a hand in revitalizing the economy. He later announces a series of deregulations that will save industry 20%. | |
| July 18, 2001 | Public protests surge as the government announces $1.5 billion in budget cuts and reductions in public aid programs required by the IMF in order for Argentina to qualify for additional loans. | |
| August 21, 2001 | The IMF agrees to $8 billion in financial aid to support Argentina's depleted currency reserves following increasing capital flight. | |
| December 1, 2001 | Government closes the banks. | |
| December 5, 2001 | IMF refuses to make a $1.26 billion loan installment amid disagreements over the content of the Argentine 2002 government budget. | |
| December 19, 2001 | Government declares a state of siege as thousands of unemployed workers riot in Buenos Aires, demanding food and the resignation of the president. | |
| December 20, 2001 | President Fernando de la Rua and his government fall. Rioting in Buenos Aires intensifies. | |
| December 29, 2001 | Peronist President Adolfo Rodriguez Saa lasts only one week as president before he too is driven from office. Saa declares the largest sovereign debt default in history: Argentina will not make interest payments on $155 billion in sovereign public debt. | |
| January 1, 2002 | Eduardo Duhalde becomes Argentina's fifth president in two weeks. He is immediately granted emergency powers to deal with the growing political and economic crisis. | |
| January 6, 2002 | In his first act as president, Duhalde devalues the peso from Ps1.00/$ to Ps1.40/$. | |
| February 1, 2002 | The supreme court of Argentina, after several weeks of political sparring with the federal government, declares the two-month-long bank closure unconstitutional, instructing the government to reopen the banks on Monday February 4. | |
| February 3, 2002 | The government, on Sunday, announces a change in the direction of Argentina's economic revisions. The peso is to be floated immediately, ending one month of an official bi-level exchange rate system. The banks are to be closed on Monday and Tuesday. All banking reserves held as U.S. dollars are to be converted to pesos at differing exchange rates. The government pursues the overthrow of the supreme court, setting the stage for a constitutional crisis for the country. | |
| March 26, 2002 | Peso floated to Ps3.50/$. | |

Whether any of the forecasting services are worth their cost depends partly on the motive for forecasting as well as the required accuracy of the forecast. For example, long-run forecasts may be motivated by a multinational firm's desire to initiate a foreign investment in Japan, or perhaps to raise long-term funds denominated in Japanese yen. Or a portfolio manager may be considering diversifying for the long term in Japanese securities. The longer the time horizon of the forecast, the more inaccurate but also the less critical the forecast is likely to be. The forecaster will typically use annual data to display long-run trends in such economic fundamentals as Japanese inflation, growth, and the BOP.

Short-term forecasts are typically motivated by a desire to hedge a receivable, payable, or dividend for perhaps a period of three months. In this case the long-run economic fundamentals may not be as important as technical factors in the marketplace, government intervention, news, and passing whims of traders and investors. Accuracy of the forecast is critical since most of the exchange rate changes are relatively small even though the day-to-day volatility may be high.

Forecasting services normally undertake fundamental economic analysis for long-term forecasts, and some base their short-term forecasts on the same basic model. Others base their short-term forecasts on technical analysis similar to that conducted in security analysis. They attempt to correlate exchange rate changes with various other variables, regardless of whether there is any economic rationale for the correlation. The chances of these forecasts being consistently useful or profitable depends on whether one believes the foreign exchange market is efficient. The more efficient the market is, the more likely it is that exchange rates are "random walks," with past price behavior providing no clues to the future. The less efficient the foreign exchange market is, the better the chance that forecasters may get lucky and find a key relationship that holds, at least for the short run. If the relationship is really consistent, however, others will soon discover it and the market will become efficient again with respect to that piece of information.

Exhibit 5.9 summarizes the various forecasting periods, regimes, and the authors' opinions on the preferred methodologies. Opinions, however, are subject to change without notice! (And remember, if the authors could predict the movement of exchange rates with regularity, we surely wouldn't write books.)

## CROSS-RATE CONSISTENCY IN FORECASTING

International financial managers must often forecast their home currency exchange rates for the set of countries in which the firm operates, not only to decide whether to hedge or to make an investment, but also as an integral part of preparing multicountry operating budgets in the home country's currency. These are the operating budgets against which the performance of foreign subsidiary managers will be judged. Checking the reasonableness of the cross rates implicit in individual forecasts acts as a reality check to the original forecasts.

To illustrate, assume the U.S. parent home office forecasts the yen-to-dollar exchange rate a year hence to be ¥105/$ and the U.K. pound sterling rate to be $1.85/£. This creates an implied spot rate one year hence of ¥194.25/£. However, both the Japanese and the British financial managers, with good reason, have forecast a spot rate one year hence of ¥190.00/£.

Obviously the two foreign subsidiary managers (forecasting ¥190.00/£) and the home office (with an implicit forecast of ¥194.25/£) cannot both be correct. The time to reconcile these conflicting forecasts is the present, not one year hence when managers

**EXHIBIT 5.9**

Exchange Rate
Forecasting in
Practice

| Forecast Period | Regime | Recommended Forecast Methods |
|---|---|---|
| **Short Run** | *Fixed Rate* | 1. Assume the fixed rate is maintained |
| | | 2. Indications of stress on fixed rate |
| | | 3. Capital controls; black market rates |
| | | 4. Indicators of government's capability to maintain fixed rate |
| | | 5. Changes in official foreign currency reserves |
| | *Floating Rate* | 1. Technical methods which capture trend |
| | | 2. Forward rates as forecasts |
| | |    a. <30 days; assume a random walk |
| | |    b. 30–90 days; forward rates |
| | | 3. 90–360 days; combine trend with fundamental analysis |
| | | 4. Fundamental analysis of inflationary concerns |
| | | 5. Government declarations and agreements regarding exchange rate goals |
| | | 6. Cooperative agreements with other countries |
| **Long Run** | *Fixed Rate* | 1. Fundamental analysis |
| | | 2. BOP management |
| | | 3. Ability to control domestic inflation |
| | | 4. Ability to generate hard currency reserves to use for intervention |
| | | 5. Ability to run trade surpluses |
| | *Floating Rate* | 1. Focus on inflationary fundamentals and PPP |
| | | 2. Indicators of general economic health such as economic growth and stability |
| | | 3. Technical analysis of long-term trends; new research indicates possibility of long-term technical "waves" |

in Japan or the United Kingdom claim that their performance against budget is better than measured by the U.S. parent. Additionally, checking the reasonableness of implied cross rates is an exercise in improving the accuracy of the forecasting process.

## FORECASTING: WHAT TO THINK?

Obviously, with the variety of theories and practices, forecasting exchange rates into the future is a daunting task. Here is a synthesis of our thoughts and experience:

- It appears from decades of theoretical and empirical studies that exchange rates do adhere to the fundamental principles and theories outlined in the previous sections. Fundamentals do apply in the long term. There is, therefore, something of a *fundamental equilibrium path* for a currency's value.

- It also seems that in the short term, a variety of random events, institutional frictions, and technical factors may cause currency values to deviate significantly from their long-term fundamental path. This is sometimes referred to as *noise*. Clearly, therefore, we might expect deviations from the long-term path not only to occur, but to occur with some regularity and relative longevity.

Exhibit 5.10 illustrates this synthesis of forecasting thought. The long-term equilibrium path of the currency — although relatively well defined in retrospect — is not always apparent in the short term. The exchange rate itself may deviate in something of a cycle or wave about the long-term path.

If market participants agree on the general long-term path and possess *stabilizing expectations*, the currency's value will periodically return to the long-term path. It is critical, however, that when the currency's value rises above the long-term path, most market participants see it as being overvalued and respond by selling the currency, causing its price to fall. Similarly, when the currency's value falls below the long-term path, market participants respond by buying the currency driving its value up. This is what is meant by *stabilizing expectations*: Market participants continually respond to deviations from the long-term path by buying or selling to drive the currency back to the long-term path.

If, for some reason, the market becomes unstable, as illustrated by the dotted deviation path in Exhibit 5.10, the exchange rate may move significantly away from the long-term path for longer periods of time. Causes of these destabilizing markets, weak infrastructure (such as the banking system), and political or social events that dictate

**EXHIBIT 5.10**

Differentiating Short-Term Noise from Long-Term Trends

## Real World Example 5.2
### FORECASTING THE DOLLAR/POUND EXCHANGE RATE (*CABLE*) IN SUMMER 2004

The following analysis was published by WellsFargo.com on June 1, 2004, arguing that the British pound could strengthen to $2.00/£ in the coming month. Did it?

*It is possible to build a scenario where GBP/USD — Cable — hits $2.00 in June. This scenario is premised on the Bank of England Monetary Policy Committee (MPC) raising rates 25bps on June 10, 6-month US:UK interest rate differentials (we use 6-month Cable forward points) widening to −325 pips and a 4% overshoot of our Cable forwards fair value model, which Cable has regularly done over the last two years. Should the MPC hike rates with the GBP trade weighted index (TWI) trading above 106.0, Cable at 2.00 becomes a real prospect.*

*We've identified a pretty solid relationship between Cable and six-month Cable forward points. The regression, using 760 data points, generates a high R-squared of 0.91. Basically, multiply the 6-month Cable forward points (now −298) by −0.00241, add it to 1.1287 and le voila, Cable fair value at 1.8470. Should a June 10 hike push those 6-month forwards out to −325 — a Cable fair value of 1.9120 is generated.*

*However, during the two-year USD bear trend, Cable has frequently overshot its fair value reading by some 4–5%, suggesting $2.00 is not out of the question.*

*Should the MPC hike rates June 10 with GBP TWI over 106.00, we wouldn't rule out a GBP buying frenzy generating $2.00 on Cable. Importantly, GBP TWI was at 106.2 in early April when the MPC voted to leave rates unchanged and cite it as a reason for not raising rates. Equally, GBP TWI was at 103.7 on May 6, when the MPC voted to raise rates 25bps. At the time, the debate was whether to do 25 or 50bps and MPC minutes show that GBP didn't feature at all in that debate. Thus a MPC rate hike June 10 with TWI over 106.0 would show that there's little the MPC can do about strong GBP and that the risks of above trend growth and an over-shooting of the two year 2.00% target remain paramount.*

*Using a Robert Rubin-style probability weighted return model (very approximate), we see a 50% chance of a move to $2.00 and 50% chance of a setback to 1.80 — so Cable looks a buy.*

Source: WellsFargo.com, June 1, 2004.

economic behaviors, are often the actions of speculators, inefficient or uncompetitive economic outcomes. *Real World Example 5.2, Forecasting the Dollar/Pound Exchange Rate*, illustrates some of the arguments frequently combined when forecasting short-term currency movements.

## EXCHANGE RATE DYNAMICS: MAKING SENSE OF MARKET MOVEMENTS

Although the various theories surrounding exchange rate determination are clear and sound, it may appear on a day-to-day basis that the currency markets do not pay much attention to the theories, they don't read the books! The difficulty is understanding which fundamentals are driving markets at which points in time.

One example of this relative confusion over exchange rate dynamics is the phenomenon known as *overshooting*. Assume that the current spot rate between the dollar and the euro, as illustrated in Exhibit 5.11, is $S_0$. The U.S. Federal Reserve announces an expansionary monetary policy which cuts U.S. dollar interest rates. If euro-denominated interest rates remain unchanged, the new spot rate expected by the exchange markets on the basis of interest differentials is $S_1$. This immediate change in the exchange rate is typical of how the markets react to *news*, distinct economic and political events which are observable. The immediate change in the value of the dollar/euro is therefore based on interest differentials.

**EXHIBIT 5.11**

Exchange Rate
Dynamics:
Overshooting

If the U.S. Federal Reserve were to announce a change in monetary policy, an expansion in money supply growth, it could potentially result in an "overshooting" exchange rate change.

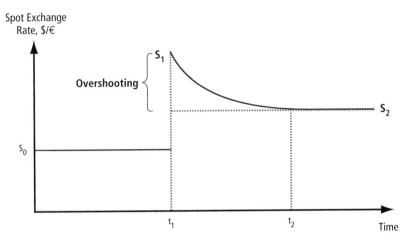

The Fed announces a monetary expansion at time $t_1$. This results immediately in lower dollar interest rates. The foreign exchange markets immediately respond to the lower dollar interest rates by driving the value of the dollar down from $S_0$ to $S_1$. This new rate is based on *interest differentials*. However, in the coming days and weeks, as the fundamental price effects of the monetary policy actions work their way through the economy, *purchasing power parity* takes hold and the market moves toward a longer-term valuation of the dollar — by time $t_2$ — of $S_2$, a weaker dollar than $S_0$, but not as weak as initially set at $S_1$.

As time passes, however, the price impacts of the monetary policy change start working their way through the economy. As price changes occur over the medium to long-term, purchasing power parity forces drive the market dynamics, and the spot rate moves from $S_1$ toward $S_2$. Although both $S_1$ and $S_2$ were rates determined by the market, they reflected the dominance of different theoretical principles. As a result, the initial lower value of the dollar of $S_1$ is often explained as an *overshooting* of the longer-term equilibrium value of $S_2$.

This is of course only one possible series of events and market reactions. Currency markets are subject to new *news* every hour of every day, making it very difficult to forecast exchange rate movements in short periods of time. In the longer term, as shown here, the markets do customarily return to fundamentals of exchange rate determination.

---

**MINI-CASE**

# Turkey's Kriz (B): Uncovered Interest Arbitrage

The Mini-Case on Turkey presented after Chapter 3 ("Turkey's Kriz (A): Deteriorating Balance of Payments"), documented the deterioration of the Turkish current account balance in the year prior to the Turkish lira crisis

— or kriz — of February 2001. As illustrated in Exhibit 1, the lira's collapse was large and sudden. Although the balance of payments current and financial accounts recorded major swings in their relative values in the year prior to

## EXHIBIT 1

**The Turkish Inflation Rate and Exchange Rate (quarterly)**

Source: International Monetary Fund, *International Financial Statistics*, October 2001, pp. 842–843. Copyright 2001 by International Monetary Fund. Reproduced with permission via Copyright Clearance Center.

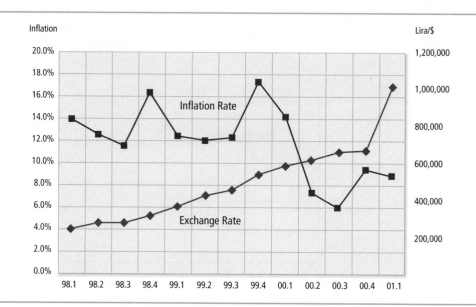

the crisis, the question remained as to the underlying causes of the crisis.

## Turkish Banking

The Turkish banking system was notoriously corrupt in the latter part of the 1990s. Bank licenses, which gave the holder the right to open commercial and investment banking operations in Turkey, were given or sold as political favors by influential members of the Turkish government. These banks, once operational, were free to go to the international marketplace and represent themselves as established and creditworthy borrowers. And borrow they did.

> *The crisis was Turkey's worst in decades. Its banks had borrowed billions of dollars at low rates, converted them to lira, and bought high-yielding Turkish government T-bills. The strategy worked until the lira lost 40% of its value in a few days. Interbank interest rates hit 7,000%. Unable to pay their dollar debts, most Turkish banks were technically insolvent.*
>
> "Crash Control for a Broken Economy," *Business Week*, August 27, 2001

Throughout 1998, 1999, and the first half of 2000, many Turkish banks borrowed large quantities of dollars outside of Turkey. The banks then converted the dollar proceeds into Turkish lira and purchased Turkish government bonds as investments. The motivation was clear: Borrowing at low dollar rates and reinvesting in much

higher government bond rates created significant profits. These profits would persist as long as the Turkish lira held its value.

But the lira's value was heavily managed by the Turkish government. Because of the relatively high inflation rates suffered throughout 1998 and 1999 (see Exhibit 1), the Turkish government had pursued a gradual, continual devaluation policy. The managed devaluation, similar to Brazil's under the Real Plan between 1994 and 1999, was not sufficient. The lira was devalued at a rate significantly less than what the inflation differentials called for.

The activities of the banks added fuel to an economy already afire. This investment structure was none other than *uncovered interest arbitrage,* as described in Chapter 4. This growing industry in interest arbitrage had a series of immediate and eventual impacts on the Turkish financial system:

- The dollar-to-lira conversion in the spot market aided in propping-up the value of the Turkish lira. As seen in Exhibit 1, the lira was managed in value against the U.S. dollar over time. Although Turkish inflation rates were substantially higher than U.S. dollar inflation, the large quantities of dollars converted into lira artificially boosted the demand for lira, raising its value (or preventing a further devaluation than what inflation would call for).

- The continuing demand for Turkish government bonds — government debt — allowed the government to fund increasing budget deficits at manageable costs. The strong demand by the banks for Turkish securities prevented the yields on government bonds from rising dramatically. It also prevented market forces from signaling to the government the dangers of its growing deficit spending and national debt.

- The growing external debt obligation of the Turkish banks, however, was an expanding threat to the stability of the banking system. Once the obligations came due, and many of the bank debts were *callable* in that the international banks could demand repayment overnight, the rush to exchange lira for dollars for debt service would drive the exchange rate down dramatically.

Turkey had, however, been quite successful in its fight against the ingrained inflationary forces. In the latter half of 2000 the inflation rate had dropped dramatically and interest rates had followed. The resulting economic boom immediately showed itself in a rapid increase in imports and the corresponding current account deficit for the year 2000. As a number of journalists noted, the country's disinflation program had been a victim of its own success.

## Economic Death Spiral

In the fall of 2000 the Turkish economy was booming, but the country's ability to service its growing international debt was in peril. In late October a major Turkish bank failed when it could not meet its foreign debt service obligations. As interest rates and inflation rates started spiraling upward once again, the Turkish government turned to the IMF for help. The banking system was saved — at least temporarily — by a $7.5 billion loan package from the IMF. (Between the fall of 1999 and the spring of 2001 the IMF committed over $11 billion to Turkey.) The IMF, as part of its loan conditions, required the government to reduce foreign indebtedness, reconstruct and clean-up the Turkish banking system, and undertake a privatization program for many state-owned industries.

But these extensive measures were much easier said than done. As the economy now slowed, the various government and financial austerity measures were politically unpopular. Turk Telecom, the state-owned, fixed-line telecommunications company, offered 33.5% ownership to any foreign or domestic investor. Not a single bid was received. An offer for controlling interest in Turkish Airlines was met by a similar lack of interest by international investors.

In December 2000 the European Union and Turkey engaged in a series of heated public debates over political and trade relations. Turkey complained that the EU was placing unfair and discriminatory barriers in its way as it aspired to EU membership. The EU responded that many of Turkey's current trade restrictions were not in the spirit of membership. Turkey explained that it was in the midst of an economic crisis and was only attempting to slow the growing current account deficit. Tensions escalated.

But in January 2001 there was some growing optimism, at least outside of Turkey, that the various reforms and initiatives could yet succeed.

> *The pending $7.5 billion IMF support package and stand by arrangement are likely to ease market concerns about the credibility of Turkey's stabilization program, particularly in view of the revitalized privatization agenda and strengthened fiscal targets for 2001. The Turkish lira has strengthened on the back of IMF funding.*
>
> *On a three-month view, however, expect the lira to return to track inflation performance suggesting a level below TL750,000 by the end of March. An outside probability of a full-blown currency devaluation — similar to that in 1993 — cannot be discounted, however.*
>
> "IMF Bailout of Turkey Appears Successful,"
> *Corporate Finance*, January 2001

## The Turkish *Kriz*

On February 18, 2001, a public argument erupted between President Ahmet Necdet Sezer and Prime Minister Bulent Ecevit over the lack of progress in removing corrupt politicians from office. President Sezer complained that the Prime Minister's efforts had been "half-hearted." The Prime Minister tried to quell international concerns by quickly renewing his commitment to the Turkish disinflation program and the ongoing initiatives to reduce political corruption, but the damage was already done.

The following day, February 19, international investors pulled over $5 billion of capital out of the country. The Turkish central bank's total foreign exchange reserves, $20 billion, was unable to sustain a defense at this rate of capital flight. On February 22 the Turkish government announced it was floating the lira. As illustrated in Exhibit 2, the lira's value immediately plummeted from TL685,000/$ to over TL1,000,000/$.

In the months that followed the Turkish lira continued to fall, and many of the country's banks collapsed. Industrial production, which had grown 2% and 1% in the third and fourth quarters of 2000, respectively, fell 20% in the first quarter of 2001. The road to economic reform and prosperity appeared to extend far into the future for the people of Turkey.

## EXHIBIT 2

The Fall of the
Turkish Lira

© 2002 by Prof.
Werner Antweiler,
University of British
Columbia, Vancouver
BC, Canada. Time
period shown
in diagram:
1/Jun/2000–
30/May/2001

**Daily Exchange Rates: Turkish Lira per U.S. Dollar**

### Case Questions

1. Was the Turkish lira's collapse the result of a balance of payments crisis, an inflation crisis, a political crisis, or an economic crisis?
2. Describe precisely how the Turkish banks were performing uncovered interest arbitrage. Do you feel this was an inappropriate investment policy?
3. How could the Turkish banks be contributing to financial crisis if they were purchasing Turkish government bonds and helping finance and support their own government?

4. Which do you think is more critical to a country such as Turkey, fighting inflation or fighting a large trade and current account deficit?
5. The quote from *Corporate Finance*, although noting the outside possibility of a devaluation, was largely positive regarding Turkey's future in January 2001. What would you have thought?

## Summary of Learning Objectives

*Examine how the supply and demand for any currency can be viewed as an asset choice issue within the portfolio of investors*

- The asset approach to forecasting suggests that whether foreigners are willing to hold claims in monetary form depends partly on relative real interest rates and partly on a country's outlook for economic growth and profitability.
- Longer-term forecasting, over one year, requires a return to the basic analysis of exchange rate fundamentals such as BOP, relative inflation rates, relative interest rates, and the long-run properties of purchasing power parity.

- Technical analysts (chartists) focus on price and volume data to determine past trends that are expected to continue into the future.
- Exchange rate forecasting in practice is a mix of both fundamental and technical forms of exchange rate analysis.

*Explore how the three major approaches to exchange rate determination — parity conditions, the balance of payments, and the asset approach — combine to explain in part the recent currency crises experienced in Asia, Russia, and Argentina*

- The Asian currency crisis was primarily a balance of payments crisis in its origins and impacts on exchange rate determination. A weak economic and financial infrastructure, corporate governance problems, and speculation were also contributing factors.

- The Russian ruble crisis of 1998 was a complex combination of speculative pressures best explained by the asset approach to exchange rate determination.

- The Argentina crisis of 2002 was probably a combination of a disequilibrium in international parity conditions (differential rates of inflation) and balance of payments disequilibrium (current account deficits combined with financial account outflows).

*Observe how forecasters combine technical analysis with the three major theoretical approaches to forecasting exchange rates*

- Longer-term forecasting, longer than one year, requires a return to the basic analysis of exchange rate fundamentals such as BOP, relative inflation rates, relative interest rates, and the long-run properties of purchasing power parity.

- Technical analysis (chartists) focus on price and volume data to determine past trends that are expected to continue into the future.

- Exchange rate forecasting in practice is a mix of both fundamental and technical forms of exchange rate analysis.

## QUESTIONS

1. **Term forecasting.** What are the major differences between short-term and long-term forecasts for
   **a.** a fixed exchange rate?
   **b.** a floating exchange rate?

2. **Exchange rate dynamics.** What is meant by the term *overshooting*? What causes it and how is it corrected?

3. **Fundamental equilibrium.** What is meant by the term *fundamental equilibrium path* for a currency value? What is *noise*?

4. **Asset market approach to forecasting.** Explain how the asset market approach can be used to forecast future spot exchange rates. How does the asset market approach differ from the BOP approach to forecasting?

5. **Technical analysis.** Explain how technical analysis can be used to forecast future spot exchange rates. How does technical analysis differ from the BOP and asset market approaches to forecasting?

6. **Forecasting services.** Numerous exchange rate forecasting services exist. Trident's CFO Maria Gonzalez is considering whether to subscribe to one of these services at a cost of $20,000 per year. The price includes online access to the forecasting services' computerized econometric exchange rate prediction model. What factors should Maria consider when deciding whether or not to subscribe?

7. **Cross-rate consistency in forecasting.** Explain the meaning of *cross-rate consistency* as used by MNEs. How do MNEs use a check of cross-rate consistency in practice?

8. **Infrastructure weakness.** Infrastructure weakness was one of the causes of the emerging market crisis in Thailand in 1997. Define infrastructure weakness and explain how it could affect a country's exchange rate.

9. **Infrastructure strength.** Explain why infrastructure strengths have helped to offset the large BOP deficits on current account in the United States.

10. **Speculation.** The emerging market crises of 1997–2002 were worsened because of rampant speculation. Do speculators cause such crises or do they simply respond to market signals of weakness? How can a government manage foreign exchange speculation?

11. **Foreign direct investment.** Swings in foreign direct investment flows into and out of emerging markets contribute to exchange rate volatility. Describe one concrete historical example of this phenomenon during the last 10 years.

12. **Thailand's crisis of 1997.** What were the main causes of Thailand's crisis of 1997? What lessons were learned and what steps were eventually taken to normalize Thailand's economy?

13. **Russia's crisis of 1998.** What were the main causes of Russia's crisis of 1998? What lessons were learned and what steps were taken to normalize Russia's economy?

14. **Argentina's crisis of 2001–2002.** What were the main causes of Argentina's crisis of 2001–2002? What lessons were learned and what steps were taken to normalize Argentina's economy?

## PROBLEMS

1. **Brazilian real.** The Brazilian real's (R$) value was R$1.21/$ on Monday January 11, 1999. Its value fell to R$1.43/$ on Friday January 15, 1999. What was the percent change in its value?

2. **Turkish lira.** The Turkish lira (TL) was officially devalued by the Turkish government in February 2001 during a severe political and economic crisis. The Turkish government announced on February 21 that the lira would be devalued by 20%. The spot exchange rate on February 20 was TL68,000/$.

   **a.** What was the exchange rate after a 20% devaluation?

   **b.** Within three days the lira had plummeted to TL100,000/$. What percent change was this from the predevaluation rate?

3. **Mexican peso.** The Mexican peso (Ps) was trading at Ps3.30/$ on December 20, 1994. It was devalued by the Mexican government to Ps5.50/$ the next day. What was the percent devaluation?

4. **Russian ruble.** The Russian ruble (R) traded at R6.25/$ on August 7, 1998. By September 10, 1998, its value had fallen to R20.00/$. What was the percent change in its value?

5. **Thai baht.** The Thai baht (Bt) was devalued by the Thai government from Bt25/$ to Bt29/$ on July 2, 1997. What was the percent devaluation of the baht?

6. **Ecuadoran sucre.** The Ecuadoran sucre (S) suffered from hyper-inflationary forces throughout 1999. Its value moved from S5,000/$ to S25,000/$. What was the percent change in its value?

7. **Forecasting the Argentine peso.** As illustrated in the graph below, the Argentine peso moved from its fixed exchange rate of Ps1.00/$ to over Ps2.00/$ in a matter of days in early January 2002. After a brief period of high volatility, the peso's value appeared to settle down into a range varying between 2.0 and 2.5 pesos per dollar.

   If you were forecasting the Argentine peso further into the future, how would you use the information in the graphic — the value of the peso freely floating in the weeks following devaluation — to forecast its future value?

   Use the following economic, financial, and business indicators from the February 3, 2003 issue of *The Economist* to answer problems 8 through 17.

**Daily Exchange Rates: Argentine Pesos per U.S. Dollar**

© 2002 by Prof. Werner Antweiler, University of British Columbia, Vancouver BC, Canada. Time period shown in diagram: 1/Jul/2000–25/Jan/2002

**Forecasting the Pan-Pacific Pyramid: Australia, Japan, and the United States**

| Country | Gross Domestic Product | | | | Industrial Production Recent Qtr | Retail Sales Recent Qtr | Unemployment Rate Recent Qtr |
|---|---|---|---|---|---|---|---|
| | Recent Qtr | 2003 | Forecast 2004e | Forecast 2005e | | | |
| Australia | 0.9% | 2.8% | 3.8% | 3.1% | −0.9% | 7.7% | 5.5% |
| Japan | 6.1% | 2.3% | 4.1% | 2.1% | 8.7% | −0.5% | 4.7% |
| United States | 4.4% | 3.2% | 4.7% | 3.6% | 6.3% | 8.5% | 5.6% |

| Country | Consumer Prices | | | Producer Prices | | Wages and Earnings | |
|---|---|---|---|---|---|---|---|
| | Year Ago | 2003 | Forecast 2004e | Latest | Year Ago | Latest | Year Ago |
| Australia | 3.4% | 2.7% | 2.3% | −1.1% | 3.0% | 5.1% | 4.4% |
| Japan | −0.1% | −0.3% | −0.1% | 1.1% | −1.1% | 0.7% | 1.8% |
| United States | 2.1% | 2.3% | 2.3% | 4.9% | 2.4% | 2.2% | 3.0% |

| Country | Money Supply Growth | Interest Rates (percent per annum) | | | | | Corporate Bonds |
|---|---|---|---|---|---|---|---|
| | | 3-month Money Market | | 2-year Govt Bonds | 10-year Govt Bonds | | |
| | | Latest | Year Ago | | Latest | Year Ago | |
| Australia | 11.0% | 5.48% | 4.62% | 5.18% | 5.90% | 4.73% | 6.66% |
| Japan | 2.0% | 0.02% | 0.01% | 0.20% | 1.87% | 0.63% | 1.93% |
| United States | 5.5% | 1.40% | 0.88% | 2.74% | 4.70% | 3.35% | 6.11% |

| Country | Trade Balance Last 12 mos (billion $) | Current Account | | | Trade-Weighted Exchange Rate (1990 = 100) | | Currency per Pound |
|---|---|---|---|---|---|---|---|
| | | Last 12 mos (billion $) | Actual 2003 (% of GDP) | Forecast 04 (% of GDP) | Jun 23 | Year Ago | Jun 23 |
| Australia | −16.8 | −$33.0 | −6.2% | −5.2% | 81.6 | 83.5 | 2.65 |
| Japan | 121.4 | $157.2 | 3.0% | 3.3% | 136.1 | 128.5 | 198 |
| United States | −568.9 | −$537.3 | −5.0% | −5.1% | 97.5 | 101.9 | 1.82 |

Source: Data abstracted from *The Economist*, June, 2004. Unless otherwise noted, percentages are percent changes over one year. Rec Qtr = recent quarter. Values for 2004e and 2005e are estimates or forecasts.

8. **Current spot rates.** What are the current spot exchange rates for the following cross-rates?

   a. Japanese yen/U.S. dollar

   b. Japanese yen/Australian dollar

   c. Australian dollar/U.S. dollar

9. **Purchasing power parity forecasts.** Using the theory of purchasing power parity, and that forecasted changes in consumer prices are the best measures of expected inflation, forecast the following spot exchanges for one year into the future:

   a. Japanese yen/U.S. dollar

   b. Japanese yen/Australian dollar

   c. Australian dollar/U.S. dollar

10. **International Fisher forecasts.** Using International Fisher and the fact that the latest two-year government bond rates are the most appropriate interest rates for applying International Fisher, forecast the following spot exchanges for one year into the future:

   a. Japanese yen/U.S. dollar

   b. Japanese yen/Australian dollar

   c. Australian dollar/U.S. dollar

11. **Implied real interest rates.** Use the latest two-year government bond rates and the forecast changes in consumer prices to forecast the real interest rates for the following:

   a. Australian dollar

   b. Japanese yen

   c. U.S. dollar

12. **Forecasting with real interest rates.** Using the real interest rates forecast in Problem 11 above, forecast the following spot exchange rates one year into the future:

   a. Japanese yen/U.S. dollar
   b. Japanese yen/Australian dollar
   c. Australian dollar/U.S. dollar

13. **Forward rates as forecasts.** Using the three-month money market interest rates listed, calculate the three-month forward rates for the following exchange rates:

   a. Japanese yen/U.S. dollar
   b. Japanese yen/Australian dollar
   c. Australian dollar/U.S. dollar

14. **Real economic activity and misery.** One of the common general measures of national economic health is sometimes referred to as the *misery index*, the sum of the country's inflation rate and unemployment rate. Using the previously calculated cross-rates (Problem 8), calculate the country's misery index and use it as a relative measure for forecasting, in the same way as inflation differentials or interest differentials are used to forecast.

   a. Japanese yen/U.S. dollar
   b. Japanese yen/Australian dollar
   c. Australian dollar/U.S. dollar

15. **Balance of payments approach.** Using the trade and current account information provided, forecast the direction of spot exchange rate movement one year into the future for the following spot exchange rates:

   a. Japanese yen/U.S. dollar
   b. Japanese yen/Australian dollar
   c. Australian dollar/U.S. dollar

   Now, in addition to the economic and financial data, look at the next two graphs Exhibits 15A and 15B, and consider how these three currency values have performed in recent years.

16. **Current Accounts and spot rates.** Given what you concluded about the direction of the spot exchange rate in Problem 8, does this directional view still fit with the recent trend exhibited by the spot exchange rate above for the Japanese yen/U.S. dollar and Australian dollar/U.S. dollar?

## EXHIBIT 15A

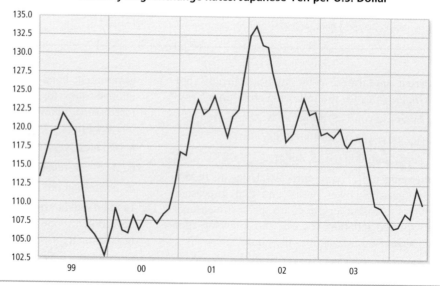

Monthly Avg. Exchange Rates: Japanese Yen per U.S. Dollar

**EXHIBIT 15B**

Monthly Avg. Exchange Rates: Australian Dollars per U.S. Dollar

17. **Exchange rate trends and bounds.** Using the graphics of the spot exchange rates for January 1999 through February 2003, determine what you believe the trend is, the mean value is, and the upper and lower bounds are to their respective rates.

## Internet Exercises

1. **Recent economic and financial data.** Use the following Web sites to obtain recent economic and financial data used for all approaches to forecasting presented in this chapter.

   Economist.com
   http://www.economist.com
   FT.com
   http://www.ft.com
   EconEdLink
   http://www.econedlink.org/datalinks/index.cfm

2. **OzForex weekly comment.** The OzForex Foreign Exchange Services Web site provides a weekly commentary on major political and economic factors and events that move current markets. Read what they expect to happen in the coming week on three major global currencies — the dollar, yen, and euro.

   OzForex
   http://www.ozforex.com.au/marketwatch.htm

3. **Exchange rates, interest rates, and global markets.** The magnitude of market data can seem overwhelming on occasion. Use the following Bloomberg markets page to organize your thoughts and your global data.

   Bloomberg Financial News
   http://www.bloomberg.com/markets

4. **National Bank of Slovakia and the Slovakia koruna.** The National Bank of Slovakia has been publishing spot and forward rates of selected currencies versus the Slovakia koruna for several years. Using the following Web site, compile spot rates, three-month forward rates, and six-month forward rates for a recent two-year period. After you have graphed the data, does it appear that

the forward rate has predicted the future direction of the spot rate?

National Bank of Slovakia
  http://www.nbs.sk/KL/INDEXA.HTM

5.  **Banque Canada and the Canadian dollar forward market.** Use the following Web site to find the latest spot and forward quotes of the Canadian dollar against the Bahamian dollar and the Brazilian real.

Banque Canada
  http://www.bankofcanada.ca/en/index.htm

CHAPTER 6

# The Foreign Exchange Market

## LEARNING OBJECTIVES

Examine the functions performed by the foreign exchange market, its participants, size, and geographic and currency composition

Distinguish between spot, forward, swap, and other types of foreign exchange financial instruments

Identify the forms of currency quotations used by currency dealers, financial institutions, and agents of all kinds when conducting foreign exchange transactions

Analyze the interaction between changing currency values, cross exchange rates, and the opportunities arising from intermarket arbitrage

The foreign exchange market provides the physical and institutional structure through which the money of one country is exchanged for that of another country, the rate of exchange between currencies is determined, and foreign exchange transactions are physically completed. *Foreign exchange* means the money of a foreign country; that is, foreign currency bank balances, banknotes, checks, and drafts. A *foreign exchange transaction* is an agreement between a buyer and seller that a fixed amount of one currency will be delivered for some other currency at a specified rate.

This chapter describes the following features of the foreign exchange market:

- Its geographical extent
- Its three main functions
- Its participants
- Its immense daily transaction volume
- Types of transactions, including spot, forward, and swap transactions
- Methods of stating exchange rates, quotations, and changes in exchange rates

## Geographical Extent of the Foreign Exchange Market

The foreign exchange market spans the globe, with prices moving and currencies trading somewhere every hour of every business day. Major world trading starts each morning in Sydney and Tokyo, moves west to Hong Kong and Singapore, passes on to Bahrain, shifts to the main European markets of Frankfurt, Zurich, and London, jumps the Atlantic to New York, goes west to Chicago, and ends in San Francisco and Los Angeles. Many large international banks operate foreign exchange trading rooms in each major geographic trading center in order to serve important commercial accounts on a 24-hour-a-day basis. Global currency trading is indeed a 24-hour-a-day process. As illustrated in Exhibit 6.1, the volume of currency transactions ebbs and flows across the globe as the major currency trading centers of London, New York, and Tokyo open and close throughout the day.

**EXHIBIT 6.1**

Measuring Foreign Exchange Market Activity: Average Electronic Conversions per Hour

Source: Federal Reserve Bank of New York, "The Foreign Exchange Market in the United States," 2001, www.ny.frb.org

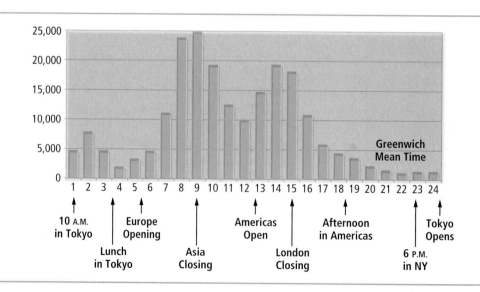

In some countries, a portion of foreign exchange trading is conducted on an official trading floor by open bidding. Closing prices are published as the official price, or "fixing," for the day, and certain commercial and investment transactions are based on this official price. Business firms in countries with exchange controls often must surrender foreign exchange earned from exports to the central bank at the daily fixing price.

Banks engaged in foreign exchange trading are connected by highly sophisticated telecommunications networks. Professional dealers and brokers obtain exchange rate quotes on desktop computer screens and communicate with each other by telephone, computer, fax, and telex. The foreign exchange departments of many nonbank business firms also use computer networks to keep in touch with the market and to seek out the best quotations. Reuters, Telerate, and Bloomberg are the leading suppliers of foreign exchange rate information and trading systems. A recent development has been the introduction of automated "matching" systems into computerized quotation systems. Many dealers think computer-executed transactions will replace other, more conventional, trading systems in the near future.

## Functions of the Foreign Exchange Market

The foreign exchange market is the mechanism by which participants transfer purchasing power between countries, obtain or provide credit for international trade transactions, and minimize exposure to the risks of exchange rate changes.

- Transfer of purchasing power is necessary because international trade and capital transactions normally involve parties living in countries with different national currencies. Each party usually wants to deal in its own currency, but the trade or capital transaction can be invoiced in only one currency. Hence one party must deal in a foreign currency.
- Because the movement of goods between countries takes time, inventory in transit must be financed. The foreign exchange market provides a source of credit. Specialized instruments, such as bankers' acceptances and letters of credit, are available to finance international trade. These documents will be explained in Chapter 20.
- The foreign exchange market provides "hedging" facilities for transferring foreign exchange risk to someone else more willing to carry risk. These facilities are explained in Chapter 8.

## Market Participants

The foreign exchange market consists of two tiers, the interbank or wholesale market, and the client or retail market. Individual transactions in the interbank market are usually for large sums that are multiples of a million U.S. dollars or the equivalent value in other currencies. By contrast, contracts between a bank and its clients are usually for specific amounts.

Five broad categories of participants operate within these two tiers: bank and non-bank foreign exchange dealers, individuals and firms conducting commercial or investment transactions, speculators and arbitragers, central banks and treasuries, and foreign exchange brokers.

## BANK AND NONBANK FOREIGN EXCHANGE DEALERS

Banks, and a few nonbank foreign exchange dealers, operate in both the interbank and client markets. They profit from buying foreign exchange at a *bid* price and reselling it at a slightly higher *ask* (also called *offer*) price. Competition among dealers worldwide narrows the spread between bid and offer and so contributes to making the foreign exchange market efficient in the same sense as in securities markets.

Dealers in the foreign exchange departments of large international banks often function as *market makers*. Such dealers stand willing at all times to buy and sell those currencies in which they specialize and thus maintain an inventory position in those currencies. They trade with other banks in their own monetary centers and with other centers around the world in order to maintain inventories within the trading limits set by bank policy. Trading limits are important because foreign exchange departments of many banks operate as profit centers, and individual dealers are compensated on a profit incentive basis.

Currency trading is quite profitable for commercial and investment banks. Many of the major currency-trading banks in the United States derive between 10% and 20% on average of their annual net income from currency trading. But currency trading is also very profitable for the bank's traders, who typically earn a bonus based on the profitability to the bank of their individual trading activities.

Small- to medium-size banks are likely to participate but not be market makers in the interbank market. Instead of maintaining significant inventory positions, they buy from and sell to larger banks to offset retail transactions with their own customers. Of course, even market-making banks do not make markets in every currency. They trade for their own account in those currencies of most interest to their customers and become participants when filling customer needs in less important currencies. *Real World Example 6.1* describes a typical foreign exchange dealer's day.

## INDIVIDUALS AND FIRMS CONDUCTING COMMERCIAL AND INVESTMENT TRANSACTIONS

Importers and exporters, international portfolio investors, MNEs, tourists, and others use the foreign exchange market to facilitate execution of commercial or investment transactions. Their use of the foreign exchange market is necessary but nevertheless incidental to their underlying commercial or investment purpose. Some of these participants use the market to "hedge" foreign exchange risk.

## SPECULATORS AND ARBITRAGERS

Speculators and arbitragers seek to profit from trading in the market itself. They operate in their own interest, without a need or obligation to serve clients or to ensure a continuous market. Where dealers seek profit from the spread between bid and offer in addition to what they might gain from changes in exchange rates, speculators seek all of their profit from exchange rate changes. Arbitragers try to profit from simultaneous exchange rate differences in different markets.

A large proportion of speculation and arbitrage is conducted on behalf of major banks by traders employed by those banks. Thus banks act both as exchange dealers and as speculators and arbitragers. (However banks seldom admit to speculating; they characterize themselves as "taking an aggressive position"!) As illustrated in *Real World Example 6.2*, there are also many fraudulent currency dealers and funds.

## Real World Example 6.1
### THE FOREIGN EXCHANGE DEALER'S DAY

How do foreign exchange dealers prepare for their working day? Foreign exchange dealing in Europe is officially opened at 8 A.M., but the dealer's work starts at least one hour earlier. Every morning, the chief dealers give their staff guidelines for their dealing activities. They will reassess their strategy on the basis of their estimation of the market over the next few months. They will also decide their tactics for the day, based on the following factors:

- Trading activities in the past few hours in New York and the Far East. Because of the time difference, banks in New York will have continued trading for several hours longer than the banks in Europe, while in the Far East the working day is already closing when the European day begins.
- New economic and political developments. Following the theoretical forces which determine exchange rates, changes in interest rates, economic indicators and monetary aggregates are the fundamental factors influencing exchange rates. Political events such as military conflicts, social unrest, the fall of a government, etc., can also influence, and sometimes even dominate, the market scene.
- The bank's own foreign exchange position.

Early in the morning, market makers use electronic information systems to catch up on any events of the past night which might impact exchange rates. Charts, graphic presentations of market movements, and screen-based rate boards allow dealers to study the latest developments in exchange rates in New York and the Far East. As soon as this preparatory work is completed, the dealers will be ready for international trades (between 8 A.M. and 5 P.M.).

The day starts with a series of telephone calls between the key market players, the aim being to sound out what intentions are. Until recently, brokers also acted as intermediaries in foreign exchange and money market operations. Nowadays, however, the Electronic Broking System (EBS) has largely replaced the activities of the brokers themselves. The original brokers used to work with minimum amounts, such as US$ 5 million, whereas the EBS allows flexible trading from US$1 to 999 million. EBS does not only deal in U.S. dollars, however. Currencies such as EUR/CHF, EUR/JPY, and EUR/GBP are also traded. This means that the continuity of rate determination is substantially higher, as a larger number of smaller amounts, previously negotiated privately between banks, now play a role in setting rates. Another advantage of this system is that the rates are always available on-screen.

Source: *Foreign Exchange and Money Market Transactions*, UBS Investment Bank, Spring 2004.

## CENTRAL BANKS AND TREASURIES

Central banks and treasuries use the market to acquire or spend their country's foreign exchange reserves as well as to influence the price at which their own currency is traded. They may act to support the value of their own currency because of policies adopted at the national level or because of commitments entered into through membership in joint float agreements, such as the European Monetary System (EMS) central bank's agreements that preceded introduction of the euro. Consequently, the motive is not to earn a profit as such, but rather to influence the foreign exchange value of their currency in a manner that will benefit the interests of their citizens. In many instances they do their job best when they willingly take a loss on their foreign exchange transactions. As willing loss takers, central banks and treasuries differ in motive and behavior from all other market participants.

## FOREIGN EXCHANGE BROKERS

Foreign exchange brokers are agents who facilitate trading between dealers without themselves becoming principals in the transaction. For this service they charge a small commission. They maintain instant access to hundreds of dealers worldwide via open

## Real World Example 6.2
### BEWARE OF FOREIGN CURRENCY TRADING FRAUDS

Have you been solicited to trade foreign currency contracts (also known as *forex*)? If so, you need to know how to spot foreign currency trading frauds. The United States Commodity Futures Trading Commission (CFTC), the federal agency that regulates commodity futures and options markets in the United States, warns consumers to take special care to protect themselves from the various kinds of frauds being perpetrated in today's financial markets, including those involving so-called *foreign currency trading*.

A new federal law, the Commodity Futures Modernization Act of 2000, makes clear that the CFTC has the jurisdiction and authority to investigate and take legal action to close down a wide assortment of unregulated firms offering or selling foreign currency futures and options contracts to the general public. In addition, the CFTC has jurisdiction to investigate and prosecute foreign currency fraud occurring in its registered firms and their affiliates.

CFTC has witnessed the increasing numbers and growing complexity of financial investment opportunities in recent years, including a sharp rise in foreign currency trading scams. While much foreign currency trading is legitimate, various forms of foreign currency trading have been touted in recent years to defraud members of the public.

### WARNING SIGNS OF FRAUD

If you are solicited by a company that claims to trade foreign currencies and asks you to commit funds for those purposes, you should be very careful. Heed the warnings below before placing your funds with any currency trading company.

1. Stay away from opportunities that sound too good to be true.
2. Avoid any company that predicts or guarantees large profits.
3. Stay away from companies that promise little or no financial risk.
4. Don't trade on margin unless you understand what it means.
5. Question firms that claim to trade in the "interbank market."
6. Be wary of sending or transferring cash on the Internet, by mail, or otherwise.
7. Currency scams often target members of ethnic minorities.
8. Be sure you get the company's performance track record.
9. Don't deal with anyone who won't give you their background.

Source: Public warning issued by the U.S. Commodities and Futures Trading Corporation. http://www.cftc.gov/opa/enf98/opaforexa15.htm: March 8, 2002.

telephone lines. At times a broker may maintain a dozen or more such lines to a single client bank, with separate lines for different currencies and for spot and forward markets.

It is a broker's business to know at any moment exactly which dealers want to buy or sell any currency. This knowledge enables the broker to find quickly an opposite party for a client without revealing the identity of either party until after a transaction has been agreed upon. Dealers use brokers for speed and because they want to remain anonymous, since the identity of participants may influence short-term quotes.

## Transactions in the Interbank Market

Transactions in the interbank market are conducted via the latest technology in telecommunications, since there is little face-to-face trading (except in those few countries still using trading floors). Complete trust between parties is crucial. Nevertheless, as described in *Real World Example 6.2*, foreign exchange trading frauds have occurred. In the United States, the Commodity Futures Modernization Act of 2000 gives the responsibility for regulating foreign exchange trading fraud to the U.S. Commodity Futures Trading Commission (CFTC).

Transactions in the foreign exchange market can be executed on a *spot*, *forward*, or *swap* basis. A broader definition of the foreign exchange market includes foreign currency options and futures (covered in Chapter 7). A *spot* transaction requires almost immediate delivery of foreign exchange. A *forward* transaction requires delivery of foreign exchange at some future date, either on an "outright" basis or through a "futures" contract. A *swap* transaction is the simultaneous exchange of one foreign currency for another.

## SPOT TRANSACTIONS

A spot transaction in the interbank market is the purchase of foreign exchange, with delivery and payment between banks to take place, normally, on the second following business day. The Canadian dollar settles with the U.S. dollar on the first following business day.

The date of settlement is referred to as the *value date*. On the value date, most dollar transactions in the world are settled through the computerized Clearing House Interbank Payments System (CHIPS) in New York, which provides for calculation of net balances owed by any one bank to another and for payment by 6:00 P.M. that same day in Federal Reserve Bank of New York funds.

A typical spot transaction in the interbank market might involve a U.S. bank contracting on a Monday for the transfer of £10,000,000 to the account of a London bank. If the spot exchange rate were $1.8420/£, the U.S. bank would transfer £10,000,000 to the London bank on Wednesday, and the London bank would transfer $18,420,000 to the U.S. bank at the same time. A spot transaction between a bank and its commercial customer would not necessarily involve a wait of two days for settlement.

## OUTRIGHT FORWARD TRANSACTIONS

An *outright forward transaction* (usually called just *forward*) requires delivery at a future value date of a specified amount of one currency for a specified amount of another currency. The exchange rate is established at the time of the agreement, but payment and delivery are not required until maturity. Forward exchange rates are normally quoted for value dates of one, two, three, six, and twelve months. Actual contracts can be arranged for other numbers of months or, on occasion, for periods of more than one year. Payment is on the second business day after the even-month anniversary of the trade. Thus a two-month forward transaction entered into on March 18 will be for a value date of May 20, or the next business day if May 20 falls on a weekend or holiday.

Note that as a matter of terminology we can speak of "buying forward" or "selling forward" to describe the same transaction. A contract to deliver dollars for euros in six months is buying euros forward for dollars and selling dollars forward for euros.

## SWAP TRANSACTIONS

A swap transaction in the interbank market is the simultaneous purchase and sale of a given amount of foreign exchange for two different value dates. Both purchase and sale are conducted with the same counterparty. A common type of swap is a *spot against forward*. The dealer buys a currency in the spot market and simultaneously sells the same amount back to the same bank in the forward market. Since this is executed as a single transaction with one counterparty, the dealer incurs no unexpected foreign exchange risk. Swap transactions and outright forwards combined made up 57% of all foreign exchange market activity in April 2004.

**FORWARD-FORWARD SWAPS.**    A more sophisticated swap transaction is called a *forward-forward swap*. A dealer sells £20,000,000 forward for dollars for delivery in, say, two months at $1.8420/£ and simultaneously buys £20,000,000 forward for delivery in three months at $1.8400/£. The difference between the buying price and the selling price is equivalent to the interest rate differential — that is, interest rate parity; between the two currencies. Thus a swap can be viewed as a technique for borrowing another currency on a fully collateralized basis.

**NONDELIVERABLE FORWARDS (NDFS).**    Created in the early 1990s, the *nondeliverable forward*, or NDF, is now a relatively common derivative offered by the largest providers of foreign exchange derivatives. NDFs possess the same characteristics and documentation requirements as traditional forward contracts except that they are settled only in U.S. dollars and the foreign currency being sold forward or bought forward is not delivered. The dollar-settlement feature reflects the fact that NDFs are contracted offshore, for example, in New York for a Mexican investor, and so are beyond the reach and regulatory frameworks of the home country governments (Mexico in this case). NDFs are used primarily for emerging market currencies — currencies which typically do not have liquid money markets or eurocurrency interest rates. Pricing of NDFs reflects basic interest differentials, as with regular forward contracts, plus an additional premium charged by the bank for dollar settlement.

## Size of the Market

The Bank for International Settlements (BIS), in conjunction with central banks around the world, conducts a survey of currency trading activity every three years. The most recent survey, conducted in April 2004, estimated *daily* global net turnover in traditional foreign exchange market activity to be $1.9 trillion. This most recent period showed dramatic growth in foreign exchange trading over that seen in April 2001. BIS data is shown in Exhibit 6.2.

**EXHIBIT 6.2**

Global Foreign Exchange Market Turnover, 1989–2004 (daily averages in April, billions of US$)

Source: Bank for International Settlements, "Triennial Central Bank Survey of Foreign Exchange and Derivatives Market Activity in April 2004," September 2004, p. 9.

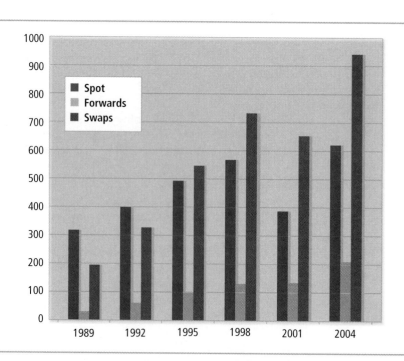

**EXHIBIT 6.3**

Geographic Distribution of Foreign Exchange Market Turnover, 1989–2004 (daily averages in April, US$ billions)

Source: Bank for International Settlements, "Triennial Central Bank Survey of Foreign Exchange and Derivatives Market Activity in April 2004," September 2004, p. 13.

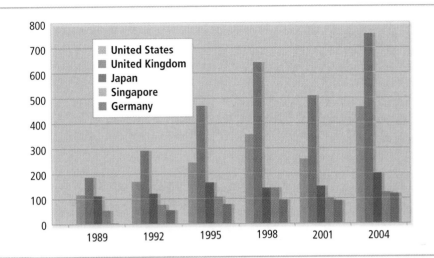

Global foreign exchange turnover in Exhibit 6.2 is divided into three categories of currency instruments: spot transactions, forward transactions, and swap transactions. All three categories of currency transactions rose between the 2001 and 2004 surveys, after diminished activity in two of the three categories between the 1998 and 2001 surveys.

Exhibit 6.3 shows the proportionate share of foreign exchange trading for the most important national markets in the world in April 2004. (Note that although the data is collected and reported on a national basis, "the United States" should largely be interpreted as "New York" due to the fact that the great majority of foreign exchange trading takes place in the major city in each country.) The United Kingdom (London) continues to be the world's major foreign exchange market in traditional foreign exchange market activity with roughly $750 billion in average daily turnover. The U.K. is followed by the United States (New York), Japan (Tokyo), Singapore, and Germany (Frankfurt). Indeed, more than half of all world foreign exchange trading takes place in just those five countries. Foreign exchange trading in Japan and Singapore each exceeds that of any European country except the United Kingdom, and Hong Kong (not shown) is sixth in the world.

Exhibit 6.4 summarizes the BIS April 2004 survey results by currency, rather than by country of traditional trading activity. Because every foreign exchange transaction involves two currencies, the data cannot logically be broken down by single currency alone. Hence the sum of the world's reported transactions comes to twice the actual turnover, and the percent of total trades for each currency totals 200%. Net global turnover in April 2004 was dominated by trading in U.S. dollars, euros, and Japanese yen. The "big three," as they are often called, were followed by the U.K. pound sterling and the Swiss franc, in that order.

## Foreign Exchange Rates and Quotations

A foreign exchange *rate* is the price of one currency expressed in terms of another currency. A foreign exchange *quotation* (or *quote*) is a statement of willingness to buy or sell at an announced rate.

**EXHIBIT 6.4**

Currency
Distribution of
Global Foreign
Exchange Market
Turnover
(percentage
shares of average
daily turnover in
April)

Source: Bank for
International
Settlements,
"Triennial Central
Bank Survey of
Foreign Exchange
and Derivatives
Market Activity
in April 2004,"
September 2004,
p. 11.

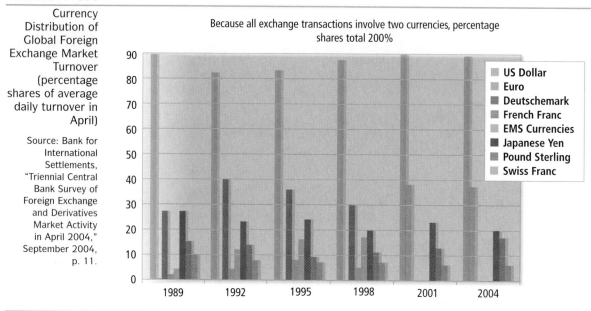

In the retail market (including newspapers and foreign exchange booths at airports), quotes are most often given as the home currency price of the foreign currency and are also given for many currency pairs. However, this practice is not uniform worldwide. As described in the next section, the professional interbank market has standardized its quotation system.

## INTERBANK QUOTATIONS

Recall from Exhibit 6.4 that most foreign exchange transactions are through the U.S. dollar. Professional dealers and brokers may state foreign exchange quotations in one of two ways: (1) the foreign currency price of one dollar, or (2) the dollar price of a unit of foreign currency. Most foreign currencies in the world are stated in terms of the number of units of foreign currency needed to buy one dollar. For example, the exchange rate between U.S. dollars and Swiss franc is normally stated

**SF1.6000/$,** read as "1.6000 Swiss francs per dollar"

This method, called *European terms,* expresses the rate as the foreign currency price of one U.S. dollar. An alternative method is called *American terms.* The same exchange rate above expressed in American terms is

**$0.6250/SF,** read as "0.6250 dollars per Swiss franc"

Under American terms, foreign exchange rates are stated as the U.S. dollar price of one unit of foreign currency. Note that European terms and American terms are reciprocals:

$$\frac{1}{SF1.600/\$} = \$0.6250/SF$$

With several exceptions, including two important ones, most interbank quotations around the world are stated in European terms. Thus, throughout the world the normal way of quoting the relationship between the Swiss franc and U.S. dollar is SF1.6000/$; this method may also be called "Swiss terms." A Japanese yen quote of ¥118.32/$ is called "Japanese terms," although the expression "European terms" is often used as the generic name for Asian as well as European currency prices of the dollar. European terms were adopted as the universal way of expressing foreign exchange rates for most (but not all) currencies in 1978 to facilitate worldwide trading through telecommunications.

As mentioned, several exceptions exist to the use of European terms quotes. The two most important are quotes for the euro and for the U.K. pound sterling. The euro, first traded in January 1999, and the U.K. pound sterling are both normally quoted in American terms; that is, the U.S. dollar price of a euro or a pound sterling. Additionally, Australian dollars and New Zealand dollars are normally quoted on American terms. Sterling is quoted as the foreign currency price of one pound for historical reasons. For centuries the British pound sterling consisted of 20 shillings, each of which had 12 pence. Multiplication and division with the nondecimal currency were difficult. The custom evolved for foreign exchange prices in London, then the undisputed financial capital of the world, to be stated in foreign currency units per pound. This practice remained even after sterling changed to decimals in 1971.

American terms are used in quoting rates for most foreign currency options and futures, as well as in retail markets that deal with tourists and personal remittances. Foreign exchange traders use nicknames for major currencies. *Cable* means the exchange rate between U.S. dollars and U.K. pound sterling, the name dating from the time when transactions in dollars and pounds were carried out over the transatlantic telegraph cable. A Canadian dollar is a *loonie*, named after the waterfowl on Canada's one-dollar coin. *Paris* means the French franc, while *kiwi* stands for the New Zealand dollar, *Aussie* for the Australian dollar, *Swissie* for Swiss francs, and *Sing dollar* for the Singapore dollar.

Currency amounts must be precise in foreign exchange conversations to avoid major blunders. Unfortunately, British and U.S. English meaning differs for the word "billion." For the British, "one billion" is 1 followed by 12 zeros: 1,000,000,000,000 or a million million. In the United States and France, where the system of numeration is based on groups of threes rather than fours, one billion is a thousand million, or 1,000,000,000. For the British a "trillion" is a million billions, while in U.S. and French usage a "trillion" is a thousand billions, the same as one British billion.[1] To avoid confusion, foreign exchange traders use the word *yard* to describe a U.S. billion.

## DIRECT AND INDIRECT QUOTES

Foreign exchange quotes are at times described as either *direct* or *indirect*. In this pair of definitions, the home or base country of the currencies being discussed is critical.

A *direct quote* is a home currency price of a unit of foreign currency, and an *indirect quote* is a foreign currency price of a unit of home currency. The form of the quote depends on what the speaker regards as home.

---

[1]*The Shorter Oxford English Dictionary on Historical Principles*, 3rd Edition, Volumes I and II, Oxford: Clarendon Press, 1973.

The foreign exchange quote SF1.6000/$ is a direct quote in Switzerland — it is the Swiss home currency (Swiss franc) price of a foreign currency (U.S. dollar). Exactly the same quotation, SF1.6000/$, is an indirect quotation when used in the United States — it is now the foreign currency (Swiss franc) price of the home currency (U.S. dollar). The reciprocal of this quote, $0.6250/SF, is a direct quote in the United States and an indirect quote in Switzerland.

The direct dollar quote against the Swiss franc, $0.6250/SF in the above example, may also be referred to as the "external value of the Swiss franc" — that is, the value of one Swiss franc outside of Switzerland. The internal value of the Swiss franc is SF1.6000/$ — the number of Swiss francs that can be purchased for one dollar.

## BID AND ASK QUOTATIONS

Interbank quotations are given as a *bid* and *ask* (also referred to as *offer*). A bid is the price (i.e., exchange rate) in one currency at which a dealer will buy another currency. An ask is the price (i.e., exchange rate) at which a dealer will sell the other currency. Dealers bid (buy) at one price and ask (sell) at a slightly higher price, making their profit from the spread between the buying and selling prices.

Bid and ask quotations in the foreign exchange markets are superficially complicated by the fact that the bid for one currency is also the offer for the opposite currency. A trader seeking to buy dollars with Swiss francs is simultaneously offering to sell Swiss francs for dollars. Assume a bank makes the quotations shown in the top half of Exhibit 6.5 for the Japanese yen. The spot quotations on the first line indicate that the bank's foreign exchange trader will buy dollars (i.e., sell Japanese yen) at the bid price of ¥118.27 per dollar. The trader will sell dollars (i.e., buy Japanese yen) at the ask price of ¥118.37 per dollar.

### EXHIBIT 6.5

Spot and Forward Quotations for the Euro and Japanese Yen

| | Term | Euro: Spot & Forward ($/€) | | | Yen: Spot & Forward (¥/$) | | |
| --- | --- | --- | --- | --- | --- | --- | --- |
| | | Mid Rates | Bid | Ask | Mid Rates | Bid | Ask |
| | Spot | 1.0899 | 1.0897 | 1.0901 | 118.32 | 118.27 | 118.37 |
| Cash rates | 1 week | 1.0903 | 3 | 4 | 118.23 | −10 | −9 |
| | 1 mo | 1.0917 | 17 | 19 | 117.82 | −51 | −50 |
| | 2 mo | 1.0934 | 35 | 36 | 117.38 | −95 | −93 |
| | 3 mo | 1.0953 | 53 | 54 | 116.91 | −143 | −140 |
| | 4 mo | 1.0973 | 72 | 76 | 116.40 | −195 | −190 |
| | 5 mo | 1.0992 | 90 | 95 | 115.94 | −240 | −237 |
| | 6 mo | 1.1012 | 112 | 113 | 115.45 | −288 | −287 |
| | 9 mo | 1.1075 | 175 | 177 | 114.00 | −435 | −429 |
| | 1 yr | 1.1143 | 242 | 245 | 112.50 | −584 | −581 |
| Swap rates | 2 yr | 1.1401 | 481 | 522 | 106.93 | −1150 | −1129 |
| | 3 yr | 1.1679 | 750 | 810 | 101.09 | −1748 | −1698 |
| | 4 yr | 1.1899 | 960 | 1039 | 96.82 | −2185 | −2115 |
| | 5 yr | 1.2102 | 1129 | 1276 | 92.91 | −2592 | −2490 |

Note: *mo* is month, *yr* is year. Mid rates are the numerical average of bid and ask.

As illustrated in Exhibit 6.5, however, the full *outright quotation* (the full price to all of its decimal points) is typically shown only for the current spot rate. Traders, however, tend to abbreviate when talking on the phone or putting quotations on a video screen. The first term, the bid, of a spot quotation may be given in full: that is, "118.27." However, the second term, the ask, will probably be expressed only as the digits that differ from the bid. Hence the bid and ask for spot yen would probably be shown as "118.27–37" on a video screen.

## EXPRESSING FORWARD QUOTATIONS ON A POINTS BASIS

The spot quotations given in the top line for each currency in Exhibit 6.5 are *outright*: ¥118.27/$ for the spot bid and ¥118.37/$ for the spot ask. The forward rates are, however, typically quoted in terms of *points*, also referred to as *cash rates* and *swap rates* depending on maturity. A point is the last digit of a quotation, with convention dictating the number of digits to the right of the decimal point. Currency prices for the U.S. dollar are usually expressed to four decimal points. Hence a point is equal to 0.0001 of most currencies. Some currencies, such as the Japanese yen shown in Exhibit 6.5, are quoted only to two decimal points. A forward quotation expressed in points is not a foreign exchange rate as such. Rather it is the difference between the forward rate and the spot rate. Consequently the spot rate itself can never be given on a points basis.

The three-month points quotations for the Japanese yen in Exhibit 6.5 are −143 bid and −140 ask. The first number (−143) refers to points away from the spot bid, and the second number (−140) to points away from the spot ask. Given the outright quotes of 118.27 bid and 118.37 ask, the outright three-month forward rates are calculated as follows:

|                              | *Bid*    | *Ask*    |
|------------------------------|----------|----------|
| Outright spot:               | ¥118.27  | ¥118.37  |
| plus points (three months)   | −1.43    | −1.40    |
| Outright forward:            | ¥116.84  | ¥116.97  |

The forward bid and ask quotations in Exhibit 6.5 for two years or longer are called *swap rates*. As mentioned earlier, many forward exchange transactions in the interbank market involve a simultaneous purchase for one date and sale (reversing the transaction) for another date. This "swap" is a way to borrow one currency for a limited time while giving up the use of another currency for the same time. In other words, it is a short-term borrowing of one currency combined with a short-term loan of an equivalent amount of another currency. The two parties could, if they wanted, charge each other interest at the going rate for each of the currencies. However it is easier for the party with the higher-interest currency to simply pay the *net* interest differential to the other. The swap rate expresses this net interest differential on a points basis rather than as an interest rate.

## FORWARD QUOTATIONS IN PERCENTAGE TERMS

As introduced in Chapter 2, forward quotations may also be expressed as the percent-per-annum deviation from the spot rate. This method of quotation facilitates comparing premiums or discounts in the forward market with interest rate differentials. However the percent premium or discount depends on which currency is the home, or base, currency. Assume the following quotations, where the dollar is the home currency:

| | Foreign currency/<br>home currency | Home currency/<br>foreign currency |
|---|---|---|
| Spot rate | ¥105.65/$ | $0.009465215/¥ |
| Three-month forward | ¥105.04/$ | $0.009520183/¥ |

**QUOTATIONS EXPRESSED IN FOREIGN CURRENCY TERMS (INDIRECT QUOTATIONS).**
When the foreign currency price of the home currency is used, the formula for the
percent-per-annum premium or discount becomes

$$f^¥ = \frac{\text{Spot} - \text{Forward}}{\text{Forward}} \times \frac{360}{n} \times 100$$

Substituting ¥/$ spot and forward rates, as well as the number of days forward (90),

$$f^¥ = \frac{105.65 - 105.04}{105.04} \times \frac{360}{90} \times 100 = +2.32\% \text{ per annum}$$

The sign is positive, again indicating that the forward yen is selling at a 2.32% per
annum premium over the dollar.

**QUOTATIONS EXPRESSED IN HOME CURRENCY TERMS (DIRECT QUOTATIONS).**
When the home currency price for a foreign currency is used, the formula for the percent premium or discount $(f^¥)$ is

$$f^¥ = \frac{\text{Forward} - \text{Spot}}{\text{Spot}} \times \frac{360}{n} \times 100$$

where $n$ is the number of days in the contract. ($n$ may also be the number of months,
in which case the numerator is 12.) Substituting the $/¥ spot and forward rates, as well
as the number of days forward (90),

$$f^¥ = \frac{0.009520183 - 0.009465215}{0.009465215} \times \frac{360}{90} \times 100 = +2.32\% \text{ per annum}$$

The sign is positive, indicating that the forward yen is selling at a 2.32% per annum premium over the dollar.

## READING NEWSPAPER QUOTATIONS

Foreign exchange rates are quoted in all major world newspapers. The manner of quotation in *The Wall Street Journal* and the *Financial Times*, the world's two major
English-language business newspapers, is shown in Exhibit 6.6. Although these quotes
for the pound are for the same day, they are not identical because of time zone differences and the banks surveyed for the quotes.

*The Wall Street Journal* gives American terms quotes under the heading "US$
equivalent" and European terms quotes under the heading "Currency per US$."
Quotes are for the last two trading days and are given on an outright basis for spot,
one-, three-, and six-month forwards. The exchange rates quoted are mid rates, the
average of the bid-ask. Quotes are for trading among banks in amounts of $1 million
or more, as quoted at 4 P.M. Eastern Time by Reuters and other sources. The *Journal*
states that retail transactions provide fewer units of foreign currency per dollar.

**EXHIBIT 6.6**

Foreign Exchange Rate Quotations on the U.S. Dollar/British Pound in the Financial Press

*The Wall Street Journal*

| | US$ Equivalent | | Currency per US$ | |
| --- | --- | --- | --- | --- |
| | **Thu** | **Wed** | **Thu** | **Wed** |
| U.K. (pound) | 1.8410 | 1.8343 | .5432 | .5452 |
| one-month forward | 1.8360 | 1.8289 | .5447 | .5468 |
| three-months forward | 1.8259 | 1.8187 | .5477 | .5498 |
| six-months forward | 1.8120 | 1.8048 | .5519 | .5541 |

Source: "Exchange Rates," *The Wall Street Journal*, Friday June 4, 2004 (quotes for Thursday June 3, 2004), p. B5.

*Financial Times*

| | **Closing Mid** | **Day's Change** |
| --- | --- | --- |
| U.K. (0.5429)    (£) | 1.8418 | −0.0015 |
| one month | 1.8368 | −0.0011 |
| three month | 1.8268 | −0.0008 |
| one year | 1.7885 | −0.0007 |

Source: "Currencies, Bonds & Interest Rates," *Financial Times*, June 4, 2004 (quotes are for June 3, 2004), p. 25.

The *Financial Times* presents the latest day's closing mid rates as well, plus the absolute change in the rate from the previous trading day's close. One-month, three-month, and one-year forward rates are quoted in direct terms, U.S. dollars per pound. The rate in parentheses next to "U.K." is the current spot rate in British pounds per U.S. dollar.

## CROSS RATES

Many currency pairs are only inactively traded, so their exchange rate is determined through their relationship to a widely traded third currency. For example, a Mexican importer needs Japanese yen to pay for purchases in Tokyo. Both the Mexican peso (MXP) and the Japanese yen (¥) are commonly quoted against the U.S. dollar. Assume the following quotes.

| Japanese yen | ¥ 110.73/$ |
| --- | --- |
| Mexican peso | MXP 11.4456/$ |

The Mexican importer can buy one U.S. dollar for 11.4456 Mexican pesos, and with that dollar buy 110.73 Japanese yen. The cross rate calculation would be

$$\frac{\text{Japanese yen/ U.S. dollar}}{\text{Mexican pesos/ U.S. dollar}} = \frac{¥110.73/\$}{\text{MXP}11.4456/\$} = ¥9.6745/\text{MXP}$$

The cross rate could also be calculated as the reciprocal

$$\frac{\text{Mexican peso/ U.S. dollar}}{\text{Japanese yen/ U.S. dollar}} = \frac{\text{MXP}11.4456/\$}{¥110.73/\$} = \text{MXP}0.1034/¥$$

**EXHIBIT 6.7**

Key Currency Cross Rates

| | Dollar | Euro | Pound | Sfranc | Peso | Yen | CdnDlr |
|---|---|---|---|---|---|---|---|
| Canada | 1.3618 | 1.6646 | 2.5071 | 1.0889 | .11898 | .01230 | — |
| Japan | 110.73 | 135.34 | 203.85 | 88.539 | 9.674 | — | 81.309 |
| Mexico | 11.4456 | 13.9899 | 21.071 | 9.1519 | — | .10336 | 8.4045 |
| Switzerland | 1.2506 | 1.5286 | 2.3024 | — | .10927 | .01129 | .9183 |
| U.K. | .54320 | .6639 | — | .4343 | .04746 | .00491 | .39886 |
| Euro | .81810 | — | 1.5062 | .65418 | .07148 | .00739 | .60075 |
| U.S. | — | 1.2223 | 1.8410 | .79960 | .08737 | .00903 | .73430 |

Reuters, as quoted in "Key Currency Cross Rates," *The Wall Street Journal*, Friday June 4, 2004. Quotes are for late New York Trading, Thursday, June 3, 2004.

Cross rates often appear in financial publications in the form of a matrix such as is shown in Exhibit 6.7. This matrix shows the amount of each currency (columns) needed to buy a unit of the currency of the country on the line (row), as quoted by *The Wall Street Journal.*

## INTERMARKET ARBITRAGE

Cross rates can be used to check on opportunities for intermarket arbitrage. Suppose the following exchange rates are quoted:

| | |
|---|---|
| Citibank quotes U.S. dollars per euro: | $1.2223/€ |
| Barclays Bank quotes U.S. dollars per pound sterling: | $1.8410/£ |
| Dresdner Bank quotes euros per pound sterling: | €1.5100/£ |

The cross rate between Citibank and Barclays is

$$\frac{\$1.8410/£}{\$1.2223/€} = €1.5062/£$$

This cross rate is not the same as Dresdner's quotation of €1.5100/£, so an opportunity exists to profit from arbitrage between the three markets. Exhibit 6.8 shows the steps in what is called *triangular arbitrage.*

A market trader with $1,000,000 can sell that sum spot to Barclays Bank for $1,000,000 ÷ $1.8410/£ = £543,183. Simultaneously these pounds can be sold to Dresdner Bank for £543,183 × €1.5100/£ = €820,206, and the trader can then immediately sell these euro to Citibank for dollars: €820,206 × $1.2223/€ = $1,002,538. The profit on one such turn is a risk-free $2,538. Such triangular arbitrage can continue until exchange rate equilibrium is reestablished; that is, until the calculated cross rate equals the actual quotation, less any tiny margin for transaction costs.

Two aspects should be noted: (1) Such arbitrage is practical only if the participants have instant access to quotes and executions. Hence, except in rare instances such arbitrage is conducted only by foreign exchange traders. Public participation is most difficult. (2) Bank traders can conduct such arbitrage without an initial sum of money, other than their bank's credit standing, because the trades are entered into and subsequently "washed" (i.e., offset) by electronic means before the normal settlement two days later.

**EXHIBIT 6.8**

Triangular
Arbitrage

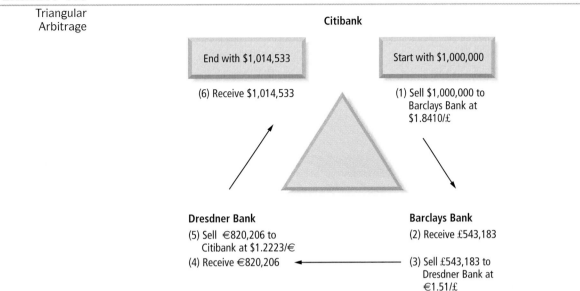

Citibank

End with $1,014,533          Start with $1,000,000

(6) Receive $1,014,533          (1) Sell $1,000,000 to
Barclays Bank at
$1.8410/£

**Dresdner Bank**          **Barclays Bank**
(5) Sell €820,206 to          (2) Receive £543,183
Citibank at $1.2223/€
(4) Receive €820,206          (3) Sell £543,183 to
Dresdner Bank at
€1.51/£

## MEASURING A CHANGE IN SPOT EXCHANGE RATES

Assume that the Swiss franc, quoted at SF1.6351/$ (which is the same as $0.61158/SF), suddenly strengthens to SF1.5000/$ (which is the same as $0.66667/SF). What is the percent increase in the dollar value of the franc, and thus in the value of Swiss franc-denominated accounts receivable or payable held by Americans? As with forward quotations in percentage form, the home currency is critical.

**QUOTATIONS EXPRESSED IN HOME CURRENCY TERMS (DIRECT QUOTATIONS).** When the home currency price for a foreign currency is used, the formula for the percent change in the foreign currency is

$$\%\Delta = \frac{\text{Ending rate} - \text{Beginning rate}}{\text{Beginning rate}} \times 100 = \frac{\$0.66667/\text{SF} - \$0.61158/\text{SF}}{\$0.61158/\text{SF}} \times 100 = +9.008\%$$

In this instance the Swiss franc is 9.0087% stronger at the ending rate. Holders of Swiss francs receivables will receive 9.008% more dollars, but those who owe Swiss francs will have to pay 9.008% more to buy them.

**QUOTATIONS EXPRESSED IN FOREIGN CURRENCY TERMS (INDIRECT QUOTATIONS).** When the foreign currency price of the home currency is used, the formula for the percent change in the foreign currency becomes

$$\%\Delta = \frac{\text{Beginning rate} - \text{Ending rate}}{\text{Ending rate}} \times 100 = \frac{\text{SF}1.6351/\$ - \text{SF}1.5000/\$}{\text{SF}1.5000/\$} \times 100 = +9.008\%$$

By both methods of calculation, the Swiss franc increased 9.008% in value relative to the dollar.

A final note of clarity on this calculation. Many students perform these two calculations and find the two very close, but still differing values. If the second calculation (or vice versa) is calculated as follows, using the precise inverse quotes, the resulting percentage change will be precisely the same, + 9.008%.

$$\%\Delta = \frac{\text{Beginning rate} - \text{Ending rate}}{\text{Ending rate}} \times 100 = \frac{\dfrac{1}{\$0.61158/\text{SF}} - \dfrac{1}{\$0.66667/\text{SF}}}{\dfrac{1}{\$0.66667/\text{SF}}} \times 100 = +9.008\%$$

## MINI-CASE

# The Venezuelan Bolivar Black Market[1]

*"Rumor has it that during the year and a half that Venezuelan President Hugo Chávez spent in jail for his role in a 1992 coup attempt against the government, he was a voracious reader. Too bad his prison syllabus seems to have been so skimpy on economics and so heavy on Machiavelli."*

*"Money Fun in the Venezuela of Hugo Chávez,"*
*The Economist*, February 13, 2004.

It's late afternoon on March 10, 2004, and Santiago opens the window of his office in Caracas, Venezuela. Immediately he is hit with the sounds rising from the plaza — cars honking, protesters banging their pots and pans, street vendors hawking their goods. Since the imposition of a new set of economic policies by President Hugo Chávez in 2002 such sights and sounds had become a fixture of city life in Caracas. Santiago sighed as he wished for the simplicity of life in the old Caracas.

Santiago's once-thriving pharmaceutical distribution business had hit hard times. Since capital controls were implemented in February 2003, dollars had been hard to come by. He had been forced to pursue various methods — methods that were more expensive and not always legal — to obtain dollars, causing his margins to decrease by 50%. To add to the strain the Venezuelan currency, the bolivar (Bs), had been recently devalued (repeatedly). This had instantly squeezed his margins as his costs had risen directly with the exchange rate. He could not find anyone to sell him dollars. His customers needed supplies and they needed them quickly, but how was he going to come up with the $30,000 — the hard currency — to pay for his most recent order?

## Political Chaos

Hugo Chávez's tenure as president of Venezuela had been tumultuous at best since his election in 1998. After repeated recalls, resignations, coups, and reappointments, the political turmoil had taken its toll on the Venezuelan economy as a whole, and its currency in particular. The short-lived success of the anti-Chávez coup in 2001, and his nearly immediate return to office, had set the stage for a retrenchment of his isolationist economic and financial policies.

On January 21, 2003, the bolivar closed at a record low — Bs1891.50/$. The next day President Chávez suspended the sale of dollars for two weeks. Nearly instantaneously, an unofficial or black market for the exchange of Venezuelan bolivars for foreign currencies (primarily U.S. dollars) sprouted. As investors of all kinds sought ways to exit the Venezuelan market, or simply to obtain the hard currency needed to continue to conduct their businesses (as was the case for Santiago), the escalating capital flight caused the black market value of the bolivar to plummet to Bs2500/$ in weeks. As markets collapsed and exchange values fell, the Venezuelan inflation rate soared to more than 30% per annum.

## Capital Controls and CADIVI

To combat the downward pressures on the bolivar, the Venezuelan government announced on February 5, 2003, the passage of the *2003 Exchange Regulations Decree*. The decree took the following actions:

1. Set the official exchange rate at Bs1596/$ for purchase (*bid*) and Bs1600/$ for sale (*offer*).

2. Established the Comisión de Administración de Divisas (CADIVI) to control the distribution of foreign exchange.
3. Implemented strict price controls to stem inflation triggered by the weaker bolivar and the exchange control-induced contraction of imports.

CADIVI was both the official means and the cheapest means by which Venezuelan citizens could obtain foreign currency. In order to receive an authorization from CADIVI to obtain dollars, an applicant was required to complete a series of forms. The applicant was then required to prove that they had paid taxes the previous three years, provide proof of business and asset ownership and lease agreements for company property, and document current Social Security payments.

Unofficially, however, there was an additional unstated requirement for permission to obtain foreign currency: that authorizations by CADIVI would be reserved for Chávez supporters. In August 2003 an anti-Chávez petition had gained widespread circulation. One million signatures had been collected. Although the government ruled that the petition was invalid, it had used the list of signatures to create a database of names and Social Security numbers that CADIVI utilized to cross-check identities when deciding who would receive hard currency. President Chávez was quoted as saying, "Not one more dollar for the *putschits*; the bolivars belong to the people."[2]

## Santiago's Alternatives

Santiago had little luck obtaining dollars via CADIVI to pay for his imports. Because he had signed the petition calling for President Chávez's removal, he had been listed in the CADIVI database as anti-Chávez, and now could not obtain permission to exchange bolivar for dollars.

The transaction in question was an invoice for $30,000 in pharmaceutical products from his U.S.–based supplier. Santiago would in turn sell to a large Venezuelan customer who would distribute the products. This transaction, however, was not the first time that Santiago had had to search out alternative sources for meeting his U.S. dollar obligations. Since the imposition of capital controls, the search for dollars had become a weekly activity for Santiago. In addition to the official process, through CADIVI, he could also obtain dollars through the *gray market*, or the *black market*.

## The Gray Market: CANTV Shares

In May 2003, three months following the implementation of the exchange controls, a window of opportunity had opened up for Venezuelans — an opportunity that allowed investors in the Caracas stock exchange to avoid the tight foreign exchange curbs. This loophole circumvented the government-imposed restrictions, by allowing investors to purchase local shares of the leading telecommunications company CANTV on the Caracas bourse, and to then convert them into dollar-denominated American Depositary Receipts (ADRs) traded on the NYSE.

The sponsor for CANTV ADRs on the NYSE was the Bank of New York, the leader in ADR sponsorship and management in the United States. The Bank of New York had suspended trading in CANTV ADRs in February after the passage of the exchange regulations decree, wishing to determine the legality of trading under the new Venezuelan currency controls. On May 26, after concluding that trading was indeed legal under the decree, the bank resumed trading in CANTV shares. CANTV's share price and trading volume soared in the following week.[3]

The share price of CANTV quickly became the primary method of calculating the implicit gray market exchange rate. For example, CANTV shares closed at Bs7945/share on the Caracas bourse on February 6, 2004. That same day, CANTV ADRs closed in New York at $18.84/ADR. Each New York ADR was equal to seven shares of CANTV in Caracas. The implied gray market exchange rate was then calculated as follows:

$$\text{Implicit Gray Market Rate} = \frac{7 \times \text{Bs7945/Share}}{\$18.84 / \text{ADR}}$$

$$= \text{Bs2952/\$}$$

The official exchange rate on that same day was Bs1598/$. This meant that the gray market rate was quoting the bolivar approximately 46% weaker against the dollar than what the Venezuelan government officially declared its currency to be worth.

Exhibit 1, on page 168, illustrates both the official exchange rate and the gray market rate (calculated using CANTV shares) for the January 2002 to March 2004 period. The divergence between the official and gray market rates beginning in February 2003 coincided with the imposition of capital controls.[4]

---

[2]"Venezuela Girds for Exchange Controls," *The Wall Street Journal* (Eastern edition), February 5, 2003, p. A14.

[3]In fact CANTV's share price continued to rise over the 2002 to 2004 period as a result of its use as an exchange rate mechanism. The use of CANTV ADRs as a method of obtaining dollars by Venezuelan individuals and organizations was typically described as "not illegal."

[4]Morgan Stanley Capital International (MSCI) announced on November 26, 2003 that it would change its standard spot rate for the Venezuelan bolivar to the notional rate based on the relationship between the price of CANTV Telefonos de Venezuela D in the local market in bolivars and the price of its ADR in U.S. dollars.

## EXHIBIT 1

Venezuelan Official and Gray Market Exchange Rates, Venezuelan Bolivar/U.S. Dollar (January 2002– March 2004)

Note: All prices and rates are Friday closing values.

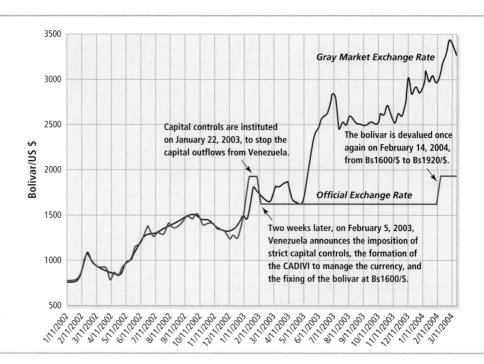

Gray Market Exchange Rate

Capital controls are instituted on January 22, 2003, to stop the capital outflows from Venezuela.

The bolivar is devalued once again on February 14, 2004, from Bs1600/$ to Bs1920/$.

Official Exchange Rate

Two weeks later, on February 5, 2003, Venezuela announces the imposition of strict capital controls, the formation of the CADIVI to manage the currency, and the fixing of the bolivar at Bs1600/$.

## The Black Market

A third method of obtaining hard currency by Venezuelans was through the rapidly expanding black market. The black market was, as is the case with black markets all over the world, essentially unseen and illegal. It was, however, quite sophisticated, using the services of a stockbroker or banker in Venezuela who simultaneously held U.S. dollar accounts offshore. The choice of a black market broker was a critical one; in the event of a failure to complete the transaction properly there was no legal recourse.

If Santiago wished to purchase dollars on the black market, he would deposit bolivars in his broker's account in Venezuela. The agreed upon black market exchange rate was determined on the day of the deposit, and usually was within a 20% band of the gray market rate derived from the CANTV share price. Santiago would then be given access to a dollar-denominated bank account outside of Venezuela in the agreed amount. The transaction took, on average, two business days to settle. The unofficial black market rate was Bs3300/$.

## Spring 2004

In early 2004 President Chávez had asked Venezuela's Central Bank to give him "a little billion" — *millardito* — of its $21 billion in foreign exchange reserves. Chávez argued that the money was actually the people's, and he

wished to invest some of it in the agricultural sector. The Central Bank refused. Not to be thwarted in its search for funds, the Chávez government announced another devaluation on February 9, 2004. The bolivar was devalued 17%, falling in official value from Bs1600/$ to Bs1920/$ (see Exhibit 1). With all Venezuelan exports of oil being purchased in U.S. dollars, the devaluation of the bolivar meant that the country's proceeds from oil exports grew by the same 17% as the devaluation itself.

The Chávez government argued that the devaluation was necessary because the bolivar was "a variable that cannot be kept frozen, because it prejudices exports and pressures the balance of payments," according to Finance Minister Tobias Nobriega. Analysts, however, pointed out that Venezuelan government actually had significant control over its balance of payments: oil was the primary export, the government maintained control over the official access to hard currency necessary for imports, and the Central Bank's foreign exchange reserves were now over $21 billion.

*It's not clear whether Mr. Chávez understands what a massive hit Venezuelans take when savings and earnings in dollar terms are cut in half in just three years. Perhaps the political-science student believes that more devalued bolivars makes everyone richer. But one unavoidable conclusion is that he recognized the devaluation as a way to pay for his*

Bolivarian "missions," government projects that might restore his popularity long enough to allow him to survive the recall, or survive an audacious decision to squelch it.

"Money Fun in the Venezuela of Hugo Chávez,"
*The Wall Street Journal* (Eastern edition),
February 13, 2004, p. A13.

## Time Was Running Out

Santiago received confirmation from CADIVI on the afternoon of March 10 that his latest application for dollars was approved and that he would receive $10,000 at the official exchange rate of Bs1920/$. Santiago attributed his good fortune to the fact that he paid a CADIVI insider

an extra 500 bolivars per dollar to expedite his request. Santiago noted with a smile that "the Chavistas need to make money too." The noise from the street seemed to be dying with the sun. It was time for Santiago to make some decisions. None of the alternatives were *bonita*, but if he was to preserve his business, dollars — at some price — had to be obtained.

## Case Questions

1. Why does a country like Venezuela impose capital controls?
2. In the case of Venezuela, what is the difference between the gray market and the black market?
3. Create a financial analysis of Santiago's choices and use it to recommend a solution to his problem.

## Summary of Learning Objectives

*Examine the functions performed by the foreign exchange market, its participants, size, and geographic and currency composition*

- The three functions of the foreign exchange market are to transfer purchasing power, provide credit, and minimize foreign exchange risk.

- The foreign exchange market is composed of two tiers: the interbank market and the client market. Participants within these tiers include bank and nonbank foreign exchange dealers, individuals and firms conducting commercial and investment transactions, speculators and arbitragers, central banks and treasuries, and foreign exchange brokers.

- Geographically, the foreign exchange market spans the globe, with prices moving and currencies traded somewhere every hour of every business day.

*Distinguish between spot, forward, swap, and other types of foreign exchange financial instruments*

- A foreign exchange *rate* is the price of one currency expressed in terms of another currency. A foreign exchange *quotation* is a statement of willingness to buy or sell currency at an announced price.

- Transactions within the foreign exchange market are executed either on a *spot* basis, requiring settlement two days after the transaction, or on a *forward* or *swap* basis, which requires settlement at some designated future date.

*Identify the forms of currency quotations used by currency dealers, financial institutions, and agents of all kinds when conducting foreign exchange transactions*

- *European terms* quotations are the foreign currency price of a U.S. dollar. *American terms* quotations are the dollar price of a foreign currency.

- Quotations can also be *direct* or *indirect*. A direct quote is the home currency price of a unit of foreign currency, while an indirect quote is the foreign currency price of a unit of home currency.

- Direct and indirect are not synonyms for American and European terms, because the home currency will change depending on who is doing the calculation, while European terms are always the foreign currency price of a dollar.

*Analyze the interaction between changing currency values, cross exchange rates, and the opportunities arising from intermarket arbitrage*

- A *cross rate* is an exchange rate between two currencies, calculated from their common relationships with a third currency. When cross rates differ from the direct rates between two currencies, intermarket arbitrage is possible.

## QUESTIONS

1. **Definitions.** Define the following terms:

   **a.** Foreign exchange market

   **b.** Foreign exchange transaction

   **c.** Foreign exchange

2. **Functions of the foreign exchange market.** What are the three major functions of the foreign exchange market?

3. **Market participants.** Identify the motive of each foreign exchange market participant for buying or selling foreign exchange.

4. **Transaction.** Define each of the following types of foreign exchange transactions:

   **a.** Spot

   **b.** Outright forward

   **c.** Forward-forward swaps

5. **Foreign exchange market characteristics.** With reference to foreign exchange turnover in 2004,

   **a.** Rank the relative size of spot, forwards, and swaps as of 2004.

   **b.** Rank the five most important geographic locations for foreign exchange turnover.

   **c.** Rank the three most important currencies of denomination.

6. **Foreign exchange rate quotations.** Define and give an example of each of the following quotes:

   **a.** Bid quote

   **b.** Ask quote

7. **Reciprocals.** Convert the following indirect quotes to direct quotes and direct quotes to indirect quotes:

   **a.** Euro: €1.22/$ (indirect quote)

   **b.** Russia: Rub 30/$ (indirect quote)

   **c.** Canada: $0.72/C$ (direct quote)

   **d.** Denmark: $0.1644/DKr (direct quote)

8. **Geographical extent of the foreign exchange market.**

   **a.** What is the geographical location of the foreign exchange market?

   **b.** What are the two main types of trading systems for foreign exchange?

   **c.** How are foreign exchange markets connected for trading activities?

9. **American and European terms.** With reference to interbank quotations, what is the difference between American terms and European terms?

10. **Direct and indirect quotes.**

   **a.** Define and give an example of a direct quote between the U.S. dollar and the Mexican peso,

where the United States is designated as the home country.

   **b.** Define and give an example of an indirect quote between the Japanese yen and the Chinese renminbi (yuan), where China is designated as the home country.

## PROBLEMS

1. **Ringgit up or down?** Before the Asian currency crisis the Malaysian ringgit traded RM2.7000/$. It currently trades at about RM3.8000/$. Did the ringgit appreciate or depreciate, and by what percentage?

2. **Forward premiums and discounts.** Use the following spot and forward quotations on the U.S. dollar/euro (U.S.$/€) exchange rate on June 28, 2004 to answer the following questions:

   **a.** Calculate the mid-rates (average) from the bid-ask quotations.

   **b.** Calculate the forward premium for all maturities using the mid-rates calculated in part (a).

| Period | Bid Rate | Ask Rate |
|--------|----------|----------|
| spot | 1.21810 | 1.21920 |
| 1 month | 1.21732 | 1.21841 |
| 2 months | 1.21679 | 1.21789 |
| 3 months | 1.21648 | 1.21758 |
| 6 months | 1.21617 | 1.21774 |
| 12 months | 1.21804 | 1.21876 |
| 24 months | 1.21021 | 1.20982 |

3. **Trading in Switzerland.** You receive the following quotes for Swiss francs against the dollar for spot, one month forward, three months forward, and six months forward.

   **1.6075 to 1.6085, 10 to 15, 14 to 22, 20 to 30**

   **a.** Calculate the outright quotes for bid and ask, and the number of points spread between each bid and ask.

   **b.** What do you notice about the spread as quotes evolve from spot toward six months? Why do you think this occurs?

4. **Yen forward premiums.** Use the following spot and forward quotations on the Japanese yen/U.S. dollar (¥/U.S.$) exchange rate on June 28, 2004 to answer the following questions:

   **a.** Calculate the mid-rates (average) from the bid-ask quotations.

   **b.** Calculate the forward premium for all maturities using the mid-rates calculated in part (a).

| Period | Bid Rate | Ask Rate |
|---|---|---|
| spot | 107.970 | 108.020 |
| 1 month | 107.816 | 107.911 |
| 2 months | 107.670 | 107.765 |
| 3 months | 107.494 | 107.609 |
| 6 months | 106.863 | 106.987 |
| 12 months | 105.391 | 105.444 |
| 24 months | 101.435 | 101.976 |

5. **Swissies forward premiums.** Using these Swiss franc/euro quotes from June 28, 2004 answer the following questions.

   a. Calculate the mid rates (average) from the bid-ask quotations given.

   b. Calculate the forward premium for all maturities using the mid rates calculated in part (a).

   c. How is the forward premium or discount changing as the maturity gets longer?

| Period | Bid Rate | Ask Rate |
|---|---|---|
| spot | 1.52200 | 1.52330 |
| 3 months | 1.51570 | 1.51701 |
| 6 months | 1.51020 | 1.51222 |
| 12 months | 1.50145 | 1.50258 |

6. **Traveling: Copenhagen to St. Petersburg.** On your post-graduation celebratory trip you are leaving Copenhagen, Denmark for St. Petersburg, Russia. Denmark's currency is the krone (Denmark, although an EU member, is not a participant in the euro). You leave Copenhagen with 10,000 Danish kroner still in your wallet. Wanting to exchange all of these for Russian rubles, you obtain the following quotes:

   Dkr 6.0729/$          R 29.070/$

   a. What is the Danish krone/Russian ruble cross rate?

   b. How many rubles will you obtain for your left-over kroner?

7. **Riskless profit on the franc.** The following exchange rates are available to you. (You can buy or sell at the stated rates.)

   | | |
   |---|---|
   | Mt. Fuji Bank | ¥120.00/$ |
   | Mt. Rushmore Bank | SF1.6000/$ |
   | Matterhorn Bank | ¥80.00/SF |

   Assume you have an initial SF10,000,000. Can you make a profit via triangular arbitrage? If so, show the steps and calculate the amount of profit in Swiss francs.

8. **Transatlantic arbitrage.** A corporate treasury with operations in New York simultaneously calls Citibank in New York City and Barclays in London. The two banks give the following quotes at the same time on the euro:

   | Citibank NY | Barclays London |
   |---|---|
   | $1.1650–70/€ | $1.1640–60/€ |

   Explain, using $1 million or its euro equivalent, how the corporate treasury could make geographic arbitrage profit with the two exchange rate quotes.

9. **Wall Street Journal quotes and premiums.** Using the *Wall Street Journal* quotes listed in Exhibit 6.6,

   a. Calculate the forward premiums or discounts for both quotation forms (US$ equivalent and currency per US$).

   b. Why are the forward premiums or discounts not identical? If you use the correct forward premium formulation, shouldn't the premiums be identical?

10. **Financial Times quotes.** Using the spot and forward quotes on the British pound from the *Financial Times* in Exhibit 6.6 in the chapter, calculate the forward premiums on the

    a. One-month forward rate

    b. Three-month forward rate

    c. One-year forward rate

11. **Venezuelan bolivar (A).** The Venezuelan government officially floated the Venezuelan bolivar (Bs) in February 2002. Within weeks, its value had moved from the pre-float fix of BS778/$ to Bs1025/$.

    a. Is this a devaluation or a depreciation?

    b. By what percentage did its value change?

12. **Venezuelan bolivar (B).** The Venezuelan political and economic crisis deepened in late 2002 and early 2003. On January 1, 2003, the bolivar was trading at Bs1400/$. By February 1, its value had fallen to Bs1950/$. Many currency analysts and forecasters were predicting that the bolivar would fall an additional 40% from its February 1 value by early summer 2003.

    a. By what percentage did the bolivar change in value in January 2003?

**b.** If the currency forecasters are correct, what would the bolivar's value be against the dollar in June 2003?

13. **Indirect quotation.** Given the following quotations when the U.S. dollar is the home currency:

Spot rate: €1.2000/$
Three-month forward rate: €1.2100/$

Calculate the forward premium on the dollar.

14. **Direct quotation on the dollar.** Given the following quotations (where the dollar is the home currency):

Spot rate: $1.8200/£
Three-month forward rate: $1.8000/£

Calculate the forward discount on the dollar.

15. **Mexican peso—European euro cross rates.** Given the following exchange rates:

Mexican peso: Ps 11.43/$
euro: €0.8404/$

Calculate the cross rate between the Mexican peso and the euro.

16. **Around the horn.** Assume the following quotes:

Citibank quotes U.S. dollars per pound at $1.8500/£
National Westminster quotes euro per pound at €1.5000/£
Deutsche Bank quotes dollars per euro at $1.2400/€

Calculate how a market trader at Citibank with $1,000,000 can make an intermarket arbitrage profit.

 **Internet Exercises**

1. **Forward quotes.** OzForex Foreign Exchange Services provides representative forward rates on a multitude of currencies online. Use the following Web site to search for forward exchange rate quotations on a variety of currencies. (Note the London, New York, and Sydney times listed on the quotation screen.)

    OzForex
    http://www.ozforex.com.au/

2. **Oanda.com currency services.** The Oanda.com company Web site has a plethora of currency-related data and services. Use the following Internet addresses to access some of these services, including the *trading game*.

    Trading game
    http://fxgame.oanda.com/
    FX History
    http://www.oanda.com/convert/fxhistory
    Currency map: illustrates country-currency movements by percentage change versus the U.S. dollar over the recent past
    http://www.oanda.com/products/fxmap
    /fxmap.shtml

3. **Emerging market currencies.** Although major currencies like the U.S. dollar and the Japanese yen dominate the headlines, there are nearly as many currencies as countries in the world. Many of these currencies are traded in extremely thin and highly regulated markets, making their convertibility suspect. Finding quotations for these currencies is sometimes very difficult. Using the Web site listed below, see how many African currency quotes you can find.

    Emerging Markets
    http://emgmkts.com/

4. **Pacific Exchange Rate Service.** The Pacific Exchange Rate Service Web site, headed up by Professor Werner Antweiler of the University of British Columbia, possesses a wealth of current information on currency exchange rates and related statistics. Use the service to plot the recent performance of currencies that have suffered significant devaluations or depreciations, such as the Argentine peso, the Venezuelan bolivar, the Turkish lira, and the Egyptian pound.

    Pacific Exchange Rate Service
    http://fx.sauder.ubc.ca/

# Foreign Currency Derivatives

## LEARNING OBJECTIVES

Examine how foreign currency futures are quoted, valued, and used for speculation purposes

Illustrate how foreign currency futures differ from forward contracts

Analyze how foreign currency options are quoted and used for speculation purposes

Consider the distinction between buying options and writing options in terms of whether profits and losses are limited or unlimited

Explain how foreign currency options are valued

Financial management of the multinational enterprise in the twenty-first century will need to consider the use of *financial derivatives*. These derivatives, so named because their values are derived from an underlying asset like a stock or a currency, are a powerful tool used in business today for two very distinct management objectives, speculation and hedging. The financial manager of an MNE may purchase these financial derivatives in order to take positions in the expectation of profit, *speculation*, or may use these instruments to reduce the risks associated with the everyday management of corporate cash flow, *hedging*. Before these financial instruments can be used effectively, however, the financial manager must understand certain basics about their structure and pricing. We will cover two common foreign currency financial derivatives in this chapter, foreign currency options and foreign currency futures. We focus here on the fundamentals of their valuation and their use for speculative purposes. Chapter 8 will describe how these foreign currency derivatives can be used to hedge commercial transactions. Chapter 14 will describe the valuation and use of interest rate swaps, the financial derivative most widely used by firms today.

A word of caution — of reservation — before we proceed further. Financial derivatives are a powerful tool in the hands of careful and competent financial managers. They can also be very destructive devices when used recklessly. The 1990s were littered with cases in which financial managers lost control of their derivatives, resulting in significant losses for their companies and occasionally outright collapse. In the right hands and with proper controls, however, financial derivatives may provide management with opportunities to enhance and protect their corporate financial performance. On the other hand, the mini-case at the end of this chapter describes how one rogue trader, Nicholas Leeson, brought down Baring Brothers & Co. through uncontrolled speculation. We begin with the relatively easier foreign currency derivative, the foreign currency future.

## Foreign Currency Futures

A *foreign currency futures contract* is an alternative to a forward contract that calls for future delivery of a standard amount of foreign exchange at a fixed time, place, and price. It is similar to futures contracts that exist for commodities (hogs, cattle, lumber, etc.), interest-bearing deposits, and gold.

Most world money centers have established foreign currency futures markets. In the United States the most important market for foreign currency futures is the International Monetary Market (IMM) of Chicago, a division of the Chicago Mercantile Exchange.

### CONTRACT SPECIFICATIONS

Contract specifications are established by the exchange on which futures are traded. For example, in the Chicago IMM, the major features that must be standardized are the following:

*Size of the contract.* Called the *notional principal*; trading in each currency must be done in an even multiple of currency units.

*Method of stating exchange rates.* "American terms" are used; that is, quotations are the U.S. dollar cost of foreign currency units, also known as direct quotes.

*Maturity date.* Contracts mature on the third Wednesday of January, March, April, June, July, September, October, or December.

*Last trading day.* Contracts may be traded through the second business day prior to the Wednesday on which they mature. Therefore, unless holidays interfere, the last trading day is the Monday preceding the maturity date.

*Collateral and maintenance margins.* The purchaser must deposit a sum as an initial margin or collateral. This requirement is similar to requiring a performance bond, and it can be met by a letter of credit from a bank, Treasury bills, or cash. In addition, a maintenance margin is required. The value of the contract is marked to market daily, and all changes in value are paid in cash daily. *Marked to market* means that the value of the contract is revalued using the closing price for the day. The amount to be paid is called the *variation margin.*

*Settlement.* Only about 5% of all futures contracts are settled by the physical delivery of foreign exchange between buyer and seller. Most often, buyers and sellers offset their original position prior to delivery date by taking an opposite position. That is, if one party buys a futures contract, that party will normally close out its position by selling a futures contract for the same delivery date. The complete buy/sell or sell/buy is called a "round turn."

*Commissions.* Customers pay a commission to their broker to execute a round turn and a single price is quoted. This practice differs from that of the interbank market, where dealers quote a bid and an offer and do not charge a commission.

*Use of a clearing house as a counterparty.* All contracts are agreements between the client and the exchange clearing house, rather than between the two clients involved. Consequently clients need not worry that a specific counterparty in the market will fail to honor an agreement. The clearing house is owned and guaranteed by all members of the exchange.

## USING FOREIGN CURRENCY FUTURES

To illustrate the use of currency futures for speculating on currency movements, we will focus on the Mexican peso futures traded on the Chicago Mercantile Exchange (CME). Exhibit 7.1 presents typical Mexican peso (Ps) futures quotations from *The Wall Street Journal*. Each contract is for 500,000 "new Mexican pesos," and is quoted in U.S. dollars per Mexican peso.

Any investor wishing to speculate on the movement of the Mexican peso versus the U.S. dollar could pursue one of the following strategies. Keep in mind that the principle of a futures contract is that if a speculator buys a futures contract, they are

**EXHIBIT 7.1**

Mexican Peso Futures, US$/Peso (CME)

Source: The *Wall Street Journal*, February 22, 2002, p. C13.

| Maturity | Open | High | Low | Settle | Change | High | Low | Open Interest |
|----------|------|------|-----|--------|--------|------|-----|---------------|
| Mar | .10953 | .10988 | .10930 | .10958 | . . . | .11000 | .09770 | 34,481 |
| June | .10790 | .10795 | .10778 | .10773 | . . . | .10800 | .09730 | 3,405 |
| Sept | .10615 | .10615 | .10610 | .10573 | . . . | .10615 | .09930 | 1,481 |

All contracts are for 500,000 new Mexican pesos. "Open" means the opening price on the day. "High" means the high price on the day. "Low" indicates the lowest price on the day. "Settle" is the closing price on the day. "Change" indicates the change in the settle price from the previous day's close. "High" and "Low" to the right of Change indicate the highest and lowest prices this specific contract (as defined by its maturity) has experienced over its trading history. "Open Interest" indicates the number of contracts outstanding.

locking in the price at which they must buy that currency on the specified future date, and if they sell a futures contract, they are locking in the price at which they must sell that currency on that future date.

**SHORT POSITIONS.**    If Amber McClain, a speculator working for International Currency Traders, believes the Mexican peso will fall in value versus the U.S. dollar by March, she could sell a March futures contract, taking a *short position*. By selling a March contract, Amber locks in the right to sell 500,000 Mexican pesos at a set price. If the price of the peso does fall by the maturity date as she expects, Amber has a contract to sell pesos at a price above their current price on the spot market. Hence, she makes a profit.

Using the quotes on Mexican peso futures in Exhibit 7.1, Amber sells one March futures contract for 500,000 pesos at the closing price, termed *settle price*, of $.10958/Ps. The value of her position at maturity — at the expiration of the futures contract in March — is then

$$\text{Value at maturity (Short position)} = -\text{Notional principal} \times (\text{Spot} - \text{Futures})$$

Note that the short position is entered into the valuation as a negative notional principal. If the spot exchange rate at maturity is $.09500/Ps, the value of her position on settlement is

$$\text{Value} = -\text{Ps}500,000 \times (\$.09500/\text{Ps} - \$.10958/\text{Ps}) = \$7,290$$

Amber's expectation proved correct: the Mexican peso fell in value versus the U.S. dollar. We could say that "Amber ends up buying at $.09500 and sells at $.10958 per peso."

All that was really required of Amber to speculate on the Mexican peso's value was that she formed an opinion on the Mexican peso's future exchange value versus the U.S. dollar. In this case, she opined that it would fall in value by the March maturity date of the futures contract.

**LONG POSITIONS.**    If Amber McClain expected the peso to rise in value versus the dollar in the near term, she could take a *long position*, by buying a March future on the Mexican peso. Buying a March future means that Amber is locking in the price at which she must buy Mexican pesos at the future's maturity date. Amber's futures contract at maturity would have the following value:

$$\text{Value at maturity (Long position)} = \text{Notional principal} \times (\text{Spot} - \text{Futures})$$

Again using the March settle price on Mexican peso futures in Exhibit 7.1, $.10958/Ps, if the spot exchange rate at maturity is $.1100/Ps, Amber has indeed guessed right. The value of her position on settlement is then

$$\text{Value} = \text{Ps}500,000 \times (\$.11000/\text{Ps} - \$.10958/\text{Ps}) = \$210$$

In this case, Amber makes a profit in a matter of months of $210 on the single futures contract. We could say that "Amber buys at $.10958 and sells at $.11000 per peso."

But what happens if Amber's expectation about the future value of the Mexican peso proves wrong? For example, if the Mexican government announces that the rate of inflation in Mexico has suddenly risen dramatically, and the peso falls to $.08000/Ps by the March maturity date, the value of Amber's futures contract on settlement is

$$\text{Value} = \text{Ps}500,000 \times (\$.08000/\text{Ps} - \$.10958/\text{Ps}) = (\$14,790)$$

In this case, Amber McClain suffers a major speculative loss. Such is the life of the currency speculator!

Futures contracts could obviously be used in combinations to form a variety of more complex positions. When we are combining contracts, however, valuation is fairly straightforward and additive in character.

## FOREIGN CURRENCY FUTURES VERSUS FORWARD CONTRACTS

Foreign currency futures contracts differ from forward contracts in a number of important ways, as shown in Exhibit 7.2. Individuals find futures contracts useful for speculation because they usually do not have access to forward contracts. For businesses, futures contracts are often considered inefficient and burdensome because the futures position is marked to market on a daily basis over the life of the contract. Although this does not require the business to pay or receive cash on a daily basis, it does result in more frequent margin calls from its financial service providers than the business typically wants.

**EXHIBIT 7.2**

Currency Futures and Forwards Compared

| Characteristic | Foreign Currency Futures | Forward Contracts |
|---|---|---|
| Size of contract | Standardized contracts per currency | Any size desired |
| Maturity | Fixed maturities, longest typically being one year | Any maturity up to one year, sometimes longer |
| Location | Trading occurs on an organized exchange | Trading occurs between individuals and banks with other banks by telecom linkages |
| Pricing | Open outcry process on the exchange floor | Prices are determined by bid and ask quotes |
| Margin/Collateral | Initial margin that is marked to market on a daily basis | No explicit collateral, but standard bank relationship necessary |
| Settlement | Rarely delivered upon; settlement normally takes place through purchase of offsetting position | Contract is normally delivered upon, although the taking of offsetting positions is possible |
| Commissions | Single commission covers both purchase and sale (roundtrip) | No explicit commission; banks earn effective commissions through the bid-ask spreads |
| Trading hours | Traditionally traded during exchange hours; some exchanges have moved to 24 hours | Negotiated by phone or Internet, 24 hours a day, through bank global networks |
| Counterparties | Unknown to each other due to the auction market structure | Parties are in direct contact in settling forward specifications |
| Liquidity | Liquid but relatively small in total sales volume and value | Liquid and relatively large in sales volume compared to futures contracts |

## Currency Options

A *foreign currency option* is a contract giving the option purchaser (the buyer) the right, but not the obligation, to buy or sell a given amount of foreign exchange at a fixed price per unit for a specified time period (until the maturity date). The most important phrase in this definition is "but not the obligation"; this means that the owner of an option possesses a valuable choice.

In many ways buying an option is like buying a ticket to a benefit concert. The buyer has the right to attend the concert, but does not have to do so. The buyer of the concert ticket risks nothing more than what she paid for the ticket. Similarly, the buyer of an option cannot lose anything more than what she paid for the option. If the buyer of the ticket decides later not to attend the concert — prior to the day of the concert, the ticket can be sold to someone else who does wish to go.

- There are two basic types of options, *calls* and *puts*. A call is an option to buy foreign currency, and a put is an option to sell foreign currency.

- The buyer of an option is termed the *holder*, while the seller of an option is referred to as the *writer* or *grantor*.

Every option has three different price elements: (1) the *exercise* or *strike price*, the exchange rate at which the foreign currency can be purchased (call) or sold (put); (2) the *premium*, which is the cost, price, or value of the option itself; and (3) the underlying or actual spot exchange rate in the market.

- An *American option* gives the buyer the right to exercise the option at any time between the date of writing and the expiration or maturity date. A *European option* can be exercised only on its expiration date, not before. Nevertheless, American and European options are priced almost the same because the option holder would normally sell the option itself before maturity. The option would then still have some "time value" above its "intrinsic value" if exercised (explained later in this chapter).

- The *premium* or option price is the cost of the option, usually paid in advance by the buyer to the seller. In the over-the-counter market (options offered by banks), premiums are quoted as a percentage of the transaction amount. Premiums on exchange-traded options are quoted as a domestic currency amount per unit of foreign currency.

- An option whose exercise price is the same as the spot price of the underlying currency is said to be *at-the-money (ATM)*. An option that would be profitable, excluding the cost of the premium, if exercised immediately is said to be *in-the-money (ITM)*. An option that would not be profitable, again excluding the cost of the premium, if exercised immediately is referred to as *out-of-the-money (OTM)*.

### FOREIGN CURRENCY OPTIONS MARKETS

In the past three decades the use of foreign currency options as a hedging tool and for speculative purposes has blossomed into a major foreign exchange activity. A number of banks in the United States and other capital markets offer flexible foreign currency options on transactions of $1 million or more. The bank market, or *over-the-counter market* as it is called, offers custom-tailored options on all major trading currencies for any time period up to one year, and in some cases, two to three years.

In December 1982, the Philadelphia Stock Exchange introduced trading in standardized foreign currency option contracts in the United States. The Chicago Mercantile Exchange and other exchanges in the United States and abroad have followed suit. Exchange-traded contracts are particularly appealing to speculators and individuals who do not normally have access to the over-the-counter market. Banks also trade on the exchanges because it is one of several ways they can offset the risk of options they have transacted with clients or other banks.

Increased use of foreign currency options is a reflection of the explosive growth in the use of other kinds of options and the resultant improvements in option pricing models. The original option pricing model developed by Black and Scholes in 1973 has been commercialized since then by numerous firms offering software programs and even built-in routines for handheld calculators. Several commercial programs are available for option writers and traders to utilize.

## OPTIONS ON THE OVER-THE-COUNTER MARKET

Over-the-counter (OTC) options are most frequently written by banks for U.S. dollars against British pounds sterling, Swiss francs, Japanese yen, Canadian dollars, and most recently, the euro.

The main advantage of over-the-counter options is that they are tailored to the specific needs of the firm. Financial institutions are willing to write or buy options that vary by amount (notional principal), strike price, and maturity. Although the over-the-counter markets were relatively illiquid in the early years, the market has grown to such proportions that liquidity is now quite good. On the other hand, the buyer must assess the writing bank's ability to fulfill the option contract. Termed *counterparty risk*, the financial risk associated with the counterparty is an increasing issue in international markets as a result of the increasing use of financial contracts like options and swaps by MNE management. Exchange-traded options are more the territory of individuals and financial institutions themselves than of business firms.

If Maria Gonzalez, the Chief Financial Officer of Trident, wishes to purchase an option in the over-the-counter market, she will normally place a call to the currency option desk of a major money center bank, specify the currencies, maturity, strike rate(s), and ask for an *indication* — a bid-offer quote. The bank will normally take a few minutes to a few hours to price the option and return the call.

## OPTIONS ON ORGANIZED EXCHANGES

Options on the physical (underlying) currency are traded on a number of organized exchanges worldwide, including the Philadelphia Stock Exchange (PHLX) and the Chicago Mercantile Exchange.

Exchange-traded options are settled through a clearing house, so that buyers do not deal directly with sellers. The clearing house is the counterparty to every option contract and it guarantees fulfillment. Clearing-house obligations are in turn the obligation of all members of the exchange, including a large number of banks. In the case of the Philadelphia Stock Exchange, clearing-house services are provided by the Options Clearing Corporation (OCC).

## CURRENCY OPTION QUOTATIONS AND PRICES

Typical quotes in *The Wall Street Journal* for options on Swiss francs are shown in Exhibit 7.3. The *Journal's* quotes refer to transactions completed on the Philadelphia Stock Exchange on the previous day. Quotations usually are available for more combinations of strike prices and expiration dates than were actually traded and thus reported in the newspaper. Currency option strike prices and premiums on the U.S. dollar are typically quoted as direct quotations on the U.S. dollar and indirect quotations on the foreign currency ($/SF, $/¥, etc.).

Exhibit 7.3 illustrates the three different prices that characterize any foreign currency option. The three prices that characterize an "August 58 ½ call option" (highlighted in Exhibit 7.3) are the following:

1. **Spot rate.** In Exhibit 7.3, "Option & Underlying" means that 58.51 cents, or $0.5851, was the spot dollar price of one Swiss franc at the close of trading on the preceding day.

2. **Exercise price.** The exercise price, or "Strike Price" listed in Exhibit 7.3, means the price per franc that must be paid if the option is exercised. The August call option on francs of 58 ½ means $0.5850/SF. Exhibit 7.3 lists nine different strike prices, ranging from $0.5600/SF to $0.6000/SF, although more were available on that date than are listed here.

3. **Premium.** The premium is the cost or price of the option. The price of the August 58 ½ call option on Swiss francs was 0.50 U.S. cents per franc, or $0.0050/SF. There was no trading of the September and December 58 ½ call on that day. The premium is the market value of the option, and therefore the terms premium, cost, price, and value are all interchangeable when referring to an option.

The August 58 ½ call option premium is 0.50 cents per franc, and in this case, the August 58 ½ put's premium is also 0.50 cents per franc. Since one option contract on the Philadelphia Stock Exchange consists of 62,500 francs, the total cost of one option contract for the call (or put in this case) is SF62,500 × $0.0050/SF = $312.50.

**EXHIBIT 7.3**

Swiss Franc Option Quotations (U.S. Cents/SF)

| Option & Underlying | Strike Price | Calls — Last Aug | Sep | Dec | Puts — Last Aug | Sep | Dec |
|---|---|---|---|---|---|---|---|
| 58.51 | 56 | – | – | 2.76 | 0.04 | 0.22 | 1.16 |
| 58.51 | 56 ½ | – | – | – | 0.06 | 0.30 | – |
| 58.51 | 57 | 1.13 | – | 1.74 | 0.10 | 0.38 | 1.27 |
| 58.51 | 57 ½ | 0.75 | – | – | 0.17 | 0.55 | – |
| 58.51 | 58 | 0.71 | 1.05 | 1.28 | 0.27 | 0.89 | 1.81 |
| 58.51 | 58 ½ | 0.50 | – | – | 0.50 | 0.99 | – |
| 58.51 | 59 | 0.30 | 0.66 | 1.21 | 0.90 | 1.36 | – |
| 58.51 | 59 ½ | 0.15 | 0.40 | – | 2.32 | – | – |
| 58.51 | 60 | – | 0.31 | – | 2.32 | 2.62 | 3.30 |

Each option = 62,500 Swiss francs. The August, September, and December listings are the option maturities or expiration dates.

## Foreign Currency Speculation

*Speculation* is an attempt to profit by trading on expectations about prices in the future. In the foreign exchange markets, speculators take an open (unhedged) position in a foreign currency and then close that position after the exchange rate has moved in — they hope — the expected direction. In the following section we analyze the manner in which speculation is undertaken in spot, forward, and options markets. It is important to understand this phenomenon because it has a major impact on our inability to accurately forecast future exchange rates. As illustrated by *Real World Example 7.1*, however, many currency speculators still get it wrong.

### SPECULATING IN THE SPOT MARKET

Hans Schmidt is a currency speculator in Zurich, Switzerland. He is willing to risk money on his own opinion about future currency prices. Hans may speculate in the spot, forward, or options markets. To illustrate, assume the Swiss franc is currently quoted as follows.

| | |
|---|---|
| Spot rate: | $0.5851/SF |
| Six-month forward rate: | $0.5760/SF |

Hans has $100,000 with which to speculate, and he believes that in six months the spot rate for the franc will be $0.6000/SF. Speculation in the spot market requires only that the speculator believe the foreign currency will appreciate in value. Hans should take the following steps.

1. Use the $100,000 today to buy SF170,910.96 spot at $0.5851/SF.

---

### Real World Example 7.1
#### ROGUE CURRENCY TRADER AT ALLIED IRISH BANK

John Rusnak, a currency trader at the U.S. Baltimore branch of Allied Irish Bank, became the newest member of the "rogue traders club" in February 2002 when it was disclosed he had lost $691 million on the bank's behalf. It seems that Mr. Rusnak failed to hedge a series of currency futures contract positions against the potential fall of the Japanese yen. Currency traders typically take positions in the spot and futures markets for expected speculative profit. To protect or "cover" their speculation, however, they typically purchase currency option contracts as insurance against their getting it wrong. The yen fell, Rusnak failed to cover, and the bank suffered the losses.

Rusnak, 37, earned an annual salary of $85,000, In addition to annual performance bonuses of between $100,000 and $150,000 per year over the past five years. Unfortunately, his rogue trades — which did not enrich him personally other than his ability to keep his job while making such bad bets — cost Allied Irish Bank greatly. As a result of the losses revealed, Allied Irish's annual earnings for 2001 were reduced to $424 million, less than half what was previously expected. The bank would also have to restate its financial results as reported to the Securities and Exchange Commission in the United States as far back as 1997.

Rusnak's losses reached such astronomical proportions as a result of a complex combination of falsified documents by him and a failure in the bank's own control and audit processes. Beginning in 1997, Rusnak had suffered continuing losses on currency positions he took for speculation purposes on behalf of the bank. Rather than acknowledge and report his losses, Rusnak wove a complex series of falsified documents that made it appear that he had been covering the positions throughout. Mr. Rusnak's services were terminated.

2. Hold the SF170,910.96 indefinitely. Although the franc is expected to rise to the target value in six months, Hans is not committed to that time horizon.

3. When the target exchange rate has been reached, sell SF170,910.96 at the new spot rate of $0.6000/SF, receiving SF170,910.96 × $0.6000/SF = $102,546.57.

This results in a profit of $2,546.57, or 2.5% on the $100,000 committed for six months (5.0% per annum). This ignores for the moment interest income on the Swiss francs and opportunity cost on the dollars.

The potential maximum gain is unlimited, while the maximum loss will be $100,000 if the francs purchased in Step 1 drop in value to zero. Having initially undertaken a spot market speculation for six months, Hans is nevertheless not bound by that target date. He may sell the francs earlier or later if he wishes.

## SPECULATING IN THE FORWARD MARKET

Forward market speculation occurs when the speculator believes that the spot price at some future date will differ from today's forward price for that same date. Success does not depend on the direction of movement of the spot rate, but on the relative position of the future spot rate and the current forward rate. Given the above data and expectations, Hans Schmidt should take the following steps.

1. Today buy SF173,611.11 forward six months at the forward quote of $0.5760/SF. Note that this step requires no outlay of cash.

2. In six months, fulfill the forward contract, receiving SF173,611.11 at $0.5760/SF for a cost of $100,000.

3. Simultaneously sell the SF173,611.11 in the spot market, at Hans' expected future spot rate of $0.6000/SF, receiving SF173,611.11 × $0.6000/SF = $104,166.67.

This is a profit of $4,166.67 ($104,166.67 − $100,000.00).

The profit of $4,166.67 cannot be related to an investment base to calculate a return on investment because the dollar funds were never needed. On the six-month anniversary Hans simply crosses the payment obligation of $100,000 with receipts of $104,166.67, and accepts a net $4,166.67. Nevertheless, some financial institutions might require him to deposit collateral as margin to ensure his ability to complete the trade.

In this particular forward speculation, the maximum loss is $100,000, the amount needed to buy francs via the forward contract. This loss would be incurred only if the value of the spot franc in six months were zero. The maximum gain is unlimited, since francs acquired in the forward market can in theory rise to an infinite dollar value.

Forward market speculation cannot be extended beyond the maturity date of the forward contract. However, if Hans wants to close out his operation before maturity, he may buy an offsetting contract. In the above example, after, say, four months Hans could sell SF173,611.11 forward two months at whatever forward price then existed. Two months after that he would close the matured six-month contract to purchase francs against the matured two-month contract to sell francs, pocketing any profit or paying up any loss. The amount of profit or loss would be fixed by the price at which Hans sold forward two months.

The example above is only one of several possible types of forward speculations and ignores any interest earned. In a spot speculation, the speculator can invest the principal amount in the foreign money market to earn interest. In the various forward speculations, a speculator who is holding cash against the risk of loss can invest those funds in the home money market. Thus relative profitability will be influenced by interest differentials.

## SPECULATING IN OPTION MARKETS

Options differ from all other types of financial instruments in the patterns of risk they produce. The option owner has the choice of exercising the option or allowing it to expire unused. The owner will exercise it only when exercising is profitable, which means only when the option is in the money. In the case of a call option, as the spot price of the underlying currency moves up, the holder has the possibility of unlimited profit. On the down side, however, the holder can abandon the option and walk away with a loss never greater than the premium paid.

## BUYER OF A CALL

The position of Hans as a buyer of a call is illustrated in Exhibit 7.4. Assume he purchases the August call option on Swiss francs described previously, the one with a strike price of 58 ½ ($0.5850/SF), and a premium of $0.005/SF. The vertical axis measures profit or loss for the option buyer at each of several different spot prices for the franc up to the time of maturity.

## EXHIBIT 7.4

Buying a Call Option on Swiss Francs

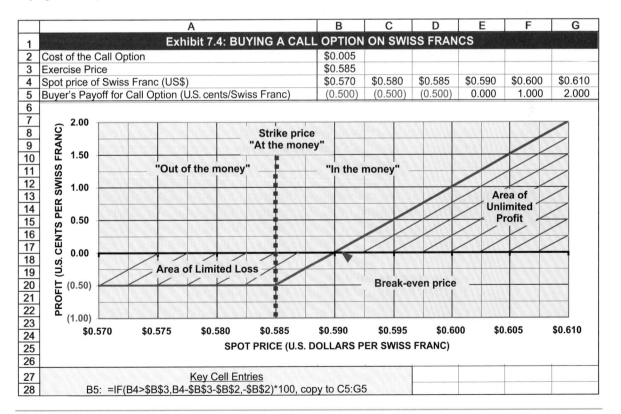

|   | A | B | C | D | E | F | G |
|---|---|---|---|---|---|---|---|
| 1 | Exhibit 7.4: BUYING A CALL OPTION ON SWISS FRANCS | | | | | | |
| 2 | Cost of the Call Option | $0.005 | | | | | |
| 3 | Exercise Price | $0.585 | | | | | |
| 4 | Spot price of Swiss Franc (US$) | $0.570 | $0.580 | $0.585 | $0.590 | $0.600 | $0.610 |
| 5 | Buyer's Payoff for Call Option (U.S. cents/Swiss Franc) | (0.500) | (0.500) | (0.500) | 0.000 | 1.000 | 2.000 |

Key Cell Entries
B5:  =IF(B4>$B$3,B4-$B$3-$B$2,-$B$2)*100, copy to C5:G5

At all spot rates below the strike price of 58.5, Hans would choose not to exercise his option. This is obvious because at a spot rate of 58.0 for example, he would prefer to buy a Swiss franc for $.580 on the spot market rather than exercising his option to buy a franc at $0.585. If the spot rate remains below 58.0 until August when the option expired, Hans would not exercise the option. His total loss would be limited to only what he paid for the option, the $0.005/SF purchase price. At any lower price for the franc, his loss would similarly be limited to the original $0.005/SF cost.

Alternatively, at all spot rates above the strike price of 58.5, Hans would exercise the option, paying only the strike price for each Swiss franc. For example, if the spot rate were 59.5 cents per franc at maturity, he would exercise his call option, buying Swiss francs for $0.585 each instead of purchasing them on the spot market at $0.595 each. He could sell the Swiss francs immediately in the spot market for $0.595 each, pocketing a gross profit of $0.010/SF, or a net profit of $0.005/SF after deducting the original cost of the option of $0.005/SF. Hans' profit, if the spot rate is greater than the strike price, with strike price $0.585, a premium of $0.005, and a spot rate of $0.595, is

$$\text{Profit} = \text{Spot Rate} - (\text{Strike Price} + \text{Premium})$$
$$= \$0.595\,/\,\text{SF} - (\$0.585\,/\,\text{SF} + \$0.005\,/\,\text{SF})$$
$$= \$0.005\,/\,\text{SF}$$

More likely, Hans would realize the profit through executing an offsetting contract on the options exchange rather than taking delivery of the currency. Because the dollar price of a franc could rise to an infinite level (off the upper right-hand side of the page in Exhibit 7.4), maximum profit is unlimited. The buyer of a call option thus possesses an attractive combination of outcomes: limited loss and unlimited profit potential.

Exhibit 7.4 is the first time we use a spreadsheet construction of an exhibit. Spreadsheets have become a very common tool in all functional areas of business management — marketing, operations, etc. — in addition to the traditional usage in finance and accounting. A number of the exhibits in this chapter and occasionally in subsequent chapters, will use a spreadsheet form for the structure of the exhibit. The purpose is to both present the important content of the exhibit and to give you some insight into how the content was constructed or calculated. We assume you are already familiar with basic spreadsheet operations; the calculation components are secondary to the purpose of the exhibit.

Note that the *break-even price* of $0.590/SF is the price at which Hans neither gains nor loses on exercise of the option. The premium cost of $0.005, combined with the cost of exercising the option of $0.585, is exactly equal to the proceeds from selling the francs in the spot market at $0.590. Note that he will still exercise the call option at the break-even price. This is so because by exercising it he at least recoups the premium paid for the option. At any spot price above the exercise price but below the break-even price, the gross profit earned on exercising the option and selling the underlying currency covers part (but not all) of the premium cost.

## WRITER OF A CALL

The position of the writer (seller) of the same call option is illustrated in Exhibit 7.5. If the option expires when the spot price of the underlying currency is below the exercise price of 58.5, the option holder does not exercise. What the holder loses, the writer gains. The writer keeps as profit the entire premium paid of $0.005/SF. Above the exercise price of 58.5, the writer of the call must deliver the underlying currency for

## EXHIBIT 7.5

Selling a Call Option on Swiss Francs

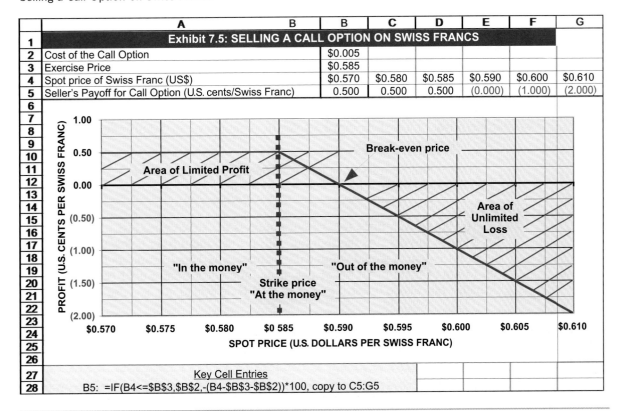

| | A | B | B | C | D | E | F | G |
|---|---|---|---|---|---|---|---|---|
| 1 | | Exhibit 7.5: SELLING A CALL OPTION ON SWISS FRANCS | | | | | | |
| 2 | Cost of the Call Option | | $0.005 | | | | | |
| 3 | Exercise Price | | $0.585 | | | | | |
| 4 | Spot price of Swiss Franc (US$) | | $0.570 | $0.580 | $0.585 | $0.590 | $0.600 | $0.610 |
| 5 | Seller's Payoff for Call Option (U.S. cents/Swiss Franc) | | 0.500 | 0.500 | 0.500 | (0.000) | (1.000) | (2.000) |

Key Cell Entries
B5:  =IF(B4<=$B$3,$B$2,-(B4-$B$3-$B$2))*100, copy to C5:G5

$0.585/SF at a time when the value of the franc is above $0.585. If the writer wrote the option "naked," that is, without owning the currency, that writer will now have to buy the currency at spot and take the loss. The amount of such a loss is unlimited and increases as the price of the underlying currency rises. Once again, what the holder gains, the writer loses, and vice versa. Even if the writer already owns the currency, the writer will experience an opportunity loss, surrendering against the option the same currency that could have been sold for more in the open market.

For example, the profit to the writer of a call option of strike price $0.585, premium $0.005, a spot rate of $0.595/SF is

$$\text{Profit} = \text{Premium} - (\text{Spot Rate} - \text{Strike Price})$$
$$= \$0.005/SF - (\$0.595/SF - \$0.585/SF)$$
$$= -\$0.005/SF$$

but only if the spot rate is greater than or equal to the strike rate. At spot rates less than the strike price, the option will expire worthless and the writer of the call option will keep the premium earned. The maximum profit that the writer of the call option can make is limited to the premium. The writer of a call option would have a rather unattractive combination of potential outcomes — limited profit potential and unlimited loss potential — but there are ways to limit such losses through other offsetting techniques.

## BUYER OF A PUT

Hans' position as buyer of a put is illustrated in Exhibit 7.6. The basic terms of this put are similar to those we just used to illustrate a call. The buyer of a put option, however, wants to be able to sell the underlying currency at the exercise price when the market price of that currency drops (not rises as in the case of a call option). If the spot price of a franc drops to, say, $0.575/SF, Hans will deliver francs to the writer and receive $0.585/SF. The francs can now be purchased on the spot market for $0.575 each and the cost of the option was $0.005/SF, so he will have a net gain of $0.005/SF.

Explicitly, the profit to the holder of a put option if the spot rate is less than the strike price, with a strike price $0.585/SF, premium of $0.005/SF, and a spot rate of $0.575/SF, is

$$\text{Profit} = \text{Strike Price} - (\text{Spot Rate} + \text{Premium})$$
$$= \$0.585/SF - (\$0.575/SF + \$0.005/SF)$$
$$= \$0.005/SF$$

The break-even price for the put option is the strike price less the premium, or $0.580/SF in this case. As the spot rate falls further and further below the strike price, the profit potential would continually increase, and Hans' profit could be unlimited (up to a maximum of $0.580/SF, when the price of a franc would be zero). At any exchange rate above the strike price of 58.5, Hans would not exercise the option and

## EXHIBIT 7.6

Buying a Put Option on Swiss Francs

| | A | B | C | D | E | F | G |
|---|---|---|---|---|---|---|---|
| 1 | Exhibit 7.6: BUYING A PUT OPTION ON SWISS FRANCS | | | | | | |
| 2 | Price of the Put Option | $0.005 | | | | | |
| 3 | Exercise Price | $0.585 | | | | | |
| 4 | Spot price of Swiss Franc (US$) | $0.560 | $0.570 | $0.580 | $0.585 | $0.590 | $0.600 |
| 5 | Buyer's Payoff for Call Option (U.S. cents/Swiss Franc) | 2.000 | 1.000 | 0.000 | (0.500) | (0.500) | (0.500) |

| | |
|---|---|
| 27 | Key Cell Entries |
| 28 | B5:  =IF(B4<=$B$3,$B$3-$B$2-B4,-$B$2)*100, copy to C5:G5 |

so would lose only the $0.005/SF premium paid for the put option. The buyer of a put option has an almost unlimited profit potential with a limited loss potential. Like the buyer of a call, the buyer of a put can never lose more than the premium paid up front.

## WRITER OF A PUT

The position of the writer who sold the put to Hans is shown in Exhibit 7.7. Note the symmetry of profit/loss, strike price, and break-even prices between the buyer and the writer of the put. If the spot price of francs drops below 58.5 cents per franc, Hans will exercise the option. Below a price of 58.5 cents per franc, the writer will lose more than the premium received from writing the option ($0.005/SF), falling below break-even. Between $0.580/SF and $0.585/SF the writer will lose part, but not all, of the premium received. If the spot price is above $0.585/SF, Hans will not exercise the option, and the option writer will pocket the entire premium of $0.005/SF.

The profit (loss) earned by the writer of a $0.585 strike price put, premium $0.005, at a spot rate of $0.575, is

$$\text{Profit (loss)} = \text{Premium} - (\text{Strike Price} - \text{Spot Rate})$$
$$= \$0.005/\text{SF} - (\$0.585/\text{SF} - \$0.575/\text{SF})$$
$$= -\$0.005/\text{SF}$$

## EXHIBIT 7.7

Selling a Put Option on Swiss Francs

| | A | B | C | D | E | F | G |
|---|---|---|---|---|---|---|---|
| 1 | Exhibit 7.7: SELLING A PUT OPTION ON SWISS FRANCS | | | | | | |
| 2 | Price of the Put Option | $0.005 | | | | | |
| 3 | Exercise Price | $0.585 | | | | | |
| 4 | Spot price of Swiss Franc (US$) | $0.560 | $0.570 | $0.580 | $0.585 | $0.590 | $0.600 |
| 5 | Seller's Payoff for Put Option (U.S. cents/SF) | (2.000) | (1.000) | 0.000 | 0.500 | 0.500 | 0.500 |
| 27 | Key Cell Entries | | | | | | |
| 28 | B5: =IF(B4<=$B$3,-$B$3+$B$2+B4,$B$2)*100, copy to C5:G5 | | | | | | |

but only for spot rates that are less than or equal to the strike price. At spot rates greater than the strike price, the option expires out-of-the-money and the writer keeps the premium. The writer of the put option has the same basic combination of outcomes available to the writer of a call: limited profit potential and unlimited loss potential.

## Option Pricing and Valuation

Exhibit 7.8 illustrates the profit/loss profile of a European-style call option on British pounds. The call option allows the holder to buy British pounds at a strike price of $1.70/£. It has a 90-day maturity. The value of this call option is actually the sum of two components:

$$\text{Total Value (Premium)} = \text{Intrinsic Value} + \text{Time Value}$$

The pricing of any currency option combines six elements. For example, this European style call option on British pounds has a premium of $0.033/£ (3.3 cents per pound) at a spot rate of $1.70/£. This premium is calculated using the following assumptions:

1. Present spot rate: $1.70/£
2. Time to maturity: 90 days
3. Forward rate for matching maturity (90 days): $1.70/£
4. U.S. dollar interest rate: 8.00% per annum
5. British pound sterling interest rate: 8.00% per annum
6. Volatility, the standard deviation of daily spot price movement: 10.00% per annum

*Intrinsic value* is the financial gain if the option is exercised immediately. It is shown by the solid red line in Exhibit 7.8, which is zero until it reaches the strike price, then rises linearly (1 cent for each 1-cent increase in the spot rate). Intrinsic value will be zero when the option is out-of-the-money — that is, when the strike price is above the market price — as no gain can be derived from exercising the option. When the spot rate rises above the strike price, the intrinsic value becomes positive because the option is always worth at least this value if exercised. On the date of maturity an option will have a value equal to its intrinsic value (zero time remaining means zero time value).

- When the spot rate is $1.74/£, the option is in-the-money and has an intrinsic value of $1.74–$1.70/£, or 4 cents per pound.
- When the spot rate is $1.70/£, the option is at-the-money and has an intrinsic value of $1.70–$1.70/£, or zero cents per pound.
- When the spot rate is $1.66/£, the option is out-of-the-money and has no intrinsic value. This is shown by the solid red line for intrinsic value lying on the horizontal axis. Only a fool would exercise this call option at this spot rate instead of buying pounds more cheaply on the spot market.

The *time value* of an option exists because the price of the underlying currency, the spot rate, can potentially move further and further into the money between the present time and the option's expiration date. Time value is shown in Exhibit 7.8 as the area between the *total value* of the option and its intrinsic value.

**EXHIBIT 7.8**

Analysis of Call Option on British Pounds with a Strike Price = $1.70/£

| | A | B | C | D |
|---|---|---|---|---|
| 1 | **Exhibit 7.8: ANALYSIS OF CALL OPTION ON BRITISH POUNDS** | | | |
| 2 | **Input Data** | | | |
| 3 | Present spot rate, $/£ | | | $1.70 |
| 4 | Strike price, $/£ | | | $1.70 |
| 5 | Time to maturity, days | | | 90 |
| 6 | Forward rate for matching maturity (90 days), $/£ | | | $1.70 |
| 7 | U.S. dollar interest rate, percent/year | | | 8.0% |
| 8 | British pound sterling interest rate, percent/year | | | 8.0% |
| 9 | Standard deviation of daily spot price movement, percent/year | | | 10.0% |
| 10 | **Effect of Spot Rate on Intrinsic, Time, and Total Value** | | | |
| 11 | | Intrinsic value, | Time value, | Total value, |
| 12 | Spot rate, $/£ | U.S. cents/£ | U.S. cents/£ | U.S. cents/£ |
| 13 | 1.65 | 0.00 | 1.37 | 1.37 |
| 14 | 1.66 | 0.00 | 1.67 | 1.67 |
| 15 | 1.67 | 0.00 | 2.01 | 2.01 |
| 16 | 1.68 | 0.00 | 2.39 | 2.39 |
| 17 | 1.69 | 0.00 | 2.82 | 2.82 |
| 18 | 1.70 | 0.00 | 3.30 | 3.30 |
| 19 | 1.71 | 1.00 | 2.82 | 3.82 |
| 20 | 1.72 | 2.00 | 2.39 | 4.39 |
| 21 | 1.73 | 3.00 | 2.01 | 5.01 |
| 22 | 1.74 | 4.00 | 1.67 | 5.67 |

| | | | |
|---|---|---|---|
| 42 | Key Cell Entries | | |
| 43 | B12: =IF(A12<$D$3,0,A12-$D$3)*100, copy to B13:B21 | | |
| 44 | C12: Calculated with option-pricing software. | | |
| 45 | D12: =B12+C12, copy to D13:D21 | | |

## EXHIBIT 7.9

The Intrinsic, Time, and Total Value Components of the 90-Day Call Option on British Pounds at Varying Spot Exchange Rates

| | Strike Price: $1.70/£ | | | | | | | | |
|---|---|---|---|---|---|---|---|---|---|
| Spot ($/£) | 1.66 | 1.67 | 1.68 | 1.69 | 1.70 | 1.71 | 1.72 | 1.73 | 1.74 |
| Intrinsic | 0.00 | 0.00 | 0.00 | 0.00 | 0.00 | 1.00 | 2.00 | 3.00 | 4.00 |
| Time | 1.67 | 2.01 | 2.39 | 2.82 | 3.30 | 2.82 | 2.39 | 2.01 | 1.67 |
| Total value | 1.67 | 2.01 | 2.39 | 2.82 | 3.30 | 3.82 | 4.39 | 5.01 | 5.67 |

Exhibit 7.9 separates the total value into intrinsic and time values for the call option depicted in Exhibit 7.8. For example, at a spot rate of $1.72/£, the option's total value is made up of 2 cents per pound intrinsic value and 2.39 cents per pound in time value, for a total value of 4.39 cents per pound.

Note that the time value component is the same in value — symmetric — as you move in either direction away from the strike price of $1.70/£. For example, the time value is 2.39 cents at spot rates of 1.68 (2 cents below strike) and 1.72 (2 cents above strike). This demonstrates the underlying principle that option pricing is based on an expected distribution of possible outcomes around the forward rate, which in this case is the same as the strike price, $1.70.

An investor will pay something today for an out-of-the-money option (i.e., zero intrinsic value) on the chance that the spot rate will move far enough before maturity to move the option in-the-money. Consequently, the price of an option is always somewhat greater than its intrinsic value, since there is always some chance that the intrinsic value will rise between the present and the expiration date.

## VOLATILITY

There are few words in the financial field more used and abused than *volatility*. *Option volatility* is defined as the standard deviation of daily percentage changes in the underlying exchange rate. Volatility is important to option value because of an exchange rate's perceived likelihood to move either into or out of the range in which the option would be exercised. If the exchange rate's volatility is rising, and therefore the risk of the option being exercised is increasing, the option premium would be increasing.

Volatility is stated in percent per annum. For example, an option may be described as having a 12.6% annual volatility. The percentage change for a single day can be found as follows:

$$\frac{12.6\%}{\sqrt{365}} = \frac{12.6\%}{19.105} = 0.66\% \text{ daily volatility}$$

For our $1.70/£ call option, an increase in annual volatility of 1 percentage point — for example from 10.0% to 11.0% — will increase the option premium from $0.033/£ to $0.036/£. The marginal change in the option premium is equal to the change in the option premium itself divided by the change in volatility:

$$\frac{\Delta \text{ premium}}{\Delta \text{ volatility}} = \frac{\$0.036/£ - \$0.033/£}{.11 - .10} = 0.30$$

The primary problem with volatility is that it is *unobservable*; it is the only input into the option pricing formula that is determined subjectively by the trader pricing the option. No single correct method for its calculation exists. The problem is one of forecasting; historical volatility is not necessarily an accurate predictor of the future volatility of the exchange rate's movement, yet there is little to go on except history.

Volatility is viewed three ways: *historic*, where the volatility is drawn from a recent period of time; *forward-looking*, where the historic volatility is altered to reflect expectations about the future period over which the option will exist; and *implied*, where the volatility is backed out of the market price of the option.

- **Historic volatility.** Historic volatility is normally measured as the percentage movement in the spot rate on a daily, 6-, or 12-hour basis over the previous 10, 30, or even 90 days.

- **Forward-looking volatility.** Alternatively, an option trader may adjust recent historic volatilities for expected market swings or events, either upward or downward.

If option traders believe that the immediate future will be the same as the recent past, the historic volatility will equal the forward-looking volatility. If, however, the future period is expected to experience greater or lesser volatility, the historic measure must be altered for option pricing.

- **Implied volatility.** Implied volatility is equivalent to having the answers to the test; implied volatilities are calculated by being backed out of the market option premium values traded. Since volatility is the only unobservable element of the option premium price, after all other components are accounted for, the residual value of volatility *implied* by the price is used.

Selected implied volatilities for a number of currency pairs on January 31, 2002, are listed in Exhibit 7.10. These volatilities are *mid-rates*, the average of the bid and ask rates quoted for option contracts. Exhibit 7.10 clearly illustrates that option volatilities vary considerably across currencies, and that the relationship between volatility and maturity (time to expiration) does not move just one direction. For example, the first exchange rate quoted, the US$/euro cross-rate, rises from a 9.0% volatility at one week

## EXHIBIT 7.10

Foreign Exchange Implied Volatility, January 31, 2002

| Currency (cross) | Symbol | Currency Option Maturity | | | | | | | |
|---|---|---|---|---|---|---|---|---|---|
| | | 1 Week | 1 Month | 2 Months | 3 Months | 6 Months | 12 Months | 2 Years | 3 Years |
| European euro | EUR | 9.0 | 9.2 | 9.4 | 9.8 | 10.5 | 10.8 | 10.9 | 10.9 |
| Japanese yen | JPY | 9.2 | 9.1 | 9.4 | 9.5 | 10.1 | 10.4 | 10.4 | 10.4 |
| Swiss franc | CHF | 9.0 | 9.2 | 9.5 | 9.9 | 10.5 | 10.8 | 10.9 | 10.9 |
| British pound | GBP | 7.3 | 7.6 | 7.8 | 8.0 | 8.5 | 8.9 | 9.1 | 9.3 |
| Canadian dollar | CAD | 7.4 | 6.8 | 6.7 | 6.5 | 6.5 | 6.4 | 6.4 | 6.3 |
| Australian dollar | AUD | 10.5 | 10.6 | 10.7 | 11.0 | 11.5 | 11.6 | 11.5 | 11.3 |
| British pound/euro | GBPEUR | 6.2 | 6.5 | 6.7 | 6.9 | 7.4 | 7.6 | 7.3 | 7.2 |
| Euro/Japanese yen | EURJPY | 10.3 | 10.3 | 10.4 | 10.7 | 11.0 | 11.2 | 11.3 | 11.3 |

Notes: These Federal Reserve Bank of New York survey ranges are for implied volatilities, mid-rates, for at-the-money options at 11:00 A.M. New York time. Quotes are for contracts of $10 million with a prime counterparty.

Source: http://ny.frb.org/pihome/statistics/vrate.shtml

to 10.9% for the three-year maturity. The US$/Canadian dollar cross-rate, however, moves in the opposite direction; from 7.4% for one week to 6.3% for the three-year maturity.

Because volatilities are the only judgmental component that the option writer contributes, they play a critical role in the pricing of options. All currency pairs have historical series that contribute to the formation of the expectations of option writers. But in the end, the truly talented option writers are those with the intuition and insight to price the future effectively.

Like all futures markets, option volatilities react instantaneously and negatively to unsettling economic and political events (or rumor). A doubling of volatility for an at-the-money option will result in an equivalent doubling of the option's price. Most currency option traders focus their activities on predicting movements of currency volatility in the short run, because short-run movements move price the most. For example, option volatilities rose significantly in the months preceding the Persian Gulf War, in September 1992 when the European Monetary System was in crisis, in 1997 after the onset of the Asian financial crisis, and in the days following the terrorist attacks on the United States in September 2001. In all instances option volatilities for major cross-currency combinations such as the SF/$ rose to nearly 20% for extended periods. As a result, premium costs rose by corresponding amounts.

In the following chapters we will illustrate how currency options can be used to reduce the risks associated with the conduct of multinational financial management. It is critical, however, that the user of any financial tool or technique — including financial derivatives — follow sound principles and practices. Many a firm has been ruined as a result of the misuse of derivatives. A word to the wise: Do not fall victim to what many refer to as the gambler's dilemma — confusing luck with talent.

## Prudence in Practice

As illustrated in *Real World Example 7.2*, major corporate financial disasters related to financial derivatives continue to be a problem in global business. As is the case with so many issues in modern society, technology is not at fault, rather human error in its use. We conclude our discussion of financial derivatives with a note of caution and humility from an essay in the *Harvard Business Review* by Peter Bernstein:

> *More than any other development, the quantification of risk defines the boundary between modern times and the rest of history. The speed, power, movement, and instant communication that characterize our age would have been inconceivable before science replaced superstition as a bulwark against risks of all kinds.*
>
> *It is hubris that we believe that we can put reliable and stable numbers on the impact of a politician's power, on the probability of a takeover boom like the one that occurred in the 1980s, on the return on the stock market over the next 2, 20, or 50 years, or on subjective factors like utility and risk aversion. It is equally silly to limit our deliberations only to those variables that do lend themselves to quantification, excluding all serious consideration of the unquantifiable. It is irrational to confuse probability with timing and to assume that an event with low probability is therefore not imminent. Such confusion, however, is by no means unusual. And it surely is naive to define discontinuity as anomaly instead of as normality; only the shape and the timing of the disturbances are hidden from us, not their inevitability.*
>
> *Finally, the science of risk management is capable of creating new risks even as it brings old risk under control. Our faith in risk management encourages us to take risk we otherwise*

## Real World Example 7.2
### A SELECT LIST OF DERIVATIVE AND MANAGERIAL DISASTERS

| Date | Company | Description |
|---|---|---|
| 1991 | Allied-Lyons (UK) | Losses of £165 million related to speculation on currency options. |
| 1993 | Shell Showa Sekiyu (Japan) | Over ¥1.5 billion in losses arising from recognition of cumulative losses on forward contracts continually rolled over between 1989 and 1993. |
| 1993 | Metallgesellschaft (Germany) | A flawed petroleum futures hedging strategy essentially caused the collapse of the organization. |
| 1994 | Codelco (Chile) | A copper futures trader for the national copper company of Chile, Codelco loses approximately 0.5% of Chile's gross domestic product for 1994 through speculative futures trading. |
| 1994 | Kashima Oil (Japan) | Hundreds of millions of yen are lost on a failed forward speculation on the Japanese yen. |
| 1994 | Procter & Gamble (U.S.), Gibson Greeting Cards (U.S.), Air Products (U.S.) Dharmala (Indonesia), | All suffer material losses in the millions of dollars on leveraged swap agreements with Bankers Trust of the United States. |
| 1995 | Barings Brothers (UK) | The oldest investment bank in London fails as a result of the losses on futures trading suffered by one trader in its Singapore office, a Mr. Nicholas Leeson. (See the mini-case below.) |
| 2002 | Allied Irish Bank (US/UK) | A rogue currency trader in the Baltimore offices of Allied Irish Bank is credited with losing more than $691 million. |

*would not take. On most counts, that is beneficial. But we should be wary of increasing the total amount of risk in the system. Research shows that the security of seat belts encourages drivers to behave more aggressively, with the result that the number of accidents rises even as the seriousness of injury in any one accident may diminish.*

Reprinted by permission of *Harvard Business Review*. Excerpt from "The New Religion of Risk Management" by Peter L. Bernstein, March–April 1996. Copyright 1996 by the Harvard Business School Publishing Corporation; all rights reserved.

## MINI-CASE

## Rogue Trader, Nicholas Leeson[1]

Nicholas Leeson was a rogue trader who reduced the value of the venerable Baring Brothers & Co (BB&Co) Bank from roughly $500 million dollars to $1.60. Leeson traded futures contracts on the Nikkei 225 and on Japanese government bonds without authorization while management at Barings, the Singapore International Monetary Exchange, the Osaka Stock Exchange, and other governing bodies in Britain and Singapore disregarded or failed to recognize the potential for financial disaster. The failure of Barings Bank provides a lesson in

[1]Abstracted from "Baring Brothers & Co., Technical Note on Rogue Trader Nicholas Leeson," by Professor Mark Griffiths, Thunderbird Case Series, A06–99–0021.

the risks and responsibilities involved in organizing and monitoring derivatives trading.

## Baring Brothers History

Baring Brothers had a long history in the London financial district with the distinction of having gone global with its operations in the eighteenth century. Founded in the late 1700s, the bank was turned into a general-banking and mercantile operation by Sir Francis Baring. During his tenure, the bank developed several lines of business: underwriting bonds, accepting deposits, and trading commodities.

Baring Brothers reached the height of its reputation after the Napoleonic Wars in Europe. The bank led the funding of the French reparations to the victors and was lauded, in 1817, by the French Duc de Richelieu, as the "sixth power in Europe," after Great Britain, France, Russia, Austria, and Prussia. Baring Brothers helped finance the Louisiana Purchase for the United States, underwrote railroad construction in Canada, and financed other projects throughout the Americas. One of those other projects was underwriting a £2 million share issue for the Buenos Aires Water Supply and Drainage Co. in 1890. The issue did not sell but Baring Brothers had already sent the money and was on the brink of failure when the Bank of England organized a consortium to bail it out.[2] Thereafter, it was known as Baring Brothers & Co.

For all its long history in cross-border transactions, the bank never grew along with the size of the markets it served. In 1995, Baring Brothers & Co. remained a small, family-controlled bank ranked 474th in the world banking market.

Barings entered the securities market in 1984 when it acquired the Far East department of Henderson Crothwaite (British stockbrokers). This new entity at Barings was called Baring Securities Ltd. (BSL). Christopher Heath, a specialist in Japanese instruments, managed to maintain independent control of Baring Securities until 1993.

During eight consecutive profitable years, everyone at Barings became accustomed to large bonuses, largely funded by profits in Baring Securities. In 1989, BSL provided £50 million of £65 million total profit for Barings. Unfortunately, the losses incurred in 1992 lead to Heath being asked to resign in March 1993.

## Nicholas Leeson

Nicholas Leeson was two days shy of his twenty-eighth birthday when his trading activities forced Baring Brothers into bankruptcy. Leeson left a note on his desk saying "I'm sorry" and bolted to Kuala Lumpur with his wife following shortly thereafter.

Nick Leeson was born in Watford, England, just outside of London. His father was a plasterer and his mother was a nurse. He was the oldest of four children. Leeson did not attend university; instead, he went directly to work in London upon completion of high school. He worked with a British bank, Coutts & Co., and then Morgan Stanley, before moving to Barings Securities London in 1989.

Nick Leeson was twenty-two years old when he was hired for the position at Baring Securities London (BSLL). BSLL was looking to fill a position settling trades completed in Japan. Leeson, who had experience at Morgan Stanley settling futures and options in Japan, was a good replacement. He worked hard, kept to himself, and was known as someone anxious to learn and eager to please. He was subsequently selected as a member of a team of four people assigned to straighten out back office problems in Jakarta.

In 1992, he was selected to run the back office for the new Baring Futures Singapore (BFS), a subsidiary that would trade futures and options. His exact responsibilities were somewhat unclear, although they did include responsibility for both the back office accounting and control functions as well as for executing clients' orders. This was when Leeson's unauthorized trading activities began. On his initiative, Leeson sat for and passed the futures-trading exam to become registered as an associated person with the Singapore International Monetary Exchange (SIMEX). He did not need the license to fulfill his responsibilities, but he did need it to execute trades. To meet his Baring's responsibilities, he only needed to take orders from clients, and pass them to a trader for execution.

In 1992, Leeson established the error account 88888 (eight is considered a lucky number by the Chinese), which, according to SIMEX investigators, he immediately began using to conceal unauthorized trading activities.[3] While a legitimate error account, numbered 99002, was known to BSLL, the 88888 account did not show on files or statements transmitted from Singapore to London. Account 88888 was known to SIMEX, but as a customer account, not as an error account. Leeson had to represent it differently to each group because he could not hide the existence of 88888 from SIMEX, and he could not explain its volume and balance to BSLL (but he could hide it from them).

## Derivatives

Since the early 1970s, derivatives have increasingly been used by firms to manage their exposure to risks. When a derivative is purchased, only part of the value of the

---

[2]Stephen Fay, *The Collapse of Barings* (New York: W.W. Norton Co. Inc., 1997), p. 10.
[3]Fay, *Collapse*, p. 94.

underlying asset is at risk, while the opportunity to benefit from favorable price fluctuations is retained. Derivatives can offer potentially enormous gains, which can lead to their use as speculative instruments. They also offer potentially debilitating losses depending on the positions taken.

Nick Leeson was trading futures and options on the Nikkei 225, an index of Japanese securities. Leeson was long Nikkei 225 futures, short Japanese government bond futures, and short both put and call options on the Nikkei index. He was betting that the Nikkei index would rise. He was wrong and ended up losing $1.39 billion. For Leeson to suffer losses of this magnitude in futures positions during January and February of 1995, he had to have held approximately one quarter of the entire open interest on the Osaka and Singapore stock exchanges. Unfortunately, since management had given such free rein to Leeson by allowing him to control both front and back office operations, this level of investment went undetected by the firm.[4]

Leeson offset any losses incurred on his long positions in Nikkei futures by writing Nikkei options. That is, when Leeson purchased futures contracts, he was required to pay cash, a margin of 15% of the contract's value to SIMEX, and when the losses on the contracts accumulated, additional margin was required because futures contracts are marked-to-market on a daily basis. However, when he wrote the options, he received cash, in the form of premiums. The premiums from the Nikkei options served two purposes: (1) they were used to hide losses created by the futures, which would otherwise have shown in BFS' financial statements, and (2) the premiums served to cover the margin calls on the futures. Leeson was able to do this due to the nature of the Japanese futures market at this time. In Japan, margin is posted on a net basis for all customers. Therefore, if many customers were short index futures, the firm can take long positions without having to post cash margin. In addition, daily settlement was one-sided. That is, losers must cover their losses daily, but winners were not permitted to withdraw gains. Therefore, it was possible to cover the firm's losses with customer gains. Another aspect of the Japanese futures market, which enabled Leeson to do this, was that the exchange did not require a separation between customer and proprietary funds. Therefore, it was impossible to distinguish between the firm's and the customers' positions.

The Nikkei 225 experienced an extended bull run throughout the late 1980s, reaching a height of close to 40,000 in 1989. By mid-1994, Leeson was convinced that since the Nikkei had fallen to half of its 1989 high, and interest rates were low, it would likely recover in the near future. He was convinced it would not fall below 19,000 and he was willing to put a lot of Baring's money at risk based on that belief. However, a rise in interest rates would hurt him and, accordingly, he took short positions in Japanese government bonds futures contracts that would pay off if interest rates rose.

Leeson's options positions were founded on his belief that volatility would be low. In fact, he had traded enough contracts by the time of the collapse that he was causing volatility to remain low. Increasingly, he had to write a larger volume of options in order to get the same amount of premiums. When it became increasingly difficult for the options' premiums to cover the margin calls on the futures, Leeson requested money from London. By February 23, 1995, BSLL had sent approximately $600 million to BFS. BSLL funded his request with little information, and with the understanding that a portion of the money was "loans to clients," as portrayed on the BFS balance sheet.

## The Losses

Leeson began trading futures in July 1992 and by the end of the month, he had bought and sold 2,051 Nikkei futures, suffering a loss of approximately $64,000 immediately.[5] By the end of the year, his losses in account 88888 were more than $3.2 million. The numbers turned somewhat in his favor by mid-1993 when the losses amounted to only $40,000. Unfortunately, Leeson intended to keep trading until his numbers were positive. By the end of 1993, the losses were approximately $30 million. At this point, Leeson wrote options for approximately $35 million to offset the futures losses and to avoid suspicion from London and the auditors. Throughout this time period, Leeson was reporting record profits, and was being heralded as a superstar.

By the end of 1994, the Nikkei had fallen to just under 20,000 and Leeson's losses approached $330 million. Meanwhile, Barings executives were expecting an estimated $20 million in profits from BFS for 1994.

Leeson's activities in the first few months of 1995 were like those of any self-respecting speculator. On January 13, 1995, the Nikkei reached 19,331 and Barings was long 3,024 Nikkei futures contracts. But, on January 17, 1995, an earthquake measuring 7.2 devastated the Japanese city of Kobe. The Nikkei plummeted below 18,840 by January 20, at which point Leeson doubled his contracts to 7,135.[6] This process continued as

[4]Hans R. Stoll, "Lost Barings: A Tale in Three Parts Concluding with a Lesson," *The Journal of Derivatives*, Fall 1995, Vol.3, No.1.
[5]Fay, *Collapse*, p. 97.
[6]*Time*, "On Going Broke," p. 44.

**EXHIBIT 1**

| KEY EVENTS: NICK LEESON & BARING BROTHERS | |
|---|---|
| 1989: | Nick Leeson is hired as a trade office clerk who settles accounts. |
| | Leeson moves to Singapore where he is responsible for the back office of Baring Futures Singapore (BFS) and the execution of clients' trades. |
| June 1992: | Leeson obtains a license to trade for BFS in the Singapore International Monetary Exchange. He is not authorized by Barings to trade beyond execution of clients' requests. |
| July 1992: | Leeson sets up the error account 88888, used to conduct unauthorized trading. |
| October 1992: | Losses in 88888 reach £4.5 million. |
| June 1993: | Losses in 88888 reach a low point of £34,000. |
| October 1993: | Leeson is given discretion by Barings to decide when and at what price to trade on behalf of Barings. Losses in 88888 are at £24.39 million. |
| 1993: | Baring Brothers & Co becomes one of the first banks to complete a solo-consolidation (merging its banking business with its securities business) under new regulations. |
| March 1994: | $40 million is lost by CS First Boston in a scheme that had the bank reimbursing a client for unauthorized money-losing derivative trades within its account. |
| April 1994: | Joseph Jett is exposed by his employer, Kidder Peabody, for $350 million of false profit. Procter & Gamble (P&G) joins the ranks of derivative losers. It loses $157 million in interest rate swaps. Bankers Trust is at the heart of the controversy. P&G refuses to pay arguing misrepresentation on the part of Banker's Trust. |
| October 1994: | Eastman Kodak loses $220 million in swaps and options. |
| August 1994: | Internal audit is conducted at BFS. It criticizes Leeson's control of back and front office activities and expresses concern over reconciliation of funds received from London. |
| Dec 1994: | Orange County loses $1.7 billion and goes bankrupt on inverse floaters. Merrill Lynch is sued and pays roughly $480 million to Orange County and fines to the SEC. |
| Dec. 31, 1994: | Losses in account 88888 exceed £208 million. Baring executives expected an estimated $20–36 million in profits for the bank from BFS. |
| Jan 11, 1995: | SIMEX sends a letter to BFS explaining that the margin for account 88888 is short $100 million. It is referred to Leeson for a response. |
| Jan. 13, 1995: | The Nikkei is at 19,331 and Barings has 3,024 Nikkei futures contracts. |
| Jan 17, 1995: | Kobe, Japan, suffers a disastrous earthquake. The damage is estimated at over $100 billion. This drives down the Nikkei, causing the value of Barings' futures positions to drop precipitously. |
| Jan 20, 1995: | Leeson doubles down to 7,135 contracts in the Nikkei, hoping for a reversal of fortune. |
| Jan 25, 1995: | The Nikkei drops below 18,000. Leeson doubles again to 17,000 (est.) contracts on Jan. 27. |
| Feb 17, 1995: | Leeson increases the number of contracts to 20,076. |
| Feb 23, 1995: | Losses approach $1.1 billion, more than twice Baring Bank's capitalization. The bank goes bankrupt and Leeson flees Singapore, two days before his twenty-eighth birthday. |

the Nikkei fell to 18,000 on February 23, 1995, and Leeson's exposure grew to more than 55,399 unhedged Nikkei futures.[7] Compounding the problem, interest rates did not rise as Leeson had expected and he was losing on the Japanese government bond futures as well.

By Friday, February 24, 1995, Barings and the world discovered that Leeson had incurred losses approaching $1.1 billion,[8] more than double the capitalization of the bank. The bank was headed toward bankruptcy. When the markets opened in Singapore and Osaka on Monday, the exchanges would declare Barings in default on its margins.

Throughout that weekend, the Bank of England hosted meetings in London to try to form a consortium to bail out Barings. Barclays Bank assumed the leadership role and was able to attain commitments for $900 million for three months. Unfortunately for Barings, no one would assume the contingent risk of additional, but as yet undiscovered losses, and the efforts failed. At the time, it was already

[7]Fay, *Collapse*, p. 275.

[8]"Report of the Board of Banking Supervision Inquiry into the Circumstances of the Collapse of Barings," Bank of England, July 18, 1995 p. 2 (hereafter referred to as Bank of England).

known that on Monday, February 27, 1995, there would be an additional $370 million in losses from Barings positions, bringing the total loss to $1.39 billion.[9] Barings was bankrupt. A detailed time line is presented in the Exhibit 1.

## Case Questions

1. What was Nick Leeson's strategy to earn trading profits on derivatives?
2. What went wrong that caused his strategy to fail?
3. Why did Nick Leeson establish a bogus error account (88888) when a legitimate account (99002) already existed?
4. Why did Barings and its auditors not discover that the error account was used by Leeson for unauthorized trading?
5. Why did none of the regulatory authorities in Singapore, Japan, and the United Kingdom discover the true use of the error account?
6. Why was Barings Bank willing to transfer large cash sums to Barings Futures Singapore?
7. Why did the attempt by the Bank of England to organize a bailout for Barings fail?
8. Suggest regulatory and management reforms that might prevent a future debacle of the type that bankrupted Barings.

## Summary of Learning Objectives

*Explain how foreign currency futures are quoted, valued, and used for speculation purposes*

- A foreign currency futures contract is an exchange-traded agreement calling for future delivery of a standard amount of foreign exchange at a fixed time, place, and price.

- Foreign currency futures contracts are in reality standardized forward contracts. Unlike forward contracts, however, trading occurs on the floor of an organized exchange rather than between banks and customers. Futures also require collateral and are normally settled through the purchase of an offsetting position.

*Illustrate how foreign currency futures differ from forward contracts*

- As summarized in Exhibit 7.2, futures differ from forward contracts by size of contract, maturity, location of trading, pricing, collateral/margin requirements, method of settlement, commissions, trading hours, counterparties, and liquidity.

- Financial managers typically prefer foreign currency forwards over futures because of forwards' simplicity of use and position maintenance. Financial speculators typically prefer foreign currency futures over forwards because of the liquidity of the futures markets.

*Analyze how foreign currency options are quoted and used for speculation purposes*

- Foreign currency options are financial contracts that give the holder the right, but not the obligation, to buy (in the case of calls) or sell (in the case of puts) a specified amount of foreign exchange at a predetermined price on or before a specified maturity date.

- The use of a currency option as a speculative device for the buyer of an option arises from the fact that an option gains in value as the underlying currency rises (for calls) or falls (for puts). The amount of loss when the underlying currency moves opposite to the desired direction is limited to the premium of the option.

- The use of a currency option as a speculative device for the writer (seller) of an option arises from the option premium. If the option — either a put or call — expires out-of-the-money (valueless), the writer of the option has earned, and retains, the entire premium.

- Speculation is an attempt to profit by trading on expectations about prices in the future. In the foreign exchange market, one speculates by taking a position in a foreign currency and then closing that position after the exchange rate has moved; a profit results only if the rate moves in the direction that the speculator expected.

[9]Martin Mayer, *The Bankers: The Next Generation* (New York: Truman Talley Books/Plume, 1997), p. 335.

*Consider the distinction between buying options and writing options in terms of whether profits and losses are limited or unlimited*

- The buyer of a call or put option has a limited loss potential and an unlimited profit potential; the buyer of a call or put cannot lose more than the option premium initially paid.

- The writer (seller) of a call or put option has a limited profit potential (the option premium earned is the limit to profit), with an unlimited loss potential of covering the option sold.

*Explain how foreign currency options are valued*

- Currency option valuation, the determination of the option's premium, is a complex combination of the current spot rate, the specific strike rate, the forward rate (which itself is dependent on the current spot rate and interest differentials), currency volatility, and time to maturity.

- The total value of an option is the sum of its intrinsic value and time value. Intrinsic value depends on the relationship between the option's strike price and the current spot rate at any single point in time, whereas time value estimates how this current intrinsic value may change — for the better — prior to the option's maturity or expiration.

## QUESTIONS

1. **Options versus futures.** Explain the difference between foreign currency *options* and *futures* and when either might be used most appropriately.

2. **Trading location for futures.** Check *The Wall Street Journal* to find where in the United States foreign exchange future contracts are traded.

3. **Futures terminology.** Explain the meaning and probable significance for international business of the following contract specifications:
   a. Specific-sized contract
   b. Standard method of stating exchange rates
   c. Standard maturity date
   d. Collateral and maintenance margins
   e. Counterparty

4. **A futures trade.** A newspaper shows the following prices for the previous day's trading in U.S. dollar-euro currency futures:

| | |
|---|---|
| Month: | December |
| Open: | 0.9124 |
| Settlement: | 0.9136 |
| Change: | +0.0027 |
| High: | 0.9147 |
| Low: | 0.9098 |
| Estimated volume: | 29,763 |
| Open interest: | 111,360 |
| Contract size: | €125,000 |

What do the above terms indicate?

5. **Puts and calls.** What is the basic difference between a *put* on British pounds sterling and a *call* on sterling?

6. **Call contract elements.** You read that exchange-traded American call options on pounds sterling having a strike price of 1.460 and a maturity of next March are now quoted at 3.67. What does this mean if you are a potential buyer?

7. **The option cost.** What happens to the premium you paid for the option in Question 6 in the event you decide to let the option expire unexercised? What happens to this amount in the event you decide to exercise the option?

8. **Buying a European option.** You have the same information as in Question 6 above, except that the pricing is for a European option. What is different?

9. **Writing options.** Why would anyone write an option, knowing that the gain from receiving the option premium is fixed but the loss if the underlying price goes in the wrong direction can be extremely large?

10. **Option valuation.** The value of an option is stated to be the sum of its *intrinsic value* and its *time value*. Explain what is meant by these terms.

## PROBLEMS

1. **Peso futures.** Amber McClain, the currency speculator we met on page 174, now sells eight June futures contracts for 500,000 pesos at the closing price quoted in Exhibit 7.1.

   a. What is the value of her position at maturity if the ending spot rate is $.12000/Ps?

   b. What is the value of her position at maturity if the ending spot rate is $.09800/Ps?

   c. What is the value of her position at maturity if the ending spot rate is $.11000/Ps?

2. **Pound futures.** Michael Polin, a currency trader for a New York investment firm, uses the British pound futures quotes below to speculate on the value of the British pound.

   a. If Michael buys 5 June pound futures, and the spot rate at maturity is $1.3980/pound, what is the value of his position?

   b. If Michael sells 12 March pound futures, and the spot rate at maturity is $1.4560/pound, what is the value of his position?

   c. If Michael buys 3 March pound futures, and the spot rate at maturity is $1.4560/pound, what is the value of his position?

   d. If Michael sells 12 June pound futures, and the spot rate at maturity is $1.3980/pound, what is the value of his position?

3. **Hans Schmidt, euro speculator.** Hans is once again speculating on the movement of currencies. Hans has $10 million to begin with, and he must state all profits at the end of any speculation in U.S. dollars. The spot rate on the euro is $1.3358/€, while the 30-day forward rate is $1.3350/€.

   a. If Hans believes the euro will continue to rise in value against the U.S. dollar, so that he expects the spot rate to be $1.3600/€ at the end of 30 days, what should he do?

   b. If Hans believes the euro will depreciate in value against the U.S. dollar, so that he expects the spot rate to be $1.2800/€ at the end of 30 days, what should he do?

4. **Hans Schmidt, Swiss franc speculator.** Similar to the situation Hans saw in the chapter, Hans believes the Swiss franc will appreciate versus the U.S. dollar in the coming three-month period. He has $100,000 to invest. The current spot rate is $0.5820/SF, the three-month forward rate is $0.5640/SF, and he expects the spot rate to reach $0.6250/SF in three months.

   a. Calculate Hans' expected profit assuming a pure spot market speculation strategy.

   b. Calculate Hans' expected profit assuming he buys or sells SF three months forward.

| British Pound Futures, US$/pound (CME) | | | | | | | | Contact = 62,500 pounds |
|---|---|---|---|---|---|---|---|---|
| **Maturity** | **Open** | **High** | **Low** | **Settle** | **Change** | **High** | **Low** | **Open Interest** |
| Mar | 1.4246 | 1.4268 | 1.4214 | 1.4228 | .0032 | 1.4700 | 1.3810 | 25,605 |
| June | 1.4164 | 1.4188 | 1.4146 | 1.4162 | .0030 | 1.4550 | 1.3910 | 809 |

Abstracted from *The Wall Street Journal*, Friday, February 22, 2002, p. C13. Quotations are for close of business on Thursday, February 21, 2002. All contracts are for 62,500 British pounds.

5. **Katya and the yen.** Katya Berezovsky works in the currency trading unit of Sumara Workers Bank in Togliatti, Russia. Her latest speculative position is to profit from her expectation that the U.S. dollar will rise significantly against the Japanese yen. The current spot rate is ¥120.00/$. She must choose between the following 90-day options on the Japanese yen:

| Option | Strike Price | Premium |
|---|---|---|
| Put on yen | ¥125/$ | $0.00003/¥ |
| Call on yen | ¥125/$ | $0.00046/¥ |

   a. Should Katya buy a put on yen or a call on yen?

   b. Using your answer to a, what is Katya's break-even price?

   c. Using your answer to a, what are Katya's gross profit and net profit (including the premium) if the spot rate at the end of the 90 days is ¥140/$?

6. **Samuel's bet.** Samuel Samosir works for Peregrine Investments in Jakarta, Indonesia. He focuses his time and attention on the U.S. dollar/Singapore dollar ($/S$) cross rate. The current spot rate is $0.6000/S$. After considerable study, he has concluded that the Singapore dollar will appreciate versus the U.S. dollar in the coming 90 days, probably to about $0.7000/S$. He has the following options on the Singapore dollar to choose from:

| Option | Strike Price | Premium |
|---|---|---|
| Put on S$ | $0.6500/S$ | $0.00003/S$ |
| Call on S$ | $0.6500/S$ | $0.00046/S$ |

**a.** Should Samuel buy a put on Singapore dollars or a call on Singapore dollars?

**b.** Using your answer to a, what is Samuel's break-even price?

**c.** Using your answer to a, what are Samuel's gross profit and net profit (including the premium) if the spot rate at the end of the 90 days is indeed $0.7000/S$?

**d.** Using your answer to a, what are Samuel's gross profit and net profit (including the premium) if the spot rate at the end of the 90 days is $0.8000/S$?

**7. How much profit—calls?** Assume a call option on euros is written with a strike price of $1.25/€ at a premium of $0.38/€) and with an expiration date three months from now. The option is for €100,000. Calculate your profit or loss should you exercise before maturity at a time when the euro is traded spot at

**a.** $1.10/€              **e.** $1.30/€

**b.** $1.15/€              **f.** $1.35/€

**c.** $1.20/€              **g.** $1.40/€

**d.** $1.25/€

**8. How much profit—puts?** Assume a put option on Japanese yen is written with a strike price of $0.008000/¥ (¥125.00/$) at a premium of 0.0080¢ per yen and with an expiration date six months from now. The option is for ¥12,500,000. Calculate your profit or loss should you exercise before maturity at a time when the yen is traded spot at

**a.** ¥110/$              **e.** ¥130/$

**b.** ¥115/$              **f.** ¥135/$

**c.** ¥120/$              **g.** ¥140/$

**d.** ¥125/$

**9. Falling Canadian dollar.** Giri Patel works for CIBC Currency Funds in Toronto. Giri is something of a *contrarian* — contrary to most forecasters, he

believes the Canadian dollar (C$) will appreciate versus the U.S. dollar over the coming 90 days. The current spot rate is $0.6750/C$. Giri may choose between the following options on the Canadian dollar:

| Option | Strike Price | Premium |
|---|---|---|
| Put on C$ | $0.7000 | $0.0003/C$ |
| Call on C$ | $0.7000 | $0.0247/C$ |

**a.** Should Giri buy a put on Canadian dollars or a call on Canadian dollars?

**b.** Using your answer to a, what is Giri's break-even price?

**c.** Using your answer to a, what are Giri's gross profit and net profit (including the premium) if the spot rate at the end of the 90 days is $0.7600/C$?

**d.** Using your answer to a, what are Giri's gross profit and net profit (including the premium) if the spot rate at the end of the 90 days is $0.8250/C$?

**10. Braveheart puts on pounds.** Andy Furstow is a speculator for a currency fund in London named Braveheart. Braveheart's clients are a collection of wealthy private investors who, with a minimum stake of £250,000 each, wish to speculate on the movement of currencies. The investors expect annual returns in excess of 25%. Although officed in London, all accounts and expectations are based in U.S. dollars.

Andy Furstow is convinced that the British pound will slide significantly — possibly to $1.3200/£ — in the coming 30 to 60 days. The current spot rate is $1.4260/£. Andy wishes to buy a put on pounds that will yield the 25% return expected by his investors. Which of the following put options would you recommend he purchase? Prove your choice is the preferable combination of strike price, maturity, and up-front premium expense.

| Strike Price | Maturity | Premium | Strike Price | Maturity | Premium |
|---|---|---|---|---|---|
| $1.36/£ | 30 days | $0.00081/£ | $1.36/£ | 60 days | $0.00333/£ |
| $1.34/£ | 30 days | $0.00021/£ | $1.34/£ | 60 days | $0.00150/£ |
| $1.32/£ | 30 days | $0.00004/£ | $1.32/£ | 60 days | $0.00060/£ |

## Pricing Currency Options on the Euro

|  | A U.S.–based firm wishing to buy or sell euros (the foreign currency) | | A European firm wishing to buy or sell dollars (the foreign currency) | |
|---|---|---|---|---|
|  | **Variable** | **Value** | **Variable** | **Value** |
| Spot rate (domestic/foreign) | $S_0$ | $1.2674 | $S_0$ | € 0.7890 |
| Strike rate (domestic/foreign) | X | $1.2500 | X | € 0.8000 |
| Domestic interest rate (% p.a.) | $r_d$ | 1.453% | $r_d$ | 2.187% |
| Foreign interest rate (% p.a.) | $r_f$ | 2.187% | $r_f$ | 1.453% |
| Time (years, 365 days) | T | 1.000 | T | 1.000 |
|    Days equivalent |  | 365.00 |  | 365.00 |
| Volatility (% p.a.) | s | 12.000% | s | 12.000% |
| Call option premium (per unit fc) | c | $0.0632 | c | € 0.0349 |
| Put option premium (per unit fc)<br>  (European pricing) | p | $0.0552 | p | € 0.0399 |
| Call option premium (%) | c | 4.99% | c | 4.42% |
| Put option premium (%) | p | 4.36% | p | 5.06% |

An Excel workbook entitled **FX Option Pricing** is downloadable from the book's Internet Web site. The workbook has four spreadsheets constructed for pricing currency options for the following five currency pairs: U.S. dollar/euro, U.S. dollar/Japanese yen, euro/Japanese yen, U.S. dollar/British pound, and euro/British pound. Use the appropriate spreadsheet from the workbook to answer the following questions.

11. **U.S. dollar/euro.** The exhibit above indicates that a one-year call option on euros at a strike rate of $1.25/€ will cost the buyer $0.0632/€, or 4.99%. But that assumed a volatility of 12.000% when the spot rate was $1.2674/€. What would that same call option cost if the volatility was reduced to 10.500% when the spot rate fell to $1.2480/€?

12. **U.S. dollar/Japanese yen.** What would be the premium expense, in home-currency, for Nakagama of Japan's purchase of an option to sell 750,000 U.S. dollars, assuming the initial values listed in the FX Option Pricing workbook?

13. **Euro/Japanese yen.** Legrand (France) is expecting to receive JPY 10.4 million in 90 days as a result of an export sale to a Japanese semiconductor firm. What will it cost, in total, to purchase an option to sell the yen at ¥0.0072/JPY?

14. **U.S. dollar/British pound.** Assuming the same initial values for the dollar/pound cross rate in the FX Option Pricing workbook, how much more would a call option on pounds be if the maturity was doubled from 90 to 180 days? What percentage increase is this for twice the length of maturity?

15. **Euro/British pound.** How would the call option premium change on the right to buy pounds with euros if the euro interest rate changed to 4.000% from the initial values listed in the FX Option Pricing workbook?

**Internet Exercises**

1. **Currency volatilities.** The single unobservable variable in currency option pricing is volatility, since volatility inputs are the expected standard deviation of the daily spot rate for the coming period of the option's maturity. Use the New York Federal Reserve Web site to obtain current currency volatilities.

   Federal Reserve Bank of New York
     http://www.ny.frb.org/

2. **Currency options and futures exchanges.** Currency options and futures are traded in many exchanges (bolsas, bourses, etc.) around the world. Using the following list of exchange Web sites as a starting point, determine exactly which currencies are traded on exchanges in the form of futures or options.

   London Stock Exchange
     http://www.londonstockexchange.com/
   Tokyo Stock Exchange
     http://www.tse.or.jp/english/
   SBF — Paris Bourse
     http://www.euronext.com/
   Bolsa de Bogota
     http://www.bolsabogota.com.co/
   Singapore Exchange
     http://www.ses.sg/

   Or, for a wider spectrum of global markets:

   Investor Map
     http://investormap.com/global.htm

# Foreign Exchange Exposure

Part 3 uses the background provided in Part 2 to analyze the task of measuring and managing foreign exchange exposure. Foreign exchange exposure is a measure of the potential that a firm's profitability, cash flow, and market value will change because of a change in exchange rates. A major responsibility of financial managers in multinational enterprises is to manage these currency exposures.

**CHAPTER 8** defines the four different types of foreign exchange exposure, namely, *transaction, operating, translation,* and *tax exposure.* It then analyzes why a firm should or should not hedge one or more of these exposures. The rest of this chapter examines specifically *transaction exposure.* This type of exposure measures changes in the value of outstanding financial obligations incurred prior to a change in exchange rates but not due to be settled until a future point in time. Typical exposures are accounts receivable and payables, including their current exposures, as well as backlog and quotation exposures. We use the Trident case to illustrate how a firm can hedge transaction exposure. The chapter concludes with an examination of how risk management is conducted in practice and a mini-case illustrating how Lufthansa attempted to hedge the transaction exposure arising from its purchase of Boeing 737s.

**CHAPTER 9** examines how a firm should measure and manage its *operating exposure.* Operating exposure measures the change in the present value of a firm resulting from a change in its future operating cash flows due to an unexpected change in exchange rates. The change in present value depends on the effect of an exchange rate change on the firm's future sales volume, prices, and costs. We use the Trident case to illustrate the change in its net present value under a variety of scenarios. We then illustrate how a firm can manage operating exposure through such strategic measures as diversifying operations and sources of financing. The chapter concludes with a description of six proactive techniques that are used to manage operating exposure in practice. These techniques are: matching currency cash flows; risk-sharing agreements; back-to-back loans; currency swaps; leads and lags; and reinvoicing centers.

**CHAPTER 10** analyzes how a firm should measure and manage its ***translation exposure.*** Translation exposure is the potential for accounting-derived changes in owners' equity and consolidated income that occur because of the need to translate foreign-currency denominated financial statements of foreign subsidiaries into a single currency to prepare worldwide consolidated financial statements. The chapter starts with a description of the current translation methods and then uses Trident Europe to illustrate use of each method. We then compare Trident's translation exposure with its operating exposure. The chapter concludes with an analysis of the use of a balance sheet hedge to offset translation exposure.

# Transaction Exposure

## LEARNING OBJECTIVES

Distinguish between the three major foreign exchange exposures experienced by firms

Identify foreign exchange transaction exposure

Analyze the pros and cons of hedging foreign exchange transaction exposure

Identify the alternatives available to a firm for managing a large and significant transaction exposure

Evaluate the institutional practices and concerns of conducting foreign exchange risk management

*Foreign exchange exposure* is a measure of the potential for a firm's *profitability, net cash flow*, and *market value* to change because of a change in exchange rates. An important task of the financial manager is to measure foreign exchange exposure and to manage it so as to maximize the profitability, net cash flow, and market value of the firm. These three components — profits, cash flows, and market value — are the key financial elements of how we view the relative success or failure of a firm. The first two — profits and cash flows — largely give rise to the third, market value. And, although the theory of finance teaches us that cash flows matter and accounting does not, any true businessperson knows that currency-related gains and losses can have destructive impacts on reported earnings. The reported earnings of any publicly traded company are fundamental to the market's opinion of that company.

## Types of Foreign Exchange Exposure

What happens to a firm when foreign exchange rates change? The effect can be measured in several ways. Exhibit 8.1 reviews the three main types of foreign exchange exposure — *transaction, operating*, and *translation* — which were first introduced in Chapter 1.

### TRANSACTION EXPOSURE

*Transaction exposure* measures changes in the value of outstanding financial obligations incurred prior to a change in exchange rates but not due to be settled until after the exchange rates change. Thus it deals with changes in cash flows that result from existing contractual obligations. The purpose of this chapter is to analyze how transaction exposure is measured and managed.

**EXHIBIT 8.1**

Conceptual Comparison of Transaction, Operating, and Translation Foreign Exchange Exposure

**Moment in time when exchange rate changes**

**Translation exposure**

Changes in reported owners' equity in consolidated financial statements caused by a change in exchange rates

**Operating exposure**

Change in expected future cash flows arising from an unexpected change in exchange rates

**Transaction exposure**

Impact of settling outstanding obligations entered into before change in exchange rates but to be settled after change in exchange rates

**Time** ⟶

## OPERATING EXPOSURE

*Operating exposure*, also called *economic exposure, competitive exposure*, or *strategic exposure*, measures the change in the present value of the firm resulting from any change in expected future operating cash flows of the firm caused by an *unexpected* change in exchange rates. The change in value depends on the effect of the exchange rate change on future sales volume, prices, and costs. Chapter 9 analyzes operating exposure.

Transaction exposure and operating exposure exist because of unexpected changes in future cash flows. The difference between the two is that transaction exposure is concerned with future cash flows already contracted for, while operating exposure focuses on expected (not yet contracted for) future cash flows that might change because a change in exchange rates has altered international competitiveness.

## TRANSLATION EXPOSURE

*Translation exposure*, also called *accounting exposure*, is the potential for accounting-derived changes in owner's equity to occur because of the need to "translate" foreign currency financial statements of foreign subsidiaries into a single reporting currency to prepare worldwide consolidated financial statements.

## TAX EXPOSURE

The tax consequence of foreign exchange exposure varies by country. As a general rule, however, only *realized* foreign exchange losses are deductible for purposes of calculating income taxes. Similarly, only *realized* gains create taxable income. *Realized* means that the loss or gain involves cash flows.

Losses from transaction exposure usually reduce taxable income in the year in which they are realized. Losses from operating exposure reduce taxable income over a series of future years. As Chapter 10 will show, losses from translation exposure are not cash losses and so are not deductible. Some steps taken to minimize one or another of the types of exposure, such as entering into a forward exchange contract, create taxable income or loss. Other steps taken to obtain the same protection have no income tax implications. Because tax exposure is determined by the country of domicile of each subsidiary, an MNE needs to plan its foreign exchange management policies to minimize the worldwide after-tax consequences of foreign exchange losses and to maximize after-tax gains. However, since many MNEs manage foreign exchange exposures centrally, gains or losses are often not matched with the country of origin.

As illustrated in *Real World Example 8.1*, however, currency exposures do not always result in losses. They may, in fact, occasionally result in gains to the firm — gains that are not the result of the firm's true operations or core competence — but from the luck and timing associated with exchange rate changes and currency movements.

## Why Hedge?

MNEs possess a multitude of cash flows that are sensitive to changes in exchange rates, interest rates, and commodity prices. These three financial price risks are the subject of the growing field of *financial risk management*. In this chapter we will focus on the sensitivity of the individual firm's future cash flows to exchange rates alone.

## Real World Example 8.1
### AMAZON.COM'S QUEST FOR PROFITS: THE ROLE OF CURRENCY GAINS/LOSSES

Jeff Bezos, the CEO of Amazon.com, had promised that Amazon would turn a profit sometime in 2001. Although most analysts and investors did not believe him, he proved them wrong as Amazon.com reported a positive operating profit of $59 million and a net income of $5 million for the fourth quarter of 2001. He had indeed delivered on his promise.

But one issue primary to all investors is the *quality* of earnings. Although there are a number of technical components to quality, one of the fundamental questions about reported earnings is whether they are *sustainable*. Did the earnings arise from operations, or from one-time asset sales, investment gains, or other nonsustainable transactions? In the case of Amazon, there was just one dimension to its quarterly profit return: the $5 million in net income was, at least in part, the result of a one-time foreign currency gain in the quarter of $16 million!

## DEFINITION OF HEDGING

Many firms attempt to manage their currency exposures through hedging. *Hedging* is the taking of a position — either acquiring a cash flow, an asset, or a contract (including a forward contract) — that will rise (or fall) in value and offset a fall (or rise) in the value of an existing position. Hedging therefore protects the owner of the existing asset from loss. However it also eliminates any gain from an increase in the value of the asset hedged against. The question remains: What is to be gained by the firm from hedging?

The value of a firm according to financial theory is the net present value of all expected future cash flows. The fact that these cash flows are *expected* emphasizes that nothing about the future is certain. If the reported currency value of many of these cash flows is altered by exchange rate changes, a firm that hedges its currency exposures reduces some of the variance in the value of its future expected cash flows. *Currency risk* can therefore be defined roughly as the variance in expected cash flows arising from unexpected exchange rate changes.

Exhibit 8.2 illustrates the distribution of expected net cash flows of the individual firm. Hedging these cash flows narrows the distribution of the cash flows about the mean of the distribution. Currency hedging reduces risk. Reduction of risk is not, however, the same as adding value or return. The value of the firm depicted in Exhibit 8.2 would be increased only if hedging actually shifted the mean of the distribution to the right. In fact, if hedging is not "free," meaning that the firm must expend resources to undertake hedging activity, then hedging will add value only if the rightward shift is sufficiently large to compensate for the cost of hedging.

## REASONS NOT TO HEDGE

Hence the key question: Is a reduction in the variability of cash flows sufficient reason for currency risk management? This question is actually a continuing debate in multinational financial management. Opponents of currency hedging commonly make the following arguments:

- Shareholders are much more capable of diversifying currency risk than the management of the firm. If shareholders do not wish to accept the currency risk of any specific firm, they can diversify their portfolios to manage the currency risk in a way that satisfies their individual preferences and risk tolerance.

**EXHIBIT 8.2**

Impact of
Hedging on the
Expected Cash
Flows of the Firm

Hedging reduces the variability of expected cash flows about the mean of the distribution.
This reduction of distribution variance is a reduction of risk.

- As noted earlier, currency risk management does not increase the expected cash flows of the firm. Currency risk management normally consumes some of a firm's resources and so reduces cash flow. The impact on value is a combination of the reduction of cash flow (which by itself lowers value) and the reduction in variance (which by itself increases value).
- Management often conducts hedging activities that benefit management at the expense of the shareholders. The field of finance called *agency theory* frequently argues that management is generally more risk-averse than shareholders. If the firm's goal is to maximize shareholder wealth, hedging is probably not in the best interest of the shareholders.
- Managers cannot outguess the market. If and when markets are in equilibrium with respect to parity conditions, the expected net present value of the hedging is zero.
- Management's motivation to reduce variability is sometimes driven by accounting reasons. Management may believe that it will be criticized more severely for incurring foreign exchange losses in its financial statements than for incurring similar or even higher cash costs in avoiding the foreign exchange loss. Foreign exchange losses appear in the income statement as a highly visible separate line item or as a footnote, but the higher costs of protection are buried in operating or interest expenses.
- Efficient-market theorists believe that investors can see through the "accounting veil" and therefore have already factored the foreign exchange effect into a firm's market valuation.

## REASONS TO HEDGE

Proponents of hedging cite the following reasons for supporting it:

- Reduction in risk in future cash flows improves the planning capability of the firm. If the firm can predict future cash flows more accurately, it may be able to undertake specific investments or activities that it might otherwise not consider.
- Reduction of risk in future cash flows reduces the likelihood that the firm's cash flows will fall below a necessary minimum. A firm must generate sufficient cash flows to make debt-service payments in order for it to continue to operate. This minimum cash flow point, often referred to as the point of *financial distress*, lies left of the center of the distribution of expected cash flows. Hedging reduces the likelihood of the firm's cash flows falling to this level.
- Management has a comparative advantage over the individual shareholder in knowing the actual currency risk of the firm. Regardless of the level of disclosure provided by the firm to the public, management always possesses an advantage in the depth and breadth of knowledge concerning the real risks and returns inherent in any firm's business.
- Markets are usually in disequilibrium because of structural and institutional imperfections, as well as unexpected external shocks (such as an oil crisis or terrorist attack). Management is in a better position than shareholders to recognize disequilibrium conditions and to take advantage of one-time opportunities to enhance firm value through *selective hedging*. "Selective hedging" refers to the hedging of large, singular, exceptional exposures or the occasional use of hedging when management has a definite expectation of the direction of exchange rates.

## Measurement of Transaction Exposure

Transaction exposure measures gains or losses that arise from the settlement of existing financial obligations whose terms are stated in a foreign currency. Transaction exposure arises from

1. Purchasing or selling on credit goods or services when prices are stated in foreign currencies
2. Borrowing or lending funds when repayment is to be made in a foreign currency
3. Being a party to an unperformed foreign exchange forward contract
4. Otherwise acquiring assets or incurring liabilities denominated in foreign currencies

The most common example of transaction exposure arises when a firm has a receivable or payable denominated in a foreign currency. As illustrated in Exhibit 8.3, the total transaction exposure consists of *quotation*, *backlog*, and *billing exposures*. A transaction exposure is actually created at the first moment the seller quotes a price in foreign currency terms to a potential buyer $(t_1)$. The quote can be verbal, as in a telephone quote, or written, as a bid or even a printed price list. The placing of an order $(t_2)$ converts the potential exposure created at the time of the quotation $(t_1)$ into actual exposure, called backlog exposure because the product has not yet been shipped or billed. Backlog

**EXHIBIT 8.3**

The Life Span of a Transaction Exposure

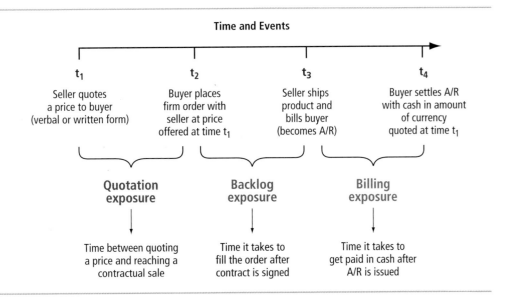

**Time and Events**

t₁ — Seller quotes a price to buyer (verbal or written form)

t₂ — Buyer places firm order with seller at price offered at time t₁

t₃ — Seller ships product and bills buyer (becomes A/R)

t₄ — Buyer settles A/R with cash in amount of currency quoted at time t₁

**Quotation exposure** — Time between quoting a price and reaching a contractual sale

**Backlog exposure** — Time it takes to fill the order after contract is signed

**Billing exposure** — Time it takes to get paid in cash after A/R is issued

exposure lasts until the goods are shipped and billed ($t_3$), at which time it becomes billing exposure. Billing exposure remains until the seller receives payment ($t_4$).

## PURCHASING OR SELLING ON OPEN ACCOUNT

Suppose that Trident Corporation sells merchandise on open account to a Belgian buyer for €1,800,000, payment to be made in 60 days. The current exchange rate is $1.2000/€, and Trident expects to exchange the euros received for €1,800,000 × $1.2000/€ = $2,160,000 when payment is received.

Transaction exposure arises because of the risk that Trident will receive something other than the $2,160,000 expected. For example, if the euro weakens to $1.1000/€ when payment is received, Trident will receive only €1,800,000 × $1.1000/€ = $1,980,000, or some $180,000 less than expected. If the euro should strengthen to $1.3000/€, however, Trident receives €1,800,000 × $1.3000/€ = $2,340,000, an increase of $180,000 over the amount expected. Thus exposure is the chance of either a loss or a gain.

Trident might have avoided transaction exposure by invoicing the Belgian buyer in dollars. Of course, if Trident attempted to sell only in dollars it might not have obtained the sale in the first place. Avoiding transaction exposure by not having a sale is counter-productive to the well-being of the firm! Even if the Belgian buyer agrees to pay in dollars, transaction exposure is not eliminated. Instead, it is transferred to the Belgian buyer, whose dollar account payable has an unknown cost in euros 60 days hence.

## BORROWING AND LENDING

A second example of transaction exposure arises when funds are borrowed or loaned, and the amount involved is denominated in a foreign currency. For example, PepsiCo's largest bottler outside of the United States in 1994 was Grupo Embotellador de

Mexico (Gemex). In mid-December, 1994, Gemex had U.S. dollar debt of $264 million. At that time Mexico's new peso (Ps) was traded at Ps3.45/US$, a pegged rate that had been maintained with minor variations since January 1, 1993, when the new currency unit was created. On December 22, 1994, the new peso was allowed to float because of economic and political events within Mexico, and in one day it sank to Ps4.65/US$. For most of the following January it traded in a range near Ps5.50/US$.

For Gemex, the increase in the peso amount of its dollar debt was:

Dollar debt in mid-December, 1994: US$264,000,000 × Ps3.45/US$=          Ps910,800,000
Dollar debt in mid-January, 1995: US$264,000,000 × Ps5.50/US$=          Ps1,452,000,000
Dollar debt increase measured in new Mexican pesos                       Ps541,200,000

The number of pesos needed to repay the dollar debt increased by 59%! In U.S. dollar terms the drop in the value of the pesos caused Gemex to need the peso-equivalent of an additional US$98,400,000 to repay. This increase in debt was the result of transaction exposure.

## OTHER CAUSES OF TRANSACTION EXPOSURE

When a firm buys a forward exchange contract, it deliberately creates transaction exposure. This risk is usually incurred to hedge an existing transaction exposure. For example, a U.S. firm might want to offset an existing obligation to purchase ¥100 million to pay for an import from Japan in 90 days. One way to offset this payment is to purchase ¥100 million in the forward market today for delivery in 90 days. In this manner the firm neutralizes any change in value of the Japanese yen relative to the dollar. If the yen increases in value, an unhedged account payable would cost more dollars, a transaction loss. The forward contract, however, has already fixed the amount of dollars needed to buy the ¥100 million. Thus the potential transaction loss (or gain) on the account payable has been offset by the transaction gain (or loss) on the forward contract.

Note that foreign currency cash balances do not create transaction exposure, even though their home-currency value changes immediately with a change in exchange rates. No legal obligation exists to move the cash from one country and currency to another. If such an obligation did exist, it would show on the books as a payable (for example, dividends declared and payable) or receivable and then be counted as part of transaction exposure. Nevertheless, the foreign exchange value of cash balances does change when exchange rates change. Such a change is reflected in the consolidated statement of cash flows and the consolidated balance sheet, as we will discuss in Chapter 10.

## CONTRACTUAL HEDGES

Foreign exchange transaction exposure can be managed by *contractual, operating,* and *financial hedges.* The main contractual hedges employ the forward, money, futures, and options markets. Operating and financial hedges use risk-sharing agreements, leads and lags in payment terms, swaps, and other strategies to be discussed in later chapters.

The term *natural hedge* refers to an offsetting operating cash flow, a payable arising from the conduct of business. A *financial hedge* refers to either an offsetting debt obligation (such as a loan) or some type of financial derivative such as an interest rate swap. It is important to distinguish hedges in the same way finance distinguishes cash flows — *operating* from *financing.*

The following case illustrates how contractual hedging techniques may protect against transaction exposure.

## Trident's Transaction Exposure

Maria Gonzalez is the chief financial officer of Trident. She has just concluded negotiations for the sale of telecommunications equipment to Regency, a British firm, for £1,000,000. This single sale is quite large in relation to Trident's present business. The sale is made in March with payment due three months later in June. Maria has collected the following financial and market information for the analysis of her currency exposure problem.

- Spot exchange rate: $1.7640/£
- Three-month forward rate: $1.7540/£ (a 2.2676% per annum discount on the pound)
- Trident's cost of capital: 12.0%
- U.K. three-month borrowing interest rate: 10.0% (or 2.5%/quarter)
- U.K. three-month investment interest rate: 8.0% (or 2.0%/quarter)
- U.S. three-month borrowing interest rate: 8.0% (or 2.0%/quarter)
- U.S. three-month investment interest rate: 6.0% (or 1.5%/quarter)
- June put option in the over-the-counter (bank) market for £1,000,000; strike price $1.75 (nearly at-the-money); 1.5% premium
- Trident's foreign exchange advisory service forecasts that the spot rate in three months will be $1.76/£.

Like many manufacturing firms, Trident operates on relatively narrow margins. Although Maria and Trident would be very happy if the pound appreciated versus the dollar, concerns center on the possibility that the pound will fall. When Maria budgeted this specific contract, she determined that its minimum acceptable margin was at a sales price of $1,700,000. The *budget rate*, the lowest acceptable dollar per pound exchange rate, was therefore established at $1.70/£. Any exchange rate below this budget rate would result in Trident actually losing money on the transaction.

Four alternatives are available to Trident to manage the exposure:

1. Remain unhedged.
2. Hedge in the forward market.
3. Hedge in the money market.
4. Hedge in the options market.

### UNHEDGED POSITION

Maria may decide to accept the transaction risk. If she believes the foreign exchange advisor, she expects to receive £1,000,000 × $1.76 = $1,760,000 in three months. However, that amount is at risk. If the pound should fall to, say, $1.65/£, she will receive only $1,650,000. Exchange risk is not one-sided, however; if the transaction is left uncovered and the pound strengthened even more than forecast by the advisor, Trident will receive considerably more than $1,760,000.

The essence of an unhedged approach is as follows.

(Today)

Do nothing.

(Three months hence)

Receive £1,000,000.
Sell £1,000,000 spot and receive
dollars at that day's spot rate.

## FORWARD MARKET HEDGE

A "forward hedge" involves a forward (or futures) contract and a source of funds to fulfill that contract. The forward contract is entered into at the time the transaction exposure is created. In Trident's case, that would be in March, when the sale to Regency was booked as an account receivable.

When a foreign currency-denominated sale such as this is made, it is booked at the spot rate of exchange existing on the booking date. In the case of Trident, the spot rate on the day it is booked as an account receivable is $1.7640/£, so the sale is recorded on Trident's books as a sale of $1,764,000. Funds to fulfill the contract will be available in June, when Regency pays £1,000,000 to Trident. If funds to fulfill the forward contract are on hand or are due because of a business operation, the hedge is considered *covered*, *perfect*, or *square* because no residual foreign exchange risk exists. Funds on hand or to be received are matched by funds to be paid.

In some situations funds to fulfill the forward exchange contract are not already available or due to be received later, but must be purchased in the spot market at some future date. Such a hedge is *open* or *uncovered*. It involves considerable risk because the hedger must take a chance on purchasing foreign exchange at an uncertain future spot rate in order to fulfill the forward contract. Purchase of such funds at a later date is referred to as "covering."

Should Trident wish to hedge its transaction exposure in the forward market, it will sell £1,000,000 forward today at the three-month forward quotation of $1.7540 per pound. This is a covered transaction in which the firm no longer has any foreign exchange risk. In three months the firm will receive £1,000,000 from the British buyer, deliver that sum to the bank against its forward sale, and receive $1,754,000. This certain sum is $6,000 less than the uncertain $1,760,000 expected from the unhedged position because the forward market quotation differs from the firm's three-month forecast. This would then be recorded on Trident's books as a foreign exchange loss of $10,000 ($1,764,000 as booked, $1,754,000 as settled).

The essence of a forward hedge is as follows.

(Today)

Sell £1,000,000
forward at $1.7540/£.

(Three months hence)

Receive £1,000,000.
Deliver £1,000,000 against
    forward sale.
Receive $1,754,000.

If Maria's forecast of future rates were identical to that implicit in the forward quotation, that is, $1.7540, expected receipts would be the same whether or not the firm hedges. However, realized receipts under the unhedged alternative could vary considerably from the certain receipts when the transaction is hedged. Believing that the forward rate is an unbiased estimate of the future spot rate does not prevent us from using the forward hedge to eliminate the risk of an unexpected change in the future spot rate.

## MONEY MARKET HEDGE

Like a forward market hedge, a money market hedge also includes a contract and a source of funds to fulfill that contract. In this instance the contract is a loan agreement. The firm seeking the money market hedge borrows in one currency and exchanges the proceeds for another currency. Funds to fulfill the contract — that is, to repay the loan — may be generated from business operations, in which case the money market hedge is covered. Alternatively, funds to repay the loan may be purchased in the foreign exchange spot market when the loan matures. In this instance the money market hedge is uncovered or open.

A money market hedge can cover a single transaction, such as Trident's £1,000,000 receivable, or repeated transactions. Hedging repeated transactions is called *matching*. It requires the firm to match the expected foreign currency cash inflows and outflows by currency and maturity. For example, if Trident had numerous sales denominated in pounds to British customers over a long period of time, it would have somewhat predictable U.K. pound cash inflows. The appropriate money market hedge technique would be to borrow U.K. pounds in an amount matching the typical size and maturity of expected pound inflows. Then, if the pound depreciated or appreciated, the foreign exchange effect on cash inflows in pounds would be approximately offset by the effect on cash outflows in pounds from repaying the pound loan plus interest.

The structure of a money market hedge resembles that of a forward hedge. The difference is that the cost of the money market hedge is determined by differential interest rates, while the cost of the forward hedge is a function of the forward rate quotation. In efficient markets, interest rate parity should ensure that these costs are nearly the same, but not all markets are efficient at all times. Furthermore, the difference in interest rates facing a private firm borrowing in two separate national markets may not be the same as the difference in risk-free government bill rates or eurocurrency interest rates in these same markets. It is the latter differential that is relevant for interest rate parity.

To hedge in the money market, Maria will borrow pounds in London at once, immediately convert the borrowed pounds into dollars, and repay the pound loan in three months with the proceeds from the sale. How much should she borrow? She will need to borrow just enough to repay both the principal and interest with the sale proceeds. The borrowing interest rate will be 10% per annum, or 2.5% for three months. Therefore, the amount to borrow now for repayment in three months is

$$\frac{£1,000,000}{1 + .025} = £975,610$$

Maria should borrow £975,610 now and in three months repay that amount plus £24,390 of interest from the sale proceeds of the account receivable. Trident would exchange the £975,610 loan proceeds for dollars at the current spot exchange rate of $1.7640/£, receiving $1,720,976 at once.

The money-market hedge, if selected by Trident, actually creates a pound-denominated liability, that is, a pound bank loan, to offset the pound-denominated asset, the account receivable. The money market hedge works as a hedge by matching assets and liabilities according to their currency of denomination. Using a simple T-account to illustrate Trident's balance sheet, we see that the loan (principal and interest payable) in British pounds offsets the pound-denominated account receivable:

| Assets | | Liabilities and Net Worth | |
|--------|--|---------------------------|--|
| Account receivable | £1,000,000 | Bank loan (principal) | £975,610 |
|  |  | Interest payable | 24,390 |
|  | £1,000,000 |  | £1,000,000 |

The loan acts as a *balance sheet hedge* — a money market hedge in this case — against the pound-denominated account receivable.

To compare the forward hedge with the money market hedge we must analyze how Trident's loan proceeds will be utilized for the next three months. Remember that the loan proceeds are received today but the forward contract proceeds are received in three months. For comparison purposes, we must calculate either the future value in three months of the loan proceeds or the present value of the forward contract proceeds. (We will use future value for pedagogical reasons, but correct use of present value would give the same comparative results.)

Because both the forward contract proceeds and the loan proceeds are relatively certain, it is possible to choose from the two alternatives the one that yields the higher dollar receipts. This result, in turn, depends on the assumed rate of investment of the loan proceeds.

At least three logical choices exist for an assumed investment rate for the loan proceeds for the next three months. First, if Trident is cash rich, the loan proceeds might be invested in U.S. dollar money market instruments that have been assumed to yield 6% per annum. Second, Maria might simply use the pound loan proceeds to substitute for an equal dollar loan that Trident would otherwise have undertaken at an assumed rate of 8% per annum. Third, Maria might invest the loan proceeds in the general operations of the firm, in which case the cost of capital of 12% per annum would be the appropriate rate. The future value of the loan proceeds at the end of three months under each of these three investment assumptions would be as follows:

| Received Today | Invested in | Rate | Future Value in Three Months |
|----------------|-------------|------|------------------------------|
| $1,720,976 | Treasury bill | 6%/yr or 1.5%/quarter | $1,746,791 |
| $1,720,976 | Debt cost | 8%/yr or 2.0%/quarter | $1,755,396 |
| $1,720,976 | Cost of capital | 12%/yr or 3.0%/quarter | $1,772,605 |

Because the proceeds in three months from the forward hedge would be $1,754,000, the money market hedge is superior to the forward hedge if Maria used the loan proceeds to replace a dollar loan (8%) or to conduct general business operations (12%). The forward hedge would be preferable if Trident merely invested the pound loan proceeds in dollar-denominated money market instruments at 6% annual interest.

A break-even investment rate can be calculated that would make Trident indifferent between the forward hedge and the money market hedge. Assume that $r$ is the unknown three-month investment rate, expressed as a decimal, that would equalize the proceeds from the forward and money market hedges. We have

$$\text{(Loan proceeds)} (1 + \text{rate}) = \text{(forward proceeds)}$$
$$\$1,720,976 (1 + r) = \$1,754,000$$
$$r = 0.0192$$

We can convert this three-month (90-day) investment rate to an annual whole percentage equivalent, assuming a 360-day financial year, as follows:

$$0.0192 \times \frac{360}{90} \times 100 = 7.68\%$$

In other words, if Maria can invest the loan proceeds at a rate higher than 7.68% per annum, she would prefer the money market hedge. If she can only invest at a rate lower than 7.68%, she would prefer the forward hedge.

The essence of the money market hedge is as follows.

(Today)

(Three months hence)

Borrow £975,610.
Exchange £975,610 for
 dollars at $1.7640/£.
Receive $1,720,976 cash.

Receive £1,000,000.
Repay £975,610 loan plus £24,390
 interest, for a total of £1,000,000.

The money market hedge therefore results in cash received up front (at the start of the period), which can then be carried forward in time for comparison with the other hedging alternatives.

Exhibit 8.4 shows the value of Trident's £1,000,000 account receivable over a range of possible ending spot exchange rates. The value of the receivable is shown uncovered, covered with a forward contract hedge, and covered with a money market hedge. Exhibit 8.4 makes it clear that the firm's view of likely exchange rate changes aids in the hedging choice. If the firm expects the exchange rate to move against Trident — to the left of $1.76/£, the money market hedge is the clearly preferred alternative. At a guaranteed value of $1,772,605, the money market hedge is by far the most profitable choice. If Trident expects the exchange rate to move in Trident's favor, to the right of $1.76/£, the choice of the hedge is more complex. Consider the following points:

- If the spot rate is expected to move to the right of $1.77/£, the unhedged alternative always provides the highest U.S. dollar value for the receivable.
- If Maria is worried that her expectations may prove incorrect, the decision to remain unhedged does not assure Trident of meeting its budgeted exchange rate of $1.70/£. This is an outcome the firm cannot afford. The possibility always exists of a major political or economic event disrupting international currency markets unexpectedly.
- If the spot rate is expected to move to the right of $1.77/£, but not far to the right, for example to $1.78/£, the expected benefits of remaining unhedged are probably outweighed by the risks of remaining unhedged. The money market hedge is still the preferred choice.

**EXHIBIT 8.4**

Valuation of Cash
Flows by Hedging
Alternative for
Trident

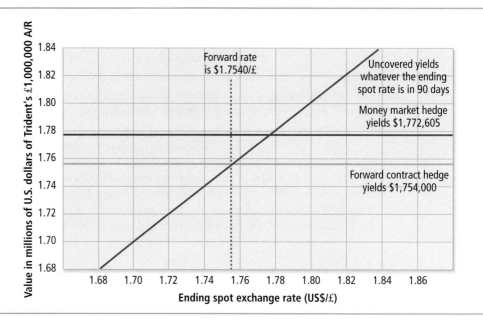

Exhibit 8.4 also helps Maria focus on exactly what she wishes she could achieve: a position that provides her protection on the downside (to the left of $1.76/£), but still allows her to benefit on the upside (to the right of $1.76/£). This is the basic advantage of an option hedge.

## OPTIONS MARKET HEDGE

Maria could also cover her £1,000,000 exposure by purchasing a put option. This technique allows her to speculate on the upside potential for appreciation of the pound while limiting downside risk to a known amount.

Given the earlier quote, Maria could purchase from her bank a three-month put option on £1,000,000 at an at-the-money (ATM) strike price of $1.75/£ and a premium cost of 1.50%. The cost of this option with strike price of $1.75, a strike price which would be considered close to forward-at-the-money, is

$$\text{(Size of option)} \times \text{(premium)} \times \text{(spot rate)} = \text{cost of option}$$
$$£1,000,000 \times 0.015 \times \$1.7640 = \$26,460$$

Because we are using future value to compare the various hedging alternatives, it is necessary to project the premium cost of the option forward three months. Once again we could justify several investment rates. We will use the cost of capital of 12% per annum or 3% per quarter. Therefore the premium cost of the put option as of June would be $26,460(1.03) = $27,254.

When the £1,000,000 is received in June, the value in dollars depends on the spot rate at that time. The upside potential is unlimited, the same as in the unhedged alternative. At any exchange rate above $1.75/£ Trident would allow its option to expire unexercised and would exchange the pounds for dollars at the spot rate. If the expected rate of $1.76/£ materializes, for example, Trident would exchange the £1,000,000 in the spot market for $1,760,000. Net proceeds would be $1,760,000 minus the $27,254 cost of the option, or $1,732,746.

In contrast to the unhedged alternative, downside risk is limited with an option. If the pound depreciates below $1.75/£, Maria would exercise her option to sell (put) £1,000,000 at $1.75/£, receiving $1,750,000 gross, but $1,722,746 net of the $27,254 cost of the option. Although this downside result is lower than the downside of the forward or money market hedges, the upside potential is not limited the way it is with those hedges. Thus, whether the option strategy is superior to a forward or money market hedge depends on the degree to which management is risk averse.

The essence of the at-the-money (ATM) option market hedge is as follows.

(Today)

Buy put option to
sell pounds at $1.75/£
Pay $26,460 for put option

(Three months hence)

Receive £1,000,000.
Either deliver £1,000,000 against put,
receiving $1,750,000, or sell £1,000,000
spot if current spot rate >$1.75/£.

We can calculate a trading range for the pound that defines the break-even points for the option compared with the other strategies. The upper bound of the range is determined by comparison with the forward rate. The pound must appreciate enough above the $1.7540/£ forward rate to cover the $0.0273/£ cost of the option. Therefore the break-even upside spot price of the pound must be $1.7540 + $0.0273 = $1.7813. If the spot pound appreciates above $1.7813/£, proceeds under the option strategy will be greater than under the forward hedge. If the spot pound ends up below $1.7813/£, the forward hedge would be superior in retrospect.

The lower bound of the range is determined by a comparison with the unhedged strategy. If the spot price falls below $1.75/£, Maria will exercise her put option and sell the proceeds at $1.75/£. The net proceeds per pound will be $1.75/£ less the $0.0273 cost of the option, or $1.7221/£. If the spot rate falls below $1.7221/£, the net proceeds from exercising the option will be greater than the net proceeds from selling the unhedged pounds in the spot market. At any spot rate above $1.7221/£, the spot proceeds from the unhedged alternative will be greater. These rates and values are summarized as follows:

| Put Option Strike Price | ATM Option $1.75/£ |
| --- | --- |
| Option cost (future value) | $27,254 |
| Proceeds if exercised | $1,750,000 |
| Minimum net proceeds | $1,722,746 |
| Maximum net proceeds | Unlimited |
| Break-even spot rate (upside) | $1.7813/£ |
| Break-even spot rate (downside) | $1.7221/£ |

## COMPARISON OF ALTERNATIVES

The four alternatives available to Maria Gonzalez and Trident are shown in Exhibit 8.5. The forward hedge yields a certain $1,754,000 in three months. The money market hedge, if the loan proceeds are invested at the 12% cost of capital, yields $1,772,605, preferable to the forward market hedge.

**EXHIBIT 8.5**

Trident's Hedging Alternatives, Including an ATM Put Option

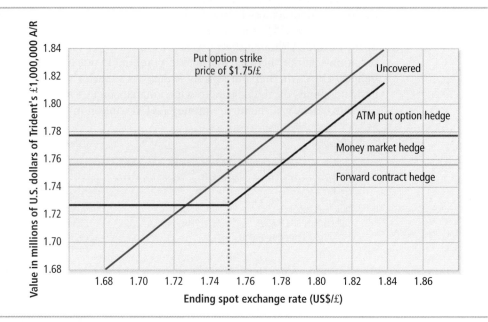

If Maria does not hedge, she can expect $1,760,000 in three months (calculated at the expected spot rate of $1.76/£). However, this sum is at risk and might be greater or smaller. Under conditions when the forward rate is accepted as the most likely future spot rate, the expected results from an unhedged position are identical to the certain results from the forward hedge. Under such circumstances the advantage of hedging over remaining unhedged is the reduction of uncertainty.

The put option offers a unique alternative. If the exchange rate moves in Trident's favor, the option offers nearly the same upside potential as the unhedged alternative except for the upfront costs. If, however, the exchange rate moves against Trident, the put option limits the downside risk to net receipts of $1,722,746.

Foreign currency options have a variety of hedging uses beyond the one illustrated here. A put option is useful to construction firms or other exporters when they must submit a fixed-price bid in a foreign currency without knowing until some later date whether their bid is successful. A put option can be used to hedge the foreign exchange risk either for the bidding period alone or for the entire period of potential exposure if the bid is won. If the bid is rejected, the loss is limited to the cost of the option. In contrast, if the risk is hedged by a forward contract and the bid is rejected, the forward contract must be reversed or eventually fulfilled at an unknown potential loss or gain. The bidder has been holding what turned out to be an uncovered forward contract.

## STRATEGY CHOICE AND OUTCOME

The preceding section compared hedging alternatives available to Trident. Trident, like all firms attempting to hedge transaction exposure, must decide on a strategy before the exchange rate changes occur. How will Maria Gonzalez of Trident choose among the alternative hedging strategies? She must select on the basis of two decision criteria: (1) the *risk tolerance* of Trident, as expressed in its stated policies; and (2) her own *view* or expectation of the direction (and distance) the exchange rate will move over the coming 90-day period.

Trident's risk tolerance is a combination of management's philosophy toward transaction exposure and the specific goals of treasury activities. Many firms believe that currency risk is simply a part of doing business internationally, and therefore start their analysis from an unhedged baseline. Other firms, however, view currency risk as unacceptable. They either start their analysis from a full forward contract cover baseline or simply mandate that all transaction exposures be fully covered by forward contracts regardless of the value of other hedging alternatives. The treasury in such firms operates as a cost or service center for the firm. On the other hand, if the treasury in a firm operates as a profit center, it might tolerate more risk.

The final choice among hedges — if Maria Gonzalez does expect the pound to appreciate — combines the firm's risk tolerance, Maria's view, and Maria's confidence in her view. Transaction exposure management with contractual hedges requires managerial judgment.

## Management of an Account Payable

The Trident case as we've discussed it so far assumes a foreign currency-denominated receivable. The management of an account payable, where the firm is required to make a foreign currency payment at a future date, is similar but not identical in form.

If Trident had a £1,000,000 account payable in 90 days, the hedging choices would appear as follows:

1. **Remain unhedged.** Trident could wait 90 days, exchange dollars for pounds at that time, and make its payment. If Trident expects the spot rate in 90 days to be $1.76/£, the payment would be expected to cost $1,760,000. This amount is, however, uncertain; the spot exchange rate in 90 days could be very different from that expected.

2. **Use forward market hedge.** Trident could buy £1,000,000 forward, locking in a rate of $1.7540/£ and a total dollar cost of $1,754,000. This is $6,000 less than the expected cost of remaining unhedged, and it is less risky. Therefore, it might be deemed preferable.

3. **Use money market hedge.** The money market hedge is distinctly different for a payable as opposed to a receivable. To implement a money market hedge in this case, Trident would exchange U.S. dollars spot and invest them for 90 days in a pound-denominated interest-bearing account. It would then use the principal and interest in British pounds at the end of the 90-day period to pay the £1,000,000 account payable.

In order to ensure that the principal and interest exactly equal the £1,000,000 due in 90 days, Trident would discount the £1,000,000 by the pound investment interest rate of 8% per annum for 90 days (2%) in order to determine the pounds needed today:

$$\frac{£1,000,000}{\left[1 + \left(.08 \times \dfrac{90}{360}\right)\right]} = £980,392.16$$

This £980,392.16 needed today would require $1,729,411.77 at the current spot rate of $1.7640/£:

$$£980,392.16 \times \$1.7640/£ = \$1,729,411.77$$

Finally, in order to compare the money market hedge outcome with the other hedging alternatives, the $1,729,411.77 cost today must be carried forward 90 days to the same future date as the other hedge choices. If the current dollar cost is carried forward at Trident's WACC of 12%, the total future value cost of the money market hedge is $1,781,294.12.

$$\$1,729,411.77 \times \left[ 1 + \left( .12 \times \frac{90}{360} \right) \right] = \$1,781,294.12$$

This is higher than the forward hedge and therefore unattractive.

4. **Use option hedge.** Trident could cover its £1,000,000 account payable by purchasing a call option on £1,000,000. A June call option on British pounds with a near at-the-money strike price of $1.75/£ would cost 1.5% (premium) or

$$£1,000,000 \times 0.015 \times \$1.7640/£ = £26,460$$

This premium, regardless of whether the call option is exercised or not, will be paid up front. Its value carried forward 90 days at the WACC of 12%, as it was in the receivable example, would raise its end-of-period cost to $27,254.

If the spot rate in 90 days is less than $1.75/£, the option would be allowed to expire and the £1,000,000 for the payable would be purchased on the spot market. The total cost of the call option hedge if the option is not exercised is theoretically smaller than any other alternative (with the exception of remaining unhedged), because the option premium is still paid and lost.

If the spot rate in 90 days exceeds $1.75/£, the call option would be exercised. The total cost of the call option hedge if exercised is as follows:

| | |
|---|---:|
| Exercise call option (£1,000,000 × $1.75/£) | $1,750,000 |
| Call option premium (carried forward 90 days) | 27,254 |
| Total maximum expense of call option hedge | $1,777,254 |

The four hedging methods of managing a £1,000,000 account payable for Trident are summarized in Exhibit 8.6. The costs of the forward hedge and money market hedge are certain. The cost of using the call option hedge is calculated as a maximum, and the cost of remaining unhedged is highly uncertain.

As with Trident's account receivable, the final hedging choice depends on the confidence of Maria's exchange rate expectations and her willingness to bear risk. The forward hedge provides the lowest cost of making the account payable payment that is certain. If the dollar strengthens against the pound, ending up at a spot rate less than $1.75/£, the call option could potentially be the lowest cost hedge. Given an expected spot rate of $1.76/£, however, the forward hedge appears to be the preferred alternative.

## Risk Management in Practice

As many different approaches to exposure management exist as there are firms. A variety of surveys of corporate risk management practices in recent years in the United States, the United Kingdom, Finland, Australia, and Germany indicate no real consensus exists regarding the best approach. The following is our attempt to assimilate the basic results of these surveys and combine them with our own personal experiences in industry.

## EXHIBIT 8.6

Valuation of Hedging Alternatives for an Account Payable

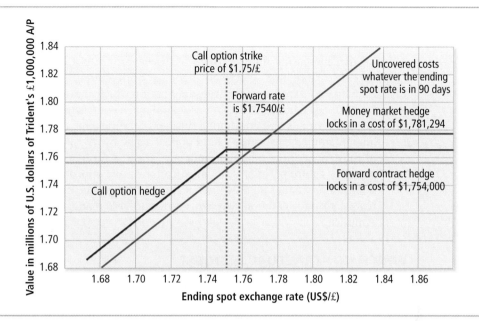

## WHICH GOALS?

The treasury function of most firms, the functional group typically responsible for transaction exposure management, is usually considered a cost center. It is not expected to add profit to the firm's bottom line (which is not the same thing as saying it is not expected to add value to the firm). Currency risk managers are expected to err on the conservative side when managing the firm's money. But, as illustrated in *Real World Example 8.2*, some MNEs have become a bit too aggressive in currency management according to the IRS.

## WHICH EXPOSURES?

Transaction exposures exist before they are actually booked as foreign currency-denominated receivables and payables. However, many firms do not allow the hedging of quotation exposure or backlog exposure as a matter of policy. The reasoning is

## Real World Example 8.2
### MANIPULATION OF CURRENCY GAINS AND LOSSES

The Internal Revenue Service (IRS) of the United States became increasingly concerned in the spring of 2002 about the possible manipulation of corporate earnings—specifically currency-related gains and losses. The government agency detected more and more companies that were creating a "circular flow of funds" in which the parent company and a foreign subsidiary would exchange cash flows for a very short time (in several cases overnight), suffering foreign exchange losses on the transactions. The losses were then used to reduce tax liabilities in the United States. The cash flows exchanged were suspicious because they reflected no underlying business reason. One set of potential solutions under consideration is the elimination of daily calculation of currency gains and losses, as well as requiring all international transactions reported for tax purposes to reflect an underlying business reason.

straightforward: Until the transaction exists on the accounting books of the firm, the probability of the exposure actually occurring is considered to be less than 100%. Conservative hedging policies dictate that contractual hedges be placed only on existing exposures.

An increasing number of firms, however, are not only actively hedging backlog exposures but also selectively hedging both quotation and anticipated exposures. Anticipated exposures are transactions for which there are — at present — no contracts or agreements between parties, but such contracts are anticipated on the basis of historical trends and continuing business relationships. Although on the surface hedging anticipated exposures would appear to be overly speculative behavior on the part of these firms, it may be that hedging expected foreign-currency payables and receivables for future periods is the most conservative approach to protect the firm's future operating revenues against unexpected exchange rate changes. Exhibit 8.7 reports the results of one of the surveys of corporate risk management conducted by Bank of America.

## WHICH CONTRACTUAL HEDGES?

As might be expected, transaction exposure management programs are generally divided along an option line: those that use options and those that do not. Firms that do not use currency options rely almost exclusively on forward contracts and money market hedges. A few firms with appreciable quantities of transaction exposure actually do no hedging at all.

**EXHIBIT 8.7**

Bank of America Corporate FX Risk Management Survey Results

Source: "Corporate America: FX Risk Management 1996," Global Capital Markets Group, Bank of America, Monograph 78, Winter 1996/97, pp. 1–3.

- **Translation Exposure Management**
  80% identify this exposure; 15% fully hedge; 15% partially or selectively hedge; 70% do not hedge; forwards used 73% of the time, options used 27%
- **Transaction Exposure**
  60% identify this exposure; 30% fully hedge; 55% partially or selectively hedge; 20% do not hedge; forwards used 83% of the time, options used 17%
- **Anticipated Exposure (*billing transaction exposure*)**
  70% identify this exposure; 2% fully hedge; 55% partially or selectively hedge; 43% do not hedge; forwards used 71% of the time, options used 29%
- **Contingent Exposure (*potential future transaction exposure*)**
  52% identify this exposure; 4% fully hedge; 11% partially or selectively hedge; 85% do not hedge; forwards used 63% of the time, options used 37%
- **Economic Exposure (*operating exposure*)**
  54% identify this exposure; 5% fully hedge; 95% do not hedge; forwards used 54% of the time, options used 46%
- **Balance Sheet Exposure (*translation exposure*)**
  30% identify this exposure; 6% fully hedge; 15% partially or selectively hedge; 78% do not hedge; forwards used 74% of the time, options used 26%
- **Income Statement Exposure (*operating exposure*)**
  44% identify this exposure; 6% fully hedge; 33% partially or selectively hedge; 61% do not hedge; forwards used 66% of the time, options used 34%
- **Firm Hedging Maturities**
  21% of hedges are for maturities of less than six months; 62% are for maturities of six months to one year; 17% are for maturities over one year
- **Functional Currency of Foreign Subsidiaries (*translation exposure*)**
  33% USD; 66% local currency

**PROPORTIONAL HEDGES.**   Many MNEs have established rather rigid transaction exposure risk management policies that mandate proportional hedging. These policies generally require the use of forward contract hedges on a percentage (for instance, 50%, 60%, or 70%) of existing transaction exposures. As the maturity of the exposures lengthens, the percentage of forward cover required decreases. The remaining portion of the exposure is then selectively hedged on the basis of the firm's risk tolerance, view of exchange rate movements, and confidence level.

Although rarely acknowledged by the firms themselves, the continual use of selective hedging programs is essentially speculation against the currency markets. Significant theoretical questions remain as to whether a firm or a financial manager can consistently predict the future direction of exchange rate movements. Gunter Dufey (the University of Michigan) once noted, "it may occasionally be possible to find money lying in the street, but I would not expect to make a living at it."

## MINI-CASE

# Lufthansa's Purchase of Boeing 737s

In January 1985 Lufthansa, the national airline of Germany, under the chairmanship of Herr Heinz Ruhnau, signed a contract with Boeing (U.S.) for the purchase of 20 Boeing 737 jets. Boeing agreed to deliver the 20 aircraft to Lufthansa's specifications in one year, January 1986. Lufthansa would have a single payment due on that date of $500 million. Given a spot exchange rate of DM3.2/$ in January 1985, this was an expected purchase of DM1.6 billion.

## The Problem

Herr Heinz Ruhnau was quite concerned over the exchange rate exposure that Lufthansa was bearing in this transaction. The U.S. dollar had been steadily appreciating in value against the deutschemark for several years. Although many currency advisors and analysts had repeatedly stated they believed the dollar to be overvalued, it had continued to climb. Herr Ruhnau agreed with the majority of the currency advisors who believed the dollar would fall soon. Herr Ruhnau also knew, however, that the size of the transaction represented too large a risk to Lufthansa if left unhedged. The current 360-day forward rate was the same as the spot rate, DM3.2/$, as a result of Eurodollar and Eurodeutschemark interest rates being the same.

But Herr Ruhnau was torn between taking the most conservative strategy of locking in a forward contract for the entire amount and following his instincts that the dollar would fall in the coming year. If the dollar did fall as he expected, he could potentially save Lufthansa millions of deutschemarks in the completion of the sale. Although Herr Ruhnau did not typically involve himself in currency management issues, the sheer size and significance of this transaction required him to make the final decision.

## The Decision

Herr Ruhnau decided to compromise. He would cover one half of the total exposure, $250 million, with a forward contract at DM3.2/$, and he would leave the other half uncovered. This would allow him to reduce his total exchange rate risk significantly, but still allow him to benefit if the dollar did indeed weaken versus the deutschemark in the coming year as he expected.

## The Outcome

In the end Herr Ruhnau's expectations proved correct. As illustrated in the exhibit, the dollar did indeed fall in the coming year—to DM2.3/$ by January of 1986. This was a spot exchange rate that had not been seen since early in 1982. Although most currency analysts had predicted the dollar to fall, most were surprised by the speed and magnitude of this change.

The total cost to Lufthansa for settlement of its payment to Boeing totaled DM1.375 billion.

Half covered with forward contract:
$250,000,000 × DM3.2/$ = DM   800,000,000
Half left uncovered:
$250,000,000 × DM2.3/$ = DM   575,000,000
Total                                 DM 1,375,000,000

The problem with the outcome was that the half of the exposure which he had covered with the forward contract resulted in a cost of DM225,000,000, higher than that left uncovered. As a result, Herr Ruhnau was heavily criticized for his handling of Lufthansa's currency exposure. He was accused of recklessly speculating with Lufthansa's money, but the speculation was seen as the forward contract, not

Lufthansa 1985–1986: What Herr Ruhnau Could and Could Not See

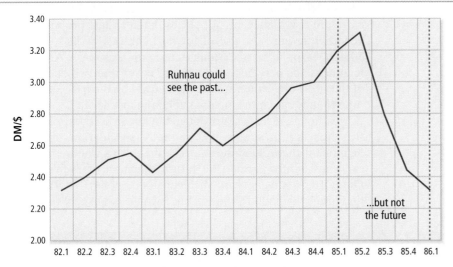

Average spot exchange rate by quarter

the amount of the dollar exposure left uncovered. Herr Ruhnau was called before the Minister of Transportation in Germany (the government authority over the national airline) to explain his actions. Discussion of his employment contract, which was due to be renewed, was postponed and eventually he was given only a short renewal. Clearly the concept of speculation takes on a completely different meaning when performance is evaluated with 20/20 hindsight!

## Case Questions

1. Do you think Heinz Ruhnau's hedging strategy made sense?
2. To what degree did he limit the upside and downside exposure of the transaction by hedging one half of it? Do you agree with his critics that he was speculating?
3. Is it fair to judge transaction exposure management effectiveness with 20/20 hindsight?

## Summary of Learning Objectives

*Distinguish between the three major foreign exchange exposures experienced by firms*

- MNEs encounter three types of currency exposure: (1) transaction exposure, (2) operating exposure, and (3) translation exposure.

- *Transaction exposure* measures gains or losses that arise from the settlement of financial obligations whose terms are stated in a foreign currency.

- *Operating exposure*, also called *economic exposure*, measures the change in the present value of the firm resulting from any change in future operating cash flows of the firm caused by an unexpected change in exchange rates.

- *Translation exposure* is the possibility that accounting-derived changes in owner's equity will occur because of the need to "translate" foreign currency financial statements of foreign subsidiaries into a single reporting currency to prepare worldwide consolidated financial statements.

*Identify foreign exchange transaction exposure*

- Transaction exposure arises from (1) purchasing or selling on credit goods or services whose prices are stated in foreign currencies; (2) borrowing or lending funds when repayment is to be made in a foreign currency; (3) being a party to an unperformed forward foreign exchange contract; and (4) otherwise acquiring assets or liabilities denominated in foreign currencies.

*Analyze the pros and cons of hedging foreign exchange transaction exposure*

- Considerable theoretical debate exists as to whether firms should hedge currency risk. Theoretically, hedging reduces the variability of the cash flows to the firm. It does not increase the cash flows to the firm. In fact, the costs of hedging may potentially lower cash flows.

*Identify the alternatives available to a firm to manage a large and significant transaction exposure*

- Transaction exposure can be managed by contractual techniques that include forward, futures, money market, and option hedges.

- The choice of which contractual hedge to use depends on the individual firm's currency risk tolerance and its expectation of the probable movement of exchange rates over the transaction exposure period.

- In general, if an exchange rate is expected to move in a firm's favor, the preferred contractual hedges are probably those which allow it to participate in some upside potential (remaining unhedged or using a currency option), but protect it against significant adverse exchange rate movements.

- In general, if the exchange rate is expected to move against the firm, the preferred contractual hedge is one which locks in an exchange rate, such as the forward contract hedge or money market hedge.

*Evaluate the institutional practices and concerns of conducting foreign exchange risk management*

- Risk management in practice requires a firm's treasury department to identify its goals. Is treasury a cost center or profit center?

- Treasury must also choose which contractual hedges it wishes to use and what proportion of the currency risk should be hedged. Additionally, treasury must determine whether the firm should buy and/or sell currency options, a historically risky strategy for some firms and banks.

## QUESTIONS

1. **Foreign exchange exposure.** Give a general definition of "foreign exchange exposure" as it relates to the operations of a multinational enterprise.

2. **Exposure types.** Explain the differences among transaction, operating, and translation exposure.

3. **Translation versus transaction exposure.** Is there any difference between translation exposure and transaction exposure? Explain.

4. **Tax exposure.** What is tax exposure and how does it relate to the triumvirate of transaction, operating, and translation exposure?

5. **Hedging.** What is a hedge?

6. **Cash flow variability.** Exhibit 8.2 in the text shows two normal distributions about a mean called expected value.

   a. What is the implication of the areas toward the center of the distributions where the hedged line is higher than the unhedged line?

   b. What is the implication of the areas toward the outlying edges of the distributions where the unhedged line is higher than the hedged line?

   c. Can an argument be made that the mean of the hedged distribution should be to the left or right of, but not the same as, the mean of the unhedged distribution? Discuss.

7. **Investor expectations.** Proponents of the efficient market hypothesis argue that an MNE should not hedge because investors can hedge themselves if they do not like the foreign exchange risks carried by the firm. Assess this argument.

8. **Creating transaction exposure.** Identify and create a hypothetical example for each of the four causes of transaction exposure.

9. **Cash balances.** Why does the holding of foreign currency cash balances not lead to transaction exposure?

10. **Natural vs. contractual hedges.** Explain the difference between a natural hedge and a contractual hedge. Give a hypothetical example of each.

11. **Risk tolerance.** What is risk tolerance? Can it be measured?

## PROBLEMS

1. **Lipitor in Indonesia.** Pfizer, the U.S.–based multinational pharmaceutical company, is evaluating an export sale of its cholesterol reduction drug, Lipitor, with a prospective Indonesian distributor. The purchase would be for 1,650 million Indonesian rupiah (Rp), which at the current spot exchange rate of Rp9,450/$, translates into nearly $175,000. Although not a big sale by Pfizer standards, company policy dictates that sales must be settled for at least a minimum gross margin, in this case, a cash settlement of $168,000 on the sale.

   The current 90-day forward rate is Rp9,950/$. Although this rate appeared unattractive, Pfizer had to contact several major banks before finding even a forward quote on the rupiah. The consensus of currency forecasters at the moment, however, is that the rupiah will hold relatively steady, possibly falling to Rp9,400 over the coming 90 to 120 days. Analyze the prospective sale and make a hedging recommendation.

2. **Embraer of Brazil.** Embraer of Brazil is one of the two leading global manufacturers of regional jets (Bombardier of Canada is the other). Regional jets are smaller than the traditional civilian airliners produced by Airbus and Boeing, seating between 50 and 100 people on average. Embraer has concluded an agreement with a regional U.S. airline to produce and deliver four aircraft one year from now for $80 million. Although Embraer will be paid in U.S. dollars, it also possesses a currency exposure of inputs — it must pay foreign suppliers $20 million for inputs one year from now (but they will be delivering the sub-components throughout the year).

The current spot rate on the Brazilian real (R$) is R$3.148/$, but it has only recently stabilized after hitting R$3.80/$ only a year ago. Forward contracts are difficult to acquire and considered expensive. Citibank Brasil has not explicitly provided Embraer a forward rate quote, but has stated that it will probably be pricing a forward off the current 4.00% U.S. dollar Eurocurrency rate and the 14.00% Brazilian government deposit note. Advise Embraer on its currency exposure.

3. **Hindustan Lever.** Unilever's subsidiary in India, Hindustan Lever, procures much of its toiletries product line from a Japanese company. Because of the shortage of working capital in India, payment terms by Indian importers are typically 180 days or longer. Hindustan Lever wishes to hedge an 8.5 million Japanese yen payable.

Although options are not available on the Indian rupee (Rs), forward rates are available against the yen. Additionally, a common practice in India is for companies like Hindustan Lever to work with a currency agent who will, in this case, lock in the current spot exchange rate in exchange for a 4.85% fee. Using the following exchange rate and interest rate data, recommend a hedging strategy.

| | |
|---|---|
| Spot rate, yen/dollar: | ¥ 120.60/$ |
| Spot rate, rupee/dollar: | Rs 47.75/$ |
| 180-day forward rate, yen/rupee: | ¥ 2.4000/Rs |
| Expected spot rate in 180 days: | ¥ 2.6000/Rs |
| 180-day rupee investment rate: | 8.000% |
| 180-day yen investment rate: | 1.500% |
| Hindustan Lever's cost of capital: | 12.00% |

4. **Mattel Toys.** Mattel is a U.S.–based company whose sales are roughly two thirds in dollars (Asia and the Americas) and one third in euros (Europe). In September Mattel delivers a large shipment of toys (primarily Barbies and Hot Wheels) to a major distributor in Antwerp.

The receivable, €30 million, is due in 90 days, standard terms for the toy industry in Europe. Mattel's treasury team has collected the following currency and market quotes. The company's foreign exchange advisors believe the euro will be at about $1.1800/€ in 90 days. Mattel's management does not use currency options in currency risk management activities. Advise Mattel on which hedging alternative is probably preferable.

| | |
|---|---|
| Spot rate: | $1.2186/€ |
| Credit Suisse 90-day forward quote: | $1.2170/€ |
| Barclays 90-day forward quote: | $1.2210/€ |
| Mattel's cost of capital: | 9.600% |
| 90-day Eurodollar interest rate: | 4.000% |
| 90-day Euroeuro interest rate: | 4.400% |
| 90-day dollar borrowing rate: | 5.600% |
| 90-day euro borrowing rate: | 6.400% |

### Tektronix

The following five problems are based on the hypothetical but typical foreign exchange transaction exposures that might be faced by Tektronix, Inc. (TEK), an actual MNE based in Beaverton, Oregon. Tek's sales in the fiscal year ending May 31, 2004 were about $1 billion. Its main products are scientific measuring instruments such as protocol analyses and simulators, network monitoring systems, transmission and cable test products, and a broad range of oscilloscopes. Part of the foreign sales were direct exports from Tek's Beaverton manufacturing and research facility. A second part of sales were passed through Tek's own foreign sales and assembly subsidiaries. A third part of sales were through joint ventures such as in Japan (Sony) and China. Tek also imported components and other materials that were used in the manufacturing operations in Beaverton. Tek's main competitors are Agilent (formerly Hewlett Packard's measuring instruments business) and Siemens (a very large German conglomerate).

5. **Tek: Italian account receivable.** Tek wishes to hedge a €4,000,000 account receivable arising from a sale to Olivetti (Italy). Payment is due in three months. Tek's Italian unit does not have ready access to local currency borrowing,

eliminating the money market hedge alternative. Citibank has offered Tek the following quotes:

| | |
|---|---|
| Spot rate: | $1.2000/€ |
| Three-month forward rate: | $1.2180/€ |

Three-month euro interest rate: 4.200% per year

Three-month put option on euros at
strike price of $1.0800/€:               3.40%

Tek's weighted average cost of capital:    9.80%

a. What are the costs of each alternative?

b. What are the risks of each alternative?

c. Which alternative should Tek choose if it prefers to play it safe?

d. Which alternative should Tek choose if it is willing to take a reasonable risk and has a directional view that the euro may be appreciating versus the dollar during the next three months?

6. **Tek: Japanese account payable.** Tek has imported components from its joint venture in Japan, Sony-Tek, with payment of ¥8,000,000 due in six months. Citibank has offered Tek the following quotes.

| | |
|---|---|
| Spot rate: | ¥108.20/$ |
| Six-month forward rate: | ¥106.20/$ |
| Six-month yen deposit rate: | 1.250% per year |
| Six-month dollar interest rate: | 4.000% per year |

Six-month call option on yen at
a strike price of ¥108/$:               2.5%

Tek's weighted average cost of capital:    9.80%

a. What are the costs of each alternative?

b. What are the risks of each alternative?

c. Which alternative should Tek choose if it is willing to take a reasonable risk and has a directional view that the yen may be depreciating versus the dollar during the next six months?

7. **Tek: British Telecom bidding.** Tek has made a £1,500,000 bid to supply and install a network monitoring system for British Telecom in Manchester, U.K. The bid is good for 30 days, at which time the winner of the bidding process will be announced. Other bidders are expected to be Agilent, Siemens, and at least two British firms. If Tek wins the bid it will have 60 days to build and install the system. During this 60-day period the £1,500,000 will be accounted for as backlog. Upon delivery and testing of the system, British Telecom will make full payment 30 days later. During this

month Tek will account for the £1,500,000 as an account receivable. Barclays Bank (U.K.) has offered Tek the following quotes:

| | |
|---|---|
| Spot rate: | $1.8418/£ |
| One-month forward rate: | 1.8368/£ |
| Four-month forward rate: | 1.8268/£ |
| One-month £ investment rate: | 4.000% per year |
| One-month £ borrowing rate: | 6.500% per year |
| Four-month £ investment rate: | 4.125% per year |
| Four-month £ borrowing rate: | 6.500% per year |

One-month put option on
pound ($1.85/£ strike):          $0.006/£ premium

Four-month put option on
pound ($1.85/£ strike):          $0.012/£ premium

Tek's weighted average cost
of capital:                              9.80%

What should Tek do to hedge this bid?

8. **Tek: Swedish price list.** Tek offers oscilloscopes and other off-the-shelf products through foreign-currency–denominated price lists. The prices are valid for three months only. One example is a Swedish price list expressed in Swedish kronor. In effect, customers are given a cost-free call option on products with a fixed dollar/krona exchange rate. During a typical three-month period, Tek could expect to sell SKr5,000,000–SKr10,000,000 worth of products based on the price list. Since the SKr/$ exchange rate is likely to change during any three-month period, Tek would like to hedge this transaction exposure (Tek's Swedish business unit does believe the krona will be strengthening versus the dollar in the coming months). Nordea Bank (Sweden) has offered Tek the following quotes:

| | |
|---|---|
| Spot rate: | SKr7.4793/$ |
| Three-month forward rate: | SKr7.4937/$ |
| Three-month krona interest rate: | 4.780% per year |
| Three-month krona borrowing rate: | 6.50% per year |
| Three-month dollar interest rate: | 4.00% per year |

Three-month put option premium on
krona @ strike price of SKr7.50/$:       2.5%

Tek's weighted average cost of capital:    9.80%

a. What are the costs of each alternative for hedging SKr5,000,000?

b. What are the risks of each alternative? How much kronor should Tek hedge if it wants to play it safe?

c. Which alternative should Tek choose if it is willing to take a reasonable risk and has a directional view that the Swedish krona will appreciate versus the U.S. dollar during the next three months?

9. **Tek: Swiss dividend payable.** Tek's European subsidiaries are formally owned by a holding company, Tek-Switzerland. Thus, the subsidiaries pay dividends to the Swiss holding company, which in turn pays dividends to Tek-Beaverton. Tek has declared a dividend of 5 million Swiss francs payable in three months from Switzerland to Tek-Beaverton. If Tek-Beaverton wishes to hedge this transaction exposure it could utilize the following quotes from Swiss Bank Corporation:

| | |
|---|---|
| Spot rate: | SFr1.2462/$ |
| Expected spot rate in three months: | SFr1.2200/$ |
| Three-month forward rate: | SFr1.2429/$ |
| Three-month Swiss franc interest rate: | 3.75% per year |
| Three-month dollar interest rate: | 4.00% per year |
| Three-month put option on SF @ strike price of SFr1.25/$: | $0.0150/SFr premium |
| Tek's weighted average of capital: | 9.80% |

What are the costs of each alternative for hedging the dividend payable? What are the risks of each alternative? Which alternative should Tek choose? Explain your assumption about Tek's motivation in choosing your suggested alternative.

10. **Northern Rainwear.** Northern Rainwear, Ltd. (Northern), a Canadian manufacturer of raincoats, does not selectively hedge its transaction exposure. Instead, if the date of the transaction is known with certainty, all foreign currency-denominated cash flows must utilize the following mandatory forward contract cover formula:

| | *Exposure Coverage Required According to Maturity* | | |
|---|---|---|---|
| | *0–90 days* | *91–180 days* | *>180 days* |
| *If Northern Is* | | | |
| paying the points forward | 75% | 60% | 50% |
| receiving the points forward | 100% | 90% | 50% |

Northern expects to receive multiple payments in Danish kroner over the next year. DKr 3,000,000 is due in 90 days; DKr 2,000,000 is due in 180 days; and DKr 1,000,000 is due in one year. Using the following spot and forward exchange rates, what

would be the amount of forward cover required by company policy by period?

| | |
|---|---|
| Spot rate: | DKr 4.70/C$ |
| Three-month forward rate: | DKr 4.71/C$ |
| Six-month forward rate: | DKr 4.72/C$ |
| One-year forward rate: | DKr 4.74/C$ |

11. **Vamo Road Industries.** Vamo Road Industries of Sarasota, Florida, is completing a new assembly plant near Guatemala City. A final construction payment of Q8,400,000 is due in six months. ("Q" is the symbol for Guatemalan *quetzals*.) Vamo uses 20% per annum as its weighted average cost of capital. Today's foreign exchange and interest rate quotations are

| | |
|---|---|
| Present spot rate: | Q7.0000/$ |
| Six-month forward rate: | Q7.1000/$ |
| Guatemalan six-month interest rate: | 14.00% per annum |
| U.S. dollar six-month interest rate: | 6.00% per annum |

Vamo's treasury manager, concerned about the Guatemalan economy, wonders if Vamo should be hedging its foreign exchange risk. The manager's own forecast is as follows:

| | |
|---|---|
| Highest expected rate: | Q8.0000/$, reflecting a significant devaluation |
| Expected rate: | Q7.3000/$ |
| Lowest expected rate: | Q6.4000/$, reflecting a strengthening of the quetzal |

What realistic alternatives are available to Vamo for making payment? Which method would you select, and why?

12. **Worldwide Travel's acquisition.** Worldwide Travel, a 100% privately owned travel company based in Honolulu, has signed an agreement to acquire a 50% ownership share of Taipei Travel, a privately owned travel agency based in Taiwan specializing in servicing inbound customers from the United States and Canada. The acquisition price is 7 million Taiwan dollars (T$7,000,000) payable in cash in three months.

Matt Morita, Worldwide Travel's owner, believes the Taiwan dollar will either remain stable or decline a little over the next three months. At the present spot rate of T$35/$, the amount of cash required is only $200,000 but even this relatively modest amount will need to be borrowed personally by Matt Morita. Taiwanese interest-bearing deposits by nonresidents are regulated by the government and are currently set at 1.5% per year. He has a credit line with Bank of Hawaii for $200,000 with a current borrowing interest rate of 8% per year. He does not believe that he can calculate a credible weighted average cost of capital since he has no stock outstanding and his competitors are all also privately owned without disclosure of their financial results. Since the acquisition would use up all his available credit, he wonders if he should hedge this transaction exposure. He has the following quotes from Bank of Hawaii:

| | |
|---|---|
| Spot rate: | T$33.40/$ |
| Three-month forward rate: | T$32.40/$ |
| Three-month dollar borrowing rate: | 6.50% per year |
| Three-month T$ deposit rate: | 1.50% per year |
| Three-month call options: | not available |

Analyze the costs and risks of each alternative, and then make a recommendation as to which alternative Morita should choose.

13. **Seattle Scientific, Inc.** Josh Miller is chief financial officer of a medium-sized Seattle-based medical device manufacturer. The company's annual sales have been growing rapidly, to $40 million, and working capital financing is a common source of concern. Josh has recently been approached by one of his major Japanese customers, Yokasa, with a new payment proposal.

Yokasa typically orders ¥12,500,000 in product every other month and pays in Japanese yen. The current payment terms extended by Seattle are 30 days, with no discounts given for early or cash payment. Yokasa has suggested that it would be willing to pay in cash — in Japanese yen — if it were given a 4.5% discount on the purchase price. Josh Miller gathered the following quotes from his bank on current spot and forward exchange rates, and estimated Yokasa's cost of capital.

| | |
|---|---|
| Spot rate: | ¥120.23/$ |
| 30-day forward rate: | ¥119.73/$ |
| 90-day forward rate: | ¥118.78/$ |
| 180-day forward rate: | ¥117.21/$ |
| Yokasa's WACC: | 8.850% |
| Seattle Scientific's WACC: | 12.500% |

a. What is Seattle Scientific's cost of hedging the yen receivable?

b. How much in U.S. dollars will Seattle Scientific receive (1) with the discount and (2) with no discount but fully covered with a forward contract?

c. If Josh were to compare the results of part (b) in present value terms, which appears to be preferable?

14. **Wilmington Chemical Company.** Wilmington Chemical Company has just purchased a shipment of phosphates from Morocco for 6,000,000, dirhams, payable in six months. Wilmington's cost of capital is 14%. The following quotes are available in the market.

| | *United States* | *Morocco* |
|---|---|---|
| Six-month interest rate for borrowing: | 6.00% p.a. | 8.00% p.a. |
| Six-month interest rate for investing: | 5.00% p.a. | 7.00% p.a. |
| Spot exchange rate: | $1.00 = 10.00 dirhams | |
| Six-month forward rate: | $1.00 = 10.40 dirhams | |

Six-month call options on 6,000,000 dirhams at an exercise price of 10.00 dirhams per dollar are available from Bank Al-Maghrub at a premium of 2%. Six-month put options on 6,000,000 dirhams at an exercise price of 10.00 dirhams per dollar are available at a premium of 3%.

Compare and contrast alternative ways that Wilmington Chemical might hedge its foreign exchange transaction exposure. What is your recommendation?

15. **Dawg-Grip, Inc.** Dawg-Grip, Inc., of Georgia just purchased a Korean company that produces plastic nuts and bolts for automobile manufacturers. The purchase price was Won7,030 million. Won1,000 million has already been paid, and the remaining Won6,030 million is due in six months. The current spot rate is Won1200/$, and the six-month forward rate is Won1260/$. Additional data:

| | |
|---|---|
| Six-month Korean interest rate: | 16.00% p.a. |
| Six-month U.S. interest rate: | 4.00% p.a. |
| Six-month call option on Korean won at W1200/$: | 3.0% premium |
| Six-month put option on Korean won at W1200/$: | 2.4% premium |

Dawg-Grip can invest at the rates given above or borrow at 2% per annum above those rates. Dawg-Grip's weighted average cost of capital is 25%. Compare alternate ways that Dawg-Grip might deal with its foreign exchange exposure. What do you recommend and why?

16. **Aqua-Pure.** Aqua-Pure is a U.S.–based company that manufactures, sells, and installs water purification equipment. On April 20 the company sold a system to the city of Nagasaki, Japan, for installation in Nagasaki's famous Glover Gardens (where Puccini's Madame Butterfly waited for the return of Lt. Pinkerton). The sale was priced in yen at ¥20,000,000, with payment due in three months. On the day of the sale the *Financial Times* published the following mid-rates for the yen:

| | |
|---|---|
| Spot exchange rate: | ¥118.255/$ (closing mid-rate) |
| One-month forward rate: | ¥117.760/$, a 5.04% p.a. premium |
| Three-month forward rate: | ¥116.830/$, a 4.88% p.a. premium |
| One-year forward rate: | ¥112.450/$, a 5.16% p.a. premium |

| Money rates (% p.a.) | United States | Japan | Differential |
|---|---|---|---|
| 1 month | 4.8750% | 0.09375% | 4.78125% |
| 3 months | 4.9375% | 0.09375% | 4.84375% |
| 12 months | 5.1875% | 0.31250% | 4.87500% |

Note: The interest rate differentials vary slightly from the forward discounts on the yen because of time differences for the quotes. The spot ¥118.255/$, for example, is a mid-point range. During April 20 the spot yen traded in London from ¥118.30/$ to ¥117.550/$.

*Additional information:* Aqua-Pure's Japanese competitors are currently borrowing yen from Japanese banks at a spread of 2 percentage points above the Japanese money rate. Aqua-Pure's weighted average cost of capital is 16%, and the company wishes to protect the dollar value of this receivable.

*Three-month options from Kyushu Bank:*
Call option on ¥20,000,000 at exercise price of
  ¥118.00/$: a 1% premium
Put option on ¥20,000,000 at exercise price of
  ¥118.00/$: a 3% premium

a. What are the costs and benefits of alternative hedges? Which would you recommend, and why?

b. What is the break-even reinvestment rate when comparing forward and money market alternatives?

17. **Botox Watch Company.** Botox Watch Company exports wristwatches to many countries, selling for local currencies to watch stores and distributors. Botox prides itself on being financially conservative. At least 70% of each individual transaction exposure is hedged, mostly in the forward market

but occasionally with options. Botox's foreign exchange policy is such that the 70% hedge may be increased up to a 120% hedge if devaluation or depreciation appears imminent.

Botox has just shipped to its major Continental European distributor. It has issued a 90-day invoice to its buyer for €1,560,000. The current spot rate is $1.2340/€, and the 90-day forward rate is $1.2460/€. Botox's treasurer, Harry Weaver, has a very good track record in predicting exchange rate movements. He currently believes the euro will weaken against the dollar in the coming 90 to 120 days, possibly to around $1.20/€.

1. Evaluate the hedging alternatives for Botox if Harry is right (Case 1: $1.20/€) and if Harry is wrong (Case 2: $1.26/€). What do you recommend?

2. What does it mean to hedge 120% of a transaction exposure?

3. What would be considered the most conservative transaction exposure management policy by a firm? How does Botox compare?

18. **Redwall Pump Company.** On March 1, Redwall Pump Company sold a shipment of pumps to Vollendam Dike Company of the Netherlands for €4,000,000, €2,000,000 payable on June 1 and €2,000,000 on September 1. Redwall derived its price quote of €4,000,000 on February 1 by dividing its normal U.S. dollar sales price of $4,320,000 by the then-current spot rate of $1.0800/€.

By the time the order was received and booked on March 1, the euro had strengthened to $1.1000/€, so the sale was in fact worth €4,000,000 × $1.1000/€ = $4,400,000. Redwall had already gained an extra $80,000 from favorable exchange rate movements! Nevertheless Redwall's director of finance now wondered if the firm should hedge against a reversal of the recent trend of the euro. Four approaches were possible:

1. *Hedge in the forward market.* The three-month forward exchange quote was $1.1060/€ and the six-month forward quote was $1.1130/€.

2. *Hedge in the money market.* Redwall could borrow euros from the Frankfurt branch of its U.S. bank at 8.00% per annum.

3. *Hedge with foreign currency options.* June put options were available at strike price of $1.1000/€ for a premium of 2.0% per contract,

and September put options were available at $1.1000/€ for a premium of 1.2%. June call options at $1.1000/€ could be purchased for a premium of 3.0%, and September call options at $1.1000/€ were available at a 2.6% premium.

4. *Do nothing.* Redwall could wait until the sales proceeds were received in June and September, hope the recent strengthening of the euro would continue, and sell the euros received for dollars in the spot market.

Redwall estimates its cost of equity capital to be 12% per annum. As a small firm, Redwall is unable to raise funds with long-term debt. U.S. T-bills yielded 3.6% per annum. What should Redwall do?

19. **Pixel's financial metrics.** Leo Srivastava is the director of finance for Pixel Manufacturing, a U.S.-based manufacturer of handheld computer systems for inventory management. Pixel's system combines a low-cost, active bar code used on inventory (the bar code tags emit an extremely low-grade radio frequency) with custom-designed hardware and software that tracks the low-grade emissions for inventory control.

Pixel has completed the sale of a bar-code system to a British firm, Grand Metropolitan (U.K.), for a total payment of £1,000,000. The following exchange rates were available to Pixel on the following dates, corresponding to the events of this specific export sale. Assume each month is 30 days.

| Date | Spot Rate ($/£) | Forward Rate ($/£) | Description |
|---|---|---|---|
| Feb 1 | 1.7850 | $F_{210} = 1.7771$ | Price quotation by Pixel (U.S.) to Grand Met (U.K.) |
| Mar 1 | 1.7465 | $F_{180} = 1.7381$ | Contract signed for the sale totaling £1,000,000 |
| Jun 1 | 1.7689 | $F_{90} = 1.7602$ | Product shipped to Grand Met |
| Aug 1 | 1.7840 | $F_{30} = 1.7811$ | Product received by Grand Met |
| Sept 1 | 1.7290 | | Grand Met makes payment of £1,000,000 |

a. Pixel's income statement will reflect the sale both as booked sales and as a potential foreign exchange gain (loss). Assume Leo decides not to hedge this transaction exposure. What is the value of the sale as booked? What is the foreign exchange gain (loss) on the sale?

b. Now assume Leo decides that he should hedge the exposure with a forward contract. The financial statements will reflect a different set of values when hedged. What is the value of the sale as booked? What is the foreign exchange gain (loss) on the sale if hedged with a forward contract?

20. **Maria Gonzalez and Trident (A).** Trident has concluded a second, larger sale of telecommunications equipment to Regency (U.K.). Total payment of £3,000,000 is due in 90 days. Maria Gonzalez has also learned that Trident will only be able to borrow in the United Kingdom at 14% per annum (due to credit concerns of the British banks). Given the following exchange rates and interest rates, what transaction exposure hedge is now in Trident's best interest?

| | |
|---|---|
| Spot rate: | $1.7620/£ |
| Expected spot rate in 90 days: | $1.7850/£ |
| 90-day forward rate: | $1.7550/£ |
| 90-day dollar deposit rate: | 6.0% per annum |
| 90-day dollar borrowing rate: | 8.0% per annum |
| 90-day pound deposit rate: | 8.0% per annum |
| 90-day pound borrowing rate: | 14.0% per annum |
| Trident's WACC: | 12.0% per annum |

Maria has also collected data on two specific options as well:

| | Strike Rate | Premium |
|---|---|---|
| 90-day put option on £: | $1.75/£ | 1.5% |
| 90-day put option on £: | $1.71/£ | 1.0% |

21. **Maria Gonzalez and Trident (B).** One year later Maria Gonzalez is still on the job at Trident. Trident's business is booming, and sales have now expanded to include exports to Germany and Japan, besides continuing sales to the United Kingdom. All export sales are invoiced in the local currency of the buyer. Maria Gonzalez will book the following sales this period:

Domestic sales: $7,300,000 (45-day credit terms)
Export sales: €2,340,000; £1,780,000; ¥125,000,000 (all export terms are 90 days)

Other income statement items are as follows:

| | |
|---|---|
| Cost of goods sold: | 65% of sales |
| G&A expenses: | 9% of sales |
| Depreciation: | $248,750 per period |
| U.S. corporate tax: | 40% of earnings before tax |
| Shares outstanding: | 1,000,000 |

Maria Gonzalez has collected the following spot rates (sales will be booked at these rates), 90-day forward rates, and 90-day forecasts by Trident's foreign exchange advisor for the three currencies:

| Spot | 90-day Forward | FX Advisor Forecast |
|------|----------------|---------------------|
| $1.5900/£ | $1.5875/£ | $1.5600/£ |
| $1.0560/€ | $1.0250/€ | $1.0660/€ |
| ¥122.43/$ | ¥120.85/$ | ¥126.00/$ |

Create a *pro forma* income statement for Trident and answer the following questions:

a. If Maria Gonzalez leaves all positions uncovered, and the final spot rates at settlement are exactly what the FX advisor had forecast, what are the foreign exchange gains (losses) for the period, and what is the final net income and earnings per share (EPS) figures?

b. If Maria Gonzalez covers all positions with full forward cover, and the final spot rates at settlement are exactly what the FX advisor forecast, what are the foreign exchange gains (losses) for the period, and the final net income and earnings per share (EPS) figures?

c. If Maria Gonzalez uses a common industry practice of covering all positions 100% with forward cover if the forward rate earns her the points, while only covering half the positions in which she is paying the forward points, what are the foreign exchange gains (losses) for the period and the final net income and earnings per share (EPS) figures, assuming the following final settlement spot rates are $1.0480/€, $1.6000/£, and ¥122.50/$?

22. **Siam Cement.** Siam Cement, the Bangkok-based cement manufacturer, suffered enormous losses during the Asian crisis in 1997. The company had been pursuing a very aggressive growth strategy in the mid-1990s, taking on massive quantities of foreign currency denominated debt (primarily U.S. dollars). When the Thai baht (B) was devalued from its pegged rate of B25.0/$ in July 1997, Siam's interest payments alone were over $900 million on its outstanding dollar debt (with an average interest rate of 8.40% on its U.S. dollar debt at that time).

Assuming Siam Cement took out a $50 million loan in June 1997 at 8.40% interest and had to repay it in one year when the spot exchange rate had stabilized at B42.0/$, what was the foreign exchange loss incurred on the transaction?

CHAPTER 9

# *Operating Exposure*

## LEARNING OBJECTIVES

Examine how operating exposure arises through unexpected changes in both operating and financing cash flows

Evaluate strategic alternatives to managing operating exposure

Detail the proactive policies firms use in managing operating exposure

This chapter extends the concept of transaction exposure, described in Chapter 8, further into time and across the multitudes of future cash flows that create the value of any multinational firm. *Operating exposure*, also called *economic exposure*, *competitive exposure*, and even *strategic exposure* on occasion, measures any change in the present value of a firm resulting from changes in future operating cash flows caused by any unexpected change in exchange rates. *Operating exposure analysis* assesses the impact of changing exchange rates on a firm's own operations over coming months and years and on its competitive position vis-á-vis other firms. The goal is to identify strategic moves or operating techniques the firm might wish to adopt to enhance its value in the face of unexpected exchange rate changes.

Operating exposure and transaction exposure are related in that they both deal with future cash flows. They differ in terms of which cash flows management considers and why those cash flows change when exchange rates change.

## Attributes of Operating Exposure

Measuring the operating exposure of a firm requires forecasting and analyzing all the firm's future individual transaction exposures together with the future exposures of all the firm's competitors and potential competitors worldwide. A simple example will clarify the point.

An MNE like Eastman Kodak (U.S.) has a number of transaction exposures at any point in time. Kodak has sales in the United States, Japan, and Europe and therefore posts a continuing series of foreign currency receivables (and payables). Sales and expenses that are already contracted for are traditional *transaction exposures*. Sales that are highly probable based on Kodak's historical business line and market share but have no legal basis yet are *anticipated transaction exposures*. (This term is used quite specifically in accounting for foreign exchange rate gains and losses.)

What if the analysis of the firm's exposure to exchange rate changes is extended even further into the future? What are the longer-term exposures of Kodak to exchange rate changes? Future exchange rate changes will not only alter the domestic currency value (U.S. dollars in this case) of the firm's foreign currency cash flows, it will change the quantity of foreign currency cash flows generated as well. Any change in Kodak's cash flows in the future depends on how competitive it is in various markets. Kodak's international competitiveness will in turn be affected by the operating exposures of its major competitors like Fuji (Japan) and Agfa (Germany). The analysis of this longer term — where exchange rate changes are unpredictable and therefore unexpected — is the goal of operating exposure analysis.

### OPERATING AND FINANCING CASH FLOWS

The cash flows of the MNE can be divided into *operating cash flows* and *financing cash flows*. Operating cash flows arise from intercompany (between unrelated companies) and intracompany (between units of the same company) receivables and payables, rent and lease payments for the use of facilities and equipment, royalty and license fees for the use of technology and intellectual property, and assorted management fees for services provided.

Financing cash flows are payments for the use of intercompany and intracompany loans (principal and interest) and stockholder equity (new equity investments and dividends). Each of these cash flows can occur at different time intervals, in different

## EXHIBIT 9.1

Financial and Operating Cash Flows Between Parent and Subsidiary

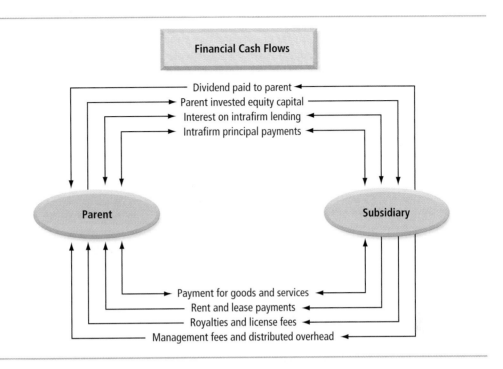

amounts, and in different currencies of denomination, and each has a different predictability of occurrence. We summarize cash flow possibilities in Exhibit 9.1.

## EXPECTED VERSUS UNEXPECTED CHANGES IN CASH FLOW

*Operating exposure* is far more important for the long-run health of a business than changes caused by transaction or translation exposure. However, operating exposure is inevitably subjective because it depends on estimates of future cash flow changes over an arbitrary time horizon. Thus it does not spring from the accounting process but rather from operating analysis. Planning for operating exposure is a total management responsibility because it depends on the interaction of strategies in finance, marketing, purchasing, and production.

An expected change in foreign exchange rates is not included in the definition of operating exposure, because both management and investors should have factored this information into their evaluation of anticipated operating results and market value. From a management perspective, budgeted financial statements already reflect information about the effect of an expected change in exchange rates. For example, under equilibrium conditions the forward rate might be used as an unbiased predictor of the future spot rate. In such a case management would use the forward rate when preparing the operating budgets, rather than assume the spot rate would remain unchanged.

Another example is that expected cash flow to amortize debt should already reflect the international Fisher effect. The level of expected interest and principal repayment should be a function of expected exchange rates rather than existing spot rates.

From an investor's perspective, if the foreign exchange market is efficient, information about expected changes in exchange rates should be widely known and thus reflected in a firm's market value. Only unexpected changes in exchange rates, or an inefficient foreign exchange market, should cause market value to change.

From a broader perspective, operating exposure is not just the sensitivity of a firm's future cash flows to unexpected changes in foreign exchange rates, but also its sensitivity to other key macroeconomic variables. This factor has been labeled as *macroeconomic uncertainty*. Chapter 4 described the parity relationships among exchange rates, interest rates, and inflation rates. However, these variables are often in disequilibrium with one another. Therefore, unexpected changes in interest rates and inflation rates could also have a simultaneous but differential impact on future cash flows. *Real World Example 9.1* illustrates macroeconomic uncertainty.

## Illustrating Operating Exposure: Trident

To illustrate the consequences of operating exposure we use Trident's European subsidiary, Trident Europe. Exhibit 9.2 presents the dilemma facing Trident Corporation as a result of an unexpected change in the value of the euro, the currency of economic consequence for the German subsidiary. Trident Corporation (U.S.) derives much of its reported profits (earnings and earnings per share — EPS — as reported to Wall Street) from its European subsidiary. If the euro unexpectedly falls in value, how will Trident Europe's revenues change (prices, in euro terms, and volumes)? How will its costs change (primarily input costs, in euro terms)? How will competitors respond? We explain the sequence of likely events over the short and medium run in the following section.

### Real World Example 9.1
#### VOLVO CAR

Volvo Car, a subsidiary of Volvo (Sweden), illustrates an MNE's sensitivity to various macroeconomic variables including exchange rates, Interest rates, and prices — that is, to macroeconomic uncertainty. Volvo Car produces most of its cars in Sweden but buys most of its inputs from Germany. The company's most important market is the United States. Top management of Volvo Car, as well as most financial analysts, believed that a depreciating Swedish krona versus the U.S. dollar, and an appreciating Swedish krona versus the deutschemark, would be beneficial to Volvo Car. Volvo Car's cash flows were statistically analyzed for their sensitivity to relevant macroeconomic variables. However, three variables explained most of the unanticipated variability of cash flows. The three variables were:

1. *The Swedish krona/deutschemark exchange rates*. A depreciating krona improved Volvo Car's cash flows.

2. *The Swedish krona short-term interest rate*. A reduction in this rate improved Volvo Car's cash flow due to increased demand for its cars.

3. *German producer prices*. An increase in these prices improved Volvo Car's cash flow.

These results reflected the fact that Volvo Car's major competitors were the German prestige car manufacturers, BMW, Mercedes, and Audi. Thus measurement of Volvo Car's long-term operating exposure depended on how its competitors were situated with respect to unexpected changes in the same key macroeconomic variables, such as foreign exchange rates, interest rates, and inflation rates. (Since this study, Volvo has been acquired by Ford.)

Source: Oxelheim, Lars, and Clas Wihlborg, "Measuring Macroeconomic Exposure: The Case of Volvo Cars," *European Financial Management*, Vol. 1, No. 3, 1995, pp. 211–263. This analysis was written before the introduction of the euro.

## EXHIBIT 9.2

Trident Corporation and Its European Subsidiary: Operating Exposure of the Parent and Its Subsidiary

An unexpected depreciation in the value of the euro alters both the competitiveness of the subsidiary and the financial results, which are consolidated with the parent company.

## BASE CASE

Trident Europe manufactures in Germany from European material and labor. Half of production is sold within Europe for euros and half is exported to non-European countries. All sales are invoiced in euros, and accounts receivable are equal to one fourth of annual sales. In other words, the average collection period is 90 days. Inventory is equal to 25% of annual direct costs. Trident Europe can expand or contract production volume without any significant change in per-unit direct costs or in overall general and administrative expenses. Depreciation on plant and equipment is €600,000 per year, and the corporate income tax in Germany is 34%.

The December 31, 2002, balance sheet and alternative scenarios are shown in Exhibit 9.3. We assume that on January 1, 2003, before any commercial activity begins, the euro unexpectedly drops 16.67% in value, from $1.2000/€ to $1.0000/€. If no devaluation had occurred, Trident Europe was expected to perform in 2003 as shown in the base case of Exhibit 9.3, generating a dollar cash flow from operations for Trident Corporation of $2,074,320.

Operating exposure depends on whether an unexpected change in exchange rates causes unanticipated changes in sales volume, sales prices, or operating costs. Following a euro devaluation, Trident Europe might choose to maintain its domestic sales prices constant in euro terms, or it might try to raise domestic prices because competing imports are now priced higher in Europe. The firm might choose to keep export prices constant in terms of foreign currencies, in terms of euros, or somewhere in between (partial pass-through). The strategy undertaken depends to a large measure on management's opinion about the price elasticity of demand. On the cost side, Trident

## EXHIBIT 9.3

Trident Europe

| | A | B | C | D | E | F |
|---|---|---|---|---|---|---|
| 1 | | Exhibit 9.3: TRIDENT EUROPE | | | | |
| 2 | | Balance Sheet Information, End of Fiscal 2002 | | | | |
| 3 | | Assets | | Liabilities and Net Worth | | | |
| 4 | Cash | € 1,600,000 | Accounts payable | | € 800,000 | |
| 5 | Accounts receivable | 3,200,000 | Short-term bank loan | | 1,600,000 | |
| 6 | Inventory | 2,400,000 | Long-term debt | | 1,600,000 | |
| 7 | Net plant and equipment | 4,800,000 | Common stock | | 1,800,000 | |
| 8 | | | Retained earnings | | 6,200,000 | |
| 9 | Sum | € 12,000,000 | Sum | | € 12,000,000 | |
| 10 | | | | Important Ratios to be Maintained and Other Data | | | | |
| 11 | | | | Accounts receivable, as percent of sales | | | 25.00% | |
| 12 | | | | Inventory, as percent of annual direct costs | | | 25.00% | |
| 13 | | | | Cost of capital (annual discount rate) | | | 20.00% | |
| 14 | | | | Income tax rate | | | 34.00% | |
| 15 | | | Base Case | Case 1 | Case 2 | Case 3 |
| 16 | | Assumptions | | | | | |
| 17 | Exchange rate, $/€ | | 1.2000 | 1.0000 | 1.0000 | 1.0000 |
| 18 | Sales volume (units) | | 1,000,000 | 1,000,000 | 2,000,000 | 1,000,000 |
| 19 | Sales price per unit | | €12.80 | €12.80 | €12.80 | €15.36 |
| 20 | Direct cost per unit | | €9.60 | €9.60 | €9.60 | €9.60 |
| 21 | | Annual Cash Flows before Adjustments | | | | | |
| 22 | Sales revenue | | € 12,800,000 | € 12,800,000 | € 25,600,000 | € 15,360,000 |
| 23 | Direct cost of goods sold | | 9,600,000 | 9,600,000 | 19,200,000 | 9,600,000 |
| 24 | Cash operating expenses (fixed) | | 890,000 | 890,000 | 890,000 | 890,000 |
| 25 | Depreciation | | 600,000 | 600,000 | 600,000 | 600,000 |
| 26 | Pretax profit | | € 1,710,000 | € 1,710,000 | € 4,910,000 | € 4,270,000 |
| 27 | Income tax expense | | 581,400 | 581,400 | 1,669,400 | 1,451,800 |
| 28 | Profit after tax | | € 1,128,600 | € 1,128,600 | € 3,240,600 | € 2,818,200 |
| 29 | Add back depreciation | | 600,000 | 600,000 | 600,000 | 600,000 |
| 30 | Cash flow from operations, in euros | | € 1,728,600 | € 1,728,600 | € 3,840,600 | € 3,418,200 |
| 31 | Cash flow from operations, in dollars | | $ 2,074,320 | $ 1,728,600 | $ 3,840,600 | $ 3,418,200 |
| 32 | | Adjustments to Working Capital for 2003 and 2007 Caused by Changes in Conditions | | | | | |
| 33 | Accounts receivable | | € 3,200,000 | € 3,200,000 | € 6,400,000 | € 3,840,000 |
| 34 | Inventory | | 2,400,000 | 2,400,000 | 4,800,000 | 2,400,000 |
| 35 | Sum | | € 5,600,000 | € 5,600,000 | € 11,200,000 | € 6,240,000 |
| 36 | Change from base conditions in 2003 | | € - | € - | € 5,600,000 | € 640,000 |
| 37 | | Year | | Year-End Cash Flows | | | | |
| 38 | | 1 (2003) | $ 2,074,320 | $ 1,728,600 | $ (1,759,400) | $ 2,778,200 |
| 39 | | 2 (2004) | $ 2,074,320 | $ 1,728,600 | $ 3,840,600 | $ 3,418,200 |
| 40 | | 3 (2005) | $ 2,074,320 | $ 1,728,600 | $ 3,840,600 | $ 3,418,200 |
| 41 | | 4 (2006) | $ 2,074,320 | $ 1,728,600 | $ 3,840,600 | $ 3,418,200 |
| 42 | | 5 (2007) | $ 2,074,320 | $ 1,728,600 | $ 9,440,600 | $ 4,058,200 |
| 43 | | Year | | Change in Year-End Cash Flows from Base Conditions | | | | |
| 44 | | 1 (2003) | na | $ (345,720) | $ (3,833,720) | $ 703,880 |
| 45 | | 2 (2004) | na | $ (345,720) | $ 1,766,280 | $ 1,343,880 |
| 46 | | 3 (2005) | na | $ (345,720) | $ 1,766,280 | $ 1,343,880 |
| 47 | | 4 (2006) | na | $ (345,720) | $ 1,766,280 | $ 1,343,880 |
| 48 | | 5 (2007) | na | $ (345,720) | $ 7,366,280 | $ 1,983,880 |
| 49 | | | | Present Value of Incremental Year-End Cash Flows | | | | |
| 50 | | | na | $ (1,033,914) | $ 2,866,106 | $ 3,742,892 |
| 51 | | | Base Case | Case 1 | Case 2 | Case 3 |
| 52 | | Key Cell Entries | | | | | |

Key Cell Entries

C22: =C$18*C19, copy to D22:F23
C24: Enter as data value, copy to D24:F24
C25: Enter as data value, copy to D25:F25
C26: =C22-SUM(C23:C25), copy to D26:F26
C27: =$E$14*C26, copy to D27:F27
C28: =C26-C27, copy to D28:F28
C29: =C25, copy to D29:F29
C30: =C28+C29, copy to D30:F30
C31: =C30*C17, copy to D31:F31

C33: =$E11*C22, copy to D33:F34
C35: =SUM(C33:C34), copy to D35:F35
C36: =C35-$C$35, copy to D36:F36
C38: =C31-C36, copy to D38:F38
C39: =C$31, copy to C38:F41
C42: =C31+C36, copy to D42:F42
D44: =D38-$C38, copy to D44:F48
D50: =NPV($E$13,D44:D48), copy to E44:F48

Europe might raise prices because of more expensive imported raw material or components, or perhaps because all domestic prices in Germany have risen and labor is now demanding higher wages to compensate for domestic inflation.

Trident Europe's domestic sales and costs might also be partly determined by the effect of the euro devaluation on demand. To the extent that the devaluation, by making prices of German goods initially more competitive, stimulates purchases of European goods in import-competing sectors of the economy as well as exports of German goods, German national income should increase. This assumes that the favorable effect of a euro devaluation on comparative prices is not immediately offset by higher domestic inflation. Thus Trident Europe might be able to sell more goods domestically because of price and income effects and internationally because of price effects.

To illustrate the effect of various postdevaluation scenarios on Trident Europe's operating exposure, consider three simple cases:

Case 1: Devaluation; no change in any variable
Case 2: Increase in sales volume, other variables remain constant
Case 3: Increase in sales price, other variables remain constant

To calculate the net change in present value under each of the scenarios, we will use a five-year horizon for any change in cash flow induced by the change in the dollar/euro exchange rate.

## CASE 1: DEVALUATION; NO CHANGE IN ANY VARIABLE

Assume that in the five years ahead no changes occur in sales volume, sales price, or operating costs. Profits for the coming year in euros will be as expected, and cash flow from operations will be €1,728,600, as shown in Exhibit 9.3. With a new exchange rate of $1.0000/€, this cash flow measured in dollars during 2003 will be €1,728,600 × $1.0000/€ = $1,728,600. Exhibit 9.3 shows that the change in year-end cash flows from the base case is $345,720 for each of the next five years (2003–2007).

Exhibit 9.3 shows that the discounted present value of this series of diminished dollar value cash flows is $1,033,914.

## CASE 2: VOLUME INCREASES; OTHER VARIABLES REMAIN CONSTANT

Assume that sales within Europe double following the devaluation because German-made telecom components are now more competitive with imports. Additionally, export volume doubles because German-made components are now cheaper in countries whose currencies have not weakened. The sales price is kept constant in euro terms because management of Trident Europe has not observed any change in local German operating costs and because it sees an opportunity to increase market share.

Exhibit 9.3 shows expected cash flow for the first year (2003) would be $3,840,600. This amount, however, is not available because a doubling of sales volume will require additional investment in accounts receivable and in inventory. Although a portion of this additional investment might be financed by increasing accounts payable, we assume additional working capital is financed by cash flow from operations.

At the end of 2003, accounts receivable will be equal to one-fourth of annual sales, or €6,400,000. This amount is twice receivables of €3,200,000 at the end of 2002, and the incremental increase of €3,200,000 must be financed from available cash. Year-end inventory would be equal to one-fourth of annual direct costs, or €4,800,000, an increase of €2,400,000 over the year-beginning level. Receivables and inventory together increase by €5,600,000. At the end of five years (2007) these incremental cash outflows will be recaptured because any investment in current assets eventually rolls back into cash.

Assuming no further change in volume, price, or costs, cash inflows for the five years would be as described in Exhibit 9.3. In this instance the devaluation causes a major drop in first-year cash flow from the $2,074,320 anticipated in 2003 without devaluation to a negative cash flow of $1,759,400. However the remaining four years' cash flow is substantially enhanced by the operating effects of the devaluation. Over time Trident Europe generates significantly more cash for its owners. The devaluation produces an operating *gain* over time, rather than an operating *loss*.

The reason that Trident Corporation is better off in Case 2 following the devaluation is that sales volume doubled while the per-unit dollar-equivalent sales price fell only 16.67% — the percent amount of the devaluation. In other words, the product faced a price elasticity of demand greater than one.

## CASE 3: SALES PRICE INCREASES; OTHER VARIABLES REMAIN CONSTANT

Assume the euro sales price is raised from €12.80 to €15.36 per unit to maintain the same U.S. dollar-equivalent price (the change offsets the depreciation of the euro). Assume further that volume remains constant in spite of this price increase; that is, customers expect to pay the same dollar-equivalent price, and local costs do not change.

Trident Europe is now better off following the devaluation than it was before because the sales price, which is pegged to the international price level, increased. However, volume did not drop. The new level of accounts receivable would be one fourth of the new sales level of €15,360,000, or €3,840,000, an increase of €640,000 over the base case. The investment in inventory is $2,400,000, which is the same as the base case because annual direct costs did not change.

Expected dollar cash flow in every year exceeds the cash flow of $2,074,320 that had been anticipated with no devaluation. The increase in working capital causes net cash flow to be only $2,778,200 in 2003, but thereafter the cash flow is $3,418,200 per year, with an additional $640,000 working capital recovered in the fifth year.

The key to this improvement is operating leverage. If costs are incurred in euros and do not increase after a devaluation, an increase in the sales price by the amount of devaluation will lead to sharply higher profits.

## OTHER POSSIBILITIES

If any portion of sales revenues were incurred in other currencies, the situation would be different. Trident Europe might leave the foreign sales price unchanged, in effect raising the euro-equivalent price. Alternatively it might leave the euro-equivalent price unchanged, thus lowering the foreign sales price in an attempt to gain volume. Of course, it could also position itself between these two extremes. Depending on elasticities and the proportion of foreign to domestic sales, total sales revenue might rise or fall.

If some or all raw material or components were imported and paid for in hard currencies, euro operating costs would increase after the devaluation of the euro. Another possibility is that local (not imported) euro costs would rise after a devaluation.

## MEASUREMENT OF LOSS

Exhibit 9.3 summarizes the change in expected year-end cash flows for the three cases and compares them with the cash flow expected should no devaluation occur (Base Case). These changes are then discounted by Trident Corporation's assumed weighted average cost of capital of 20% to obtain the present value of the gain (loss) on operating exposure.

In Case 1, in which nothing changes after the euro is devalued, Trident Corporation incurs an operating loss with a present value of $1,033,914. In Case 2, in which volume doubled with no price change after devaluation, Trident Corporation experienced an operating gain with a present value of $2,866,106. In Case 3, in which the euro sales price was increased and volume did not change, the present value of the operating gain from devaluation was $3,742,892. An almost infinite number of combinations of volume, price, and cost could follow any devaluation, and any or all of them might take effect immediately after a devaluation or only after the passage of some time.

# Strategic Management of Operating Exposure

The objective of both operating and transaction exposure management is to anticipate and influence the effect of unexpected changes in exchange rates on a firm's future cash flows, rather than merely hoping for the best. To meet this objective, management can *diversify the firm's operating and financing base*. Management can also *change the firm's operating and financing policies*.

The key to managing operating exposure at the strategic level is for management to recognize a disequilibrium in parity conditions when it occurs and to be prepositioned to react in the most appropriate way. This task can best be accomplished if a firm *diversifies* internationally both its operating and its financing bases. Diversifying operations means diversifying sales, location of production facilities, and raw material sources. Diversifying the financing base means raising funds in more than one capital market and in more than one currency.

A diversification strategy permits the firm to react either actively or passively, depending on management's risk preference, to opportunities presented by disequilibrium conditions in the foreign exchange, capital, and product markets. Such a strategy does not require management to predict disequilibrium but only to *recognize* it when it occurs. It does require management to consider how competitors are prepositioned with respect to their own operating exposures. This knowledge should reveal which firms would be helped or hurt competitively by alternative disequilibrium scenarios.

## DIVERSIFYING OPERATIONS

If a firm's operations are diversified internationally, management is prepositioned both to recognize disequilibrium when it occurs and to react competitively. Consider the case where purchasing power parity is temporarily in disequilibrium. Although the disequilibrium may have been unpredictable, management can often recognize its symptoms as soon as they occur. For example, management might notice a change in comparative costs in the firm's own plants located in different countries. It might also observe changed profit margins or sales volume in one area compared to another, depending on price and income elasticities of demand and competitors' reactions.

Recognizing a temporary change in worldwide competitive conditions permits management to make changes in operating strategies. Management might make marginal shifts in sourcing raw materials, components, or finished products. If spare capacity exists, production runs can be lengthened in one country and reduced in another. The marketing effort can be strengthened in export markets where the firm's products have become more price competitive because of the disequilibrium condition.

Even if management does not actively distort normal operations when exchange rates change, the firm should experience some beneficial portfolio effects. The variability of its cash flows is probably reduced by international diversification of its production, sourcing, and sales because exchange rate changes under disequilibrium conditions are likely to increase the firm's competitiveness in some markets while reducing it in others. In that case operating exposure would be neutralized. *Real World Example 9.2* shows Goodyear's response to the Mexican peso devaluation through a timely shift in operating strategy.

In contrast to the internationally diversified MNE, a purely domestic firm might be subject to the full impact of foreign exchange operating exposure even though it does not have foreign currency cash flows. For example, it could experience intense import competition in its domestic market from competing firms producing in countries with undervalued currencies.

A purely domestic firm does not have the option to react to an international disequilibrium condition in the same manner as an MNE. In fact, a purely domestic firm will not be positioned to recognize that a disequilibrium exists because it lacks comparative data from its own internal sources. By the time external data are available from published sources, it is often too late to react. Even if a domestic firm recognizes the disequilibrium, it cannot quickly shift production and sales into foreign markets in which it has had no previous presence.

## DIVERSIFYING FINANCING

If a firm diversifies its financing sources, it will be prepositioned to take advantage of temporary deviations from the international Fisher effect. If interest rate differentials do not equal expected changes in exchange rates, opportunities to lower a firm's cost of capital will exist. However, to be able to switch financing sources, a firm must

## Real World Example 9.2
### GOODYEAR'S RESPONSE TO THE MEXICAN PESO'S DEVALUATION

When Goodyear's manager in Mexico heard on his car radio on December 20, 1994, that the peso had crashed, he met with his managers immediately to assess the damage. Within days, he figured that domestic demand for Goodyear tires would plunge more than 20%, or 3,000 a day. His choices: lay off workers or find new export markets — right away, before his warehouse overflowed.

His team members, aided by the Goodyear Tire and Rubber company headquarters in Akron, Ohio, not only found enough export buyers to make up for what turned out to be a 3,500-tire drop in domestic sales, they also found spots to sell 1,600 more, setting an output record at the plant some 15 miles north of Mexico City. A factory that had imported supplies but exported not a single tire in 1992 now shipped away half its production, mostly to the United States but also to South America and Europe. The company quickly moved from being a net importer to being a net exporter.

already be well known in the international investment community, with banking contacts firmly established. Once again, this is not an option for a domestic firm that has limited its financing to one capital market.

Although we recommend diversification as a strategy for foreign exchange risk management, such a strategy has a potentially favorable impact on other risks as well. In particular, it could reduce the variability of future cash flows due to domestic business cycles, provided these are not perfectly correlated with international cycles. It could increase the availability of capital, and reduce its cost, by diversifying such risks as restrictive capital market policies or government borrowing competition in the capital market. It could mitigate political risks such as expropriation, war, blocked funds, or unfavorable changes in laws that reduce or eliminate profitability. The list of advantages from international diversification can even be extended to such areas as spreading the risk of technological obsolescence and reducing portfolio risk in the context of the capital asset pricing model. Now we are verging on the diversification strategy theme that appears throughout the rest of this book.

Constraints exist that may limit the feasibility of a diversification strategy for foreign exchange risk management or one of the other risks just mentioned. For example, the technology of a particular industry may require such large economies of scale that it is not economically feasible to diversify production locations. Firms in this industry could still diversify sales and financing sources, however. On the other hand, a firm may be too small or too unknown to attract international equity investors or lenders. Yet it could at least diversify its sales internationally. Thus a diversification strategy can be implemented only as far as is feasible.

## Proactive Management of Operating Exposure

Operating and transaction exposures can be *partially managed* by adopting operating or financing policies that offset anticipated foreign exchange exposures. Six of the most commonly employed proactive policies are:

1. Matching currency cash flows
2. Risk-sharing agreements
3. Back-to-back or parallel loans
4. Currency swaps
5. Leads and lags
6. Reinvoicing centers

### MATCHING CURRENCY CASH FLOWS

One way to offset an anticipated continuous long exposure to a particular currency is to acquire debt denominated in that currency. Exhibit 9.4 depicts the exposure of a U.S. firm with continuing export sales to Canada. In order to compete effectively in Canadian markets, the firm invoices all export sales in Canadian dollars. This policy results in a continuing receipt of Canadian dollars month after month. If the export sales are part of a continuing supplier relationship, the long Canadian dollar position is relatively predictable and constant. This endless series of transaction exposures could of course be continually hedged with forward contracts or other contractual hedges, as discussed in the previous chapter.

**EXHIBIT 9.4**

Matching: Debt
Financing as a
Financial Hedge

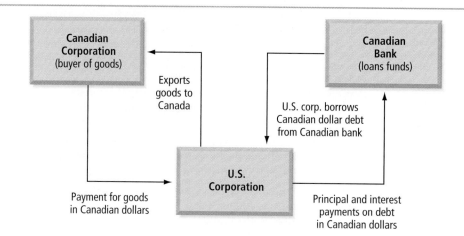

**Exposure:** The sale of goods to Canada creates a foreign
currency exposure from the inflow of Canadian dollars.

**Hedge:** The Canadian dollar debt payments act as a financial
hedge by requiring debt service, an outflow of Canadian dollars.

But what if the firm sought out a continual use, an outflow, for its continual inflow of Canadian dollars? If the U.S. firm were to acquire part of its debt-capital in the Canadian dollar markets, it could use the relatively predictable Canadian dollar cash inflows from export sales to service the principal and interest payments on Canadian dollar debt and be *cash flow matched*. The U.S.–based firm has hedged an operational cash inflow by creating a financial cash outflow, and so it does not have to actively manage the exposure with contractual financial instruments such as forward contracts. This form of hedging, sometimes referred to as *matching*, is effective in eliminating currency exposure when the exposure cash flow is relatively constant and predictable over time.

The list of potential matching strategies is nearly endless. A second alternative would be for the U.S. firm to seek out potential suppliers of raw materials or components in Canada as a substitute for U.S. or other foreign firms. The firm would then possess not only an operational Canadian dollar cash inflow, the receivable, but also a Canadian dollar operational cash outflow, a payable. If the cash flows were roughly the same in magnitude and timing, the strategy would be a *natural hedge*. The term *natural* refers to operating-based activities of the firm.

A third alternative, often referred to as *currency switching*, would be to pay foreign suppliers with Canadian dollars. For example, if the U.S. firm imported components from Mexico, the Mexican firms themselves might welcome payment in Canadian dollars because they are short Canadian dollars in their multinational cash flow network.

## CURRENCY CLAUSES: RISK-SHARING

An alternative arrangement for managing a long-term cash flow exposure between firms with a continuing buyer-supplier relationship is *risk-sharing*. Risk-sharing is a contractual arrangement in which the buyer and seller agree to "share" or split currency movement impacts on payments between them. If the two firms are interested in a long-term relationship based on product quality and supplier reliability and not on the whims of the currency markets, a cooperative agreement to share the burden of currency risk management may be in order.

If Ford's North American operations import automotive parts from Mazda (Japan) every month, year after year, major swings in exchange rates can benefit one party at the expense of the other. Ford is a major stockholder of Mazda, but it does not exert control over its operations. Therefore, the risk-sharing agreement is particularly appropriate; transactions between the two are both intercompany and intracompany. A risk-sharing agreement solidifies the partnership. One potential solution would be for Ford and Mazda to agree that all purchases by Ford will be made in Japanese yen at the current exchange rate, as long as the spot rate on the date of invoice is between, say, ¥115/$ and ¥125/$. If the exchange rate is between these values on the payment dates, Ford agrees to accept whatever transaction exposure exists (because it is paying in a foreign currency). If, however, the exchange rate falls outside this range on the payment date, Ford and Mazda will *share* the difference equally.

For example, Ford has an account payable of ¥25,000,000 for the month of March. If the spot rate on the date of invoice is ¥110/$, the Japanese yen would have appreciated versus the dollar, causing Ford's costs of purchasing automotive parts to rise. Since this rate falls outside the contractual range, Mazda would agree to accept a total payment in Japanese yen which would result from a difference of ¥5/$ (i.e., ¥115 − ¥110). Ford's payment would be:

$$\left[ \frac{¥25,000,000}{¥115.00/\$ - \dfrac{¥5.00/\$}{2}} \right] = \frac{¥25,000,000}{¥112.50/\$} = \$222,222.22$$

Ford's total payment in Japanese yen would be calculated using an exchange rate of ¥112.50/$, and saves Ford $5,050.51. At a spot rate of ¥110/$, Ford's costs for March would be $227,272.73. The risk-sharing agreement between Ford and Mazda allows Ford to pay $222,222.22, a savings of $5,050.51 over the cost without risk sharing (this "savings" is a reduction in an increased cost, not a true cost reduction.) Both parties therefore incur costs and benefits from exchange rate movements outside the specified band. Note that the movement could just as easily have been in Mazda's favor if the spot rate had moved to ¥130/$.

The risk-sharing arrangement is intended to smooth the impact on both parties of volatile and unpredictable exchange rate movements. Of course a sustained appreciation of one currency versus the other would require the negotiation of a new sharing agreement, but the ultimate goal of the agreement is to alleviate currency pressures on the continuing business relationship. Risk-sharing agreements like these have been in use for nearly 50 years on world markets. They became something of a rarity during the 1960s when exchange rates were relatively stable under the Bretton Woods Agreement. But with the return to floating exchange rates in the 1970s, firms with long-term customer-supplier relationships across borders have returned to some old ways of maintaining mutually beneficial long-term trade.

## BACK-TO-BACK LOANS

A *back-to-back loan*, also referred to as a *parallel loan* or *credit swap*, occurs when two business firms in separate countries arrange to borrow each other's currency for a specific period of time. At an agreed terminal date they return the borrowed currencies.

The operation is conducted outside the foreign exchange markets, although spot quotations may be used as the reference point for determining the amount of funds to be swapped. Such a swap creates a covered hedge against exchange loss, since each company, on its own books, borrows the same currency it repays. Back-to-back loans are also used at a time of actual or anticipated legal limitations on the transfer of investment funds to or from either country.

The structure of a typical back-to-back loan is illustrated in Exhibit 9.5. A British parent firm wanting to invest funds in its Dutch subsidiary locates a Dutch parent firm that wants to invest funds in the United Kingdom. Avoiding the exchange markets entirely, the British parent lends pounds to the Dutch subsidiary in the United Kingdom, while the Dutch parent lends euros to the British subsidiary in the Netherlands. The two loans would be for equal values at the current spot rate and for a specified maturity. At maturity the two separate loans would each be repaid to the original lender, again without any need to use the foreign exchange markets. Neither loan carries any foreign exchange risk, and neither loan normally needs the approval of any governmental body regulating the availability of foreign exchange for investment purposes.

Parent company guarantees are not needed on the back-to-back loans because each loan carries the right of offset in the event of default of the other loan. A further agreement can provide for maintenance of principal parity in case of changes in the spot rate between the two countries. For example, if the pound dropped by more than, say, 6% for as long as 30 days, the British parent might have to advance additional pounds to the Dutch subsidiary to bring the principal value of the two loans back to parity. A similar provision would protect the British if the euro should weaken. Although this parity provision might lead to changes in the amount of home currency each party must lend during the period of the agreement, it does not increase foreign exchange risk, because at maturity all loans are repaid in the same currency loaned.

**EXHIBIT 9.5**

Using a Back-to-Back Loan for Currency Hedging

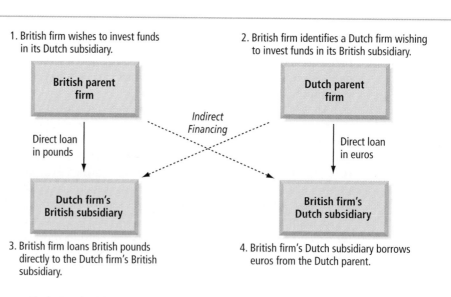

The back-to-back loan provides a method for parent-subsidiary cross-border financing without incurring direct currency exposure.

There are two fundamental impediments to widespread use of the back-to-back loan. First, it is difficult for a firm to find a partner, termed a *counterparty*, for the currency, amount, and timing desired. Secondly, a risk exists that one of the parties will fail to return the borrowed funds at the designated maturity — although this risk is minimized because each party to the loan has, in effect, 100% collateral, albeit in a different currency. These disadvantages have led to the rapid development and wide use of the currency swap.

## CURRENCY SWAPS

A *currency swap* resembles a back-to-back loan except that it does not appear on a firm's balance sheet. As we noted briefly in Chapter 6, the term *swap* is widely used to describe a foreign exchange agreement between two parties to exchange a given amount of one currency for another and, after a period of time, to give back the original amounts swapped. Care should be taken to clarify which of the many different swaps is being referred to in a specific case.

In a currency swap, a firm and a swap dealer or swap bank agree to exchange an equivalent amount of two different currencies for a specified period of time. Currency swaps can be negotiated for a wide range of maturities up to at least 10 years. If funds are more expensive in one country than another, a fee may be required to compensate for the interest differential. The swap dealer or swap bank acts as a middleman in setting up the swap agreement.

A typical currency swap first requires two firms to borrow funds in the markets and currencies in which they are best known. For example, a Japanese firm would typically borrow yen on a regular basis in its home market. If, however, the Japanese firm were exporting to the United States and earning U.S. dollars, it might wish to construct a *matching cash flow hedge* which would allow it to use the U.S. dollars earned to make regular debt-service payments on U.S. dollar debt. If, however, the Japanese firm is not well known in the U.S. financial markets, it may have no ready access to U.S. dollar debt.

One way in which it could, in effect, borrow dollars, is to participate in a *cross-currency swap* (see Exhibit 9.6). The Japanese firm could swap its yen-denominated debt service payments with another firm which has U.S. dollar-debt service payments. This swap would have the Japanese firm "paying dollars" and "receiving yen." The Japanese firm would then have dollar-debt service without actually borrowing U.S. dollars. Simultaneously, a U.S. corporation could actually be entering into a cross-currency swap in the opposite direction — "paying yen" and "receiving dollars." The swap dealer is taking the role of a middleman.

Swap dealers arrange most swaps on a blind basis, meaning that the initiating firm does not know who is on the other side of the swap arrangement — the counterparty. The firm views the dealer or bank as its counterparty. Because the swap markets are dominated by the major money center banks worldwide, the counterparty risk is acceptable. Because the swap dealer's business is arranging swaps, the dealer can generally arrange for the currency, amount, and timing of the desired swap.

Accountants in the United States treat the currency swap as a foreign exchange transaction rather than as debt and treat the obligation to reverse the swap at some later date as a forward exchange contract. Forward exchange contracts can be matched against assets, but they are entered in a firm's footnotes rather than as balance sheet items. The result is that both translation and operating exposures are avoided, and neither a long-term receivable nor a long-term debt is created on the balance sheet. The

**EXHIBIT 9.6**

Using a Cross-
Currency Swap to
Hedge Currency
Exposure

Both the Japanese corporation and the U.S. corporation would like to enter into a
cross-currency swap that would allow them to use foreign currency cash inflows
to service debt.

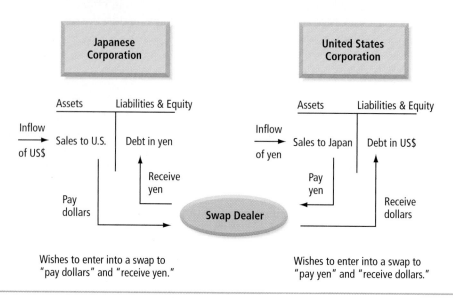

Wishes to enter into a swap to
"pay dollars" and "receive yen."

Wishes to enter into a swap to
"pay yen" and "receive dollars."

risk of changes in currency rates to the implied collateral in a long-term currency swap
can be treated with a clause similar to the maintenance-of-principal clause in a back-
to-back loan. If exchange rates change by more than some specified amount, say 10%,
an additional amount of the weaker currency might have to be advanced.

After being introduced on a global scale in the early 1980s, currency swaps have
grown to be one of the largest financial derivative markets in the world. Chapter 14
will provide a detailed explanation of the theory and application of currency swaps in
the context of interest rate risk management.

## LEADS AND LAGS: RETIMING THE TRANSFER OF FUNDS

Firms can reduce both operating and transaction exposure by accelerating or deceler-
ating the timing of payments that must be made or received in foreign currencies. *To
lead* is to pay early. A firm holding a soft currency or that has debts denominated in a
hard currency will lead by using the soft currency to pay the hard currency debts as
soon as possible. The object is to pay the currency debts before the soft currency drops
in value. *To lag* is to pay late. A firm holding a hard currency and having debts denominated in a soft currency will lag by paying those debts late, hoping that less of the hard
currency will be needed. If possible, firms will also lead and lag their collection of
receivables, collecting soft foreign currency receivables early and collecting hard foreign currency receivables later.

Leading and lagging can be done between related firms (intracompany) or with
independent firms (intercompany). Assuming that payments will be made eventually,
leading or lagging always results in changing the cash and payables position of one
firm, with the reverse effect on the other firm.

**INTRACOMPANY LEADS AND LAGS.**   Leading and lagging between related firms is more feasible because they presumably embrace a common set of goals for the consolidated group. Furthermore, the many periodic payments between units of an MNE provide opportunities for many types of leads or lags. Because opportunities for leading or lagging payments depend on the requirement for payments of this nature, the device is more readily adaptable to a company that operates on an integrated worldwide basis. If each unit functions as a separate and self-sufficient entity, the motivation for leading or lagging diminishes. In the case of financing cash flows with foreign subsidiaries, there is an additional motivation for early or late payments to position funds for liquidity reasons. For example, a subsidiary which is allowed to lag payments to the parent company is in reality borrowing from the parent.

Because the use of leads and lags is an obvious technique for minimizing foreign exchange exposure and for shifting the burden of financing, many governments impose limits on the allowed range. Terms allowed by governments are often subject to negotiation when a good argument can be presented. Thus some limits are subject to exceptions. For example, in the past Italy has placed no limit on export and import lags on trade payments with other OECD countries. However, a 180-day limit on export lags and a five-year limit on import lags was applied to trade with non-OECD countries.

**INTERCOMPANY LEADS AND LAGS.**   Leading or lagging between independent firms requires the time preference of one firm to be imposed to the detriment of the other firm. For example, Trident Europe may wish to lead in collecting its Brazilian accounts receivable that are denominated in real because it expects the real to drop in value compared with the euro. But why should the Brazilian customers prepay their accounts payable? Credit in real was part of the inducement for them to purchase from Trident Europe to begin with. The only way the Brazilians would be willing to pay their accounts payable early would be for the German creditor to offer a discount about equal to the forward discount on the real or, in equilibrium, the difference between Brazilian and German interest rates for the period of prepayment. In equilibrium this "discount" would eliminate the benefit to Trident Europe of collecting the "soft" currency earlier.

## REINVOICING CENTERS

A *reinvoicing center* is a separate corporate subsidiary that serves as a type of middleman between the parent or related unit in one location and all foreign subsidiaries in a geographic region. Manufacturing subsidiaries sell goods to distribution subsidiaries of the same firm only by selling to a reinvoicing center, which in turn resells to the distribution subsidiary. Title passes to the reinvoicing center, but the physical movement of goods is direct from the manufacturing plant, in this case Trident USA, to the foreign subsidiary, Trident Brazil. Thus the reinvoicing center handles paperwork but has no inventory.

As depicted in Exhibit 9.7, the U.S. manufacturing unit of Trident Corporation invoices the firm's reinvoicing center — located within the corporate headquarters facilities in Los Angeles — in U.S. dollars. However, the actual goods are shipped directly to Trident Brazil. The reinvoicing center in turn resells to Trident Brazil in Brazilian real. Consequentially, all operating units deal only in their own currency, and all transaction exposure lies with the reinvoicing center.

To avoid accusations of profit-shifting through transfer pricing, most reinvoicing centers resell at cost plus a small commission for their services. The resale price is

**EXHIBIT 9.7**

Use of a
Reinvoicing
Center

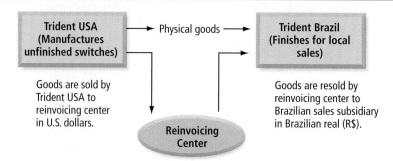

1. Trident USA ships goods directly to the Brazilian subsidiary.

2. The invoice by Trident USA, which is denominated in U.S. dollars, is passed to the reinvoicing center.

3. The reinvoicing center takes legal title to the goods.

4. The reinvoicing center invoices Trident Brazil in Brazilian real, repositioning the currency exposure from both operating units to the reinvoicing center.

frequently the manufacturer's price times the forward exchange rate for the date on which payment from the buyer is expected, although other combinations are possible. The commission covers the cost of the reinvoicing center, but does not shift profits away from operating subsidiaries.

There are three basic benefits arising from the creation of a reinvoicing center:

1. **Managing foreign exchange exposure.**  The formation of the center allows the management of all foreign exchange transaction exposure for intracompany sales to be located in one place. Reinvoicing center personnel can develop a specialized expertise in choosing which hedging technique is best at any moment, and they are likely to obtain more competitive foreign exchange quotations from banks because they are dealing in larger transactions.

2. **Guaranteeing the exchange rate for future orders.**  By guaranteeing the exchange rate for future orders, the reinvoicing center can set firm local currency costs in advance. This enables distribution subsidiaries to make firm bids to unrelated final customers, and to protect against the exposure created by a backlog of unfilled orders. Backlog exposure does not appear on the corporate books because the sales are not yet recorded. Sales subsidiaries can focus on their marketing activities and their performance can be judged without distortion because of exchange rate changes.

3. **Managing intra-subsidiary cash flows.**  The center can manage intra-subsidiary cash flows, including leads and lags of payments. With a reinvoicing center all subsidiaries settle intracompany accounts in their local currencies. The reinvoicing center need only hedge residual foreign exchange exposure.

The main disadvantage is one of cost relative to benefits received. One additional corporate unit must be created, and a separate set of books must be kept. The initial setup cost can be high because existing order-processing procedures must be reprogrammed. The center will have an impact on the tax status and customs duties of all subsidiaries, as well as on the amount of foreign exchange business directed to local banks in each country. Establishment of a reinvoicing center is likely to bring increased scrutiny by tax authorities to be sure that it is not functioning as a tax haven. Consequently a variety of professional costs will be incurred for tax and legal advice, in addition to the costs of personnel operating the center.

## Contractual Approaches: Hedging the Unhedgeable

Some MNEs now attempt to hedge their operating exposure with contractual strategies. Firms like Eastman Kodak (U.S.) and Merck (U.S.) have undertaken long-term currency option positions hedges designed to offset lost earnings from adverse exchange rate changes. This hedging of what many of these firms refer to as *strategic exposure* or *competitive exposure* seems to fly in the face of traditional theory.

The ability of firms to hedge the "unhedgeable" is dependent upon *predictability*: (1) the predictability of the firm's future cash flows and (2) the predictability of the firm's competitor's responses to exchange rate changes. Although the management of many firms may believe they are capable of predicting their own cash flows, few in practice feel capable of accurately predicting competitor response.

Merck is an example of a firm whose management feels capable of both. The company possesses relatively predictable long-run revenue streams due to the product-niche nature of the pharmaceuticals industry. As a U.S.-based exporter to foreign markets, markets in which sales levels by product are relatively predictable and prices are often regulated by government, Merck can accurately predict net long-term cash flows in foreign currencies five and ten years into the future. Merck has a relatively undiversified operating structure. It is highly centralized in terms of where research, development, and production costs are located. Merck's managers feel Merck has no real alternatives but contractual hedging if it is to weather long-term unexpected exchange rate changes. Merck has purchased over-the-counter (OTC) long-term put options on foreign currencies versus the U.S. dollar as insurance against potential lost earnings from exchange rate changes. In Merck's case, the predictability of competitor response to exchange rate changes is less pertinent given the niche-market nature of pharmaceutical products.

Eastman Kodak is another MNE that has in the past undertaken contractual hedging of its operating exposure. Kodak management believes its markets are largely price-driven and is aware that its major competitor, Fuji, has a Japanese cost base. If the U.S. dollar were to strengthen in the medium to long term, Kodak's market share in the United States and in foreign markets would decline. Kodak leadership also believes that whatever sales Kodak loses, its competitors will gain. Kodak has therefore also purchased long-term put options on foreign currencies, which would replace long-term earnings if the value of the U.S. dollar rose unexpectedly.

The magnitude of the option position depends on the nature of desired replacement. For example, if Kodak wished to insure only the lost net earnings from exchange rate–induced losses, the option position would be considerably smaller than a position attempting to replace gross sales revenues. Given the premium expenses associated with long-term put option positions of this type, replacing earnings is preferred to replacing sales.

A significant question remains as to the true effectiveness of hedging operating exposure with contractual hedges. The fact remains that even after feared exchange rate movements and put option position payoffs have occurred, the firm is competitively disadvantaged. The capital outlay required for the purchase of such sizeable put option positions is capital not used for the potential diversification of operations, which in the long run might have more effectively maintained the firm's global market share and international competitiveness.

# Toyota's European Operating Exposure

It was January 2002, and Toyota Motor Europe Manufacturing (TMEM) had a problem. More specifically, Mr. Toyoda Shuhei, the new President of TMEM, had a problem. He was on his way to Toyota Motor Company's (Japan) corporate offices outside Tokyo to explain the continuing losses of European manufacturing and sales operations. The CEO of Toyota Motor Company, Mr. Hiroshi Okuda, was expecting a proposal from Mr. Shuhei to reduce and eventually eliminate these losses. The situation was intense given that TMEM was the only major Toyota subsidiary losing money.

## Toyota and Auto Manufacturing

Toyota Motor Company was the number-one automobile manufacturer in Japan, the third largest manufacturer in the world by unit sales (5.5 million units or one auto every six seconds), but number eight in sales in continental Europe. The global automobile manufacturing industry, like many industries, had been experiencing continued consolidation in recent years as margins were squeezed, economies of scale and scope pursued, and global sales slowed.

Toyota was no different. It had continued to rationalize its manufacturing along regional lines and to increase the amount of local manufacturing in North America. In 2001 over 60% of Toyota's North American sales were

locally manufactured. But Toyota's European sales were nowhere close to this yet. Most of Toyota's automobile and truck manufacturing for Europe was still done in Japan. In 2001 only 26% of the autos sold in Europe were manufactured in Europe (including the U.K.), the remainder being imported from Japan (see Exhibit 1).

Toyota Motor Europe sold 634,000 automobiles in 2000. Europe was the second-largest foreign market for Toyota, second only to North America. TMEM expected significant growth in European sales and was planning to expand European manufacturing and sales to 800,000 units by 2005. But for fiscal 2001 the unit reported operating losses of ¥9.897 billion ($82.5 million at ¥120/$). TMEM had three assembly plants in the United Kingdom, one plant in Turkey, and one in Portugal. In November 2000 Toyota Motor Europe announced publicly that it would not generate profits for the next two years due to the weakness of the euro.

Toyota had recently introduced a new model to the European market, the Yaris, which was proving very successful. The Yaris, a super-small vehicle with a 1,000cc engine, had sold more than 180,000 units in 2000. Although the Yaris had been specifically designed for the European market, the decision had been made early on to manufacture it in Japan.

**EXHIBIT 1**

Toyota Motor's European Currency Operating Structure

## Currency Exposure

One source of the continuing operating losses suffered by TMEM was the falling value of the euro. Throughout 1999 and the first half of 2000 the yen strengthened against the euro (Exhibit 2). Although the euro regained some ground in late 2000, it remained relatively weak.

As demonstrated in Exhibit 1, the cost base for most of the autos sold within the Continental European market was the Japanese yen.

As the yen rose against the euro, costs increased significantly when measured in euro terms. If Toyota wished to preserve its price competitiveness in the European market, it had to absorb most of the exchange rate changes, suffering reduced or negative margins on both completed cars and key subcomponents shipped to its European manufacturing centers. Deciding to manufacture the Yaris in Japan had only exacerbated the problem.

## EXHIBIT 2

Daily Exchange Rates: Japanese Yen per Euro

## Management Response

Toyota management was not sitting passively by. In 2001 they had started up some assembly operations in Valenciennes, France. Although Valenciennes still constituted a relatively small percentage of total European sales as of January 2002, Toyota planned to continue to expand its capacity and capabilities to source about 25% of European sales by 2004. Assembly of the Yaris was scheduled to be moved to Valenciennes in 2002. The continuing problem, however, was that it was an assembly facility, meaning that much of the expensive value-added content of the autos being assembled was still based in either Japan or the United Kingdom.

Mr. Shuhei, with the approval of Mr. Okuda, had also initiated a local sourcing and procurement program for the United Kingdom manufacturing operations. TMEM wished to decrease the number of key components imported from Toyota Japan to reduce the currency exposure of the U.K. unit. But again, the continuing problem of the euro's weakness against the British pound, as shown in Exhibit 3, reduced the effectiveness of even this solution.

## EXHIBIT 3

Daily Exchange Rates: British Pounds per Euro

## Case Questions

1. Why do you think Toyota waited so long to move much of its manufacturing for European sales to Europe?
2. If Britain were to join the European Monetary Union, would the problem be resolved? How likely do you think it is that Britain will join?
3. If you were Mr. Shuhei, how would you categorize your problems and solutions? What was a short-term and what was a long-term problem?
4. What measures would you recommend Toyota Europe take to resolve the continuing operating losses?

## MINI-CASE

# Porsche Exposed

*BMW says that its decisions on where it locates production are driven by market needs, not currency considerations. Yet it has created natural hedges for itself by producing cars in America and Britain. By incurring costs in these markets, it greatly reduces the currency translation problem. Rival Porsche makes most of its cars in Germany, so its costs are mostly in euros. Yet a large chunk of its revenues come from sales of its sports cars in America. Lacking BMW's natural hedge, Porsche uses financial hedging to minimise the short-term impact of currency swings.*

"Grappling with the Strong Euro,"
*The Economist*, June 5, 2003, p. 53

It was January 2004 and Porsche — the legendary manufacturer of performance sports cars — wished to reevaluate its exchange rate strategy. Porsche's management had always been unconcerned about the opinions of the equity markets, but its currency hedging strategy was becoming something of a lightning rod for criticism. Although the currency hedging results had been positive, many experts believed that Porsche had simply been "more lucky than good." There was a growing nervousness among analysts that the company was actually speculating on currency movements, and that was not in the best interests of shareholders. Analysts were estimating that more than 40% of earnings were to come from currency hedging. Porsche's president and CEO, Dr. Wendelin Wiedeking, now wished to revisit the company's exposure management strategy.

## Foreign Currency Exposure

*Even if we sell a few or no cars at all in the U.S. we make money . . . because we bought dollars cheap which we now sell expensively. Our hedging is extremely good; we are calculating with levels which are significantly below current levels, and today I know what I will get for the dollar in 2006. I am very relaxed.*

Dr. Wiedeking in *Capital*, 2nd quarter, 2003

*Porsche has the heaviest U.S. exposure (and this is increasing), yet it has the lowest level of natural hedging in the sector. Porsche's earnings will have a 43% contribution from hedging contracts in 2003/04E, the highest in the sector.*

*Porsche*, Citigroup Smith Barney,
September 24, 2003, p. 5

Among European-based automakers, BMW, Mercedes, Porsche, and Volkswagen were clearly the most exposed to exchange rate changes (primarily the dollar/euro). As illustrated by Exhibit 1, Porsche possessed the largest mismatch between where their automobiles were produced and where they were sold. With 42% of global sales in NAFTA markets, and an additional 11% in the United Kingdom, Porsche possessed no manufacturing or assembly cost basis in the country markets of more than 50% of global sales.

All the European automakers, however, were cognizant and concerned over corporate currency exposures. BMW and Mercedes had recently announced plans to increase the amount of what analysts were calling *natural hedging* (the matching of dollar revenues with dollar costs). BMW planned to double the capacity of its Spartanburg, South Carolina manufacturing facility. Mercedes had similarly announced a capacity expansion for its Alabama manufacturing facility, while considering the down-sizing of its Magna Steyr, Germany operations. Volkswagen's (VW) continuing strategy to hedge its U.S.

**EXHIBIT 1**

United Kingdom and NAFTA Sales and Production of Selected European Automakers as a Percent of Global Results, 2002

| Automaker | United Kingdom | | NAFTA | |
| --- | --- | --- | --- | --- |
| | Sales | Production | Sales | Production |
| BMW | 11% | 15% | 26% | 11% |
| Fiat | 6% | 0% | 0% | 0% |
| Mercedes | 9% | 0% | 19% | 7% |
| Peugeot | 12% | 6% | 0% | 0% |
| Porsche | 11% | 0% | 42% | 0% |
| Renault | 9% | 0% | 1% | 1% |
| Volkswagen | 7% | 0% | 13% | 7% |

Source: Company reports, authors' estimates.

dollar exposure was a bit different. VW believed that if it increased its operating cost base in Brazil it would be uniquely positioned to manage its U.S. dollar risks. In that pursuit, VW had announced it would be assembling all of its Bora line and the Fox small car in Brazil, roughly 4% of VW's group output.

Porsche's exposure was clear — it was a global brand with a single-currency cost base. The company produced in only two countries, Germany and Finland (the Boxster was assembled under a licensing agreement with Valmet of Finland). Both were euro-denominated economies. Porsche believed that the quality of its engineering and manufacturing were at the core of its brand, and leadership had not been willing to move production beyond the existing European footprint.[1]

This meant that Porsche's sales outside of the eurozone were essentially export sales, and the resulting currency exposure significant, posing a considerable risk to sales and profits. Porsche's sales by currency in 2002/03 were estimated as: European euro (€) 45%; U.S. dollar ($) 40%, British pound sterling (£) 10%, Japanese yen (¥) 3%, and Swiss franc (Sfr) 2%.[2] Sensitivity to exchange rates was heightened by the lack of local content in the final auto sale.

Porsche, like some of its European counterparts, had suffered the rather whimsical swings in the value of the dollar over the years. The company's aversion to dollar exposures was founded in the reality of the losses suffered in 1992 and 1993, when the combined global recession and weak dollar had caused Porsche's sales to drop 38% in one year. The memory of the resulting losses was a lasting one. Since that time, with new leadership and new business and financial aggressiveness, Porsche had implemented a corporate-level currency management program which had both centralized Treasury functions and hedged its foreign currency exposures.

Porsche's leadership had taken a very aggressive currency hedging strategy beginning in 2001 when the euro was at a record low against the U.S. dollar. With 40% of all sales in North America, and that percentage expected to climb with the growth of the Cayenne, the company had purchased a series of put options on the U.S. dollar. These options would allow Porsche, if it desired, to exchange the U.S. dollars generated through North American sales into euros at specific exchange rates in the future. Described as a medium-term strategy, the

company had continued to increase its put option hedge purchases throughout 2002 and early 2003 so that it was 100% hedged for sales through the 2006 model year.

To actually implement the strategy Porsche created a three-year rolling portfolio of put options. Hedging net dollar exposures out three years required the company to not only forecast sales and subsequent exposures out three years, but to continually carry options possessing notional principals of a full three years of net exposure. The cost (option premiums) of an option portfolio of this size and maturity was not trivial.

Porsche had expected the dollar to fall in value (euro to rise). It therefore purchased put options with strike prices beginning at $0.90/€, and rising in subsequent years to $1.00/€. Only time would tell whether the put option strike rates chosen would provide significant profitability and protection. By locking in put option strike rates at the time of the euro's historical weakness, Porsche had acquired affordable protection against a strengthening euro for years to come — which was what Porsche both expected and feared. The gains from the hedging strategy were already materializing in 2002/03, and were expected to be even more substantial in the coming year. As illustrated in Exhibit 2, the impact of hedging activities on the basic earnings of the firm (EBIT margins) had not always been this successful.

But now there was growing sentiment that the derivative hedging strategy employed by Porsche was a second-best solution. But they did wish to take a serious look at U.S. dollar debt financing and exchange rate pass-through strategies.

**Dollar debt.** Porsche utilized nearly zero debt. Long-term debt as a percentage of assets topped 5% for the first time in 2002/03, and that was largely temporary. The company's superior operating cash flows had proven more than adequate to support aggressive capital expenditure and expansion in recent years, funding all investing activities internally and still allowing a growing accumulation of cash balances. In fact, cash and cash equivalent balances reached a record level of €1.7 billion at the end of the most recent fiscal year.

Porsche's view on debt was also rather extreme compared to that held by many other major automobile manufacturers. To quote CFO Holger Härter: "We learnt the hard way that banks are there for you when you don't need them, and when you do need them, they're nowhere

---

[1]This mini-case is abstracted with permission by the authors from *Porsche Exposed*, by Michael H. Moffet and Barbara S. Petitt, Thunderbird Case A06-04-0004.

[2]Porsche's gross U.S. dollar revenues had been growing rapidly in recent years. The 2003/04 year had ended with $1.836 billion in gross dollar revenues (auto, financing, and engineering services combined), up from $1.60 billion in 2001/02 and $1.75 billion in 2002/03. Although it varied from year to year, because the company also had some local expenses (in U.S. dollars), the net dollar exposure varied between 70% and 72% of the gross amount.

**EXHIBIT 2**

Impact of
Porsche's
Treasury Profits
on EBIT Margins

Source:
CreditSuisse/First
Boston, December
13, 2003, p. 47, p.
70. Values for
2003/04 are
estimates.

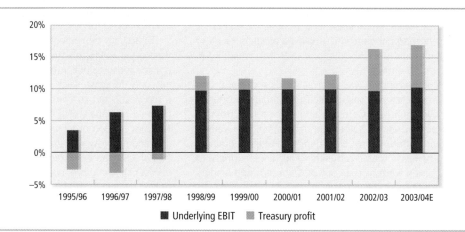

to be seen."[3] This anti-debt philosophy was also consistent with the emphasis placed by Porsche on both cash flow and cash balances. Again, in the words of CFO Härter: "We need to optimize all of the cash we generate so that we're able to continue to finance our growth ourselves, and have the confidence that if anything happens in the future that is beyond our control, we'll always be able to survive. That's absolutely essential." Although long-term dollar denominated debt was readily available to a company of Porsche's healthy financial condition, debt was clearly anathema to current management.

**Exchange rate pass-through.**  Exchange rate pass-through, the process of passing through all or part of exchange rate changes to the final customer in price, was probably very product-specific for Porsche. The 911 series was largely considered price-inelastic, and could probably accommodate additional local currency (primarily U.S. dollar) price increases and maintain sales volumes. The Boxster, competing in a very price-intensive market segment, probably could not. And although the Cayenne had debuted at a very high level, Porsche was moving quickly to introduce the lower-powered, lower-priced version immediately, fearing the higher price segment of the market was not a growth segment. All three vehicle platforms enjoyed at least attractive EBIT margins — some excessive compared to that of nearly every other auto manufacturer in the world. This portfolio could probably absorb some continued currency-induced pricing pressures in North America, but not the magnitudes some were forecasting for the euro's change against the dollar. Clearly, if the euro continued to rise, Porsche would be unable to absorb all of its movement in prices — margins would have to fall in North America.

Consider the latest addition to the stable of 911 thoroughbreds, the 911 Carrera 4S Cabriolet. A 320 horsepower, 3.6 liter six-cylinder engine convertible, the new Cabriolet had a top speed of 280 kilometers per hour and could go from zero-to-100 km/hr in 5.3 seconds. It was priced at €85,900, not including value-added tax (VAT) or other country-specific taxes. Simultaneously, Porsche planned to price the new Cabriolet at $93,200 (July 2003):

$$\text{Price}^{\$} = \text{Price}^{€} \times \text{Spot Rate}^{\$/€}$$

Which implied a rate of $1.0850/€ when rearranging the equation and plugging in the specific currency-based prices:

$$\text{Spot Rate}^{\$/€} = \frac{\text{Price}^{\$}}{\text{Price}^{€}} = \frac{\$93,200}{€85,900} = \$1.0850/€$$

This was a considerably stronger dollar than what was available on the open market at that time, the July 2003 monthly average of $1.1362/€ (about 4.5%). If the margins on the new Cabriolet were to be close to the similarly priced 911 Targa, which was currently averaging a 10.1% EBIT margin, these exchange rate changes and differentials from market could be quickly eliminated if not passed through to the dollar price. With the euro expected to rise to anywhere between $1.25/€ and $1.35/€ by July of 2004, Wiedeking and his staff did not believe even the 911's prices could be pushed up by those percentages that quickly.

In fact, Porsche's current belief was to not attempt to compete on price, but on quality and quantity. Porsche did not wish to let price clear the market. Its current contingency plans included production stops and production shifting. CEO Wiedeking was quite open about Porsche's

[3]Kersnar, Janet, "Hot Wheels," *CFO Europe.com*, November 2002.

ability to *stop* the Boxster production line within five hours of a simple phone call under the production agreement with Valmet. Over the longer run, Porsche was considering shifting a large proportion of Boxster production from Valmet in Finland to Porsche's own Stuttgart facilities, shifting 911 production over to Boxster as 911 sales dropped. This would allow the company to sustain its operating margins under shifting product demand changes.

Wiedeking and Holger did not make a practice of concerning themselves with the opinions or speculations of analysts. But many analysts were now separating Porsche's results into *underlying* versus *treasury*. For example, one investment banking firm had recently decomposed Porsche's forward-looking PE ratio into 18 *underlying* and 14 *treasury*, rather than crediting the firm with an aggregate PE of 32. Wiedeking and Holger sat down to debate their current strategy once again.

## Case Questions

1. Do you believe that Porsche's management is appropriately concerned with shareholder wealth? Does Porsche's ownership structure work to the benefit or detriment of public shareholders?

2. In your opinion is Porsche's current currency hedging strategy protecting it from adverse exchange rate changes? Will it work as well in the long run as in the short run? Evaluate the other hedging strategies available to the firm and compare and contrast alternatives.

3. Do you think Porsche's currency hedging strategy reflects a particular bias of management and ownership regarding shareholder value creation? Do you believe that Porsche can continue to predict the future movement of the euro?

## Summary of Learning Objectives

*Examine how operating exposure arises through unexpected changes in both operating and financing cash flows*

- *Foreign exchange exposure* is a measure of the potential for a firm's profitability, net cash flow, and market value to change because of a change in exchange rates. The three main types of foreign exchange risk are *operating*, *transaction*, and *translation exposures*.

- *Operating exposure* measures the change in value of the firm that results from changes in future operating cash flows caused by an unexpected change in exchange rates.

*Evaluate strategic alternatives to managing operating exposure*

- Strategies for the management of operating exposure emphasize the structuring of firm operations in order to create matching streams of cash flows by currency. This is termed *natural hedging*.

- The objective of operating exposure management is to anticipate and influence the effect of unexpected changes in exchange rates on a firm's future cash flow, rather than being forced into passive reaction to such changes. This task can best be accomplished if a firm diversifies internationally both its operations and its financing base.

*Detail the proactive policies available to firms for managing operating exposure*

- Proactive policies include matching currency of cash flow, currency risk-sharing clauses, back-to-back loan structures, and cross-currency swap agreements.

- Contractual approaches (i.e., options and forwards) have occasionally been used to hedge operating exposure but are costly and possibly ineffective.

## QUESTIONS

1. **By any other name.** Operating exposure has other names. What are they, and what do the words in these names suggest about the nature of operating exposure?

2. **Exposure type comparison.** From a cash flow measurement perspective, what is the major difference between losses from transaction exposure and from operating exposure?

3. **Intracompany cash flows.** What are the differences between operating cash flows and financial cash flows from parent to subsidiary or vice versa? List several cash flows in both categories and indicate why that flow takes place.

4. **Expected exchange rate changes.** Why do unexpected exchange rate changes contribute to

operating exposure, but expected exchange rate changes do not?

5. **Macroeconomic uncertainty.** What is *macroeconomic uncertainty* and how does it relate to measuring operating exposure?

6. **Who owns whom?** *The Economist* (December 1–7, 2001, p. 4 of "Survey" insert) reported on a French company that had a subsidiary in India. The Indian subsidiary in turn had its own subsidiary back in France. How would you conjecture the operating exposure to the international French firm of an unexpected devaluation of the Indian rupee relative to the euro?

7. **Strategic responses.** What strategic responses can a multinational firm make to avoid loss from its operating exposure?

8. **Proactive policies to offset foreign exchange exposure.** A fine line exists between fully anticipated exchange rate changes and possible-but-not-assured exchange rate changes. If management believes an exchange rate change might take place but cannot estimate the timing or amount of such change, what might management do to alleviate the possible consequences of such an uncertain devaluation?

9. **Paradox?** The possibility of a gain or loss on operating exposure offset by an opposite loss or gain on transaction exposure may appear contradictory. Explain why, when the currency in which a foreign subsidiary operates falls in value, the parent firm may experience both an operating gain and a transaction loss.

10. **Subsidiary borrowing from parent.** Newly established foreign subsidiaries are often financed with debt supplied by the parent, perhaps because a new subsidiary has no financial credit record or worthiness of its own, or maybe because the parent firm can acquire capital more cheaply. As soon as the subsidiary is operational, however, parent firms usually encourage or require their subsidiaries to arrange their own local debt financing. How would this approach serve as a natural hedge for most subsidiaries?

## PROBLEMS

1. **Trident Europe: Case 4.** Trident Europe (Exhibit 9.3) decides not to change its domestic price of

€12.80 per unit within Europe, but to raise its export price (in euros) from €12.80 per unit to €15.36 per unit, thus preserving its original dollar equivalent price of $15.36 per unit. Volume in both markets remains the same because no buyer perceives that the price has changed.

a. What is the impact on cash flow?

b. What is the impact on working capital needed?

c. What is the impact on the present value approach to measuring operating exposure?

2. **Trident Europe: Case 5.** Trident Europe (Exhibit 9.3) finds that domestic costs increase in proportion to the drop in value of the euro because of local inflation and a rise in the cost of imported raw materials and components. This rise in costs (+ 20%) applies to all cash costs, including direct costs and fixed cash operating costs. However, it does not apply to depreciation. Because of the increase in its costs Trident Europe increases its sales price in euros from €12.80 per unit to €15.36 per unit.

a. What is the impact on cash flow?

b. What is the impact on working capital needed?

c. What is the impact on the present-value approach to measuring operating exposure?

3. **Denver Plumbing Company (A).** Denver Plumbing Company exports toilet bowls to China. Sales are currently 1,000,000 units per year at the renminbi equivalent of $24 each. The Chinese renminbi has been trading at Rmb8.27/$, but a Hong Kong advisory service predicts the renminbi will drop in value next week to Rmb10.00/$, after which it will remain unchanged for at least a decade.

   Accepting this forecast as given, Denver Plumbing Company faces a pricing decision in the face of the impending devaluation: It may either (1) maintain the same renminbi price and in effect sell for fewer dollars, in which case Chinese volume will not change, or (2) maintain the same dollar price, raise the renminbi price in China to offset the devaluation, and experience a 10% drop in unit volume. Direct costs are 75% of the U.S. sales price.

a. What would be the short-run (one-year) impact of each pricing strategy?

b. Which do you recommend?

4. **Denver Plumbing Company (B).** Assume the same facts as in Denver Plumbing Company (A) above. Additionally, financial management believes that if it maintains the same renminbi sales price, volume will increase at 12% per annum for eight years. Dollar costs will not change. At the end of 10 years, Denver Plumbing's patent expires and it will no longer export to China. After the renminbi is devalued to Rmb10.00/$, no further devaluations are expected.

   If Denver Plumbing raises the renminbi price so as to maintain its dollar price, volume will increase at only 1% per annum for eight years, starting from the lower initial base of 900,000 units. Again dollar costs will not change and at the end of eight years Denver Plumbing will stop exporting to China. Denver Plumbing's weighted average cost of capital is 10%. Given these considerations, what should be Denver Plumbing's pricing policy? Explain.

5. **Hawaiian Macadamia Nuts.** Hawaiian Macadamia Nuts, based in Hilo, Hawaii, exports Macadamia nuts worldwide. The Japanese market is its biggest export market, with average annual sales invoiced in yen to Japanese customers of ¥1,200,000,000. At the present exchange rate of ¥125/$ this is equivalent to $9,600,000. Sales are relatively equally distributed during the year. They show up as a ¥250,00,000 account receivable on Hawaiian Macadamia Nuts' balance sheet. Credit terms to each customer allow for 60 days before payment is due. Monthly cash collections are typically ¥100,000,000.

   Hawaiian Macadamia Nuts would like to hedge its yen receipts, but it has too many customers and transactions to make it practical to sell each receivable forward. It does not want to use options because they are considered to be too expensive for this particular purpose. Therefore, they have decided to use a "matching" hedge by borrowing yen.

   a. How much should Hawaiian Macadamia Nuts borrow in yen?

   b. What should be the terms of payment on the yen loan?

6. **Cellini Fashionwear's risk-sharing.** Cellini Fashionwear, based in New York City, imports leather coats from Boselli Leather Goods, a reliable and longtime supplier based in Buenos Aires, Argentina. Payment is in Argentine pesos. When the peso lost its parity with the U.S. dollar in January 2002 it collapsed in value to Ps4.0/$ by October 2002. The outlook was for a further decline in the peso's value. Since both Cellini Fashionwear and Boselli Leather Goods wanted to continue their relationship they agreed on a risk-sharing arrangement. As long as the spot rate on the date of an invoice is between Ps3.5/$ and Ps4.5/$, Cellini Fashionwear will pay based on the spot rate. If the exchange rate falls outside this range they will share the difference equally with Boselli Leather Goods. The risk-sharing agreement will last for six months, at which time the exchange rate limits will be reevaluated. Cellini Fashionwear contracts to import leather coats from Boselli Leather Goods for Ps8,000,000 or $2,000,000 at the current spot rate of Ps4.0/$ during the next six months.

   a. If the exchange rate changes immediately to Ps6.00/$ what will be the dollar cost of six months of imports to Cellini Fashionwear?

   b. At Ps6.0/$ what will be the peso export sales of Boselli Leather Goods to Cellini Fashionwear?

7. **Autocars, Ltd.** Autocars, Ltd., of Coventry, England, manufactures British style sports cars, a number of which are exported to New Zealand for payment in pounds sterling. The distributor sells the sports cars in New Zealand for New Zealand dollars. The New Zealand distributor is unable to carry all of the foreign exchange risk, and would not sell Autocar models unless Autocar could share some of the foreign exchange risk. Autocars has agreed that sales for a given model year will initially be priced at a "base" spot rate between the New Zealand dollar and pound sterling set to be the spot mid-rate at the beginning of that model year. As long as the actual exchange rate is within ±5% of that base rate, payment will be made in pounds sterling. I.e., the New Zealand distributor assumes all foreign exchange risk. However if the spot rate at time of shipment falls outside of this ±5% range, Autocars will share equally (i.e., 50/50) the difference between the actual spot rate and the base rate. For the current model year the base rate is NZ$1.6400/£.

**a.** What are the outside ranges within which the New Zealand importer must pay at the then-current spot rate?

**b.** If Autocar ships 10 sports cars to the New Zealand distributor at a time when the spot exchange rate is NZ$1.7000/£, and each car has an invoice cost of £12,000, what will be the cost to the distributor in New Zealand dollars? How many pounds will Autocar receive, and how does this compare with Autocar's expected sales receipts of £12,000 per car?

**c.** If Autocars ships the same 10 sports cars to New Zealand at a time when the spot exchange rate is NZ$1.6500/£, how many New Zealand dollars will the distributor pay? How many pounds will Autocars receive?

**d.** Does a risk-sharing agreement such as this one shift the currency exposure from one party of the transaction to the other?

**e.** Why is such a risk-sharing agreement of benefit to Autocar? To the New Zealand distributor?

**8. High-Profile Printers, Inc. (A).** High-Profile Printers, Inc. (HPP) of the United States exports computer printers to Brazil, whose currency, the real (symbol R$) has been trading at R$3.40/US$. Exports to Brazil are currently 50,000 printers per year at the real equivalent of $200 each. A strong rumor exists that the real will be devalued to R$4.00/$ within two weeks by the Brazilian government. Should the devaluation take place, the real is expected to remain unchanged for another decade.

Accepting this forecast as given, HPP faces a pricing decision which must be made before any actual devaluation: HPP may either 1) maintain the same real price and in effect sell for fewer dollars, in which case Brazilian volume will not change, or 2) maintain the same dollar price, raise the real price in Brazil to compensate for the devaluation, and experience a 20% drop in volume. Direct costs in the United States are 60% of the U.S. sales price.

What would be the short-run (one-year) implication of each pricing strategy? Which do you recommend?

**9. High-Profile Printers, Inc. (B).** Assume the same facts as in High-Profile Printers (A). HPP also believes that if it maintains the same price in Brazilian real as a permanent policy, volume will

increase at 10% per annum for six years. Dollar costs will not change. At the end of six years HPP's patent expires and it will no longer export to Brazil. After the real is devalued to R$4.00/US$ no further devaluation is expected.

If HPP raises the price in real so as to maintain its dollar price, volume will increase at only 4% per annum for six years, starting from the lower initial base of 40,000 units. Again dollar costs will not change, and at the end of six years HPP will stop exporting to Brazil.

HPP's weighted average cost of capital is 12%. Given these considerations, what do you recommend for HPP's pricing policy? Justify your recommendation.

**10. Hedging Hogs: Risk-Sharing at Harley Davidson.** Harley-Davidson (USA) reportedly uses risk sharing agreements with its own foreign subsidiaries and with independent foreign distributors. Because these foreign units typically sell to their local markets and earn local currency, Harley would like to ease their individual currency exposure problems by allowing them to pay for merchandise from Harley (USA) in their local functional currency.

The spot rate between the U.S. dollar and the Australian dollar on January 1 is A$1.2823/US$. Assume that Harley uses this rate as the basis for setting its *central rate* or base exchange rate for the year at A$1.2800/US$. Harley agrees to price all contracts to Australian distributors at this exact exchange rate as long as the current spot rate on the order date is within ±2.5% of this rate. If the spot rate falls outside of this range, but is still within ±5% of the central rate, Harley will "share" equally (i.e., "50/50") the difference between the new spot rate and the neutral boundary with the distributor.

**a.** What are the specific exchange rates at the boundaries of the neutral and risk-sharing zones?

**b.** If Harley (USA) ships a motorcycle (a "hog") with an invoice of $8,500 to Australia, and the exchange rate on the order date is A$1.3442/US$, what is the price in Australian dollars?

**c.** If Harley (USA) ships the same hog to Australia, and the exchange rate on the order date is A$1.2442/US$, what is the price in Australian dollars to the foreign distributor?

**Internet Exercises**

1. **Operating exposure: recent examples.** Using the following major periodicals as starting points, find a current example of a firm with a substantial operating exposure problem. To aid in your search, you might focus on businesses having major operations in countries with recent currency crises, either through depreciation or major home currency appreciation.

   *Financial Times*
   http://www.ft.com/
   *The Economist*
   http://www.economist.com/
   *The Wall Street Journal*
   http://www.wsj.com/

2. **SEC Edgar Files.** In order to analyze an individual firm's operating exposure more carefully, it is necessary to have more detailed information available than in the normal annual report. Choose a specific firm with substantial international operations, for example Coca-Cola or PepsiCo, and search the Security and Exchange Commission's Edgar Files for more detailed financial reports of your firm's international operations.

   Search SEC Edgar Archives
   http://www.sec.gov/cgi-bin/srch-edgar

# *Translation Exposure*

## LEARNING OBJECTIVES

Demonstrate how translation practices result in a foreign exchange exposure for the multinational enterprise

Explain the meaning behind the designation of a foreign subsidiary's functional currency

Illustrate the theoretical and practical differences between the two primary methods of converting foreign currency denominated financial statements into the reporting currency of the parent company

Compare translation exposure with operating exposure

Analyze the costs and benefits of managing translation exposure

*Translation exposure*, also called *accounting exposure*, arises because financial statements of foreign subsidiaries — which are stated in foreign currency — must be restated in the parent's reporting currency for the firm to prepare consolidated financial statements. Foreign subsidiaries of U.S. companies, for example, must restate local euro, pound, yen, etc., statements into U.S. dollars so the foreign values can be added to the parent's U.S. dollar-denominated balance sheet and income statement. This accounting process is called "translation." Translation exposure is the potential for an increase or decrease in the parent's net worth and reported net income caused by a change in exchange rates since the last translation.

Although the main purpose of translation is to prepare consolidated statements, translated statements are also used by management to assess the performance of foreign subsidiaries. Although such assessment might be performed from the local currency statements, restatement of all subsidiary statements into the single "common denominator" of one currency facilitates management comparison.

## Overview of Translation

Translation in principle is quite simple. Foreign currency financial statements must be restated in the parent company's reporting currency for consolidation purposes. If the same exchange rate were used to remeasure each and every line item on the individual statement (income statement and balance sheet), there would be no imbalances resulting from the remeasurement. But if a different exchange rate were used for different line items on an individual statement, an imbalance would result.

Why would we use a different exchange rate in remeasuring different line items? Because translation principles in many countries are often a complex compromise between historical and current market valuation. Historical exchange rates may be used for certain equity accounts, fixed assets, and inventory items, while current exchange rates may be used for current assets, current liabilities, income, and expense items. The question, then, is what — if anything — is to be done with the imbalance? It is taken to either current income or equity reserves.

Translation methods differ by country along two overall dimensions, as well as by individual account. One dimension is a difference in the way a foreign subsidiary is characterized based on its degree of independence of the parent firm. The second dimension is the definition of which currency is most important for the foreign subsidiary's operations.

### SUBSIDIARY CHARACTERIZATION

Most countries today specify the translation method used by a foreign subsidiary based on the subsidiary's business operations. For example, a foreign subsidiary's business can be categorized as either an *integrated foreign entity* or a *self-sustaining foreign entity*. An integrated foreign entity is one that operates as an extension of the parent company, with cash flows and general business lines that are highly interrelated with those of the parent. A self-sustaining foreign entity is one that operates in the local economic environment independent of the parent company. The differentiation is important to the logic of translation. A foreign subsidiary should be valued principally in terms of the currency that is the basis of its economic viability.

It is not unusual to find two different foreign subsidiaries of a single company that have different characters. For example, a U.S.–based manufacturer that produces subassemblies in the United States which are then shipped to a Spanish subsidiary for finishing, assembly, and resale in the European Union would likely characterize the Spanish subsidiary as an *integrated foreign entity*. The dominant currency of economic operation is likely the U.S. dollar. That same U.S. parent may, however, also own an agricultural marketing business in Venezuela which has few cash flows or operations related to the U.S. parent company (or U.S. dollar). The Venezuelan subsidiary may purchase almost all materials and expend all costs of operations in Venezuelan bolivar, while selling exclusively in Venezuela. Because the Venezuelan subsidiary's operations are independent of its parent, and its functional currency is the Venezuelan bolivar, it would be classified as a *self-sustaining foreign entity*.

## FUNCTIONAL CURRENCY

A foreign subsidiary's *functional currency* is the currency of the primary economic environment in which the subsidiary operates and in which it generates cash flows. In other words, it is the dominant currency used by that foreign subsidiary in its day-to-day operations. It is important to note that the geographic location of a foreign subsidiary and its functional currency may be different. The Singapore subsidiary of a U.S. firm may find that its functional currency is the U.S. dollar (integrated subsidiary), the Singapore dollar (self-sustaining subsidiary), or a third currency such as the British pound (also a self-sustaining subsidiary).

The United States, rather than distinguishing a foreign subsidiary as either integrated or self-sustaining, follows a parallel approach that requires that the functional currency of the subsidiary be determined. Current U.S. translation practices are delineated in *Statement of Financial Accounting Standards Number 52*, usually referred to as FAS#52. It was issued by the Financial Accounting Standards Board (FASB) in December 1981, superseding FAS#8, which had been in effect since 1975. The FASB defines approved accounting practices for U.S. firms.

Management must evaluate the nature and purpose of each of its individual foreign subsidiaries to determine the appropriate functional currency for each. Exhibit 10.1 lists the indicators the FASB uses in determining the functional currency of a foreign subsidiary. If a foreign subsidiary of a U.S.–based company is determined to have the U.S. dollar as its functional currency, it is essentially an extension of the parent company (equivalent to the integrated foreign entity designation used by most countries). If, however, the functional currency of the foreign subsidiary is determined to be different from the U.S. dollar, the subsidiary is considered a separate entity from the parent (equivalent to the self-sustaining entity designation).

## Translation Methods

Two basic methods for the translation of foreign subsidiary financial statements are employed worldwide, the *current rate method* and the *temporal method*. Regardless of which method is employed, a translation method must not only designate at what exchange rate individual balance sheet and income statement items are remeasured, but also designate where any imbalance is to be recorded (typically either in current income or in an equity reserve account in the balance sheet). The significance of this decision is that imbalances passed through the income statement affect the firm's current reported income, while imbalances transferred directly to the balance sheet do not.

## EXHIBIT 10.1

Economic Indicators for Determining the Functional Currency

According to the Financial Accounting Standards Board (FASB), the following economic indicators should be used to determine the functional currency of any foreign subsidiary:

**A. Cash flow indicators**

(1) Foreign Currency — Cash flows related to the foreign entity's individual assets and liabilities are primarily in the foreign currency and do not impact the parent company's cash flows.

(2) Parent's Currency — Cash flows related to the foreign entity's individual assets and liabilities directly impact the parent's cash flows on a current basis and are readily available for remittance to the parent company.

**B. Sales price indicators**

(1) Foreign Currency — Sales prices for the foreign entity's products are not primarily responsive on a short-term basis to changes in exchange rates but are determined more by local competition or by local government regulation.

(2) Parent's Currency — Sales prices for the foreign entity's products are primarily responsive on a short-term basis to changes in exchange rates; for example, sales prices are determined more by worldwide competition or by international prices.

**C. Sales market indicators**

(1) Foreign Currency — There is an active local sales market for the foreign entity's products, although there might also be significant amounts of exports.

(2) Parent's Currency — The sales market is mostly in the parent's country or sales contracts are denominated in the parent's currency.

**D. Expense indicators**

(1) Foreign Currency — Labor, materials, and other costs for the foreign entity's products or services are primarily local costs, even though there might also be imports from other countries.

(2) Parent's Currency — Labor, materials, and other costs for the foreign entity's products or services, on a continuing basis, are primarily costs for components obtained from the country in which the parent company is located.

**E. Financing indicators**

(1) Foreign Currency — Financing is primarily denominated in foreign currency, and funds generated by the foreign entity's operations are sufficient to service existing and normally expected debt obligations.

(2) Parent's Currency — Financing is primarily from the parent or other dollar-denominated obligations, or funds generated by the foreign entity's operations are not sufficient to service existing and normally expected debt obligations without the infusion of additional funds from the parent. Infusion of additional funds from the parent for expansion is not a factor, provided funds generated by the foreign entity's expanded operations are expected to service that additional financing.

**F. Intercompany transactions and arrangements indicators**

(1) Foreign Currency — There is a low volume of intercompany transactions and there is not an extensive interrelationship between the operations of the foreign entity and the parent company. However, the foreign entity's operations may rely on the parent's subsidiaries' competitive advantages, such as patents and trademarks.

(2) Parent's Currency — There is a high volume of intercompany transactions and there is an extensive interrelationship between the foreign entity and the parent company. Additionally, the parent's currency generally would be the functional currency if the foreign entity is a device or shell corporation for holding investments, obligations, intangible assets, etc., that could readily be carried on the parent's or an affiliate's books.

Reprinted with permission of the FASB.

## CURRENT RATE METHOD

The current rate method is the most prevalent in the world today. Under this method, all financial statement line items are translated at the "current" exchange rate with few exceptions. Line items include

- *Assets and liabilities.* All assets and liabilities are translated at the current rate of exchange; that is, at the rate of exchange in effect on the balance sheet date.
- *Income statement items.* All items, including depreciation and cost of goods sold, are translated at either the actual exchange rate on the dates the various revenues, expenses, gains, and losses were incurred or at an appropriately weighted average exchange rate for the period.
- *Distributions.* Dividends paid are translated at the exchange rate in effect on the date of payment.
- *Equity items.* Common stock and paid-in capital accounts are translated at historical rates. Year-end retained earnings consist of the original year-beginning retained earnings plus or minus any income or loss for the year.

Gains or losses caused by translation adjustments are *not* included in the calculation of consolidated net income. Rather, translation gains or losses are reported separately and accumulated in a separate equity reserve account (on the consolidated balance sheet) with a title such as *cumulative translation adjustment* (CTA). A multitude of different names are used for this reserve account adjustment. In Spain, for example, the CTA is termed the *diferencias de conversión*. If a foreign subsidiary is later sold or liquidated, translation gains or losses of past years accumulated in the CTA account are reported as one component of the total gain or loss on sale or liquidation. The total gain or loss is reported as part of the net income or loss for the time period in which the sale or liquidation occurs. This is the subject of the mini-case, "LaJolla Engineering Services," at the end of this chapter.

The biggest advantage of the current rate method is that the gain or loss on translation does not pass through the income statement but goes directly to a reserve account. This eliminates the variability of reported earnings due to foreign exchange translation gains or losses. A second advantage of the current rate method is that the relative proportions of individual balance sheet accounts remain the same. Hence the process of translation does not distort such balance sheet ratios as the current ratio or the debt-to-equity ratio. The main disadvantage of the current rate method is that it violates the accounting principle of carrying balance sheet accounts at historical cost. For example, foreign assets purchased with dollars and then recorded on a subsidiary's statements at their foreign currency historical cost are translated back into dollars at a different rate. Thus, they are reported in the consolidated statement in dollars at something other than their historical dollar cost.

## TEMPORAL METHOD

Under the temporal method, specific assets and liabilities are translated at exchange rates consistent with the timing of the item's creation. The *temporal method* assumes that a number of individual line item assets such as inventory and net plant and equipment are restated regularly to reflect market value. If these items were not restated but were instead carried at historical cost, the temporal method becomes the *monetary/*

*nonmonetary method* of translation, a form of translation that is still used by a number of countries today. Line items include

- *Monetary assets* (primarily cash, marketable securities, accounts receivable, and long-term receivables) and *monetary liabilities* (primarily current liabilities and long-term debt) are translated at current exchange rates.
- *Nonmonetary assets and liabilities* (primarily inventory and fixed assets) are translated at historical rates.
- *Income statement items* are translated at the average exchange rate for the period, except for items such as depreciation and cost of goods sold that are directly associated with nonmonetary assets or liabilities. These accounts are translated at their historical rate.
- *Distributions*. Dividends paid are translated at the exchange rate in effect on the date of payment.
- *Equity items*. Common stock and paid-in capital accounts are translated at historical rates. Year-end retained earnings consist of the original year-beginning retained earnings plus or minus any income or loss for the year, plus or minus any imbalance from translation, as explained next.

Under the temporal method, gains or losses resulting from remeasurement are carried directly to current consolidated income and not to equity reserves. Hence foreign exchange gains and losses arising from the translation process do introduce volatility to consolidated earnings.

The basic advantage of the temporal method is that foreign nonmonetary assets are carried at their original cost in the parent's consolidated statement. In most countries this approach is consistent with the original cost treatment of domestic assets of the parent firm. In practice, however, if some foreign accounts are translated at one exchange rate while others are translated at different rates, the resulting translated balance sheet will not balance. Hence there is a need for a "plug" to remove what has been called the "dangling debit or credit." The true nature of the gain or loss created by use of such a plug is open to question. Unrealized foreign exchange gains or losses are included in quarterly primary *earnings per share* (EPS), thus increasing variability of reported earnings.

## U.S. TRANSLATION PROCEDURES

As mentioned previously, the United States differentiates foreign subsidiaries on the basis of functional currency, not subsidiary characterization. The result, however, is equivalent. Exhibit 10.2 illustrates the translation procedures used by U.S.–based companies under current U.S. generally accepted accounting principles (GAAP). As shown in Exhibit 10.2:

- If the financial statements of the foreign subsidiary of a U.S. company are maintained in U.S. dollars, translation is not required.
- If the financial statements of the foreign subsidiary are maintained in the local currency and the local currency is the functional currency, they are translated by the *current rate method*.
- If the financial statements of the foreign subsidiary are maintained in the local currency and the U.S. dollar is the functional currency, they are remeasured by the

## EXHIBIT 10.2

Procedure Flowchart for U.S. Translation Practices

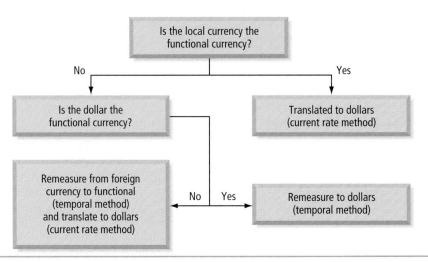

**Purpose: Foreign currency financial statements must be translated into U.S. dollars**

If the financial statements of the foreign subsidiary are expressed in a foreign currency, the following determinations need to be made.

Is the local currency the functional currency?

No — Yes

Is the dollar the functional currency?

Translated to dollars (current rate method)

Remeasure from foreign currency to functional (temporal method) and translate to dollars (current rate method)

No   Yes

Remeasure to dollars (temporal method)

*temporal method.* (Terminology can be tricky; under U.S. accounting and translation practices, use of the current rate method is termed *translation* while use of the temporal method is termed *remeasurement.*)

• If the financial statements of foreign subsidiaries of U.S. companies are maintained in the local currency and neither the local currency nor the dollar is the functional currency, then the statements must first be remeasured into the functional currency by the temporal method, and then translated into dollars by the current rate method.

## HYPERINFLATION COUNTRIES

FAS#52 has a special provision for translating statements of foreign subsidiaries of U.S. companies operating in countries where cumulative inflation has been approximately 100% or more over a three-year period. Financial statements of these subsidiaries must be translated into the reporting currency using the temporal method.

The rationale is to correct the problem of the "disappearing asset." If the current rate were used, depreciation would be understated relative to replacement costs, profits would be overstated in real terms, and the book value of plant and equipment would eventually nearly disappear from the balance sheet as its value diminished in reporting currency terms. Translating plant, equipment, and depreciation expenses at the historical exchange rate yields a higher asset value in the reporting currency than would use of the current (depreciated) exchange rate. This leads to a less distorted income statement and balance sheet. In effect, FAS#52 declares the functional currency of subsidiaries in hyperinflation countries to be the reporting currency (U.S. dollars for U.S. firms).

The hyperinflation standard has precedence in business practice.

> When a country is plagued with hyperinflation, it often uses the U.S. dollar or other hard currency as its de facto functional currency for actual transactions regardless of accounting standards. For example, most Israeli retailers in 1982 priced their merchandise in U.S. dollars, not shekels. In the face of triple-digit inflation, they cannot change their prices every other day. The U.S. dollar becomes the unit of account. Also, when an Israeli holds U.S. dollars and the shekel is devalued, his holding in dollars remains the same, whereas if he holds currency in shekels and the shekel is devalued, his holding declines in purchasing power. The U.S. dollar becomes the storehouse of value. Consistent with the mercantile practice of businessmen in highly inflationary economies, the FASB promulgates the accounting standard that the home currency becomes the functional currency when inflation is rampant; otherwise the local currency is the functional currency. Accounting standards-setting simply is patterned after accepted business practice.
>
> Russell A. Taussig, "Impact of SFAS 52 on the Translation of Foreign Financial Statements of Companies in Highly-Inflationary Economies," *Journal of Accounting, Auditing, and Finance,* Winter 1983, pp. 145–176.

In summary, U.S. translation practices require the parent company to first determine the functional currency of the foreign subsidiary, which then dictates whether the subsidiary's financial statements will be translated by the current rate method or remeasured by the temporal method. A final point of emphasis: The selection of the functional currency is determined by the economic realities of the subsidiary's operations and is not a discretionary management decision on preferred procedures or elective outcomes. Since many U.S.–based multinationals have numerous foreign subsidiaries, some U.S. dollar–functional and some foreign currency–functional, foreign currency gains and losses may be both passing through current consolidated income and/or accruing in equity reserves.

## INTERNATIONAL TRANSLATION PRACTICES

As illustrated in Exhibit 10.3, many of the world's largest industrial countries — as well as the relatively newly formed International Accounting Standards Committee (IASC) — follow the same basic translation procedure:

- A foreign subsidiary is an *integrated foreign entity* or a *self-sustaining foreign entity*.
- Integrated foreign entities are typically remeasured using the *temporal method* (or some slight variation thereof).
- Self-sustaining foreign entities are translated at the *current rate method*, also termed the *closing-rate method*.

## Translation Example: Trident Europe

Let us continue the example of Trident from Chapter 9, focusing here on its European subsidiary. We will also illustrate translation by the temporal method in order to show the very arbitrary nature of a translation gain or loss. Selection of the accounting method is the major factor in determining the magnitude of gain or loss. The example that follows deals with balance sheet translation only. The somewhat more complex procedures for translating income statements are described in international accounting texts.

## EXHIBIT 10.3

Comparison of Translation Methods Employed in Selected Countries

| Country | Integrated Foreign Entity | Self-Sustaining Foreign Entity |
|---|---|---|
| United States | Financial statements are remeasured using the temporal method with adjustments included in current net income. | Current rate method. Translation adjustments are reported as a separate component of shareholders' equity. |
| International | Temporal method. Translation adjustments are included in net income currently, except that translation adjustments on long-term monetary items may be deferred and amortized over the life of the item. | Current rate method. Translation adjustments are reported as a separate component of shareholders' equity. |
| Australia | Temporal method. Translation adjustments are included in current net income. | Current rate method. Translation adjustments are reported as a separate component of shareholders' equity. |
| Canada | Temporal method. Translation adjustments are included in current net income. | Current rate method. Translation adjustments are reported as a separate component of shareholders' equity. |
| France | Temporal method. Translation adjustments are included in current net income. | Current rate method. Translation adjustments are reported as a separate component of shareholders' equity. |
| Germany | Temporal method or current rate method is acceptable. Translation adjustments are included in net income currently if the temporal method is used and as a separate component if the current rate method is used. | Same as for integrated foreign entity. |
| Japan | Temporal method. Adjustments related to foreign subsidiaries are reported separately as an asset or a liability; adjustments related to divisions or branches are included in current net income. | Same as for integrated foreign entity. |
| Netherlands | Temporal method. Translation adjustments are included in current net income. The current rate method is used if the entity utilizes current value accounting. | Current rate method. Translation adjustments are reported as a separate component of shareholders' equity. |
| United Kingdom | Temporal method. Translation adjustments are included in current net income. | Current rate method. Translation adjustments are reported as a separate component of shareholders' equity. |

Source: *Survey of International Accounting Practices*, Arthur Andersen & Co., Coopers & Lybrand, Deloitte & Touche, Ernst & Young, KPMG Peat Marwick, and Price Waterhouse, 1991.

The functional currency of Trident Europe is the euro, and the reporting currency of its parent, Trident Corporation, is the U.S. dollar. Assume the following:

1. Plant and equipment and long-term debt were acquired and common stock issued by Trident Europe some time in the past when the exchange rate was $1.2760/€. Although the euro never traded at this rate against the dollar, the historic deutschemark rate in use at the time the initial investment was made must be converted to a "historic euro rate" which, in effect, backdates euro rates against the deutschemark.

2. Inventory currently on hand was purchased or manufactured during the immediately prior quarter when the average exchange rate was \$1.2180/€. At the close of business on Monday, December 31, 2001, the current spot exchange rate was \$1.2000/€.

3. When business reopened on January 2, 2002, after the New Year holiday, the euro had dropped 16.67% in value versus the dollar to \$1.0000/€.

The example will also look at the consequences had the euro strengthened by 10% overnight to \$1.3200/€.

## CURRENT RATE METHOD

The top half of Exhibit 10.4 illustrates translation loss using the current rate method. Assets and liabilities on the predepreciation balance sheet are translated at the current exchange rate of \$1.1600/€. Capital stock is translated at the historical rate of \$1.2760/€, and retained earnings are translated at a composite rate that is equivalent to having each past year's addition to retained earnings translated at the exchange rate in effect in that year.

The sum of retained earnings and the cumulative translation adjustment (CTA) account must "balance" the liabilities and net worth section of the balance sheet with the asset side. For this hypothetical text example we have assumed the two amounts used for the December 31, 2001, balance sheet. The assumption does not affect the final measure of the increase in the CTA account because the retained earnings account is carried over at whatever arbitrary amount is assigned for this example.

As shown in the top half of Exhibit 10.4, the "just before depreciation" dollar translation reports an accumulated translation loss from prior periods of \$136,800. This balance is the cumulative gain or loss from translating euro statements into dollars in prior years, and it had been carried separately in the CTA account. Statements from 1998 and earlier would have originally been deutschemark statements, translated into euros after January 1, 1999, when the euro was introduced.

After the 16.67% depreciation, Trident Corp. translates assets and liabilities at the new exchange rate of \$1.0000/€. Equity accounts, including retained earnings, are translated just as they were before depreciation, and as a result the cumulative translation loss increases to \$1,736,800. The increase of \$1,600,000 in this account (from a cumulative loss of \$136,800 to a new cumulative loss of \$1,736,800) is the translation loss measured by the current rate method.

This translation loss is a decrease in equity, measured in the parent's reporting currency, of net exposed assets. An *exposed asset* is an asset whose value drops with the depreciation of the functional currency and rises with an appreciation of that currency. *Net* exposed assets in this context means exposed assets minus exposed liabilities. Net exposed assets are positive (that is, "long") if exposed assets exceed exposed liabilities. They are negative ("short") if exposed assets are smaller than exposed liabilities.

Exposure can be measured by creating a before-and-after translated balance sheet, as in Exhibit 10.4. A simpler method is to multiply net exposed assets by the percentage amount of depreciation. We did this calculation for the current rate method in the left column of Exhibit 10.5, which illustrates that a 16.67% depreciation of the euro means that net exposed assets of \$9,600,000 lose 16.67% of their value, a translation loss of \$1,600,000.

Suppose instead that the euro had appreciated. If, by the end of the year, the euro had appreciated from \$1.2000/€ to \$1.3200/€, the appreciation would be 10%. The effect of this appears in Panel B of Exhibit 10.5, which starts with the same net exposed

**EXHIBIT 10.4**

Trident Europe: Translation Loss Just After Depreciation of the Euro

|  | In Euros | $/€ | December 31, 2001 Just Before Depreciation | $/€ | January 2, 2002 Just After Depreciation |
|---|---|---|---|---|---|
| **Current Rate Method** | | | | | |
| Cash | €1,600,000 | 1.2000 | $1,920,000 | 1.0000 | $1,600,000 |
| Accounts receivable | 3,200,000 | 1.2000 | 3,840,000 | 1.0000 | 3,200,000 |
| Inventory | 2,400,000 | 1.2000 | 2,880,000 | 1.0000 | 2,400,000 |
| Net plant and equipment | 4,800,000 | 1.2000 | 5,760,000 | 1.0000 | 4,800,000 |
|  | €12,000,000 |  | $14,400,000 |  | $12,000,000 |
| Accounts payable | € 800,000 | 1.2000 | $960,000 | 1.0000 | $800,000 |
| Short-term bank loan | 1,600,000 | 1.2000 | 1,920,000 | 1.0000 | 1,600,000 |
| Long-term debt | 1,600,000 | 1.2000 | 1,920,000 | 1.0000 | 1,600,000 |
| Common stock | 1,800,000 | 1.2760 | 2,296,800 | 1.2000 | 2,296,800 |
| Retained earnings | 6,200,000 | (a) | 7,440,000 | 1.2000(b) | 7,440,000 |
| Translation adjustment (CTA) | — | — | (136,800) | — | (1,736,800) |
|  | €12,000,000 |  | $14,400,000 |  | $12,000,000 |
| **Temporal Method** | | | | | |
| Cash | €1,600,000 | 1.2000 | $1,920,000 | 1.0000 | $1,600,000 |
| Accounts receivable | 3,200,000 | 1.2000 | 3,840,000 | 1.0000 | 3,200,000 |
| Inventory | 2,400,000 | 1.2180 | 2,923,200 | 1.2180 | 2,923,200 |
| Net plant and equipment | 4,800,000 | 1.2760 | 6,124,800 | 1.2760 | 6,124,800 |
|  | €12,000,000 |  | $14,808,000 |  | $13,848,000 |
| Accounts payable | € 800,000 | 1.2000 | $960,000 | 1.0000 | $800,000 |
| Short-term bank loan | 1,600,000 | 1.2000 | 1,920,000 | 1.0000 | 1,600,000 |
| Long-term debt | 1,600,000 | 1.2000 | 1,920,000 | 1.0000 | 1,600,000 |
| Common stock | 1,800,000 | 1.2760 | 2,296,800 | 1.2760 | 2,296,800 |
| Retained earnings | 6,200,000 | (a) | 7,711,200 | (b) | 7,711,200 |
| Translation gain (loss) | — | — | — | (c) | (160,000) |
|  | €12,000,000 |  | $14,808,000 |  | $13,848,000 |

[a] Dollar retained earnings before depreciation are the cumulative sum of additions to retained earnings of all prior years, translated at exchange rates in each year. See text for assumptions used in this example.

[b] Translated into dollars at the same rate as before depreciation of the euro.

[c] Under the temporal method, the translation loss of $160,000 would be closed into retained earnings via the income statement rather than left as a separate line item shown here. Hence, under the temporal method, ending retained earnings would actually be $7,711,200 − $160,000 = $7,551,200.

assets calculated in Panel A. Under the current rate method, the U.S. parent would have a translation gain of $960,000.

## TEMPORAL METHOD

Translation of the same accounts under the temporal method shows the arbitrary nature of any gain or loss from translation. This is illustrated in the bottom half of Exhibit 10.4. Monetary assets and monetary liabilities in the predepreciation euro balance sheet are translated at the current rate of exchange, but other assets and the

## EXHIBIT 10.5

Trident Europe: Translation Loss or Gain: Comparison of Current Rate and Temporal Methods

**Panel A: Depreciation of the euro, from $1.2000/€ to $1.0000/€ (−16.67%)**

| | Current Rate Method | Temporal Method |
|---|---|---|
| **Exposed Assets** | | |
| Cash | $1,920,000 | $1,920,000 |
| Accounts receivable | 3,840,000 | 3,840,000 |
| Inventory | 2,880,000 | not exposed |
| Net plant and equipment | 5,760,000 | not exposed |
| Total exposed assets ("A") | $14,400,000 | $5,760,000 |
| **Exposed Liabilities** | | |
| Accounts payable | $960,000 | $960,000 |
| Short-term bank loan | 1,920,000 | 1,920,000 |
| Long-term debt | 1,920,000 | 1,920,000 |
| Total exposed liabilities ("L") | $4,800,000 | $4,800,000 |
| Gain (loss) if euro depreciates | | |
| Net exposed assets ("A" − "L") | $9,600,000 | $960,000 |
| Times amount of depreciation | × (0.1667) | × (0.1667) |
| Translation gain (loss) | ($1,600,000) | ($160,000) |

**Panel B: Appreciation of the euro, from $1.2000/€ to $1.3200/€ (+10.00%)**

| | | |
|---|---|---|
| Gain (loss) if euro appreciates | | |
| Net exposed assets ("A" − "L") | $9,600,000 | $960,000 |
| Times amount of appreciation | × 0.1000 | × 0.1000 |
| Translation gain (loss) | $960,000 | $96,000 |

equity accounts are translated at their historic rates. For Trident Europe, the historical rate for inventory differs from that for net plant and equipment because inventory was acquired more recently.

Under the temporal method, translation losses are not accumulated in a separate equity account but passed directly through each quarter's income statement. Thus in the dollar balance sheet translated before depreciation, retained earnings were the cumulative result of earnings from all prior years translated at historical rates in effect each year, plus translation gains or losses from all prior years. In Exhibit 10.4, no translation loss appears in the predepreciation dollar balance sheet because any losses would have been closed to retained earnings.

The effect of the 16.67% depreciation is to create an immediate translation loss of $160,000. This amount is shown as a separate line item in Exhibit 10.4 in order to focus attention on it for this textbook example. Under the temporal method, this translation loss of $160,000 would pass through the income statement, reducing reported net income and reducing retained earnings. Ending retained earnings would in fact be $7,711,200 minus $160,000, or $7,551,200. Other countries using the temporal method do not necessarily require gains and losses to pass through the income statement.

When translation loss is viewed in terms of changes in the value of exposed accounts, as in the right column of Exhibit 10.5, the loss under the temporal method is 16.67% of net exposed assets of $960,000, or $160,000. If the euro should appreciate

10%, the translation gain to the U.S. parent would be $96,000, as shown at the bottom of the right column in Exhibit 10.5.

## MANAGERIAL IMPLICATIONS

In Exhibits 10.4 and 10.5, translation loss or gain is larger under the current rate method because inventory and net plant and equipment, as well as all monetary assets, are deemed exposed. When net exposed assets are larger, gains or losses from translation are also larger.

The managerial implications of this fact are very important. If management expects a foreign currency to depreciate, it could minimize translation exposure by reducing net exposed assets. If management anticipates an appreciation of the foreign currency, it should increase net exposed assets to benefit from a gain.

Depending on the accounting method of the moment, management might select different assets and liabilities for reduction or increase. Thus "real" decisions about investing and financing might be dictated by which accounting technique is required, when in fact the method of reporting should be neutral in its influence on operating and financing decisions.

## Comparing Translation Exposure with Operating Exposure

Translation gains or losses in the event of a currency depreciation are compared with the operating gains or losses from Chapter 9 Exhibit 9.3 in Exhibit 10.6. Obviously translation gains or losses can be quite different from operating gains or losses, not only in magnitude but also in sign. A manager focusing only on translation losses, in a situation such as Trident Europe, might avoid doing business in Germany because of the likelihood of such a loss. The manager might fear losing a bonus tied to reported profits, or possibly losing a job if the investment in Germany were made and the income statement reported severe translation losses back to the home office.

Operating exposure presents an entirely different view of the same situation. As summarized in Exhibit 10.6, Germany and Europe became more (not less) desirable locations for investment because of the *operating* consequences that followed depreciation in two of the three cases shown here. This illustrates the importance of focusing decisions primarily on the operating consequences of changes in exchange rates and only secondarily on the accounting-based measurements of performance.

**EXHIBIT 10.6**

Comparison of Translation Exposure with Operating Exposure, Depreciation of Euro from $1.200/€ to $1.0000/€ for Trident Europe

| Exposure | Amount | Gain or Loss |
|---|---|---|
| **Translation Exposure** (Exhibits 10.4 and 10.5) | | |
| Current rate method | ($1,600,000) | **Loss** on translation |
| Temporal method | ($160,000) | **Loss** on translation |
| **Operating Exposure** (in present value terms; Exhibit 9.3) | | |
| Case 1: Depreciation of euro | ($1,033,914) | **Loss** on operations |
| Case 2: Volume doubles | $2,866,106 | **Gain** on operations |
| Case 3: Sales price increases | $3,742,892 | **Gain** on operations |

## Managing Translation Exposure

The main technique to minimize translation exposure is called a *balance sheet hedge*. Some firms have attempted to hedge translation exposure in the forward market. Such action amounts to speculating in the forward market in the hope that a cash profit will be realized to offset the noncash loss from translation. Success depends on a precise prediction of future exchange rates, for such a hedge will not work over a range of possible future spot rates. In addition, such a hedge will increase the tax burden, since the profit from the forward hedge (i.e., speculation) is taxable, but the translation loss does not reduce taxable income.

### BALANCE SHEET HEDGE DEFINED

A balance sheet hedge requires an equal amount of *exposed* foreign currency assets and liabilities on a firm's consolidated balance sheet. If this can be achieved for each foreign currency, net translation exposure will be zero. A change in exchange rates will change the value of exposed liabilities in an equal amount but in a direction opposite to the change in value of exposed assets. If a firm translates by the temporal method, a zero net exposed position is called *monetary balance*. Complete monetary balance cannot be achieved under the current rate method because total assets would have to be matched by an equal amount of debt, but the equity section of the balance sheet must still be translated at historic exchange rates.

The cost of a balance sheet hedge depends on relative borrowing costs. If foreign currency borrowing costs, after adjusting for foreign exchange risk, are higher than parent currency borrowing costs, the balance sheet hedge is costly, and vice versa. Normal operations, however, already require decisions about the magnitude and currency denomination of specific balance sheet accounts. Thus balance sheet hedges are a compromise in which the denomination of balance sheet accounts is altered, perhaps at a cost in terms of interest expense or operating efficiency, to achieve some degree of foreign exchange protection.

### BALANCE SHEET HEDGE ILLUSTRATED

To illustrate a balance sheet hedge, let us return again to the translation exposure previously identified for Trident Europe and its parent, Trident Corporation. Earlier data from Exhibit 10.4 is restated in a different format in Exhibit 10.7.

Trident Europe expects the euro to drop 16.67% in value from its year-beginning value to a new exchange rate of $1.0000/€. Under the current rate method, the expected loss is 16.67% of the exposure of $9,600,000, or $1,600,000. Under the temporal method, the expected loss is 16.67% of the exposure of $960,000, or $160,000.

To achieve a balance sheet hedge, Trident Corporation must either (1) reduce exposed euro assets without simultaneously reducing euro liabilities or (2) increase euro liabilities without simultaneously increasing euro assets. One way to do this is to exchange existing euro cash for dollars. If Trident Europe does not have large euro cash balances, it can borrow euros and exchange the borrowed euros for dollars. Another subsidiary could borrow euros and exchange them for dollars. That is, the essence of the hedge is for the parent or any of its subsidiaries to create euro debt and exchange the proceeds for dollars.

**CURRENT RATE METHOD.**    Under the current rate method, Trident Europe should borrow as much as €8,000,000. The initial effect of this first step is to increase both an

## EXHIBIT 10.7

Trident Europe,
Balance Sheet
Exposure

| | Balance Sheet Accounts | Current Rate Exposure | Temporal Exposure |
|---|---|---|---|
| **Assets** | | | |
| Cash | €1,600,000 | €1,600,000 | €1,600,000 |
| Accounts receivable | 3,200,000 | 3,200,000 | 3,200,000 |
| Inventory | 2,400,000 | 2,400,000 | |
| Net plant and equipment | 4,800,000 | 4,800,000 | |
| Total assets | €12,000,000 | | |
| Exposed assets | | €12,000,000 | €4,800,000 |
| | | | |
| **Liabilities and capital** | | | |
| Accounts payable | €800,000 | €800,000 | €800,000 |
| Short-term bank debt | 1,600,000 | 1,600,000 | 1,600,000 |
| Long-term debt | 1,600,000 | 1,600,000 | 1,600,000 |
| Capital stock | 1,800,000 | | |
| Retained earnings | 6,200,000 | | |
| Total liabilities and net worth | €12,000,000 | | |
| Exposed liabilities | | €4,000,000 | €4,000,000 |
| Net exposed assets in euros | | €8,000,000 | €800,000 |
| Times exchange rate ($/€) | | × 1.2000 | × 1.2000 |
| Net exposed assets in dollars | | $9,600,000 | $960,000 |
| Times amount of devaluation | | × 0.1667 | × 0.1667 |
| Expected translation gain (loss) | | $(1,600,000) | $(160,000) |

exposed asset (cash) and an exposed liability (notes payable) on the balance sheet of Trident Europe, with no immediate effect on net exposed assets. The required follow-up step can take two forms: (1) Trident Europe can exchange the acquired euros for U.S. dollars and hold those dollars itself, or (2) it can transfer the borrowed euros to Trident Corporation, perhaps as a euro dividend or as repayment of intracompany debt. Trident Corporation could then exchange the euros for dollars. In some countries, of course, local monetary authorities will not allow their currency to be so freely exchanged.

Another possibility would be for Trident Corporation or a sister subsidiary to borrow the euros, thus keeping the euro debt entirely off Trident Europe's books. However, the second step is still essential to eliminate euro exposure; the borrowing entity must exchange the euros for dollars or other unexposed assets. Any such borrowing should be coordinated with all other euro borrowings to avoid the possibility that one subsidiary is borrowing euros to reduce translation exposure at the same time as another subsidiary is repaying euro debt. (Note that euros can be "borrowed," by simply delaying repayment of existing euro debt; the goal is to increase euro debt, not borrow in a literal sense.)

**TEMPORAL METHOD.** If translation is by the temporal method, only the much smaller amount of €800,000 need be borrowed. As before, Trident Europe could use the proceeds of the loan to acquire U.S. dollars. However, Trident Europe could also use the proceeds to acquire inventory or fixed assets in Europe. Under the temporal method these assets are not regarded as exposed and do not drop in dollar value when the euro depreciates.

## WHEN IS A BALANCE SHEET HEDGE JUSTIFIED?

If a firm's subsidiary is using the local currency as the functional currency, the following circumstances could justify when to use a balance sheet hedge:

- The foreign subsidiary is about to be liquidated, so that the value of its CTA would be realized.
- The firm has debt covenants or bank agreements that state the firm's debt/equity ratios will be maintained within specific limits.
- Management is evaluated on the basis of certain income statement and balance sheet measures that are affected by translation losses or gains.
- The foreign subsidiary is operating in a hyperinflationary environment.

If a firm is using the parent's home currency as the functional currency of the foreign subsidiary, all transaction gains/losses are passed through to the income statement. Hedging this consolidated income to reduce its variability may be important to investors and bond rating agencies. *Real World Example 10.1* describes an alternative hedging of accounting results, foreign currency-denominated income.

## Real World Example 10.1
### HEDGING THE EURO AWAY

In the year 2000 a number of major U.S. multinationals grew increasingly concerned over the sliding value of the euro. Given the significant contribution of continental profits earned in euros, the declining value of the euro versus the dollar represented a continuing degradation of potential reported profits. Some, like Coca-Cola Company, hedged the dollar value of their projected euro earnings. The hedges protected the dollar value of their euro earnings, and as a result, the companies suffered no material declines in consolidated earnings. Others, however, like Goodyear and Caterpillar, suffered double-digit percentage reductions in consolidated earnings as a result of the unhedged euro decline.

**The Impact of the Falling Value of the Euro on Selected U.S.–Based Multinationals**

| Company | Operating Income 3rd Qtr 2000 (Millions) | Reduction Because of Euro (Percent) |
|---|---|---|
| Goodyear | $68 | 30% |
| Caterpillar | $294 | 12% |
| McDonald's | $910 | 5% |
| Kimberly-Clark | $667 | 2.5% |

Source: "Business Won't Hedge the Euro Away," *Business Week*, December 4, 2000.

Although a number of companies have admittedly been able to prevent their consolidated earnings from being hurt by falling foreign currencies — for a quarter or a series of quarters, at least — it is still highly controversial for a firm to expend resources and acquire hedging positions with forwards and swaps to hedge accounting results.

## CHOICE BETWEEN MINIMIZING TRANSACTION OR TRANSLATION EXPOSURE

Management will find it almost impossible to offset both translation and transaction exposure at the same time. Reduction of one exposure usually changes the amount of the other exposure. For example, the easiest way to offset translation exposure is to require the parent and all subsidiaries to denominate all exposed assets and liabilities in the parent's reporting currency. For U.S. firms and their subsidiaries, all assets and liabilities would be held in dollars. Such a firm would have no translation exposure, but each subsidiary would have its own transaction exposure.

To illustrate, assume that a U.S. parent company instructs its Japanese subsidiary to bill an export to the parent in dollars. The account receivable on the Japanese subsidiary's books is shown as the yen equivalent of the dollar amount, and yen profit is recorded at the time of sale. If, before the parent pays dollars to the Japanese subsidiary, the yen appreciates 5%, the parent still pays only the contracted dollar amount. The Japanese subsidiary receives 5% fewer yen than were expected and booked as profit. Hence the Japanese subsidiary will experience a 5% foreign exchange loss on its dollar-denominated accounts receivable. Lower yen profit will eventually be translated into lower dollar profit when the subsidiary's income statement is consolidated with that of the parent. Eventually the consolidated U.S.–based MNE will show a foreign exchange loss — in dollars!

Similar reasoning will show that if a firm chooses to eliminate transaction exposure, translation exposure might even be increased. The easiest way to be rid of transaction exposure is to require the parent and all subsidiaries to denominate all accounts subject to transaction exposure in its local currency. Thus every subsidiary would avoid transaction gains or losses. However, each subsidiary would be creating net translation exposure by being either long or short in terms of local currency — exposed assets or liabilities. The consolidated financial statement of the parent firm would show translation exposure in each local currency.

As a general matter, firms seeking to reduce both types of exposure usually reduce transaction exposure first. They then recalculate translation exposure (which may have changed), and decide if any residual translation exposure can be reduced without creating more transaction exposure. Taxes complicate the decision to seek protection against transaction or translation exposure. Transaction losses are normally considered "realized" losses and are therefore deductible from pretax income. However, translation losses are only "paper" losses, involving no cash flows, and are not deductible from pretax income. It is highly debatable whether protective techniques that necessitate cash payments, and so reduce net cash flow, should be incurred to avoid noncash losses.

# LaJolla Engineering Services

Meaghan O'Conner had inherited a larger set of problems in the Engineering Equipment Division than she had ever expected.[1] After taking over as the CFO of the division in March 2004, Meaghan had discovered that LaJolla's Engineering Equipment Division's Latin American subsidiaries were the source of recent losses and growing income threats. The rather unusual part of the growing problem was that both the losses and the threats were arising from currency translation.

## Latin American Subsidiaries

LaJolla was a multinational engineering services company with an established reputation in electrical power system design and construction. Although most of LaJolla's business was usually described as "services," and therefore using or owning few real assets, that was not the case with the Engineering Equipment Division. This specific business unit was charged with owning and operating the very high-cost and specialized heavy equipment involved in certain electrical power transmission and distribution system construction. In Meaghan's terminology, she was in charge of the "Big Iron" in a company of consultants.

LaJolla's recent activity had been focused in four countries, Argentina, Jamaica, Venezuela, and Mexico. And unfortunately, the last few years had not been kind to the value of these currencies — particularly against the U.S. dollar. Each of LaJolla's subsidiaries in these countries was local currency functional. Each subsidiary generated the majority of its revenues from local service contracts, and many of the operating expenses were also local. But each of the units had invested in some of the specialized equipment — the so-called Big Iron — which had led to *net exposed assets* when LaJolla had completed its consolidation of foreign activities each year for financial reporting purposes. The translation gains and losses (mostly losses in recent years as the Argentine peso, Jamaican dollar, Venezuelan bolivar, and Mexican peso had weakened against the U.S. dollar), had accumulated in the cumulative translation adjustment line item on the company's consolidated books. But the problem had become more real of late.

Ordinarily, these translation losses would not have been a large managerial issue for LaJolla and Meaghan, except for a minor document filing error in Argentina in the fall of 2003. LaJolla, like many multinational companies operating in Argentina in recent years, had simply given up on conducting any real business of promise in the severely depressed post-crisis Argentina. It had essentially closed up shop there in the summer of 2003. But its legal counsel in Buenos Aires had made a mistake. Instead of ceasing current operations and mothballing the existing assets of LaJolla Engineering

Argentina, the local counsel had filed papers stating that LaJolla was liquidating the business. Although it seemed a minor distinction, according to U.S. GAAP and FAS52, LaJolla would now have to realize in current earnings the cumulative translation losses which had grown over the years from the Argentine business. And these were substantial: $7 million in losses in the fourth quarter of 2003. LaJolla's management had not been happy.

## LaJolla 2004

As a result of this recent experience, LaJolla was taking a close look at all of the translation gains and losses of its various business units worldwide. Once again, the company's Latin American operations were the focal point, as collectively many of the Latin currencies had weakened recently against the dollar, although the dollar itself was quite weak against the euro. Jamaica, Venezuela, and Mexico each posed their individual problems and challenges, but all posed translation adjustment threats to LaJolla.

**Jamaica.** The company had been fairly concerned about the Jamaican business and its contracts from the very beginning.[2] The company had initially agreed to take all revenues in Jamaican dollars (sealing the local currency functional currency designation), but after the fall of the Jamaican dollar in early 2003 (Exhibit 1), the company had

## EXHIBIT 1

**Monthly Avg. Exchange Rates: Jamaican Dollars per U.S. Dollar**

[1]This case concerns a real company. The names and countries have been changed to preserve confidentiality.

[2]All exchange rate diagrams courtesy of the Pacific Exchange Rate Service (http://fx.sauder.ubc.ca), a service for academic research and teaching; © 2004 by Prof. Werner Antweiler, University of British Columbia, Vancouver BC, Canada. Time period shown in each diagram is 1/Jan/2000–9/Mar/2004.

renegotiated a risk-sharing agreement. The agreement restructured the relationship to one where, although LaJolla would continue to be paid in local currency, the two companies would share any changes in the exchange rate beginning in the fourth quarter of 2003 when establishing the charges as invoiced. Regardless, the continuing decline of the Jamaican dollar had created substantial translation losses for LaJolla in Jamaica.

**Mexico.** Although the Mexican peso had been quite stable for a number of years, it clearly had started to slide against the dollar in 2002 and 2003 (Exhibit 2). Meaghan had become particularly frustrated with the Mexican situation the deeper she looked into it. LaJolla had only initiated the subsidiary's operations in Mexico in early 2000, yet the reported translation losses from Mexico had grown much more rapidly than what she would have expected. She had also become quite agitated when she realized that the financial reports coming from her Mexican offices were seemingly "writing-up" the translation losses every quarter. When she had asked questions, first by phone and then later in person, her local financial controller simply stopped talking (she was working through an interpreter), claiming they simply did not understand her questions. Meaghan was no beginner in international finance, and she knew that Mexican financial statements did regularly index foreign currency denominated accounts in line with government published indexes of asset values related to currencies. She wondered if the indexing could be at the source of the rapid growth in translation losses.

**Venezuela.** The continuing political crisis in Venezuela surrounding the presidency of Hugo Chavez had taken its toll on the Venezuelan Bolivar (Exhibit 3). Not only was LaJolla suffering declining U.S. dollar proceeds from its Venezuelan operations, but it had continued to suffer severe late payments from the various government agencies which the company was exclusively providing services to. The average invoice was now taking more than 180 days to be settled, and the bolivar's decline had added to the losses. Translation losses were accumulating here, again from a subsidiary whose functional currency was the local currency. The LaJolla controller in Venezuela had faxed her a proposal that would involve changing the currency used for the books in Venezuela to U.S. dollars, as well as a suggestion that they consider moving the subsidiary offshore for accounting and consolidation purposes (meaning out of Venezuela). He had suggested either the Cayman Islands or the Netherlands Antilles just off the coast.

All in all, Meaghan was beginning to think she made a big mistake when she had accepted the promotion to CFO of this division. She turned her eyes once more to look out over the Pacific and ponder what alternatives she might have to manage these exposures, and what — if anything — she should do immediately.

## EXHIBIT 2

### Monthly Avg. Exchange Rates: Mexican Pesos per U.S. Dollar

© 2004 by Prof. Werner Antweiler, University of British Columbia, Vancouver BC, Canada.

## EXHIBIT 3

### Monthly Avg. Exchange Rates: Venezuelan Bolivars per U.S. Dollar

© 2004 by Prof. Werner Antweiler, University of British Columbia, Vancouver BC, Canada.

## Case Questions

1. Do you believe Meaghan O'Connor should spend time and resources attempting to manage translation losses, what many consider purely an accounting phenomenon?

2. How would you characterize or structure your analysis of each of the individual country threats to LaJolla? What specific features of their individual problems seem to be intertwined with currency issues?

3. What would you recommend that Meaghan do?

## Summary of Learning Objectives

*Demonstrate how translation practices result in a foreign exchange exposure for the multinational enterprise*

- Translation exposure results from translating foreign currency denominated statements of foreign subsidiaries into the parent's reporting currency so the parent can prepare consolidated financial statements. Translation exposure is the potential for loss or gain from this translation process.

*Explain the meaning behind the designation of a foreign subsidiary's functional currency*

- A foreign subsidiary's functional currency is the currency of the primary economic environment in which the subsidiary operates and in which it generates cash flows. In other words, it is the dominant currency used by that foreign subsidiary in its day-to-day operations.

*Illustrate the theoretical and practical differences between the two primary methods of converting foreign currency denominated financial statements into the reporting currency of the parent company*

- The two basic procedures for translation used in most countries today are the current rate method and the temporal method.

- Technical aspects of translation include questions about when to recognize gains or losses in the income statement, the distinction between functional and reporting currency, and the treatment of subsidiaries in hyperinflation countries.

*Compare translation exposure with operating exposure*

- Translation gains and losses can be quite different from operating gains and losses, not only in magnitude but in sign. Management may need to determine which is of greater significance prior to deciding which exposure is to be managed first.

*Analyze the costs and benefits of managing translation exposure*

- The main technique for managing translation exposure is a balance sheet hedge. This calls for having an equal amount of exposed foreign currency assets and liabilities.

- Even if management chooses to follow an active policy of hedging translation exposure, it is nearly impossible to offset both transaction and translation exposure simultaneously. If forced to choose, most managers will protect against transaction losses because these are realized cash losses, rather than protect against translation losses.

## QUESTIONS

1. **By any other name.** What does the word *translation* mean? Why is translation exposure sometimes called *accounting exposure*?

2. **Converting financial assets.** In the context of preparing consolidated financial statements, are the words *translate* and *convert* synonyms?

3. **The central problem.** What is the central problem in consolidating the financial statements of a foreign subsidiary?

4. **Self-sustaining subsidiaries.** What is the difference between a *self-sustaining foreign subsidiary* and an *integrated foreign subsidiary*?

5. **Functional currency.** What is a *functional currency*? What is a *nonfunctional currency*?

6. **Translating assets.** What are the major differences in translating assets between the current rate method and the temporal method?

7. **Translating liabilities.** What are the major differences in translating liabilities between the current rate method and the temporal method?

8. **Hyperinflation.** What is hyperinflation and what are its consequences for translating foreign financial statements?

9. **Foreign exchange losses by any other name.** What are the primary differences among losses from transaction exposure, operating exposure, and translation exposure?

10. **Reacting to potential losses.** How should financial managers react to any differences between potential losses from operating exposure and translation exposure?

11. **Trident and a strong dollar.** During the year ahead the U.S. dollar is expected to appreciate vis-à-vis the euro. How might this affect the reported

consolidated earnings of Trident and its operating subsidiary in Germany?

12. **Trident and a weak dollar.** During the year ahead the U.S. dollar is expected to weaken vis-à-vis the euro. How might this affect the reported consolidated earnings of Trident and its operating subsidiary in Germany?

## PROBLEMS

1. **Montevideo Products, S.A.** Montevideo Products, S.A., is the Uruguayan subsidiary of a U.S. manufacturing company. Its balance sheet for January 1 follows. The January 1 exchange rate between the U.S. dollar and the peso Uruguayo ($U) is $U15/US$.

### Montevideo Products, S.A.
### Balance Sheet, January 1,
### thousands of pesos Uruguayo

| Assets | |
| --- | --- |
| Cash | $U60,000 |
| Accounts receivable | 120,000 |
| Inventory | 120,000 |
| Net plant and equipment | 240,000 |
| | $U540,000 |

| Liabilities and Net Worth | |
| --- | --- |
| Current liabilities | $U30,000 |
| Long-term debt | 90,000 |
| Capital stock | 300,000 |
| Retained earnings | 120,000 |
| | $U540,000 |

a. Determine Montevideo's contribution to the translation exposure of its parent on January 1, using the current rate method.

b. Calculate Montevideo's contribution to its parent's translation loss if the exchange rate on December 31 is $U20/US$. Assume all peso Uruguayo accounts remain as they were at the beginning of the year.

2. **Siam Toys, Ltd.** Siam Toys, Ltd., is the Thai subsidiary of a U.S. toy manufacturer. Siam Toys manufactures plastic injection molding equipment for making toy cars. Sales are primarily in the United States and Europe. Siam Toys' balance sheet in thousands of Thai bahts (B) as of March 31 is as follows:

### Siam Toys, Ltd.
### Balance Sheet, March 31, thousands of Thai bahts

| Assets | |
| --- | --- |
| Cash | B24,000 |
| Accounts receivable | 36,000 |
| Inventory | 48,000 |
| Net plant and equipment | 60,000 |
| | B168,000 |

| Liabilities and Net Worth | |
| --- | --- |
| Accounts payable | B18,000 |
| Bank loans | 60,000 |
| Common stock | 18,000 |
| Retained earnings | 72,000 |
| | B168,000 |

Exchange rates for translating Siam Toy's balance sheet into U.S. dollars are

B40.00/$ April 1 exchange rate after 25% devaluation.

B30.00/$ March 31 exchange rate, before 25% devaluation. All inventory was acquired at this rate.

B20.00/$ Historic exchange rate at which plant and equipment were acquired.

The Thai baht dropped in value from B30/$ to B40/$ between March 31 and April 1. Assuming no change in balance sheet accounts between these two days, calculate the gain or loss from translation by both the current rate method and the temporal method. Explain the translation gain or loss in terms of changes in the value of exposed accounts.

3. **Egyptian Ingot, Ltd.** Egyptian Ingot, Ltd., is the Egyptian subsidiary of Trans-Mediterranean Aluminum, a British multinational that fashions automobile engine blocks from aluminum. Trans-Mediterranean's home reporting currency is the British pound.

Egyptian Ingot's December 31 balance sheet is shown below. At the date of this balance sheet the exchange rate between Egyptian pounds and British pounds sterling was £E5.50/UK£.

**Assets**

| | |
|---|---|
| Cash | £E16,500,000 |
| Accounts receivable | 33,000,000 |
| Inventory | 49,500,000 |
| Net plant and equipment | 66,000,000 |
| | £E165,000,000 |

**Liabilities and Net Worth**

| | |
|---|---|
| Accounts payable | £E24,750,000 |
| Long-term debt | 49,500,000 |
| Invested capital | 90,750,000 |
| | £E165,000,000 |

**a.** What is Egyptian Ingot's contribution to the translation exposure of Trans-Mediterranean on December 31, using the current rate method?

**b.** Calculate the translation exposure loss to Trans-Mediterranean if the exchange rate at the end of the following quarter is £E6.00/£. Assume all balance sheet accounts are the same at the end of the quarter as they were at the beginning.

**4. Trident Europe (A).** Using facts in this chapter for Trident Europe, assume the exchange rate on January 2, 2002, in Exhibit 10.4 dropped in value from $1.2000/€ to $0.9000/€ rather than to $1.0000/€. Recalculate Trident Europe's translated balance sheet for January 2, 2002 with the new exchange rate using the current rate method.

**a.** What is the amount of translation gain or loss?

**b.** Where should the gain or loss appear in the financial statements?

**5. Trident Europe (B).** Using facts in this chapter for Trident Europe, assume, as in Question 4, that the exchange rate on January 2, 2002, in Exhibit 10.4 dropped in value from $1.2000/€ to $0.9000/€ rather than to $1.0000/€. Recalculate Trident Europe's translated balance sheet for January 2, 2002, with the new exchange rate using the temporal rate method.

**a.** What is the amount of translation gain or loss?

**b.** Where should the gain or loss appear in the financial statements?

**c.** Why does the translation loss or gain under the temporal method differ from the loss or gain under the current rate method?

**6. Trident Europe (C).** Using facts in this chapter for Trident Europe, assume the exchange rate on January 2, 2002, in Exhibit 10.4 appreciated from $1.2000/€ to $1.5000/€. Calculate Trident Europe's translated balance sheet for January 2, 2002, with the new exchange rate using the current rate method.

**a.** What is the amount of translation gain or loss?

**b.** Where should the gain or loss appear in the financial statements?

**7. Trident Europe (D).** Using facts in this chapter for Trident Europe, assume, as in Question 6, that the exchange rate on January 2, 2002, in Exhibit 10.4 appreciated from $1.2000/€ to $1.5000/€. Calculate Trident Europe's translated balance sheet for January 2, 2002, with the new exchange rate using the temporal method.

**a.** What is the amount of translation gain or loss?

**b.** Where should the gain or loss appear in the financial statements?

## Internet Exercises

**1. Changing translation practices: FASB.** The Financial Accounting Standards Board (FASB) promulgates standard practices for the reporting of financial results by companies in the United States. It also often leads the way in the development of new practices and emerging issues around the world. One major issue today is the valuation and reporting of financial derivatives and derivative agreements by firms. Use the

FASB's home page and the Web sites of several of the major accounting firms and other interest groups around the world to see current proposed accounting standards and the current state of reaction to the proposed standards.

FASB home page
   http://raw.rutgers.edu/raw/fasb/
Treasury Management Association
   http://www.tma.org/

2.  **Nestlé's financial statements and exchange rates.** Using Nestlé's Web sites, check current press releases for recent financial results, including what the company reports as the primary currencies and average exchange rates used for translation of international financial results during the most recent period.

    Nestlé: The World Food Company
      http://www.nestle.com/

# Financing the Global Firm

Part 4 examines how a firm can use the global capital market to minimize its cost of capital and maximize its access to capital. A firm needs to achieve a global cost and availability of capital in order to compete successfully in both its domestic and foreign markets.

**CHAPTER 11** starts with a review of how we can compute a firm's cost of capital, using Trident's weighted average cost of capital as an illustration. Next we examine the role played by international portfolio investors in determining whether or not a firm can achieve a lower a global cost and a greater availability of capital. Then we examine the link between cost and availability of capital, namely, the effect of market liquidity and market segmentation. We continue with a detailed illustrative case showing how Novo Industri, a Danish MNE, was able to achieve a lower global cost and greater availability of capital despite being located in an illiquid and segmented Danish capital market. We conclude by comparing the cost of capital for MNEs with that of their domestic counterparts.

**CHAPTER 12** examines how a firm can source its equity in global capital markets. Management must first design a strategy to gain access to the world's most liquid equity markets. Access should improve the liquidity of a firm's equity shares and thereby lower its weighted average cost of capital. An important milestone occurs when a firm cross-lists its shares on one or more foreign stock exchanges. An even more important milestone is for the firm to sell some of its equity to foreign investors. We analyze the barriers a firm must overcome if it is to be successful at cross-listing and selling equity abroad. The chapter concludes with a description of alternative instruments that a firm can use to sell its equity in foreign markets.

**CHAPTER 13** describes how a firm wishing to minimize its cost of capital must maintain a financial structure that balances debt and equity in a manner that is acceptable to its shareholders and creditors. An MNE, in particular, must consider how to maintain access to global capital markets, reduce risk through international diversification, minimize foreign exchange risk due to raising foreign currency-denominated debt, and meet the expectations of international portfolio investors. An MNE must also consider how to finance its foreign subsidiaries and structure their balance sheets. Next we describe the various debt instruments that an MNE can use to tap global debt markets, including syndicated bank loans, Euronotes, and international bonds.

**CHAPTER 14** explains how financial managers of all firms, whether domestic or multinational, must manage interest rate risk. Interest rate risk affects both the liability and asset side of a firm's balance sheet. On the liability side of the balance sheet, a firm's interest rate risk is affected by credit risk and repricing risk on floating rate loans. We describe three important interest rate risk management instruments, namely forward rate agreements, interest rate futures, and interest rate swaps. We use the Trident case to illustrate how a firm can swap from a fixed interest rate cash flow obligation to a floating rate obligation and vice versa. Next we show how Trident can use a currency swap to switch from floating rate dollars to fixed rate Swiss francs, and then unwind this swap at a later date. The chapter concludes with an illustrative case of an actual three-way back-to-back cross-currency swap.

# Global Cost and Availability of Capital

## LEARNING OBJECTIVES

Show how a firm headquartered in a country with an illiquid and segmented capital market achieves a lower global cost and greater availability of capital

Analyze the link between cost and availability of capital

Evaluate the effect of market liquidity and segmentation on the cost of capital

Compare the weighted average cost of capital for an MNE with that of its domestic counterpart

How can firms tap global capital markets for the purpose of minimizing their cost of capital and maximizing capital's availability? Why should they do so?

Global integration of capital markets has given many firms access to new and cheaper sources of funds beyond those available in their home markets. These firms can then accept more long-term projects and invest more in capital improvements and expansion. If a firm resides in a country with illiquid and/or segmented capital markets, it can achieve this lower global cost and greater availability of capital by a properly designed and implemented strategy. The dimensions of the cost and availability of capital are illustrated in Exhibit 11.1. The impact of firm-specific characteristics, market liquidity for the firm's securities, and the definition and effect of market segmentation on the prices of a firm's capital are the subject of most of this chapter.

A firm that must source its long-term debt and equity in a *highly illiquid domestic securities market* will probably have a relatively high cost of capital and will face limited availability of such capital, which in turn will lower its competitiveness both internationally and vis-à-vis foreign firms entering its home market. This category of firms includes both firms resident in emerging countries, where the capital market remains undeveloped, and firms too small to gain access to their own national securities markets. Many family-owned firms find themselves in this category because they choose not to utilize securities markets to source their long-term capital needs.

Firms resident in industrial countries with *small capital markets* often source their long-term debt and equity at home in these partially liquid domestic securities markets. The firms' cost and availability of capital is better than that of firms in countries with illiquid capital markets. However, if these firms can tap the highly liquid global markets, they can also strengthen their competitive advantage in sourcing capital.

Firms resident in countries with *segmented capital markets* must devise a strategy to escape dependence on that market for their long-term debt and equity needs. A

## EXHIBIT 11.1

Dimensions of the Cost and Availability of Capital Strategy

**Local Market Access**                    **Global Market Access**

*Firm-Specific Characteristics*

| Firm's securities appeal only to domestic investors | Firm's securities appeal to international portfolio investors |

*Market Liquidity for Firm's Securities*

| Illiquid domestic securities market and limited international liquidity | Highly liquid domestic market and broad international participation |

*Effect of Market Segmentation on Firm's Securities and Cost of Capital*

| Segmented domestic securities market that prices shares according to domestic standards | Access to global securities market that prices shares according to international standards |

national capital market is segemented if the required rate of return on securities in that market differs from the required rate of return on securities of comparable expected return and risk traded on other securities markets. Capital markets become segmented because of such factors as excessive regulatory control, perceived political risk, anticipated foreign exchange risk, lack of transparency, asymmetric availability of information, cronyism, insider trading, and many other market imperfections.

Firms constrained by any of the above conditions must develop a strategy to escape their own limited capital markets and source some of their long-term capital abroad. This chapter will first review how a firm calculates its weighted average cost of capital when international portfolio investors are able to invest in its equity and debt securities. Trident Corporation will be our example.

The second section of this chapter analyzes how a firm can attract international portfolio investors to its securities. This ability depends on firm-specific characteristics, a regulatory environment that permits unrestricted cross-border investment flows, and a financial strategy that creates market liquidity and global pricing for the firm's securities, whether or not its domestic market is segmented from other capital markets.

The third section focuses on the link between the cost and availability of capital. Achieving this link requires improving market liquidity for the firm's securities and escaping from a segmented domestic market. If the firm is successful in implementing these strategies, it will reduce its weighted average cost of capital and increase its availability.

The fourth section analyzes whether MNEs have reduced their cost of capital below that of their comparable domestic competitors.

## Weighted Average Cost of Capital

A firm normally finds its weighted average cost of capital (WACC) by combining the cost of equity with the cost of debt in proportion to the relative weight of each in the firm's optimal long-term financial structure. More specifically,

$$k_{WACC} = k_e \frac{E}{V} + k_d(1-t)\frac{D}{V}$$

where

$k_{WACC}$ = weighted average after-tax cost of capital
$k_e$ = risk-adjusted cost of equity
$k_d$ = before-tax cost of debt
$t$ = marginal tax rate
$E$ = market value of the firm's equity
$D$ = market value of the firm's debt
$V$ = total market value of the firm's securities $(D + E)$

### COST OF EQUITY

The *capital asset pricing model* (CAPM) approach is to define the cost of equity for a firm by the following formula:

$$k_e = k_{rf} + \beta_j(k_m - k_{rf})$$

where

| | |
|---|---|
| $k_e$ | = expected (required) rate of return on equity |
| $k_{rf}$ | = rate of interest on risk-free bonds (Treasury bonds, for example) |
| $\beta_j$ | = coefficient of *systematic risk* for the firm |
| $k_m$ | = expected (required) rate of return on the market portfolio of stocks |

*Systematic risk* is a function of the total variability of expected returns of the firm's stock relative to the market index ($k_m$) and the degree to which the variability of expected returns of the firm is correlated to the expected returns on the market index. More formally,

$$\beta_j = \frac{\rho_{jm}\sigma_j}{\sigma_m}$$

where $\beta_j$ (*beta*) is the measure of systematic risk for security j, $\rho$ (*rho*) is the correlation between security j and the market; $\sigma_j$ (*sigma*) is the standard deviation of the return on firm j; and $\sigma_m$ (*sigma*) is the standard deviation of the market return.

*Beta* will have a value of less than 1.0 if the firm's returns are less volatile than the market, 1.0 if the same as the market, or greater than 1.0 if more volatile — or risky — than the market. CAPM analysis assumes that the required return estimated is an indication of what more is necessary to keep an investor's capital invested in the equity considered. If the equity's return does not reach the expected return, CAPM assumes that individual investors will liquidate their holdings.

## COST OF DEBT

The normal procedure for measuring the cost of debt requires a forecast of interest rates for the next few years, the proportions of various classes of debt the firm expects to use, and the corporate income tax rate. The interest costs of the different debt components are then averaged according to their proportion in the debt structure. This before-tax average, $k_d$, is then adjusted for corporate income taxes by multiplying it by the expression (1 − tax rate), to obtain $k_d(1 - t)$, the weighted average after-tax cost of debt.

The weighted average cost of capital is normally used as the risk-adjusted discount rate whenever a firm's new projects are in the same general risk class as its existing projects. On the other hand, a project-specific required rate of return should be used as the discount rate if a new project differs from existing projects in business or financial risk.

## TRIDENT'S WEIGHTED AVERAGE COST OF CAPITAL

Maria Gonzalez, Trident's CFO, calculates Trident's weighted average cost of capital to be 12.28%, as shown in Exhibit 11.2.

She believes that Trident's cost of capital is already at a global level. It is fully competitive with Trident's main rivals in the telecommunications hardware industry segment worldwide, which are mainly headquartered in the United States, the United Kingdom, Canada, Finland, Sweden, Germany, Japan, and the Netherlands. Their shares are listed on prominent stock exchanges and international portfolio investors can freely trade in their shares. Trident itself is listed on the very liquid NASDAQ. The key to Trident's favorable global cost and availability of capital is its ability to attract and hold the international portfolio investors that own its stock.

**EXHIBIT 11.2**

Calculation of Trident's Weighted Average Cost of Capital

## Cost of Equity ($k_e$) Inputs

| | |
|---|---|
| $k_{rf}$ = 5.000% | $k_{rf}$ is the risk-free rate of interest estimated by using the U.S. Treasury bond rate. |
| $k_m$ = 15.000% | $k_m$ is the expected rate of return on the market portfolio held by a well-diversified global investor. Over 40% of Trident's stock is held by foreign portfolio investors, as part of their globally diversified portfolios. Trident's U.S. investors also typically hold globally diversified portfolios. |
| $\beta$ = 1.2 | $\beta$ is Trident's estimate of its own systematic risk using the correlation of Trident's returns with those of the market ($\rho$), Trident's standard deviation ($\sigma_{Trd}$), and the market's standard deviation ($\sigma_m$). |

The cost of equity is then:

$$k_e = k_{rf} + \beta\,(k_m - k_{rf}) = 5.000\% + 1.2\,(15.000\% - 5.000\%) = 17.000\%.$$

## Cost of Debt ($k_d$) Inputs

| | |
|---|---|
| $k_d$ = 8.000% | $k_d$ is the before-tax cost of debt estimated by observing the current yield on Trident's outstanding bonds combined with bank debt. |
| t = 35% | t is the U.S. corporate income tax rate. |

The after-tax cost of debt is then:

$$k_d\,(1 - t) = 8.000\,(1 - 0.35\,) = 8.000\,(\,0.65\,) = 5.200\%.$$

## Financial Structure

| | |
|---|---|
| E/V = 60% | E/V is the equity ratio, the percentage of Trident's securities (E + D) that is equity. |
| D/V = 40% | D/V is the debt ratio, the percentage of Trident's securities (E + D) that is debt (bonds and bank loans). |
| V = 100% | V is the market value of Trident's securities (E + D). |

The *weighted average cost* of capital ($k_{WACC}$) is then:

$$k_{WACC} = k_e \frac{E}{V} + k_d(1-t)\frac{D}{V} = 17.00\%(.60) + 5.20\%(.40) = 12.28\%.$$

## CALCULATING EQUITY RISK PREMIUMS IN PRACTICE

In practice calculating a firm's equity risk premium is more controversial. Although the capital asset pricing model (CAPM) has now become very widely accepted in global business as the preferred method of calculating the cost of equity for a firm, there is rising debate over what numerical values should be used in its application, especially the equity risk premium. The *equity risk premium* is the average annual return of the market expected by investors over and above riskless debt, the term ($k_m - k_{rf}$). The mini-case at the end of the chapter shows how Nestlé (Switzerland) could use the international CAPM to calculate its cost of equity.

**EQUITY RISK PREMIUM HISTORY.**    The field of finance does agree that a cost of equity calculation should be forward-looking, meaning that the inputs to the equation should represent what is expected to happen over the relevant future time horizon. As is typically the case, however, practitioners use historical evidence as the basis for their

**EXHIBIT 11.3**

Equity Risk Premiums Around the World, 1900–2002

| | Relative to Bills | | | Relative to Bonds | | |
|---|---|---|---|---|---|---|
| | Geometric Mean | Arithmetic Mean | SD | Geometric Mean | Arithmetic Mean | SD |
| Australia | 6.8 | 8.3 | 17.2 | 6.0 | 7.6 | 19.0 |
| Belgium | 2.2 | 4.4 | 23.1 | 2.1 | 3.9 | 20.2 |
| Canada | 4.2 | 5.5 | 16.8 | 4.0 | 5.5 | 18.2 |
| Denmark | 2.2 | 3.8 | 19.6 | 1.5 | 2.7 | 16.0 |
| France | 6.4 | 8.9 | 24.0 | 3.6 | 5.8 | 22.1 |
| Germany | 3.9 | 9.4 | 35.5 | 5.7 | 9.0 | 28.8 |
| Ireland | 3.6 | 5.5 | 20.4 | 3.2 | 4.8 | 18.5 |
| Italy | 6.3 | 10.3 | 32.5 | 4.1 | 7.6 | 30.2 |
| Japan | 6.1 | 9.3 | 28.0 | 5.4 | 9.5 | 33.3 |
| The Netherlands | 4.3 | 6.4 | 22.6 | 3.8 | 5.9 | 21.9 |
| South Africa | 5.9 | 7.9 | 22.2 | 5.2 | 6.8 | 19.4 |
| Spain | 2.8 | 4.9 | 21.5 | 1.9 | 3.8 | 20.3 |
| Sweden | 5.2 | 7.5 | 22.2 | 4.8 | 7.2 | 2.5 |
| Switzerland | 3.2 | 4.8 | 18.8 | 1.4 | 2.9 | 17.5 |
| United Kingdom | 4.2 | 5.9 | 20.1 | 3.8 | 5.1 | 17.0 |
| United States | 5.3 | 7.2 | 19.8 | 4.4 | 6.4 | 20.3 |
| Average | 4.5 | 6.9 | 22.8 | 3.8 | 5.9 | 21.6 |
| World | 4.4 | 5.7 | 16.5 | 3.8 | 4.9 | 15.0 |

Source: Elroy Dimson, Paul Marsh, and Mike Stanton, "Global Evidence on the Equity Risk Premium," *Journal of Applied Corporate Finance*, vol. 15, no. 4, 2003, p. 31. The equity risk premium is measured as 1 + equity rate of return divided by 1 + risk-free return, minus 1. The statistics reported in this table are based on 103 annual observations for each country, except Germany, which excludes 1922–1923, when bill and bondholders experienced returns of –100% due to hyperinflation. The row labeled "Average" is a simple, unweighted average of the statistics for the 16 individual countries. The row marked "World" is for the world index. SD is standard deviation.

forward-looking projections. The current debate begins with a debate over what has happened in the past.

Exhibit 11.3 presents the results of a large study originally completed in 2001, but updated in 2003. The study calculates the equity risk premium in 16 different developed countries for the 1900–2002 period. There are clearly significant differences in equity returns over time by country. Comparing arithmetic returns, Italy was the highest (10.3%) with Germany (9.4%) and Japan (9.3%) following. Denmark, with an average arithmetic return of only 3.8%, had the lowest premium. The United States had an average arithmetic return of 7.2%, while the United Kingdom had 5.9%. The average return for the 16 listed countries was 6.9%. The world, as defined by the authors of the study, had an arithmetic return of 5.7%.

There is less debate regarding the use of arithmetic returns over geometric returns. The mean arithmetic return is simply the average of the annual percentage changes in capital appreciation plus dividend distributions. This is a rate of return calculation with which every business student is familiar. The mean geometric return, however, is a more specialized calculation that takes into account only the beginning and ending values over an extended period of history. It then calculates the annual average rate of compounded growth to get from the beginning to the end, without paying attention to

**EXHIBIT 11.4**

Arithmetic Versus
Geometric
Returns:
A Sample
Calculation

| Year | 1 | 2 | 3 | 4 | 5 | Mean |
|------|---|---|---|---|---|------|
| Share price | 10 | 12 | 10 | 12 | 14 | |
| Arithmetic change | | +20.00% | −16.67% | +20.00% | +16.67% | +10.00% |
| Geometric change | | +8.78% | +8.78% | +8.78% | +8.78% | + 8.78% |

Arithmetic change is calculated year-by-year as $[P_2/P_1 - 1]$. The simple average of the series is the mean. The geometric change is calculated using only the beginning and ending values, 10 and 14, and the geometric root of $[(14/10)^{1/4} - 1]$ is found (the G is in reference to four periods of change). The geometric change assumes reinvested compounding, whereas the arithmetic mean only assumes point-to-point investment.

the specific path taken in between. Exhibit 11.4 provides a simple example of how the two methods would differ for a very short historical series of stock prices.

Arithmetic returns capture the year-to-year volatility in markets, which geometric returns do not. For this reason, most practitioners prefer the arithmetic, as it embodies more of the volatility so often characteristic of equity markets globally. Note that the geometric return will in all but a few extreme circumstances yield a smaller mean return.

**THE UNITED STATES LOOKING FORWARD.**    The debate over which equity risk premium to use in practice was highlighted in this same study by looking at what equity risk premiums are being recommended for the United States by a variety of sources. As illustrated in Exhibit 11.5, a hypothetical firm with a beta of 1.0 (estimated market risk equal to that of the market) might have a cost of equity as low as 9.000% and as high as 12.800% using this set of alternative values. Note that here the authors used geometric returns, not arithmetic returns.

How important is it for a company to accurately predict its cost of equity? The corporation must annually determine which potential investments it will accept and reject due to its limited capital resources. If the company is not accurately estimating its cost of equity — and therefore its general cost of capital — it will not be accurately estimating the net present value of potential investments if it uses its own cost of capital as the basis for discounting expected cash flows.

**EXHIBIT 11.5**

Alternative
Estimates of Cost
of Equity for a
Hypothetical U.S.
Firm Assuming
$\beta = 1$ and $k_{rf} = 4\%$

| Source | Equity Risk Premium | Cost of Equity | Differential |
|--------|--------------------|--------------|--------------|
| Ibbotson | 8.800% | 12.800% | 3.800% |
| Finance textbooks | 8.500% | 12.500% | 3.500% |
| Investor surveys | 7.100% | 11.100% | 2.100% |
| Dimson, et al. | 5.000% | 9.000% | Baseline |

Source: Equity risk premium quotes from "Stockmarket Valuations: Great Expectations," *The Economist*, January 31, 2002.

## The Demand for Foreign Securities: The Role of International Portfolio Investors

Gradual deregulation of equity markets during the past three decades not only elicited increased competition from domestic players but also opened up markets to foreign competitors. International portfolio investment and cross-listing of equity shares on foreign markets have become commonplace.

What motivates portfolio investors to purchase and hold foreign securities in their portfolio? The answer lies in an understanding of "domestic" portfolio theory and how it has been extended to handle the possibility of global portfolios. More specifically, it requires an understanding of the principles of portfolio risk reduction, portfolio rate of return, and foreign currency risk. These principles are explained in detail in Chapter 15.

Both domestic and international portfolio managers are *asset allocators*. Their objective is to maximize a portfolio's rate of return for a given level of risk, or to minimize risk for a given rate of return. International portfolio managers can choose from a larger bundle of assets than portfolio managers limited to domestic-only asset allocations. As a result, internationally diversified portfolios often have a higher expected rate of return, and they nearly always have a lower level of portfolio risk, since national securities markets are imperfectly correlated with one another.

Portfolio asset allocation can be accomplished along many dimensions depending on the investment objective of the portfolio manager. For example, portfolios can be diversified according to the type of securities. They can be composed of stocks only or bonds only or a combination of both. They also can be diversified by industry or by size of capitalization (small-cap, mid-cap, and large-cap stock portfolios).

For our purposes, the most relevant dimensions are diversification by country, geographic region, stage of development, or a combination of these (global). An example of diversification by country is the Korea Fund. It was at one time the only vehicle for foreign investors to hold South Korean securities, but foreign ownership restrictions have more recently been liberalized. A typical regional diversification would be one of the many Asian funds. These performed exceptionally well until the "bubble" burst in Japan and Southeast Asia during the last years of the 1990s. Portfolios composed of emerging market securities are examples of diversification by stage of development. They are composed of securities from different countries, geographic regions, and stage of development.

## The Link Between Cost and Availability of Capital

Trident's weighted average cost of capital (WACC) was calculated assuming that equity and debt capital would always be available at the same required rate of return even if Trident's capital budget expands. This is a reasonable assumption considering Trident's excellent access through the NASDAQ to international portfolio investors in global capital markets. It is a bad assumption, however, for firms resident in illiquid or segmented capital markets, small domestic firms, and family-owned firms resident in any capital market. We will now examine how market liquidity and market segmentation can affect a firm's cost of capital. This is followed by an illustrative case showing how Novo Industri A/S, a Danish firm, was able to overcome the disadvantages of being resident in an illiquid and segmented market.

## IMPROVING MARKET LIQUIDITY

Although no consensus exists about the definition of *market liquidity*, we can observe market liquidity by noting the degree to which a firm can issue a new security without depressing the existing market price, as well as the degree to which a change in price of its securities elicits a substantial order flow. *Real World Example 11.1* elaborates on the definition and concept of market liquidity in a U.S. context.

In the domestic case an underlying assumption is that total availability of capital to a firm at any time is determined by supply and demand in the domestic capital markets. A firm should always expand its capital budget by raising funds in the same proportion as its optimal financial structure. As its budget expands in absolute terms, however, its marginal cost of capital will eventually increase. In other words, a firm can only tap the capital market for some limited amount in the short run before suppliers of capital balk at providing further funds, even if the same optimal financial structure is preserved. In the long run this may not be a limitation, depending on market liquidity.

In the multinational case a firm is able to improve market liquidity by raising funds in the euromarkets (money, bond, and equity), by selling security issues abroad, and by tapping local capital markets through foreign subsidiaries. Such activity should logically expand the capacity of an MNE to raise funds in the short run over what might have been raised if the firm were limited to its home capital market. This situation assumes that the firm preserves its optimal financial structure.

## MARKET SEGMENTATION

If all capital markets are fully integrated, securities of comparable expected return and risk should have the same required rate of return in each national market after adjusting for foreign exchange risk and political risk. This definition applies to both equity and debt, although it often happens that one or the other may be more integrated than its counterpart.

Capital market segmentation is a financial market imperfection caused mainly by government constraints, institutional practices, and investor perceptions. The most important imperfections are

- Asymmetric information between domestic and foreign-based investors
- High securities transaction costs
- Foreign exchange risks
- Political risks
- Corporate governance differences
- Regulatory barriers

Market imperfections do not necessarily imply that national securities markets are inefficient. A national securities market can be *efficient* in a domestic context and yet segmented in an international context. According to finance theory, a market is efficient if security prices in that market reflect all available relevant information and adjust quickly to any new relevant information. Therefore the price of an individual security reflects its "intrinsic value" and any price fluctuations will be "random walks" around this value. Market efficiency assumes that transaction costs are low, that many participants are in the market, and that these participants have sufficient financial strength to move security prices. Empirical tests of market efficiency show that most major national markets are reasonably efficient.

# Real World Example 11.1
## MARKET LIQUIDITY

Liquidity is a slippery concept. The New York Stock Exchange says its specialists provide the most liquidity, and that dispersing trading in NYSE stocks would be bad for everyone. Electronic marketplaces like Archipelago Exchange, Instinet, and Island say their systems are highly liquid. But the debate is confused. Steps that increase liquidity in certain circumstances could dry it up in others. Here's a primer:

**What is liquidity?** It's the ability to buy or sell assets quickly without affecting their price. An asset is "liquid" if you can turn it into cash quickly and still get a good price for it.

**What about liquidity in stocks?** Liquidity takes on two very different appearances depending on whether markets are calm or in crisis. In calm markets, liquidity is something that pleases traders by reducing how much prices move against them when they buy or sell. In contrast, when a market suffers a crisis, such as major bad news, liquidity is what keeps trading from drying up entirely. By stepping in to buy when others won't, "liquidity providers" can quell panic that makes it impossible to sell at any price.

**Explain calm-market liquidity first.** For small investors, it's mostly about what traders call "narrow spreads." Middlemen make profits by buying shares at a low price and selling them at a higher price. Competition narrows that gap — or spread — so more of the benefits of trading go to the customers than to the middlemen. Big investors also care about rapid execution of their trades, since often they try to profit from short-term price fluctuations. And they care about "market depth." Markets are deep when it's possible to buy lots of shares in a short period without causing a shortage that forces the price up, or to sell without flooding the market and forcing the price down.

**Does liquidity dry up in calm markets when trading gets split up among many venues?** You would think so. But research by Roger D. Huang, finance professor at the University of Notre Dame's Mendoza College of Business, shows that spreads between the highest bids and lowest offers on NASDAQ stocks have narrowed since electronic communications networks (ECNS) began competing with NASDAQ market makers. Often, he reported in a study in the *Journal of Finance* last

year, it's the ECNs that post the best prices. And Huang believes it's still possible to buy and sell large blocks of stock efficiently by splitting orders up among multiple trading venues.

**So who needs the NYSE specialists and the NASDAQ market makers?** In calm markets, they're probably not essential. But they play a crucial role when markets suffer a shock. NYSE specialists are obligated to maintain orderly markets when prices are falling by buying shares with their own money. NASDAQ market makers are also supposed to post bids as well as offers for the shares they trade at all times, although their obligations are less stringent.

**How can a handful of specialists and market makers make any difference?** Think of them as levers for the Federal Reserve, which is the lender of last resort in crises. In 1987, the Federal Reserve was worried that the October stock market crash would touch off a wave of defaults and damage the entire economy. To get the market functioning again, it urged big banks to lend money to technically insolvent specialists and market makers so that they could continue trading, says Douglas W. Diamond, finance professor at the University of Chicago's Graduate School of Business. In turn, the Fed promised the banks they could borrow from it without restraint.

**Couldn't the Fed do the same thing with electronic communications networks?** No, because ECNs simply match buyers and sellers, without trading for their own accounts. If markets seized up, the Fed would not know where to direct loans to re-liquefy potential buyers and restart markets.

**So, what should be done?** The people who are redesigning markets with an eye toward improving calm-market liquidity should keep in mind the importance of maintaining liquidity in times of crisis. That may mean preserving some of the rules that allow NYSE specialists to be profitable, such as the trade-through rule, which requires orders to flow to the NYSE if its specialists are providing the best price. Take away the specialists' profits, and they may not be around the next time a crisis strikes.

Source: Peter Coy, "The Ups and Downs of Market Liquidity and the Different Ways Both Specialists and Electronic Exchanges Affect It," *Business Week*, Nov. 3, 2003, p. 104.
© 2003 The McGraw-Hill Companies. All Rights Reserved.

An efficient national securities market might very well correctly price all securities traded in that market on the basis of information available to the investors who participate in that market. However, if that market is segmented, foreign investors would not be participants. Thus securities in the segmented market would be priced on the basis of domestic rather than international standards.

In the rest of this chapter and the next chapter we will use the term *MNE* to describe all firms that have access to a global cost and availability of capital. This includes qualifying MNEs, whether they are located in highly developed or emerging markets. It also includes large firms that are not multinational but have access to global capital markets. They too could be located in highly developed or emerging capital markets. We will use the term *domestic firm* (DF) for all firms that do not have access to a global cost and availability of capital, no matter where they are located.

Availability of capital depends on whether a firm can gain liquidity for its debt and equity securities and a price for those securities based on international rather than national standards. In practice this means that the firm must define a strategy to attract international portfolio investors and thereby escape the constraints of its own illiquid or segmented national market.

## THE EFFECT OF MARKET LIQUIDITY AND SEGMENTATION

The degree to which capital markets are illiquid or segmented has an important influence on a firm's marginal cost of capital and thus on its weighted average cost of capital. The marginal cost of capital is the weighted average cost of the next currency unit raised. This is illustrated in Exhibit 11.6, which shows the transition from a domestic to a global marginal cost of capital.

Exhibit 11.6 shows that the MNE has a given marginal return on capital at different budget levels, represented in the line MRR. This demand is determined by ranking potential projects according to net present value or internal rate of return. Percentage rate of return to both users and suppliers of capital is shown on the vertical scale. If the firm is limited to raising funds in its domestic market, the line $MCC_D$ shows the marginal domestic cost of capital (vertical axis) at various budget levels (horizontal axis). Remember that the firm continues to maintain the same debt ratio as it expands its budget, so that financial risk does not change. The optimal budget in the domestic case

**EXHIBIT 11.6**

Market Liquidity, Segmentation, and the Marginal Cost of Capital

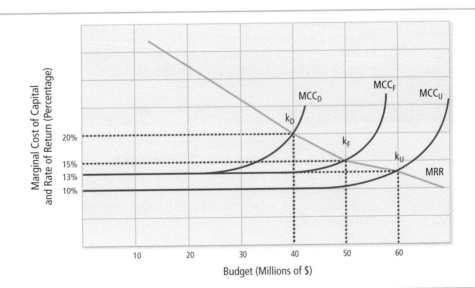

is $40 million, where the marginal return on capital (MRR) just equals the marginal cost of capital ($MCC_D$). At this budget the marginal domestic cost of capital, $k_D$, would be equal to 20%.

If the MNE has access to additional sources of capital outside an illiquid domestic capital market, the marginal cost of capital should shift to the right (the line $MCC_F$). In other words, foreign markets can be tapped for long-term funds at times when the domestic market is saturated because of heavy use by other borrowers or equity issuers, or when it is unable to absorb another issue of the MNE in the short run. Exhibit 11.6 shows that by a tap of foreign capital markets the firm has reduced its marginal international cost of capital, $k_F$ to 15%, even while it raises an additional $10 million. This statement assumes that about $20 million is raised abroad, since only about $30 million could be raised domestically at a 15% marginal cost of capital.

If the MNE is located in a capital market that is both illiquid and segmented, the line $MCC_U$ represents the decreased marginal cost of capital if it gains access to other equity markets. As a result of the combined effects of greater availability of capital and international pricing of the firm's securities, the marginal cost of capital, $k_U$, declines to 13% and the optimal capital budget climbs to $60 million.

Most of the tests of market segmentation suffer from the usual problem for models — namely, the need to abstract from reality in order to have a testable model. In our opinion a realistic test would be to observe what happens to a single security's price when it has been traded only in a domestic market, is "discovered" by foreign investors, and then is traded in a foreign market. Arbitrage should keep the market price equal in both markets. However, if during the transition we observe a significant change in the security's price uncorrelated with price movements in either of the underlying securities markets, we can infer that the domestic market was segmented.

In academic circles tests based on case studies are often considered to be "casual empiricism," since no theory or model exists to explain what is being observed. Nevertheless, something may be learned from such cases, just as scientists learn from observing nature in an uncontrolled environment. Furthermore, case studies that preserve real-world complications may illustrate specific kinds of barriers to market integration and ways in which they might be overcome.

Unfortunately, few case studies have been documented in which a firm has "escaped" from a segmented capital market. In practice, escape usually means being listed on a foreign stock market such as New York or London, and/or selling securities in foreign capital markets. We will illustrate something more specific by using the example of Novo Industri A/S, a Danish firm.[1]

## Illustrative Case: Novo Industri A/S (Novo)

Novo is a Danish multinational firm which produces industrial enzymes and pharmaceuticals (mostly insulin). In 1977, Novo's management decided to "internationalize" its capital structure and sources of funds. This decision was based on the observation that the Danish securities market was both illiquid and segmented from other capital markets. In particular, the lack of availability and high cost of equity capital in Denmark resulted in Novo having a higher cost of capital than its main multinational

[1]The Novo case material is a condensed version of Arthur Stonehill and Kåre B. Dullum, *Internationalizing the Cost of Capital in Theory and Practice: The Novo Experience and National Policy Implications*, Copenhagen: Nyt Nordisk Forlag Arnold Busck, 1982; and New York: Wiley, 1982. Reprinted with permission.

competitors, such as Eli Lilly (U.S.), Miles Laboratories (U.S. — a subsidiary of Bayer, Germany), and Gist Brocades (Netherlands).

Apart from the cost of capital, Novo's projected growth opportunities signaled the eventual need to raise new long-term capital beyond what could be raised in the illiquid Danish market. Since Novo is a technology leader in its specialties (insulin and industrial enzymes), planned capital investments in plant, equipment, and research could not be postponed until internal financing from cash flow became available. Novo's competitors would preempt any markets not served by Novo.

Even if an equity issue of the size required could have been raised in Denmark, the required rate of return would have been unacceptably high. For example, Novo's price/earnings ratio was typically around 5; that of its foreign competitors was well over 10. Yet Novo's business and financial risk appeared to be about equal to that of its competitors. A price/earnings ratio of 5 appeared appropriate for Novo only within a domestic Danish context when Novo was compared with other domestic firms of comparable business and financial risk.

If Denmark's securities markets were integrated with world markets, one would expect foreign investors to rush in and buy "undervalued" Danish securities. In that case firms like Novo would enjoy an international cost of capital comparable to that of their foreign competitors. Strangely enough, no Danish governmental restrictions existed that would have prevented foreign investors from holding Danish securities. Therefore one must look for investor perception as the main cause of market segmentation in Denmark at that time.

At least six characteristics of the Danish equity market were responsible for market segmentation: (1) asymmetric information base of Danish and foreign investors, (2) taxation, (3) alternative sets of feasible portfolios, (4) financial risk, (5) foreign exchange risk, and (6) political risk.

## ASYMMETRIC INFORMATION

Certain institutional characteristics of Denmark caused Danish and foreign investors to be uninformed about each other's equity securities. The most important information barrier was a Danish regulation that prohibited Danish investors from holding foreign private sector securities. Therefore Danish investors had no incentive to follow developments in foreign securities markets or to factor such information into their evaluation of Danish securities. As a result, Danish securities might have been priced correctly in the efficient market sense relative to one another, considering the Danish information base, but priced incorrectly considering the combined foreign and Danish information base. Another detrimental effect of this regulation was that foreign securities firms did not locate offices or personnel in Denmark, since they had no product to sell. Lack of a physical presence in Denmark reduced the ability of foreign security analysts to follow Danish securities.

A second information barrier was lack of enough Danish security analysts following Danish securities. Only one professional Danish securities analysis service was published (Børsinformation), and that was in the Danish language. A few Danish institutional investors employed in-house analysts, but their findings were not available to the public. Almost no foreign security analysts followed Danish securities because they had no product to sell and the Danish market was too small (small-country bias).

Other information barriers included language and accounting principles. Naturally, financial information was normally published in Danish, using Danish accounting principles. A few firms, such as Novo, published English versions, but

almost none used U.S. or British accounting principles or attempted to show any rec-
onciliation with such principles.

## TAXATION

Danish taxation policy had all but eliminated investment in common stock by individuals. Until a tax law change in July 1981, capital gains on shares held for over two years
were taxed at a 50% rate. Shares held for less than two years, or for "speculative" purposes, were taxed at personal income tax rates, with the top marginal rate being 75%.
In contrast, capital gains on bonds were tax free. This situation resulted in bonds being
issued at deep discounts because the redemption at par at maturity was considered a
capital gain. Thus most individual investors held bonds rather than stocks. This factor
reduced the liquidity of the stock market and increased the required rate of return on
stocks if they were to compete with bonds.

## FEASIBLE SET OF PORTFOLIOS

Because of the prohibition on foreign security ownership, Danish investors had a very
limited set of securities from which to choose a portfolio. In practice, Danish institutional portfolios were composed of Danish stocks, government bonds, and mortgage
bonds. Since Danish stock price movements are closely correlated with each other,
Danish portfolios possessed a rather high level of systematic risk. In addition, government policy had been to provide a relatively high real rate of return on government
bonds after adjusting for inflation. The net result of taxation policies on individuals,
and attractive real yields on government bonds was that required rates of return on
stocks were relatively high by international standards.

From a portfolio perspective, Danish stocks provided an opportunity for foreign
investors to diversify internationally. If Danish stock price movements were not closely
correlated with world stock price movements, inclusion of Danish stocks in foreign
portfolios should reduce these portfolios' systematic risk. Furthermore, foreign
investors were not subject to the high Danish income tax rates because they are normally protected by tax treaties that typically limit their tax to 15% on dividends and
capital gains. As a result of the international diversification potential, foreign investors
might have required a lower rate of return on Danish stocks than Danish investors,
other things being equal. However, other things were not equal because foreign
investors perceived Danish stocks to carry more financial, foreign exchange, and political risk than their own domestic securities.

## FINANCIAL, FOREIGN EXCHANGE, AND POLITICAL RISKS

Financial leverage utilized by Danish firms was relatively high by U.S. and U.K. standards
but not abnormal for Scandinavia, Germany, Italy, or Japan. In addition, most of the debt
was short term with variable interest rates. Just how foreign investors viewed financial
risk in Danish firms depended on what norms they followed in their home countries. We
know from Novo's experience in tapping the Eurobond market in 1978 that Morgan
Grenfell, its British investment banker, advised Novo to maintain a debt ratio (debt/total
capitalization) closer to 50% rather than the traditional Danish 65% to 70%.

Foreign investors in Danish securities are subject to foreign exchange risk.
Whether this is a plus or minus factor depends on the investor's home currency, perception about the future strength of the Danish krone, and its impact on a firm's operating exposure. Through personal contacts with foreign investors and bankers, Novo's

management did not believe foreign exchange risk was a factor in Novo's stock price because its operations were perceived as being well-diversified internationally.

With respect to political risk, Denmark was perceived as a stable Western democracy but with the potential to cause periodic problems for foreign investors. In particular, Denmark's national debt was regarded as too high for comfort, although this judgment had not yet shown up in the form of risk premiums on Denmark's Eurocurrency syndicated loans.

## THE ROAD TO GLOBALIZATION

Although Novo's management in 1977 wished to escape from the shackles of Denmark's segmented and illiquid capital market, many barriers had to be overcome. It is worthwhile to describe some of these obstacles, because they typify the barriers faced by other firms from segmented markets that wish to internationalize their capital sources.

**CLOSING THE INFORMATION GAP.**   Novo had been a family-owned firm from its founding in the 1920s by the two Pedersen brothers until 1974, when it went public and listed its "B" shares on the Copenhagen Stock Exchange. The "A" shares were held by the Novo Foundation; the "A" shares were sufficient to maintain voting control. However, Novo was essentially unknown in investment circles outside of Denmark. To overcome this disparity in the information base, Novo increased the level of its financial and technical disclosure in both Danish and English versions.

The information gap was further closed when Morgan Grenfell successfully organized a syndicate to underwrite and sell a $20 million convertible Eurobond issue for Novo in 1978. In connection with this offering Novo listed its shares on the London Stock Exchange to facilitate conversion and to gain visibility. These twin actions were the key to dissolving the information barrier and, of course, they also raised a large amount of long-term capital on favorable terms, which would have been unavailable in Denmark.

Despite the favorable impact of the Eurobond issue on availability of capital, Novo's cost of capital actually increased when Danish investors reacted negatively to the potential dilution effect of the conversion right. During 1979, Novo's share price declined from around Dkr300 per share to around Dkr220 per share.

**THE BIOTECHNOLOGY BOOM.**   During 1979, a fortuitous event occurred. Biotechnology began to attract the interest of the U.S. investment community, with several sensationally oversubscribed stock issues by such start-up firms as Genentech and Cetus. Thanks to the aforementioned domestic information gap, Danish investors were unaware of these events and continued to value Novo at a low price/earnings ratio of 5, compared with over 10 for its established competitors and 30 or more for these new potential competitors.

In order to profile itself as a biotechnology firm with a proven track record, Novo organized a seminar in New York City on April 30, 1980. Soon after the seminar a few sophisticated individual U.S. investors began buying Novo's shares and convertibles through the London Stock Exchange. Danish investors were only too happy to supply this foreign demand. Therefore, despite relatively strong demand from U.S. and British investors, Novo's share price increased only gradually, climbing back to the Dkr300 level by mid-summer. However, during the following months foreign interest began to snowball, and by the end of 1980 Novo's stock price had reached the Dkr600 level. Moreover, foreign investors had increased their proportion of share ownership from virtually nothing to around 30%. Novo's price/earnings ratio had risen to around 16, which was now in line with that of its international competitors but not with the Danish market. At this point one must conclude that Novo had succeeded in internationalizing its cost of capital. Other Danish securities remained locked in a segmented capital market. Exhibit 11.7 shows that the movement in the Danish stock market in general did not parallel the rise in Novo's share price, nor could it be explained by movement in the U.S. or U.K. stock markets as a whole.

**DIRECTED SHARE ISSUE IN THE UNITED STATES.**    During the first half of 1981, under the guidance of Goldman Sachs and with the assistance of Morgan Grenfell and Copenhagen Handelsbank, Novo prepared a prospectus for SEC registration of a U.S. share offering and eventual listing on the New York Stock Exchange. The main barriers encountered in this effort, which would have general applicability, were connected with preparing financial statements that could be reconciled with U.S. accounting principles and the higher level of disclosure required by the SEC. In particular, industry segment reporting was a problem both from a disclosure perspective and an accounting perspective because the accounting data were not available internally in that format. As it turned out, the investment barriers in the U.S. were relatively tractable, although expensive and time consuming to overcome.

The more serious barriers were caused by a variety of institutional and governmental regulations in Denmark. The latter were never designed so that firms could issue shares at market value, since Danish firms typically issued stock at par value with preemptive rights. By this time, however, Novo's share price, driven by continued foreign buying, was so high that virtually nobody in Denmark thought it was worth the price which foreigners were willing to pay. In fact, prior to the time of the share issue in July 1981 Novo's share price had risen to over Dkr1500, before settling down to a

**EXHIBIT 11.7**

Novo's B-Share Prices Compared with Stock Market Indices

Source: *Internationalizing the Cost of Capital: The Novo Experience and National Policy Implications*, Arthur I. Stonehill and Kåre B. Dullum, ©1982 John Wiley & Sons. Reproduced with permission.

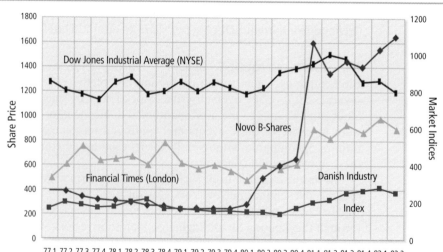

level around Dkr1400. Foreign ownership had increased to over 50% of Novo's shares outstanding!

**STOCK MARKET REACTIONS.**   One final piece of evidence on market segmentation can be gleaned from the way Danish and foreign investors reacted to the announcement of the proposed $61 million U.S. share issue on May 29, 1981. Novo's share price dropped 156 points the next trading day in Copenhagen, equal to about 10% of its market value. As soon as trading started in New York, the stock price immediately recovered all of its loss. The Copenhagen reaction was typical for an illiquid market. Investors worried about the dilution effect of the new share issue, because it would increase the number of shares outstanding by about 8%. They did not believe that Novo could invest the new funds at a rate of return which would not dilute future earnings per share. They also feared that the U.S. shares would eventually flow back to Copenhagen if biotechnology lost its glitter.

The U.S. reaction to the announcement of the new share issue was consistent with what one would expect in a liquid and integrated market. U.S. investors viewed the new issue as creating additional demand for the shares as Novo became more visible due to the selling efforts of a large aggressive syndicate. Furthermore, the marketing effort was directed at institutional investors who were previously underrepresented among Novo's U.S. investors. They had been underrepresented because U.S. institutional investors want to be assured of a liquid market in a stock in order to be able to get out, if desired, without depressing the share price. The wide distribution effected by the new issue, plus SEC registration and a New York Stock Exchange listing, all added up to more liquidity and a global cost of capital.

**EFFECT ON NOVO'S WEIGHTED AVERAGE COST OF CAPITAL.**   During most of 1981 and the years thereafter Novo's share price was driven by international portfolio investors transacting on the New York, London, and Copenhagen stock exchanges. This reduced Novo's weighted average cost of capital and lowered its marginal cost of capital. Novo's systematic risk was reduced from its previous level, which was determined by nondiversified (internationally) Danish institutional investors and the Novo Foundation. However, its appropriate debt ratio level was also reduced to match the standards expected by international portfolio investors trading in the U.S., U.K., and other important markets. In essence, the U.S. dollar became Novo's functional currency when being evaluated by international investors. Theoretically, its revised weighted average cost of capital should have become a new reference hurdle rate when evaluating new capital investments in Denmark or abroad.

Other firms that follow Novo's strategy are also likely to have their weighted average cost of capital become a function of the requirements of international portfolio investors. Firms resident in some of the emerging market countries have already experienced "dollarization" of trade and financing for working capital. This phenomenon might be extended to long-term financing and the weighted average cost of capital.

The Novo experience has been described in hopes that it can be a model for other firms wishing to escape from segmented and illiquid home equity markets. In particular MNEs based in emerging markets often face barriers and lack of visibility similar to what Novo faced. They could benefit by following Novo's proactive strategy employed to attract international portfolio investors. However, a word of caution is advised. Novo had an excellent operating track record and a very strong worldwide market niche in two important industry sectors. This record continues to attract investors in Denmark and abroad. Other companies would also need to have such a favorable track record to attract foreign investors.

## Globalization of Securities Markets

During the 1980s numerous other Nordic and other European firms followed Novo's example. They cross-listed on major foreign exchanges such as London and New York. They placed equity and debt issues in major securities markets. In most cases they were successful in lowering their WACC and increasing its availability.

During the 1980s and 1990s national restrictions on cross-border portfolio investment were gradually eased under pressure from the Organisation for Economic Cooperation and Development (OECD), a consortium of most of the world's most industrialized countries. Liberalization of European securities markets was accelerated because of the European Union's efforts to develop a single European market without barriers. Emerging nation markets followed suit, as did the former East Bloc countries after the breakup of the Soviet Union. Emerging national markets have often been motivated by the need to source foreign capital to finance large-scale privatization.

At the present time market segmentation has been significantly reduced, although the liquidity of individual national markets remains limited. Most observers believe that for better or for worse we have achieved a global market for securities. The good news is that many firms have been assisted to become MNEs because they now have access to a global cost and availability of capital. The bad news is that the correlation among securities markets has increased, thereby reducing, but not eliminating, the benefits of international portfolio diversification. Globalization of securities markets has also led to more volatility and speculative behavior as shown by the emerging market crises of the 1995–2001 period, and the collapse of high tech in the following year.

### CORPORATE GOVERNANCE AND THE COST OF CAPITAL

Would global investors be willing to pay a premium for a share in a good corporate governance company? A recent study of Norwegian and Swedish firms measured the impact of foreign board membership (Anglo-American) on firm value. They summarized their findings as follows:

> *Using a sample of firms with headquarters in Norway or Sweden the study indicates a significantly higher value for firms that have outsider Anglo-American board member(s), after a variety of firm-specific and corporate governance related factors have been controlled for. We argue that this superior performance reflects the fact that these companies have successfully broken away from a partly segmented domestic capital market by "importing" an Anglo-American corporate governance system. Such an "import" signals a willingness on the part of the firm to expose itself to improved corporate governance and enhances its reputation in the financial market.[2]*

[2]Lars Oxelheim and Trond Randøy, "The impact of foreign board membership on firm value," *Journal of Banking and Finance*, vol. 27, no. 12, 2003, p. 2369.

## STRATEGIC ALLIANCES

Strategic alliances are normally formed by firms that expect to gain synergies from one or more of the following joint efforts. They might share the cost of developing technology, or pursue complementary marketing activities. They might gain economies of scale or scope or a variety of other commercial advantages. However, one synergy that may sometimes by overlooked is the possibility for a financially strong firm to help a financially weak firm to lower its cost of capital by providing attractively priced equity or debt financing. This is illustrated in the *Real World Example 11.2* on the strategic alliance between Bang & Olufsen and Philips.

In Chapters 12 through 14 we will describe the experiences of firms that have successfully tapped global securities markets and the financial strategies and instruments they have used.

# Real World Example 11.2
## BANG & OLUFSEN AND PHILIPS N.V.

One excellent example of financial synergy that lowered a firm's cost of capital was provided by the cross-border strategic alliance of Philips N.V. of the Netherlands and Bang & Olufsen (B&O) of Denmark in 1990. Philips N.V. is one of the largest multinational firms in the world and the leading consumer electronics firm in Europe. B&O is a small European competitor but with a nice niche at the high end of the audiovisual market.

Philips was a major supplier of components to B&O, a situation it wished to continue. It also wished to join forces with B&O in the upscale consumer electronics market, where Philips did not have the quality image enjoyed by B&O. Philips was concerned that financial pressure might force B&O to choose a Japanese competitor for a partner. That would be very unfortunate. B&O had always supported Philips' political efforts to gain EU support to make the few remaining European-owned consumer electronics firms more competitive than their strong Japanese competitors.

### B&O's Motivation

B&O was interested in an alliance with Philips to gain more rapid access to its new technology and assistance in converting that technology into B&O product applications. B&O wanted assurance of timely delivery of components at volume discounts from Philips itself, as well as access to Philip's large network of suppliers under the terms enjoyed by Philips. Equally important, B&O wanted to get an equity infusion from Philips to strengthen its own shaky financial position. Despite its commercial artistry, in recent years B&O had been only marginally profitable, and its

publicly traded shares were considered too risky to justify a new public equity issue either in Denmark or abroad. It had no excess borrowing capacity.

### The Strategic Alliance

A strategic alliance was agreed upon that would give each partner what it desired commercially. Philips agreed to invest DKK342 million (about $50 million) to increase the equity of B&O's main operating subsidiary. In return it received a 25% ownership of the expanded company.

When B&O's strategic alliance was announced to the public on May 3, 1990, the share price of B&O Holding, the listed company on the Copenhagen Stock Exchange, jumped by 35% in two days. It remained at that level until the Gulf War crisis temporarily depressed B&O's share price. The share price has since recovered and the expected synergies eventually materialized. B&O eventually bought back its shares from Philips at a price that had been predetermined at the start.

In evaluating what happened, we recognize that an industrial purchaser might be willing to pay a higher price for a firm that will provide it some synergies than would a portfolio investor who does not receive these synergies. Portfolio investors are only pricing firms' shares based on the normal risk versus return tradeoff. They cannot normally anticipate the value of synergies that might accrue to the firm from an unexpected strategic alliance partner. The same conclusion should hold for a purely domestic strategic alliance, but this example happens to be a cross-border alliance.

## The Cost of Capital for MNEs Compared with Capital for Domestic Firms

Is the weighted average cost of capital for MNEs higher or lower than for their domestic counterparts? The answer is a function of the marginal cost of capital, the relative after-tax cost of debt, the optimal debt ratio, and the relative cost of equity.

### AVAILABILITY OF CAPITAL

We saw earlier in this chapter that international availability of capital to MNEs, or to other large firms that can attract international portfolio investors, may allow them to lower their cost of equity and debt compared with most domestic firms. In addition, international availability permits an MNE to maintain its desired debt ratio, even when significant amounts of new funds must be raised. In other words, an MNE's marginal cost of capital is constant for considerable ranges of its capital budget. This statement is not true for most domestic firms. They must either rely on internally generated funds or borrow in the short and medium term from commercial banks.

### FINANCIAL STRUCTURE, SYSTEMATIC RISK, AND THE COST OF CAPITAL FOR MNEs

Theoretically MNEs should be in a better position than their domestic counterparts to support higher debt ratios because their cash flows are diversified internationally. The probability of a firm's covering fixed charges under varying conditions in product, financial, and foreign exchange markets should improve if the variability of its cash flows is minimized.

By diversifying cash flows internationally, the MNE might be able to achieve the same kind of reduction in cash flow variability as portfolio investors receive from diversifying their security holdings internationally. The same argument applies — namely, that returns are not perfectly correlated between countries. For example, in 2000 Japan was in recession but the United States was experiencing rapid growth. Therefore we might have expected returns, on either a cash flow or an earnings basis, to be depressed in Japan and favorable in the United States. An MNE with operations located in both these countries could rely on its strong U.S. cash inflow to cover debt obligations, even if its Japanese subsidiary produced weak net cash inflows.

Despite the theoretical elegance of this hypothesis, empirical studies have come to the opposite conclusion.[3] Despite the favorable effect of international diversification of cash flows bankruptcy risk was only about the same for MNEs as for domestic firms. However, MNEs faced higher agency costs, political risk, foreign exchange risk, and asymmetric information. These have been identified as the factors leading to lower debt ratios and even a higher cost of long-term debt for MNEs. Domestic firms rely much more heavily on short and intermediate debt, which lie at the low cost end of the yield curve.

Even more surprising, one study found that MNEs have a higher level of systematic risk than their domestic counterparts.[4] The same factors caused this phenomenon

---

[3]Kwang Chul Lee and Chuck C. Y. Kwok, "Multinational Corporations vs. Domestic Corporations: International Environmental Factors and Determinants of Capital Structure," *Journal of International Business Studies*, Summer 1988, pp. 195–217.

[4]David M. Reeb, Chuck C. Y. Kwok, and H. Young Back, "Systematic Risk of the Multinational Corporation," *Journal of International Business Studies*, Second Quarter 1998, pp. 263–279.

as caused the lower debt ratios for MNEs. The study concluded that the increased standard deviation of cash flows from internationalization more than offset the lower correlation from diversification.

As we stated earlier in this chapter, the systematic risk term, $\beta_j$, is defined as

$$\beta_j = \frac{\rho_{jm}\sigma_j}{\sigma_m}$$

where $\rho_{jm}$ is the correlation coefficient between security j and the market; $\sigma_j$ is the standard deviation of the return on firm j; and $\sigma_m$ is the standard deviation of the market return. The MNE's systematic risk could increase if the decrease in the correlation coefficient, $\rho_{jm}$, due to international diversification, is more than offset by an increase in $\sigma_j$, the standard deviation due to the aforementioned risk factors. This conclusion is consistent with the observation that many MNEs use a higher hurdle rate to discount expected foreign project cash flows. In essence, they are accepting projects they consider to be riskier than domestic projects, thus potentially skewing upward their perceived systematic risk. At the least, MNEs need to earn a higher rate of return than their domestic equivalents in order to maintain their market value.

A more recent study found that internationalization actually allowed emerging market MNEs to carry a higher level of debt and lowered their systematic risk.[5] This occurred because the emerging market MNEs are investing in more stable economies abroad, a strategy that lowers their operating, financial, foreign exchange, and political risks. The reduction in risk more than offsets their increased agency costs and allows the emerging market MNEs to enjoy higher leverage and lower systematic risk than their U.S.–based MNE counterparts.

## Solving a Riddle: Is the Weighted Average Cost of Capital for MNEs Really Higher Than for Their Domestic Counterparts?

The riddle is that the MNE is supposed to have a lower marginal cost of capital (MCC) than a domestic firm because of the MNE's access to a global cost and availability of capital. On the other hand, the empirical studies we mentioned show that the MNE's weighted average cost of capital (WACC) is actually higher than for a comparable domestic firm because of agency costs, foreign exchange risk, political risk, asymmetric information, and other complexities of foreign operations.

The answer to this riddle lies in the link between the cost of capital, its availability, and the opportunity set of projects. As the opportunity set of projects increases, eventually the firm needs to increase its capital budget to the point where its marginal cost of capital is increasing. The optimal capital budget would still be at the point where the rising marginal cost of capital equals the declining rate of return on the opportunity set of projects. However, this would be at a higher weighted average cost of capital than would have occurred for a lower level of the optimal capital budget.

To illustrate this linkage Exhibit 11.8 shows the marginal cost of capital given different optimal capital budgets. Assume that there are two different demand schedules based on the opportunity set of projects for both the MNE and domestic counterpart (DC).

[5]Chuck C. Y. Kwok, and David M. Reeb, "Internationalization and Firm Risk: An Upstream-Downstream Hypothesis," *Journal of International Business Studies,* vol. 31, no. 4, 2000, pp. 611–630.

**EXHIBIT 11.8**

The Cost of
Capital for the
MNE and
Domestic
Counterpart
Compared

The line $MRR_{DC}$ depicts a modest set of potential projects. It intersects the line $MCC_{MNE}$ at 15% and a $100 million budget level. It intersects the $MCC_{DC}$ at 10% and a $140 million budget level. At these low budget levels the $MCC_{MNE}$ has a higher MCC and probably weighted average cost of capital than its domestic counterpart (DC), as discovered in the recent empirical studies.

The line $MRR_{MNE}$ depicts a more ambitious set of projects for both the MNE and its domestic counterpart. It intersects the line $MCC_{MNE}$ still at 15% and a $350 million budget. However, it intersects the $MCC_{DC}$ at 20% and a budget level of $300 million. At these higher budget levels the $MCC_{MNE}$ has a lower MCC and probably weighted average cost of capital than its domestic counterpart, as predicted earlier in this chapter.

In order to extend this conclusion to the general case, we would need to know under what conditions a domestic firm would be willing to undertake the optimal capital budget despite its increasing the firm's marginal cost of capital. At some point the MNE might also have an optimal capital budget at the point where its MCC is rising.

Empirical studies show that neither mature domestic firms nor MNEs are typically willing to assume the higher agency costs or bankruptcy risk associated with higher MCCs and capital budgets. In fact, most mature firms demonstrate some degree of corporate wealth maximizing behavior. They are somewhat risk averse and tend to avoid returning to the market to raise fresh equity. They prefer to limit their capital budgets to what can be financed with free cash flows. Indeed, they have a so-called pecking order that determines which sources of funds they tap and in what order. This behavior motivates shareholders to monitor management more closely. They tie management's compensation to stock performance (options). They may also require other types of contractual arrangements that are collectively part of agency costs.

In conclusion, if both MNEs and domestic firms do actually limit their capital budgets to what can be financed without increasing their MCC, then the empirical findings that MNEs have higher WACC stands. If the domestic firm has such good growth opportunities that it chooses to undertake growth despite an increasing marginal cost of capital, then the MNE would have a lower WACC. Exhibit 11.9 summarizes these conclusions.

## EXHIBIT 11.9

**Do MNEs Have a Higher or Lower WACC Than Their Domestic Counterparts?**

Is $MNE_{wacc}$ > or < $Domestic_{wacc}$?

$$k_{WACC} = k_e \left[ \frac{Equity}{Value} \right] + k_d (1-t) \left[ \frac{Debt}{Value} \right]$$

Empirical studies indicate MNEs have a lower debt/capital ratio than domestic counterparts, indicating MNEs have a higher cost of capital.

And MNEs seem to have a lower average cost of debt than domestic counterparts, indicating MNEs have a lower cost of capital.

The cost of equity required by investors is higher for multinational firms than for domestic firms. Possible explanations are higher levels of *political risk*, *foreign exchange risk*, and *higher agency costs* of doing business in a multinational managerial environment. However, at relatively high levels of the optimal capital budget, the MNE would have a lower cost of capital.

---

## MINI-CASE

# Nestlé: An Application of the International CAPM

In theory, the primary distinction in the estimation of the cost of equity for an individual firm using an internationalized version of the CAPM is the definition of the market and a recalculation of the firm's beta for that market. The case of Nestlé (Switzerland) provides an illustration of the possible impact of this globalization of portfolios.

Nestlé, the Swiss-based multinational firm that produces and distributes a variety of confectionery products, serves as an excellent example of how the international investor may view the global cost of capital differently from a domestic investor.[6]

Estimating the required return on Nestlé, a prospective Swiss investor might assume a risk-free return of 3.3% (index of Swiss government bond issues, in Swiss francs), an average return on a portfolio of Swiss equities of 10.2% (*Financial Times Swiss Index*, in Swiss francs), and a $\beta_{Nestlé}$ of 0.885. An investor would then expect Nestlé to yield 9.4065% for the coming year.

$$k_e^{Nestlé} = k_{rf} + (k_m - k_{rf})\beta_{Nestlé} = 3.3 + (10.2 - 3.3)0.885 = 9.4065\%$$

One problem with this traditional domestic CAPM approach is that it assumes investors in the Swiss market, and potentially in Nestlé, hold portfolios limited to stocks available in the Swiss market alone — a purely domestic portfolio. If Swiss investors held internationally diversified portfolios instead, both the expected market return ($k_m$), and the beta estimate for Nestlé ($\beta_{Nestlé}$) would be defined and determined differently.

A Swiss investor may hold a global portfolio, rather than a domestic portfolio. Given the trends toward deregulation and integration of international capital markets, the Swiss investor's portfolio expectations would be more accurately represented by a global portfolio index rather than by a purely domestic index.

We follow Stulz's (1995) preference here for describing the internationally diversified portfolio as the global portfolio rather than the world portfolio. The distinction is important. The world portfolio is an index of all securities in the world. However, even with the increasing trend of deregulation and financial integration, a number of securities markets still remain segmented or restricted in their

[6]René Stulz, "The Cost of Capital in Internationally Integrated Markets: The Case of Nestle," *European Financial Management*, vol. 1, no. 1, March 1995, pp. 11–22.

access. Those securities actually available to an investor are the *global portfolio*.

In the case of Nestlé, for the same time period as before, a global portfolio index such as the *Financial Times* index in Swiss francs (FTA-Swiss) would show a market return of 13.7% (as opposed to the domestic Swiss index return of 10.2%). In addition, a beta for Nestlé estimated on Nestlé's returns versus the global portfolio index would be much smaller, 0.585 (as opposed to the 0.885 found previously). An internationally diversified Swiss investor would expect a return on Nestlé of

$$k_e^{Nestlé} = k_{rf} + (k_m - k_{rf})\beta_{Nestlé} = 3.3 + (13.7 - 3.3)0.585 = 9.384\%$$

Admittedly, there is not a lot of difference in the end. Exhibit 1 summarizes the values and results of the comparison. However, given the magnitude of change in both the values of the market return average and the beta for the firm, it is obvious that the final result could easily have varied by several hundred basis points. The proper construction of the investor's portfolio and the proper portrayal of the investor's perceptions of risk and opportunity cost are clearly important to identifying the global cost of a company's equity capital.

## Case Questions

1. There are a multitude of barriers to the free and open movement of capital across boundaries. How would these barriers affect professional investors and portfolio managers with respect to new information regarding the return and risk prospects of individual securities globally?
2. Given such market imperfections as limitations on trading, illiquidity, and lack of perfect information in many emerging markets, is there any way to measure or define an international or global portfolio?
3. The international CAPM uses the risk-free rate of interest as its base. Under what conditions could you calculate a risk-free rate of return globally?

## EXHIBIT 1

| Estimating the Global Cost of Equity for Nestlé (Switzerland) | Domestic Portfolio for Swiss Investor | Global Portfolio for Swiss Investor |
| --- | --- | --- |
| | $k_{rf}$ = 3.3% (Swiss bond index yield) | $k_{rf}$ = 3.3% (Swiss bond index yield) |
| | $k_m$ = 10.2% (Swiss market portfolio in SF) | $k_m$ = 13.7% (*Financial Times* Global index in SF) |
| | $\beta_{Nestlé}$ = 0.885 (Nestlé versus Swiss market portfolio) | $\beta_{Nestlé}$ = 0.585 (Nestlé versus FTA-Swiss index) |

$$k_{Nestlé} = k_{rf} + (k_m - k_{rf}) \beta_{Nestlé}$$

| Required return on Nestlé: | Required return on Nestlé: |
| --- | --- |
| $k_e^{Nestlé}$ = 9.4065% | $k_e^{Nestlé}$ = 9.3840% |

Source: All values are taken from René Stulz, "The Cost of Capital in Internationally Integrated Markets: The Case of Nestlé," *European Financial Management*, vol. 1, no. 1, March 1995, pp. 11–22.

## Summary of Learning Objectives

*Show how a firm headquartered in a country with an illiquid and segmented capital market achieves a lower global cost of capital and greater availability of capital*

- Gaining access to global capital markets should allow a firm to lower its cost of capital. A firm can improve access to global capital markets by increasing the market liquidity of its shares and by escaping from segmentation of its home capital market.

*Analyze the link between cost and availability of capital*

- The cost and availability of capital is directly linked to the degree of market liquidity and segmentation. Firms having access to markets with high liquidity and a low level of segmentation should have a lower cost of capital and greater ability to raise new capital.

- A firm is able to increase its market liquidity by raising debt in the Euromarket, by selling security issues in individual national capital markets and as euroequities, and by tapping local capital markets through foreign subsidiaries. Increased market liquidity causes the marginal cost of capital line to "flatten out to the right." This results in the firm's being able to raise more capital at the same low marginal cost of capital, thereby justifying its investing in more capital projects. The key is to attract international portfolio investors.

*Evaluate the effect of market liquidity and segmentation on the cost of capital*

- A national capital market is segmented if the required rate of return on securities in that market differs from the required rate of return on securities of comparable expected return and risk that are traded on other national securities markets. Capital market segmentation is a financial market imperfection caused by government constraints and investor perceptions. The most important imperfections are (1) asymmetric information, (2) transaction costs, (3) foreign exchange risk, (4) corporate governance differences, (5) political risk, and (6) regulatory barriers.

- Segmentation results in a higher cost of capital and less availability of capital.

- If a firm is resident in a segmented capital market, it can escape from this market by sourcing its debt and equity abroad. The result should be a lower marginal cost of capital, improved liquidity for its shares, and a larger capital budget. The experience of Novo served as a model for firms resident in small or emerging markets that are partially segmented and illiquid.

*Compare the weighted average cost of capital for an MNE with that of its domestic counterpart*

- Whether MNEs have a lower cost of capital than their domestic counterparts depends on their optimal financial structures, systematic risk, availability of capital, and the level of the optimal capital budget.

## QUESTIONS

1. **Dimensions of the cost and availability of capital.** Global integration has given many firms access to new and cheaper sources of funds beyond those available in their home markets. What are the dimensions of a strategy to capture this lower cost and greater availability of capital?

2. **Benefits.** What are the benefits of achieving a lower cost and greater availability of capital?

3. **Definitions.** Define the following terms:
   a. Systematic risk
   b. Unsystematic risk
   c. Beta (in the capital asset pricing model)

4. **Equity risk premiums.**
   a. What is an equity risk premium?
   b. What is the difference between calculating an equity risk premium using arithmetic returns compared to geometric returns?
   c. In Exhibit 11.3, why are arithmetic mean risk premiums always higher than geometric mean risk premiums?

5. **Portfolio investors.** Both domestic and international portfolio managers are *asset allocators*.
   a. What is their portfolio management objective?
   b. What is the main advantage that international portfolio managers have compared to portfolio managers who are limited to domestic-only asset allocation?

6. **Dimensions of asset allocation.** Portfolio asset allocation can be accomplished along many dimensions depending on the investment objective of the portfolio manager. Identify the various dimensions.

7. **Market liquidity.**
   a. Define what is meant by *market liquidity*.
   b. What are the main disadvantages of being located in an illiquid market?
   c. If a firm is limited to raising funds in its domestic capital market, what happens to its marginal cost of capital as it expands?
   d. If a firm can raise funds abroad, what happens to its marginal cost of capital as it expands?

8. **Market segmentation.**
   a. Define *market segmentation*.
   b. What are the six main causes of market segmentation?
   c. What are the main disadvantages of being located in a segmented market?

9. **Market liquidity and segmentation effects.** What is the effect of market liquidity and segmentation on a firm's cost of capital?

10. **Novo Industri (A).** Why did Novo believe its cost of capital was too high compared to its competitors' cost? Why did Novo's relatively high cost of capital create a competitive disadvantage?

11. **Novo Industri (B).** Novo believed that the Danish capital market was segmented from world capital markets. Explain the six characteristics of the Danish equity market that were responsible for its segmentation.

12. **Novo Industri (C).**

    a. What was Novo's strategy to internationalize its cost of capital?

    b. What is the evidence that Novo's strategy succeeded?

13. **Emerging markets.** It has been suggested that firms located in illiquid and segmented emerging markets could follow Novo's proactive strategy to internationalize their own cost of capital. What are the preconditions that would be necessary to succeed in such a proactive strategy?

14. **Cost of capital for MNEs compared to domestic firms.** Theoretically MNEs should be in a better position than their domestic counterparts to support higher debt ratios because their cash flows are diversified internationally. However, recent empirical studies have come to the opposite conclusion. These studies also concluded that MNEs have higher betas than their domestic counterparts.

    a. According to these empirical studies why do MNEs have lower debt ratios than their domestic counterparts?

    b. According to these empirical studies why do MNEs have higher betas than their domestic counterparts?

15. **The riddle.** The riddle is an attempt to explain under what conditions an MNE would have a higher or lower debt ratio and beta than its domestic counterpart. Explain and diagram what these conditions are.

16. **Emerging market MNEs.** Apart from improving liquidity and escaping from a segmented home market, why might emerging market MNEs further lower their cost of capital by listing and selling equity abroad?

## PROBLEMS

1. **Houston Oil Company.** Houston Oil Company's cost of debt is 7%. The risk-free rate of interest is 3%. The expected return on the market portfolio is 8%. After depletion allowances, Houston's effective tax rate is 25%. Its optimal capital structure is 60% debt and 40% equity.

    a. If Houston's beta is estimated at 1.1, what is Houston's weighted average cost of capital?

    b. If Houston's beta is estimated at 0.8, significantly lower because of the continuing profit prospects in the global energy sector, what is Houston's weighted average cost of capital?

2. **Trident's cost of capital.** Exhibit 11.2 showed the calculation of Trident's weighted average cost of capital. Assuming that financial conditions have worsened, and using the following current data, recalculate

    a. Trident's cost of equity

    b. Trident's cost of debt

    c. Trident's weighted average cost of capital

    $k_{rf} = 4.000\%$     $k_m = 9.000\%$     $\beta = 1.3$

    $k_d = 7.000\%$     $T = 30\%$     $E/V = 50\%$

    $D/V = 50\%$     $V = 100\%$

3. **Sunshine Pipelines, Inc.** Sunshine Pipelines, Inc., is a large U.S. natural gas pipeline company that wants to raise $120 million to finance expansion. Sunshine wants a capital structure that is 50% debt and 50% equity. Its corporate combined federal and state income tax rate is 40%.

    Sunshine finds that it can finance in the domestic U.S. capital market at the following rates. Both debt and equity would have to be sold in multiples of $20 million, and these cost figures show the component costs, each, of debt and equity if raised half by equity and half by debt.

| | Cost of Domestic Equity | Cost of Domestic Debt |
|---|---|---|
| Up to $40 million of new capital | 12% | 8% |
| $41 million to $80 million of new capital | 18% | 12% |
| Above $80 million | 22% | 16% |

A London bank advises Sunshine that U.S. dollars could be raised in Europe at the following costs, also in multiples of $20 million while maintaining the 50/50 capital structure.

|  | Cost of European Equity | Cost of European Debt |
|---|---|---|
| Up to $40 million of new capital | 14% | 6% |
| $41 million to $80 million of new capital | 16% | 10% |
| Above $80 million | 24% | 18% |

Each increment of cost would be influenced by the total amount of capital raised. That is, if Sunshine first borrowed $20 million in the European market at 6% and matched this with an additional $20 million of equity, additional debt beyond this amount would cost 12% in the United States and 10% in Europe. The same relationship holds for equity financing.

a. Calculate the lowest average cost of capital for each increment of $40 million of new capital, where Sunshine raises $20 million in the equity market and an additional $20 million in the debt market at the same time.

b. If Sunshine plans an expansion of only $60 million, how should that expansion be financed? What will be the weighted average cost of capital for the expansion?

4. **Tata's cost of capital.** Tata is the largest and most successful specialty goods company in India. It has not entered the North American marketplace yet, but it is considering establishing manufacturing and distribution facilities in the United States through a wholly owned subsidiary. It has approached two investment banking advisors, Goldman Sachs and Bank of New York, for estimates of what its costs of capital would be several years into the future when it planned to list its American subsidiary on a U.S. stock exchange. Using the following assumptions by the two advisors, calculate the prospective costs of debt, equity, and the WACC for Tata U.S.

| Capital Cost Component | Symbol | Goldman Sachs | Bank of NY |
|---|---|---|---|
| Risk-free rate of interest | $k_{rf}$ | 3.0% | 3.0% |
| Average equity market return | $k_m$ | 9.0% | 12.0% |
| Estimated cost of debt, single-A | $k_d$ | 7.5% | 7.8% |
| Estimated correlation of Tata with market | $\rho_{jm}$ | 0.90 | 0.85 |
| Estimated standard deviation of Tata's returns | $\sigma_j$ | 24.0% | 30.0% |
| Estimated standard deviation of market's returns | $\sigma_m$ | 18.0% | 22.0% |
| Recommended debt to capital structure | D/V | 35% | 40% |
| Recommended equity to capital structure | E/V | 65% | 60% |
| Estimated effective U.S. tax rate | t | 35% | 35% |

5. **Country equity risk premiums.** Using the century of equity market data presented in Exhibit 11.3, answer the following questions.

a. Which country had the largest differential between the arithmetic mean and geometric mean?

b. If a Swiss firm were attempting to calculate its cost of equity using this data, assuming a risk-free rate of 2.0% and a security beta of 1.4, what would be its estimated cost of equity using both the arithmetic and geometric means for the equity risk premium?

6. **Cargill's cost of capital.** Cargill is generally considered to be the largest privately held company in the world. Headquartered in Minneapolis, Minnesota, the company has been averaging sales of over $50 billion per year over the past 5-year period. Although the company does not have publicly traded shares, it is still extremely important for it to calculate its weighted average cost of capital properly in order to make rational decisions on new investment proposals.

|  | Company A | Company B | Cargill |
|---|---|---|---|
| Company sales | $4.5 billion | $26 billion | $50 billion |
| Company's beta | 0.86 | 0.78 | ?? |
| Credit rating | AA | A | AA |
| Weighted average cost of debt | 6.885% | 7.125% | 6.820% |
| Debt to total capital | 34% | 41% | 28% |
| International sales/sales | 12% | 26% | 45% |

Assuming a risk-free rate of 2.5%, an effective tax rate of 40%, and a market risk premium of 5.5%, estimate the weighted average cost of capital first for companies A and B, and then make a "guestimate" of what you believe a comparable WACC would be for Cargill.

7. **The Tombs.** You have joined your friends at the local watering hole, *The Tombs*, for your weekly debate on international finance. The topic this week is whether the cost of equity can ever be cheaper than the cost of debt. The group has chosen Brazil in the mid-1990s as the subject of the debate. One of the group members has the following table of data, which is then the subject of analysis.

| Brazilian Economic Performance | 1995 | 1996 | 1997 | 1998 | 1999 |
|---|---|---|---|---|---|
| Inflation rate (IPC) | 23.2% | 10.0% | 4.8% | −1.0% | 10.5% |
| Bank lending rate (CDI) | 53.1% | 27.1% | 24.7% | 29.2% | 30.7% |
| Exchange rate (reais/$) | 0.972 | 1.039 | 1.117 | 1.207 | 1.700 |
| Stock market index (Bovespa) | 16.0% | 28.0% | 30.2% | −33.5% | 151.9% |

Larry argues that "its all about *expected* versus *delivered*. You can talk about what equity investors expect, but they often find that what is delivered for years at a time is so small — even sometimes negative — that in effect the cost of equity is cheaper than the cost of debt."

Mohammed — he goes by Mo — interrupts: "But you're missing the point. The cost of capital is what the investor *requires* in compensation for the risk taken going *into* the investment. If he doesn't end up getting it, and that was happening here, then he pulls his capital out and walks."

Curly is the theoretician. "Ladies, this is not about empirical results; it is about the fundamental concept of risk-adjusted returns. An investor in equities knows he will reap returns only after all compensation has been made to debt-providers. He is therefore always subject to a higher level of risk to his return than debt instruments, and as the *capital asset pricing model* states, equity investors set their expected returns as a risk-adjusted factor over and above the returns to risk-free instruments."

At this point Larry and Mo simply stare at Curly, pause, and order another beer. Using the Brazilian data presented, comment on this week's debate at The Tombs.

*Sushmita-Chen and the riddle. Use the following information to answer Questions 8 through 10.*

*Sushmita-Chen is an American conglomerate that is actively debating the impact of international diversification of its operations on its capital structure and cost of capital. The firm is planning on reducing consolidated debt after diversification.*

| | Symbol | Before Diversification | After Diversification |
|---|---|---|---|
| Debt-to-capital ratio | D/V | 38% | 32% |
| Equity-to-capital ratio | E/V | 62% | 68% |
| Corporate tax rate | t | 35% | 35% |
| Correlation of S-C's returns with market | $\rho_{jm}$ | 0.88 | 0.76 |
| Standard deviation of S-C's returns | $\sigma_j$ | 28.0% | 26.0% |
| Standard deviation of market's returns | $\sigma_m$ | 18.0% | 18.0% |
| Market risk premium | $k_m - k_{rf}$ | 5.50% | 5.50% |
| Corporate cost of debt | $k_d$ | 7.20% | 7.00% |
| Risk-free rate of interest | $k_{rf}$ | 3.00% | 3.00% |

8. **Sushmita-Chen's cost of equity.** Senior management at Sushmita-Chen is actively debating the implications of diversification on its cost of equity. Although both parties agree that the company's returns will be less correlated with the reference market return in the future, the financial advisors believe that the market will assess an additional 3.0% risk premium for "going international" to the basic CAPM cost of equity. Calculate Sushmita-Chen's cost of equity before and after international diversification of its operations, with and without the hypothetical additional risk premium, and comment on the discussion.

9. **Sushmita-Chen's WACC.** Calculate the weighted average cost of capital for Sushmita-Chen before and after international diversification.

   a. Did the reduction in debt costs reduce the firm's WACC? How would you describe the impact of international diversification on its costs of capital?

   b. Adding the hypothetical risk premium to the cost of equity introduced in Question 8 (an added 3.0% to the cost of equity because of international diversification), what is the firm's WACC?

10. **Sushmita-Chen's WACC and effective tax rate.** Many MNEs have greater ability to control and reduce their effective tax rates when expanding international operations. If Sushmita-Chen was able to reduce its consolidated effective tax rate from 35% to 32%, what would be the impact on its WACC?

**Internet Exercises**

1. **International diversification via mutual funds.** All major mutual fund companies now offer a variety of internationally diversified mutual funds. The degree of international composition across funds, however, differs significantly. Use the Web sites listed below, and any others of interest, to distinguish between diversification degrees and methodologies.

   Fidelity
      http://www.fidelity.com/funds/
   T. Rowe Price
      http://www.troweprice.com/
   Merrill Lynch
      http://www.ml.com/
   Scudder
      http://www.scudder.com/
   Kemper Funds
      http://www.kemperfunds.com

2. **Center for Latin American Capital Markets Research.** Although most of the Latin American markets have suffered significant falls in trading following the Mexican peso crisis of December 1994 and the Brazilian real in January 1999, many of these markets may still be some of the most "undervalued" markets in the world. If you were given the task of investing US$1 million in a single equity market in Latin American or South America, which one would you invest in? Use the World Wide Web to find recent market performance statistics to support your choice.

   Center for Latin American Capital Markets Research
      http://users.netrus.net/gmorles/

3. **Novo Industri.** Novo Industri A/S merged with Nordisk Gentofte in 1989. Nordisk Gentofte was Novo's main European competitor. The combined company, now called Novo Nordisk, has become the leading producer of insulin worldwide. Its main competitor is still Eli Lilly of the United States. Using standard investor information, and the Web site for Novo Nordisk and Eli Lilly, determine whether during the most recent five years Novo Nordisk has maintained a cost of capital competitive with Eli Lilly. In particular examine the P/E ratios, share prices, debt ratios, and betas. Try to calculate each firm's actual cost of capital.

   Novo Nordisk
      http://www.novonordisk.com
   Eli Lilly and Company
      http://www.lilly.com
   BigCharts.com
      http://bigcharts.marketwatch.com

4. **Cost of capital calculator.** Ibbotson Associates of Chicago is one of the leading providers of quantitative estimates of the cost of capital across markets. Use the following Web site — specifically the *Cost of Capital Center* — to prepare an overview of the major theoretical approaches and the numerical estimates they yield for cross-border costs of capital.

   Ibbotson Associates
      http://www.ibbotson.com

# *Sourcing Equity Globally*

## LEARNING OBJECTIVES

Design a strategy to source equity globally

Analyze the motivations and goals of a firm cross-listing its shares on foreign equity markets

Analyze the motivations and goals of a firm issuing new equity shares on foreign equity markets

Recognize the many barriers to effective penetration of foreign equity markets through cross-listing and selling equity abroad

Identify the various financial instruments that can be used to source equity in the global equity markets

Chapter 11 analyzed why gaining access to global capital markets should lower a firm's marginal cost of capital and increase its availability by improving the market liquidity of its shares and by overcoming market segmentation. In order to implement such a lofty goal it is necessary to start by designing a strategy that will ultimately attract international investors. This involves identifying and choosing among alternative paths to access global markets. It also usually requires some restructuring of the firm, improving the quality and level of its disclosure, and making its accounting and reporting standards more transparent to potential foreign investors. The Novo case in Chapter 11 is a good illustration of the steps that need to be taken and barriers that might be faced.

A focus of this chapter is on firms resident in less liquid or segmented markets. They are the ones that need to tap liquid and unsegmented markets in order to attain the global cost and availability of capital. These firms are typically resident in emerging market countries and many of the smaller industrial country markets. Firms resident in the United States and United Kingdom already have full access to their own domestic liquid and unsegmented markets. Although they too source equity and debt abroad, it is unlikely to have as favorable an impact on their cost and availability of capital. In fact, sourcing funds abroad is often motivated only by the need to fund large foreign acquisitions rather than existing domestic or foreign operations.

This chapter starts with the design of a strategy to source both equity and debt capital globally. It then describes depositary receipts. These are the most important instruments that facilitate cross-border trading in securities. The chapter then continues with the specifics of cross-listing and selling equity issues abroad. (Selling of debt issues abroad is delayed until the next chapter.) It concludes with an analysis of alternative instruments to source equity abroad.

## Designing a Strategy to Source Equity Globally

Designing a capital sourcing strategy requires management to agree upon a long-run financial objective and then choose among the various alternative paths to get there. Exhibit 12.1 is a visual presentation of alternative paths to the ultimate objective of attaining a global cost and availability of capital.

Normally the choice of paths and implementation is aided by an early appointment of an investment bank as official advisor to the firm. Investment bankers are in touch with potential foreign investors and what they are currently requiring. They can also help navigate the various institutional requirements and barriers that must be satisfied. Their services include advising if, when, and where a cross-listing should be initiated. They usually prepare the required stock prospectus if an equity issue is desired, help to price the issue, and maintain an aftermarket to prevent the share price from falling below its initial price.

### ALTERNATIVE PATHS

Most firms raise their initial capital in their own domestic market (see Exhibit 12.1). They may be tempted to skip the intermediate steps and drop to the bottom line, a Euroequity issue in global markets. This is when a good investment bank advisor will offer a reality check. Most firms that have only raised capital in their domestic market are not well enough known to attract foreign investors. Remember from Chapter 11 that Novo was advised by its investment bankers to start with a convertible Eurobond

**EXHIBIT 12.1**

Alternative Paths to Globalize the Cost and Availability of Capital

Source: Oxelheim, Stonehill, Randøy, Vikkula, Dullum, and Modén, *Corporate Strategies in Internationalising the Cost of Capital*, Copenhagen Business School Press, 1998, p. 119.

Copyright Copenhagen Business School Press, 1998. ISBN: 87-630-0067-9, www.cbspress.dk

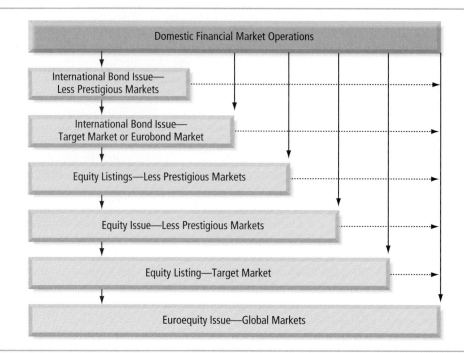

issue and simultaneously cross-list their shares (and the bonds) in London. This was despite the fact that Novo had an outstanding track record with respect to growth, profitability, and dominance of two worldwide market niches (insulin and industrial enzymes).

Exhibit 12.1 shows that most firms should start sourcing abroad with an international bond issue. The bond issue could be placed on a less prestigious foreign market, followed by an international bond issue in a target market or in the Eurobond market. The next step might be to cross-list and issue equity in one of the less prestigious markets so as to attract international investor attention. The next step could be to cross-list shares on a highly liquid prestigious foreign stock exchange such as London (LSE), NYSE, or NASDAQ. The ultimate step would be to place a directed equity issue in a prestigious target market or a Euroequity issue in global equity markets.

## DEPOSITARY RECEIPTS

*Depositary receipts* (depositary shares) are negotiable certificates issued by a bank to represent the underlying shares of stock, which are held in trust at a foreign custodial bank. Global depositary receipts (GDRs) refer to certificates traded outside the United States. American depositary receipts (ADRs) refer to certificates traded in the United States and denominated in U.S. dollars. ADRs are sold, registered, and transferred in the United States in the same manner as any share of stock, with each ADR representing some multiple of the underlying foreign share. This multiple allows the ADRs to possess a price per share appropriate for the U.S. market (typically between $20 and $50 per share) even if the price of the foreign share is inappropriate when converted to U.S. dollars directly. Exhibit 12.2 illustrates the underlying issuance structure of an ADR.

**EXHIBIT 12.2**

Mechanics of
American
Depositary
Receipts (ADRs)

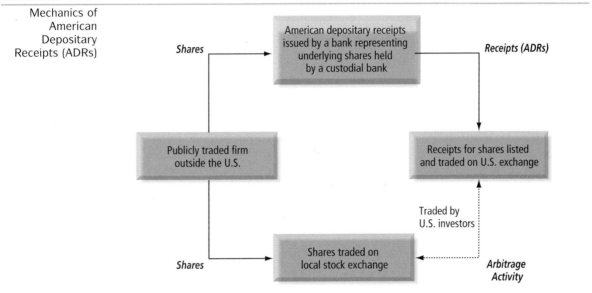

ADRs can be exchanged for the underlying foreign shares, or vice versa, so arbitrage keeps foreign and U.S. prices of any given share the same after adjusting for transfer costs. For example, investor demand in one market will cause a price rise there, which will cause an arbitrage rise in the other market even when investors there are not as bullish on the stock.

ADRs convey certain technical advantages to U.S. shareholders. Dividends paid by a foreign firm are passed to its custodial bank and then to the bank that issued the ADR. The issuing bank exchanges the foreign currency dividends for U.S. dollars and sends the dollar dividend to the ADR holders. ADRs are in registered form, rather than in bearer form. Transfer of ownership is facilitated because it is done in the United States in accordance with U.S. laws and procedures. In the event of death of a shareholder, the estate need not to go through probate in a foreign court system. Normally, trading costs are lower than when buying or selling the underlying shares in their home market. Settlement is usually faster in the United States. Withholding taxes are simpler because they're handled by the depositary bank.

ADRs are either *sponsored* or *unsponsored*. Sponsored ADRs are created at the request of a foreign firm wanting its shares traded in the United States. The firm applies to the Securities and Exchange Commission (SEC) and a U.S. bank for registration and issuance of ADRs. The foreign firm pays all costs of creating such sponsored ADRs. If a foreign firm does not seek to have its shares traded in the United States but U.S. investors are interested, a U.S. securities firm may initiate creation of the ADRs. Such an ADR would be unsponsored, but the SEC still requires that all new ADR programs must have approval by the firm itself even if it is not a sponsored ADR.

Exhibit 12.3 summarizes the characteristics of ADRs in the United States. It shows three levels of commitment, distinguished by the necessary accounting standards, SEC registration requirement, time to completion, and costs. Level I ("over the counter" or pink sheets) is the easiest to satisfy. It facilitates trading in foreign securities that have been acquired by U.S. investors but the securities are not registered with the SEC. It is the least costly approach but might have a minimal impact on liquidity.

**EXHIBIT 12.3**

Characteristics of
Depositary
Receipt Programs
Traded in the
United States

| | Level I | Level II | Level III | 144a |
|---|---|---|---|---|
| Primary exchange | OTC pink sheets | NYSE, AMEX, or NASDAQ | NYSE, AMEX, or NASDAQ | PORTAL |
| Accounting standards | Home country standards | U.S. GAAP | U.S. GAAP | Home country standards |
| SEC registration | Exempt | Full registration | Full registration | Exempt |
| Share issuance | Existing shares only (public offering) | Existing shares only (public offering) | New equity capital raised (public offering) | New equity capital raised (private offering) |
| Time to completion | 10 weeks | 10 weeks | 14 weeks | 16 days |
| Costs | $25,000 | $200,000–$700,000 | $500,000–$2,000,000 | $250,000–$500,000 |

Foreign securities traded in the U.S. are required to perform periodic reporting under the 1934 Exchange Act, provided that the company's equity securities are held of record by 500 or more persons, of which 300 or more are U.S. residents. This requires quarterly reporting, filing the form 20-F in U.S. generally accepted accounting principles. Level I and 144a DRs are eligible for a 12g3-2(b) exemption from this requirement, and only have to supply to the SEC copies of information that the company makes public in its home country. Privately placed depositary receipts are also eligible for the 12g3-2(b) exemption. They trade between qualified institutional buyers under SEC Rule 144a, which provides a safe harbor exemption from the registration requirements of the Securities Act of 1933. Source: *Global Offerings of Depositary Receipts, A Transaction Guide*, The Bank of New York: 1995. Reprinted in Darius P. Miller, "The Market Reaction to International Cross-Listings: Evidence from Depositary Receipts," *Journal of Financial Economics*, vol. 51, 1999, p.103–123.

Level II applies to firms that want to list existing shares on the NYSE, ASE, or NASDAQ markets. They must meet the full registration requirements of the SEC. This means reconciling their financial accounts with those used under U.S. GAAP. This raises the cost considerably. Level III applies to the sale of a new equity issued in the United States. It too requires full registration with the SEC and an elaborate stock prospectus. This is the most expensive alternative but is the most likely to improve the stock's liquidity and escape from home market segmentation. So-called 144a programs are described later in this chapter.

## Foreign Equity Listing and Issuance

According to the alternative paths depicted in Exhibit 12.1, a firm needs to choose one or more stock market on which to cross-list its shares and sell new equity. Just where to go depends mainly on the firm's specific motives and the willingness of the host stock market to accept the firm. By cross-listing and selling its shares on a foreign stock exchange a firm typically tries to accomplish one or more of the following objectives:

- Improve the liquidity of its existing shares and support a liquid secondary market for new equity issues in foreign markets.
- Increase its share price by overcoming mispricing in a segmented and illiquid home capital market.
- Increase the firm's visibility and political acceptance to its customers, suppliers, creditors, and host governments.
- Establish a secondary market for shares used to acquire other firms in the host market.

• Create a secondary market for shares that can be used to compensate local management and employees in foreign subsidiaries.

## IMPROVING LIQUIDITY

Quite often foreign investors have acquired a firm's shares through normal brokerage channels, even though the shares are not listed in the investor's home market or not traded in the investor's preferred currency. Cross-listing is a way to encourage such investors to continue to hold and trade these shares, thus marginally improving secondary market liquidity. This is usually done through ADRs.

Firms domiciled in countries with small illiquid capital markets often outgrow those markets and are forced to raise new equity abroad. Listing on a stock exchange in the market in which these funds are to be raised is typically required by the underwriters to insure post-issue liquidity in the shares.

The introductory section of this chapter suggested that firms start by cross-listing in a less prestigious market followed by an equity issue in that market (see Exhibit 12.1). In order to maximize liquidity, however, the ideal is to cross-list and issue equity in a prestigious market and eventually to be able to offer a global equity issue.

## GLOBAL REGISTERED SHARE (GRS)

Similar to ordinary shares, GRSs have the added benefit of being able to be traded on equity exchanges around the globe in a variety of currencies. ADRs, however, are quoted only in U.S. dollars and are traded only in the United States. GRSs can, theoretically, be traded with the sun, following markets as they open and close around the globe around the clock. The shares are traded electronically, therefore eliminating the specialized forms and depositaries required by share forms like ADRs.

GRSs are not really a recent innovation. They are in fact nearly identical to the structure used for cross-border trading of Canadian company securities in the U.S. for decades. Over 70 Canadian firms are listed on the NYSE, and all of these shares trade as ordinary shares in both their home market in Canada and the U.S. market.

According to the NYSE, dealing fees levied on ADRs cost investors between 3 and 5 cents per share per trade. By comparison, GRSs carry a flat cost of $5 per trade, regardless of the quantity of shares traded. For foreign corporations expecting or hoping to become widely traded securities for large institutional investors, the flat rate per trade for GRSs may increase their cost efficiency. A two-way electronic linkage between the Depositary Trust Company in the United States and the Deutsche Börse Clearing Company in Germany facilitates the efficient quoting, trading, and settlement of shares in the respective currencies as shown in Exhibit 12.4.

In October 2001 Deutsche Bank (DB) of Germany chose to list on the New York Stock Exchange via GRSs. Many critics argued that by listing through GRSs Deutsche Bank would experience lower trading in their shares. This lower-trading expectation was based on DaimlerChrysler's GRS experiences in 1998, as described in the mini-case at the end of this chapter.

## SIZE AND LIQUIDITY OF THE MARKET

Exhibit 12.5 describes selected stock exchange size and market liquidity statistics for end of year 2002. In order to maximize liquidity, it is desirable to cross-list and/or sell equity in the most liquid market. The column in Exhibit 12.5 entitled "Value of Share

**EXHIBIT 12-4**

Global Registered
Shares

German Equity System → **German investors** can trade in equities listed on any of the three exchanges, but quoted in local currency (€)

Electronic Linkages

Swiss Equity System → **Swiss investors** can trade in equities listed on any of the three exchanges, but quoted in local currency (SFR)

Electronic Linkages

New York Stock Exchange → **U.S. and Canadian investors** can trade in equities listed on any of the three exchanges, but quoted in local currency, the US$ in the U.S. and the C$ in Canada

**EXHIBIT 12.5**

Selected Stock Exchange Size Characteristics and Market Liquidity, End 2002

| Exchanges | Type* | Number of companies | | Value of Share Trading (millions of US$) |
|---|---|---|---|---|
| | | Domestic | Foreign | |
| NYSE | TSV | 1894 | 472 | 10,311,156 |
| NASDAQ | REV | 3268 | 381 | 7,254,594 |
| LSE | REV | 1892 | 382 | 4,001,340 |
| Euronext | REV | 1114 | na | 1,988,359 |
| Tokyo | TSV | 2119 | 34 | 1,564,244 |
| Deutsche Börse (Ger) | TSV | 715 | 219 | 1,212,302 |
| Spain | TSV | 986 | 29 | 653,229 |
| Italy | REV | 288 | 7 | 634,635 |
| Swiss Exchange | REV | 258 | 140 | 599,749 |
| Taiwan | TSV | 638 | 3 | 633,632 |
| Korea | TSV | 679 | 0 | 596,632 |

na = Not available

Source: World Federation of Exchanges: Statistics, http://www.world-exchanges.org/.

*Type indicates the method by which exchanges define and compile turnover. Trading System View (TSV) counts as turnover only those transactions which pass through their trading systems or which take place on the exchange's trading floor. Regulated Environment Review (REV) exchanges include in their turnover figures all transactions, with no distinction between on- and off-market, or transactions made into foreign markets reported on the national market.

Trading" is one indicator of the overall ability of the market to provide liquidity and availability of capital.

- The NYSE, NASDAQ, and LSE are clearly the most liquid markets.

- The NYSE, NASDAQ, and LSE have the largest number of foreign listings— 472, 381, and 382, respectively.

The number of listed foreign firms on the NYSE is largest among the global exchanges (472), and the individual trading volume of these firms is typically quite large relative to their home markets. For example, Telefonos de Mexico was the most actively traded stock on the NYSE in the mid-1990s. However, the trading volume of the foreign companies listed on the LSE was higher than for foreign companies listed on the NYSE (not shown in exhibit).

Deutsche Börse (Germany) and Euronext (the merged markets of Amsterdam, Brussels, and Paris) have fairly liquid markets for domestic shares but a much lower level of liquidity for trading foreign shares. On the other hand, Deutsche Börse and Euronext are quite appropriate target markets for firms resident in the EU, especially those that have adopted the euro. They are also used as supplementary cross-listing locations for firms that are already cross-listed on LSE, NYSE, or NASDAQ.

Tokyo has fallen on hard times. It is now only fifth in trading volume. It is a nearly total flop as a location for foreign firms to gain liquidity and had only 34 foreign firms cross-listed in 2002, compared with 67 in 1996.

## THE NEW YORK STOCK EXCHANGE (NYSE) COMPARED WITH THE LONDON STOCK EXCHANGE (LSE)

If we compare the NYSE with the LSE, we note that liquidity in the most actively traded shares is similar, but the NYSE is a more liquid market for the least popular shares. Transaction costs as measured by spreads are lower on the NYSE. The LSE spreads are roughly comparable to the spreads on NASDAQ. On the other hand, the cost of listing and disclosure requirements are less onerous on the LSE than on the NYSE. In terms of fairness, the NYSE is superior because orders are executed chronologically, whereas on the LSE one has to shop from dealer to dealer. Crisis management by specialists has been more effective in practice on the NYSE than on any other exchange, including LSE. Despite the more favorable liquidity attributes of the NYSE, nearly as many foreign firms list on the LSE as on the NYSE. We must conclude that the ease and cost of listing, the lower required disclosure levels, and the less frequent reporting requirements have tilted the scale toward the LSE for firms that might have trouble overcoming these barriers. However, for those firms that are willing to pay the price, a listing on the NYSE should improve the liquidity of their shares more than could be achieved with a similar listing elsewhere.

Although overall market liquidity is shown in Exhibit 12.5, additional characteristics contribute to the liquidity of individual stocks. These include market-making activities, transaction costs, fairness, and crisis management. At one end of the spectrum is the NYSE, where assigned specialists are responsible for ensuring a liquid, low-cost, fair, and orderly market. At the other end of the spectrum is the LSE, where *market makers*, formerly called *jobbers*, voluntarily make an active market in some but not all listed shares. Which system is better is in dispute. At the moment, corporate goverance issues on the NYSE are being attacked and reforms are being made.

## Effect of Cross-Listing and Equity Issuance on Share Price

### CROSS-LISTING

Does merely cross-listing on a foreign stock exchange have a favorable impact on share prices? It depends on the degree to which markets are segmented.

If a firm's home capital market is segmented, the firm could theoretically benefit by cross-listing in a foreign market if that market values the firm or its industry more than does the home market. This was certainly the situation experienced by Novo when it listed on the NYSE in 1981 (see Chapter 11). However, most capital markets are becoming more integrated with global markets. Even emerging markets are less segmented than they were just a few years ago.

As early as the period from 1969 to 1982, when markets were more segmented than today, a research study found a positive share price effect for foreign firms that listed on the NYSE, AMEX, or NASDAQ.[1] A later study found that share prices increased for foreign firms that cross-listed their shares in ADR form on the NYSE and AMEX during the period from 1982 to 1992.[2] The authors concluded that cross-listing in the United States enhanced share value by reducing the overall effect of segmentation among different national securities markets.

A more recent and most comprehensive study consisted of 181 firms from 35 countries that instituted their first ADR program in the United States during the period from 1985 to 1995.[3] The author measured the stock price impact of the announcement of a cross-listing in the United States and found significant positive abnormal returns around the announcement date. These were retained in the period immediately following. As expected, the study showed that the abnormal returns were greater for firms resident in emerging markets with a low level of legal barriers to capital flows, than for firms resident in developed markets. Firms resident in emerging markets with heavy restrictions on capital flows received some abnormal returns, but not as high as firms resident in the other markets. This was due to the perceived limited liquidity of firms resident in markets with too many restrictions on capital flows.

Finally, a still more recent study concluded as follows:

> At the end of 1997, foreign companies with shares cross-listed in the U.S. had Tobin's q ratios that were 16.5% higher than the q ratios of non-cross-listed firms from the same country. The valuation difference is statistically significant and reaches 37% for those companies that list on major U.S. exchanges, even after controlling for a number of firm and country characteristics. We suggest that a U.S. listing reduces the extent to which controlling shareholders can engage in expropriation and thereby increases the firm's ability to take advantage of growth opportunities. We show that growth opportunities are more highly valued for firms that choose to cross-list in the U.S., particularly those from countries with poorer investor rights.[4]

Tobin's q in this study is defined as follows: "For the numerator we take the book value of total assets, subtract the book value of equity, and add the market value of equity. For the denominator we use the book value of total assets."[5]

## EQUITY ISSUANCE

It is well known that the combined impact of a new equity issue undertaken simultaneously with a cross-listing has a more favorable impact on stock price than cross-listing alone. This occurs because the new issue creates an instantly enlarged shareholder

[1]Gordon J. Alexander, Cheol S. Eun, and S. Janakiramanan, "International Listings and Stock Returns: Some Empirical Evidence," *Journal of Financial and Quantitative Analysis*, vol. 23, no. 2, June 1988, pp. 135–151.

[2]Anant K. Sundaram and Dennis E. Logue, "Valuation Effects of Foreign Company Listings on U.S. Exchanges," *Journal of International Business Studies*, vol. 27, no. 1, first quarter 1996, pp. 67–88.

[3]Darius P. Miller, "The Market Reaction to International Cross-Listings: Evidence from Depositary Receipts," *Journal of Financial Economics*, vol. 51, 1999, pp. 102–123.

[4]Craig Doidge, G. Andrew Karolyi, and René M. Stulz, "Why Are Foreign Firms Listed in the U.S. Worth More?" *Journal of Financial Economics*, vol. 71, 2004, p. 205.

[5]Ibid., p. 216.

base. Marketing efforts by the underwriters prior to the issue engender higher levels of visibility. Post-issue efforts by the underwriters to support at least the initial offering price also reduce investor risk.

The study of 181 firms cross-listing in the United States contained 30 firms that initiated new equity issues (Level III ADRs). The author found a statistically significant abnormal return for these firms, even higher than for the firms that just cross-listed (Levels I and II). Furthermore, the highest abnormal return was for Chilean firms (8.23%). The Chilean market has one of the highest levels of restrictions affecting foreign investors. Since it is well known that stock prices react negatively to new domestic issues in the United States, something truly significant must be happening when foreign ADRs are sold in the United States.

Even U.S. firms can benefit by issuing equity abroad. A recent study of U.S. firms that issued equity abroad concluded that increased name recognition and accessibility from global equity issues leads to increased investor recognition and participation in both the primary and secondary markets.[6] Moreover, the ability to issue global shares can validate firm quality by reducing the information asymmetry between insiders and investors. Another conclusion was that U.S. firms may seize a window of opportunity to switch to global offerings when domestic demand for their shares is weak. Finally, the study found that U.S. firms announcing global equity offerings have significantly less negative market reactions by about one percentage point than what would have been expected had they limited their issues to the domestic market.

## INCREASING VISIBILITY AND POLITICAL ACCEPTANCE

MNEs list in markets where they have substantial physical operations. Commercial objectives are to enhance corporate image, advertise trademarks and products, get better local press coverage, and become more familiar with the local financial community in order to raise working capital locally.

Political objectives might include the need to meet local ownership requirements for a multinational firm's foreign joint venture. Local ownership of the parent firm's shares might provide a forum for publicizing the firm's activities and how they support the host country. This objective is the most important one for Japanese firms. The Japanese domestic market has both low-cost capital and high availability. Therefore Japanese firms are not trying to increase the stock price, the liquidity of their shares, or the availability of capital.

## INCREASING POTENTIAL FOR SHARE SWAPS WITH ACQUISITIONS

Firms that follow a strategy of growth by acquisition are always looking for creative ways to fund these acquisitions rather than paying cash. Offering their shares as partial payment is considerably more attractive if those shares have a liquid secondary market. In that case the target's shareholders have an easy way to convert their acquired shares to cash if they do not prefer a share swap. However, a share swap is often attractive as a tax-free exchange.

[6]Congsheng Wu and Chuck C. Y. Kwok, "Why Do U.S. Firms Choose Global Equity Offerings?" *Financial Management*, Summer 2002, pp. 47–65.

## COMPENSATING MANAGEMENT AND EMPLOYEES

If an MNE wishes to use stock options and share purchase compensation plans for local management and employees, local listing would enhance the perceived value of such plans. It should reduce transaction and foreign exchange costs for the local beneficiaries.

# Barriers to Cross-Listing and Selling Equity Abroad

Although a firm may decide to cross-list and/or sell equity abroad, certain barriers exist. The most serious barriers are the future commitment to providing full and transparent disclosure of operating results and balance sheets as well as a continuous program of investor relations.

## THE COMMITMENT TO DISCLOSURE AND INVESTOR RELATIONS

A decision to cross-list must be balanced against the implied increased commitment to full disclosure and a continuing investor relations program. For firms resident in the Anglo-American markets, listing abroad might not appear to be much of a barrier. For example, the SEC's disclosure rules for listing in the United States are so stringent and costly that any other market's rules are mere child's play. Reversing the logic, however, non–U.S. firms must really think twice before cross-listing in the United States. Not only are the disclosure requirements breathtaking, but continuous timely quarterly information is required by U.S. regulators and investors. As a result, the foreign firm must provide a costly continuous investor relations program for its U.S. shareholders, including frequent "road shows" and the time-consuming personal involvement of top management.

## DISCLOSURE IS A DOUBLE-EDGED SWORD

The U.S. school of thought is that the worldwide trend toward requiring fuller, more transparent, and more standardized financial disclosure of operating results and balance sheet positions may have the desirable effect of lowering the cost of equity capital. As we observed in 2002, lack of full and accurate disclosure, and poor transparency worsened the U.S. stock market decline as investors fled to safer securities such as U.S. government bonds. This action increased the equity cost of capital for all firms. The other school of thought is that the U.S. level of required disclosure is an onerous, costly burden. It chases away many potential listers, thereby narrowing the choice of securities available to U.S. investors at reasonable transaction costs.

A study of 203 internationally traded shares concluded that there is a statistically significant relationship between the level of financial disclosure required and the markets on which the firms chose to list.[7] The higher the level of disclosure required, the less likely that a firm would list in that market. However, for those firms that do list despite the disclosure and cost barriers, the payoff could be needed access to additional equity funding of a large factory or an acquisition in the United States. Daimler Benz took the painful step of cross-listing on the NYSE prior to raising equity in the United States to fund a new auto plant and, as it turned out later, to merge with Chrysler Corporation.

---

[7]Shahrokh M. Saudagaran and Gary C. Biddle, "Foreign Listing Location: A Study of MNEs and Stock Exchanges in Eight Countries," *Journal of International Business Studies*, vol. 26, no. 2, second quarter 1995, pp. 319–341.

## Alternative Instruments to Source Equity in Global Markets

Alternative instruments to source equity in global markets include the following:

- Sale of a *directed public share issue* to investors in a target market
- Sale of a *Euroequity public issue* to investors in more than one market, including both foreign and domestic markets
- Private placements under SEC Rule 144A
- Sale of shares to *private equity funds*
- Sale of shares to a foreign firm as part of a *strategic alliance*

### DIRECTED PUBLIC SHARE ISSUES

A *directed public share issue* is defined as one that is targeted at investors in a single country and underwritten in whole or in part by investment institutions from that country. The issue might or might not be denominated in the currency of the target market. The shares might or might not be cross-listed on a stock exchange in the target market.

The $61 million U.S. share issue by Novo in 1981 (Chapter 11) was a good example of a successful directed share issue that both improved the liquidity of Novo's shares and lowered its cost of capital. Novo repeated this success in 1983 with a $100 million share issue at $53 per share (ADR), compared with $36 per share two years earlier.

A directed share issue might be motivated by a need to fund acquisitions or major capital investments in a target foreign market. This is an especially important source of equity for firms that reside in smaller capital markets and that have outgrown that market. A foreign share issue, plus cross-listing, can provide it with improved liquidity for its shares and the means to use those shares to pay for acquisitions.

Nycomed, a small but well-respected Norwegian pharmaceutical firm, is an example of this type of motivation for a directed share issue combined with cross-listing. Its commercial strategy for growth was to leverage its sophisticated knowledge of certain market niches and technologies within the pharmaceutical field by acquiring other promising firms that possess relevant technologies, personnel, or market niches. Europe and the United States have provided fertile hunting grounds. The acquisitions were paid for partly with cash and partly with shares. Norway is too small a home capital market to fund these acquisitions for cash or to provide a liquid enough market to minimize Nycomed's marginal cost of capital.

Nycomed responded to the challenge by selling two successful directed share issues abroad. In June 1989 it cross-listed on the LSE (quoted on SEAQ International) and raised the equivalent of about $100 million in equity from foreign investors there. Then in June 1992 it cross-listed on the NYSE and raised about $75 million with a share issue directed at U.S. investors. Nycomed eventually merged with Amersham, a British firm, and moved its headquarters to the United Kingdom.

### EUROEQUITY PUBLIC ISSUE

The gradual integration of the world's capital markets and increased international portfolio investment has spawned the emergence of a very viable Euroequity market. A firm can now issue equity underwritten and distributed in multiple foreign equity markets, sometimes simultaneously with distribution in the domestic market. The same financial institutions that had previously created an infrastructure for the Euronote and Eurobond markets (described in detail in Chapter 13) were responsible for the Euroequity market. The term "euro" does not imply that the issuers or investors are located in Europe, nor does it mean the shares are sold in euros. It is a generic term for international securities issues originating and being sold anywhere in the world.

The largest and most spectacular issues have been made in conjunction with a wave of privatizations of government-owned enterprises. The Thatcher government in the United Kingdom created the model when it privatized British Telecom in December 1984. That issue was so large that it was necessary and desirable to sell *tranches* to foreign investors in addition to the sale to domestic investors. A tranche is an allocation of shares, typically to underwriters that are expected to sell to investors in their designated geographic markets. The objective is both to raise the funds and to ensure post-issue worldwide liquidity. Unfortunately, in the case of British Telecom the issue was, in retrospect, underpriced. Most of the foreign shares, especially those placed in the United States, flowed back to London, leaving a nice profit behind for the U.S. underwriters and investors. Nevertheless, other large British privatization issues followed British Telecom, most notably British Steel in 1988.

Euroequity privatization issues have been particularly popular with international portfolio investors because most of the firms are very large, with excellent credit ratings and profitable quasi-government monopolies at the time of privatization. The British privatization model has been so successful that numerous others have followed. One of the largest Euroequity issues was made by Deutsche Telecom AG. It was privatized by an initial public offering of $13.3 billion in November 1996.

Even government-owned firms in emerging capital markets have implemented privatization with the help of foreign tranches.

- Telefonos de Mexico, the giant Mexican telephone company, completed a $2 billion Euroequity issue in 1991. U.S.-based Southwestern Bell became a 10% shareholder, as did numerous other foreign institutional and individual investors. Telefonos de Mexico has a very liquid listing on the NYSE.

- One of the largest Euroequity offerings by a firm resident in an illiquid market was the 1993 sale of shares for $3.04 billion by YPF Sociedad Anónima, Argentina's state-owned oil company. About 75% of its shares were placed in tranches outside of Argentina, with 46% in the United States alone. Its underwriting syndicate represented a virtual who's who of the world's leading investment banks.

It appears that many of the privatized firms have performed well after being privatized. A recent study of privatization concluded that privatized firms showed strong performance improvements without reducing employment security. The firms in the study had been fully or partially privatized via public equity issues during the period from 1961 to 1990. After privatization, the firms increased real sales, raised capital investment levels, improved efficiency, and expanded their employment. With respect to financial performance, their profitability improved, debt levels were lowered, and dividend payments increased.[8]

## PRIVATE PLACEMENT UNDER SEC RULE 144A

One type of directed issue with a long history as a source of both equity and debt is the private placement market. A *private placement* is the sale of a security to a small set of qualified institutional buyers. The investors are traditionally insurance companies and

---

[8]William L. Megginson, Robert C. Nash, and Mathias Van Randenborgh, "The Financial and Operating Performance of Newly Privatized Firms: An International Empirical Analysis," *Journal of Finance*, June 1994, pp. 403–452.

investment companies. Since the securities are not registered for sale to the public, investors have typically followed a "buy and hold" policy. In the case of debt, terms are often custom designed on a negotiated basis. Private placement markets now exist in most countries.

As noted in Exhibit 12.3, in April 1990 the SEC approved Rule 144A. It permits qualified institutional buyers (QIBs) to trade privately placed securities without the previous holding period restrictions and without requiring SEC registration.

A *qualified institutional buyer* is an entity (except a bank or a savings and loan) that owns and invests on a discretionary basis $100 million in securities of non-affiliates. Banks and savings and loans must meet this test but also must have a minimum net worth of $25 million. The SEC has estimated that about 4,000 QIBs exist, mainly investment advisors, investment companies, insurance companies, pension funds, and charitable institutions.

Simultaneously, the SEC modified its Regulation S to permit foreign issuers to tap the U.S. private placement market through an SEC Rule 144A issue, also without SEC registration. A screen-based automated trading system called PORTAL was established by the National Association of Securities Dealers (NASD) to support the distribution of primary issues and to create a liquid secondary market for these unregistered private placements.

Since SEC registration has been identified as the main barrier to foreign firms wishing to raise funds in the United States, SEC Rule 144A placements are proving attractive to foreign issuers of both equity and debt securities. Atlas Copco, the Swedish multinational engineering firm, was the first foreign firm to take advantage of SEC Rule 144A. It raised $49 million in the United States through an ADR equity placement as part of its larger $214 million Euroequity issue in 1990. Since then several billion dollars a year have been raised by foreign issuers with private equity placements in the United States. However, it does not appear that such placements have a favorable effect on either liquidity or stock price.[9]

## PRIVATE EQUITY FUNDS

Many mature family-owned firms resident in emerging markets are unlikely to qualify for a global cost and availability of capital even if they follow the strategy suggested in this chapter. Although they might be consistently profitable and growing, they are still too small, too invisible to foreign investors, lacking in managerial depth, and unable to fund the up-front costs of a globalization strategy. For these firms, private equity funds may be a solution.

*Private equity funds* are usually limited partnerships of institutional and wealthy individual investors that raise their capital in the most liquid capital markets, especially the United States. They then invest the private equity fund in mature, family-owned firms located in emerging markets. The investment objective is to help these firms to restructure and modernize in order to face increasing competition and the growth of new technologies. Sometimes they fund family-owned firms that need to be connected with foreign MNEs, joint venture partners, or strategic alliances. They also can fund privatized government-owned firms.

Private equity funds differ from traditional venture capital funds. The latter usually operate mainly in highly developed countries. They typically invest in high-tech start-ups with the goal of exiting the investment with an initial public offering (IPO) placed in those same highly liquid markets. Very little venture capital is available in

[9]Narjess Boubakri and Jean Claude Cosset, "The Financial and Operating Performance of Newly Privatized Firms: Evidence from Developing Countries," *The Journal of Finance*, vol. 53, no. 3, June 1998, pp. 1081–1110. This same conclusion was reached in the slightly more recent study by Miller 1999, op. cit.

emerging markets, partly because it would be difficult to exit with an IPO in an illiquid market. The same exiting problem faces the private equity funds, but they appear to have a longer time horizon. They invest in already mature and profitable companies. They are content with growing companies through better management and mergers with other firms.

The Exxel Group is an example of a successful private equity fund. Its founder and CEO, Juan Navarro, has been called the "buyout king of Argentina." From 1991 to 2002 the firm invested $4.8 billion in 74 companies in Argentina. In line with its mission, the company has continued to pursue full operational control over all acquisitions in order to implement its superior managerial, industrial, and market knowledge to create shareholder value. As illustrated in the *Real World Example 12.1*, however, even an innovative firm such as the Exxel Group cannot avoid an economic crisis like that suffered by Argentina from 2001 to 2002.

## STRATEGIC ALLIANCES

Strategic alliances are normally formed by firms that expect to gain synergies from one or more of the following joint efforts. They might share the cost of developing technology, or pursue complementary marketing activities. They might gain economies of scale or scope or a variety of other commercial advantages. However, one synergy that may sometimes be overlooked is the possibility that a financially strong firm can help a financially weak firm lower its cost of capital by providing attractively priced equity or debt financing. This was illustrated in *Real World Example 11.2* on the strategic alliance between Bang & Olufsen and Philips.

---

### Real World Example 12.1
#### PRIVATE EQUITY IN ARGENTINA AND THE ARGENTINE CRISIS

It used to be relatively easy for private equity investors to cash out of their Latin American holdings through the public equity markets. But last year [2001], not a single Latin American-based company conducted an initial public offering and only a handful of companies undertook secondary listings. Exxel Group managed to secure a multinational buyer for its stake in the Argentine Supermercados Norte supermarket chain. And in April, when Exxel was struggling to meet interest payments on some $688 million in debt, executed an impressive exit when it sold its remaining 49% stake in Norte to the French supermarket company Carrefour for $263 million. Selling an Argentine company last year in itself was a notable feat and Exxel's divestment wins *LatinFinance*'s private equity deal of the year for its innovative structure.

Source: Adapted from "Cash Out to Carrefour," *Latin Finance*, February 2002.

---

## MINI-CASE

# Deutsche Bank's Global Registered Shares

*With the globalization of financial markets, the increased operations of multinational companies in multiple markets around the world, and the explosion in cross-border merger-and-acquisition activity, there is a growing need for a single class of security to be traded among investors worldwide. In response to the changing environment, several non-U.S. companies have, or are considering, issuing*

*NYSE Global Shares as an alternative to American Depositary Receipts (ADRs).*

"NYSE Global Shares Growing a New Class of Security," www.NYSE.com.

Since 1927 foreign companies have listed their shares on the New York Stock Exchange by issuing American depositary receipts, or ADRs. Foreign companies have found the ADR a very corporate-friendly system by which foreign corporations could reach investors in the New York equity capital markets. But in October 2001 Deutsche Bank (DB) of Germany chose to list on the New York Stock Exchange via global registered shares (GRSs). Many critics argued that by listing through GRSs Deutsche Bank would experience lower trading in their shares. The question floating among many international analysts was why the bank had chosen GRSs over ADRs.

Deutsche Bank may have learned the ropes of GRSs through services it provides to another GRS issuer, Celanese AG. Celanese AG (Germany) had listed GRSs in New York in October 1999, allowing its stockholders to trade shares simultaneously in Frankfurt and New York. Celanese uses a single global share registry to provide a database that is updated daily on all ownership and account balances. The registry is maintained by Registrar Services, a subsidiary of Deutsche Bank in Frankfurt, Germany. That registry combines a registry of North American activities maintained by Mellon Investor Services and the Germany-based registry maintained by Deutsche Bank.

Celanese global shares are traded on the Frankfurt stock exchange, and quoted and settled in euros. Celanese's GRSs listed in New York are quoted and settled in U.S. dollars, like ADRs, allowing investors a local-currency form of a foreign-incorporated equity.

## The DaimlerChrysler Experience

In November 1998 DaimlerChrysler AG (Germany) surprised the global equity markets by being the first company to list on the NYSE using GRSs rather than ADRs. (Prior to Daimler's merger with Chrysler it had enjoyed a relatively liquid level of trading on the New York Stock Exchange using ADRs.) The acclaim surrounding the GRS listing was short-lived, however, as evidence grew the following year that trading activity in the combined DaimlerChrysler shares (New York Stock Exchange symbol DCX) was much weaker than hoped. A study conducted by Andrew Karolyi of Ohio State University published in early 2000 indicated that only 5% of the transactions in Daimler's shares were traded via the GRS listing on the NYSE.[10]

[10]G. Andrew Karolyi, *DaimlerChrysler AG, The First Truly Global Share,* Fisher College of Business, Ohio State University, working paper, May 2002.

Although it is difficult to explain all of the forces at work in DaimlerChrysler's share trading, the GRSs listing rather than ADRs is considered a major one. Another major factor is that the newly combined company was actually dropped from Standard & Poor's 500 Index when the index was rebalanced.

## EXHIBIT 1

### The DaimlerChrysler GRS Experience

*Average daily trading prior to Daimler-Chrysler merger:*

| | | |
|---|---|---|
| Daimler Benz | Frankfurt | $777 million |
| Chrysler Corporation | New York | $100 million |

*Average daily trading post-merger for DCX joint listing:*

| | | |
|---|---|---|
| DaimlerChrysler | Frankfurt | $1 billion |
| DaimlerChrysler GRSs | | |
| December 1998 | New York | $200 million |
| February 1999 | New York | $100 million |

Of the 10 European companies listing on the NYSE in 2001, only Deutsche Bank chose to use GRSs rather than ADRs. The seven others — including Siemens, BASF, and Novartis — claim to have seriously considered GRSs, but concluded that the initial costs of ADRs were substantially lower and their liquidity in the American marketplace greater. Although there are few explicit up-front costs associated specifically with GRS listings, traditional German firms have issued much of their equity in bearer form. Prior to being able to issue GRSs, the firms would need to go through the process of registration of shares for trading via the electronic linkages with New York. Deutsche Bank, evidently as part of its preparations, had issued registered shares in Frankfurt in 1999.

## Case Questions

1. Do you believe the differences between ADRs and GRSs are real or cosmetic? Why?
2. Why do you think Deutsche Bank would proceed with a GRS listing when so many others have not?
3. What do you think Deutsche Bank concluded from DaimlerChrysler's experience with GRSs?

## Summary of Learning Objectives

*Design a strategy to source equity globally*

- Designing a capital sourcing strategy requires management to agree on a long-run financial objective.

- The firm must then choose among the various alternative paths to get there, including where to cross-list its shares, where to issue new equity, and the form the equity should take.

*Analyze the motivations and goals of a firm cross-listing its shares on foreign equity markets*

A firm cross-lists its shares on foreign stock exchanges for one or more of the following reasons:

- To improve the liquidity of its existing shares by using depositary receipts
- To increase its share price by overcoming mispricing by a segmented, illiquid home capital market
- To support a new equity issue sold in a foreign market
- To establish a secondary market for shares used in acquisitions
- To increase the firm's visibility and political acceptability to its customers, suppliers, creditors, and host governments
- To create a secondary market for shares that will be used to compensate local management and employees in foreign subsidiaries

*Analyze the motivations and goals of a firm issuing new equity shares on foreign equity markets*

- If it is to support a new equity issue or to establish a market for share swaps, the target market should also be the listing market.
- If it is to increase the firm's commercial and political visibility or to compensate local management and employees, it should be the markets in which the firm has significant operations.
- The major liquid stock markets are the NYSE, NASDAQ, LSE, Euronext, Tokyo, and Deutsche Börse.
- The choice among these six markets depends on its size and the sophistication of its market-making activities, including competitive transaction costs and competent crisis management.

*Recognize the many barriers to effective penetration of foreign equity markets through cross-listing and selling equity abroad*

- The most serious barriers are the future commitment to providing full and transparent disclosure of operating results and balance sheets as well as a continuous program of investor relations
- Non–U.S. firms must think twice before cross-listing in the United States. Not only are the disclosure requirements onerous, but continuous timely quarterly information is required by U.S. regula-

tors and investors. As a result, the foreign firm must provide a costly, continuous investor relations program for its U.S. shareholders, including frequent "road shows" and the time-consuming personal involvement of top management.

*Identify the various financial instruments that can be used to source equity in the global equity markets*

A firm can lower its cost of capital and increase its liquidity by selling its shares to foreign investors in a variety of forms:

- Sale of a directed share issue to investors in one particular foreign equity market
- Sale of a Euroequity share issue to foreign investors simultaneously in more than one market, including foreign and domestic markets
- Private placement under SEC Rule 144A
- Sale of shares to private equity funds
- Sale of shares to a foreign firm as part of a strategic alliance

## QUESTIONS

1. **Designing a strategy to source equity globally.** Exhibit 12.1 illustrates alternative paths to globalizing the cost and availability of capital. Identify the specific steps in Exhibit 12.1 that were taken by Novo Industri (Chapter 11), in chronological order, to gain an international cost and availability of capital.

2. **Depositary receipts — definitions.** Define the following terms:
   a. ADRs
   b. GDRs
   c. Sponsored depositary receipts
   d. Unsponsored depositary receipts

3. **ADRs.** Distinguish between the three levels of commitment for ADRs traded in the United States.

4. **Foreign equity listing and issuance.** Give five reasons why a firm might cross-list and sell its shares on a very liquid stock exchange.

5. **Cross-listing abroad.** What are the main reasons a U.S. firm might cross-list abroad?

6. **Implementing a strategy to source equity globally.** Using the stock exchange characteristics shown in Exhibit 12.5, design a chronological strategy to

source equity globally for an MNE located in the following home markets:

   **a.** Mexico

   **b.** Portugal

   **c.** Hong Kong

   **d.** Chile

7. **Barriers to cross-listing.** What are the main barriers to cross-listing abroad?

8. **Alternative instruments.** What are five alternative instruments that can be used to source equity in global markets?

9. **Directed public share issue.**

   **a.** Define what is meant by a "directed public share issue."

   **b.** Why did Novo choose to make a $61 million directed public share issue in the United States in 1981?

10. **Euroequity public share issue.** Define what is meant by a "Euroequity public share issue."

11. **Private placement under SEC Rule 144A.**

   **a.** What is SEC Rule 144A?

   **b.** Why might a foreign firm choose to sell its equity in the United States under SEC Rule 144A?

12. **Private equity funds.**

   **a.** What is a private equity fund?

   **b.** How do private equity funds differ from traditional venture capital firms?

   **c.** How do private equity funds raise their own capital, and how does this action give them a competitive advantage over local banks and investment funds?

13. **Strategic alliances.**

   **a.** Why do firms form international strategic alliances?

   **b.** Why can an international strategic alliance lower a firm's cost of capital?

## PROBLEMS

In Chapter 11 we described how Novo Industri A/S (Novo) increased its stock price by sevenfold between April, 1980 and July, 1981. Its strategy was to be discovered by international portfolio investors and sell equity and list in both London and New York. The next six problems ask you to determine just how the dramatic increase in Novo's stock price theoretically should have lowered Novo's cost of capital after the new securities issues in London and New York.

Prior to April, 1980, Novo's stock price was determined by the norms of the Danish stock market, since nearly all shareholders were Danish, mostly institutional investors. Novo's stock price hovered around Dkr200 with a price-earnings ratio of 5, typical of the Danish stock market. After April, 1980, Novo's stock price was increasingly determined by the norms of international portfolio investors, especially from the United States and United Kingdom. By the time Novo sold its $61 million equity issue and listed on the New York Stock Exchange, its stock price had increased to Dkr1400 and its P/E ratio to 16, typical of the U.S. and U.K. stock markets.

Problems 1 through 6 relate to Novo. Problems 7 through 10 relate to HangSung, a hypothetical Korean chaebol that also experienced a domestic cost of capital that became an international cost of capital after issuing equity abroad.

1. **Novo's cost of equity prior to April, 1980.** Assuming that the following data apply, calculate Novo's cost of equity.

| | |
|---|---|
| Danish $k_{rf}$ = 10.0% | Denmark purposely maintained high real rates of interest to protect its exchange rate. |
| Novo's $\beta$ = 1.0 | The Danish market did not distinguish between growth stocks and other industrial stocks; their share prices all moved together. |
| Danish $k_m$ = 18.0% | The required return on stocks was quite high due to competition with high real interest rates and lack of international diversification by Danish investors caused by Danish legal restrictions. |

2. **Novo's WACC prior to April, 1980.** Assume that the following data apply:

| | |
|---|---|
| $k_d$ = 12.0% | Novo's cost of debt |
| $k_e$ = 18.0% | Novo's cost of equity |
| E/V = 30% | Novo's equity-to-capital ratio |
| D/V = 70% | Novo's debt-to-capital ratio |
| V = 100% | Total market value of Novo's securities, D + E |
| t = 40% | Novo's effective tax rate |

**a.** What was Novo's weighted average cost of capital?

**b.** How did this affect its capital budget?

3. **Novo's cost of equity after April, 1981.** Assuming the following data now apply, calculate Novo's cost of equity.

International $k_{rf}$ = 8.0%

International $\beta_{Novo}$ = 0.8

International $k_m$ = 12.0%

International portfolio investors dominated the trading activity in Novo's stock. Most of the volume was executed on the New York Stock Exchange. Therefore we use international norms rather than Danish norms.

4. **Novo's WACC after July, 1981.** Assume that the following data apply:

$k_d$ = 10.0%    Novo's new cost of debt due to a lower debt ratio

$k_e$ = 11.2%    Novo's cost of equity

E/V = 50%    Novo's equity-to-capital ratio; international investors required a lowered debt ratio than the previous 70%

D/V = 50%    Novo's new lower debt-to-capital ratio

V = 100%    Total market value of Novo's securities, D + E

t = 40%    Novo's effective tax rate

**a.** What was Novo's weighted average cost of capital?

**b.** How did this affect its capital budget?

5. **Novo's cost of equity in 2004.** Answer the following questions assuming the following:

International $k_{rf}$ = 4.0%    Risk-free interest rates had fallen due to the slow economic growth in much of the world

International $\beta_{Novo}$ = 0.8

International $k_m$ = 8.0%    The poor performance of stocks worldwide during the last three years had reduced expected returns

What was Novo's cost of equity?

6. **Novo's WACC in early 2004.** Assume that the following data apply:

$k_d$ = 6.0%    Novo's new cost of debt due to overall lower interest rates

$k_e$ = 7.2%    Novo's cost of equity

E/V = 50%    Novo's equity-to-capital ratio

D/V = 50%    Novo's debt-to-capital ratio

V = 100%    Total market value of Novo's securities, D + E

t = 40%    Novo's effective tax rate

**a.** What was Novo's weighted average cost of capital?

**b.** How did this affect its capital budget?

*Emerging Market Conglomerate: HangSung, a Korean chaebol.* Use the following data to answer Problems 7 through 10.

7. **HangSung before equity issue abroad.** Assume the following data applied to HangSung before it raised equity abroad. What was HangSung's cost of equity?

Korean    $k_{rf}$ = 10.0%

HangSung's    $\beta$ = 1.0

Korean $k_m$    = 14.0%

8. **HangSung's WACC before equity issue abroad.** Assume the following data applied to HangSung before it raised equity abroad. What was HangSung's WACC?

$k_d$ = 12.0%    HangSung's cost of debt

$k_e$ = 14.0%    HangSung's cost of equity

E/V = 20%    HangSung's equity-to-capital ratio; Korean chaebols have relatively high debt and low equity ratios by international standards

D/V = 80%    HangSung's debt-to-capital ratio

V = 100%    Total market value of HangSung's securities, D + E

t = 30%    HangSung's effective tax rate

9. **HangSung after equity issue abroad in 2004.** Assume the following data applied to HangSung after it raised equity abroad. What was its cost of equity?

International $k_{rf}$ = 4.0%

International $\beta_{HangSung}$ = 0.7

International $k_m$ = 8.0%

10. **HangSung's WACC after equity issue abroad in 2004.** Assume the following data applied to HangSung after it raised equity abroad.

$k_d = 6.0\%$   HangSung's new cost of debt was lower to due to overall lower interest rates, but also because it had lowered its very high debt ratio

$k_e = 6.8\%$   HangSung's cost of equity

$E/V = 40\%$   HangSung's equity-to-capital ratio

$D/V = 60\%$   HangSung's debt-to-capital ratio

$V = 100\%$   Total market value of HangSung's securities, $D + E$

$t = 30\%$   HangSung's effective tax rate

a. What was HangSung's WACC in 2004?

b. How did this affect its capital budget?

## Internet Exercises

1. **American depositary receipts.** American depositary receipts (ADRs) now make up more than 10% of all equity trading on U.S. stock exchanges. As more companies based outside of the United States list on U.S. markets, the need to understand the principal forces that drive ADR values increases with each trading day. Begin with Deutsche Morgan Grenfell's detailed description of the ADR process and current ADR trading activity:

   a. Prepare a briefing for senior management in your firm encouraging them to consider internationally diversifying the firm's liquid asset portfolio with ADRs.

   b. Identify whether the ADR program level (I, II, III, 144A) has any significance to which securities you believe the firm should consider.

   Deutsche Morgan Grenfell
     http://www.adr-dmg.com
   Bank of New York
     http://www.bankofny.com/
   JP Morgan's ADR Center
     http://adr.com
   Stock City
     http://www.stockcity.com/

2. **Institutional ownership of ADRs.** Use the JP Morgan ADR center Web site to find the largest individual owners of major ADRs traded in New York. Include Nokia, Telefonos de Mexico, Toyota, Siemens, and Philips in your search.

   JP Morgan's ADR Center
     http://adr.com

3. **Stock exchanges.** Exhibit 12.5 presents some data on selected stock exchanges.

   a. Using the same source Web site as the exhibit, compare the stock exchanges shown in Exhibit 12.5 by market capitalization and concentration of 5% most-capitalized and most-traded domestic companies.

   b. Expand Exhibit 12.5 on your own by adding the less liquid stock markets listed on the Web site.

   c. Highlight your own country's stock market data if you are from a country not shown in Exhibit 12.5.

   World Federation of Exchanges: Statistics
     http://www.world-exchanges.org/

# Financial Structure and International Debt

## LEARNING OBJECTIVES

Extend the theory of optimal financial structure to the multinational enterprise (MNE)

Analyze the factors that, in practice, determine the financial structure of foreign subsidiaries within the context of the MNE

Evaluate the various internal and external sources of funds available for the financing of foreign subsidiaries

Identify the relevant characteristics of different international debt instruments in financing both the MNE itself and its various foreign subsidiary components

Apply the strategies of project financing to the funding of large global projects with unique characteristics

We must modify the theory of optimal financial structure considerably to encompass the multinational firm. This chapter starts with a brief review of the domestic theory of optimal financial structure. We follow this with an analysis of the complexities involved in finding an optimal financial structure for an MNE. The next section highlights the unique complexities that influence the optimal financial structure for foreign subsidiaries of MNEs. The chapter continues with an analysis of the alternative debt instruments that an MNE can utilize to achieve an optimal financial structure. We follow this with an analysis of how Trident Corporation and its subsidiaries are financed. The chapter concludes with an examination of how MNEs can use a project finance structure to fund large and unique international projects.

## Optimal Financial Structure

After many years of debate, most finance theorists are now in agreement about whether an optimal financial structure exists for a firm, and if so, how it can be determined. The great debate between the so-called traditionalists and the Modigliani and Miller school of thought has apparently ended in a compromise. When taxes and bankruptcy costs are considered, a firm has an optimal financial structure determined by that particular mix of debt and equity that minimizes the firm's cost of capital for a given level of business risk. If the business risk of new projects differs from the risk of existing projects, the optimal mix of debt and equity would change to recognize trade-offs between business and financial risks.

Exhibit 13.1 illustrates how the cost of capital varies with the amount of debt employed. As the debt ratio, defined as total debt divided by total assets at market values, increases, the overall cost of capital ($K_{WACC}$) decreases because of the heavier weight of low-cost debt $[K_d(1-t)]$ compared to high-cost equity ($K_e$). The low cost of debt is, of course, due to the tax deductibility of interest shown by the term $(1-t)$.

**EXHIBIT 13.1**

The Cost of Capital and Financial Structure

Partly offsetting the favorable effect of more debt is an increase in the cost of equity ($K_e$), because investors perceive greater financial risk. Nevertheless, the overall weighted average after-tax cost of capital ($K_{WACC}$) continues to decline as the debt ratio increases, until financial risk becomes so serious that investors and management alike perceive a real danger of insolvency. This result causes a sharp increase in the cost of new debt and equity, thus increasing the weighted average cost of capital. The low point on the resulting U-shaped cost of capital curve, which is at 14% in Exhibit 13.1, defines the debt ratio range in which the cost of capital is minimized.

Most theorists believe that the low point is actually a rather broad, flat area encompassing a wide range of debt ratios, 30% to 60% in Exhibit 13.1, where little difference exists in the cost of capital. They also believe that, at least in the United States, the range of the flat area and the location of a particular firm's debt ratio within that range are determined by such variables as (1) the industry in which it competes, (2) volatility of its sales and operating income, and (3) the collateral value of its assets.

## Optimal Financial Structure and the MNE

The domestic theory of optimal financial structures needs to be modified by four more variables in order to accommodate the case of the MNE. These variables, in order of appearance, are: (1) the availability of capital, (2) diversification of cash flows, (3) foreign exchange risk, and (4) the expectations of international portfolio investors.

### AVAILABILITY OF CAPITAL

Chapter 11 demonstrated that access to capital in global markets allows an MNE to lower its cost of equity and debt compared with most domestic firms. It also permits an MNE to maintain its desired debt ratio, even when significant amounts of new funds must be raised. In other words, a multinational firm's marginal cost of capital is constant for considerable ranges of its capital budget. This statement is not true for most small domestic firms because they do not have access to the national equity or debt markets. They must either rely on internally generated funds or borrow for the short and medium term from commercial banks.

Multinational firms domiciled in countries that have illiquid capital markets are in almost the same situation as small domestic firms unless they have gained a global cost and availability of capital. They must rely on internally generated funds and bank borrowing. If they need to raise significant amounts of new funds to finance growth opportunities, they may need to borrow more than would be optimal from the viewpoint of minimizing their cost of capital. This is equivalent to saying that their *marginal cost of capital is increasing at higher budget levels*.

### RISK REDUCTION THROUGH INTERNATIONAL DIVERSIFICATION OF CASH FLOWS

As explained in Chapter 11, the theoretical possibility exists that multinational firms are in a better position than domestic firms to support higher debt ratios because their cash flows are diversified internationally. The probability of a firm's covering fixed charges under varying conditions in product, financial, and foreign exchange markets should increase if the variability of its cash flows is minimized.

By diversifying cash flows internationally, the MNE might be able to achieve the same kind of reduction in cash flow variability as portfolio investors receive from diversifying their security holdings internationally. Returns are not perfectly correlated between countries.

In contrast, a domestic German firm would not enjoy the benefit of cash flow international diversification but would have to rely entirely on its own net cash inflow from domestic operations. Perceived financial risk for the German firm would be greater than for a multinational firm because the variability of its German domestic cash flows could not be offset by positive cash flows elsewhere in the world.

As introduced in Chapter 11, the diversification argument has been challenged by empirical research findings that MNEs in the United States actually have lower debt ratios than their domestic counterparts. The agency costs of debt were higher for the MNEs, as were political risks, foreign exchange risks, and asymmetric information.

## FOREIGN EXCHANGE RISK AND THE COST OF DEBT

When a firm issues foreign currency denominated debt, its effective cost equals the after-tax cost of repaying the principal and interest in terms of the firm's own currency. This amount includes the nominal cost of principal and interest in foreign currency terms, adjusted for any foreign exchange gains or losses.

For example, if a U.S.–based firm borrows Sfr1,500,000 for one year at 5.00% interest, and during the year the franc appreciates from an initial rate of Sfr1.5000/\$ to Sfr1.4400/\$, what is the dollar cost of this debt ($k_d^\$$)? The dollar proceeds of the initial borrowing are calculated at the current spot rate of Sfr1.5000/\$:

$$\frac{Sfr1,500,000}{Sfr1.5000/\$} = \$1,000,000$$

At the end of one year the U.S.–based firm is responsible for repaying the Sfr1,500,000 principal plus 5.00% interest, or a total of Sfr1,575,000. This repayment, however, must be made at an ending spot rate of Sfr1.4400/\$:

$$\frac{Sfr1,500,000 \times 1.05}{Sfr1.4400/\$} = \$1.093,750$$

The actual dollar cost of the loan's repayment is not the nominal 5.00% paid in Swiss franc interest, but 9.375%.

$$\frac{\$1,093,750}{\$1,000,000} = 1.09375$$

The dollar cost is higher than expected due to appreciation of the Swiss franc against the U.S. dollar.

This total home-currency cost is actually the result of the combined percentage cost of debt and percentage change in the foreign currency's value. We can find the total cost of borrowing Swiss francs by a U.S. dollar-based firm, $k_d^\$$, by multiplying one plus the Swiss franc interest expense, $k_d^{Sfr}$, by one plus the percentage change in the Sfr/\$ exchange rate, $s$:

$$k_d^\$ = \left[ \left( 1 + k_d^{Sfr} \right) \times \left( 1 + s \right) \right] - 1$$

where $k_d^{Sfr} = 5.00\%$ and $s = 4.1667\%$. The percentage change in the value of the Swiss franc versus the U.S. dollar, when the home currency is the U.S. dollar, is

$$\frac{S_1 - S_2}{S_2} \times 100 = \frac{Sfr1.5000/\$ - Sfr1.4400/\$}{Sfr1.4400/\$} \times 100 = +4.1667\%$$

The total expense, combining the nominal interest rate and the percentage change in the exchange rate, is

$$k_d^\$ = \left[ \left( 1 + .0500 \right) \times \left( 1 + .041667 \right) \right] - 1 = .09375, \text{ or } 9.375\%$$

The total percentage cost of capital is 9.375%, not simply the foreign currency interest payment of 5%. The after-tax cost of this Swiss franc denominated debt, when the U.S. income tax rate is 34%, is

$$k_d^\$ \left( 1 - t \right) = 9.375\% \times 0.66 = 6.1875\%$$

The firm would report the added 4.1667% cost of this debt in terms of U.S. dollars as a foreign exchange transaction loss, and it would be deductible for tax purposes.

**BORROWING WITH 20/20 HINDSIGHT.**     MNEs have discovered that borrowing foreign currency denominated bonds on a long-term basis creates considerable exposure to transaction gains or losses. Exhibit 13.2 compares a sample of foreign currency denominated bonds issued by firms in a wide variety of countries during 1989–1990 as shown in columns (1) and (2). Column (3) shows the firm's expected cost in home currency terms at the time of issuance. Column (4) shows that about 10 years later — June 1, 1999 — the realized cost was different from the expected cost (again, in home currency terms). Column (5) shows the difference between expected and realized costs, which were of course due to changes in exchange rates. Note that foreign exchange exposure worked both favorably (negative differences) and unfavorably (positive

**EXHIBIT 13.2**

Costs of Borrowing in Foreign Currency Denominated Bonds (percentage)

| Issuer | (1)<br>Home<br>Country | (2)<br>Date of<br>Issue | (3)<br>Costs of Funds<br>Time of Issue (%) | (4)<br>Cost of Funds<br>as of 6/1/99 (%) | (5)<br>Cost<br>Differences (%) |
|---|---|---|---|---|---|
| Deutsche Bank Finance | Germany | 5/24/89 | 9.59 | 7.24 | −2.35 |
| Republic of Austria | Austria | 7/10/89 | 8.46 | 6.73 | −1.73 |
| Den Danske Bank | Denmark | 2/16/89 | 9.93 | 8.46 | −1.47 |
| Electricite de France | France | 4/18/89 | 9.50 | 8.22 | −1.28 |
| Japan Finance Corp. | Japan | 4/4/89 | 9.63 | 8.70 | −0.93 |
| British Telecom Finance | Britain | 7/13/89 | 8.46 | 8.33 | −0.13 |
| Alcan Aluminum Ltd. | Canada | 7/20/89 | 9.89 | 11.38 | +1.49 |
| Finnish Export Credit Ltd. | Finland | 2/1/89 | 9.68 | 12.16 | +2.48 |
| Banca Commerciale Italiana | Italy | 3/10/89 | 9.37 | 12.07 | +2.70 |
| Government of Malaysia | Malaysia | 9/19/90 | 10.29 | 13.10 | +2.81 |
| Kingdom of Thailand | Thailand | 8/1/89 | 8.70 | 11.87 | +3.17 |
| Republic of Turkey | Turkey | 8/30/89 | 10.25 | 84.11 | +73.86 |

Source: Steven M. Dawson, based on calculation methods in "Eurobond Currency Selection: Hindsight," *Financial Executive*, November 1993, p. 73. "Cost of Funds: Time of Issue" is the expected home currency cost given coupon, new issue price, and maturity. "Cost of Funds as of 6/1/99" is cost in home country currency given the U.S. bank transfer exchange rate at time of each interest or principal payment. Payments after June 1, 1999, are assumed made at the June 1 exchange rate.

differences) for the sample firms. And note specifically the disastrous impact of Turkey's currency devaluation on its cost of funds in home currency terms: +73.86%!

## EXPECTATIONS OF INTERNATIONAL PORTFOLIO INVESTORS

The last two chapters highlighted the fact that the key to gaining a global cost and availability of capital is attracting and retaining international portfolio investors. Their expectations for a firm's debt ratio and overall financial structures are based on global norms that have developed over the past 30 years. Because a large proportion of international portfolio investors are based in the most liquid and unsegmented capital markets, such as the United States and the United Kingdom, their expectations tend to predominate and override individual national norms. Therefore, regardless of other factors, if a firm wants to raise capital in global markets, it must adopt global norms that are close to the U.S. and U.K. norms. Debt ratios up to 60% appear to be acceptable. Any higher debt ratio is more difficult to sell to international portfolio investors.

## Financial Structure of Foreign Subsidiaries

If we accept the theory that minimizing the cost of capital for a given level of business risk and capital budget is an objective that should be implemented from the perspective of the consolidated MNE, then the financial structure of each subsidiary is relevant only to the extent that it affects this overall goal. In other words, an individual subsidiary does not really have an independent cost of capital. Therefore its financial structure should not be based on an objective of minimizing it.

Financial structure norms for firms vary widely from one country to another but cluster for firms domiciled in the same country. This statement is the conclusion of a long line of empirical studies that have investigated the question, from 1969 to the present. Most of these international studies concluded that country-specific environmental variables are key determinants of debt ratios. Among these variables are historical development, taxation, corporate governance, bank influence, existence of a viable corporate bond market, attitude toward risk, government regulation, availability of capital, and agency costs.

Many other institutional differences also influence debt ratios in national capital markets, but firms trying to attract international portfolio investors must pay attention to debt ratio norms those investors expect. Since many international portfolio investors are influenced by the debt ratios that exist in the Anglo-American markets, there is a trend toward more global conformity. MNEs and other large firms dependent on attracting international portfolio investors are beginning to adopt similar debt ratio standards, even if domestic firms continue to use national standards. *Real World Example 13.1* illustrates one of the recent ways in which equity is injected into subsidiaries, the *equity carve-out*.

### LOCAL NORMS AND THE FINANCIAL STRUCTURE OF LOCAL SUBSIDIARIES

Within the constraint of minimizing its consolidated worldwide cost of capital, should an MNE take differing country debt ratio norms into consideration when determining its desired debt ratio for foreign subsidiaries? For definition purposes the debt considered here should be only that borrowed from sources outside the MNE. This debt would include local and foreign currency loans as well as Eurocurrency loans. The

## Real World Example 13.1
### EQUITY CARVE-OUTS

The sale of a minority equity interest in a subsidiary, typically 20% or less, is termed an equity carve-out. The purpose of equity carve-outs is to raise equity capital for subsidiary operations without risking loss of control. The popular storyline on equity carve-outs has been that firms could increase their share price and their equity capital base without sacrificing control. Evidence from a recent study, however, indicates that this is not the case.

The study, by McKinsey, of 200 major carve-outs in Europe and the United States for the 1990–2001 period found that only 10% of carve-outs raised the parents' share price by more than 12%. And, to make matters worse, in the two years following the initial public offering of subsidiary shares most carve-outs actually destroyed shareholder value. There was, however, one important exception: when the long-term path of the carve-out was to create a fully independent company — a spin-off — the carve-outs significantly outperformed the S&P 500 company returns.

The study found that the long-term ownership of carve-outs demonstrated declining parent control. Five years following the carve-out, only 8% of carve-outs continued to exist as public companies clearly controlled by a parent — 50% or more

control (8% more were controlled by parents holding less than 50%). An additional 31% of the carve-outs were held by parents with a stake of less than 25%, and third parties had either acquired or merged with 30% of the carve-outs.

**Equity Carve-Outs Five Years Out**

| | |
|---|---:|
| Acquired or merged | 39% |
| Repurchased by parent | 11% |
| De-listed | 3% |
| Independent (>75% public) | 31% |
| Remained parent-controlled | 16% |
| Total | 100% |

Although there are a variety of reasons for the relative failure of equity carve-outs to build sustainable shareholder value, the primary problem appears to be the basic conflict between giving the subsidiary adequate independence versus the potential competitive conflicts between the subsidiaries and parents (frequently finding themselves bidding against one another in the marketplace).

Source: Abstracted from "When Carve-Outs Make Sense," by André Annema, William C. Fallon, and Marc H. Goedhart, *The McKinsey Quarterly*, 2002, no. 2, and "Doing the Spin-Out," by Patricia Anslinger, Sheila Bonini, and Michael Patsalos-Fox, *The McKinsey Quarterly*, 2000, no. 1, pp. 98–105. Study covered 204 carve-outs with a value exceeding $50 million announced prior to January 1, 1998 for the January 1990 to May 2001 period.

reason for this definition is that parent loans to foreign subsidiaries are often regarded as equivalent to equity investment both by host countries and by investing firms. A parent loan is usually subordinated to other debt and does not create the same threat of insolvency as an external loan. Furthermore, the choice of debt or equity investment is often arbitrary and subject to negotiation between host country and parent firm.

**MAIN ADVANTAGES OF LOCALIZATION.**     The main advantages of a finance structure for foreign subsidiaries that conforms to local debt norms are as follows:

- A localized financial structure reduces criticism of foreign subsidiaries that have been operating with too high a proportion of debt (judged by local standards), often resulting in the accusation that they are not contributing a fair share of risk capital to the host country. At the other end of the spectrum, a localized financial structure would improve the image of foreign subsidiaries that have been operating with too little debt and thus appear to be insensitive to local monetary policy.

- A localized financial structure helps management evaluate return on equity investment relative to local competitors in the same industry. In economies where interest rates are relatively high as an offset to inflation, the penalty paid reminds management of the need to consider price level changes when evaluating investment performance.

- In economies where interest rates are relatively high because of a scarcity of capital, and real resources are fully utilized (full employment), the penalty paid for borrowing local funds reminds management that unless return on assets is greater than the local price of capital — that is, negative leverage — they are probably misallocating scarce domestic real resources such as land and labor. This factor may not appear relevant to management decisions, but it will certainly be considered by the host country in making decisions with respect to the firm.

**MAIN DISADVANTAGES OF LOCALIZATION.**   The main disadvantages of localized financial structures are as follows:

- An MNE is expected to have a comparative advantage over local firms in overcoming imperfections in national capital markets through better availability of capital and the ability to diversify risk. Why should it throw away these important competitive advantages to conform to local norms established in response to imperfect local capital markets, historical precedent, and institutional constraints that do not apply to the MNE?
- If each foreign subsidiary of an MNE localizes its financial structure, the resulting consolidated balance sheet might show a financial structure that does not conform to any particular country's norm. The debt ratio would be a simple weighted average of the corresponding ratio of each country in which the firm operates. This feature could increase perceived financial risk and thus the cost of capital for the parent, but only if two additional conditions are present:

  1. The consolidated debt ratio is pushed completely out of the discretionary range of acceptable debt ratios in the flat area of the cost of capital curve, shown previously in Exhibit 13.1.
  2. The MNE is unable to offset high debt in one foreign subsidiary with low debt in other foreign or domestic subsidiaries at the same cost. If the international Fisher effect is working, replacement of debt should be possible at an equal after-tax cost after adjusting for foreign exchange risk. On the other hand, if market imperfections preclude this type of replacement, the possibility exists that the overall cost of debt, and thus the cost of capital, could increase if the MNE attempts to conform to local norms.

- The debt ratio of a foreign subsidiary is only cosmetic, because lenders ultimately look to the parent and its consolidated worldwide cash flow as the source of repayment. In many cases debt of subsidiaries must be guaranteed by the parent firm. Even if no formal guarantee exists, an implied guarantee usually exists because almost no parent firm would dare to allow a subsidiary to default on a loan. If it did, repercussions would surely be felt with respect to the parent's own financial standing, with a resulting increase in its cost of capital.

**COMPROMISE SOLUTION.**   In our opinion a compromise position is possible. Both multinational and domestic firms should try to minimize their overall weighted average cost of capital for a given level of business risk and capital budget, as finance theory suggests. However, if debt is available to a foreign subsidiary at equal cost to that which could be raised elsewhere, after adjusting for foreign exchange risk, then localizing the foreign subsidiary's financial structure should incur no cost penalty and yet would also enjoy the advantages listed above.

## FINANCING THE FOREIGN SUBSIDIARY

In addition to choosing an appropriate financial structure for foreign subsidiaries, financial managers of multinational firms need to choose among alternative sources of funds to finance foreign subsidiaries. Sources of funds available to foreign subsidiaries can be classified as *internal to the MNE* and *external to the MNE*.

Ideally the choice among the sources of funds should minimize the cost of external funds after adjusting for foreign exchange risk. The firm should choose internal sources in order to minimize worldwide taxes and political risk. Simultaneously, the firm should ensure that managerial motivation in the foreign subsidiaries is geared toward minimizing the firm's consolidated worldwide cost of capital, rather than the foreign subsidiary's cost of capital. Needless to say, this task is difficult if not impossible, and the tendency is to place more emphasis on one variable at the expense of others.

**INTERNAL SOURCES OF FUNDING.** Exhibit 13.3 provides an overview of the *internal* sources of financing for foreign subsidiaries. In general, although the equity provided by the parent is required, it is frequently kept to legal and operational mini-

## EXHIBIT 13.3

Internal Financing of the Foreign Subsidiary

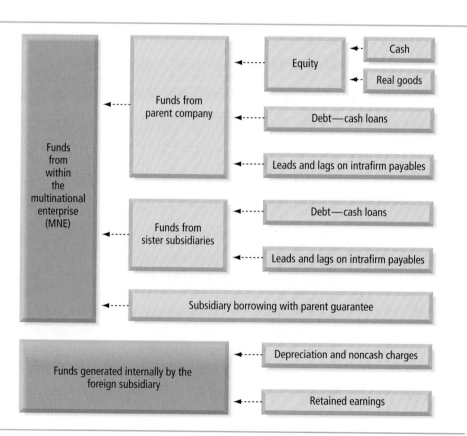

mums to reduce risk of invested capital. Equity investment can take the form of either *cash* or *real goods* (machinery, equipment, inventory, and the like).

Debt is the preferable form of subsidiary financing, but access to local host country debt is limited in the early stages of a foreign subsidiary's life. Without a history of proven operational capability and debt service capability, the foreign subsidiary must acquire its debt from the parent company or sister subsidiaries (initially) and from unrelated parties with a parental guarantee (after operations have been initiated).

Once the operational and financial capabilities of the foreign subsidiary have been established, its ability to generate funds internally may become critical for the subsidiary's future growth. In special cases in which the subsidiary may be operating in a highly segmented market, such as an emerging market nation considered to be risky by the international investment and banking communities, the subsidiary's ability to generate its own funds from internal sources is important. These sources combine retained earnings, depreciation, and other noncash expenses. (A *noncash expense* is a deductible item such as depreciation, but the "expense" as a cash flow never leaves the firm.)

**EXTERNAL SOURCES OF FUNDING.**    Exhibit 13.4 provides an overview of the sources of foreign subsidiary financing *external* to the MNE. The sources are first decomposed into three categories: debt from the parent's country, debt from countries outside the parent's country, and local equity. Debt acquired from external parties in the parent's country reflects the lenders' familiarity with and confidence in the parent company itself, although the parent is in this case not providing explicit guarantees for the repayment of the debt.

Local currency debt, that is, debt acquired in the host country of the foreign subsidiary's residence, is particularly valuable to the foreign subsidiary that has substantial local currency cash inflows arising from its business activities. Local currency debt

**EXHIBIT 13.4**

External Financing of the Foreign Subsidiary

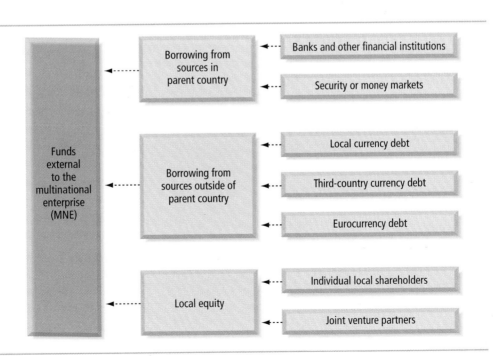

provides a foreign exchange financial hedge, matching currency of inflow with currency of outflow. Gaining access to local currency debt often takes time and patience by foreign subsidiary management in establishing operations and developing a local market credit profile. And in the case of many emerging markets, local currency debt is in short supply for all borrowers, local or foreign.

## International Debt Markets

The international debt markets offer the borrower a variety of different maturities, repayment structures, and currencies of denomination. The markets and their many different instruments vary by source of funding, pricing structure, maturity, and subordination or linkage to other debt and equity instruments. Exhibit 13.5 provides an overview of the three basic categories described in the following sections, along with their primary components as issued or traded in the international debt markets today. The three major sources of debt funding on the international markets are *international bank loans and syndicated credits*, the *Euronote market*, and the *international bond market*.

An MNE will normally need debt in a variety of maturities, payment structures, and currencies, therefore often using all three markets in addition to its traditional domestic funding base. The following sections describe the basic attributes of these markets and instruments, as well as their relative advantages and disadvantages for meeting the funding needs of the individual MNE.

### BANK LOANS AND SYNDICATED CREDITS

**INTERNATIONAL BANK LOANS.**   International bank loans have traditionally been sourced in the Eurocurrency markets. Eurodollar bank loans are also called *Eurodollar credits* or simply *Eurocredits*. The latter title is broader because it encom-

---

**EXHIBIT 13.5**

International Debt Markets and Instruments

passes nondollar loans in the Eurocurrency market. The key factor attracting both depositors and borrowers to the Eurocurrency loan market is the narrow interest rate spread within that market. The difference between deposit and loan rates is often less than 1%.

**EUROCREDITS.**   Eurocredits are bank loans to MNEs, sovereign governments, international institutions, and banks denominated in Eurocurrencies and extended by banks in countries other than the country in whose currency the loan is denominated. The basic borrowing interest rate for Eurodollar loans has long been tied to the London Interbank Offered Rate (LIBOR), which is the deposit rate applicable to interbank loans within London. Eurodollars are lent for both short- and medium-term maturities, with transactions for six months or less regarded as routine. Most Eurodollar loans are for a fixed term with no provision for early repayment.

**SYNDICATED CREDITS.**   The syndication of loans has enabled banks to spread the risk of very large loans among a number of banks. Syndication is particularly important because many large MNEs need credit in excess of a single bank's loan limit. A *syndicated bank credit* is arranged by a lead bank on behalf of its client. Before finalizing the loan agreement, the lead bank seeks the participation of a group of banks, with each participant providing a portion of the total funds needed. The lead manager bank will work with the borrower to determine the amount of the total credit, the floating-rate base and spread over the base rate, maturity, and fee structure for managing the participating banks. The periodic expenses of the syndicated credit are composed of two elements:

1. The actual interest expense of the loan, normally stated as a spread in basis points over a variable-rate base such as LIBOR.

2. The commitment fees paid on any unused portions of the credit. The spread paid over LIBOR by the borrower is considered the *risk premium*, reflecting the general business and financial risk applicable to the borrower's repayment capability.

*Real World Example 13.2* illustrates the pricing common to the syndicated loan markets, including interest expenses and the commitment and investment banking fees.

## EURONOTE MARKET

The Euronote market is the collective term used to describe short- to medium-term debt instruments sourced in the Eurocurrency markets. Although a multitude of differentiated financial products exists, they can be divided into two major groups — *underwritten facilities* and *nonunderwritten facilities*. Underwritten facilities are used for the sale of Euronotes in a number of different forms. Nonunderwritten facilities are used for the sale and distribution of *Euro-commercial paper* (ECP) and *Euro medium-term notes* (EMTNs).

**EURONOTE FACILITIES.**   A major development in international money markets is the establishment of facilities for sales of short-term, negotiable, promissory notes — *Euronotes.* Among the facilities for their issuance are revolving underwriting facilities (rufs), note issuance facilities (nifs), and standby note issuance facilities (snifs). These facilities are provided by international investment and commercial banks. The euronote is a substantially cheaper source of short-term funds than syndicated loans because the notes are placed directly with the investor public, and the securitized and

## Real World Example 13.2
### PRICING AND STRUCTURE OF A SYNDICATED EUROCREDIT

**Borrower:** Irish Aerospace, GPA Airbus, GPA Fokker, GPA Jetprop, GPA Rolls

**Amount:** US$1.25 billion; Revolving loans/guarantees/letters of credit

**Terms:** Eight years at 93.75 basis points over LIBOR, with a margin of 7/8% for GPA Airbus drawings

**Arranger:** Citicorp Investment Bank

**Lead Managers and Underwriters:** Citibank, Chase Investment Bank, Toronto-Dominion Bank, Citibank (Channel Islands) for a syndicate of Japanese leasing companies, Credit Suisse, Societe Generale (London), Amsterdam-Rotterdam Bank, Bank of Nova Scotia, Bank of Tokyo International, Daiwa Bank, IBJ, Irish Intercontinental

A typical syndicated loan of this type would have up-front fees totaling 1.5% of the principal. The fees would be divided between three groups: (1) the lead arranger bank(s), which organizes the loan and participants; (2) the lead managing and underwriting banks, which aid in the syndication of the loan; and (3) the participating banks, which actually provide the capital.

If the 1.5% total fee was subdivided equally among the three groups, the proceeds of the loan after expenses of issuance and arrangement are

$$\$1,250,000,000 - \left[(0.005+0.005+0.005)\right.$$

$$\left. \times \$1,250,000,000\right] = \$1,231,250,000$$

The debt service payments over the eight-year period prior to principal repayment are LIBOR + 93.75 basis points; assuming an initial LIBOR rate of 9.00% (reset every six months for semi-annual debt service payments)

$$\left[\frac{0.0900+0.009375}{2}\right] \times \$1,250,000,000 = \$62,109,375$$

The effective annual cost is thus

$$\left[\frac{\$62,109,375}{\$1,231,250,000}\right] \times 2 \times 100 = 10.09\%$$

The syndicated credit will cost Irish Aerospace 10.09% at the current LIBOR rate of 9.000%.

---

underwritten form allows the ready establishment of liquid secondary markets. The banks receive substantial fees initially for their underwriting and placement services.

**EURO-COMMERCIAL PAPER (ECP).**    Euro-commercial paper (ECP), like commercial paper issued in domestic markets around the world, is a short-term debt obligation of a corporation or bank. Maturities are typically one, three, and six months. The paper is sold normally at a discount or occasionally with a stated coupon. Although the market is capable of supporting issues in any major currency, over 90% of issues outstanding are denominated in U.S. dollars.

**EURO MEDIUM-TERM NOTES (EMTNS).**    The Euro medium-term note is the latest major entrant to the world's debt markets. The EMTN effectively bridges the maturity gap between ECP and the longer-term and less flexible international bond. Although many of the notes were initially underwritten, most EMTNs are now nonunderwritten.

The rapid initial growth of the EMTN market followed directly on the heels of the same basic instrument that began in the U.S. domestic market when the U.S. Securities and Exchange Commission (SEC) instituted Rule #415, allowing companies to obtain *shelf registrations* for debt issues. What this means is that once the registration is obtained, the corporation can issue notes on a continuous basis without having to obtain new registrations for each additional issue. This in turn allows a firm to sell short- and medium-term notes through a much cheaper and more flexible issuance facility than ordinary bonds.

The EMTN's basic characteristics are similar to those of a bond, with principal, maturity, and coupon structures and rates being comparable. The EMTN's typical maturities range from as little as nine months to a maximum of 10 years. Coupons are typically paid semiannually, and coupon rates are comparable to similar bond issues. The EMTN does, however, have three unique characteristics. First, the EMTN is a facility, allowing continuous issuance over a period of time, unlike a bond issue which is essentially sold all at once. Second, because EMTNs are sold continuously, in order to make debt service (coupon redemption) manageable, coupons are paid on set calendar dates regardless of the date of issuance. Finally, EMTNs are issued in relatively small denominations, from $2 million to $5 million, making medium-term debt acquisition much more flexible than the large minimums customarily needed in the international bond markets.

## INTERNATIONAL BOND MARKET

The international bond market sports a rich array of innovative instruments created by imaginative investment bankers, who are unfettered by the usual controls and regulations governing domestic capital markets. Indeed, the international bond market rivals the international banking market in terms of the quantity and cost of funds provided to international borrowers. All international bonds fall within two generic classifications, *Eurobonds* and *foreign bonds*. The distinction between categories is based on whether the borrower is a domestic or a foreign resident, and whether the issue is denominated in the local currency or a foreign currency.

**EUROBONDS.**    A *Eurobond* is underwritten by an international syndicate of banks and other securities firms, and is sold exclusively in countries other than the country in whose currency the issue is denominated. For example, a bond issued by a firm resident in the United States, denominated in U.S. dollars, but sold to investors in Europe and Japan (not to investors in the United States), would be a Eurobond.

Eurobonds are issued by multinational corporations, large domestic corporations, sovereign governments, governmental enterprises, and international institutions. They are offered simultaneously in a number of different national capital markets, but not in the capital market or to residents of the country in whose currency the bond is denominated. Almost all Eurobonds are in bearer form with call provisions and sinking funds.

The syndicate that offers a new issue of Eurobonds might be composed of underwriters from a number of countries, including European banks, foreign branches of U.S. banks, banks from offshore financial centers, investment and merchant banks, and nonbank securities firms.

- **The straight fixed-rate issue.** The straight fixed-rate issue is structured like most domestic bonds, with a fixed coupon, set maturity date, and full principal repayment upon final maturity. Coupons are normally paid annually, rather than semiannually, primarily because the bonds are bearer bonds and annual coupon redemption is more convenient for the holders.

- **The floating-rate note (FRN).** The floating-rate note (FRN) was the new instrument of fashion on the international bond scene in the early 1980s. The FRN normally pays a semiannual coupon which is determined using a variable-rate base. A typical coupon would be set at some fixed spread over LIBOR. This structure, like most variable-rate interest-bearing instruments, is designed to allow investors to shift more of the interest-rate risk of a financial investment to the borrower. It was a popular instrument in the early 1980s when world markets were characterized by relatively high and unpredictable interest rates. Although many FRNs have fixed maturities, a number of major issues since 1985 are perpetuities. The principal will never be repaid. Thus they provide many of the same financial functions as equity.

- **The equity-related issue.** The most recent major addition to the international bond markets is the equity-related issue. The equity-related international bond resembles the straight fixed-rate issue in practically all price and payment characteristics, with the added feature that it is convertible to stock prior to maturity at a specified price per share (or alternatively, number of shares per bond). The borrower is able to issue debt with lower coupon payments due to the added value of the equity conversion feature.

 **FOREIGN BONDS.**    A *foreign bond* is underwritten by a syndicate composed of members from a single country, sold principally within that country, and denominated in the currency of that country. The issuer, however, is from another country. A bond issued by a firm resident in Sweden, denominated in dollars, and sold in the United States to U.S. investors by U.S. investment bankers, would be a foreign bond. Foreign bonds have nicknames: foreign bonds sold in the United States are "Yankee bonds"; foreign bonds sold in Japan are "Samurai bonds"; and foreign bonds sold in the United Kingdom are "Bulldogs."

## UNIQUE CHARACTERISTICS OF EUROBOND MARKETS

Although the Eurobond market evolved at about the same time as the Eurodollar market, the two markets exist for different reasons, and each could exist independently of the other. The Eurobond market owes its existence to several unique factors, some of which have changed recently. Three of the original factors still of importance are absence of regulatory interference, less stringent disclosure practices, and favorable tax treatment.

**ABSENCE OF REGULATORY INTERFERENCE.**    National governments often impose tight controls on foreign issuers of securities denominated in the local currency and sold within their national boundaries. However, governments in general have less stringent limitations for securities denominated in foreign currencies and sold within their markets to holders of those foreign currencies. In effect, Eurobond sales fall outside the regulatory domain of any single nation.

**LESS STRINGENT DISCLOSURE.**    Disclosure requirements in the Eurobond market are much less stringent than those of the Securities and Exchange Commission (SEC) for sales within the United States. U.S. firms often find that the registration costs of a Eurobond offering are less than those of a domestic issue and that less time is needed to bring a new issue to market. Non–U.S. firms often prefer Eurodollar bonds over bonds sold within the United States because they do not wish to undergo the costs, and disclosure, needed to register with the SEC. However, the SEC has relaxed disclosure requirements for certain private placements (Rule #144A), which has improved the attractiveness of the U.S. domestic bond and equity markets.

**FAVORABLE TAX STATUS.**    Eurobonds offer tax anonymity and flexibility. Interest paid on Eurobonds is generally not subject to an income withholding tax. As one might expect, Eurobond interest is not always reported to tax authorities. Eurobonds are usually issued in bearer form, meaning that the name and country of residence of the owner is not on the certificate. To receive interest, the bearer cuts an interest coupon from the bond and turns it in at a banking institution listed on the issue as a paying agent. European investors are accustomed to the privacy provided by bearer bonds and are very reluctant to purchase registered bonds, which require holders to reveal their names before they receive interest. Bearer bond status, of course, is also tied to tax avoidance.

## RATING OF EUROBONDS AND OTHER INTERNATIONAL ISSUES

Purchasers of Eurobonds do not rely only on bond-rating services or on detailed analyses of financial statements. The general reputation of the issuing corporation and its underwriters has been a major factor in obtaining favorable terms. For this reason, larger and better-known MNEs, state enterprises, and sovereign governments are able to obtain the lowest interest rates. Firms whose names are better known to the general public, possibly because they manufacture consumer goods, are often believed to have an advantage over equally qualified firms whose products are less widely known.

Rating agencies, such as Moody's and Standard & Poor's (S&P), provide ratings for selected international bonds for a fee. Moody's ratings for international bonds imply the same creditworthiness as for domestic bonds of U.S. issuers. Moody's limits its evaluation to the issuer's ability to obtain the necessary currency to repay the issue according to the original terms of the bond. The agency excludes any assessment of risk to the investor caused by changing exchange rates. Exhibit 13.6 lists Moody's sovereign ceilings for foreign-currency ratings by country in August 1999.

Moody's rates international bonds upon request of the issuer. Based on supporting financial statements and other material obtained from the issuer, it makes a preliminary rating and then informs the issuer who has an opportunity to comment. After Moody's determines its final rating, the issuer may decide not to have the rating published. Consequently a disproportionately large number of published international ratings fall into the highest categories, since issuers about to receive a lower rating do not allow publication.

Moody's review of political risk includes study of the government system, the social environment, and the nation's external relations. Its review of economic risk looks at debt burden, international liquidity, balance of payments flexibility, economic structure, growth performance, economic management, and economic outlook. Moody's also evaluates the bonds of sovereign-supported entities by looking first at their creditworthiness on a stand-alone basis and then at the extent to which sovereign support either enhances or diminishes the borrower's financial strength. Credit ratings are critical to borrowers and investors alike. An MNE's credit rating determines its cost of funds.

Exhibit 13.7 summarizes the structure and size of the global bond market for end-of-year 2001. These statistics provide a degree of perspective on the many bond instruments used globally, and specifically, by whom. Interestingly, the United States, when combining the government and corporate sectors, comprises more than half — 51.8% to be precise — of the total global bond market. The United States also dominates the foreign bond market (59.5%) and the Eurobond market (61.7%). The United Kingdom, however, although making up a rather small portion of the total global bond market, has a significant presence in both the foreign (17.7%) and Eurobond markets (10.6%), living up to its heritage as the home of many global organizations, as well as serving as host to the largest international financial center, London.

## EXHIBIT 13.6

Moody's Investors Service's Sovereign Ceilings for Foreign-Currency Ratings for Selected Countries (August 1999)

| Country | Bonds & Notes L.T. | S.T. | Bank Deposits L.T. | S.T. | Country | Bonds & Notes L.T. | S.T. | Bank Deposits L.T. | S.T. |
|---|---|---|---|---|---|---|---|---|---|
| Argentina | Ba3 | P-1 | Aaa | P-1 | Lithuania | Ba1 | NP | Ba2 | NP |
| Australia | Aa2 | P-1 | Aa2 | P-1 | Luxembourg | WR | WR | WR | WR |
| Brazil | B2 | NP | Caa1 | NP | Malaysia | Baa3 | NP | Baa1 | NP |
| Bulgaria | B2 | NP | B3 | NP | Mexico | Ba2* | NP | B1* | NP |
| Canada | Aa2 | P-1 | Aa2 | P-1 | New Zealand | Aa2 | P-1 | Aa2 | P-1 |
| Cayman Islands | Aa3 | P-1 | Aa3 | P-1 | Norway | Aaa | P-1 | Aaa | P-1 |
| Chile | Baa1 | P-2 | Baa1 | P-2 | Oman | Baa2 | P-2 | Baa2 | P-2 |
| China | A3 | P-2 | Baa2 | P-3 | Pakistan | Caa1 | NP | Ca | NP |
| Colombia | Baa3 | — | Ba1 | NP | Peru | Ba3 | NP | B1 | NP |
| Croatia | Baa3 | P-3 | Ba1 | NP | Philippines | Ba1 | NP | Ba2 | NP |
| Czech Republic | Baa1 | P-2 | Baa1 | P-2 | Poland | Baa3 | — | Ba1 | NP |
| Denmark | Aa1 | P-1 | Aa1 | P-1 | Romania | B3 | NP | Caa1 | NP |
| Euroland | Aaa | P-1 | Aaa | P-1 | Russia | B3 | NP | Ca | NP |
| Greece | A2 | P-2 | A2 | P-2 | Singapore | Aa1 | P-1 | Aa1 | P-1 |
| Hong Kong | A3 | P-1 | A3 | P-1 | Slovakia | Ba1 | NP | Ba2 | NP |
| Hungary | Baa1 | P-2 | Baa1 | P-2 | Slovenia | A3 | P-2 | A3 | P-2 |
| Iceland | Aa3 | P-1 | Aa3 | P-1 | South Africa | Baa3 | — | Ba1 | NP |
| India | Ba2 | NP | Ba3 | NP | Sweden | Aa2 | P-1 | Aa2 | P-1 |
| Indonesia | B3 | NP | Ca | NP | Switzerland | Aaa | P-1 | Aaa | P-1 |
| Israel | A3 | P-2 | A3 | P-2 | Taiwan | Aa3 | P-1 | Aa3 | P-1 |
| Japan | Aa1 | P-1 | Aa1 | P-1 | Thailand | Ba1 | NP | B1 | NP |
| Kazakhstan | B1 | NP | B2 | NP | United States | Aaa | P-1 | Aaa | P-1 |
| Korea | Baa3 | NP | Baa2 | NP | Uruguay | Baa3 | P-3 | Baa3 | P-3 |
| Kuwait | Baa1 | P-2 | Baa1 | P-2 | United Kingdom | Aaa | P-1 | Aaa | P-1 |
| | | | | | Venezuela | B2 | NP | Caa1 | NP |

Source: Moody's Investors Services, http:www.moodys.com/repldata/ratings/ratsov.htm.

* Under review for possible upgrading.

All EU-12 members of the euro (euroland) are rated together. Long-term bond ratings, from highest to lowest: Aaa, Aa, and A are highest grade (investment grade); Baa, Ba, and B are medium-grade (speculative grade); Caa, Ca, and C are poorest grade. Moody's also applies numerical modifiers (1, 2, and 3) within each rating classification, with 1 being in the higher end of the rating grade. Short-term ratings, from highest to lowest, are P-1, P-1, P-3, and NP (not prime).

Access to debt capital is, however, still a function of basic societal norms. Religion itself may play a part in the use and availability of debt capital. *Real World Example 13.3* (page 356) illustrates one area rarely seen by Westerners: Islamic Finance.

## Project Financing

One of the hottest topics in international finance today is project finance. *Project finance* is the arrangement of financing for long-term capital projects, large in scale, long in life, and generally high in risk. This is a very general definition, however, because many forms and structures fall under this generic heading.

**EXHIBIT 13.7**

Size and Structure of the Global Bond Market, 2001 (nominal value, billions of U.S. dollars)

| Country | Total Out-standing (bil US$) | % World Bond Market (bil US$) | Government (bil US$) | Government % of Gov | Corporate (bil US$) | Corporate % of Corp | Foreign (bil US$) | Foreign % of For | Eurobond (bil US$) | Eurobond % of Euro |
|---|---|---|---|---|---|---|---|---|---|---|
| United States | 17,090.9 | 51.8% | 8,588.8 | 48.2% | 5,174.9 | 53.2% | 486.8 | 59.5% | 2,840.4 | 61.7% |
| Euroland | 6,466.9 | 19.6% | 3,127.1 | 17.6% | 2,690.0 | 27.6% | - | 0.0% | 649.8 | 14.1% |
| Japan | 5,305.2 | 16.1% | 3,938.7 | 22.1% | 854.6 | 8.8% | 61.0 | 7.5% | 450.9 | 9.8% |
| United Kingdom | 1,081.6 | 3.3% | 390.9 | 2.2% | 55.6 | 0.6% | 145.1 | 17.7% | 490.0 | 10.6% |
| Canada | 514.4 | 1.6% | 356.0 | 2.0% | 111.0 | 1.1% | 0.4 | 0.0% | 47.1 | 1.0% |
| Switzerland | 261.6 | 0.8% | 49.6 | 0.3% | 82.1 | 0.8% | 110.4 | 13.5% | 19.5 | 0.4% |
| Denmark | 252.3 | 0.8% | 67.9 | 0.4% | 175.5 | 1.8% | - | 0.0% | 8.9 | 0.2% |
| Australia | 182.7 | 0.6% | 57.2 | 0.3% | 86.2 | 0.9% | 9.9 | 1.2% | 29.4 | 0.6% |
| Sweden | 128.6 | 0.4% | 60.2 | 0.3% | 60.7 | 0.6% | 3.9 | 0.5% | 3.8 | 0.1% |
| Norway | 47.7 | 0.1% | 20.5 | 0.1% | 22.2 | 0.2% | 0.5 | 0.1% | 4.6 | 0.1% |
| New Zealand | 16.6 | 0.1% | 10.7 | 0.1% | - | 0.0% | - | 0.0% | 5.9 | 0.1% |
| Sub total | $31,348.5 | 95.1% | $16,667.6 | 93.6% | $9,312.8 | 95.7% | $818.0 | 100.0% | $4,550.3 | 98.8% |
| *Emerging Markets* | | | | | | | | | | |
| Asia | 1,000.7 | 3.0% | 538.8 | 3.0% | 419.0 | 4.3% | na | | 42.9 | 0.2% |
| Latin America | 391.6 | 1.2% | 389.1 | 2.2% | na | | na | | 2.5 | 0.0% |
| E. Europe, Middle East, and Africa | 231.3 | 0.7% | 220.1 | 1.2% | na | | na | | 11.2 | 0.1% |
| Total | $32,972.1 | 100.0% | $17,815.6 | 100.0% | $9,731.8 | 100.0% | $818.0 | 100.0% | $4,606.9 | 100.0% |
| Percent of total | | 100.0% | | 54.0% | | 29.5% | | 2.5% | | 14.0% |

Source: "Size and Structure of the World Bond Market, 2002," Merrill Lynch, Global Fixed Income Research Team, April 2002, p. 4. All data is for calendar year-end and is collected from national sources for government, corporate, and foreign markets. Eurobond data is from the Bank for International Settlements. Euroland data is from the European Central Bank. Government sector includes bonds issued by the central government, quasi-government, and agencies.

Project finance is not new. Examples go back centuries and include many famous early international businesses such as the Dutch East India Company and the British East India Company. These entrepreneurial importers financed their trade ventures to Asia on a voyage-by-voyage basis, with each voyage's financing being like venture capital; investors would be repaid when the shipper returned and the fruits of the Asian marketplace were sold at the docks to Mediterranean and European merchants. If all went well, the individual shareholders of the voyage were paid in full.

Project finance is used widely today by MNEs in the development of large-scale infrastructure projects in China, India, and many other emerging markets. Although each individual project has unique characteristics, most are highly leveraged transactions, with debt making up more than 60% of the total financing. Equity is a small component of project financing for two reasons: first, the simple scale of the investment project often precludes a single investor or even a collection of private investors from being able to fund it; second, many of these projects involve subjects traditionally funded by governments — such as electrical power generation, dam building, highway construction, energy exploration, production, and distribution.

This level of debt, however, places an enormous burden on cash flow for debt service. Therefore, project financing usually requires a number of additional levels of risk reduction. The lenders involved in these investments must feel secure that they will be

## Real World Example 13.3
### ISLAMIC FINANCE

There was a time when religious restrictions meant that Islamic finance was a limited affair. Recently, however, all sorts of sophisticated financial products have sprung up that conform to at least some interpretations of sharia (Islamic law). On October 20, the Bahrain Monetary Agency announced that Citi Islamic Bank and its American Parent, Citigroup, would arrange a $250 million Islamic bond issue, its first to be offered to investors outside the Gulf. Sharia Funds, another American outfit, is working with Islamic scholars on the first hedge funds compliant with the Koran, to be launched by December. HSBC is set to offer Islamic insurance products in Britain next year.

Western institutions' keenness is easily understood: Although the size of the market is hard to assess, most estimates say that the assets of those who might invest in Islamic financial products amount to around $250 billion. The difficulty is that Islamic finance is inseparable from sharia and must therefore follow different rules from those underpinning conventional financial products.

Broadly, three sharia rules set Islamic finance apart. First and most straightforward is a bar on involvement with industries considered sinful, such as gambling, alcohol, and pig meat. Second is a strict ban on *riba*, loosely translated as interest. Third is an injunction to avoid *gharar* — roughly, excessive risk-taking and uncertainty. So such standard products as interest-earning savings account are not allowed. Nor might insur-ance be, on a strict reading, because of uncertainty over whether and how much policies will pay out, and because premiums might be invested unacceptably.

Most Islamic credit transactions are constructed on a notion of partnerships in which risk and profit are shared. For instance, depositors in "investment accounts" in Islamic banks earn a profit share on their deposits, rather than interest. Instead of providing a loan for a car or a washing machine, a supplier of finance will buy the product on a customer's behalf and then sell it on to him at a profit. Islamic mortgages consist of similar, if more complicated, transactions with built-in mark-ups that are considered to be rent, not interest. Often, the profit margins on all these transactions are based on market interest rates.

These practices, though widespread, are controversial. Much more so are recent innovations such as Islamic hedge funds, which are devising trading techniques based on controversial interpretations of sharia. The growing use of structured finance to insulate Muslim investors from interesting-bearing debt transactions is also drawing criticism from some scholars. There may be a backlash. Mr. El-Gamal points out that Malaysia, which has a fairly sophisticated Islam money market, has become more conservative recently, owing to the rejection by the Arab world and Pakistan of this type of trading.

Source: Abstracted from "Finance and Economics: West Meets East; Islamic Finance," *The Economist*. October 25, 2003, vol. 369, no. 8347, p. 93.

repaid; bankers are not by nature entrepreneurs and do not enjoy entrepreneurial returns from project finance.

Four basic properties are critical to the success of project financing.

1. **Separability of the project from its investors.** The project is established as an individual legal entity, separate from the legal and financial responsibilities of its individual investors. This not only protects the assets of equity investors; it provides a controlled platform upon which creditors can evaluate the risks associated with the singular project. The ability of the project's cash flows to service all the debt itself assures that the debt service payments will be automatically allocated by and from the project itself (and not from a decision by management within an MNE).

2. **Long-lived and capital-intensive singular projects.** Not only must the individual project be separable and large in proportion to the financial resources of its owners, its business line must be singular in its construction, operation, and size (capacity). The size is set at inception and is seldom, if ever, changed over the project's life.

3. **Cash flow predictability from third-party commitments.** An oil field or electric power plant produces a homogeneous commodity product that can yield predictable cash flows if third-party commitments to take or pay can be established.

Nonfinancial costs of production need to be controlled over time, usually through long-term supplier contracts with price adjustment clauses based on inflation. The predictability of net cash inflows to long-term contracts eliminates much of the individual project's business risk, allowing the financial structure to be heavily debt-financed and still safe from financial distress.

The predictability of the project's revenue stream is essential in securing project financing. Typical contract provisions intended to ensure adequate cash flow normally include the following clauses: quantity and quality of the project's output; a pricing formula that enhances the predictability of adequate margin to cover operating costs and debt service payments, and a clear statement of the circumstances that permit significant changes in the contract, such as *force majeure* or adverse business conditions.

4. **Finite projects with finite lives.** Even with a longer-term investment, it is critical that the project have a definite ending point at which all debt and equity have been repaid. Because the project is a standalone investment whose cash flows go directly to the servicing of its capital structure, and not to reinvestment for growth or other investment alternatives, investors of all kinds need assurances that the project's returns will be attained in a finite period. There is no capital appreciation, but only cash flow.

Examples of project finance include some of the largest individual investments undertaken in the past three decades, such as British Petroleum's financing of its interest in the North Sea and the Trans-Alaska Pipeline. The Trans-Alaska Pipeline was a joint venture between Standard Oil of Ohio, Atlantic Richfield, Exxon, British Petroleum, Mobil Oil, Philips Petroleum, Union Oil, and Amerada Hess. Each of these projects cost $1 billion or more and represented capital expenditures that no single firm would or could attempt to finance. Yet, through a joint venture arrangement, the higher-than-normal risk absorbed by the capital employed could be managed.

## MINI-CASE

# Tirstrup BioMechanics (Denmark): Raising Dollar Debt

*The objects of a financier are, then, to secure an ample revenue; to impose it with judgment and equality; to employ it economically; and, when necessity obliges him to make use of credit, to secure its foundations in that instance, and for ever, by the clearness and candor of his proceedings, the exactness of his calculations, and the solidity of his funds.*

Edmund Burke (1729–1797)

Although it was still August, Julie Harbjerg bent over against the first chill of autumn and hurried up Copenhagen's Strøget — the historic cobblestoned pedestrian street that begins at the City Hall and extends through the heart of the old city. She tried to keep her mind clear so that she could properly evaluate the various financing proposals that had been discussed in previous weeks with the many bankers who had visited Copenhagen. As assistant treasurer (international) for Tirstrup BioMechanics of Denmark, Julie was responsible for the initial assessment of financing proposals for Tirstrup's international investments.

In 2003 the Tirstrup Group's products encompassed a full array of electromechanical medical devices. The product line included cardiac rhythm devices, pacing systems, and implantable defibrillators. A major corporate objective was to reduce Tirstrup's dependency on cardiac products. In 2003 60% of its estimated US$2.1 billion sales (kr6.6044/$) were outside Denmark, although 85% of the Group's $2.4 billion in assets remained in the country.

Tirstrup was considering an acquisition of $410 million in the United States, and Julie Harbjerg was responsible for constructing a financing package. Tirstrup had roughly

$30 million in cash on hand, and the seller had offered to carry a note for $75 million of the total. The note would be for five years at 7.50% per annum. Julie's boss, Knut Wicksell, director of finance, felt that funding should be such that repayment was deferred for at least seven years. Since Tirstrup had been burned during the last rise in short-term rates, it was generally understood that management's goal was to increase the proportion of fixed-rate debt. Julie had already been told by Wicksell that any equity issuance was out of the question.

Back in the office, Julie looked at the three U.S. dollar choices that she had previously considered and double-checked her all-in-cost (AIC) calculations again (see Exhibit 1).

- **Eurodollar bond.** Probably the most obvious choice to finance a U.S. acquisition was a Eurodollar bond. The bankers felt that Tirstrup's name was sufficiently well known in Europe that it could float a $100 million dollar Eurobond at a fixed rate of 5.60% (12-year maturity). Fees would probably total 2%.
- **Private placement in the United States.** Several bankers had recommended a private placement of debt with an institutional investor in the United States. Nordeabank felt that their New York specialists could

place as much as $200 million of Tirstrup's paper in this manner. The immediate cost would be about 5.3%, a little bit higher than a public issue in the United States (a *Yankee bond*), but the fees were significantly lower — about 7/8% of the principal.

- **Yankee bond.** As noted, Tirstrup could issue a bond in the United States. The problem was that the company currently had no real operations in the United States and had very little name recognition as a borrower. Bankers expected the company to pay about 5.75% for a seven-year issuance, with an additional 1.5% in up-front fees.

In addition to the dollar-denominated issuances, Julie was also considering two nondollar-denominated issuances, one euro and one Danish kroner.

- **€-denominated Eurobond.** Dresdner Bank (Germany) had recommended a euro-denominated Eurobond for €100 million, $112 million at that day's exchange rate of $1.1160/€. The amount would be higher if the euro strengthened, as many economists expected would happen soon. Tirstrup would have to pay 4.80%, probably about 5.0% all-in for seven-year euro funds after the 2% fees were paid
- **Danish kroner bond.** Tirstrup's primary Copenhagen bank assured her that they could float an issue of

## EXHIBIT 1

The All-in-Cost of the Debt Financing Alternatives

|  | Private Placement | US$ Eurobond | Yankee Bond | Euro-Eurobond | Danish Kroner |
|---|---|---|---|---|---|
| Principal (millions) | $200.000 | $100,000 | $100.000 | € 100.000 | kr 650.000 |
| Maturity (years) | 10 | 12 | 7 | 7 | 7 |
| Fixed Rate (per annum) | 6.500% | 5.600% | 5.750% | 4.800% | 4.650% |
| Fees (of principal) | 0.875% | 2.000% | 1.500% | 2.000% | 1.500% |
| Year | Cash Flows | Cash Flows | Cash Flows | Cash Flows | Cash Flows |
| 0 | $198.250 | $98.000 | $98.500 | € 98.000 | kr 640.250 |
| 1 | ($11.000) | ($5.600) | ($5.750) | – € 4.800 | (kr 30.225) |
| 2 | ($11.000) | ($5.600) | ($5.750) | – € 4.800 | (kr 30.225) |
| 3 | ($11.000) | ($5.600) | ($5.750) | – € 4.800 | (kr 30.225) |
| 4 | ($11.000) | ($5.600) | ($5.750) | – € 4.800 | (kr 30.225) |
| 5 | ($11.000) | ($5.600) | ($5.750) | – € 4.800 | (kr 30.225) |
| 6 | ($11.000) | ($5.600) | ($5.750) | – € 4.800 | (kr 30.225) |
| 7 | ($11.000) | ($5.600) | ($105.750) | – € 104.800 | (kr 680.225) |
| 8 | ($11.000) | ($5.600) | | | |
| 9 | ($11.000) | ($5.600) | | | |
| 10 | ($211.000) | ($5.600) | | | |
| 11 | | ($5.600) | | | |
| 12 | | ($105.600) | | | |
| All-in-cost (AIC) | 5.617% | 5.836% | 6.019% | 5.147% | 4.908% |

Note: All-in-cost is calculated as the internal rate of return of the complete series of cash flows associated with the issuance, including proceeds net of fees and complete repayment of principal and interest.

kr650 million (approximately $98.4 million at the current spot rate of kr6.6044/$). The issue would be limited to about seven years, and her bankers assured her that the fees would be "as low as 1.5%."

Julie began to organize her thoughts — and her spreadsheets. She wanted to be able to recommend a package of financing that would meet the company's needs and minimize cost and risk. She then began to sketch out a funding matrix which would combine all elements in one form — one which would focus, after all fees and spreads, on the all-in-cost of capital (AIC). Exhibit 1 summarizes her calculations.

## Case Questions

1. Which of the many debt characteristics — currency, maturity, cost, fixed versus floating rate — do you believe are of the highest priority for Julie and Tirstrup?
2. Does the currency of denomination depend on the currency of the parent or the currency of the business unit which will be responsible for servicing the debt?
3. Exhibit 1 is Julie's spreadsheet analysis of what she considers relevant choices. Using these, what would you recommend as a financing package?

## Summary of Learning Objectives

*Extend the theory of optimal financial structure to the multinational enterprise (MNE)*

- The domestic theory of optimal financial structures needs to be modified by four variables in order to accommodate the case of the MNE. These variables are (1) the availability of capital, (2) diversification of cash flows, (3) foreign exchange risk, and (4) the expectations of international portfolio investors.

- A multinational firm's marginal cost of capital is constant for considerable ranges of its capital budget. This statement is not true for most small domestic firms because they do not have access to the national equity or debt markets.

- By diversifying cash flows internationally, the MNE may be able to achieve the kind of reduction in cash flow variability that portfolio investors receive from diversifying their security holdings internationally.

- When a firm issues foreign currency denominated debt, its effective cost equals the after-tax cost of repaying the principal and interest in terms of the firm's own currency. This amount includes the nominal cost of principal and interest in foreign currency terms, adjusted for any foreign exchange gains or losses.

- Therefore, regardless of other factors, if a firm wants to raise capital in global markets, it must adopt global norms that are close to the U.S. and U.K. norms. Debt ratios up to 60% appear to be acceptable. Any higher debt ratio is more difficult to sell to international portfolio investors.

*Analyze the factors that, in practice, determine the financial structure of foreign subsidiaries within the context of the MNE*

- A compromise position between minimizing the global cost of capital and conforming to local capital norms (localization) is possible when determining the financial structure of a foreign subsidiary. Both multinational and domestic firms should try to minimize their overall weighted average cost of capital for a given level of business risk and capital budget, as finance theory suggests.

- The debt ratio of a foreign subsidiary is in reality only cosmetic, because lenders ultimately look to the parent and its consolidated worldwide cash flow as the source of repayment. In many cases debt of subsidiaries must be guaranteed by the parent firm.

*Evaluate the various internal and external sources of funds available for the financing of foreign subsidiaries*

- The international debt markets offer the borrower a variety of different maturities, repayment structures, and currencies of denomination. The markets and their many different instruments vary by source of funding, pricing structure, maturity, and subordination or linkage to other debt and equity instruments.

- The three major sources of debt funding on the international markets are *international bank loans and syndicated credits*, the *Euronote market*, and the *international bond market*.

*Identify the relevant characteristics of different international debt instruments in financing both the MNE itself and its various foreign subsidiary components*

- Eurocurrency markets serve two valuable purposes: (1) Eurocurrency deposits are an efficient and convenient money market device for holding excess corporate liquidity and (2) the Eurocurrency market is a major source of short-term bank loans to finance corporate working capital needs, including the financing of imports and exports.

- Three original factors in the evolution of the Eurobond markets are still of importance: absence of regulatory interference, less stringent disclosure practices, and favorable tax treatment.

*Apply the strategies of project financing to the funding of large global projects with unique characteristics*

- Project finance is used widely today in the development of large-scale infrastructure projects in many emerging markets. Although each individual project has unique characteristics, most are highly leveraged transactions, with debt making up more than 60% of the total financing. Equity is a small component of project financing for two reasons: first, the scale of the investment project often prevents a single investor or even a collection of private investors from being able to fund it; second, many of these projects are of a kind traditionally funded by governments — such as electrical power generation, dam building, highway construction, and energy exploration, production, and distribution.

## QUESTIONS

1. **Objective.** What, in simple wording, is the objective sought by finding an optimal capital structure?

2. **Varying debt proportions.** As debt in a firm's capital structure is increased from no debt to a significant proportion of debt (say, 60%), what tends to happen to the cost of debt, to the cost of equity, and to the overall weighted average cost of capital?

3. **Availability of capital.** How does the availability of capital influence the theory of optimal capital structure for a multinational enterprise?

4. **Diversified cash flows.** If a multinational firm is able to diversify its sources of cash inflow so as to receive those flows from several countries and in several currencies, do you think that tends to increase or decrease its weighted average cost of capital?

5. **Ex-post cost of borrowing.** Exhibit 13.2 in the text shows that Deutsche Bank borrowed funds at a nominal cost of 9.59% per annum, but at a later date that debt was selling to yield 7.24%. Near the other extreme, the Kingdom of Thailand borrowed funds at a nominal cost of 8.70% but after the fact found the debt was sold in the market at a yield of 11.87%. What caused the changes, in this case in opposite directions, and what might management do to benefit (as Deutsche Bank did) rather than suffer (as the Kingdom of Thailand did)?

6. **Local norms.** Should foreign subsidiaries of multinational firms conform to the capital structure norms of the host country or to the norms of their parent's country? Discuss.

7. **Argentina.** In January 2002 the government of Argentina broke away from its currency board system that had tied the peso to the U.S. dollar and devalued the peso from APs1.0000/$ to APs1.40000$. This caused some Argentine firms with dollar-denominated debt to go bankrupt. Should a U.S. or European parent in good financial health "rescue" its Argentine subsidiary, which would otherwise go bankrupt because of Argentine political and economic management in the four or five years prior to January 2002? Assume the parent has not entered into a formal agreement to guarantee the debt of its Argentine subsidiary.

8. **Internal financing.** What is the difference between "internal" financing and "external" financing for a subsidiary? List three types of internal financing and three types of external financing available to a foreign subsidiary.

9. **Eurodollars.** Which of the following are Eurodollars and which are not?

   a. A U.S. dollar deposit owned by a German corporation and held in Barclay's Bank in London

   b. A U.S. dollar deposit owned by a German corporation and held in Bank of America's office in London

   c. A U.S. dollar deposit owned by a German corporation and held in Sumitomo Bank in Tokyo

   d. A U.S. dollar deposit owned by a German corporation and held in Citibank in New York

**e.** A U.S. dollar deposit owned by a German corporation and held in the New York branch of Deutsche Bank

**f.** A U.S. dollar deposit owned by a U.S. resident and held in Overseas Banking Corporation in Singapore

**g.** A U.S. dollar deposit owned by a U.S. resident and held in the New York branch of Deutsche Bank

**h.** A deposit of euros in Paribas Bank in Paris

**i.** A deposit of euros in Citibank in New York

**j.** A deposit of Australian dollars in Paribas Bank in Paris

10. **Eurodollar deposits.** Why would anyone, individual or corporation, want to deposit U.S. dollars in a bank outside of the United States when the natural location for such deposits would be a bank within the United States?

11. **Define the following terms:**
    **a.** LIBOR
    **b.** Euro LIBOR
    **c.** Eurocredits
    **d.** Syndicated bank credits

12. **International debt instruments.** Bank borrowing has long been the manner by which corporations and governments borrowed funds for short periods of time. What, then, is the advantage over bank borrowing for each of the following?
    **a.** Syndicated loans
    **b.** Euronotes
    **c.** Euro-Commercial Paper
    **d.** Euro Medium-Term Notes
    **e.** International bonds

13. **Euro versus foreign bonds.** What is the difference between a Eurobond and a foreign bond, and why do two types of international bonds exist?

14. **Separation.** In project financing, the project is a legal entity separate from the corporations that are the equity owners. Why?

15. **Singular project.** In the context of project financing, what is a "long-lived, capital-intensive, singular project"?

16. **Predictability.** Predictability of future cash flows is essential to induce creditors to participate in project financing. How does financial leverage increase the risk in highly leveraged projects, and how do the creators of investments financed by project financing manage to reduce the volatility of future cash flows?

17. **Infinite lives.** Why do projects with infinite lives and grandiose growth projects not appeal to creditors who would engage in project financing, whereas those attributes are normally very desirable in a corporate investment?

18. **Maximizing present value.** Do the equity investors in investments based on project financing seek to maximize the present value of their investment, or are they compensated by some other manner?

## PROBLEMS

1. **Tuba City Manufacturing, Inc.** Tuba City Manufacturing, Inc, a U.S. multinational company, has the following debt components in its consolidated capital section:

| | |
|---|---|
| U.S. dollar-denominated 25-year bonds at 6.00% | $10,000,000 |
| U.S. dollar-denominated 5-year Euronotes at 4.00% | $4,000,000 |
| Euro-denominated 10-year bonds at 5.00% | €6,000,000 |
| Yen-denominated 20-year bonds at 2% | ¥750,000,000 |
| Common stock | $35,000,000 |
| Retained earnings | $15,000,000 |

Tuba City's finance staff estimates their cost of equity to be 20%. Current exchange rates are

| | |
|---|---|
| European euros | $1.24/€ |
| British pounds sterling | $1.86/£ |
| Japanese yen | ¥109/$ |

Income taxes are 30% around the world after allowing for credits. Calculate Tuba City's weighted average cost of capital. Are any assumptions implicit in your calculation?

2. **Pacific Group (USA).** Pacific Group, a private equity firm headquartered out of Houston, Texas, borrows £3,000,000 for one year at 9% interest, and during the year the pound depreciates from $1.86/£ to $1.75/£. What is the dollar cost of this debt?

3. **Hartford Associates (USA).** Hartford Associates, a U.S.–based investment partnership, borrows €80,000,000 at a time when the exchange rate is $1.22/€. The entire principal is to be repaid in three years, and interest is 6% per annum, paid annually in euros. The euro is expected to depreciate vis à vis the dollar at 3% per annum. What is the effective cost of this loan for Hartford?

4. **Quatrefoil Construction Company.** Quatrefoil Construction Company consists of a U.S. parent and wholly owned subsidiaries in Malaysia (Q-Malaysia) and Mexico (Q-Mexico). Selected portions of their nonconsolidated balance sheets, translated into U.S. dollars, are shown below.

*Q-Malaysia (accounts in ringgits)*

| | |
|---|---|
| Long-term debt | RM 11,400,000 |
| Shareholders' equity | RM 15,200,000 |

*Q-Mexico (accounts in pesos)*

| | |
|---|---|
| Long-term debt | Ps 20,000,000 |
| Shareholders' equity | Ps 60,000,000 |

*Quatrefoil Construction Company*

| | |
|---|---|
| Investment in subsidiaries | |
| In Q-Malaysia | $4,000,000 |
| In Q-Mexico | 6,000,000 |

*Nonconsolidated Balance Sheet — Selected Items Only)*

| | |
|---|---|
| Parent long-term debt | $ 12,000,000 |
| Common stock | 5,000,000 |
| Retained earnings | 20,000,000 |

Current exchange rates are

| | |
|---|---|
| Malaysia: | RM3.80/$ |
| Mexico: | Ps 10/$ |

What are the debt and equity proportions in Quatrefoil's consolidated balance sheet?

5. **Grupo Bimbo de Mexico.** Grupo Bimbo, although Mexican by incorporation, evaluates all business results, including financing costs, in U.S. dollars. The company needs to borrow $100,000,000 — or the foreign currency equivalent — for four years. For all issues, interest is payable once per year, at the end of the year. Available alternatives are

   a. Sell Japanese yen bonds at par yielding 3% per annum. The current exchange rate is ¥106/$, and the yen is expected to strengthen against the dollar by 2% per annum.

   b. Sell euro-denominated bonds at par yielding 7% per annum. The current exchange rate is $1.1960/€, and the euro is expected to weaken against the dollar by 2% per annum.

   c. Sell U.S. dollar bonds at par yielding 5% per annum.

   Which course of action do you recommend Grupo Bimbo take and why?

6. **Zermatt Air (Switzerland).** Zermatt Air retains $12 million from tickets sold to U.S. dollar holders, after paying fuel and landing costs associated with its frequent flights between Washington Dulles Airport in the United States and Geneva, Switzerland. These funds are currently deposited in Mid-Manhattan Bank in New York City, where they are earning 5.00% per annum. Docklands Bank in London pays 5.50% interest on Eurodollar deposits, and Zermatt Air decides to move its funds from New York to London.

   a. Show journal entries (debits and credits) on the books of Zermatt Air, Mid-Manhattan Bank, and Docklands Bank to reflect this transfer.

   b. By how much have bank deposits of the U.S. bank changed?

   c. What happens if Docklands Bank invests the dollars in long-term U.S. government bonds?

7. **Gas du Ardennes.** Gas du Ardennes, a European gas company, is borrowing US$800,000,000 via a syndicated Eurocredit for six years at 80 basis points over LIBOR. LIBOR for the loan will be reset every six months. The funds will be provided by a syndicate of eight leading investment bankers, which will charge up-front fees totaling 1.2% of the principal amount. What is the effective interest cost for the first year if LIBOR is 8.00% for the first six months and 7.00% for the second six months?

8. **River Thames Insurance Company.** River Thames Insurance Company plans to sell $1,000,000 of Euro-commercial paper with a 60-day maturity, discounted to yield 6.0% per annum. What will be the immediate proceeds to River Thames Insurance?

9. **Mediterranean Alliance, S.A.** Mediterranean Alliance, S.A., is raising funds via a Euro medium-term note with the following characteristics.

   Coupon rate: 8.00% payable semiannually on June 30 and December 31

   Date of issuance: February 28, 2003

Maturity: August 31, 2005

How much in dollars will Mediterranean Alliance, S.A., receive for each $1,000 note sold?

10. **Yunnan Airlines.** Yunnan Airlines, headquartered in Kunming, China, needs US$5,000,000 for one year to finance working capital. The airline has two alternatives for borrowing:

   **a.** Borrow US$5,000,000 in Eurodollars in London at 9.00% per annum

**b.** Borrow HK$39,000,000 in Hong Kong at 7.00% per annum, and exchange these Hong Kong dollars at the present exchange rate of HK$7.8/US$ for U.S. dollars.

At what ending exchange rate would Yunnan Airlines be indifferent between borrowing U.S. dollars and borrowing Hong Kong dollars?

## Internet Exercises

1. **Sovereign credit ratings criteria.** The evaluation of credit risk and all other relevant risks associated with the multitude of borrowers on world debt markets requires a structured approach to international risk assessment. Check both Standard & Poor's and Moody's criteria described in depth on their Web sites to differentiate the various risks (local currency risk, default risk, currency risk, transfer risk, etc.) with major sovereign ratings worldwide.

   Standard & Poor's
   http://www2.standardandpoors.com/servlet/
   Satellite?pagename=sp/Page/HomePg
   Moody's
   http://www.moodys.com/

2. **Brady bonds and emerging markets.** Emerging markets have repeatedly been beaten down with every major international financial crisis, whether it be the Mexican peso (1994), the Thai baht (1997), the Russian ruble (1998), or the Brazilian real (1999). Use the Web sites listed below to prepare an analysis of why these markets come under such severe pressure when a crisis occurs somewhere else in the world.

   Brady Network
   http://www.bradynet.com/
   Brady Bond Primer
   http://www.emgmkts.com/research/
   bradydef.htm

# Interest Rate and Currency Swaps

## LEARNING OBJECTIVES

Define interest rate risk and demonstrate how can it be managed

Describe interest rate swaps and show how they can be used to manage interest rate risk

Show how interest rate swaps and cross-currency swaps can be used to manage both foreign exchange risk and interest rate risk at the same time

This chapter fine-tunes the analysis of the optimal financial structure for a multinational enterprise (MNE). In Chapter 13 we analyzed the financial structure of MNEs from the perspective of an optimal capital structure — debt versus equity. In this chapter we profile the optimal strategies for managing interest rate and currency risks associated with an MNE's capital structure. Our main tools are interest rate and currency swaps. Moreover, many of the same tools we observed earlier in foreign exchange risk management have parallels in interest rate and currency risk management.

The management of financial risks — exchange rates, interest rates, and commodity prices — is a rapidly expanding area of multinational financial management. All three of these financial prices introduce risk into the cash flows of the firm. The identification, measurement, and management of interest rate risk now receive roughly the same level of attention and effort as foreign exchange risk did just a few years ago.

# Defining Interest Rate Risk

All firms — domestic or multinational, small or large, leveraged or unleveraged — are sensitive to interest rate movements in one way or another. Although a variety of interest rate risks exist in theory and industry, this book focuses on the financial management of the nonfinancial firm. Hence our discussion is limited to the interest rate risks associated with the multinational firm. The interest rate risks of financial firms, such as banks, are not covered here.

The single largest interest rate risk of the nonfinancial firm is debt service. The debt structure of the MNE will possess differing maturities of debt, different interest rate structures (such as fixed versus floating rate), and different currencies of denomination. Interest rates are currency-specific. Each currency has its own interest rate yield curve and credit spreads for borrowers. Therefore, the multicurrency dimension of interest rate risk for the MNE is a serious concern. As illustrated in Exhibit 14.1, even the interest rate calculations vary on occasion across currencies and countries.

The second most prevalent source of interest rate risk for the MNE lies in its holdings of interest-sensitive securities. Unlike debt, which is recorded on the right-hand side of the firm's balance sheet, the marketable securities portfolio of the firm appears on the left-hand side. Marketable securities represent potential earnings or interest

## EXHIBIT 14.1

**International Interest Rate Calculations**

International interest rate calculations differ by the number of days used in the period's calculation and the definition of how many days there are in a year (for financial purposes). The following example highlights how the different methods result in different one-month payments of interest on a $10 million loan, 5.500% per annum interest, for an exact period of 28 days.

|  |  |  | $10 million @ 5.500% per annum | |
| --- | --- | --- | --- | --- |
| **Practice** | **Day Count in Period** | **Days/Year** | **Days Used** | **Interest Payment** |
| International | Exact number of days | 360 | 28 | $42,777.78 |
| British | Exact number of days | 365 | 28 | $42,191.78 |
| Swiss (Eurobond) | Assumed 30 days/month | 360 | 30 | $45,833.33 |

Adapted from "Hedging Instruments for Foreign Exchange, Monday Market, and Precious Metals," Union Bank of Switzerland, pp. 41–42.

inflows to the firm. Ever-increasing competitive pressures have pushed financial managers to tighten their management of both the left and right sides of the firm's balance sheet.

Whether it is on the left or right side, the *reference rate* of interest calculation merits special attention. A *reference rate* — for example, U.S. dollar LIBOR — is the rate of interest used in a standardized quotation, loan agreement, or financial derivative valuation. LIBOR, the London Interbank Offered Rate, is by far the most widely used and quoted, as described in Chapter 2. It is officially defined by the British Bankers Association (BBA). U.S. dollar LIBOR is the mean of 16 multinational banks' interbank offered rates as sampled by the BBA at approximately 11 A.M. London time in London. Similarly, the BBA calculates the Japanese yen LIBOR, euro LIBOR, and other currency LIBOR rates at the same time in London from samples of banks.

The interbank interest rate market is not, however, confined to London. Most major domestic financial centers construct their own interbank offered rates for local loan agreement purposes. These rates include PIBOR (Paris Interbank Offered Rate), MIBOR (Madrid Interbank Offered Rate), SIBOR (Singapore Interbank Offered Rate), and FIBOR (Frankfurt Interbank Offered Rate), to name but a few. Exhibit 14.2 illustrates the close relationship between LIBOR and other short-term interest rates and deposit rates.

### EXHIBIT 14.2

U.S. Dollar-
Denominated
Interest Rates
(February 2004)

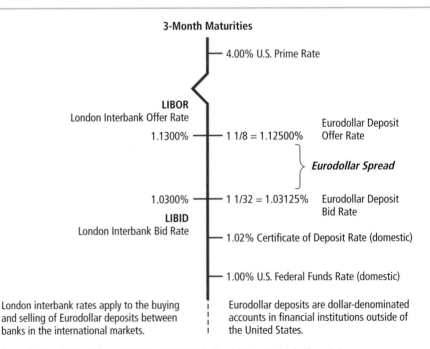

London interbank rates apply to the buying and selling of Eurodollar deposits between banks in the international markets.

Eurodollar deposits are dollar-denominated accounts in financial institutions outside of the United States.

Source: *The Financial Times,* February 10, 2004, p. 27. © 2004 The Financial Times. Reprinted with permission.

# Management of Interest Rate Risk

## THE MANAGEMENT DILEMMA

Before they can manage interest rate risk, treasurers and financial managers of all types must resolve a basic management dilemma: the balance between risk and return. Treasury has traditionally been considered a service center (cost center) and is therefore not expected to take positions that incur risk in the expectation of profit. Treasury activities are rarely managed or evaluated as profit centers. Treasury management practices are therefore predominantly conservative, but opportunities to reduce costs or actually earn profits are not to be ignored. History, however, is littered with examples in which financial managers have strayed from their fiduciary responsibilities in the expectation of profit. Unfortunately, much of the time they have realized only loss. Losses on derivatives by specific companies have already been chronicled in Chapter 7. The many derivative disasters, combined with the wider use of financial derivatives, has helped more and more firms realize the value of well-constructed policy statements such as those in Exhibit 14.3.

Both foreign exchange and interest rate risk management must focus on managing existing or anticipated cash flow exposures of the firm. As in foreign exchange exposure management, the firm cannot undertake informed management or hedging strategies without forming expectations — a *directional* and/or *volatility view* — of interest rate movements. Fortunately, interest rate movements have historically shown more stability and less volatility than exchange rates. Financial management has frequently found it valuable to err on the conservative side, adding to the predictability of commitments and cash flows. This conservativism in turn improves the strategic decision-making capability of the firm. Finally, similar to exchange rate risks, the question still exists as to whether stockholders want management to hedge interest rate risk or prefer to diversify the risk away through their ownership of other securities.

Once management has formed expectations about future interest rate levels and movements, it must choose the appropriate implementation, a path which includes the selective use of various techniques and instruments.

## EXHIBIT 14.3

**Treasury Policy Statements**

The major derivative disasters of the 1990s highlighted the need for the proper construction and implementation of corporate financial management policy statements. Policy statements are, however, frequently misunderstood by those writing and enforcing them. A few helpful fundamentals may be in order.

- *A policy is a rule, not a goal.* A policy is intended to limit or restrict management actions, not set priorities or goals. For example, "Thou shalt not write uncovered options" is a policy. "Management will pursue the lowest cost of capital at all times" is a goal.

- *A policy is intended to restrict some subjective decision-making.* Although at first glance this aspect seems to indicate that management is not to be trusted, it is actually intended to make management's decision-making easier in potentially harmful situations.

- *A policy is intended to establish operating guidelines independently of staff.* Although many policies may appear overly restrictive given the specific talents of financial staff, the fiduciary responsibility of the firm needs to be maintained independently of the specific personnel on-board. Changes in personnel frequently place new managers in uncomfortable and unfamiliar surroundings. Errors in judgment may result. Proper policy construction provides a constructive and protective base for management's learning curve.

## CREDIT RISK AND REPRICING RISK

Prior to describing the management of the most common interest rate pricing risks, it is important to distinguish between credit risk and repricing risk. *Credit risk*, sometimes termed *roll-over risk*, is the possibility that a borrower's creditworth, at the time of renewing a credit, is reclassified by the lender. This can result in changing fees, changing interest rates, altered credit line commitments, or even denial. *Repricing risk* is the risk of changes in interest rates charged (earned) at the time a financial contract's rate is reset.

Consider the following three different debt strategies being considered by a corporate borrower. Each is intended to provide $1 million in financing for a three-year period.

- Strategy 1: Borrow $1 million for three years at a fixed rate of interest.
- Strategy 2: Borrow $1 million for three years at a floating rate, LIBOR + 2%, to be reset annually.
- Strategy 3: Borrow $1 million for one year at a fixed rate, then renew the credit annually.

Although the lowest cost of funds is always a major selection criteria, it is not the only one. If the firm chooses strategy 1, it assures itself of the funding for the full three years at a known interest rate. It has maximized the predictability of cash flows for the debt obligation. What it has sacrificed, to some degree, is the ability to enjoy a lower interest rate in the event that interest rates fall over the period. Of course, it has also eliminated the risk that interest rates could rise over the period, increasing debt servicing costs.

Strategy 2 offers what strategy 1 did not, flexibility (repricing risk). It too assures the firm of full funding for the three-year period. This eliminates credit risk. Repricing risk is, however, alive and well in strategy 2. If LIBOR changes dramatically by the second or third year, the LIBOR rate change is passed through fully to the borrower. The spread, however, remains fixed (reflecting the credit standing that has been locked in for the full three years). Flexibility comes at a cost in this case, the risk that interest rates could go up as well as down.

Strategy 3 offers more flexibility and more risk. First, the firm is borrowing at the shorter end of the yield curve. If the yield curve is positively sloped, as is commonly the case in major industrial markets, the base interest rate should be lower. But the short end of the yield curve is also the more volatile. It responds to short-term events in a much more pronounced fashion than longer-term rates. The strategy also exposes the firm to the possibility that its credit rating may change dramatically by the time for credit renewal, for better or worse. Noting that credit ratings in general are established on the premise that a firm can meet its debt-service obligations under worsening economic conditions, firms that are highly creditworthy (investment rated grades) may view strategy 3 as a more relevant alternative than do firms of lower quality (speculative grades). This is not a strategy for firms that are financially weak.

Although the above example gives only a partial picture of the complexity of funding decisions within the firm, it demonstrates the many ways credit risks and repricing risks are inextricably intertwined. The expression *interest rate exposure* is a complex concept, and the proper measurement of the exposure prior to its management is critical. We now proceed to describe the interest rate risk of the most common form of corporate debt, floating rate loans.

## TRIDENT'S FLOATING RATE LOANS

Floating rate loans are a widely used source of debt for firms worldwide. They are also the source of the single largest and most frequently observed corporate interest rate exposure.

Exhibit 14.4 depicts the costs and cash flows for a three-year floating rate loan taken out by Trident Corporation. The loan of US$10 million will be serviced with annual interest payments and total principal repayment at the end of the three-year period.

- The loan is *priced* at U.S. dollar LIBOR + 1.500% (note that the cost of money, interest, is often referred to as *price*). The LIBOR base will be reset each year on an agreed-upon date (say two days prior to payment). Whereas the LIBOR component is truly floating, the spread of 1.500% is actually a fixed component of the interest payment, which is known with certainty for the life of the loan.
- When the loan is drawn down initially, at year zero, an up-front fee of 1.500% is charged by the lender. This fee results in a reduction in the net proceeds of the loan by US$150,000. Although the loan agreement states the amount as $10,000,000 and Trident is required to repay it in full, the actual net proceeds to the firm are only $9,850,000.
- Trident will not know the actual interest cost of the loan until the loan has been completely repaid. Maria Gonzalez, the CFO of Trident, may forecast what

## EXHIBIT 14.4

Trident Corporation's Costs and Cash Flows in Servicing a Floating Rate Loan

The expected interest rates and cash flows associated with a three-year $10,000,000 floating rate loan. Trident pays an initiation fee of 1.500% of principal up front (which reduces proceeds).

| Loan Interest Rates | Year 0 | Year 1 | Year 2 | Year 3 | |
|---|---|---|---|---|---|
| LIBOR (floating) | 5.000% | 5.000% | 5.000% | 5.000% | |
| Spread (fixed) | | 1.500% | 1.500% | 1.500% | |
| Total interest payable | | 6.500% | 6.500% | 6.500% | |
| **Interest cash flows on loan** | | | | | |
| LIBOR (floating) | | ($500,000) | ($500,000) | ($500,000) | |
| Spread (fixed) | | (150,000) | (150,000) | (150,000) | |
| Total interest | | ($650,000) | ($650,000) | ($650,000) | |
| Loan proceeds (repayment) | $9,850,000 | | | ($10,000,000) | |
| Total loan cash flows | $9,850,000 | ($650,000) | ($650,000) | ($10,650,000) | |
| IRR of total cash flows | 7.072% | | All-in-cost (AIC) | | |
| **Sensitivities to LIBOR** | **LIBOR (yr 0)** | **LIBOR (yr 1)** | **LIBOR (yr 2)** | **LIBOR (yr 3)** | **AIC** |
| Baseline case above | 5.000% | 5.000% | 5.000% | 5.000% | 7.072% |
| LIBOR rises 25 basis points/yr | | 5.250% | 5.500% | 5.750% | 7.565% |
| LIBOR falls 25 basis points/yr | | 4.750% | 4.500% | 4.250% | 6.578% |

Note: The effective cost of funds (before-tax) for Trident, all-in-cost (AIC), is found by determining the internal rate of return (IRR) of the total cash flows associated with the loan. The AIC of the original loan agreement, without fees, is 6.500%.

LIBOR will be for the life of the loan, but she will not know with certainty until all payments have been completed. This uncertainty is not only an interest rate risk, but it is also an actual cash flow risk associated with the interest payment. (A fixed interest rate loan has *interest rate risk*, in this case opportunity cost, which does not put actual cash flows at risk.)

Exhibit 14.4 illustrates the *all-in-costs* (AIC) of the loan under a number of different sensitivities. The AIC is found by calculating the internal rate of return (IRR) of the total cash flows for repayment. The baseline analysis assumes that LIBOR remains at 5.000% for the life of the loan. Including the up-front fees, the AIC to Trident is 7.072% (or 6.500% flat without fees). If, however, LIBOR were to rise steadily over the three-year period by 25 basis points (0.25%) per year, the AIC of the loan would rise to 7.565%. If LIBOR were to fall by the same 25 basis points per year, the AIC would fall to 6.578%. We must remember, however, that only the LIBOR component of the loan price creates cash flow risk.

If Trident Corporation decided, after it had taken out the loan, that it wished to manage the interest rate risk associated with the loan agreement, it would have a number of management alternatives:

- **Refinancing.** Trident could go back to its lender and restructure and refinance the entire agreement. This is not always possible and it is often expensive.
- **Forward rate agreements (FRAs).** Trident could lock in the future interest rate payments with FRAs, much the same way that exchange rates are locked in with forward contracts.
- **Interest rate futures.** Although companies rarely use foreign currency futures for foreign exchange risk management, interest rate futures have gained substantially more acceptance. Trident could lock in the future interest rate payments by taking an interest rate futures position.
- **Interest rate swaps.** Trident could enter into an additional agreement with a bank or swap dealer in which it exchanged cash flows in such a way that the interest rate payments on the floating rate loan would become fixed.

## FORWARD RATE AGREEMENTS

A *forward rate agreement* (FRA) is an interbank-traded contract to buy or sell interest rate payments on a notional principal. These contracts are settled in cash. The buyer of an FRA obtains the right to lock in an interest rate for a desired term that begins at a future date. The contract specifies that the seller of the FRA will pay the buyer the increased interest expense on a nominal sum (the notional principal) of money if interest rates rise above the agreed rate, but the buyer will pay the seller the differential interest expense if interest rates fall below the agreed rate. Maturities available are typically 1, 3, 6, 9, and 12 months, much like traditional forward contracts for currencies.

For example, Trident may decide that it wishes to lock in the first interest payment (due at the end of the year 1), so it buys an FRA that locks in a total interest payment of 6.500%. If LIBOR rises above 5.000% by the end of year 1, Trident would receive a cash payment from the FRA seller that would reduce the interest rate to 5.000%. Similarly, if LIBOR were to fall during year 1 to below 5.000% (not what Maria Gonzalez expects to happen), Trident would make a cash payment to the seller of the FRA, effectively raising its LIBOR payment to 5.000% and the total loan interest to 6.500%.

Like foreign currency forward contracts, FRAs are useful on individual exposures. They are contractual commitments of the firm that allow little flexibility to enjoy favorable movements, such as when LIBOR is falling as was just described. Firms also use FRAs if they plan to invest in securities at future dates but fear that interest rates might fall prior to the investment date. Because of the limited maturities and currencies available, however, FRAs are not widely used outside the largest industrial economies and currencies.

## INTEREST RATE FUTURES

Unlike foreign currency futures, *interest rate futures* are relatively widely used by financial managers and treasurers of nonfinancial companies. Their popularity stems from the relatively high liquidity of the interest rate futures markets, their simplicity of use, and the rather standardized interest rate exposures most firms possess. The two most widely used futures contracts are the Eurodollar futures traded on the Chicago Mercantile Exchange (CME) and the U.S. Treasury Bond Futures of the Chicago Board of Trade (CBOT). Interestingly, the third-largest volume of a traded futures contract in the latter 1990s was the U.S. dollar/Brazilian real currency futures contract traded on the Bolsa de Mercadorias y Futuros in Brazil.

To illustrate the use of futures for managing interest rate risks we will focus on the three-month Eurodollar futures contracts. Exhibit 14.5 presents Eurodollar futures for two years (they actually trade 10 years into the future).

The yield of a futures contract is calculated from the *settlement price*, which is the closing price for that trading day. For example, a financial manager examining the Eurodollar quotes in Exhibit 14.5 for a March 2003 contract would see that the *settlement price* on the previous day was 94.76, an annual yield of 5.24%:

$$\text{Yield} = (100.00 - 94.76) = 5.24\%$$

Since each contract is for a three-month period (quarter) and a notional principal of $1 million, each basis point is actually worth $2,500 (.01 × $1,000,000 × 90/360).

If Maria Gonzalez were interested in hedging a floating rate interest payment due in March 2003, she would need to *sell a future,* to take a *short position.* This strategy is referred to as a short position because Maria is selling something she does not own (as in shorting common stock). If interest rates rise by March — as Maria fears — the

**EXHIBIT 14.5**

Eurodollar Futures Prices

| Maturity | Open | High | Low | Settle | Yield | Open Interest |
|---|---|---|---|---|---|---|
| June 02 | 94.99 | 95.01 | 94.98 | 95.01 | 4.99 | 455,763 |
| Sept | 94.87 | 94.97 | 94.87 | 94.96 | 5.04 | 535,932 |
| Dec | 94.60 | 94.70 | 94.60 | 94.68 | 5.32 | 367,036 |
| Mar 03 | 94.67 | 94.77 | 94.66 | 94.76 | 5.24 | 299,993 |
| June | 94.55 | 94.68 | 94.54 | 94.63 | 5.37 | 208,949 |
| Sept | 94.43 | 94.54 | 94.43 | 94.53 | 5.47 | 168,961 |
| Dec | 94.27 | 94.38 | 94.27 | 94.36 | 5.64 | 130,824 |

Typical presentation by *The Wall Street Journal.* Only regular quarterly maturities shown. All contracts are for $1 million; points of 100%. Open interest is number of contracts outstanding.

futures price will fall and she will be able to close the position at a profit. This profit will roughly offset the losses associated with rising interest payments on her debt. If she is wrong, however, and interest rates actually fall by the maturity date, causing the futures price to rise, Maria will suffer a loss that will wipe out the "savings" derived by making a lower floating rate interest payment than she expected. So by selling the March 2003 futures contract, she will be locking in an interest rate of 5.24%.

Obviously interest rate futures positions could be — and are on a regular basis — purchased purely for speculative purposes. Although that is not the focus of the managerial context here, the example shows how any speculator with a directional view on interest rates could take positions in expectations of profit.

As mentioned previously, the most common interest rate exposure of the nonfinancial firm is interest payable on debt. Such exposure is not, however, the only interest rate risk. As more and more firms aggressively manage their entire balance sheet, the interest earnings from the left-hand side are under increasing scrutiny. If financial managers are expected to earn higher interest on interest-bearing securities, they may well find a second use of the interest rate futures market: to lock in future interest earnings. Exhibit 14.6 provides an overview of these two basic interest rate exposures and the strategies needed to manage interest rate futures.

## INTEREST RATE SWAPS

Swaps are contractual agreements to exchange or *swap* a series of cash flows. These cash flows are most commonly the interest payments associated with debt service, such as the floating rate loan described above.

- If the agreement is for one party to swap its fixed interest rate payment for the floating interest rate payments of another, it is termed an *interest rate swap*.
- If the agreement is to swap currencies of debt service obligation — for example, Swiss franc interest payments in exchange for U.S. dollar interest payments — it is termed a *currency swap*.
- A single swap may combine elements of both interest rate and currency swaps.

In any case, however, the swap serves to alter the firm's cash flow obligations, as in changing floating rate payments into fixed rate payments associated with an existing debt obligation. The swap itself is not a source of capital, but rather an alteration of the

**EXHIBIT 14.6**

Interest Rate Futures Strategies for Common Exposures

| Exposure | Futures Action | Interest Rates | Position Outcome |
|---|---|---|---|
| Paying interest on future date | Sell a future (short position) | If rates go up | Futures price falls; short earns a profit |
| | | If rates go down | Futures price rises; short earns a loss |
| Earning interest on future date | Buy a future (long position) | If rates go up | Futures price falls; long earns a loss |
| | | If rates go down | Futures price rises; long earns a profit |

cash flows associated with payment. What is often termed the *plain vanilla swap* is an agreement between two parties to exchange fixed rate for floating rate financial obligations. This type of swap forms the largest single financial derivative market in the world.

The two parties may have various motivations for entering into the agreement. For example, a very common position is as follows. A corporate borrower of good credit standing has existing floating rate debt service payments. The borrower, after reviewing current market conditions and forming expectations about the future, may conclude that interest rates are about to rise. In order to protect the firm against rising debt-service payments, the company's treasury may enter into a swap agreement to *pay fixed/receive floating*. This means the firm will now make fixed rate interest payments and receive from the swap counterparty floating rate interest payments. The floating rate payments that the firm receives are used to service the debt obligation of the firm, so the firm, on a net basis, is now making fixed rate interest payments. Using derivatives it has synthetically changed floating rate debt into fixed rate debt. It has done so without going through the costs and intricacies of refinancing existing debt obligations.

Similarly, a firm with fixed rate debt that expects interest rates to fall can change fixed rate debt to floating rate debt. In this case, the firm would enter into a *pay floating/receive fixed* interest rate swap. Exhibit 14.7 presents a summary table of the recommended interest rate swap strategies for firms holding either fixed rate debt or floating rate debt.

The cash flows of an interest rate swap are interest rates applied to a set amount of capital (*notional principal*). For this reason they are also referred to as *coupon swaps*. Firms entering into interest rate swaps set the notional principal so that the cash flows resulting from the interest rate swap cover their interest rate management needs.

Interest rate swaps are contractual commitments between a firm and a swap dealer and are completely independent of the interest rate exposure of the firm. That is, the firm may enter into a swap for any reason it sees fit and then swap a notional principal that is less than, equal to, or even greater than the total position being managed. For example, a firm with a variety of floating rate loans on its books may enter into interest rate swaps for only 70% of the existing principal, if it wishes.

The reason for entering into a swap, and the swap position the firm enters into, is purely at management's discretion. It should also be noted that the interest rate swap market is filling a gap in market efficiency. If all firms had free and equal access to capital markets, regardless of interest rate structure or currency of denomination, the swap market would most likely not exist. The fact that the swap market not only exists but flourishes and provides benefits to all parties is in some ways the proverbial "free lunch," due to comparative advantage.

**EXHIBIT 14.7**

Interest Rate Swap Strategies

| Position | Expectation | Interest Rate Swap Strategy |
|----------|-------------|------------------------------|
| Fixed rate debt | Rates to go up | Do nothing |
| | Rates to go down | Pay floating/Receive fixed |
| Floating rate debt | Rates to go up | Pay fixed/Receive floating |
| | Rates to go down | Do nothing |

## COMPARATIVE ADVANTAGE

Companies of different credit quality are treated differently by the capital markets. For example, Unilever (U.K.) and Xerox (U.S.) are both in the market for $30 million of debt for a five-year period. Unilever has a AAA credit rating (the highest) and therefore has access to both fixed and floating rate interest debt at attractive rates. Unilever would prefer to borrow at floating rates, since it already has fixed rate funds and wishes to increase the proportion of its debt portfolio which is floating. Xerox has a BBB credit rating (the lowest major category of investment-grade debt ratings) and would prefer to raise the debt at fixed rates of interest. Although Xerox has access to both fixed rate and floating rate funds, the fixed rate debt is considered expensive. The firms, through Citibank, could actually borrow in their relatively advantaged markets and then swap their debt service payments. This is illustrated in Exhibit 14.8.

## IMPLEMENTATION OF THE INTEREST RATE SWAP

Each company first borrows in the market in which it has relative comparative advantage. As illustrated in Exhibit 14.8, Unilever can borrow fixed rate funds 1.000% cheaper than Xerox (7.000% as opposed to 8.000%), and can borrow floating rate funds $1/2$% cheaper ($1/4$% relative to Xerox's $3/4$%). This means that Unilever's *relative comparative advantage* is to borrow fixed rate funds, and therefore Xerox should borrow floating rate funds.

1. Unilever borrows at the fixed rate of 7.000% per annum, and then enters into a *receive fixed pay floating* interest rate swap with Citibank. The bank then agrees to make the debt service payments of 7.000% on behalf of Unilever for the life of the swap agreement (five years).

2. Unilever agrees in turn to pay Citibank a floating rate of interest, one-year LIBOR, enabling it to make debt service payments on a floating rate basis, which it prefers. The interest rate it negotiates with Citibank is lower than the rate it could have acquired on its own.

**EXHIBIT 14.8**

Comparative Advantage and Structuring a Swap Agreement

Rates available to Unilever
Borrow fixed: 7.000%
Borrow floating: LIBOR + $1/4$%

Rates available to Xerox
Borrow fixed: 8.000%
Borrow floating: LIBOR + $3/4$%

3. Xerox borrows at the floating rate of LIBOR + ³/₄%, and then swaps the payments with Citibank. Citibank agrees to service the floating rate debt payments on behalf of Xerox.

4. Xerox agrees in turn to pay Citibank a fixed rate of interest, 7.875%, enabling Xerox to make fixed rate debt service payments — which it prefers — but at a lower cost of funds than it could have acquired on its own.

## BENEFITS OF THE INTEREST RATE SWAP

Unilever borrowed funds at 7.000% fixed rate. It has now entered into a swap agreement in which it will pay floating, LIBOR + 0%, in return for Citibank making its 7.000% interest payments on its debt. Unilever then has the following combined interest payments:

| | | |
|---|---|---|
| Unilever borrows at fixed rates: | (7.000%) | |
| Swaps *fixed for floating* rates: | + 7.000% | Receives fixed |
| | (LIBOR) | Pays floating |
| Net interest (debt + swap) | (LIBOR) | |

Xerox borrowed funds at LIBOR + ³/₄%, a floating rate of interest. It has now entered into a swap agreement to swap *floating for fixed*, meaning that it will receive a floating rate of LIBOR + ¹/₄% and pay a fixed rate of interest, 7.875%.

| | | |
|---|---|---|
| Xerox borrows at floating rates: | (LIBOR + ³/₄%) | |
| Swaps *floating for fixed* rates: | + LIBOR + ³/₄% | Receives floating |
| | (7.875%) | Pays fixed |
| Net interest (debt + swap) | (7.875%) | |

Each of the borrowers benefits from the interest rate swap by being able to borrow capital in the preferred interest rate structure and at a lower rate than obtainable on their own.

| | *Unilever (U.K.)* | *Xerox (U.S.)* |
|---|---|---|
| If borrowing directly | LIBOR + ¹/₄ % | 8.000% |
| If borrowing through swap | LIBOR + 0% | 7.875% |
| Savings | + ¹/₄% | + 0.125% |

How is this possible? Each benefits as a result of the specialization of each borrower acquiring funds in their market of preferred access, and then exchanging interest payment streams, redistributing the benefits of specialization. However, pitfalls do exist. Even sophisticated financial executives can misunderstand the risks involved in more complex interest swaps as illustrated by *Real World Example 14.1*, which describes failed proprietary swap agreements between Procter & Gamble and Bankers Trust.

## Trident Corporation: Swapping to Fixed Rates

Trident Corporation's existing floating rate loan is now the source of some concern to Maria Gonzalez. Recent events have led her to believe that interest rates, specifically LIBOR, may be rising in the three years ahead. Because the loan agreement is relatively new (Trident is still in the first year of the loan and has yet to make an interest payment), refinancing is considered too expensive at this point. Maria believes that a *pay fixed/receive floating* interest rate swap may be the better alternative for fixing future interest rates now. Upon contacting several of its primary banks, Trident is

## Real World Example 14.1
### CAVEAT EMPTOR, PROCTER & GAMBLE'S SWAPS

Procter & Gamble (U.S.) is an extremely large and sophisticated multinational firm, with operations in over 100 countries. In 1993 P&G had a number of interest rate swap agreements maturing with Bankers Trust (U.S.), and wished to replace them. Bankers Trust, knowing its client's appetite for risk, suggested and sold to P&G a number of *proprietary* swap agreements.

But P&G did not understand the formula or how it was to be applied. It turned out that the proprietary swap formulas were extremely sensitive to interest rate increases. Each 1% increase in the Treasury yield increased P&G's payment by more than 17% of the swap's notional principal per year.

P&G lost over $163 million in 1993 (before tax) on swap agreements with Bankers Trust by the time the agreements were closed. The losses were a direct result of the over 2% increase in Treasury rates in the spring of 1993 and the proprietary pricing mechanisms of the agreements. It seems that buying financial derivatives is like buying any product: *caveat emptor* (buyer beware) still applies.

quoted a fixed rate of 5.750% against LIBOR. If Trident enters into the swap agreement, for the next three years it will receive LIBOR and pay out 5.750% on a notional principal of $10 million. A quick analysis of the combined existing loan and pay fixed/receive floating swap undertaken by Trident's treasury group is presented in Exhibit 14.9.

The swap agreement does not replace the existing loan agreement; it supplements it. Trident is still responsible for making all payments on the floating rate loan. Note that the swap agreement applies only to the interest payments on the loan and does not include the principal repayment. The portion of the debt service payment that Trident is concerned about — the LIBOR base rate — would now be offset by the

## EXHIBIT 14.9

Trident Corporation's Interest Rate Swap to Pay Fixed/Receive Floating

| Loan Interest Rates | Variability | Year 1 | Year 2 | Year 3 |
|---|---|---|---|---|
| LIBOR (floating) | Could go up or down | − 5.000% | − 5.000% | − 5.000% |
| Spread (fixed) | Fixed | − 1.500% | − 1.500% | − 1.500% |
| Total interest payable | | − 6.500% | − 6.500% | − 6.500% |
| **Swap Interest Rates** | | | | |
| Pay fixed | Fixed | − 5.750% | − 5.750% | − 5.750% |
| Receive floating LIBOR | Could go up or down | + 5.000% | + 5.000% | + 5.000% |
| **Combined Loan and Swap Position** | | | | |
| LIBOR on loan | Paying | − 5.000% | − 5.000% | − 5.000% |
| Spread (fixed) | Paying | − 1.500% | − 1.500% | − 1.500% |
| Pay fixed on swap | Paying | − 5.750% | − 5.750% | − 5.750% |
| Receive floating LIBOR on swap | Receiving | + 5.000% | + 5.000% | + 5.000% |
| Net interest due after swap | Net payment | − 7.250% | − 7.250% | − 7.250% |

Note: On the date the interest rate swap agreement is made the actual LIBOR rates for all years (1, 2, and 3), are unknown. However, on the basis of the expectations of swap traders, the present value of the floating rate cash flow streams and fixed rate cash flow streams are equal on the agreement date.

receipt of a cash flow of LIBOR from the swap bank. This arrangement leaves Trident responsible for payment of the 1.500% fixed spread on the loan plus the fixed payment to the swap bank of 5.750%. These payments combine to create a total fixed interest rate payment of 7.250% on the $10 million debt, as illustrated in Exhibit 14.9.

The question that remains for Maria Gonzalez is whether this is a good deal. Trident now has a fixed rate debt of $10 million for three years. If current market rates quoted to Trident by its lenders are at fixed rates above 7.250%, the answer is *yes*. Trident would be well advised to secure the swap agreement now, assuming its goal is to lock in fixed rates of interest for the coming three years.

## Currency Swaps

Since all swap rates are derived from the yield curve in each major currency, the fixed to floating rate interest rate swap existing in each currency allows firms to swap across currencies. Exhibit 14.10 lists typical swap rates for the euro, the U.S. dollar, the Japanese yen, and the Swiss franc. These swap rates are based on the government security yields in each of the individual currency markets, plus a credit spread applicable to investment grade borrowers in the respective markets.

Note that the swap rates in Exhibit 14.10 are not rated or categorized by credit ratings. This is so because the swap market itself does not carry the credit risk associated with individual borrowers. We saw that in the previous interest rate swap example

### EXHIBIT 14.10

Interest Rate and Currency Swap Quotes

| Years | Euro-€ Bid | Euro-€ Ask | Swiss franc Bid | Swiss franc Ask | U.S. dollar Bid | U.S. dollar Ask | Japanese yen Bid | Japanese yen Ask |
|---|---|---|---|---|---|---|---|---|
| 1 | 2.99 | 3.02 | 1.43 | 1.47 | 5.24 | 5.26 | 0.23 | 0.26 |
| 2 | 3.08 | 3.12 | 1.68 | 1.76 | 5.43 | 5.46 | 0.36 | 0.39 |
| 3 | 3.24 | 3.28 | 1.93 | 2.01 | 5.56 | 5.59 | 0.56 | 0.59 |
| 4 | 3.44 | 3.48 | 2.15 | 2.23 | 5.65 | 5.68 | 0.82 | 0.85 |
| 5 | 3.63 | 3.67 | 2.35 | 2.43 | 5.73 | 5.76 | 1.09 | 1.12 |
| 6 | 3.83 | 3.87 | 2.54 | 2.62 | 5.80 | 5.83 | 1.33 | 1.36 |
| 7 | 4.01 | 4.05 | 2.73 | 2.81 | 5.86 | 5.89 | 1.55 | 1.58 |
| 8 | 4.18 | 4.22 | 2.91 | 2.99 | 5.92 | 5.95 | 1.75 | 1.78 |
| 9 | 4.32 | 4.36 | 3.08 | 3.16 | 5.96 | 5.99 | 1.90 | 1.93 |
| 10 | 4.42 | 4.46 | 3.22 | 3.30 | 6.01 | 6.04 | 2.04 | 2.07 |
| 12 | 4.58 | 4.62 | 3.45 | 3.55 | 6.10 | 6.13 | 2.28 | 2.32 |
| 15 | 4.78 | 4.82 | 3.71 | 3.81 | 6.20 | 6.23 | 2.51 | 2.56 |
| 20 | 5.00 | 5.04 | 3.96 | 4.06 | 6.29 | 6.32 | 2.71 | 2.76 |
| 25 | 5.13 | 5.17 | 4.07 | 4.17 | 6.29 | 6.32 | 2.77 | 2.82 |
| 30 | 5.19 | 5.23 | 4.16 | 4.26 | 6.28 | 6.31 | 2.82 | 2.88 |
| LIBOR | 3.0313 | 3.0938 | 1.3125 | 1.4375 | 4.9375 | 5.0625 | 0.1250 | 0.2188 |

Typical presentation by *The Financial Times*. Bid and ask spreads as of close of London business. US$ is quoted against three-month LIBOR; Japanese yen against six-month LIBOR; Euro and Swiss franc against six-month LIBOR.

when Trident, which borrowed on its own at LIBOR plus a spread of 1.500% (the spread representing the credit spread specific to the borrower), swapped out of the LIBOR component only. The fixed spread, a credit risk premium, was still borne by the firm itself. For example, lower-rated firms may pay spreads of 3% or 4% over LIBOR, while some of the world's largest and most financially sound MNEs may actually raise capital at rates of LIBOR –0.40%. The swap market does not differentiate the rate by the participant; all swap at fixed rates versus LIBOR in the respective currency.

The usual motivation for a currency swap is to replace cash flows scheduled in an undesired currency with flows in a desired currency. The desired currency is probably the currency in which the firm's future operating revenues (inflows) will be generated. Firms often raise capital in currencies in which they do not possess significant revenues or other natural cash flows. The reason they do so is cost; specific firms may find capital costs in specific currencies attractively priced to them under special conditions. Having raised the capital, however, the firm may wish to swap its repayment into a currency in which it has future operating revenues.

The utility of the currency swap market to an MNE and government institutions is significant. An MNE wishing to swap a 10-year fixed 6.04% U.S. dollar cash flow stream could swap to 4.46% fixed in euro, 3.30% fixed in Swiss francs, or 2.07% fixed in Japanese yen. It could swap from fixed dollars not only to fixed rates, but also to floating LIBOR rates in the various currencies as well. All are possible at the rates quoted in Exhibit 14.10.

*Real World Example 14.2* illustrates how a government, Ecuador, utilized currency swaps to help its development.

## Trident Corporation: Swapping Floating Dollars into Fixed Rate Swiss Francs

We return to Trident Corporation to demonstrate how to use a currency swap. After raising $10 million in floating rate financing, and subsequently swapping into fixed rate payments, Trident decides that it would prefer to make its debt service payments in Swiss francs. Trident had recently signed a sales contract with a Swiss buyer that will be paying francs to Trident over the next three-year period. This would be a natural inflow of Swiss francs for the coming three years, and Trident may decide it wishes to match the currency of denomination of the cash flows through a currency swap.

Trident Corporation now enters into a three-year *pay Swiss francs and receive U.S. dollars* currency swap. Both interest rates are fixed. Trident will pay 2.01% (ask rate) fixed Swiss franc interest, and receive 5.56% (bid rate) fixed U.S. dollars.

As illustrated in Exhibit 14.11, the three-year currency swap entered into by Trident is different from the plain vanilla interest rate swap described above in two important ways:

1. The spot exchange rate in effect on the date of the agreement establishes what the notional principal is in the target currency. The target currency is the currency Trident is swapping into, in this case the Swiss franc. The $10,000,000 notional principal converts to a Sfr15,000,000 notional principal. This is the principal used to establish the actual cash flows Trident is committing to making (2.01% × Sfr15,000,000 = Sfr301,500).

2. The notional principal itself is part of the swap agreement. In the interest rate swaps described previously, both interest payment cash flows were based on the

same U.S. dollar notional principal. Hence, there was no need to include the principal in the agreement. In a currency swap, however, because the notional principals are denominated in two different currencies, and the exchange rate between those two currencies may change over the life of the swap, the notional principals are actually part of the swap agreement.

## Real World Example 14.2
### ECUADORIAN DEBT-FOR-DEVELOPMENT

In the early 1990s several countries introduced unique programs that used some of the basic concepts of cross-currency swaps to both reduce their existing foreign currency debts and promote internal development programs. These countries had borrowed large quantities of U.S. dollar denominated debt in the prior decade, and were now attempting to find ways this debt could be reduced.

Ecuador introduced a Debt-for-Development Program in 1990. This program allowed foreign not-for-profit institutions like universities to exchange their U.S. dollars for local currency denominated debt — Ecuadorian sucre bonds in this case. The dollars received from the universities would then be used to pay off the outstanding debt. The universities would then sell the local currency bonds for cash. The cash was then used to run student study programs in Ecuador. The cash could not, however, be exchanged in the currency markets for dollars or any other currency, since this would cause additional downward pressures on the value of the sucre, which Ecuador was trying to avoid.

The mechanics of the swap program were not, however, without risk. For example, Harvard University actually purchased the Ecuadorian debt from banks in New York City. It was able to buy these at a discounted rate, say $0.20 per $1.00 of face value debt. (The discount was the result of Ecuador's difficulty in paying off the debt, which was only expected to worsen.) This discounted price then allowed Harvard to effectively "multiply" its financial resources by a factor of 5 (1/.2). Harvard would then present the bonds to the Ecuadorian government in Quito, where the authorities would exchange the dollar bonds for sucre bonds. Harvard then immediately sold the bonds on the open market for cash. The cash received was substantially larger than what Harvard could have obtained by simply exchanging U.S. dollars for Ecuadorian sucre in the foreign exchange market.

Other countries introduced similar programs for the same reasons during this time. Costa Rica introduced a debt-for-environment program in which Costa Rican foreign currency debt could be exchanged for local currency resources that could be expended only for environmental projects within Costa Rica. Chile had a number of debt-for-equity swap programs in which debt holders (e.g., major banks around the world) could exchange their bonds, which were in default, for equity shares in Chilean corporations.

## EXHIBIT 14.11

Trident Corporation's Currency Swap: Pay Swiss Francs and Receive U.S. Dollars

| Swap component | Year 0 | Year 1 | Year 2 | Year 3 |
|---|---|---|---|---|
| Trident will receive fixed US$ at this rate: | | 5.56% | 5.56% | 5.56% |
| On a notional principal of: | $10,000,000 | | | |
| Cash flows Trident will receive: | | $556,000 | $556,000 | $10,556,000 |
| Exchange rate | Sfr.1.5000/$ | | | |
| Trident will pay fixed Sfr at rate: | | 2.01% | 2.01% | 2.01% |
| On a notional principal of: | Sfr15,000,000 | | | |
| Cash flows Trident will pay: | | Sfr301,500 | Sfr301,500 | Sfr15,301,500 |

The pay fixed US$ rate of 5.56% is the three-year bid rate in Exhibit 14.10. The receive fixed Swiss franc rate of 2.01% is the three-year ask rate from Exhibit 14.10. Once Trident Corporation determines the notional principal of $10,000,000, the current spot rate is used to determine the notional principal for the Swiss franc side of the swap (or vice versa depending on Trident's goals). The present value of each side of the swap at inception is $10,000,000 (Sfr15,000,000).

At the time of the swap's inception, both positions have the same net present value. Trident's swap commits it to three future cash payments in Swiss francs. In turn it will receive three payments in U.S. dollars. The payments are set. Financial accounting practices will require Trident to regularly track and value its position, *mark-to-market* the swap, on the basis of current exchange rates and interest rates. If after the swap is initiated the Swiss franc appreciates versus the dollar, and Trident is paying francs, Trident will record a loss on the swap for accounting purposes. (Similarly, the swap dealer's side of the transaction will record a gain.) At the same time, if interest rates in Swiss franc markets rise, and Trident's swap commits it to a fixed rate of 2.01%, then a gain will result from the interest component of the swap's value. In short, gains and losses on the swap, at least for accounting purposes, will persist throughout the swap's life.

The currency swaps described here are nonamortizing swaps. A *nonamortizing swap* repays the entire principal at maturity, rather than over the life of the swap agreement. Swap dealers will of course be more than happy to provide the firm with the form of its choice. We use nonamortizing swap examples throughout this chapter for simplicity of presentation.

## TRIDENT CORPORATION: UNWINDING SWAPS

As with all original loan agreements, it may happen that at some future date the partners to a swap may wish to terminate the agreement before it matures. If, for example, after one year Trident Corporation's Swiss sales contract is terminated, Trident will no longer need the swap as part of its hedging program. Trident could terminate or *unwind* the swap with the swap dealer.

Unwinding a currency swap requires the discounting of the remaining cash flows under the swap agreement at current interest rates, then converting the target currency (Swiss francs here) back to the home currency of the firm (U.S. dollars for Trident). If Trident has two payments remaining on the swap agreement of Sfr301,500 and Sfr15,301,500 (an interest-only payment, and a principal and interest payment), and the two-year fixed rate of interest for francs is now 2.000%, the present value of Trident's commitment in Swiss francs is

$$PV(Sfr) = \frac{Sfr\,301{,}500}{(1.020)^1} + \frac{Sfr15{,}301{,}500}{(1.020)^2} = Sfr15{,}002{,}912$$

At the same time, the present value of the remaining cash flows on the dollar side of the swap is determined using the current two-year fixed dollar interest rate, which is now 5.500%:

$$PV(\$) = \frac{\$556{,}000}{(1.055)^1} + \frac{\$10{,}556{,}000}{(1.055)^2} = \$10{,}011{,}078$$

Trident's currency swap, if unwound at this time, would yield a present value of net inflows (what it receives under the swap) of $10,011,078 and a present value of outflows (what it pays under the swap) of Sfr15,002,912. If the spot exchange rate is now Sfr1.4650/$, the net settlement of this currency swap will be

$$Settlement = \$10{,}011{,}078 = \frac{Sfr15{,}002{,}912}{Sfr1.4650/\$} = (\$229{,}818)$$

Trident makes a cash payment to the swap dealer of $229,818 to terminate the swap. Trident lost on the swap, largely as a result of the appreciation of the Swiss franc (the interest rates barely changed). Since Trident had promised to pay in the currency which is now stronger in value — the franc — unwinding the swap is costly. The swap, however, was entered into as a hedge rather than as a financial investment.

## Counterparty Risk

*Counterparty risk* is the potential exposure any individual firm bears that the second party to any financial contract will be unable to fulfill its obligations under the contract's specifications. Concern over counterparty risk has risen in the interest rate and currency swap markets as a result of a few large and well-publicized swap defaults. The rapid growth in the currency and interest rate financial derivatives markets has actually been accompanied by a surprisingly low default rate to date, particularly in a global market that is, in principle, unregulated.

Counterparty risk has long been one of the major factors that favor the use of exchange-traded rather than over-the-counter derivatives. Most exchanges, like the Philadelphia Stock Exchange for currency options or the Chicago Mercantile Exchange for Eurodollar futures, are themselves the counterparty to all transactions. This allows all firms a high degree of confidence that they can buy or sell exchange-traded products quickly, and with little concern over the credit quality of the exchange itself. Financial exchanges typically require a small fee of all traders on the exchanges, to fund insurance funds created expressly for the purpose of protecting all parties. Over-the-counter products, however, are direct credit exposures to the firm because the contract is generally between the buying firm and the selling financial institution. Most financial derivatives in today's world financial centers are sold or brokered only by the largest and soundest financial institutions. This structure does not mean, however, that firms can enter continuing agreements with these institutions without some degree of real financial risk and concern.

A firm entering into a currency or interest rate swap agreement retains ultimate responsibility for the timely servicing of its own debt obligations. Although a swap agreement may constitute a contract to exchange U.S. dollar payments for euro payments, the firm that actually holds the dollar debt is still legally responsible for payment. The original debt remains on the borrower's books. In the event a swap counterparty does not make the payment as agreed, the firm legally holding the debt is still responsible for debt service. In the event of such a failure, the euro payments would be stopped, by the right of *offset*, and the losses associated with the failed swap would be mitigated.

The real exposure of an interest or currency swap is not the total notional principal, but the mark-to-market values of differentials in interest or currency interest payments (replacement cost) since the inception of the swap agreement. This differential is similar to the change in swap value discovered by unwinding a swap. This amount is typically only 2% to 3% of the notional principal.

## Illustrative Case: A Three-Way Back-to-Back Cross-Currency Swap

Individual firms often find special demands for their debt in select markets, allowing them to raise capital at several basis points lower there than in other markets. Thus a growing number of firms are confronted with debt service in currencies that are not

A Three-Way
Back-to-Back
Cross-Currency
Swap

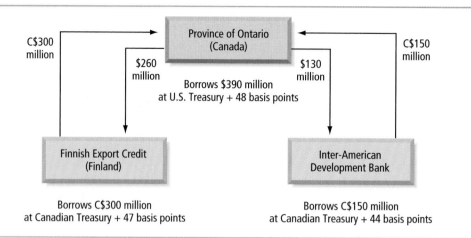

normal for their operations. The result has been a use of debt issuances coupled with swap agreements from inception. The three-way borrowing plus swap structure depicted in Exhibit 14.12 between a Canadian province, a Finnish export agency, and a multilateral development bank is a case in point.

The Finnish Export Credit agency (FEC), the Province of Ontario, Canada, and the Inter-American Development Bank all possessed ready access to particular sources of capital but wished debt service in another. The investment banking house of Goldman Sachs as matchmaker brought all parties together and aided in the negotiation of both borrowing rates and swap rates.

- FEC had not raised capital in the Canadian dollar Euromarkets before this and would be well received if borrowing there. FEC, however, had a need for increased debt service payments in U.S. dollars at this time, not Canadian dollars.
- Province of Ontario (Canada) needed Canadian dollars, but due to the size of the provincial borrowings in the recent past, it knew that further issues would push up the cost of funds. The province was, however, considered an attractive credit risk by the U.S. dollar market.
- Inter-American Development Bank (IADB), like FEC, had a need for additional U.S. dollar-denominated debt service. It had already raised the majority of its capital in the dollar markets, but it was a welcome newcomer to the Canadian dollar market.

Each borrower determined its initial debt amounts and maturities expressly with the needs of the currency swap in mind. Then, in conjunction with Goldman Sachs, each negotiated the best pricing for its individual debt commitments. Simultaneous with debt issuance and placement, the three parties swapped the proceeds and debt service payment streams for their desired debt profiles. Each party was therefore able to issue debt in the market in which its debt would be well received (thus at lower cost) and then swap into the desired currency. All parties borrowed where they had a comparative advantage and then swapped into their desired currency at a lower all-in-cost than they could have achieved by direct debt issuance in that currency.

MINI-CASE

# McDonald's Corporation's British Pound Exposure

McDonald's Corporation has investments in over 100 countries. It considers its equity investment in foreign subsidiaries to be at risk, subject to hedging depending on the individual country, currency, and market.

## British Subsidiary as an Exposure

McDonald's parent company has three different pound-denominated exposures arising from ownership and operation of its British subsidiary.

- First, the British subsidiary has equity capital, which is a pound-denominated asset of the parent company.
- Second, in addition to the equity capital invested in the British subsidiary, the parent company provides intra-company debt in the form of a four-year £125 million loan. The loan is denominated in British pounds and carries a fixed 5.30% per annum interest payment.
- Third, the British subsidiary pays a fixed percentage of gross sales in royalties to the parent company. This too is pound-denominated. The three different exposures sum to a significant exposure problem for McDonald's.

An additional technical detail further complicates the situation. When the parent company makes an intracompany loan to the British subsidiary, it must designate — according to U.S. accounting and tax law practices — whether the loan is considered to be *permanently invested* in that country. (Although on the surface it seems illogical to consider four years "permanent," the parent company could continually roll the loan over and never actually repay it.) If it is not considered permanent, the foreign exchange gains and losses related to the loan flow directly to the parent company's profit and loss statement, according to FAS#52. If, however, the loan is designated as permanent, the foreign exchange gains and losses related to the intracompany loan flow only to the cumulative translation adjustment (CTA) on the consolidated balance sheet. To date, McDonald's has chosen to designate the loan as *permanent*. The functional currency of the British subsidiary for consolidation purposes is the local currency, the British pound.

Anka Gopi is both Manager for Financial Markets/Treasury and a McDonald's shareholder. She is currently reviewing the existing hedging strategy employed by McDonald's against the pound exposure. The company has been hedging the pound exposure by entering into a cross-currency U.S. dollar/British pound sterling swap. The current swap is a seven-year swap to receive dollars and pay pounds. Like all cross-currency swaps, the agreement requires McDonald's-U.S. to make regular pound-denominated interest payments and a bullet principal repayment (notional principal) at the end of the swap agreement. McDonald's considers the large notional principal payment a hedge against the equity investment in its British subsidiary.

According to FAS#52, a company may elect to take the interest associated with a foreign currency denominated loan and carry that directly to the parent company's P&L. This has been done in the past, and McDonald's has benefitted from the inclusion of this interest payment.

FAS#133, *Accounting for Derivative Instruments and Hedging Activities*, issued in June 1998, was originally intended to be effective for all fiscal quarters within fiscal years beginning after June 15, 1999 (for most firms this meant January 1, 2000). The new standard, however, was so complex and potentially of such material influence to U.S.–based MNEs that the Financial Accounting Standards Board has been approached by dozens of major firms and asked to postpone mandatory implementation. The standard's complexity, combined with the workloads associated with Y2K (year 2000) risk controls, persuaded the Financial Accounting Standards Board to delay FAS#133's mandatory implementation date indefinitely.

Anka Gopi wishes to consider the potential impact of FAS#133 on the hedging strategy currently employed. Under FAS#133, the firm will have to mark-to-market the entire cross-currency swap position, including principal, and carry this to *other comprehensive income* (OCI). OCI, however, is actually a form of income required under U.S. GAAP and reported in the footnotes to the financial statements, but not the income measure used in reported earnings per share. Although McDonald's has been carrying the interest payments on the swap to income, it has not previously had to carry the present value of the swap principal to OCI. In Anka's eyes, this poses a substantial material risk to OCI.

Anka Gopi also wishes to reconsider the current strategy. She begins by listing the pros and cons of the current strategy, comparing these to alternative strategies, and then deciding what if anything should be done about it at this time.

## Case Questions

1. How does the cross-currency swap effectively hedge the three primary exposures McDonald's has relative to its British subsidiary?
2. How does the cross-currency swap hedge the long-term equity exposure in the foreign subsidiary?
3. Should Anka — and McDonald's — worry about OCI?

## Summary of Learning Objectives

*Define interest rate risk and demonstrate how can it be managed*

- The single largest interest rate risk of the nonfinancial firm is debt service. The debt structure of the MNE will possess differing maturities of debt, different interest rate structures (such as fixed versus floating rate), and different currencies of denomination.

- The increasing volatility of world interest rates, combined with the increasing use of short-term and variable-rate debt by firms worldwide, has led many firms to actively manage their *interest rate risks*.

- The primary sources of interest rate risk to a multinational nonfinancial firm are short-term borrowing and investing, as well as long-term sources of debt.

- The techniques and instruments used in interest rate risk management in many ways resemble those used in currency risk management: the tried and true methods of lending and borrowing.

- The primary instruments and techniques used for interest rate risk management include forward rate agreements (FRAs), interest rate futures, and interest rate swaps.

*Describe interest rate swaps and show how they can be used to manage interest rate risk*

- The interest rate and currency swap markets allow firms that have limited access to specific currencies and interest rate structures to gain access at relatively low costs. This in turn allows these firms to manage their currency and interest rate risks more effectively.

*Show how interest rate swaps and cross-currency swaps can be used to manage both foreign exchange risk and interest rate risk at the same time*

- A cross-currency interest rate swap allows a firm to alter both the currency of denomination of cash flows in debt service and the fixed-to-floating or floating-to-fixed interest rate structure.

## QUESTIONS

1. **Triumvirate of risks.** Define and explain the three main financial risks facing a multinational enterprise.

2. **Reference rates.** What is an interest reference rate and how is it used to set rates for individual borrowers?

3. **Risk and return.** Some corporate treasury departments are organized as service centers (cost centers), while others are set up as profit centers. What is the difference and what are the implications for the firm?

4. **Forecast types.** What is the difference between a specific forecast and a directional forecast?

5. **Policy statements.** Explain the difference between a goal statement and a policy statement.

6. **Credit and repricing risk.** From the point of view of a borrowing corporation, what are credit and repricing risks? Explain steps a company might take to minimize both.

7. **Forward rate agreement.** How can a business firm that has borrowed on a floating rate basis use a forward rate agreement to reduce interest rate risk?

8. **Eurodollar futures.** The newspaper reports that a given June Eurodollar future settled at 93.55. What was the annual yield?

9. **Defaulting on an interest rate swap.** Smith Company and Jones Company enter into an interest rate swap, with Smith paying fixed interest to Jones, and Jones paying floating interest to Smith. Smith now goes bankrupt and so defaults on its remaining interest payments. What is the financial damage to Jones Company?

10. **Currency swaps.** Why would one company with interest payments due in pounds sterling want to swap those payments for interest payments due in U.S. dollars?

11. **Counterparty risk.** How does organized exchange trading in swaps remove any risk that the counterparty in a swap agreement will not complete the agreement?

## PROBLEMS

1. **Cisneros, S.A.** Cisneros S.A., a Venezuelan company, wishes to borrow $5,000,000 for eight weeks. A rate of 4.00% per annum is quoted by potential lenders in New York, Great Britain, and Switzerland using, respectively, international, British, and the Swiss-Eurobond definitions of interest (day count conventions). From which source should Cisneros borrow?

2. **Rankine Corporation.** Rankine Corporation of Australia seeks to borrow US$30,000,000 in the Eurodollar market. Funding is needed for two years. Investigation leads to three possibilities:

   - Rankine Corporation could borrow the US$30,000,000 for two years at a fixed 5% rate of interest.

   - Rankine Corporation could borrow the US$30,000,000 at LIBOR + 1.5%. LIBOR is currently 3.5%, and the rate would be reset every six months.

   - Rankine Corporation could borrow the US$30,000,000 for one year only at 4.5%. At the end of the first year Rankine Corporation would have to negotiate for a new one-year loan.

   Compare the alternatives and make a recommendation.

3. **Raid Gauloises.** Raid Gauloises is a rapidly growing French sporting goods and adventure racing outfitter. The company has decided to borrow €20,000,000 via a Euroeuro floating rate loan for four years. Raid must decide between two competing loan offerings from two of its banks.

   Banque de Paris has offered the four-year debt at euro LIBOR + 2.00% with an up-front initiation fee of 1.8%. Banque de Sorbonne, however, has offered euro LIBOR + 2.5%, a higher spread, but with no loan initiation fees up front, for the same term and principal. Both banks reset the interest rate at the end of each year.

   Euro LIBOR is currently 4.00%. Raid's economist forecasts that LIBOR will rise by 0.5% each year. Banque de Sorbonne, however, officially forecasts euro LIBOR to begin trending upward at the rate of 0.25% per year. Raid Gauloises's cost of capital is 11%. Which loan proposal do you recommend for Raid Gauloises?

4. **Felini Motors.** Felini Motors of Italy recently took out a four-year €5 million loan on a floating rate basis. It is now worried, however, about rising interest costs. Although it had initially believed interest rates in the euro zone would be trending downward, recent economic indicators show growing inflationary pressures. Analysts are predicting that the European Central Bank will slow monetary growth, driving interest rates up.

   Felini is now considering whether to seek some protection against a rise in euro LIBOR, and is considering a forward rate agreement (FRA) with an insurance company. According to the agreement Felini would pay to the insurance company at the end of each year the difference between its initial interest cost at LIBOR + 2.50% (6.50%) and any fall in interest cost due to a fall in LIBOR. Conversely, the insurance company would pay to Felini 70% of the difference between Felini's initial interest cost and any increase in interest costs caused by a rise in LIBOR.

   Purchase of the floating rate agreement will cost $100,000, paid at the time of the initial loan. What are Felini's annual financing costs now if LIBOR rises? If LIBOR falls? Felini uses 12% as its weighted average cost of capital. Do you recommend that Felini purchase the FRA?

5. **John Jones.** John Jones must pay floating rate interest three months from now. He wants to lock in these interest payments by buying an interest rate futures contract. Interest rate futures for three months from now settled at 93.07, for a yield of 6.93% per annum. If the floating interest rate three months from now is 6.00%, what did John Jones gain or lose? If it is 8.00% what did John Jones gain or lose?

6. **Cañon Candy Company.** Mary Martin, the treasurer of Cañon Candy Company believes interest rates are going to rise, so she wants to swap her future floating rate interest payments for fixed rates. At present she is paying LIBOR + 2% per annum on $5,000,000 of debt for the next two years, with payments due semiannually. LIBOR is currently 4.00% per annum. Ms. Martin has just made an interest payment, so the next payment is due six months from today.

   Ms. Martin finds that she can swap her current floating rate payments for fixed payments of

7.00% per annum. (Cañon Candy's weighted average cost of capital is 12%, which Ms. Martin calculates to be 6% per six-month period, compounded semiannually.)

**a.** If LIBOR rises at the rate of 50 basis points per six-month period, starting tomorrow, how much does Ms. Martin save or cost her company by making this swap?

**b.** If LIBOR falls at the rate of 25 basis points per six-month period, starting tomorrow, how much does Ms. Martin save or cost her company by making this swap?

7. **Xavier and Zulu.** Xavier Manufacturing and Zulu Products each seek funding at the lowest possible cost. Xavier would prefer the flexibility of floating rate borrowing, while Zulu wants the security of fixed rate borrowing. Xavier is the more creditworthy company. They face the following rate structure. Xavier, with the better credit rating, has lower borrowing costs in both types of borrowing:

|  | Xavier | Zulu |
|---|---|---|
| Credit rating | AAA | BBB |
| Fixed rate cost of borrowing | 8% | 12% |
| Floating rate cost of borrowing | LIBOR + 1% | LIBOR + 2% |

Xavier wants floating rate debt, so it could borrow at LIBOR + 1%. However, it could borrow fixed at 8% and swap for floating rate debt. Zulu wants fixed rate, so it could borrow fixed at 12%. However, it could borrow floating at LIBOR + 2% and swap for fixed rate debt. What should each company do?

8. **Trident's Cross-Currency Swap: Sfr for US$.** Trident entered into a three-year cross-currency interest rate swap, described in the chapter, to receive U.S. dollars and pay Swiss francs. Trident, however, decided to unwind the swap after one year, thereby having two years left on the settlement costs of unwinding the swap after one year. Repeat the calculations for unwinding, but assume that the following rates now apply:

| | |
|---|---|
| Two-year Swiss franc interest rate | 5.20% per annum |
| Two-year U.S. dollar interest rate | 2.20% per annum |
| Spot exchange rate | SF1.5560/$ |

9. **Trident's Cross-Currency Swap: Yen for Euros.** Using the same table of swap rates (Exhibit 14.10), assume Trident enters into a swap agreement to receive euros and pay Japanese yen, on a notional principal of €5,000,000. The spot exchange rate at the time of the swap is ¥104/€.

**a.** Calculate all principal and interest payments, in both euros and yen, for the life of the swap agreement. (Use Exhibit 14.11 as a guide.)

**b.** Assume that one year into the swap agreement Trident decides it wishes to unwind the swap agreement and settle it in euros. Assuming that a two-year fixed rate of interest on the Japanese yen is now 0.80%, and a two-year fixed rate of interest on the euro is now 3.60%, and the spot rate of exchange is now ¥114/€, what is the net present value of the swap agreement? Who pays whom what?

10. **Delphi.** Delphi is the U.S.-based automotive parts supplier which was spun off from General Motors in 2000. With annual sales of over $26 billion, the company has expanded its markets far beyond the traditional automobile manufacturers in the pursuit of a more diversified sales base. As part of the general diversification effort, the company wishes to diversify the currency of denomination of its debt portfolio as well. Assume Delphi enters into a $50 million seven-year cross-currency interest rate swap to do just that — pay euros and receive dollars. Using the data in Exhibit 14.12:

**a.** Calculate all principal and interest payments in both currencies for the life of the swap.

**b.** Assume that three years later Delphi decides to unwind the swap agreement. If four-year fixed rates of interest in euros have now risen to 5.35% and four-year fixed rate dollars have fallen to 4.40%, and the current spot exchange rate is $1.02/€, what is the net present value of the swap agreement? Who pays who what?

**Internet Exercises**

1. **Current interest rates and yield curves.** Use the New York Federal Reserve Bank's Web site to find recent interest rates on all maturities of U.S. dollar-denominated debt issues. Historical data is also available so that it is relatively easy to plot how the Treasury's Constant Maturity yields have changed from week to week and month to month for maturities varying between three months and 10 years.

    Federal Reserve Bank of New York
    http://www.ny.frb.org/
    Board of Governors of the Federal Reserve
    http://www.federalreserve.gov/releases

2. **The International Swaps and Derivatives Association (ISDA).** The ISDA is the primary global organization that attempts to both standardize the use of interest rate and cross-currency swaps and track the market's size. Use ISDA's Web site to find out which type of interest rate derivative is growing the fastest.

    International Swaps and Derivatives Association
    http://www.isda.org

3. **Emerging markets and debt.** The emerging markets of Latin America, Eastern Europe, Africa, and Asia are where many firms are now expanding operations and therefore creating new demands for debt. Use the following Web sites to learn more about the instruments and markets of many emerging markets, including the most recent quotes on Brady Bonds, one of the most widely traded emerging market debt instruments in the world.

    Emerging Markets Companion
    http://www.emgmkts.com/
    J.P. Morgan Chase
    http://www.jpmorgan.com/

# Foreign Investment Decisions

Part 5 analyzes how a firm transitions from the international trade stage to become a full-blown multinational firm. At this point, you have completed the prerequisite steps to acquire enough knowledge about international operations before diving in. In Part 1 you learned to understand the global financial environment in which all firms live. In Part 2 you studied how foreign exchange rates are determined and how foreign exchange markets and instruments function. In Part 3 you discovered how to measure and manage foreign exchange exposure. In Part 4 you analyzed why a firm needs to gain a global cost and availability of capital if it is to compete successfully both in its domestic and international markets. Now it is time to take the next step.

**CHAPTER 15** shows how an MNE and an international portfolio investor can reduce their risk through international diversification. Since an MNE needs to attract and retain international portfolio investors in order to gain its global cost and availability of capital, risk reduction through international diversification is important to both parties. Because the theory of international portfolio diversification has a much-studied theoretical and empirical base, we use it as the basis for understanding the benefits of diversification, both for MNEs and for investors. Although we build on domestic portfolio theory, we need to add the foreign exchange risk introduced by holding foreign currency-denominated securities in the portfolio.

**CHAPTER 16** analyzes the theory and strategy that leads a firm to foreign direct investment. You will learn how the *theory of comparative advantage* is the basis for international trade. However, market imperfections create a rationale for the existence of multinational enterprises. You then learn why firms become multinational, where they choose to locate, and how they determine their modes of foreign involvement.

**CHAPTER 17** shows you how to adjust for political risk in foreign investments. We separate risks into three categories: (1) *firm-specific risks*; (2) *country-specific risks*; and (3) *global-specific risks*. Firm-specific risks include governance risks that stem from goal conflicts with host countries. Country-specific risks stem from host country policies that reduce a firm's ability to transfer freely its funds in and out of the host country. However, country-specific risks also arise from cultural and institutional differences. Global risks arise from terrorism activities, the current antiglobalization movement, environmental concerns, poverty, and cyber attacks.

**CHAPTER 18** introduces the foreign complexities that you must consider when undertaking a capital budgeting analysis of a foreign project. You learn that a foreign project should be analyzed both from the project's own viewpoint and from its parent's viewpoint. An illustrative case, "Cemex Enters Indonesia," illustrates how you should value a foreign project and recognize through sensitivity analysis the various political and foreign exchange risks. The chapter concludes with an introduction to the newly important field of real option analysis.

# International Portfolio Theory and Diversification

## LEARNING OBJECTIVES

Separate total risk of a portfolio into two components, diversifiable and nondiversifiable

Demonstrate how both the diversifiable and non-diversifiable risks of an investor's portfolio may be reduced through international diversification

Explore how foreign exchange risk affects the individual investor investing internationally

Define the optimal domestic portfolio and the optimal international portfolio

Review the recent history of equity market performance globally, including the degree to which the markets are more or less correlated in their movements

Examine the question of whether markets appear to be more or less integrated over time

This chapter explores how application of portfolio theory can reduce risks of asset portfolios held by MNEs, and risks incurred by MNEs in general from internationally diversified activities. In the first part of the chapter we extend portfolio theory from the domestic to the international business environment. Then we show how the risk of a portfolio, whether it be a securities portfolio or the general portfolio of activities of the MNE, is reduced through international diversification. The second part of the chapter details the theory and application of international portfolio theory and presents recent empirical results of the risk-return tradeoffs of internationally diversified portfolios. The third and final section explores international diversification's impact on the cost of capital for the MNE.

## International Diversification and Risk

The case for international diversification of portfolios can be decomposed into two components: the potential risk reduction benefits of holding international securities, and the potential added foreign exchange risk.

### PORTFOLIO RISK REDUCTION

We first focus only on risk. The risk of a portfolio is measured by the ratio of the variance of the portfolio's return relative to the variance of the market return. This is the *beta* of the portfolio. As an investor increases the number of securities in a portfolio, the portfolio's risk declines rapidly at first, then asymptotically approaches the level of *systematic risk* of the market. A fully diversified domestic portfolio would have a beta of 1.0. This is illustrated in Exhibit 15.1.

**EXHIBIT 15.1**

Portfolio Risk Reduction Through Diversification

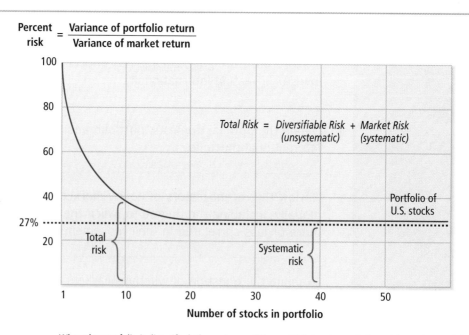

When the portfolio is diversified, the variance of the portfolio's return relative to the variance of the market's return (beta) is reduced to the level of systematic risk — the risk of the market itself.

Exhibit 15.1 illustrates portfolio risk reduction for the U.S. economy. It shows that a fully diversified U.S. portfolio is only about 27% as risky as a typical individual stock. This relationship implies that about 73% of the risk associated with investing in a single stock is diversifiable in a fully diversified U.S. portfolio. Although we can reduce risk substantially through portfolio diversification, it is not possible to eliminate it totally because security returns are affected by a common set of factors — a set we characterize as the market.

The total risk of any portfolio is therefore composed of *systematic risk* (the market) and *unsystematic risk* (the individual securities). Increasing the number of securities in the portfolio reduces the unsystematic risk component leaving the systematic risk component unchanged.

Exhibit 15.2 illustrates the incremental gains of diversifying both domestically and internationally. The lowest line in Exhibit 15.2 (portfolio of international stocks) represents a portfolio in which foreign securities have been added. It has the same overall risk shape as the U.S. stock portfolio, but it has a lower portfolio beta. This means that the international portfolio's market risk is lower than that of a domestic portfolio. This situation arises because the returns on the foreign stocks are closely correlated not with returns on U.S. stocks, but rather with a global beta. We will return to the concept of a global beta in the third section of this chapter.

## FOREIGN EXCHANGE RISK

The foreign exchange risks of a portfolio, whether it be a securities portfolio or the general portfolio of activities of the MNE, are reduced through international diversification. The construction of internationally diversified portfolios is both the same as

**EXHIBIT 15.2**

Portfolio Risk Reduction Through International Diversification

$$\text{Percent risk} = \frac{\text{Variance of portfolio return}}{\text{Variance of market return}}$$

Portfolio of U.S. stocks

Portfolio of international stocks

Number of stocks in portfolio

*When the portfolio is diversified internationally, the portfolio's beta — the level of systematic risk that cannot be diversified away — is lowered.*

and different than creating a traditional domestic portfolio. Internationally diversified portfolios are the same in principle because the investor is attempting to combine assets that are less than perfectly correlated, reducing the total risk of the portfolio. In addition, by adding assets outside the home market — assets that previously were not available to be averaged into the portfolio's expected returns and risks — the investor is tapping into a larger pool of potential investments.

But international portfolio construction is also different in that when the investor acquires assets or securities outside the investor's home-country market, the investor may also be acquiring a foreign currency-denominated asset. This is not always the case. For example, many U.S.–based investors routinely purchase and hold Eurodollar bonds (on the secondary market only; it is illegal during primary issuance), which would not pose currency risk to the U.S.–based investor for they are denominated in the investor's home currency. Thus the investor has actually acquired *two* additional assets — the currency of denomination and the asset subsequently purchased with the currency — one asset in principle, but two in expected returns and risks.

**JAPANESE EQUITY EXAMPLE.**    A numerical example can illustrate the difficulties associated with international portfolio diversification and currency risk. A U.S.-based investor takes US$1,000,000 on January 1, 2002, and invests in a share traded on the Tokyo Stock Exchange (TSE). On January 1, 2002, the spot exchange rate is ¥130.00/$. The US$1 million therefore yields ¥130,000,000. The investor uses ¥130,000,000 to acquire shares on the Tokyo Stock Exchange at ¥20,000 per share, acquiring 6,500 shares, and holds the shares for one year.

At the end of one year the investor sells the 6,500 shares at the market price, which is now ¥25,000 per share; the shares have risen ¥5,000 per share in price. The 6,500 shares at ¥25,000 per share yield proceeds of ¥162,500,000.

The Japanese yen are then changed back into the investor's home currency, the U.S. dollar, at the spot rate of ¥125.00/$ in effect on January 1, 2003. This results in total U.S. dollar proceeds of $1,300,000.00. The total return on the investment is then

$$\frac{US\$1,300,000 - US\$1,000,000}{US\$1,000,000} = 30.00\%$$

The total U.S. dollar return is actually a combination of the return on the Japanese yen (which in this case was positive) and the return on the shares listed on the Tokyo Stock Exchange (which was also positive). This value is expressed by isolating the percentage change in the share price ($r^{shares}$) in combination with the percentage change in the currency value ($r^{¥/\$}$):

$$R^{\$} = \left[\left(1 + r^{¥/\$}\right)\left(1 + r^{shares, ¥}\right)\right] - 1$$

In this case the value of the Japanese yen, in the eyes of a U.S.–based investor, rose 4.00% (from ¥130/$ to ¥125/$), while the shares traded on the Tokyo Stock Exchange rose 25.00%. The total investment return in U.S. dollars is therefore

$$R^{\$} = \left[(1 + .0400)(1 + .2500)\right] - 1 = .3000 \text{ or } 30.00\%$$

Obviously the risk associated with international diversification, when it includes currency risk, is inherently more complex than that of domestic investments. You should also see, however, that the presence of currency risk may alter the correlations associated with securities in different countries and currencies, providing portfolio

## Real World Example 15.1
### SHOULD FUND MANAGERS HEDGE CURRENCY RISK?

The impact of the decline of the euro in 2000 on globally diversified portfolios reawakened the debate among portfolio managers as to whether currency components and their risks within the portfolios should be hedged. The decline of the euro over the year 2000, a drop of 19.6%, severely damaged the returns of many international portfolios.

The major international stock index used by most portfolio managers to benchmark performance is the Morgan Stanley Capital International European, Australian, Far Eastern (EAFE) Index. The EAFE index fell 14.17% in 2000. If the currency component of the index was removed (effectively hedged), the index fell only 4.38%.

For example, the Artisan Fund does not practice currency hedging by principle. It believes that the currency risk component of an international portfolio is part and parcel to the principle of international diversification. The problem, however, is that the fund was exposed to the slide of the euro throughout 2000 and its investors suffered. Fund managers who argue against hedging are quick to point out that many of the world's major currencies experience large swings, frequently moving back in the opposite direction, sometimes quickly, in subsequent periods.

Other funds, like Janus Worldwide, used forward contracts and options to completely hedge their portfolios against currency fluctuations. They argue that removing the currency movements from the portfolio returns allows the fund to focus purely on stock-picking, the traditional competence of the fund manager. For example, Tweedy, Browne Company's Global Fund rose 12.4% in 2000, out-performing 95% of similar international funds sold to U.S.–based investors. According to the fund's manager, currency hedging added approximately 10 percentage points to the performance of the fund.

Still other funds practice selective hedging, removing the risk associated with the currencies which the fund managers and its currency analysts feel are the most at risk in the current period. In the end it is a matter of taste. Similar to the question of whether financial managers should hedge or not hedge their transaction exposures, the debate over hedging currency components of international portfolios will continue.

composition and diversification possibilities that domestic investment and portfolio construction may not. *Real World Example 15.1* details the debate regarding foreign exchange risk.

In conclusion:

- International diversification benefits induce investors to demand foreign securities (the so-called *buy-side*).
- If the addition of a foreign security to the portfolio of the investor aids in the reduction of risk for a given level of return, or if it increases the expected return for a given level of risk, then the security adds value to the portfolio.
- A security that adds value will be demanded by investors. Given the limits of the potential supply of securities, increased demand will bid up the price of that security, resulting in a lower cost of capital for the issuing firm. The firm issuing the security, the *sell-side*, is therefore able to raise capital at a lower cost.

## Internationalizing the Domestic Portfolio

We first review the basic principles of traditional domestic portfolio theory to aid in our identification of the incremental changes introduced through international diversification. We then illustrate how diversifying the portfolio internationally alters the potential set of portfolios available to the investor.

## THE OPTIMAL DOMESTIC PORTFOLIO

Classic portfolio theory assumes a typical investor is risk-averse. This means that an investor is willing to accept some risk but is not willing to bear unnecessary risk. *The typical investor is therefore in search of a portfolio that maximizes expected portfolio return per unit of expected portfolio risk.*

The domestic investor may choose among a set of individual securities in the domestic market. The near infinite set of portfolio combinations of domestic securities form the *domestic portfolio opportunity set* shown in Exhibit 15.3. The set of portfolios formed along the extreme left edge of the domestic portfolio opportunity set is termed the *efficient frontier*. It represents the optimal portfolios of securities that possess the minimum expected risk for each level of expected portfolio return. The portfolio with the minimum risk among all those possible is the *minimum risk domestic portfolio* ($MR_{DP}$).

The individual investor will search out the optimal domestic portfolio (DP) which combines the risk-free asset and a portfolio of domestic securities found on the efficient frontier. He or she begins with the risk-free asset with return of $R_f$ (and zero expected risk), and moves out along the security market line until reaching portfolio DP. This portfolio is defined as the optimal domestic portfolio because it moves out into risky space at the steepest slope — maximizing the slope of expected portfolio return over expected risk — while still touching the opportunity set of domestic portfolios. This line is called the *capital market line*, and portfolio theory assumes an investor who can borrow and invest at the risk-free rate can move to any point along this line.

Note that the optimal domestic portfolio is not the portfolio of minimum risk ($MR_{DP}$). A line stretching from the risk-free asset to the minimum risk domestic portfolio would have a lower slope than the capital market line, and the investor would not

**EXHIBIT 15.3**

Optimal Domestic
Portfolio
Construction

An investor may choose a portfolio of assets enclosed by the *domestic portfolio opportunity set*. The *optimal domestic portfolio* is found at DP, where the capital market line is tangent to the domestic portfolio opportunity set. The domestic portfolio with the minimum risk is designated $MR_{DP}$.

be receiving as great an expected return (vertical distance) per unit of expected risk (horizontal distance) as that found at DP.

## INTERNATIONAL DIVERSIFICATION

Exhibit 15.4 illustrates the impact of allowing the investor to choose among an internationally diversified set of potential portfolios. The *internationally diversified portfolio opportunity set* shifts leftward of the purely domestic opportunity set. At any point on the efficient frontier of the internationally diversified portfolio opportunity set, the investor can find a portfolio of lower expected risk for each level of expected return.

It is critical to be clear as to exactly why the internationally diversified portfolio opportunity set is of lower expected risk than comparable domestic portfolios. The gains arise directly from the introduction of additional securities and/or portfolios which are of less than perfect correlation with the securities and portfolios within the domestic opportunity set.

For example, Sony Corporation is listed on the Tokyo Stock Exchange. Sony's share price derives its value from both the individual business results of the firm and the market in which it trades. If either or both are not perfectly positively correlated to the securities and markets available to a U.S.–based investor, then that investor would observe the opportunity set shift shown in Exhibit 15.4.

## THE OPTIMAL INTERNATIONAL PORTFOLIO

The investor can now choose an optimal portfolio that combines the same risk-free asset as before with a portfolio from the efficient frontier of the internationally diversified portfolio opportunity set. The *optimal international portfolio*, IP, is again found by locating that point on the capital market line (internationally diversified) which

**EXHIBIT 15.4**

The Internationally Diversified Portfolio Opportunity Set

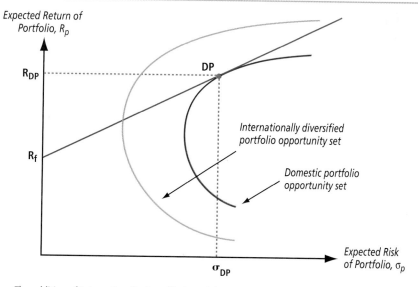

The addition of internationally diversified portfolios to the total opportunity set available to the investor shifts the total portfolio opportunity set left, providing lower expected risk portfolios for each level of expected portfolio return.

**EXHIBIT 15.5**

The Gains from
International
Portfolio
Diversification

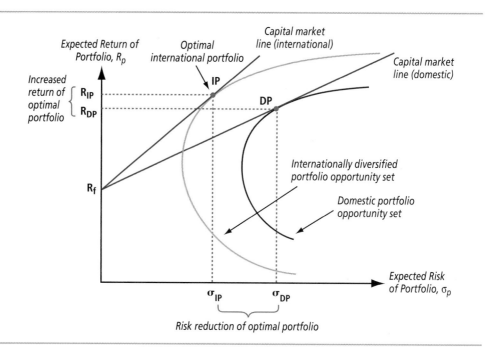

extends from the risk-free asset return of $R_f$ to a point of tangency along the internationally diversified efficient frontier. We illustrate this in Exhibit 15.5.

The benefits of international diversification are now obvious. The investor's optimal portfolio IP possesses both higher expected portfolio return ($R_{IP} > R_{DP}$), and lower expected portfolio risk ($\sigma_{IP} < \sigma_{DP}$), than the purely domestic optimal portfolio. The optimal international portfolio is superior to the optimal domestic portfolio.

## THE CALCULATION OF PORTFOLIO RISK AND RETURN

An investor may reduce investment risk by holding risky assets in a portfolio. As long as the asset returns are not perfectly positively correlated, the investor can reduce risk because some of the fluctuations of the asset returns will offset each other.

**TWO-ASSET MODEL.** Let us assume Trident's CFO Maria Gonzalez is considering investing Trident Corporation's marketable securities in two different risky assets, an index of the U.S. equity markets and an index of the German equity markets. The two equities are characterized by the following expected returns (the mean of recent returns) and expected risks (the standard deviation of recent returns):

|  | Expected Return | Expected Risk ($\sigma$) |
|---|---|---|
| United States equity index (US) | 14% | 15% |
| German equity index (GER) | 18% | 20% |
| Correlation coefficient ($\rho_{US\text{-}GER}$) | 0.34 | |

If the weights of investment in the two assets are $w_{US}$ and $w_{GER}$ respectively, and $w_{US} + w_{GER} = 1$, the risk of the portfolio ($\sigma_p$), usually expressed in terms of the standard deviation of the portfolio's expected return, is given by the following equation:

$$\sigma_P = \sqrt{w_{US}^2\sigma_{US}^2 + w_{GER}^2\sigma_{GER}^2 + 2w_{US}w_{GER}\rho_{US\text{-}GER}\sigma_{US}\sigma_{GER}}$$

where $\sigma_{US}^2$ and $\sigma_{GER}^2$ are the squared standard deviations of the expected returns of risky assets in the United States and Germany (the variances), respectively. The Greek letter *rho*, $\rho_{US\text{-}GER}$, is the correlation coefficient between the two market returns over time.

We now plug in the values for the standard deviations of the United States (15%) and Germany (20%), and the correlation coefficient of 0.34. Assuming that Maria initially wishes to invest 40% of her funds in the United States (0.40), and 60% of her funds in German equities (0.60), the expected risk of the portfolio will be

$$\sigma_P = \sqrt{(0.40)^2(0.15)^2 + (0.60)^2(0.20)^2 + 2(0.40)(0.60)(0.34)(0.15)(0.20)}$$

which, when reduced, is

$$\sqrt{0.0036 + 0.0144 + 0.0049} = 0.151 \approx 15.1\%$$

Note that the portfolio risk is *not* the weighted average of the risks of the individual assets. As long as the correlation coefficient ($\rho$) is smaller than 1.0, some of the fluctuations of the asset returns will offset each other, resulting in risk reduction. The lower the correlation coefficient, the greater the opportunity for risk diversification.

We obtain the expected return of the portfolio with the following equation:

$$E(R_P) = w_{US}E(R_{US}) + w_{GER}E(R_{GER})$$

where $E(R_p)$, $E(R_{US})$, and $E(R_{GER})$ are the expected returns of the portfolio, the U.S. equity index, and the German equity index, respectively. Using the expected returns for the United States (14%) and German (18%) equity indexes above, we find the expected return of the portfolio to be

$$E(R_P) = (0.4)(0.14) + (0.6)(0.18) = 0.164 \approx 16.4\%$$

**ALTERING THE WEIGHTS.**   Before Maria finalizes the desired portfolio, she wishes to evaluate the impact of changing the weights between the two equity indexes on the expected risk and expected returns of the portfolio. Using weight increments of 0.5, she graphs the alternative portfolios in the customary portfolio risk-return graphic. Exhibit 15.6 illustrates the result.

The different portfolios possible using different weights with the two equity assets provides Maria some interesting choices. The two extremes, the greatest expected return and the minimum expected risks, call for very different weight structures. The greatest expected return is, as we would expect from the original asset expectations, 100% German in composition. The minimum expected risk portfolio, with approximately 15.2% expected risk, is made up of approximately 70% U.S. and 30% German securities.

**MULTIPLE ASSET MODEL.**   We can generalize the above equations to a portfolio consisting of multiple assets. The portfolio risk is

$$\sigma_P = \sqrt{\sum_{i=1}^{N} w_i^2\sigma_j^2 + \sum_{i=1}^{N-1}\sum_{j=i+1}^{N} w_i w_j \rho_{ij}\sigma_i\sigma_j}$$

**EXHIBIT 15.6**

Alternative
Portfolio Profiles
Under Varying
Asset Weights

and the portfolio expected return is

$$E\left(R_P\right) = \sum_{i=1}^{N} w_i E\left(R_i\right)$$

where N stands for the total number of assets included in the portfolio.

By allowing investors to hold foreign assets, we substantially enlarge the feasible set of investments; higher return can be obtained at a given level of risk, or lower risk can be attained at the same level of return.

## National Markets and Asset Performance

As demonstrated in the previous section, asset portfolios are traditionally constructed of both interest bearing risk-free assets and risky assets. Exhibit 15.7 presents the performance of major individual national markets by asset category — bills, bonds, and equities — for the twentieth century (1900–2000). Risks and returns are presented on a real basis.

Exhibit 15.7 demonstrates that, at least for the 100-year period ending in 2000, the risk of investing in equity assets has been rewarded with substantial returns. U.S. equities delivered an inflation-adjusted mean return of 8.7%, versus mean returns of 2.1% on bonds and 1.0% on Treasury bills. But the U.S. market is also not exceptional, and in fact, equity markets in Australia, Germany, Japan, South Africa, and Sweden all exhibited higher mean returns for the century. It is also interesting to note that equity returns for all 16 countries listed demonstrated positive mean returns, the lowest being 4.8% in Belgium, and the highest being 9.9% in Sweden.

As demonstrated by *Real World Example 15.2*, however, average performances over extended periods of time may be misleading, as they have a tendency to smooth returns which during the time of the crisis would indeed take an investor's breath away!

**EXHIBIT 15.7**

Real Returns and Risks on the Three Major Asset Classes, Globally, 1900–2000

| Country | Equities (%) | | Bonds (%) | | Bills (%) | |
|---|---|---|---|---|---|---|
| | Mean | S.D. | Mean | S.D. | Mean | S.D. |
| Australia | 9.0 | 17.7 | 1.9 | 13.0 | 0.6 | 5.6 |
| Belgium | 4.8 | 22.8 | 0.3 | 12.1 | 0.0 | 8.2 |
| Canada | 7.7 | 16.8 | 2.4 | 10.6 | 1.8 | 5.1 |
| Denmark | 6.2 | 20.1 | 3.3 | 12.5 | 3.0 | 6.4 |
| France | 6.3 | 23.1 | 0.1 | 14.4 | −2.6 | 11.4 |
| Germany | 8.8 | 32.3 | 0.3 | 15.9 | 0.1 | 10.6 |
| Ireland | 7.0 | 22.2 | 2.4 | 13.3 | 1.4 | 6.0 |
| Italy | 6.8 | 29.4 | −0.8 | 14.4 | −2.9 | 12.0 |
| Japan | 9.3 | 30.3 | 1.3 | 20.9 | −0.3 | 14.5 |
| The Netherlands | 7.7 | 21.0 | 1.5 | 9.4 | 0.8 | 5.2 |
| South Africa | 9.1 | 22.8 | 1.9 | 10.6 | 1.0 | 6.4 |
| Spain | 5.8 | 22.0 | 1.9 | 12.0 | 0.6 | 6.1 |
| Sweden | 9.9 | 22.8 | 3.1 | 12.7 | 2.2 | 6.8 |
| Switzerland | 6.9 | 20.4 | 3.1 | 8.0 | 1.2 | 6.2 |
| United Kingdom | 7.6 | 20.0 | 2.3 | 14.5 | 1.2 | 6.6 |
| United States | 8.7 | 20.2 | 2.1 | 10.0 | 1.0 | 4.7 |

Source: Abstracted from Elroy Dimson, Paul Marsh, and Mike Staunton, *Triumph of the Optimists, 101 Years of Global Investment Returns*, Princeton University Press, 2002, p. 60. "Mean" is arithmetic mean; "S.D." is standard deviation of mean returns. Bond and bill statistics for Germany exclude the years 1922–1923; Swiss equities begin 1911.

## Real World Example 15.2
### EQUITY MARKET CRISES IN THE TWENTIETH CENTURY

The largest equity market losses in the past century were primarily related to war and terrorism, and their associated economic devastation.

| Country | Event | Equity Market Losses (real returns, %) |
|---|---|---|
| U.S. | Terrorist attacks, September 11, 2001 | −14% |
| U.S. | October 1987 stock market crash | −23% |
| U.S. | Bear market, 2000–2001 | −37% |
| U.S. | Wall Street crash of 1929 | −60% |
| U.K. | Bear market, 1973–1974 | −71% |
| Germany | World War II, 1945–1948 | −91% |
| Japan | World War II, 1944–1947 | −97% |

Source: Elroy Dimson, Paul Marsh, and Mike Staunton, *Triumph of the Optimists, 101 Years of Global Investment Returns*, Princeton University Press, 2002, p. 58.

The true benefits of global diversification, however, arise from the fact that the returns of different stock markets around the world are not perfectly positively correlated. Because there are different industrial structures in different countries and because different economies do not exactly follow the same business cycle, we expect smaller return correlations between investments in different countries than between investments within a given country.

Exhibit 15.8 reports correlation coefficients between world equity markets for 1900–2000. The correlation coefficients in the lower bottom left of the exhibit are for the entire period, 1900–2000, while the upper top right of the exhibit are for the 1996–2000 period. The relatively low correlation coefficients among returns for the 16 countries for either period indicates great potential for international diversification. The returns, for the sake of comparison, have all been converted to the same currency basis (in this case the U.S. dollar) and are corrected for inflation.

As noted by the authors of the study, the correlations seem to be "plausible and linked to geography and distance" as national markets that are contiguous or near-contiguous seemingly demonstrate the higher correlation coefficients for the century. For example, among the lower bottom left correlation coefficients, the highest correlations are those between the United States and Canada (.80) and Ireland and the United Kingdom (.73).

The correlation coefficients among national equity markets in the upper top right of Exhibit 15.8, correlations for the 1996–2000 period, are noticeably higher than those for the entire century. The mean correlation coefficient for the entire century was 0.36, while that of the 1996–2000 period was 0.50. Although only for the most recent time segment, and one in which global equity market performance could have been atypical

## EXHIBIT 15.8

Correlation Coefficients Between World Equity Markets, 1900–2000

*Upper Top Right*: Correlations based on 60 months of real dollar returns, 1996–2000, from FTSE World (Ireland and South Africa) and MSCI (all others).

*Lower Bottom Left*: Correlations based on 101 years of real dollar returns, 1900–2000.

| | World | U.S. | UK | Swi | Swe | Spa | Saf | Neth | Jap | Ita | Ire | Ger | Fra | Den | Can | Bel | Aus |
|---|---|---|---|---|---|---|---|---|---|---|---|---|---|---|---|---|---|
| World | | .93 | .77 | .59 | .62 | .67 | .54 | .73 | .68 | .52 | .69 | .69 | .73 | .57 | .82 | .54 | .69 |
| U.S. | .85 | | .67 | .44 | .46 | .53 | .46 | .57 | .49 | .40 | .66 | .56 | .56 | .46 | .78 | .45 | .57 |
| UK | .70 | .55 | | .58 | .44 | .63 | .31 | .71 | .42 | .39 | .73 | .58 | .59 | .57 | .57 | .59 | .56 |
| Swi | .68 | .50 | .62 | | .39 | .60 | .19 | .72 | .36 | .45 | .57 | .53 | .64 | .58 | .35 | .63 | .37 |
| Swe | .62 | .44 | .42 | .54 | | .63 | .38 | .63 | .34 | .49 | .27 | .76 | .76 | .44 | .61 | .29 | .44 |
| Spa | .41 | .25 | .25 | .36 | .37 | | .35 | .63 | .32 | .64 | .50 | .64 | .75 | .56 | .51 | .55 | .54 |
| Saf | .55 | .43 | .49 | .39 | .34 | .26 | | .30 | .44 | .24 | .31 | .42 | .37 | .25 | .62 | .10 | .66 |
| Neth | .57 | .39 | .42 | .51 | .43 | .28 | .29 | | .39 | .59 | .63 | .74 | .77 | .64 | .55 | .70 | .46 |
| Jap | .45 | .21 | .33 | .29 | .39 | .40 | .31 | .25 | | .18 | .33 | .25 | .36 | .24 | .50 | .17 | .59 |
| Ita | .54 | .37 | .43 | .52 | .39 | .41 | .41 | .32 | .34 | | .33 | .55 | .71 | .50 | .40 | .51 | .38 |
| Ire | .58 | .38 | .73 | .70 | .42 | .35 | .42 | .46 | .29 | .43 | | .42 | .45 | .49 | .54 | .57 | .50 |
| Ger | .30 | .12 | −.01 | .22 | .09 | −.03 | .05 | .27 | .06 | .016 | .03 | | .83 | .61 | .57 | .59 | .46 |
| Fra | .62 | .36 | .45 | .54 | .44 | .47 | .38 | .48 | .25 | .52 | .53 | .19 | | .63 | .60 | .66 | .48 |
| Den | .57 | .38 | .40 | .51 | .56 | .34 | .31 | .50 | .46 | .38 | .55 | .22 | .45 | | .55 | .54 | .30 |
| Can | .80 | .80 | .55 | .48 | .53 | .27 | .54 | .34 | .30 | .37 | .41 | .13 | .35 | .46 | | .30 | .65 |
| Bel | .58 | .38 | .40 | .57 | .43 | .40 | .29 | .60 | .25 | .47 | .49 | .26 | .68 | .42 | .35 | | .30 |
| Aus | .66 | .47 | .66 | .51 | .50 | .28 | .56 | .41 | .28 | .43 | .62 | .04 | .47 | .42 | .62 | .35 | |

Source: Elroy Dimson, Paul Marsh, and Mike Staunton, *Triumph of the Optimists, 101 Years of Global Investment Returns*, Princeton University Press, 2002, p. 115. Reprinted by permission of Princeton University Press.

given the dot.com bubble in select industrial markets, the coefficients do indicate a higher degree of market performance integration.[1]

Additional multiple regression studies undertaken by the authors of the study found that when the twentieth century was divided in half "there was no discernible relationship between the two half centuries." They went on to determine that "it would not have been possible to predict correlations for 1950–2000 from those estimated from annual data over the first half-century."[2]

## MARKET PERFORMANCE ADJUSTED FOR RISK: THE SHARPE AND TREYNOR PERFORMANCE MEASURES

Although the previous two exhibits provided some insights into the long-term historical performance of individual national markets and key assets, they do not provide a complete picture of how returns and risks must be considered in combination. Exhibit 15.9 presents summary statistics for the monthly returns across 18 major equity markets for the 1977–1996 period. In addition to the traditional measures of individual market performance of mean return and standard deviation (for risk), the individual national market's beta to the global portfolio is reported as well as two measures of risk-adjusted returns, the Sharpe and Treynor measures.

Investors should examine returns by the amount of return per unit of risk accepted, rather than in isolation (as in simply mean risks and returns). For example, in Exhibit 15.9, the Hong Kong market had the highest average monthly return at 1.50%, but also the highest risk, a standard deviation of 9.61%. (A major contributing factor to its high volatility was, perhaps, the political uncertainty about the future of the British colony after 1997.)

To consider both risk and return in evaluating portfolio performance, we introduce two measures in Exhibit 15.9, the *Sharpe measure* (SHP) and the *Treynor measure* (TRN). The Sharpe measure calculates the average return over and above the risk-free rate of return per unit of portfolio risk:

$$\text{Sharpe measure} = \text{SHP}_i = \frac{\overline{R}_i - R_f}{\sigma_i}$$

where $R_i$ is the average return for portfolio i during a specified time period, $R_f$ is the average risk-free rate of return, and $\sigma_i$ is the risk of portfolio i. The Treynor measure is very similar, but instead of using the standard deviation of the portfolio's total return as the measure of risk, it utilizes the portfolio's beta, $\beta_i$, the systematic risk of the portfolio, as measured against the world market portfolio:

$$\text{Treynor measure} = \text{TRN}_i = \frac{\overline{R}_i - R_f}{\beta_i}$$

The Sharpe measure indicates on average how much excess return (above risk-free rate) an investor is rewarded per unit of portfolio risk the investor bears.

Though the equations of the Sharpe and Treynor measures look similar, the difference between them is important. If a portfolio is perfectly diversified (without any unsystematic risk), the two measures give similar rankings because the total portfolio risk is equivalent to the systematic risk. If a portfolio is poorly diversified, it is possible

[1]Elroy Dimson, Paul Marsh, and Mike Staunton, *Triumph of the Optimists, 101 Years of Global Investment Returns*, Princeton University Press, 2002, p. 115–116.

[2]Ibid., p. 116.

## EXHIBIT 15.9

Summary Statistics of the Monthly Returns for 18 Major Stock Markets, 1977–1996
(all returns converted into U.S. dollars and include all dividends paid)

| | Mean Return (%) | Standard Deviation (%) | Beta $(\beta_i)$ | Sharpe M. $(SHP_i)$ | Treynor M. $(TRN_i)$ |
|---|---|---|---|---|---|
| Australia | 1.00 | 7.44 | 1.02 | 0.078 | 0.0057 |
| Austria | 0.77 | 6.52 | 0.54 | 0.055 | 0.0066 |
| Belgium | 1.19 | 5.53 | 0.86 | 0.141 | 0.0091 |
| Canada | 0.82 | 5.34 | 0.93 | 0.076 | 0.0044 |
| Denmark | 0.99 | 6.25 | 0.68 | 0.092 | 0.0085 |
| France | 1.18 | 6.76 | 1.08 | 0.113 | 0.0071 |
| Germany | 0.97 | 6.17 | 0.84 | 0.089 | 0.0065 |
| Hong Kong | 1.50 | 9.61 | 1.09 | 0.113 | 0.0100 |
| Italy | 0.96 | 7.57 | 0.89 | 0.071 | 0.0061 |
| Japan | 1.08 | 6.66 | 1.21 | 0.099 | 0.0055 |
| Netherlands | 1.39 | 4.93 | 0.89 | 0.197 | 0.0109 |
| Norway | 1.00 | 7.94 | 1.02 | 0.073 | 0.0057 |
| Singapore | 1.09 | 7.50 | 1.01 | 0.090 | 0.0057 |
| Spain | 0.83 | 6.81 | 0.94 | 0.060 | 0.0044 |
| Sweden | 1.37 | 6.67 | 0.97 | 0.143 | 0.0099 |
| Switzerland | 1.10 | 5.39 | 0.86 | 0.127 | 0.0080 |
| United Kingdom | 1.35 | 5.79 | 1.06 | 0.162 | 0.0089 |
| United States | 1.01 | 4.16 | 0.82 | 0.143 | 0.0072 |
| Average | 1.09 | 6.51 | 0.93 | 0.107 | 0.0073 |

The results are computed with stock market data from Morgan Stanley's *Capital International Perspectives*, monthly.

for it to show a high ranking on the basis of the Treynor measure, but a lower ranking on the basis of the Sharpe measure. The difference is attributable to the low level of portfolio diversification. The two measures, therefore, provide complementary but different information.

**HONG KONG EXAMPLE.** The mean return for Hong Kong in Exhibit 15.9 was 1.5%. If we assume the average risk-free rate was 5% per year during this period (or 0.42% per month), the Sharpe measure would be calculated as

$$SHP_{HKG} = \frac{\overline{R}_i - R_f}{\sigma_i} = \frac{0.015 - 0.0042}{0.0961} = 0.113$$

For each unit (%) of portfolio total risk an investor bore, the Hong Kong market rewarded the investor with a monthly excess return of 0.113% in 1977–1996.
Alternatively, the Treynor measure was

$$TRN_{HKG} = \frac{\overline{R}_i - R_f}{\beta_i} = \frac{0.015 - 0.0042}{1.09} = 0.0100$$

Though the Hong Kong market had the second highest Treynor measure, its Sharpe measure was ranked eighth, indicating that the Hong Kong market portfolio was not very well diversified from the world market perspective. Instead, the highest ranking belonged to the Netherlands market, which had the highest Sharpe (0.197) and Treynor (0.0109) measures.

Does this mean that a U.S. investor would have been best rewarded by investing in the Netherlands market over this period? The answer is yes if the investor were allowed to invest in only one of these markets. It would definitely have been better than staying home in the U.S. market, which had a Sharpe measure of 0.143 for the period. However, if the investor were willing to combine these markets in a portfolio, the performance would have been even better. Since these market returns were not perfectly positively correlated, further risk reduction was possible through diversification across markets.

## ARE MARKETS INCREASINGLY INTEGRATED?

It is often said that as capital markets around the world become more and more integrated, the benefits of diversification will be reduced. To examine this question, we break the 20-year sample period of 1977–1996 into halves: 1977–1986 and 1987–1996. The date 1986 coincides with the official movement toward a single Europe. At this time most EU countries deregulated their securities markets — or at least began the process of removing remaining restrictions on the free flow of capital across the borders.

Exhibit 15.10 reports selected stock markets' correlation coefficients with the United States for each subperiod. Only the Danish-U.S. market correlation actually fell from the first to the second period. The Canadian-U.S. correlation rose from an already high 0.66 to 0.77 in the latter period. Similarly, the correlations between the United States and both Singapore and the United Kingdom rose to 0.66 and 0.67, respectively.

The overall picture is that the correlations have increased over time. The answer to the question, "Are markets increasingly integrated?" is most likely yes. However, although capital market integration has decreased some benefits of international portfolio diversification, the correlation coefficients between markets are still far from 1.0. There are still plenty of risk-reducing opportunities for international portfolio diversification.

**EXHIBIT 15.10**

Comparison of Selected Correlation Coefficients Between Stock Markets for Two Time Periods (dollar returns)

| Correlation to United States | 1977–1986 | 1987–1996 | Change |
|---|---|---|---|
| Canada | 0.66 | 0.77 | +0.11 |
| Denmark | 0.26 | 0.18 | −0.08 |
| France | 0.37 | 0.55 | +0.18 |
| Germany | 0.24 | 0.42 | +0.18 |
| Hong Kong | 0.13 | 0.61 | +0.48 |
| Japan | 0.16 | 0.26 | +0.10 |
| Singapore | 0.31 | 0.66 | +0.35 |
| Switzerland | 0.38 | 0.47 | +0.09 |
| United Kingdom | 0.40 | 0.67 | +0.27 |

Correlation coefficients computed from data from Morgan Stanley's *Capital International Perspectives*.

## MINI-CASE

# Strategic Currency Hedging[3]

*Strategic currency hedging policy can be an important risk-control measure for funds with international assets. Passive currency exposure can be seen as a source of risk with no compensating risk premium. Hedging currency exposure removes return component that is a source of expected risk but not expected return. Leaving assets unhedged could be the correct policy decision, but it should not be the default position. The decision should be based on a systematic analysis of the costs and benefits of currency hedging. Given that currency adds risk, has zero expected excess return over long periods of time, and is relatively inexpensive to hedge, it is puzzling that the international investors' default position is not 100% hedged rather than the industry norm of 0% hedged.*

"Currency Management: Strategies to Add Alpha and Reduce Risk," Andrew Dales and Richard Meese, *Investment Insights*, Barclays Global Investment, October 2003, Volume 6, Issue 7, p. 2.

Sean O'Connor was in his second analytical rotation in the management training program at Zenex Securities. He had been assigned to the international equities division for the past three months, and had now been given the task of reviewing the theory and evidence related to active currency management of internationally diversified portfolios.

Sean was reviewing an article that maintained there were at least three basic arguments supporting active currency management. First, unlike equity markets like the New York Stock Exchange, many of the participants who trade daily in the global currency markets are not trading for a profit. Corporate hedgers are trading for hedging purposes; central banks trade in pursuit of a variety of macroeconomic goals. Unlike many other financial markets that meet modern financial efficiency criteria, there is no real consensus of the proper valuation

model(s) for currencies. This means that there is a much greater possibility that currency values could deviate for long periods of time from their correct value.

Finally, and quite promisingly, a number of recent studies had indicated that active currency managers do indeed add value to their portfolio performance. Exhibit 1 reports the result of one recent study following 19 active currency managers over a seven-year period. As shown, even at the 75th percentile, active currency managers have had on average positive performance in four of the seven years.

Sean's review of the studies also reconfirmed a simple but extremely important element of active currency management: The currency strategy must be considered separately from the bond or equity strategy of any portfolio. These markets move on the basis of very different drivers at different points in time, by country. Exhibit 2 was also quite convincing on this point, as the separable returns and risks on equities and currency pairs for a select set of equity markets were distinct. And, just as importantly, the Sharpe ratios for the hedged versus unhedged portfolios were largely the same. So, in the end, a blanket policy of hedging all currency risk seemingly does not change the risk-return tradeoff appreciably.

## Case Questions

1. According to Exhibit 1, were a significant number of portfolio managers consistently able to add value to international portfolios through active (selective) currency management over the time period studied?
2. According to Exhibit 2, would the international investor in an Australia portfolio be better off, on average, with a completely hedged or unhedged portfolio?
3. If you were Sean, what would you conclude from this specific study?

## EXHIBIT 1

| Russell/Mellon Survey of 19 Active Managers, Ending June 30, 2003 | Annualized Active Return in Percent Per Annum | | | | | | |
|---|---|---|---|---|---|---|---|
| Percentile | 1 year | 2 years | 3 years | 4 years | 5 years | 6 years | 7 years |
| 25th | 3.14 | 3.13 | 1.64 | 1.14 | 0.94 | 0.95 | 1.25 |
| Median | 1.01 | 0.77 | 1.04 | 0.40 | 0.44 | 0.63 | 0.83 |
| 75th | −0.07 | 0.22 | 0.36 | −0.01 | −0.04 | 0.31 | 0.36 |
| Mean | 1.05 | 0.98 | 0.80 | 0.46 | 0.35 | 0.63 | 1.07 |

Source: Russell/Mellon Analytical Services, LLC, as quoted by Barclays.

[3]This mini-case is fictional. Many of the arguments and concepts utilized are based on "Currency Management: Strategies to Add Alpha and Reduce Risk," by Andrew Dales and Richard Meese, *Investment Insights*, Barclays Global Investment, October 2003, vol. 6, no. 7.

**EXHIBIT 2**

Annual Historical Excess Returns, Annual Risk, and Sharpe Ratios for Selected Equities and Currencies, January 1978 to February 2003

| Asset | Country | Average excess return (%) | Annual risk (%) | Sharpe ratio |
|---|---|---|---|---|
| Equities | Australia | 4.22 | 19.30 | 0.22 |
| | Canada | 3.33 | 17.70 | 0.19 |
| | Japan | 2.34 | 18.60 | 0.13 |
| | U.K. | 3.73 | 17.00 | 0.22 |
| | U.S. | 5.85 | 15.70 | 0.37 |
| Forward currency | AUD/USD | 0.62 | 9.99 | 0.06 |
| | CAD/USD | 0.34 | 4.81 | 0.07 |
| | JPY/USD | 0.74 | 12.70 | 0.06 |
| | GBP/USD | (1.15) | 11.10 | (0.10) |
| Unhedged international equities | Australia | 4.44 | 15.60 | 0.28 |
| | Canada | 4.07 | 13.90 | 0.29 |
| | Japan | 5.62 | 17.90 | 0.31 |
| | U.K. | 2.70 | 16.50 | 0.16 |
| | U.S. | 3.23 | 17.00 | 0.19 |
| Hedged international equities | Australia | 3.30 | 14.10 | 0.23 |
| | Canada | 3.37 | 14.00 | 0.23 |
| | Japan | 4.17 | 14.40 | 0.29 |
| | U.K. | 3.62 | 14.00 | 0.26 |
| | U.S. | 2.98 | 14.80 | 0.20 |

Source: Adapted from Barclays, op cit, p. 7.

## Summary of Learning Objectives

*Separate total risk of a portfolio into two components, diversifiable and nondiversifiable*

- The total risk of any portfolio is composed of *systematic* (the market) and *unsystematic* (the individual securities) risk. Increasing the number of securities in the portfolio reduces the unsystematic risk component.

*Demonstrate how both the diversifiable and non-diversifiable risks of an investor's portfolio may be reduced through international diversification*

- An internationally diversified portfolio has a lower portfolio beta. This means that the portfolio's market risk is lower than that of a domestic portfolio. This situation arises because the returns on the foreign stocks are closely correlated not with returns on U.S. stocks, but rather with a global beta.

- Investors construct internationally diversified portfolios in an attempt to combine assets which are less than perfectly correlated, reducing the total risk of the portfolio. In addition, by adding assets outside the home market, the investor has now tapped into a larger pool of potential investments.

*Explore how foreign exchange risk affects the individual investor investing internationally*

- International portfolio construction is also different in that when the investor acquires assets or securities outside the investor's home-country market, the investor may also be acquiring a foreign currency denominated asset.

- The investor has actually acquired two additional assets — the currency of denomination and the asset subsequently purchased with the currency — one asset in principle, but two in expected returns and risks.

- The foreign exchange risks of a portfolio, whether it be a securities portfolio or the general portfolio of activities of the MNE, are reduced through international diversification.

*Define the optimal domestic portfolio and the optimal international portfolio*

- The individual investor will search out the *optimal domestic portfolio* (DP), which combines the risk-free asset and a portfolio of domestic securities found on the efficient frontier. The investor begins with the risk-free asset with return of $R_f$ (and zero expected risk) and moves out along the capital market line until reaching portfolio DP.

- This portfolio is called the *optimal domestic portfolio* because it moves out into risky space at the steepest slope — maximizing the slope of expected portfolio return over expected risk — while still touching the opportunity set of domestic portfolios.

- The *optimal international portfolio*, IP, is found by finding that point on the capital market line (internationally diversified) which extends from the risk-free asset return of $R_f$ to a point of tangency along the internationally diversified efficient frontier.

- The investor's optimal portfolio IP possesses both higher expected portfolio return ($R_{IP} > R_{DP}$), and lower expected portfolio risk ($\sigma_{IP} < \sigma_{DP}$), than the purely domestic optimal portfolio. The optimal international portfolio is superior to the optimal domestic portfolio.

*Review the recent history of equity market performance globally, including the degree to which the markets are more or less correlated in their movements*

- Risk reduction is possible through international diversification because the returns of different stock markets around the world are not perfectly positively correlated.

- Because there are different industrial structures in different countries and because different economies do not exactly follow the same business cycle, we expect smaller return correlations between investments in different countries than between investments within a given country.

- The relatively low correlation coefficients among returns of 18 major stock markets around the world in the 20-year period from 1977 to 1996 indicates great potential for international diversification.

*Examine the question of whether markets appear to be more or less integrated over time*

- The overall picture is that the correlations have increased over time.

- Nevertheless, 91 of the 153 correlations (59%) and the overall mean (0.46) were still below 0.5 in 1987–1996. The answer to the question, "Are markets increasingly integrated?" is yes.

- However, although capital market integration has decreased some benefits of international portfolio diversification, the correlation coefficients between markets are still far from 1.0. There are still plenty of risk-reducing opportunities for international portfolio diversification.

## QUESTIONS

1. **Diversification benefits.** How does the diversification of a portfolio change its expected returns and expected risks? Is this in principle any different for internationally diversified portfolios?

2. **Risk reduction.** What types of risk are present in a diversified portfolio? Which type of risk remains after the portfolio has been diversified?

3. **Measurement of risk.** How, according to portfolio theory, is the risk of the portfolio measured exactly?

4. **Market risk.** If all national markets have market risk, is all market risk the same?

5. **Currency risk.** The currency risk associated with international diversification is a serious concern for portfolio managers. Is it possible for currency risk ever to benefit the portfolio's return?

6. **Optimal domestic portfolio.** Define in words (without graphics) how the optimal domestic portfolio is constructed.

7. **Minimum risk portfolios.** If the primary benefit of portfolio diversification is risk reduction, is the investor always better off choosing the portfolio with the lowest expected risk?

8. **International risk.** Many portfolio managers, when asked why they do not internationally diversify their portfolios, answer that "the risks are not worth the expected returns." Using the theory of international diversification, how would you evaluate this statement?

9. **Correlation coefficients.** The benefits of portfolio construction, domestically or internationally, arise from the lack of correlation among assets and markets. The increasing globalization of business is expected to change these correlations over time. How do you believe they will change and why?

10. **Relative risk and return.** Conceptually, how do the Sharpe and Treynor performance measures define risk differently? Which do you believe is a more useful measure in an internationally diversified portfolio?

11. **International equities and currencies.** As the newest member of the asset allocation team in your firm, you constantly find yourself being quizzed by your fellow group members. The topic this morning is international diversification. One analyst asks you the following question:

    *Security prices are driven by a variety of factors, but corporate earnings are clearly one of the primary drivers. And corporate earnings — on average — follow business cycles. Exchange rates, as they taught you back in college, reflect the market's assessment of the growth prospects for the economy behind the currency. So if securities go up with the business cycle, and currencies go up with the business cycle, why do we see currencies and securities prices across the globe not going up and down together?*

    Answer her question.

12. **Are MNEs global investments?** Firms with operations and assets across the globe, true MNEs, are in many ways as international in composition as the most internationally diversified portfolio of unrelated securities. Why do investors not simply invest in MNEs traded on their local exchanges and forego the complexity of purchasing securities traded on foreign exchanges?

13. **ADRs versus direct holdings.** When you are constructing your portfolio, you know you want to include Cementos de Mexico (Mexico) in it, but you cannot decide whether you wish to hold it in the form of ADRs traded on the NYSE or directly through purchases on the Mexico City Bolsa.

    a. Does it make any difference in regard to currency risk?

    b. List the pros and cons of ADRs and direct purchases.

c. What would you recommend if you were an asset investor for a corporation with no international operations or internationally diversified holdings?

## PROBLEMS

1. **Investing on the DAX.** Giri Iyer is European analyst and strategist for Tristar Funds, a New York–based mutual fund company. Giri is currently evaluating the recent performance of shares in Pacific Wietz, a publicly traded specialty chemical company in Germany listed on the Frankfurt DAX. The baseline investment amount used by Tristar is $100,000. He gathers the following quotes:

    | Element | Jan 1 Purchase | Dec 31 Sale | Distributions |
    | --- | --- | --- | --- |
    | Share price | €135.00 | €157.60 | €15.00 |
    | Exchange rate | $1.0660/€ | $1.1250/€ | — |

    a. What was the return on the security in local currency terms?

    b. What was the return on the security in U.S. dollar terms?

    c. Does this mean it was a good investment for a local investor, a U.S.-based investor, or both?

2. **Portfolio risk and return: Boeing and Unilever.** An investor is evaluating a two-asset portfolio of the following two securities:

    | Security | Expected Return (percent) | Std. Dev. (percent) |
    | --- | --- | --- |
    | Boeing (U.S.) | 18.6 | 22.8 |
    | Unilever (U.K.) | 16.0 | 24.0 |

    a. If the two securities have a correlation of +.6, what is the expected risk and return for a portfolio that is equally weighted?

    b. If the two securities have a correlation of +.6, what is the expected risk and return for a portfolio that is 70% Boeing and 30% Unilever?

    c. If the two securities have a correlation of +.6, what is the expected risk and return for a portfolio that is optimally weighted? Determine the weights that minimize the combined risk.

3. **Sharpe and Treynor performance measures.**  Assume the U.S. dollar returns (monthly averages) are as follows for three Baltic republics.

Calculate the Sharpe and Treynor measures of market performance.

| Country | Mean Return | Standard Deviation | Risk-Free Rate | Beta |
|---------|-------------|--------------------|----------------|------|
| Estonia | 1.12% | 16.00% | 0.42% | 1.65 |
| Latvia | 0.75% | 22.80% | 0.42% | 1.53 |
| Lithuania | 1.60% | 13.50% | 0.42% | 1.20 |

4. **Anglo and American equity fund.** An investor is evaluating a two-asset portfolio of the following two securities:

| Security | Expected Return (percent) | Std. Dev. (percent) |
|----------|---------------------------|---------------------|
| Anglo Equities | 12.5 | 26.4 |
| American Equities | 10.8 | 22.5 |

a. If the two equity funds have a correlation of +.72, what is the expected risk and return for the following three portfolio weightings?

   Portfolio A:  75% Anglo, 25% American
   Portfolio B:  50% Anglo, 50% American
   Portfolio C:  25% Anglo, 75% American

b. Which of the portfolios is preferable? On what basis?

*Eastbridge Technology (London Stock Exchange).* Eastbridge Technology is an information technology services provider. It currently operates primarily within the European marketplace, and therefore is not active or traded on any North American stock exchange. The company's share price and dividend distributions have been as follows in recent years:

| | 6/30/00 | 6/30/01 | 6/30/02 | 6/30/03 |
|---|---------|---------|---------|---------|
| Share price (£) | 37.40 | 42.88 | 40.15 | 44.60 |
| Dividend (£) | 1.50 | 1.60 | 1.70 | 1.80 |
| Spot exchange rate ($/£) | 1.4650 | 1.4260 | 1.4896 | 1.5546 |

5. **Eastbridge Technology: British pound-based investors.** Using the data above, calculate the annual average capital appreciation rate on Eastbridge shares, as well as the average total return (including dividends) to a British pound-based investor holding the shares for the entire period shown.

6. **Eastbridge Technology: U.S. dollar-based investors (A).** Using the data above, calculate the annual average total return (including dividends) to a U.S. dollar-based investor holding the shares for the entire period shown. Assume an investment of $100,000.

7. **Eastbridge Technology: U.S.-dollar-based investors (B).** Using the data above — but assuming an exchange rate that began at $1.4650/£ in June 2000 and then consistently appreciated versus the U.S. dollar 3.0% per year for the entire period — calculate the annual average total return (including dividends) to a U.S. dollar-based investor holding the shares for the entire period shown.

8. **Brazilian investors diversify.** The Brazilian economy in 2001 and 2002 had gone up and down. The Brazilian *real* (R$) had been declining since 1999 (when it was floated). Investors wished to diversify internationally — into U.S. dollars for the most part — to protect themselves against the domestic economy and currency. A large private investor had, in April 2002, invested R$500,000 in Standard & Poor's 500 Indexes, which are traded on the American Stock Exchange (AMSE: SPY). The beginning and ending index prices and exchange rates between the real and the dollar were as follows:

| | 4/10/2002 | 4/10/2003 |
|---|-----------|-----------|
| Share price of SPY (US$) | 112.60 | 87.50 |
| Exchange rate (R$/$) | 2.27 | 3.22 |

a. What was the return on the index fund for the year to a U.S.-based investor?

b. What was the return to the Brazilian investor for the one-year holding period? If the Brazilian investor could have invested locally in Brazil in an interest bearing account guaranteeing 12%, would that have been better than the American diversification strategy?

9. **Russian-U.S. equity portfolio (A).** An investor is evaluating a two-asset portfolio that combines a U.S. equity fund with a Russian equity fund. The expected returns, risks, and correlation coefficients for the coming one-year period are as follows:

| Security | Expected Return (percent) | Expected Risk (percent) |
|----------|---------------------------|-------------------------|
| U.S. equity fund | 10.50 | 18.60 |
| Russian equity fund | 16.80 | 36.00 |

Assuming the expected correlation coefficient is 0.52 for the coming year, which weights (use increments of 5% such as 95/5, 90/10) result in the best tradeoff between expected risk and expected return?

10. **Russian-U.S. equity portfolio (B).** Rework the previous problem, but assume that you have reduced the expected correlation coefficient from 0.52 to 0.38. Which weights (use increments of 5% such as 95/5, 90/10) result in the best tradeoff between expected risk and expected return?

 ## Internet Exercises

1. **International diversification via mutual funds.** All major mutual fund companies now offer a variety of internationally diversified mutual funds. The degree of international composition across funds, however, differs significantly. Use the Web sites listed below, and any others of interest, to

   **a.** distinguish between international funds, global funds, worldwide funds, and overseas funds.

   **b.** determine how international funds have been performing, in U.S. dollar terms, relative to mutual funds offering purely domestic portfolios.

   Fidelity
   http://www.fidelity.com/funds
   T. Rowe Price
   http://www.troweprice.com
   Merrill Lynch
   http://www.ml.com
   Scudder
   http://www.scudder.com
   Kemper Funds
   http://www.Kemperfunds.com

2. **Center for Latin American Capital Markets Research.** Because most of the Latin American markets suffered significant declines in market value following the Mexican peso crisis of December 1994, many of these markets may still be some of the most undervalued markets in the world. If you were given the task of investing US$1 million in a single equity market in Latin America, which one would you choose? Use the World Wide Web to find recent market performance statistics to support your choice.

   Center for Latin American Capital
   http://users.netrus.net/gmorles/

# Foreign Direct Investment Theory and Strategy

## LEARNING OBJECTIVES

Show why the theory of comparative advantage is the theoretical justification for international trade

Analyze how market imperfections create a rationale for the existence of multinational enterprises

Explain why firms become multinational

Demonstrate how key competitive advantages support MNEs' strategy to originate and sustain direct foreign investment

Show how the OLI Paradigm provides a theoretical foundation for the globalization process

Identify factors and forces that must be considered in the determination of where multinational enterprises invest

Illustrate the managerial and competitive dimensions of the alternative methods for foreign investment

Trident officially became a multinational enterprise (MNE), as shown in Exhibit 1.3 in Chapter 1, when it seized the opportunity to establish a greenfield market-seeking manufacturing subsidiary in Hamburg, Germany (Trident Europe). This was followed by a market-seeking acquisition in Sao Paulo, Brazil (Trident Brazil), and a production efficiency-seeking joint venture in Shanghai, China (Trident China). The strategy that firms like Trident undertake to become an MNE is the subject of this chapter. More specifically, we analyze the decision whether, where, and how to undertake *foreign direct investment* (FDI).

The internationalization process itself, however, begins with international trade. This chapter first reviews the theory of comparative advantage, the theoretical foundation of trade. Only after highlighting the limitations of international trade is it possible to understand why firms move beyond the geographic boundaries of their home country in order to license or manufacture abroad, that is, to engage in foreign direct investment.

The second section of the chapter analyzes how market imperfections create a rationale for the existence of multinational enterprises. Here we explain what motivates firms to become multinational. We then demonstrate how key competitive advantages support a firm's strategy to undertake direct foreign investment. We follow this by showing how the *OLI Paradigm* provides a theoretical foundation for foreign direct investment. Then we analyze how a firm decides where to invest abroad through various types of foreign involvement. At the end of the chapter is a mini-case on how one company pursued the global licensing of its product.

## The Theory of Comparative Advantage

The *theory of comparative advantage* provides a basis for explaining and justifying international trade in a model world assumed to enjoy free trade, perfect competition, no uncertainty, costless information, and no government interference. The theory contains the following features:

- Exporters in Country A sell goods or services to unrelated importers in Country B.

- Firms in Country A specialize in making products that can be produced relatively efficiently, given Country A's endowment of factors of production, that is, land, labor, capital, and technology. Firms in Country B do likewise, given the factors of production found in Country B. In this way the total combined output of A and B is maximized.

- Because the factors of production cannot be moved freely from Country A to Country B, the benefits of specialization are realized through international trade.

- The way the benefits of the extra production are shared depends on the *terms of trade*, the ratio at which quantities of the physical goods are traded. Each country's share is determined by supply and demand in perfectly competitive markets in the two countries. Neither Country A nor Country B is worse off than before trade, and typically both are better off, albeit perhaps unequally.

## AN EXAMPLE OF COMPARATIVE ADVANTAGE

For an example of the benefits of free trade based on comparative advantage, assume that Thailand is more efficient than Brazil at producing sports shoes and stereo equipment. With one unit of production (a mix of land, labor, capital, and technology), efficient Thailand can produce either 12 shipping containers (ctrs) of shoes or 6 shipping containers of stereo equipment. Brazil, being less efficient in both, can produce only 10 containers of shoes or 2 containers of stereo equipment with one unit of input. These production capabilities are as follows:

|  | Production Capability | |
|---|---|---|
|  | Containers of sports shoes | Containers of stereo equipment |
| Thailand (1,000 production units) | 12/unit | 6/unit |
| Brazil (1,000 production units) | 10/unit | 2/unit |

A production unit in Thailand has an *absolute advantage* over a production unit in Brazil in both shoes and stereo equipment. Nevertheless, Thailand has a larger *relative advantage* over Brazil in producing stereo equipment (6 to 2) than shoes (12 to 10). As long as these ratios are unequal, comparative advantage exists.

Assume that no trade takes place, and each country divides its own production units between shoes and stereo equipment. Each country elects to allocate 300 production units to shoes and 700 production units to stereo equipment, resulting in the production and consumption outcomes in the top of Exhibit 16.1.

Now assume complete specialization. Thailand produces only stereo equipment and Brazil produces only shoes. World production would be higher for both shoes and stereo equipment, as illustrated by the bottom half of Exhibit 16.1.

Clearly the world in total is better off because there are now 10,000 containers of shoes — instead of just 6,600. And there are 6,000 containers of stereo equipment — instead of just 5,600. But distribution is quite distorted. The Thais now tap only bare feet to their music, and the Brazilians dance through Carnival with good shoes but no recorded music!

**EXHIBIT 16.1**

The Theory of Comparative Advantage: A Numerical Example of Brazil and Thailand

**Production If No Trade**

|  | Shoe Production | Stereo Production |
|---|---|---|
| Thailand produces and consumes | 300 × 12 = 3,600 ctrs | 700 × 6 = 4,200 ctrs |
| Brazil produces and consumes | 300 × 10 = 3,000 | 700 × 2 = 1,400 |
| Total world production and consumption | 6,600 ctrs | 5,600 ctrs |

**Complete Specialization**

|  | Shoe Production | Stereo Production |
|---|---|---|
| Thailand produces only stereo equipment |  | 1,000 × 6 = 6,000 ctrs |
| Brazil produces only shoes | 1,000 × 10 = 10,000 ctrs | _____ |
| Total world production and consumption | 10,000 ctrs | 6,000 ctrs |

**EXHIBIT 16.2**

Trade at Thailand's Domestic Price

*For each container of stereo equipment exported, Thailand imports two containers of shoes from Brazil.*

| | Shoe Production plus/minus trade | Stereo Production plus/minus trade |
|---|---|---|
| Thailand produces 6,000 containers of stereo equipment and exports 1,800 containers | 0 + 3,600 = 3,600 ctrs | 6,000 − 1,800 = 4,200 ctrs |
| Brazil produces 10,000 containers of shoes and exports 3,600 containers | 10,000 − 3,600 = 6,400 | 0 + 1,800 = 1,800 |
| World production and consumption | 10,000 ctrs | 6,000 ctrs |

Trade can resolve this distribution problem. Assume initially that trade between Thailand and Brazil takes place at the ratio of two containers of shoes for one container of stereo equipment. This exchange rate of two containers of shoes for one container of stereo equipment is Thailand's domestic price; that is, the ratio of trade within Thailand should it produce both items and not engage in international trade. Assume further that Thailand exports 1,800 containers of stereo equipment to Brazil and imports 3,600 containers of shoes from Brazil. The situation would be as depicted in Exhibit 16.2.

At this price all gains go to Brazil, which consumes 6,400 containers of shoes (instead of 3,000 with no trade) and consumes 1,800 containers of stereo equipment (instead of 1,400 with no trade). Thailand's consumption, 3,600 containers of shoes and 4,200 containers of stereos, is just as it was with no trade. Thailand has gained nothing from trade at this price, although it has lost nothing either!

Assume now that trade takes place at Brazil's domestic price of five containers of shoes for each container of stereo equipment. This is illustrated in Exhibit 16.3. At Brazil's internal price, all gains go to Thailand, which now consumes 7,000 containers of shoes (instead of 3,600 with no trade) and 4,600 containers of stereo equipment (instead of 4,200 with no trade). Brazil's consumption, 3,000 containers of shoes and 1,400 containers of stereo equipment, is the same as with no trade. Brazil has gained nothing from trade at this price — although neither has it lost anything.

**EXHIBIT 16.3**

Trade at Brazil's Domestic Price

*For each container of stereo equipment exported, Thailand imports five containers of shoes from Brazil.*

| | Shoe Production plus/minus trade | Stereo Production plus/minus trade |
|---|---|---|
| Thailand produces 6,000 containers of stereo equipment and exports 1,400 containers | 0 + 7,000 = 7,000 ctrs | 6,000 − 1,400 = 4,600 ctrs |
| Brazil produces 10,000 containers of shoes and exports 7,000 containers | 10,000 − 7,000 = 3,000 | 0 + 1,400 = 1,400 |
| World production and consumption | 10,000 ctrs | 6,000 ctrs |

**EXHIBIT 16.4**

Trade at a Price
Reached by Free
Bargaining

*For each container of stereo equipment exported, Thailand imports four containers of shoes from Brazil.*

|  | Shoe Production plus/minus trade | Stereo Production plus/minus trade |
|---|---|---|
| Thailand produces 6,000 containers of stereo equipment and exports 1,600 containers | 0 + 6,400 = 6,400 ctrs | 6,000 − 1,600 = 4,400 ctrs |
| Brazil produces 10,000 containers of shoes and exports 6,400 containers | 10,000 − 6,400 = 3,600 | 0 + 1,600 = 1,600 |
| World production and consumption | 10,000 ctrs | 6,000 ctrs |

Now let trade take place at a price in between Thailand's domestic price of 2-to-1 and Brazil's domestic price of 5-to-1. Assume that free bargaining leads to a price of 4-to-1, as seen in Exhibit 16.4.

At any price between the boundaries of 2-to-1 and 5-to-1, both countries benefit from specializing and trading. At a 4-to-1 price Thailand consumes 2,800 more containers of shoes as well as 200 more containers of stereo equipment than it has consumed with no trade. Brazil consumes 600 more containers of shoes as well as 200 more containers of stereo equipment than it has consumed with no trade. Total combined production of both shoes and stereo equipment has increased through the specialization process, and it only remains for the exchange ratio to determine how this larger output is distributed between the two countries.

## LIMITATIONS OF COMPARATIVE ADVANTAGE

Although international trade might have approached the comparative advantage model during the nineteenth century, it certainly does not today, for the following reasons.

- Countries do not appear to specialize only in those products that could be most efficiently produced by that country's particular factors of production. Instead, governments interfere with comparative advantage for a variety of economic and political reasons, such as to achieve full employment, economic development, national self-sufficiency in defense-related industries, and protection of an agricultural sector's way of life. Government interference takes the form of tariffs, quotas, and other nontariff restrictions.

- At least two of the factors of production — capital and technology — now flow directly and easily between countries, rather than only indirectly through traded goods and services. This direct flow occurs between related subsidiaries and affiliates of multinational firms, as well as between unrelated firms via loans, and license and management contracts, as we will discuss later in this chapter.

- Modern factors of production are more numerous than in this simple model. Factors considered in the location of production facilities worldwide include local and managerial skills, a dependable legal structure for settling contract disputes, research and development competence, educational levels of available workers, energy resources, consumer demand for brand-name goods, mineral and raw material availability, access to capital, tax differentials, supporting infrastructure (roads, ports, communication facilities), and possibly others.

- Although the terms of trade are ultimately determined by supply and demand, the process by which the terms are set is different from that visualized in traditional trade theory. They are determined partly by administered pricing in oligopolistic markets.

- Comparative advantage shifts over time as less developed countries become more developed and realize their latent opportunities. For example, over the past 150 years comparative advantage in producing cotton textiles has shifted from the United Kingdom to the United States, to Japan, to Hong Kong, to Taiwan, and to China.

- The classical model of comparative advantage did not really address certain other issues such as the effect of uncertainty and information costs, the role of differentiated products in imperfectly competitive markets, and economies of scale.

Nevertheless, although the world is a long way from the classical trade model, the general principle of comparative advantage is still valid. The closer the world gets to true international specialization, the more world production and consumption can be increased, provided the problem of equitable distribution of the benefits can be solved to the satisfaction of consumers, producers, and political leaders. Complete specialization, however, remains an unrealistic limiting case, just as perfect competition is a limiting case in microeconomic theory.

## SUPPLY CHAIN OUTSOURCING: COMPARATIVE ADVANTAGE TODAY

Comparative advantage is still a relevant theory to explain why particular countries are most suitable for exports of goods and services that support the global supply chain of both MNEs and domestic firms. The comparative advantage of the twenty-first century, however, is based more on services and their cross-border facilitation by telecommunications and the Internet. The source of a nation's comparative advantage, however, still is created from the mixture of its own labor skills, access to capital, and technology.

Many locations for supply chain outsourcing exist today. Exhibit 16.5 presents a geographical overview of this modern reincarnation of trade-based comparative advantage. To prove that these countries should specialize in the activities shown you would need to know how costly the same activities would be in the countries that are importing these services compared to their own other industries. Remember that it takes a *relative advantage* in costs, not just an *absolute advantage*, to create *comparative advantage*.

For example, India has developed a highly efficient and low-cost software industry. This industry supplies not only the creation of custom software, but also call centers for customer support and other information technology services. The Indian software industry is composed of subsidiaries of MNEs and of independent companies.

If you own a Compaq computer and call the customer support center number for help, you are highly likely to reach a call center in India. Answering your call will be a knowledgeable Indian software engineer or programmer who will walk you through

**EXHIBIT 16.5**

Global Outsourcing of Comparative Advantage

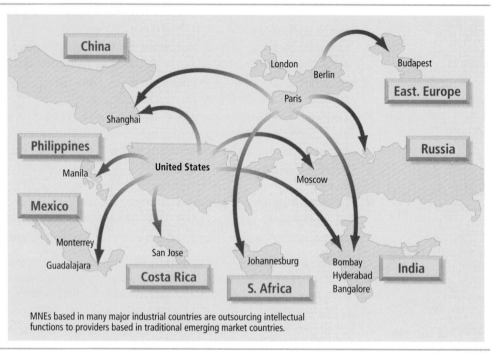

MNEs based in many major industrial countries are outsourcing intellectual functions to providers based in traditional emerging market countries.

your problem. India has a large number of well-educated, English-speaking technical experts who are paid only a fraction of the salary and overhead earned by their U.S. counterparts. The overcapacity and low cost of international telecommunication networks today further enhances the comparative advantage of an Indian location.

As illustrated by *Real World Example 16.1*, the extent of global outsourcing is already reaching out to every corner of the globe. From financial back offices in Manila to information technology engineers in Hungary, modern telecommunications now take business activities to labor, rather than labor migrating to the places of business.

## Market Imperfections: A Rationale for the Existence of the Multinational Firm

Trident and other MNEs strive to take advantage of imperfections in national markets for products, factors of production, and financial assets. Imperfections in the market for products translate into market opportunities for MNEs. Large international firms are better able to exploit such competitive factors as economies of scale, managerial and technological expertise, product differentiation, and financial strength than are their local competitors. In fact, MNEs thrive best in markets characterized by international oligopolistic competition, where these factors are particularly critical. In addition, once MNEs have established a physical presence abroad, they are in a better position than purely domestic firms to identify and implement market opportunities through their own internal information network.

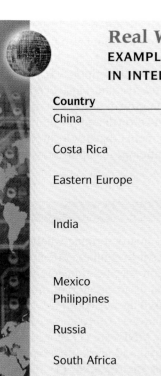

## Real World Example 16.1
### EXAMPLES OF GLOBAL OUTSOURCING OF COMPARATIVE ADVANTAGE IN INTELLECTUAL SKILLS

| Country | Activity |
|---|---|
| China | Chemical, mechanical, and petroleum engineering services; business and product development centers for companies like GE |
| Costa Rica | Call centers for Spanish-speaking consumers in many industrial markets; Accenture has IT support and back-office operations call centers. |
| Eastern Europe | American and IT service providers operate call centers for customer and business support in Hungary, Poland, and the Czech Republic, and Romanian and Bulgarian centers for German-speaking IT customers in Europe |
| India | Software engineering and support; call centers for all types of computer and telecom services; medical analysis and consultative services; Indian companies such as Tata, Infosys, and Wipro are already global leaders in IT design, implementation, and support. |
| Mexico | Automotive engineering and electronic sector services |
| Philippines | Financial and accounting services; architecture services; telemarketing and graphic arts |
| Russia | Software and engineering services; R&D centers for Boeing, Intel, Motorola, and Nortel |
| South Africa | Call and user support services for French, English, and German-speaking consumers throughout Europe |

Source: Abstracted from "Is Your Job Next?" *Business Week,* February 3, 2003.

## WHY DO FIRMS BECOME MULTINATIONAL?

Strategic motives drive the decision to invest abroad and become an MNE. These motives can be summarized under the following five categories.

1. **Market seekers** produce in foreign markets either to satisfy local demand or to export to markets other than their home market. U.S. automobile firms manufacturing in Europe for local consumption are an example of market-seeking motivation. Trident's foreign subsidiaries fall into this category.

2. **Raw material seekers** extract raw materials wherever they can be found, either for export or for further processing and sale in the country in which they are found — the *host country*. Firms in the oil, mining, plantation, and forest industries fall into this category.

3. **Production efficiency seekers** produce in countries where one or more of the factors of production are underpriced relative to their productivity. Labor-intensive production of electronic components in Taiwan, Malaysia, and Mexico is an example of this motivation.

4. **Knowledge seekers** operate in foreign countries to gain access to technology or managerial expertise. For example, German, Dutch, and Japanese firms have purchased U.S.-located electronics firms for their technology.

5. **Political safety seekers** acquire or establish new operations in countries that are considered unlikely to expropriate or interfere with private enterprise. For example, Hong Kong firms invested heavily in the United States, United Kingdom, Canada, and Australia in anticipation of the consequences of China's 1997 takeover of the British colony.

The five types of strategic considerations just described are not mutually exclusive. Forest products firms seeking wood fiber in Brazil, for example, would also find a large Brazilian market for a portion of their output.

In industries characterized by worldwide oligopolistic competition, each of the above strategic motives should be subclassified into *proactive* and *defensive* investments. Proactive investments are designed to enhance the growth and profitability of the firm itself. Defensive investments are designed to deny growth and profitability to the firm's competitors. Examples of the latter are investments that try to preempt a market before competitors can get established there, or attempt to capture raw material sources in order to deny them to competitors.

## Sustaining and Transferring Competitive Advantage

In deciding whether to invest abroad, management must first determine whether the firm has a sustainable competitive advantage that enables it to compete effectively in the home market. The competitive advantage must be firm-specific, transferable, and powerful enough to compensate the firm for the potential disadvantages of operating abroad (foreign exchange risks, political risks, and increased agency costs).

Based on observations of firms that have successfully invested abroad, we can conclude that some of the competitive advantages enjoyed by MNEs are (1) economies of scale and scope arising from their large size; (2) managerial and marketing expertise; (3) superior technology owing to their heavy emphasis on research; (4) financial strength; (5) differentiated products; and sometimes (6) competitiveness of their home markets.

### ECONOMIES OF SCALE AND SCOPE

Economies of scale and scope can be developed in production, marketing, finance, research and development, transportation, and purchasing. In each of these areas there are significant competitive advantages to being large, whether size is due to international or domestic operations. Production economies can come from the use of large-scale automated plant and equipment or from an ability to rationalize production through worldwide specialization. For example, some automobile manufacturers, such as Ford, rationalize manufacturing by producing engines in one country, transmissions in another, and bodies in another and assembling still elsewhere, with the location often being dictated by comparative advantage.

Marketing economies occur when firms are large enough to use the most efficient advertising media to create worldwide brand identification, as well as to establish worldwide distribution, warehousing, and servicing systems. Financial economies derive from access to the full range of financial instruments and sources of funds, such as the Eurocurrency, Euroequity, and Eurobond markets. In-house research and development programs are typically restricted to large firms because of the minimum-size threshold for establishing a laboratory and scientific staff. Transportation economies accrue to firms that can ship in carload or shipload lots. Purchasing economies come from quantity discounts and market power.

### MANAGERIAL AND MARKETING EXPERTISE

Managerial expertise includes skill in managing large industrial organizations from both a human and a technical viewpoint. It also encompasses knowledge of modern analytical techniques and their application in functional areas of business. Managerial expertise can be developed through prior experience in foreign markets. In most empirical studies multinational firms have been observed to export to a market before establishing a production facility there. Likewise, they have prior experience sourcing raw materials and human capital in other foreign countries either through imports, licensing, or FDI. In this manner the MNEs can partially overcome the supposed superior local knowledge of host country firms.

## ADVANCED TECHNOLOGY

Advanced technology includes both scientific and engineering skills. It is not limited to MNEs, but firms in the most industrialized countries have had an advantage in terms of access to continuing new technology spin-offs from the military and space programs. Empirical studies have supported the importance of technology as a characteristic of MNEs.

## FINANCIAL STRENGTH

As discussed in Chapter 11, companies demonstrate financial strength by achieving and maintaining a global cost and availability of capital. This is a critical competitive cost variable that enables them to fund FDI and other foreign activities. MNEs that are resident in liquid and unsegmented capital markets are normally blessed with this attribute. However, MNEs that are resident in small industrial or emerging market countries can still follow a proactive strategy of seeking foreign portfolio and corporate investors.

Small- and medium-size firms often lack the characteristics that attract foreign (and maybe domestic) investors. They are too small or unattractive to achieve a global cost of capital. This limits their ability to fund FDI, and their higher marginal cost of capital reduces the number of foreign projects that can generate the higher required rate of return.

## DIFFERENTIATED PRODUCTS

Firms create their own firm-specific advantages by producing and marketing differentiated products. Such products originate from research-based innovations or heavy marketing expenditures to gain brand identification. Furthermore, the research and marketing process continues to produce a steady stream of new differentiated products. It is difficult and costly for competitors to copy such products, and they always face a time lag if they try. Having developed differentiated products for the domestic home market, the firm may decide to market them worldwide, a decision consistent with the desire to maximize return on heavy research and marketing expenditures.

## COMPETITIVENESS OF THE HOME MARKET

A strongly competitive home market can sharpen a firm's competitive advantage relative to firms located in less competitive home markets. This phenomenon is known as the "diamond of national advantage." The diamond has four components, as illustrated in Exhibit 16.6.[1]

A firm's success in competing in a particular industry depends partly on the availability of factors of production (land, labor, capital, and technology) appropriate for

[1]Michael Porter, *The Competitive Advantage of Nations*, London: Macmillan Press, 1990.

**EXHIBIT 16.6**

Determinants of National Competitive Advantage: Porter's Diamond

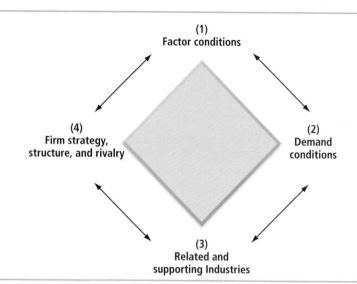

that industry. Countries that are either naturally endowed with the appropriate factors or able to create them will probably spawn firms that are both competitive at home and potentially so abroad. For example, a well-educated work force in the home market creates a competitive advantage for firms in certain high-tech industries.

Firms facing sophisticated and demanding customers in the home market are able to hone their marketing, production, and quality control skills. Japan is such a market.

Firms in industries that are surrounded by a critical mass of related industries and suppliers will be more competitive because of this supporting cast. For example, electronic firms located in centers of excellence, such as in the San Francisco Bay area, are surrounded by efficient, creative suppliers and enjoy access to educational institutions at the forefront of knowledge.

A competitive home market forces firms to fine-tune their operational and control strategies for their specific industry and country environment. Japanese firms learned how to organize to implement their famous just-in-time inventory control system. One key was to use numerous subcontractors and suppliers that were encouraged to locate near the final assembly plants.

In some cases home country markets have not been large or competitive, but MNEs located there have nevertheless developed global niche markets served by foreign subsidiaries. Global competition in oligopolistic industries substitutes for domestic competition. For example, a number of MNEs resident in Scandinavia, Switzerland, and the Netherlands fall in this category. Some of these are Novo Nordisk (Denmark), Norske Hydro (Norway), Nokia (Finland), L.M. Ericsson (Sweden), Astra (Sweden), ABB (Sweden/Switzerland), Roche Holding (Switzerland), Royal Dutch Shell (the Netherlands), Unilever (the Netherlands), and Philips (the Netherlands).

Emerging market countries have also spawned aspiring global MNEs in niche markets even though they lack competitive home country markets. Some of these are traditional exporters in natural resource fields such as oil, agriculture, and minerals, but they are in transition to becoming MNEs. They typically start with foreign sales subsidiaries, joint ventures, and strategic alliances. Examples are Petrobras (Brazil), YPF

(Argentina), and Cemex (Mexico). Another category of firms is those that have been recently privatized in the telecommunications industry. Examples are Telefonos de Mexico and Telebras (Brazil). Still others started as electronic component manufacturers but are making the transition to manufacturing abroad. Examples are Samsung Electronics (Korea) and Acer Computer (Taiwan).

## The OLI Paradigm and Internalization

The OLI Paradigm (Buckley and Casson, 1976; Dunning, 1977) is an attempt to create an overall framework to explain why MNEs choose FDI rather than serve foreign markets through alternative modes such as licensing, joint ventures, strategic alliances, management contracts, and exporting.[2]

The *OLI Paradigm* states that a firm must first have some competitive advantage in its home market — "O" or *owner-specific* — that can be transferred abroad if the firm is to be successful in foreign direct investment. Second, the firm must be attracted by specific characteristics of the foreign market — "L" or *location-specific* — that will allow it to exploit its competitive advantages in that market. Third, the firm will maintain its competitive position by attempting to control the entire value chain in its industry — "I" or *internalization*. This leads it to foreign direct investment rather than licensing or outsourcing.

### DEFINITIONS

The "O" in OLI stands for owner-specific advantages. As described earlier, a firm must have competitive advantages in its home market. These must be firm-specific, not easily copied, and in a form that allows them to be transferred to foreign subsidiaries. For example, economies of scale and financial strength are not necessarily firm-specific because they can be achieved by many other firms. Certain kinds of technology can be purchased, licensed, or copied. Even differentiated products can lose their advantage to slightly altered versions, given enough marketing effort and the right price.

The "L" in OLI stands for location-specific advantages. These factors are typically market imperfections or genuine comparative advantages that attract FDI to particular locations. These factors might include a low-cost but productive labor force, unique sources of raw materials, a large domestic market, defensive investments to counter other competitors, or centers of technological excellence.

The "I" in OLI stands for internalization. According to the theory, the key ingredient for maintaining a firm-specific competitive advantage is possession of proprietary information and control of the human capital that can generate new information through expertise in research. Needless to say, once again large research-intensive firms are most likely to fit this description.

Minimizing transactions costs is the key factor in determining the success of an internalization strategy. Wholly-owned FDI reduces the agency costs that arise from asymmetric information, lack of trust, and the need to monitor foreign partners, suppliers, and financial institutions. Self-financing eliminates the need to observe specific debt covenants on foreign subsidiaries that are financed locally or by joint venture

---

[2]Peter J. Buckley, and Mark Casson, *The Future of the Multinational Enterprise*, London: McMillan, 1976; and John H. Dunning, "Trade Location of Economic Activity and the MNE: A Search for an Eclectic Approach," in *The International Allocation of Economic Activity*, Bertil Ohlin, Per-Ove Hesselborn, and Per Magnus Wijkman, eds., New York: Holmes and Meier, 1977, pp. 395–418.

**EXHIBIT 16.7**

Finance-Specific Factors and the OLI Paradigm: "X" indicates a connection between FDI and finance-specific strategies

| | Ownership Advantages | Location Advantages | Internalization Advantages |
|---|:---:|:---:|:---:|
| *Proactive Financial Strategies* | | | |
| 1. Gaining and maintaining a global cost and availability of capital | | | |
| • Competitive sourcing of capital globally | X | X | |
| • Strategic preparatory cross-listing | X | | |
| • Providing accounting and disclosure transparency | X | | |
| • Maintaining competitive commercial and financial banking relationships | X | | |
| • Maintaining a competitive credit rating | X | X | X |
| 2. Negotiating financial subsidies and/or reduced taxation to increase free cash flow | X | X | |
| 3. Reducing financial agency cost through FDI | | | X |
| 4. Reducing operating and transaction exposure through FDI | X | | |
| *Reactive Financial Strategies* | | | |
| 1. Exploiting undervalued or overvalued exchange rates | | X | |
| 2. Exploiting undervalued or overvalued stock prices | | X | |
| 3. Reacting to capital control that prevents the free movement of funds | | X | |
| 4. Minimizing taxation | | X | X |

Source: Reprinted from *International Business Review*, Vol. 10, Lars Oxelheim, Arthur Stonehill and Trond Randøy, "On the Treatment of Finance Specific Factors Within the OLI Paradigm," pages 381–398, ©2001, with permission from Elsevier Science.

partners. If a multinational firm has a low global cost and high availability of capital, why share it with joint venture partners, distributors, licensees, and local banks, all of which probably have a higher cost of capital?

## THE FINANCIAL STRATEGY

Financial strategies are directly related to the OLI Paradigm in explaining FDI, as shown in Exhibit 16.7. Proactive financial strategies can be controlled in advance by the MNE's financial managers. These include strategies necessary to gain an advantage from lower global cost and greater availability of capital and were explained in detail in Part 4. Other proactive financial strategies are negotiating financial subsidies and/or reduced taxation to increase free cash flows, reducing financial agency costs through FDI, and reducing operating and transaction exposure through FDI.

Reactive financial strategies, as illustrated in Exhibit 16.7, depend on discovering market imperfections. For example, the MNE can exploit misaligned exchange rates and stock prices. It also needs to react to capital controls that prevent the free movement of funds and react to opportunities to minimize worldwide taxation.

## Deciding Where to Invest

The decision about where to invest abroad is influenced by behavioral factors. The decision about where to invest abroad for the first time is not the same as the decision about where to reinvest abroad. A firm learns from its first few investments abroad and what it learns influences subsequent investments.

In theory, a firm should identify its competitive advantages. Then it should search worldwide for market imperfections and comparative advantage until it finds a country where it expects to enjoy a competitive advantage large enough to generate a risk-adjusted return above the firm's hurdle rate.

In practice, firms have been observed to follow a sequential search pattern as described in the behavioral theory of the firm. Human rationality is bounded by one's ability to gather and process all the information that would be needed to make a perfectly rational decision based on all the facts. This observation lies behind two related behavioral theories of FDI. They are described next as the *behavioral approach* and *international network theory*.

## BEHAVIORAL APPROACH TO FDI

The behavioral approach to analyzing the FDI decision is typified by the so-called Swedish School of economists.[3] The Swedish School has rather successfully explained not just the initial decision to invest abroad but also later decisions to reinvest elsewhere and to change the structure of a firm's international involvement over time. Based on the internationalization process of a sample of Swedish MNEs, the economists observed that these firms tended to invest first in countries that were not too far distant in psychic terms. *Close psychic distance* defined countries with a cultural, legal, and institutional environment similar to Sweden's, such as Norway, Denmark, Finland, Germany, and the United Kingdom. The initial investments were modest in size to minimize the risk of an uncertain foreign environment. As the Swedish firms learned from their initial investments, they became willing to take greater risks with respect to both the psychic distance of the countries and the size of the investments.

## MNES IN A NETWORK PERSPECTIVE

As the Swedish MNEs grew and matured, so did the nature of their international involvement. Today each MNE is perceived as being a member of an international network, with nodes based in each of the foreign subsidiaries, as well as the parent firm itself. Centralized (hierarchical) control has given way to decentralized (heterarchical) control. Foreign subsidiaries compete with each other and with the parent for expanded resource commitments, thus influencing the strategy and reinvestment decisions. Many of these MNEs have become political coalitions with competing internal and external networks. Each subsidiary (and the parent) is embedded in its host country's network of suppliers and customers. It is also a member of a worldwide network based on its industry. Finally, it is a member of an organizational network under the nominal control of the parent firm. Complicating matters still further is the possibility that the parent itself may have evolved into a *transnational firm*, one that is owned by a coalition of investors located in different countries.[4]

Asea Brown Boveri (ABB) is an example of a Swedish-Swiss firm that has passed through the international evolutionary process all the way to being a transnational firm. ABB was formed through a merger of Sweden-based ASEA and Switzerland-based Brown Boveri in 1991. Both firms were already dominant players internationally in the electrotechnical and engineering industries. ABB has literally hundreds of foreign subsidiaries, which are managed on a very decentralized basis. ABB's "flat"

---

[3]John Johansen, and F. Wiedersheim-Paul, "The Internationalization of the Firm: Four Swedish Case Studies," *Journal of Management Studies*, vol. 12, no. 3, 1975; and John Johansen and Jan Erik Vahlne, "The Internationalization of the Firm: A Model of Knowledge Development and Increasing Foreign Market Commitments," *Journal of International Business Studies*, vol. 8, no. 1, 1977.

[4]Mats Forsgren, *Managing the Internationalization Process: The Swedish Case*, London: Routledge, 1989.

organization structure and transnational ownership encourage local initiative, quick response, and decentralized FDI decisions. Although overall strategic direction is the legal responsibility of the parent firm, foreign subsidiaries play a major role in all decision making. Their input in turn is strongly influenced by their own membership in their local and worldwide industry networks.

## How to Invest Abroad: Modes of Foreign Involvement

The globalization process for a firm like Trident includes a sequence of decisions regarding where production is to occur, who is to own or control intellectual property, and who is to own the actual production facilities. Exhibit 16.8 provides a roadmap to explain this FDI sequence.

### EXPORTING VERSUS PRODUCTION ABROAD

There are several advantages to limiting a firm's activities to exports. *Exporting* has none of the unique risks facing FDI, joint ventures, strategic alliances, and licensing. Political risks are minimal. Agency costs, such as monitoring and evaluating foreign units, are avoided. The amount of front-end investment is typically lower than in other modes of foreign involvement. Foreign exchange risks remain, however.

The fact that a significant share of exports (and imports) are executed between MNEs and their foreign subsidiaries and affiliates further reduces the risk of exports compared to other modes of involvement. For example, *Real World Example 16.2* shows the extent of exports and imports from U.S.–based MNEs to their foreign subsidiaries and affiliates.

### EXHIBIT 16.8

The FDI Sequence: Foreign Presence and Foreign Investment

Source: Adapted from Gunter Dufey and R. Mirus, "Foreign Direct Investment: Theory and Strategic Considerations," unpublished, University of Michigan, 1985. Reprinted with permission from the authors. All Rights Reserved.

## Real World Example 16.2
### KEEPING IT IN THE FAMILY: AMERICAN EXPORTS TO AND IMPORTS FROM AMERICAN-OWNED AFFILIATES ABROAD (BILLIONS OF US$)

|  | Intracompany | Intercompany | Total |
|---|---|---|---|
| **All countries** | | | |
| Exports | 145.5 | 24.5 | 170.0 |
| Imports | 123.9 | 19.4 | 143.3 |
| Balance | 21.6 | 5.1 | 26.7 |
| **High-income countries** | | | |
| Exports | 129.0 | 20.8 | 149.9 |
| Imports | 54.0 | 15.1 | 129.1 |
| Balance | 35.0 | 5.7 | 40.7 |
| **Middle-income countries** | | | |
| Exports | 28.9 | 5.4 | 34.3 |
| Imports | 31.5 | 1.9 | 33.4 |
| Balance | −2.6 | 3.5 | 0.8 |
| **Low-income countries** | | | |
| Exports | 1.6 | 0.2 | 1.8 |
| Imports | 1.8 | 0.4 | 2.2 |
| Balance | −0.2 | −0.2 | −0.4 |

Source: Edward M. Graham, Institute for International Economics, as cited in "Globalisation and Its Critics: A Survey of Globalisation," *The Economist*, September 29, 2001, p. 9. © 2001 The Economist Newspaper Ltd. All Rights Reserved. Reprinted with permission. Further reproduction prohibited. www.economist.com

There are also disadvantages. A firm is not able to internalize and exploit the results of its research and development as effectively as if it invested directly. The firm also risks losing markets to imitators and global competitors that might be more cost efficient in production abroad and distribution. As these firms capture foreign markets, they might become so strong that they can export back into the domestic exporter's own market. Remember that defensive FDI is often motivated by the need to prevent this kind of predatory behavior as well as to preempt foreign markets before competitors can get started.

## LICENSING AND MANAGEMENT CONTRACTS VERSUS CONTROL OF ASSETS ABROAD

*Licensing* is a popular method for domestic firms to profit from foreign markets without the need to commit sizable funds. Since the foreign producer is typically wholly-owned locally, political risk is minimized. In recent years a number of host countries have demanded that MNEs sell their services in "unbundled form" rather than only through FDI. Such countries would like their local firms to purchase managerial expertise and knowledge of product and factor markets through management contracts, and purchase technology through licensing agreements.

The main disadvantage of licensing is that license fees are likely to be lower than FDI profits, although the return on the marginal investment might be higher. Other disadvantages include

- Possible loss of quality control
- Establishment of a potential competitor in third-country markets

- Possible improvement of the technology by the local licensee, which then enters the original firm's home market
- Possible loss of opportunity to enter the licensee's market with FDI later
- Risk that technology will be stolen
- High agency costs

MNEs have not typically used licensing of independent firms. On the contrary, most licensing arrangements have been with their own foreign subsidiaries or joint ventures. License fees are a way to spread the corporate research and development cost among all operating units and a means of repatriating profits in a form more acceptable to some host countries than dividends.

*Management contracts* are similar to licensing insofar as they provide for some cash flow from a foreign source without significant foreign investment or exposure. Management contracts probably lessen political risk because repatriation of managers is easy. International consulting and engineering firms traditionally conduct their foreign business on the basis of a management contract.

Whether licensing and management contracts are cost effective compared to FDI depends on the price host countries will pay for the unbundled services. If the price were high enough, many firms would prefer to take advantage of market imperfections in an unbundled way, particularly in view of the lower political, foreign exchange, and business risks. Because we observe MNEs continuing to prefer FDI, we must assume that the price for selling unbundled services is still too low.

Why is the price of unbundled services too low? The answer may lie in the synergy created when services are bundled as FDI in the first place. Managerial expertise is often dependent on a delicate mix of organizational support factors that cannot be transferred abroad efficiently. Technology is a continuous process, but licensing usually captures only the technology at a particular point in time. Most important of all, however, economies of scale cannot be sold or transferred in small bundles. By definition they require large-scale operations. A relatively large operation in a small market can hardly achieve the same economies of scale as a large operation in a large market.

Despite the handicaps, some MNEs have successfully sold unbundled services. An example is sales of managerial expertise and technology to the OPEC countries. In this case, however, the OPEC countries are both willing and able to pay a price high enough to approach the returns on FDI (bundled services) while receiving only the lesser benefits of the unbundled services.

## JOINT VENTURE VERSUS WHOLLY-OWNED SUBSIDIARY

A *joint venture* is here defined as shared ownership in a foreign business. A foreign business unit that is partially owned by the parent company is typically termed a *foreign affiliate*. A foreign business unit that is 50% or more owned (and therefore controlled) by the parent company is typically designated a *foreign subsidiary*. A joint venture would therefore typically fall into the categorization of being a foreign affiliate but not a foreign subsidiary.

A joint venture between an MNE and a host country partner is a viable strategy if, and only if, the MNE finds the right local partner. Some of the obvious advantages of having a compatible local partner are as follows:

1. The local partner understands the customs, mores, and institutions of the local environment. An MNE might need years to acquire such knowledge on its own with a wholly-owned greenfield subsidiary.

2. The local partner can provide competent management, not just at the top but also at the middle levels of management.
3. If the host country requires that foreign firms share ownership with local firms or investors, 100% foreign ownership is not a realistic alternative to a joint venture.
4. The local partner's contacts and reputation enhance access to the host country's capital markets.
5. The local partner may possess technology that is appropriate for the local environment or perhaps can be used worldwide.
6. The public image of a firm that is partially locally owned may improve its sales possibilities if the purpose of the investment is to serve the local market.

Despite this impressive list of advantages, joint ventures are not as common as wholly-owned foreign subsidiaries because MNEs fear interference by the local partner in certain critical decision areas. Indeed, what is optimal from the viewpoint of the local venture may be suboptimal for the multinational operation as a whole. The most important potential conflicts or difficulties are these:

1. Political risk is increased rather than reduced if the wrong partner is chosen. Imagine the standing of joint ventures undertaken with the family or associates of Suharto in Indonesia or Slobodan Milosevic in Serbia just before their overthrow. The local partner must be credible and ethical or the venture is worse off for being a joint venture.
2. Local and foreign partners may have divergent views about the need for cash dividends, or about the desirability of growth financed from retained earnings versus new financing.
3. Transfer pricing on products or components bought from or sold to related companies creates a potential for conflict of interest.
4. Control of financing is another problem area. An MNE cannot justify its use of cheap or available funds raised in one country to finance joint venture operations in another country.
5. Ability of a firm to rationalize production on a worldwide basis can be jeopardized if such rationalization would act to the disadvantage of local joint venture partners.
6. Financial disclosure of local results might be necessary with locally traded shares, whereas if the firm is wholly-owned from abroad such disclosure is not needed. Disclosure gives nondisclosing competitors an advantage in setting strategy.

Valuation of equity shares is difficult. How much should the local partner pay for its share? What is the value of contributed technology, or of contributed land in a country like China where all land is state owned? It is highly unlikely that foreign and host country partners have similar opportunity costs of capital, expectations about the required rate of return, or similar perceptions of appropriate premiums for business, foreign exchange, and political risks. Insofar as the venture is a component of the portfolio of each investor, its contribution to portfolio return and variance may be quite different for each.

## GREENFIELD INVESTMENT VERSUS ACQUISITION

A *greenfield investment* is defined as establishing a production or service facility starting from the ground up, that is, from a green field. A cross-border acquisition, in contrast, is defined as the purchase of an existing foreign-based firm or facility. The advantages and disadvantages of these modes of international involvement are contrasted in the chapter on cross-border mergers and acquisitions available on the book's Web site.

## STRATEGIC ALLIANCES

The term *strategic alliance* conveys different meanings to different observers. In one form of cross-border strategic alliance, two firms exchange a share of ownership with one another. A strategic alliance can be a takeover defense if the prime purpose is for a firm to place some of its stock in stable and friendly hands. If that is all that occurs, it is just another form of portfolio investment.

In a more comprehensive strategic alliance, in addition to exchanging stock, the partners establish a separate joint venture to develop and manufacture a product or service. Numerous examples of such strategic alliances can be found in the automotive, electronics, telecommunications, and aircraft industries. Such alliances are particularly suited to high-tech industries where the cost of research and development is high and timely introduction of improvements is important.

A third level of cooperation might include joint marketing and servicing agreements in which each partner represents the other in certain markets. Some observers believe such arrangements begin to resemble the cartels prevalent in the 1920s and 1930s. Because they reduce competition, cartels have been banned by international agreements and many national laws.

## MINI-CASE

# Benecol's Global Licensing Agreement

In November 1996, a Finnish company by the name of Raisio introduced a revolutionary new product into supermarkets across Finland — a cholesterol-reducing margarine called Benecol. Deriving its name from *bene* from the Latin for good, and *col* for cholesterol, the margarine could potentially reduce a regular consumer's blood cholesterol levels by 14–15%. All that was needed was for the consumer to consume a few grams of the margarine roughly three times a day — essentially with meals.

Although priced at roughly three times the price of most other margarine products, Raisio could not keep store shelves stocked with the level of immediate demand. The global potential for the product was thought to be enormous. Raisio, traditionally a relatively quiet share on the Helsinki Stock Exchange, skyrocketed in the following months.

The problem, however, was that Raisio itself was primarily a regional producer of industrial chemicals and foodstuffs, with margarine being its only retail product. Simultaneously, there were a number of potential competitive products in various stages of pipeline development around the world by large and capable companies like Novartis and Unilever. Raisio quickly came to the conclusion that if it were to reap the benefits of Benecol quickly and effectively in the global marketplace, it would need a global partner.

After continued negotiations, in March 1997 Raisio signed a global licensing agreement with McNeil Consumer Products, a healthcare products subsidiary of Johnson & Johnson (USA). The global licensing agreement gave exclusive rights to McNeil for the global distribution and sale of all products containing Benecol. The licensing agreement had three key elements, as described in the following exhibit.

The agreement made Raisio responsible for ensuring an adequate supply of stanol ester for all McNeil product needs. Raisio would have no other responsibilities under the agreement, other than the usual commitments associated with continued product development, testing, and certification. McNeil would be responsible for product development, manufacturing, regulatory approvals for national and international distribution, and marketing globally.

### Global Licensing: Agreement Between Raisio (Finland) and McNeil Consumer Products (USA)

1. Raisio would provide at an agreed-upon price all stanol ester (the key chemical ingredient of Benecol) which McNeil would use in producing all Benecol-based products;
2. Raisio would receive a royalty calculated as a percentage of the retail sales price of all Benecol products sold in any marketplace outside of Finland (the exact royalty rate was not disclosed, but is thought to be about 5%);
3. Raisio would receive a series of milestone payments from McNeil totaling roughly $60 million from 1997 to 1999.

## Case Questions

1. How does the global licensing agreement split *risk* and *return*, in a financial sense, between Raisio and McNeil?
2. How will the returns to Raisio accrue over the short-to-medium-to-long term under the agreement, assuming the product is met with relative success?

3. What are some of the possible motivations to Raisio and McNeil behind a *milestone agreement*? Assume the milestone payments are agreed-upon payments from McNeil to Raisio if
   a. Raisio successfully completes the expansion of its manufacturing capabilities for stanol ester.
   b. McNeil successfully introduces Benecol products in major industrial markets, overcoming regulatory hurdles or reaching specific sales goals.

## *Summary of Learning Objectives*

*Show why the theory of comparative advantage is the theoretical justification for international trade*

- The theory of comparative advantage is based on one country possessing a relative (not absolute) advantage in the production of goods intensive in either land, labor, or capital compared to another country.

*Analyze how market imperfections create a rationale for the existence of multinational enterprises*

- Imperfections in national markets for products, factors of production, and financial assets translate into market opportunities for MNEs.

*Explain why firms become multinational*

- Strategic motives drive the decision to invest abroad and become an MNE. Firms could be seeking new markets, raw material sources, production efficiency locations, access to state-of-the-art knowledge, or political safety.

*Demonstrate how key competitive advantages support MNEs' strategy to originate and sustain direct foreign investment*

- In order to invest abroad a firm must have a sustainable competitive advantage in the home market. This must be strong enough and transferable enough to overcome the disadvantages of operating abroad.
- Competitive advantages stem from economies of scale and scope arising from large size, managerial and marketing expertise, superior technology, financial strength, differentiated products, and competitiveness of the home market.

*Show how the OLI Paradigm provides a theoretical foundation for the globalization process*

- The OLI Paradigm is an attempt to create an overall framework to explain why MNEs choose FDI rather than serve foreign markets through alternative modes, such as licensing, joint ventures, strategic alliances, management contracts, and exporting.
- Finance-specific strategies are directly related to the OLI Paradigm, including both proactive and reactive financial strategies.

*Identify factors and forces that must be considered in the determination of where multinational enterprises invest*

- The decision about where to invest is influenced by economic and behavioral factors, as well as the stage of a firm's historical development.
- Psychic distance plays a role in determining the sequence of FDI and later reinvestment. As firms learn from their early investments they venture further afield and are willing to risk larger commitments.
- The most internationalized firms can be viewed from a network perspective. The parent firm and each of the foreign subsidiaries are members of networks. The networks are composed of relationships within a worldwide industry, within the host countries with suppliers and customers, and within the multinational firm itself.

*Illustrate the managerial and competitive dimensions of the alternative methods for foreign investment*

- Exporting avoids political risk but not foreign exchange risk. It requires the least up-front investment but it might eventually lose markets to imitators and global competitors that might be more cost efficient in production abroad and distribution.

- Alternative (to wholly-owned foreign subsidiaries) modes of foreign involvement exist. They include joint venture, strategic alliances, licensing, management contracts, and traditional exporting.

- Licensing enables a firm to profit from foreign markets without a major front-end investment. However, disadvantages include limited returns, possible loss of quality control and potential of establishing a future competitor.

- The success of a joint venture depends primarily on the right choice of a partner. For this reason and a number of issues related to possible conflicts in decision making between a joint venture and a multinational parent, the wholly-owned foreign subsidiary approach is more common.

## QUESTIONS

1. **Evolving into multinationalism.** As a firm evolves from purely domestic into a true multinational enterprise, it must consider (a) its competitive advantages, (b) where it wants to locate production, (c) the type of control it wants to have over any foreign operations, and (d) how much monetary capital to invest abroad. Explain how each of these four considerations is important to the success of foreign operations.

2. **Theory of comparative advantage.** What is the essence of the theory of comparative advantage?

3. **Market imperfections.** MNEs strive to take advantage of market imperfections in national markets for products, factors of production, and financial assets. Large international firms are better able to exploit such imperfections. What are their main competitive advantages?

4. **Strategic motives for foreign direct investment (FDI).**

   a. Summarize the five main motives that drive the decision to initiate FDI.

   b. Match these motives with the following MNEs:

   General Motors (USA)
       Royal Dutch Shell (Netherlands/UK)

   Kentucky Fried Chicken (USA)
       Jardine Matheson (Hong Kong)

   Apple Computer (USA)
       NEC (Japan)

5. **Competitive advantage.** In deciding whether to invest abroad, management must first determine whether the firm has a sustainable competitive advantage that enables it to compete effectively in the home market. What are the necessary characteristics of this competitive advantage?

6. **Economies of scale and scope.** Explain briefly how economies of scale and scope can be developed in production, marketing, finance, research and development, transportation, and purchasing.

7. **Competitiveness of the home market.** A strongly competitive home market can sharpen a firm's competitive advantage relative to firms located in less competitive markets. This phenomenon is known as Porter's "diamond of national advantage." Explain what is meant by the "diamond of national advantage."

8. **OLI Paradigm.** The OLI Paradigm is an attempt to create an overall framework to explain why MNEs choose FDI rather than serve foreign markets through alternative modes.

   a. Explain what is meant by the "O" in the OLI Paradigm.

   b. Explain what is meant by the "L" in the OLI Paradigm.

   c. Explain what is meant by the "I" in the OLI Paradigm.

9. **Financial links to OLI.** Financial strategies are directly related to the OLI Paradigm.

   a. Explain how *proactive* financial strategies are related to OLI.

   b. Explain how *reactive* financial strategies are related to OLI.

10. **Where to invest.** The decision about where to invest abroad is influenced by behavioral factors

    a. Explain the *behavioral approach* to FDI.

    b. Explain the *international network theory* explanation of FDI.

11. **Exporting versus producing abroad.** What are the advantages and disadvantages of limiting a firm's activities to exporting compared to producing abroad?

12. **Licensing and management contracts versus producing abroad.** What are the advantages and disadvantages of licensing and management contracts compared to producing abroad?

13. **Joint venture versus wholly-owned production subsidiary.** What are the advantages and disadvantages of forming a joint venture to serve a foreign market compared to serving that market with a wholly-owned production subsidiary?

14. **Greenfield investment versus acquisition.** What are the advantages and disadvantages of serving a foreign market through a greenfield foreign direct investment compared to an acquisition of a local firm in the target market?

15. **Cross-border strategic alliance.** The term "cross-border strategic alliance" conveys different meanings to different observers. What are these meanings?

## PROBLEMS

*Comparative Advantage.* Problems 1–5 illustrate an example of trade induced by comparative advantage. They assume that China and France each have 1,000 production units. With one unit of production (a mix of land, labor, capital, and technology), China can produce either 10 containers of toys or 7 cases of wine. France can produce either 2 cases of toys or 7 cases of wine. Thus, a production unit in China is five times as efficient compared to France when producing toys, but equally efficient when producing wine. Assume at first that no trade takes place. China allocates 800 production units to building toys and 200 production units to producing wine. France allocates 200 production units to building toys and 800 production units to producing wine.

1. **Production and consumption.** What is the production and consumption of China and France without trade?

2. **Specialization.** Assume complete specialization, where China produces only toys and France produces only wine. What would be the effect on total production?

3. **Trade at China's domestic price.** China's domestic price is 10 containers of toys equals 7 cases of wine. Assume China produces 10,000 containers of toys and exports 2,000 to France. Assume France produces 7,000 cases of wine and exports 1,400 cases to China. What happens to total production and consumption?

4. **Trade at France's domestic price.** France's domestic price is 2 containers of toys equals 7 cases of wine. Assume China produces 10,000 containers of toys and exports 400 containers to France. Assume France in turn produces 7,000 cases of wine and exports 1,400 cases to China. What happens to total production and consumption?

5. **Trade at negotiated mid-price.** The mid-price for exchange between France and China can be calculated as follows:

|  | Toys |  | Wine |
|---|---|---|---|
| China's domestic price | 10 | to | 7 |
| France's domestic price | 2 | to | 7 |
| Negotiated mid-price | 6 | to | 7 |

What happens to total production and consumption?

## Internet Exercises

1. **International capital flows: public and private.** Major multinational organizations (some of which are listed below) attempt to track the relative movements and magnitudes of global capital investment. Using these Web sites and others you may find, prepare a two-page executive briefing on the question of whether capital generated in the industrialized countries is finding its way to the less-developed and emerging markets. Is there some critical distinction between less-developed and emerging?

The World Bank
   http://www.worldbank.org/
Organisation for Economic Co-operation and Development
   http://www.oecd.org/
European Bank for Reconstruction and Development
   http://www.ebrd.org/

2. **International management and strategy consultancies.** The management consulting industry has been a primary resource for MNEs throughout

the world in the 1990s to design and develop their corporate strategies. The following firm Web sites provide some insight into the industry, the job opportunities available for professionals in consulting, as well as some interesting features such as The Boston Consulting Group's online interactive case study.

A.T. Kearney
  http://www.atkearney.com/

Bain & Company
  http://www.bain.com/
Booz Allen Hamilton
  http://www.bah.com/
The Boston Consulting Group
  http://www.bcg.com/
McKinsey & Company
  http://www.mckinsey.com/

# Political Risk Assessment and Management

## LEARNING OBJECTIVES

Define and classify foreign political risks

Analyze firm-specific risks

Examine country-specific risks

Identify global-specific risks

This chapter starts by defining political risks by classifying them on three levels: firm-specific, country-specific, or global-specific. The next section examines how an MNE can assess political risk by predicting each of these levels of risk. This is followed by a detailed discussion of firm-specific risks related to corporate governance and goal conflict. Then comes an analysis of one of the two main categories of country-specific risk called transfer risk. The following section describes the other main category of country-specific risk, namely, culture and institutional risks. This chapter ends with an analysis of global-specific risks, such as terrorism and other actions that are worldwide in origin rather than specific to a particular country.

## Defining Political Risk

In order for an MNE to identify, measure, and manage its political risks, it needs to define and classify these risks. Exhibit 17.1 classifies the political risks facing MNEs as being firm-specific, country-specific, or global-specific.

- *Firm-specific risks*, also known as *micro risks*, are those political risks that affect the MNE at the project or corporate level. *Governance risk,* due to goal conflict between an MNE and its host government, is the main political firm-specific risk. (An MNE also faces business risks and foreign exchange risks, which are covered extensively in other sections of this book).
- *Country-specific risks*, also known as *macro risks*, are those political risks that also affect the MNE at the project or corporate level but originate at the country level. The two main political risk categories at the country level are *transfer risk* and *cultural and institutional risks*. Transfer risk concerns mainly the problem of blocked funds, but also peripherally sovereign credit risk (covered elsewhere in this book). Cultural and institutional risks spring from ownership structure, human

**EXHIBIT 17.1**

Classification of
Political Risks

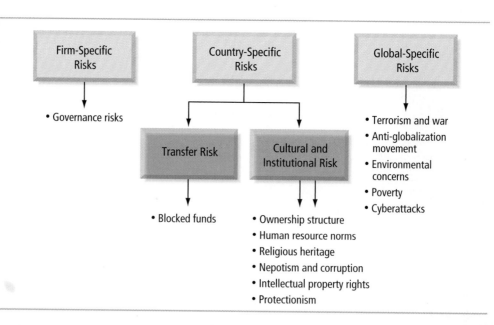

resource norms, religious heritage, nepotism and corruption, intellectual property rights, and protectionism.

- *Global-specific risks* are those political risks that affect the MNE at the project or corporate level but originate at the global level. Examples are terrorism, the anti-globalization movement, environmental concerns, poverty, and cyberattacks.

This method of classification differs sharply from the traditional method that classifies risks according to the disciplines of economics, finance, political science, sociology, and law. We prefer our classification system because it is easier to relate the identified political risks to existing and recommended strategies to manage these risks.

## Assessing Political Risk

How can multinational firms anticipate government regulations that, from the firm's perspective, are discriminatory or wealth depriving? Normally a twofold approach is utilized. At the macro level, firms attempt to assess a host country's political stability and attitude toward foreign investors. At the micro level, firms analyze whether their firm-specific activities are likely to conflict with host-country goals as evidenced by existing regulations. The most difficult task, however, is to anticipate changes in host-country goal priorities, new regulations to implement reordered priorities, and the likely impact of such changes on the firm's operations.

### PREDICTING FIRM-SPECIFIC RISK (MICRO RISK)

From the viewpoint of a multinational firm, assessing the political stability of a host country is only the first step, since the real objective is to anticipate the effect of political changes on activities of a specific firm. Indeed, different foreign firms operating within the same country may have very different degrees of vulnerability to changes in host-country policy or regulations. One does not expect a Kentucky Fried Chicken franchise to experience the same risk as a Ford manufacturing plant.

The need for firm-specific analyses of political risk has led to a demand for tailor-made studies undertaken in-house by professional political risk analysts. This demand is heightened by the observation that outside professional risk analysts rarely even agree on the degree of macro-political risk that exists in any set of countries.

In-house political risk analysts relate the macro risk attributes of specific countries to the particular characteristics and vulnerabilities of their client firms. Mineral extractive firms, manufacturing firms, multinational banks, private insurance carriers, and worldwide hotel chains are all exposed in fundamentally different ways to politically inspired restrictions. Even with the best possible firm-specific analysis, MNEs cannot be sure that the political or economic situation will not change. Thus it is necessary to plan protective steps in advance to minimize the risk of damage from unanticipated changes.

### PREDICTING COUNTRY-SPECIFIC RISK (MACRO RISK)

Macro political risk analysis is still an emerging field of study. Political scientists in academia, industry, and government study country risk for the benefit of multinational firms, government foreign policy decision makers, and defense planners.

Political risk studies usually include an analysis of the historical stability of the country in question, evidence of present turmoil or dissatisfaction, indications of economic stability, and trends in cultural and religious activities. Data are usually assembled by reading local newspapers, monitoring radio and television broadcasts, reading publications from diplomatic sources, tapping the knowledge of outstanding expert consultants, contacting other business persons who have had recent experience in the host country, and finally conducting on-site visits.

Despite this impressive list of activities, the prediction track record of business firms, the diplomatic service, and the military has been spotty at best. When one analyzes trends, whether in politics or economics, the tendency is to predict an extension of the same trends into the future. It is a rare forecaster who is able to predict a cataclysmic change in direction. Who predicted the overthrow of Ferdinand Marcos in the Philippines? Indeed, who predicted the collapse of communism in the Soviet Union and the Eastern European satellites? Who predicted the fall of President Suharto in Indonesia in 1998, or Saddam Hussein in 2004?

Despite the difficulty of predicting country risk, the MNE must still attempt to do so in order to prepare itself for the unknown. A number of institutional services provide updated country risk ratings on a regular basis. A sample of these rating for selected countries is shown in Exhibit 17.2.

## EXHIBIT 17.2

Country Risk Ratings for Selected Countries

| Risk Ratings | Indonesia | Finland | Brazil | Russia | Mexico |
|---|---|---|---|---|---|
| Currency unit | rupiah | euro | real | ruble | peso |
| Arrangement | floating | EMU | floating | managed float | floating |
| *S&P Rating* | CCC+ | AA | B+ | SD | BB |
| *Moody's Rating* | B3 | Aaa | B2 | B3 | B2 |
| *Fitch ICA* | B− | AAA | B | CCC | BB |
| *Economist Intelligence Unit*: | | | | | |
| Rating | D | B | D | D | C |
| Score | 67 | 35 | 62 | 79 | 53 |
| *Euromoney*: | | | | | |
| Rank | 88 | 12 | 76 | 161 | 47 |
| Score | 36.4 | 90.9 | 41.7 | 20.9 | 55.2 |
| *Institutional Investor*: | | | | | |
| Rank | 86 | 14 | 65 | 104 | 49 |
| Score | 27.9 | 82.2 | 37.4 | 20.0 | 46.0 |
| Trend | Negative | Positive | Negative | Negative | Positive |
| *International Country Risk Guide*: | | | | | |
| Political | 42.0 | 90.0 | 66.0 | 54.0 | 69.0 |
| Financial | 22.0 | 39.0 | 31.5 | 25.5 | 31.0 |
| Economic | 18.0 | 45.5 | 33.0 | 18.5 | 35.0 |
| *Milken Institute Capital Access Index*: | | | | | |
| Score | 37.8 | | 61.65 | 57.81 | 61.65 |
| Quantitative | 56.6 | | 52.38 | 71.15 | 52.38 |
| Risk measures | 26.3 | | 29.41 | 43.59 | 31.25 |
| Qualitative | 0.0 | | 36.36 | 31.03 | 34.76 |
| *Overseas Private Invest Corp*. | Yes | No | Yes | Yes | No |

Adapted by authors from the sources listed above. All values for March 1999. Each of these institutional services has its own regularly updated publications that were used to prepare this table.

## PREDICTING GLOBAL-SPECIFIC RISK

Predicting global-specific risk is even more difficult than predicting the other two types of political risk. Nobody predicted the surprise attacks on the World Trade Center and the Pentagon in the United States on September 11, 2001. On the other hand, the aftermath of this attack — the war on global terrorism, increased U.S. homeland security, and the destruction of part of the terrorist network in Afghanistan — was predictable. Nevertheless, we have come to expect future surprise terrorist attacks. U.S.–based MNEs are particularly exposed to not only al Qaeda but also to other unpredictable groups willing to use terror or mob action to promote such diverse causes as anti-globalization, environmental protection, and even anarchy.

Since there is a great need to predict terrorism, we can expect to see a number of new indices, similar to country-specific indices, but devoted to ranking different types of terrorist threats, their locations, and potential targets.

# Firm-Specific Risks

The firm-specific risks which confront MNEs include foreign exchange risks and governance risks. The various business and foreign exchange risks were detailed in Chapters 8, 9, and 10. We focus our discussion here on governance risks.

## GOVERNANCE RISKS

As introduced in Chapter 1, *governance risk* is the ability to exercise effective control over an MNE's operations within a country's legal and political environment. For an MNE, however, governance is a subject similar in structure to consolidated profitability — it must be addressed for the individual business unit and subsidiary, as well as for the MNE as a whole.

The most important type of governance risk for the MNE on the subsidiary level arises from a goal conflict between bona fide objectives of host governments and the private firms operating within their spheres of influence. Governments are normally responsive to a constituency of their citizens. Firms are responsive to a constituency of their owners and other stakeholders. The valid needs of these sets of constituents need not be the same, but governments set the rules. Consequently, governments impose constraints on the activities of private firms as part of their normal administrative and legislative functioning.

Historically, conflicts between objectives of MNEs and host governments have arisen over such issues as the firm's impact on economic development, perceived infringement on national sovereignty, foreign control of key industries, sharing or non-sharing of ownership and control with local interests, impact on a host country's balance of payments, influence on the foreign exchange value of its currency, control over export markets, use of domestic versus foreign executives and workers, and exploitation of national resources. Attitudes about conflicts are often colored by views about free enterprise versus state socialism, the degree of nationalism or internationalism present, or the place of religious views in determining appropriate economic and financial behavior.

The best approach to goal conflict management is to anticipate problems and negotiate understandings ahead of time. Different cultures apply different ethics to the question of honoring prior contracts, especially when they were negotiated with a previous administration. Nevertheless, prenegotiation of all conceivable areas of conflict provides a better basis for a successful future for both parties than does overlooking the possibility that divergent objectives will evolve over time. Prenegotiation often includes negotiating investment agreements, buying investment insurance and guarantees, and designing risk-reducing operating strategies to be used after the foreign investment decision has been made.

## NEGOTIATING INVESTMENT AGREEMENTS

An *investment agreement* spells out specific rights and responsibilities of both the foreign firm and the host government. The presence of MNEs is as often sought by development-seeking host governments as a particular foreign location sought by an MNE. All parties have alternatives and so bargaining is appropriate.

An investment agreement should spell out policies on financial and managerial issues, including the following:

- The basis on which fund flows, such as dividends, management fees, royalties, patent fees, and loan repayments, may be remitted
- The basis for setting transfer prices
- The right to export to third-country markets
- Obligations to build, or fund, social and economic overhead projects, such as schools, hospitals, and retirement systems
- Methods of taxation, including the rate, the type, and the means by which the rate base is determined
- Access to host-country capital markets, particularly for long-term borrowing
- Permission for 100% foreign ownership versus required local ownership (joint venture) participation
- Price controls, if any, applicable to sales in the host-country markets
- Requirements for local sourcing versus import of raw materials and components
- Permission to use expatriate managerial and technical personnel, and to bring them and their personal possessions into the country free of exorbitant charges or import duties
- Provision for arbitration of disputes
- Provisions for planned divestment, should such be required, indicating how the going concern will be valued and to whom it will be sold

## INVESTMENT INSURANCE AND GUARANTEES: OPIC

MNEs can sometimes transfer political risk to a home-country public agency through an investment insurance and guarantee program. Many developed countries have such programs to protect investments by their nationals in developing countries.

The U.S. investment insurance and guarantee program is managed by the government-owned Overseas Private Investment Corporation (OPIC). OPIC's stated purpose is to mobilize and facilitate the participation of U.S. private capital and skills in the economic and social progress of less developed friendly countries and areas, thereby complementing the developmental assistance of the United States. OPIC offers insurance coverage for four separate types of political risk, which have their own specific definitions for insurance purposes:

- *Inconvertibility* is the risk that the investor will not be able to convert profits, royalties, fees, or other income, as well as the original capital invested, into dollars.

- *Expropriation* is the risk that the host government takes a specific step that for one year prevents the investor or the foreign subsidiary from exercising effective control over use of the property.
- *War, revolution, insurrection, and civil strife* coverage applies primarily to the damage of physical property of the insured, although in some cases inability of a foreign subsidiary to repay a loan because of a war may be covered.
- *Business income* coverage provides compensation for loss of business income resulting from events of political violence that directly cause damage to the assets of a foreign enterprise.

## OPERATING STRATEGIES AFTER THE FDI DECISION

Although an investment agreement creates obligations on the part of both foreign investor and host government, conditions change and agreements are often revised in the light of such changes. The changed conditions may be economic, or they may be the result of political changes within the host government. The firm that sticks rigidly to the legal interpretation of its original agreement may well find that the host government first applies pressure in areas not covered by the agreement and then possibly reinterprets the agreement to conform to the political reality of that country. Most MNEs, in their own self-interest, follow a policy of adapting to changing host-country priorities whenever possible.

The essence of such adaptation is anticipating host-country priorities and making the activities of the firm of continued value to the host country. Such an approach assumes the host government acts rationally in seeking its country's self-interest and is based on the idea that the firm should initiate reductions in goal conflict. Future bargaining position can be enhanced by careful consideration of policies in production, logistics, marketing, finance, organization, and personnel.

**LOCAL SOURCING.**    Host governments may require foreign firms to purchase raw material and components locally as a way to maximize value-added benefits and to increase local employment. From the viewpoint of the foreign firm trying to adapt to host-country goals, local sourcing reduces political risk, albeit at a tradeoff with other factors. Local strikes or other turmoil may shut down the operation and such issues as quality control, high local prices because of lack of economies of scale, and unreliable delivery schedules become important. Often the MNE lowers political risk only by increasing its financial and commercial risk.

**FACILITY LOCATION.**    Production facilities may be located so as to minimize risk. The natural location of different stages of production may be resource-oriented, footloose, or market-oriented. Oil, for instance, is drilled in and around the Persian Gulf, Russia, Venezuela, and Indonesia. No choice exists for where this activity takes place. Refining, on the other hand, is footloose: A refining facility can be moved easily to another location or country. Whenever possible, oil companies have built refineries in politically safe countries, such as Western Europe, or small islands (such as Singapore or Curaçao), even though costs might be reduced by refining nearer the oil fields. They have traded reduced political risk and financial exposure for possibly higher transportation and refining costs.

**CONTROL OF TRANSPORTATION.**    Control of transportation has been an important means to reduce political risk. Oil pipelines that cross national frontiers, oil tankers, ore carriers, refrigerated ships, and railroads have all been controlled at times to influence the bargaining power of nations and companies.

**CONTROL OF TECHNOLOGY.**    Control of key patents and processes is a viable way to reduce political risk. If a host country cannot operate a plant because it does not have technicians capable of running the process, or of keeping up with changed technology, abrogation of an investment agreement with a foreign firm is unlikely. Control of technology works best when the foreign firm is steadily improving its technology.

**CONTROL OF MARKETS.**    Control of markets is a common strategy to enhance a firm's bargaining position. As effective as the OPEC cartel was in raising the price received for crude oil by its member countries in the 1970s, marketing was still controlled by the international oil companies. OPEC's need for the oil companies limited the degree to which its members could dictate terms. In more recent years OPEC members have established some marketing outlets of their own, such as Kuwait's extensive chain of Q8 gas stations in Europe.

Control of export markets for manufactured goods is also a source of leverage in dealings between MNEs and host governments. The MNE would prefer to serve world markets from sources of its own choosing, basing the decision on considerations of production cost, transportation, tariff barriers, political risk exposure, and competition. The selling pattern that maximizes long-run profits from the viewpoint of the world-wide firm rarely maximizes exports, or value added, from the perspective of the host countries. Some will argue that if the same plants were owned by local nationals and were not part of a worldwide integrated system, more goods would be exported by the host country. The contrary argument is that self-contained local firms might never obtain foreign market share because they lack economies of scale on the production side and are unable to market in foreign countries.

**BRAND NAME AND TRADEMARK CONTROL.**    Control of a brand name or trademark can have an effect almost identical to that of controlling technology. It gives the MNE a monopoly on something that may or may not have substantive value but quite likely represents value in the eyes of consumers. Ability to market under a world brand name is valuable for local firms and thus represents an important bargaining attribute for maintaining an investment position.

**THIN EQUITY BASE.**    Foreign subsidiaries can be financed with a thin equity base and a large proportion of local debt. If the debt is borrowed from locally owned banks, host-government actions that weaken the financial viability of the firm also endanger local creditors.

**MULTIPLE-SOURCE BORROWING.**    If the firm must finance with foreign source debt, it may borrow from banks in a number of countries rather than just from home country banks. If, for example, debt is owed to banks in Tokyo, Frankfurt, London, and New York, nationals in a number of foreign countries have a vested interest in keeping the borrowing subsidiary financially strong. If the multinational is U.S.–owned, a fallout between the United States and the host government is less likely to cause the local government to move against the firm if it also owes funds to these other countries.

## Country-Specific Risks: Transfer Risk

Country-specific risks affect all firms, domestic and foreign, that are resident in a host country. Exhibit 17.3 presents a taxonomy of most of the contemporary political risks and firm strategies that emanate from a specific country location. The main country-specific political risks are *transfer risk* and *cultural and institutional risks*.

### BLOCKED FUNDS

*Transfer risk* is defined as limitations on the MNE's ability to transfer funds into and out of a host country without restrictions. When a government runs short of foreign exchange and cannot obtain additional funds through borrowing or attracting new foreign investment, it usually limits transfers of foreign exchange out of the country, a restriction known as *blocked funds*. In theory, this does not discriminate against foreign-owned firms because it applies to everyone; in practice, foreign firms have more at stake because of their foreign ownership. Depending on the size of a foreign exchange shortage, the host government might simply require approval of all transfers of funds abroad, thus reserving the right to set a priority on the use of scarce foreign exchange in favor of necessities rather than luxuries. In very severe cases the government might make its currency nonconvertible into other currencies, thereby fully blocking transfers of funds abroad. In between these positions are policies that restrict the size and timing of dividends, debt amortization, royalties, and service fees.

MNEs can react to the potential for blocked funds at three stages.

1. Prior to making an investment, a firm can analyze the effect of blocked funds on expected return on investment, the desired local financial structure, and optimal links with subsidiaries.

## EXHIBIT 17.3

Management Strategies for Country-Specific Risks

**Transfer Risk**

**Cultural and Institutional Risk**

**Blocked Funds**
- Preinvestment strategy to anticipate blocked funds
- Fronting loans
- Creating unrelated exports
- Obtaining special dispensation
- Forced reinvestment

**Ownership Structure**
- Joint venture

**Religious Heritage**
- Understand and respect host country religious heritage

**Nepotism and Corruption**
- Disclose bribery policy to both employees and clients
- Retain a local legal advisor

**Human Resource Norms**
- Local management and staffing

**Intellectual Property**
- Legal action in host country courts
- Support worldwide treaty to protect intellectual property rights

**Protectionism**
- Support government actions to create regional markets

2. During operations a firm can attempt to move funds through a variety of repositioning techniques.

3. Funds that cannot be moved must be reinvested in the local country in a manner that avoids deterioration in their real value because of inflation or exchange depreciation.

## PREINVESTMENT STRATEGY TO ANTICIPATE BLOCKED FUNDS

Management can consider blocked funds in their capital budgeting analysis. Temporary blockage of funds normally reduces the expected net present value and internal rate of return on a proposed investment. Whether the investment should nevertheless be undertaken depends on whether the expected rate of return, even with blocked funds, exceeds the required rate of return on investments of the same risk class. Preinvestment analysis also includes the potential to minimize the effect of blocked funds by financing with local borrowing instead of parent equity, swap agreements, and other techniques to reduce local currency exposure and thus the need to repatriate funds. Sourcing and sales links with subsidiaries can be predetermined so as to maximize the potential for moving blocked funds.

## MOVING BLOCKED FUNDS

What can a multinational firm do to transfer funds out of countries having exchange or remittance restrictions? At least six popular strategies are used:

1. Providing alternative conduits for repatriating funds (analyzed in Chapter 21)
2. Transfer pricing goods and services between related units of the MNE (analyzed in Chapter 20)
3. Leading and lagging payments (described in Chapter 8)
4. Using fronting loans
5. Creating unrelated exports
6. Obtaining special dispensation

**FRONTING LOANS.**   A *fronting loan* is a parent-to-subsidiary loan channeled through a financial intermediary, usually a large international bank. Fronting loans differ from parallel or back-to-back loans, discussed in Chapter 9. The latter are offsetting loans between commercial businesses arranged outside the banking system. Fronting loans are sometimes referred to as *link financing*.

In a direct intracompany loan a parent or sister subsidiary loans directly to the borrowing subsidiary, and at a later date the borrowing subsidiary repays the principal and interest. In a fronting loan, by contrast, the "lending" parent or subsidiary deposits funds in, say, a London bank, and that bank loans the same amount to the borrowing subsidiary in the host country. From the London bank's point of view the loan is risk-free, because the bank has 100% collateral in the form of the parent's deposit. In effect the bank fronts for the parent — hence the name *fronting loan*. Interest paid by the borrowing subsidiary to the bank is usually slightly higher than the rate paid by the bank to the parent, allowing the bank a margin for expenses and profit.

The bank chosen for the fronting loan is usually in a neutral country, away from both the lender's and the borrower's legal jurisdiction. Use of fronting loans increases chances for repayment should political turmoil occur between the home and host countries. Government authorities are more likely to allow a local subsidiary to repay a loan to a large international bank in a neutral country than to allow the same subsidiary to repay a loan directly to its parent. To stop payment to the international bank would hurt the international credit image of the country, whereas to stop payment to the parent corporation would have minimal impact on that image and might even provide some domestic political advantage.

**CREATING UNRELATED EXPORTS.**   Another approach to blocked funds that bene-fits both the subsidiary and host country is the creation of unrelated exports. Because the main reason for stringent exchange controls is usually a host country's persistent inability to earn hard currencies, anything an MNE can do to create new exports from the host country helps the situation and provides a potential means to transfer funds out.

Some new exports can often be created from present productive capacity with little or no additional investment, especially if they are in product lines related to existing operations. Other new exports may require reinvestment or new funds, although if the funds reinvested consist of those already blocked, little is lost in the way of opportunity costs.

**SPECIAL DISPENSATION.**   If all else fails and the multinational firm is investing in an industry that is important to the economic development of the host country, the firm may bargain for special dispensation to repatriate some portion of the funds that oth-erwise would be blocked. Firms in "desirable" industries such as telecommunications, semiconductor manufacturing, instrumentation, pharmaceuticals, or other research and high-technology industries may receive preference over firms in mature industries. The amount of preference received depends on bargaining among the informed par-ties, the government and the business firm, either of which is free to back away from the proposed investment if unsatisfied with the terms.

**SELF-FULFILLING PROPHECIES.**   In seeking escape routes for blocked funds — or for that matter in trying to position funds through any of the techniques discussed in this chapter — the MNE may increase political risk and cause a change from partial blockage to full blockage. The possibility of such a self-fulfilling cycle exists any time a firm takes action that, no matter how legal, thwarts the underlying intent of politically motivated controls. In the statehouses of the world, as in the editorial offices of the local press and TV, MNEs and their subsidiaries are always a potential scapegoat.

**FORCED REINVESTMENT.**   If funds are indeed blocked from transfer into foreign exchange, they are by definition reinvested. Under such a situation the firm must find local opportunities that will maximize rate of return for a given acceptable level of risk.

If blockage is expected to be temporary, the most obvious alternative is to invest in local money market instruments. Unfortunately, in many countries such instruments are not available in sufficient quantity or with adequate liquidity. In some cases gov-ernment treasury bills, bank deposits, and other short-term instruments have yields that are kept artificially low relative to local rates of inflation or probable changes in exchange rates. Thus the firm often loses real value during the period of blockage.

If short- or intermediate-term portfolio investments, such as bonds, bank time deposits, or direct loans to other companies, are not possible, investment in additional production facilities may be the only alternative. Often this investment is what the host country is seeking by its exchange controls, even if the existence of exchange controls is by itself counterproductive to the idea of additional foreign investment. Examples of forced direct reinvestment can be cited for Peru, where an airline invested in hotels and in maintenance facilities for other airlines; for Turkey, where a fish canning company constructed a plant to manufacture cans needed for packing the catch; and for Argentina, where an automobile company integrated vertically by acquiring a transmission manufacturing plant previously owned by a supplier.

If investment opportunities in additional production facilities are not available, funds may simply be used to acquire other assets expected to increase in value with local inflation. Typical purchases might be land, office buildings, or commodities that are exported to global markets. Even inventory stockpiling might be a reasonable investment, given the low opportunity cost of the blocked funds.

## Country-Specific Risks: Cultural and Institutional Risks

When investing in some of the emerging markets, MNEs that are resident in the most industrialized countries face serious risks because of cultural and institutional differences. Among many such differences are

- Differences in allowable ownership structures
- Differences in human resource norms
- Differences in religious heritage
- Nepotism and corruption in the host country
- Protection of intellectual property rights
- Protectionism

### OWNERSHIP STRUCTURE

Historically, many countries have required that MNEs share ownership of their foreign subsidiaries with local firms or citizens. Thus, joint ventures were the only way an MNE could operate in some host countries. Prominent countries that used to require majority local ownership were Japan, Mexico, China, India, and Korea. This requirement has been eliminated or modified in more recent years by these countries and most others. However, firms in certain industries are still either excluded from ownership completely or must accept being a minority owner. These industries are typically related to national defense, agriculture, banking, or other sectors that are deemed critical for the host nation. Even the United States would not welcome foreign ownership of large key defense-related firms such as Boeing Aircraft.

The risks involved in controlling foreign joint ventures were described in Chapter 16. Potential limitations on an MNE's operating decisions make foreign joint ventures less desirable than wholly-owned foreign subsidiaries, exporting, licensing, contract production, strategic alliances, and other alternative forms of serving foreign markets.

### HUMAN RESOURCE NORMS

MNEs are often required by host countries to employ a certain proportion of host country citizens rather than staffing mainly with foreign expatriates. It is often very difficult to fire local employees due to host country labor laws and union contracts. This lack of flexibility to downsize in response to business cycles affects both MNEs and their local competitors. It also qualifies as a country-specific risk.

Cultural differences can also inhibit an MNE's staffing policies. For example, it is somewhat difficult for a woman manager to be accepted by local employees and managers in many Middle Eastern countries. The most extreme example of discrimination against women has been highlighted in Afghanistan while the Taliban were in power. Since the Taliban's downfall in late 2001, several women have been suggested for important government roles. It is expected that the private sector in Afghanistan will also reintegrate women into the workforce.

## RELIGIOUS HERITAGE

The current hostile environment for MNEs in some Middle Eastern countries such as Iran, Iraq, and Syria is being fed by some extremist Muslim clerics who are enraged about the continuing violence in Israel and the occupied Arab territories. However, the root cause of these conflicts is a mixture of religious fervor for some and politics for others. Although it is popular to blame the Muslim religion for its part in fomenting the conflict, a number of Middle Eastern countries, such as Egypt, Saudi Arabia, and Jordan, are relatively passive when it comes to *jihads*. Jihads are calls for Muslims to attack the infidels (Jews and Christians). Osama bin Laden's call for jihad against the United States has not generated any great interest on the part of moderate Muslims. Indeed one Muslim country, Turkey, has had a secular government for many decades. It strongly supported efforts to rid the world of bin Laden.

Despite religious differences, MNEs have operated successfully in emerging markets, especially in extractive and natural resource industries, such as oil, natural gas, minerals, and forest products. The main MNE strategy is to understand and respect the host country's religious traditions.

## NEPOTISM AND CORRUPTION

MNEs must deal with endemic nepotism and corruption in a number of important foreign investment locations. Indonesia was famous for nepotism and corruption under the now-deposed Suharto government. Nigeria, Kenya, Uganda, and a number of other African countries had a history of nepotism and corruption after they threw out their colonial governments after World War II. China and Russia have recently launched well-publicized crackdowns on those practices.

Bribery is not limited to emerging markets. It is also a problem in even the most industrialized countries, including the United States and Japan. In fact, the United States has an antibribery law that would imprison any U.S. business executive found guilty of bribing a foreign government official. This law was passed in reaction to an attempt by Lockheed Aircraft to bribe a Japanese Prime Minister.

**TI'S CORRUPTION PERCEPTION INDEX.**   Transparency International (TI) publishes a monthly newsletter on corruption in international business. TI's Corruption Perception Index for 2002 is shown in Exhibit 17.4. This index is based on the level of corruption as perceived by persons working for MNEs and financial institutions. Thus it is an index not of actual corruption, but rather of perceptions. The score is based on an integrity ranking, where 10 equals an entirely clean country and 0 a country in which business transactions are entirely dominated by kickbacks, extortion, bribery, and similar practices. The standard deviation measures the dispersions of opinion.

**MANAGING BRIBERY.**   MNEs are caught in a dilemma. Should they employ bribery if their local competitors use this strategy? Alternative strategies are

- Refuse bribery outright, or else demands will quickly multiply.

## EXHIBIT 17.4

Transparency International's Corruption Perception Index, 2002

| Country Rank | Country | CPI 2002 score | Standard deviation | Country Rank | Country | CPI 2002 score | Standard deviation |
|---|---|---|---|---|---|---|---|
| 1 | Finland | 9.7 | 0.4 | 52 | Czech Republic | 3.7 | 0.8 |
| 2 | Denmark | 9.5 | 0.3 | | Latvia | 3.7 | 0.2 |
| | New Zealand | 9.5 | 0.2 | | Morocco | 3.7 | 1.8 |
| 4 | Iceland | 9.4 | 0.4 | | Slovak Republic | 3.7 | 0.6 |
| 5 | Singapore | 9.3 | 0.2 | | Sri Lanka | 3.7 | 0.4 |
| | Sweden | 9.3 | 0.2 | 57 | Colombia | 3.6 | 0.7 |
| 7 | Canada | 9.0 | 0.2 | | Mexico | 3.6 | 0.6 |
| | Luxembourg | 9.0 | 0.5 | 59 | China | 3.5 | 1.0 |
| | Netherlands | 9.0 | 0.3 | | Dominican Rep. | 3.5 | 0.4 |
| 10 | United Kingdom | 8.7 | 0.5 | | Ethiopia | 3.5 | 0.5 |
| 11 | Australia | 8.6 | 1.0 | 62 | Egypt | 3.4 | 1.3 |
| 12 | Norway | 8.5 | 0.9 | | El Salvador | 3.4 | 0.8 |
| | Switzerland | 8.5 | 0.9 | 64 | Thailand | 3.2 | 0.7 |
| 14 | Hong Kong | 8.2 | 0.8 | | Turkey | 3.2 | 0.9 |
| 15 | Austria | 7.8 | 0.5 | 66 | Senegal | 3.1 | 1.7 |
| 16 | USA | 7.7 | 0.8 | 67 | Panama | 3.0 | 0.8 |
| 17 | Chile | 7.5 | 0.9 | 68 | Malawi | 2.9 | 0.9 |
| 18 | Germany | 7.3 | 1.0 | | Uzbekistan | 2.9 | 1.0 |
| | Israel | 7.3 | 0.9 | 70 | Argentina | 2.8 | 0.6 |
| 20 | Belgium | 7.1 | 0.9 | 71 | Cote d'Ivoire | 2.7 | 0.8 |
| | Japan | 7.1 | 0.9 | | Honduras | 2.7 | 0.6 |
| | Spain | 7.1 | 1.0 | | India | 2.7 | 0.4 |
| 23 | Ireland | 6.9 | 0.9 | | Russia | 2.7 | 1.0 |
| 24 | Botswana | 6.4 | 1.5 | | Tanzania | 2.7 | 0.7 |
| 25 | France | 6.3 | 0.9 | | Zimbabwe | 2.7 | 0.5 |
| | Portugal | 6.3 | 1.0 | 77 | Pakistan | 2.6 | 1.2 |
| 27 | Slovenia | 6.0 | 1.4 | | Philippines | 2.6 | 0.6 |
| 28 | Namibia | 5.7 | 2.2 | | Romania | 2.6 | 0.8 |
| 29 | Estonia | 5.6 | 0.6 | | Zambia | 2.6 | 0.5 |
| | Taiwan | 5.6 | 0.8 | 81 | Albania | 2.5 | 0.8 |
| 31 | Italy | 5.2 | 1.1 | | Guatemala | 2.5 | 0.6 |
| 32 | Uruguay | 5.1 | 0.7 | | Nicaragua | 2.5 | 0.7 |
| 33 | Hungary | 4.9 | 0.5 | | Venezuela | 2.5 | 0.5 |
| | Malaysia | 4.9 | 0.6 | 85 | Georgia | 2.4 | 0.7 |
| | Trinidad & Tobago | 4.9 | 1.5 | | Ukraine | 2.4 | 0.7 |
| 36 | Belarus | 4.8 | 1.3 | | Vietnam | 2.4 | 0.8 |
| | Lithuania | 4.8 | 1.9 | 88 | Kazakhstan | 2.3 | 1.1 |
| | South Africa | 4.8 | 0.5 | 89 | Bolivia | 2.2 | 0.4 |
| | Tunisia | 4.8 | 0.8 | | Cameroon | 2.2 | 0.7 |
| 40 | Costa Rica | 4.5 | 0.9 | | Ecuador | 2.2 | 0.3 |
| | Jordan | 4.5 | 0.7 | | Haiti | 2.2 | 1.7 |
| | Mauritius | 4.5 | 0.8 | 93 | Moldova | 2.1 | 0.6 |
| | South Korea | 4.5 | 1.3 | | Uganda | 2.1 | 0.3 |
| 44 | Greece | 4.2 | 0.7 | 95 | Azerbaijan | 2.0 | 0.3 |
| 45 | Brazil | 4.0 | 0.4 | 96 | Indonesia | 1.9 | 0.6 |
| | Bulgaria | 4.0 | 0.9 | | Kenya | 1.9 | 0.3 |
| | Jamaica | 4.0 | 0.4 | 98 | Angola | 1.7 | 0.2 |
| | Peru | 4.0 | 0.6 | | Madagascar | 1.7 | 0.7 |
| | Poland | 4.0 | 1.1 | | Paraguay | 1.7 | 0.2 |
| 50 | Ghana | 3.9 | 1.4 | 101 | Nigeria | 1.6 | 0.6 |
| 51 | Croatia | 3.8 | 0.2 | 102 | Bangladesh | 1.2 | 0.7 |

Source: Transparency International, http://www.transparency.org/cpi/2002/cpi2002.en.html © 2002 Transparency International. Reprinted with permission.

- Retain a local advisor to diffuse demands by local officials, customs agents, and other business partners.
- Do not count on the justice system in many emerging markets, because Western-oriented contract law may not agree with local norms.
- Educate both management and local employees about whatever bribery policy the firm intends to follow.

## INTELLECTUAL PROPERTY RIGHTS

Rogue businesses in some host countries have historically infringed on the *intellectual property rights* of both MNEs and individuals. *Intellectual property rights* grant the exclusive use of patented technology and copyrighted creative materials. Examples of patented technology are unique manufactured products, processing techniques, and prescription pharmaceutical drugs. Examples of copyrighted creative materials are software programs, educational materials (textbooks), and entertainment products (music, film, art).

MNEs and individuals need to protect their intellectual property rights through the legal process. However, courts in some countries have historically not done a fair job of protecting intellectual property rights of anyone, much less of foreign MNEs. In those countries the legal process is costly and subject to bribery.

The agreement on Trade-Related Aspects of Intellectual Property Rights (TRIPS) to protect intellectual property rights has recently been ratified by most major countries. China signed the treaty as one of the conditions it needed to meet to join the World Trade Organization (WTO) in 2001. It remains to be seen whether host governments are strong enough to enforce their official efforts to stamp out intellectual piracy. Complicating this task is the thin line that exists between the real item being protected and look-alikes or generic versions of the same item.

## PROTECTIONISM

*Protectionism* is defined as the attempt by a national government to protect certain of its designated industries from foreign competition. Industries that are protected are usually related to defense, agriculture, and "infant" industries.

**DEFENSE.** Even though the United States is a vocal proponent of open markets, a foreign firm proposing to buy Lockheed Missile Division or other critical defense suppliers would not be welcome. The same attitude exists in many other countries, such as France, which has always wanted to maintain an independent defense capability.

**AGRICULTURE.** Agriculture is another sensitive industry. No MNE would be foolish enough as to attempt to buy agricultural properties, such as rice operations, in Japan. Japan has desperately tried to maintain an independent ability to feed its population. Agriculture is the "Mother Earth" industry that most countries want to protect for their own citizens.

**INFANT INDUSTRIES.** The traditional protectionist argument is that newly emerging industries need protection from foreign competition until they can get firmly established. The infant industry argument is usually directed at limiting imports but not necessarily MNEs. In fact most host countries encourage MNEs to establish operations in industries that do not presently exist in the host country. Sometimes the host country offers foreign MNEs infant-industry status for a limited number of years. This status could lead to tax subsidies, construction of infrastructure, employee training, and other aids to help the MNE get started. Host countries are especially interested in attracting MNEs that promise to export, either to their own foreign subsidiaries elsewhere or to unrelated parties.

**TARIFF BARRIERS.**　　The traditional methods for countries to implement protectionist barriers were through tariff and nontariff regulations. Negotiations under the General Agreements on Tariffs and Trade (GATT) have greatly reduced the general level of tariffs over the past decades. This process continues today under the auspices of the WTO. However, many nontariff barriers remain.

**NON-TARIFF BARRIERS.**　　Nontariff barriers, which restrict imports by something other than a financial cost, are often difficult to identify because they are promulgated as health, safety, or sanitation requirements. A list of the major types of nontariff barriers would include those shown in Exhibit 17.5.

**STRATEGIES TO MANAGE PROTECTIONISM.**　　MNEs have only a very limited ability to overcome host country protectionism. However, MNEs do enthusiastically support efforts to reduce protectionism by joining together in regional markets. The best examples of regional markets are the European Union (EU), the North American Free Trade Association (NAFTA), and the Latin American Free Trade Association (MERCOSUR). Among the objectives of regional markets are elimination of internal trade barriers, such as tariffs and nontariff barriers, as well as the free movement of citizens for employment purposes. External trade barriers still exist.

The EU is trying to become a "United States of Europe," with a single internal market without barriers. It is not quite there, although the European Monetary Union and the euro have almost eliminated monetary policy differences. The EU still tolerates differences in fiscal policies, legal systems, and cultural identities. In any case, the movement toward regional markets is very favorable for MNEs serving those markets with foreign subsidiaries.

## ENRON INTERNATIONAL

Enron was introduced in Chapter 1 as the poster boy of failed corporate governance. However, country-specific risks also played a role in Enron's eventual demise. A particular problem was its overly aggressive direct investment activities in emerging markets. *Real World Example 17.1* illustrates some of Enron International's problems.

**EXHIBIT 17.5**

Types of Non-Tariff Barriers

1. Specific limitations on trade, which either limit the amount of imports directly or establish import procedures that make importing more difficult
2. Customs and administrative entry procedures, which include inconsistent procedures for valuation, classification, of documents, or assessing fees
3. Unduly stringent or discriminating standards imposed in the name of protecting health, safety, and quality
4. Governmental participation in trade
5. Charges on imports
6. Other nontariff barriers

Source: Adapted from material in A. D. Cao, "Non-Tariff Barriers to U.S. Manufactured Exports," *Columbia Journal of World Business*, Summer 1980, pp. 93–102.

## Real World Example 17.1
### ENRON INTERNATIONAL IN INDIA

Enron International, first under John Wing and later under Rebecca Mark, signed and sealed new power and pipeline projects at a breakneck pace. The difference was that by the time Enron International grew to size and influence in the mid-1990s under Rebecca Mark, projects recognized earnings up front using the same mark-to-market accounting as employed in the trading businesses. These projects committed Enron's capital resources for years to come, and in many cases, locked in cash flow shortfalls for as many years as well. In the rush to sign and deliver deals, inadequate due diligence became common, overly aggressive bidding promised unprofitable margins, and a growing disdain for the costs and complexity of project execution characterized deals. Deals were done at the expense of delivery.

Enron Development would often sign and book deals which later proved to be dead in the water. Accounting rules required that projects which were no longer in progress be written down in current earnings. Enron Development fought these write-offs at every turn. Rich Kinder had instructed the unit that these unrecognized losses, called "snowballs" within Enron, be kept below $90 million in total. In early 1996, however, they soared to over $200 million.

The Dabhol, India project was a microcosm of Enron's business model. In December 1993, after roughly 18 months of negotiations, Enron Development signed a long-term power sales contract with the electricity board of Maharashtra, India (MSEB). Enron would build a 2,000-megawatt natural gas-fueled power plant at an estimated cost of $2.8 billion. The Maharashtra energy board agreed to buy 90% of the power produced by the plant at a U.S. dollar-denominated price for a minimum of 20 years. From the very beginning, problems mounted. It took Rebecca Mark more than two years and millions of dollars in negotiations, court cases, and contract restructurings to get the financing in place. Within months a change in the Maharashtra government resulted in an outpouring of project opposition. Once again, Mark went into overdrive for months of negotiations and renegotiations. Finally, on February 23, 1996, a new contract was signed between Enron and the MSEB. By December financing was in place and the project's construction resumed. But opposition continued, and it became clear that the MSEB would never be willing or able to pay for the power (estimated at over $30 billion for the project life).

The project was dead. In the words of one Wall Street analyst on Enron's India activities, "I've never been to another country where every single person hates one company." Phase I of the project was operational for only a short period of time, and Phase II (as of December 2003) is still only 80% complete. The Dabhol power plant today is considered a failure for everyone involved but Rebecca Mark. Mark earned bonuses for both the original deal and the successful renegotiation. In 1996 Enron International generated 15% of Enron's total earnings, and was expected to grow at double-digit rates for years to come. Rebecca Mark was named CEO of Enron International. Many people believed that Rebecca Mark would be Enron's next CEO, but she left in 2000, selling here 1.4 million shares for $79.5 million.

## Global-Specific Risks

Global-specific risks faced by MNEs have come to the forefront in recent years. Exhibit 17.6 summarizes some of these risks and the strategies that can be used to manage them. The most visible recent risk was, of course, the attack by terrorists on the twin towers of the World Trade Center in New York on September 11, 2001. Many MNEs had major operations in the World Trade Center and suffered heavy casualties among their employees. In addition to terrorism, other global-specific risks include the anti-globalization movement, environmental concerns, poverty in emerging markets, and cyberattacks on computer information systems.

### TERRORISM AND WAR

Although the World Trade Center attack and its aftermath, the war in Afghanistan and Iraq, have affected nearly everyone in the world, many other acts of terrorism have been committed in recent years. More terrorist acts are expected to occur in the future.

**EXHIBIT 17.6**

Management
Strategies for
Global-Specific
Risks

**Terrorism and War**
- Support government efforts to fight terrorism and war
- Crisis planning
- Cross-border supply chain integration

**Anti-Globalization**
- Support government efforts to reduce trade barriers
- Recognize that MNEs are the targets

**Environmental Concerns**
- Show sensitivity to environmental concerns
- Support government efforts to maintain a level playing field for pollution controls

**Poverty**
- Provide stable, relatively well-paying jobs
- Establish the strictest of occupational safety standards

**Cyberattacks**
- No effective strategy except Internet security efforts
- Support government anti-cyberattack efforts

*MNE movement toward multiple primary objectives:*
*Profitability, Sustainable Development, Corporate Social Responsibility*

Particularly exposed are the foreign subsidiaries of MNEs and their employees. As mentioned earlier, foreign subsidiaries are especially exposed to war, ethnic strife, and terrorism because they are symbols of their respective parent countries.

No MNE has the tools to avert terrorism. Hedging, diversification, insurance, and the likes are not suited to the task. Therefore, MNEs must depend on governments to fight terrorism and protect their foreign subsidiaries (and now even the parent firm). In return, governments expect financial, material, and verbal support from MNEs to support antiterrorist legislation and proactive initiatives to destroy terrorist cells wherever they exist.

## CRISIS PLANNING

MNEs can be subject to damage by being in harm's way. Nearly every year one or more host countries experience some form of ethnic strife, outright war with other countries, or terrorism. It seems that foreign MNEs are often singled out as symbols of oppression because they represent their parent country, especially if it is the United States.

Resolving war and ethnic strife is beyond the ability of MNEs. Instead, they need to take defensive steps to limit the damage. *Crisis planning* has become a major activity for MNEs at both the foreign subsidiary and parent firm levels. Crisis planning means educating management and other employees about how to react to various scenarios of violence. For example, MNE units must know how to stay in communication with each other; how to protect the MNE's property; how to escape the country; and how to protect themselves by maintaining a low profile.

## CROSS-BORDER SUPPLY CHAIN INTEGRATION

The drive to increase efficiency in manufacturing has driven many MNEs to adopt just-in-time (JIT) near-zero inventory systems. Focusing on *inventory velocity*, the speed at which inventory moves through a manufacturing process, arriving only as needed and not before, has allowed these MNEs to generate increasing profits and cash flows with less capital being bottled-up in the production cycle. This finely tuned supply chain system, however, is subject to significant political risk if the supply chain extends across borders.

**SUPPLY CHAIN INTERRUPTIONS.**    Consider the cases of Dell Computer, Ford Motor Company, Dairy Queen, Apple Computer, Herman Miller, and The Limited in the days following the terrorist attacks of September 11, 2001. An immediate result was the grounding of all aircraft into or out of the United States. Similarly, the land (Mexico and Canada) and sea borders of the United States were also shut down and not reopened for several days in some specific sites. Ford Motor Company shut down five of its manufacturing plants in the days following September 11 because of inadequate inventories of critical automotive inputs supplied from Canada. Dairy Queen experienced such significant delays in key confectionary ingredients many of its stores were also temporarily closed.

Dell Computer, with one of the most highly acclaimed and admired virtually integrated supply chains, depends on computer parts and subassembly suppliers and manufacturers in Mexico and Canada to fulfill its everyday assembly and sales needs. In recent years Dell has carried less than three full days sales of total inventory — by cost-of-goods value. Suppliers are integrated electronically with Dell's order fulfillment system, and they deliver required components and subassemblies as sales demands require. But with the closure of borders and grounding of air freight, the company was brought to a near standstill because of its supply chain's reliance on the ability to treat business units and suppliers in different countries as if they were all part of a single seamless political unit.

As a result of these newly learned lessons, many MNEs are now evaluating the degree of exposure their supply chains possess in regard to cross-border stoppages or other cross-border political events. These companies are not, however, about to abandon JIT. It is estimated that U.S. companies alone have saved more than $1 billion a year in inventory carrying costs by using JIT methods over the past decade. This substantial benefit is now being weighed against the costs and risks associated with the post-September 11 supply chain interruptions.

To avoid suffering a similar fate in the future, manufacturers, retailers, and suppliers are now employing a range of tactics:

- **Inventory management.** Manufacturers and assemblers are considering carrying more buffer inventory in order to hedge against supply and production-line disruptions. Retailers, meanwhile, should think about the timing and frequency of their replenishment. Rather than stocking up across the board, companies are focusing on the most critical parts to the product or service, and on those components that are uniquely available only from international sources.
- **Sourcing.** Manufacturers are now being more selective about where the critical inputs to their products come from. Although sourcing strategies will have to vary by location, firms are attempting to work more closely with existing suppliers to minimize cross-border exposures and reduce the potential costs with future stoppages.
- **Transportation.** Retailers and manufacturers alike are reassessing their cross-border shipping arrangements. For example, many inputs that currently are carried by passenger flights may be precluded from cohabitation on these flights in the

future. Although the mode of transportation employed is a function of value, volume, and weight, many firms are now reassessing whether higher costs for faster shipment balance out the more tenuous their delivery under airline stoppages from either labor, terrorist, or even bankruptcy disruptions in the future.

*Real World Example 17.2* illustrates how many of the security policies adopted by the U.S. government also have an impact on the efficiency of supply chain management.

## ANTI-GLOBALIZATION MOVEMENT

During the past decade there has been a growing negative reaction by some groups to reduced trade barriers and efforts to create regional markets, particularly to NAFTA and the European Union. NAFTA has been vigorously opposed by those sectors of the labor movement that could lose jobs to Mexico. Opposition within the European Union centers on loss of cultural identity, dilution of individual national control as new members are admitted, overcentralization of power in a large bureaucracy in Brussels, and most recently the disappearance of individual national currencies in mid-2002, when the euro became the only currency in 12 of the 15 member nations.

The anti-globalization movement has become more visible following riots in Seattle during the 2001 annual meeting of the World Trade Organization. Anti-globalization forces were not solely responsible for these riots, or for subsequent riots in Quebec and Prague in 2001. Other disaffected groups, such as environmentalists and even anarchists, joined in to make their causes more visible.

MNEs do not have the tools to combat anti-globalism. Indeed, they are blamed for fostering the problem in the first place. Once again, MNEs must rely on governments and crisis planning to manage these risks.

## Real World Example 17.2
### INTERNATIONAL SUPPLY CHAIN SECURITY: TIME IS MONEY

Many new and evolving border security laws and guidelines will have a hand in slowing import processing times at the U.S. border. To protect businesses from these events, U.S. importers must navigate through a variety of new security initiatives, including the following:

| | |
|---|---|
| C-TPAT | **The Custom-Trade Partnership Against Terrorism.** A U.S. Customs program designed to encourage companies across the supply chain to voluntarily self-assess and strengthen security practices to protect the United States against the risk of terrorist activity via product and conveyance tampering on import shipments. |
| CSI | **Container Security Initiative.** A U.S. Customs program focusing on securing ocean-going containers by engaging the authorities of certain foreign ports shipping the highest volumes of container traffic into the United States in a way that will facilitate early detection of potential security problems. |
| FAST | **Free and Secure Trade.** A joint U.S.-Canada program designed to expedite customs clearance of goods moving across the northern border through specially designated FAST lanes for qualified goods by qualified shippers. |
| CIP | **Carrier Initiative Program.** A voluntary U.S. Customs and carrier program designed to prevent smuggling of narcotics on air, sea, and land commercial conveyances. |
| BASC | **Business Anti-Smuggling Coalition.** A business-led initiative designed to complement the CIP program by combating contraband smuggling via commercial trade and eliminate the contamination of legitimate business shipments by criminal hands. |

Source: Adapted from "The New Era of International Supply Chain Security," *World Trade*, November 2002, pp. 56–57. Used with permission.

## ENVIRONMENTAL CONCERNS

MNEs have been accused of exporting their environmental problems to other countries. The accusation is that MNEs frustrated by pollution controls in their home country have relocated these activities to countries with weaker pollution controls. Another accusation is that MNEs contribute to the problem of global warming. However, that accusation applies to all firms in all countries. It is based on the manufacturing methods employed by specific industries and on consumers' desire for certain products such as large automobiles and sport vehicles that are not fuel efficient.

Once again, solving environmental problems is dependent on governments passing legislation and implementing pollution control standards. In 2001, the Kyoto Treaty, which attempted to reduce global warming, was ratified by most nations, with the notable exception of the United States. However, the United States has promised to combat global warming using its own strategies. The United States objected to provisions in the worldwide treaty that allowed emerging nations to follow less restrictive standards, while the economic burden would fall on the most industrialized countries, particularly the United States.

## POVERTY

MNEs have located foreign subsidiaries in countries plagued by extremely uneven income distribution. At one end is an elite class of well-educated, well-connected, and productive persons. At the other end of the spectrum is a very large class of persons living at or below the poverty level. They lack education, social and economic infrastructure, and political power.

MNEs might be contributing to this disparity by employing the elite class to manage their operations. On the other hand, MNEs are creating relatively stable and well-paying jobs for those who were otherwise unemployed and living below the poverty level. Despite being accused of supporting sweatshop conditions, MNEs usually compare favorably to their local competitors. For example, Nike, one of the targeted MNEs, usually pays better, provides more fringe benefits, maintains higher safety standards, and educates their workforce to allow personnel to advance up the career ladder. Of course, Nike cannot manage a country's poverty problems overall, but it can improve conditions for some persons.

## CYBERATTACKS

The rapid growth of the Internet has fostered a whole new generation of scam artists and cranks that disrupt the usefulness of the World Wide Web. This is both a domestic and an international problem. MNEs can face costly cyberattacks because of their visibility and the complexity of their internal information systems.

At this point in time, we know of no uniquely international strategies that MNEs can use to combat cyberattacks. MNEs are using the same strategies to manage foreign cyberattacks as they use for domestic attacks. Once again, they must rely on governments to control cyberattacks.

## GOVERNANCE, RIGHTS, AND THE FUTURE

The first years of the twenty-first century have seen a rebirth in society's reflections on business. One of the most audible debates has been that regarding sustainable development, the principle that economic development today should not compromise the ability of future generations to achieve and enjoy similar standards of living. Although sustainable development initially focused on environmental concerns, it has evolved to include equal concerns which "incorporate the ambition for a just and caring society."[1] Although these debates have typically remained within areas of economic development, the debate in business circles has centered on corporate social responsibility. *Real World Example 17.3* illustrates corporate social responsibility in practice. The mini-case below describes how Starbucks Coffee manages its social responsibility in practice.

## Real World Example 17.3
### CORPORATE SUSTAINABILITY

Recent reports from the Danish pharmaceuticals group Novo Nordisk and Carrefour, the French food retailer, demonstrate the potentially wide practical impact of a company's commitment to sustainability.

Novo Nordisk (*Reporting on the Triple Bottom Line 2001*) identifies a wide range of indicators that measure its impact on the environment, people, and societies. Examples of areas covered include animal welfare, water and energy use efficiency, and compliance with regulatory limits. The report stresses the need to involve and educate employees; work internationally; define targets and report annually; balance financial, environmental, social, and health policies in the business decision processes; and conduct dialogue and partnerships with stakeholders.

The operational impact at Carrefour (*Sustainability Report 2001*) involves everything from fostering fair trade — the report cites 54 tons of Carrefour organic coffee sold in France last year that was bought in Mexico for 30 percent more than the market price — to reducing atmospheric emissions from cold storage units and a commitment to eliminate genetically modified organisms from animal feed in the company's product lines.

Source: Excerpted from "Measuring the Impact of a New Approach," *Financial Times*, Monday August 19, 2002, p. 5. © 2002 The Financial Times. Reprinted with permission.

## MINI-CASE

# Globalization and Starbucks Coffee[2]

*Starbucks defines corporate social responsibility as conducting our business in ways that produce social, environmental and economic benefits to the communities in which we operate. In the end, it means being responsible to our stakeholders.*

*There is growing recognition of the need for corporate accountability. Consumers are demanding more than "product" from their favorite brands. Employees are choosing to work for companies with strong values. Shareholders are more inclined to invest in businesses with outstanding corporate reputations. Quite simply, being socially responsible is not only the right thing to do; it can distinguish a company from its industry peers.*

*Corporate Social Responsibility Annual Report*
Starbucks Coffee, Fiscal 2001, p. 3.

Starbucks found itself, somewhat to its surprise, an early target of the anti-globalism movement. Like McDonald's before it, it appeared to be yet another American cultural imperialist, bringing a chain-store sameness to all countries everywhere. Like McDonald's, Starbucks found that its uniquely defined brand and experience did not have to conform to local cultural norms, but could exist alongside traditional practices, creating its own market and successfully altering some consumer behaviors.

Unlike McDonald's, however, Starbucks was the purveyor of a commodity, coffee, that was priced and sold on global markets. Coffee was sourced from hundreds of thousands of small growers in Central and South America, many of whom were severely impoverished by all global income and purchasing power standards. As coffee prices plummeted in the late 1990s, companies like Starbucks were criticized for benefitting from lower cost sourcing and for their unwillingness to help improve the economic conditions of the coffee growers.

[1]Dickson, Tim, "The Financial Case for Behaving Responsibly," *Financial Times*, August 19, 2002, p. 5.

[2]This illustrative case is adapted from "Planet Starbucks (A)" by Professors Michael H. Moffett and Kannan Ramaswamy, Thunderbird Case Series, A06-02-0000, 2003. Copyright © 2003 Thunderbird — The Garvin School of International Management. All Rights Reserved.

## Procurement

Coffee was traditionally bought and sold using *market pricing*, which means buying from wholesalers at a global market price — the so-called New York C. Since Starbucks purchased only arabica bean premium grade coffee, *green coffee*, it always paid a premium above New York C. Both New York C prices and the premium, however, moved up and down with global market conditions. Traditional robusta bean purchases by mass-market labels were made on the wholesale markets through brokers and buyers.

Starbucks, however, preferred to purchase using *outright pricing*, in which the price was negotiated directly with owners of small and medium-sized farms, cutting out the segment of the supply chain which the wholesalers (called *coyotes* in Central and South America) usually occupied. In principle, a greater proportion of the price went directly to the producers, assuring a higher return to the small farmer. In addition to the pricing structure, Starbucks was also attempting to break from traditional market practices of always buying in the cash market. The company was moving aggressively to purchase more and more of its coffee under long-term contract guaranteeing prices to growers over multiple crop years.

## Coffee Prices

The single biggest problem was the price of coffee itself. As illustrated by Exhibit 1, the global price of arabica coffee had been extremely volatile over the previous 20 years. In fact, arabica beans had been as high as $1.50/lb (annual average, they had been significantly higher on a daily and weekly basis) as recently as 1994. The price in recent years had plummeted, as more and more coffee production came on to the market, creating a substantial excess supply. This was an obvious benefit to coffee consumers, including Starbucks. The growers, however, most of whom had small farms of 7 hectares or less, were now receiving prices nearly 40 cents/lb, when average production costs were 77 cents/lb. Although this was not the fault or responsibility of Starbucks (it was estimated to use less than 1% of the world's annual coffee crop), the company was criticized for paying less than a living wage to its growers.

By 2001 Starbucks had implemented a multitude of programs to pursue its program for corporate social responsibility (CSR) and pursue sustainable economic development for the people in its supply chain. Not wishing to own the supply chain, Starbucks arrived at a strategy that was a complex combination of altered business practices in procurement, direct support to the coffee growers, and the formation of brands that would provide conduits for consumers wishing to support CSR initiatives. Exhibit 2 provides a brief overview of some of these programs.

## Conduit Brand Development

Much of the growing pressure on all multinational companies for sustainable development and social responsibility arose directly from consumer segments. In an effort to provide a direct conduit for these consumer demands, Starbucks had initiated a company program called *Commitment to Origins* "dedicated to creating a sustainable growing environment in coffee originating countries." Under the program Starbucks had introduced Shade Grown Mexico coffee and Fair Trade Certified coffee.

Shade Grown Mexico coffee was introduced in 1998 in partnership with Conservation International (CI), a non-profit environmental organization. Coffee purchased by Starbucks from CI's Conservation Coffee Program was

---

**EXHIBIT 1**

Arabica Bean Coffee Prices, 1981–2001

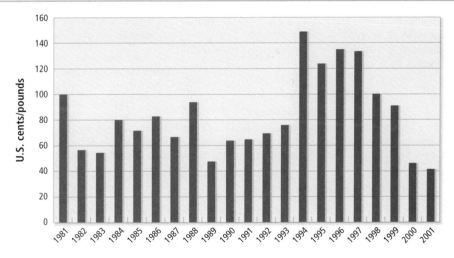

Source: International Coffee Organization (ICO), www.ico.org.

**EXHIBIT 2**

Starbucks' CSR
Programs
Focusing on
Coffee Growers

*Starbucks' coffee buyers work with coffee wholesalers and directly with small farmers and farm cooperatives in procurement*

Infrastructure, including schools, clinics, and coffee processing facilities

Supplemental funding for farm credit programs to support farm capital needs

Contributions to CARE, the nonprofit international relief organization

**Shade Grown Mexico Brand** Partnership formed in 1998, encourages production of shade-grown coffee using ecologically sound growing practices to promote bio-diversity and to financially support farms employing these practices (with Conservation International, CI)

**Fair Trade Certified Brand** Partnership in which Starbucks promises consumers that the farmers who produced the coffee beans were paid a guaranteed minimum price that helps support a better life for farm families (with TransFair USA)

cultivated under the canopy of shade trees in origin countries. This practice was considered ecologically sound and helped support bio-diversity. Shade Grown Mexico coffee purchases had grown from 304,000 pounds in 2000 to an estimated 1.5 million pounds in 2002.[3] Shade Grown Mexico coffee had been selectively introduced in Starbucks stores in North America and through online sales at starbucks.com.

Beginning in 2000, Starbucks began working with TransFair USA, a nonprofit organization which provided independent certification for all Fair Trade coffee in the United States.[4]

*The concept of Fair Trade addressed the question of the just distribution of the burdens and benefits of trade. The Fair Trade movement argues that when most of the customers' purchasing dollar goes to the retailer, the marketer, the wholesaler, and the speculator and very little goes to the laborer or the farmer, something is wrong with the mutual benefits of the exchanges, particularly when those who provide the product have earnings that do not even cover subsistence costs.[5]*

Although Starbucks had introduced *Fair Trade* coffee in North American stores, and promoted it through various

[3] Starbucks' commitment to CI was established on an annual basis. Starbucks had renewed its partnership in 2000 for a three-year period, agreeing to purchase at least 200,000 pounds of shade grown coffee annually. Starbucks has also noted that growers of Shade Grown Mexico coffee received price premiums of 60% over local coffee prices in fiscal 2001.

[4] TransFair USA is associated with Equal Exchange, a Fair Trade organization promoting socially responsible business practices with coffee growers in Central and Latin America.

[5] John Kohls and Sandra L. Christensen, "The Business Responsibility for Wealth Distribution in a Globalized Political-Economy: Merging Moral Economics and Catholic Social Teaching," *Journal of Business Ethics*, February 2002, p. 12.

brochures and promotions ("Coffee of the Day" monthly), it continued to be heavily criticized for not expanding the program faster. In October 2001 the company expanded its commitments, agreeing to purchase at least one million pounds of Fair Trade certified coffee, meeting its quality requirements in the following 12 to 18 months.

Both of these product brand programs allowed consumers wishing to support these sustainable development initiatives to express their interest through purchasing. But Fair Trade certified coffee was higher cost, by definition, and that cost premium was reflected in the retail price.[6] Both Fair Trade and Shade Grown Mexico coffees were 20% to 25% more expensive compared to Starbucks' traditional blends (whole bean coffee sales).

Starbucks was a regular and growing giver, supporting relief organizations such as CARE, the nonprofit international relief organization, as well as providing direct support to farmers and farm communities around the world.[7] For example, Starbucks had contributed $43,000 in 2001 to the construction of a health clinic and school in Guatemala and a health clinic in East Timor. The company was also providing aid in a variety of ways to the improvement of coffee processing facilities in a number of the countries of origin.

The anti-globalization movement continued to focus much of its efforts on Starbucks. Plummeting coffee prices on world markets in 2001 and 2002 had led to more and more pressure on Starbucks to increase the prices it paid to growers. Starbucks chairman Howard Shultz became the increasing target of mail, fax, and e-mail campaigns to pressure Starbucks into more proactive policies for grower income support (see Exhibit 3). Although Starbucks had actively pursued a number of corporate social responsibility initiatives, it was accused of polishing its image more than truly working to improve the lives of those its existence depended on, the coffee growers.

---

**EXHIBIT 3**

Cyberattack: The
Starbucks
Campaign

*Participate in the Organic Consumers Association*
*"Global Week of Action Against Starbucks," September 21–28.*

*In October 2001, Starbucks made a commitment to buy 1 million more pounds of Fair Trade coffee and brew Fair Trade coffee once a month. Don't let Starbucks stop there — Send a Free Fax to demand that Starbucks brew Fair Trade Coffee of the Day EVERY WEEK!*

The coffee industry is in crisis. Coffee prices are at an all-time low, remaining below $.50 since August with no increase in sight. This means that farmers are becoming even more impoverished, going further into debt and losing their land. Meanwhile coffee companies such as Starbucks have not lowered consumer prices but are pocketing the difference, even taking into account the quality premiums in the specialty industry.

The Fair Trade Labeling Organizations International recently released figures that show a total production by groups on the Fair Trade Coffee Register of 165,000,000 pounds in year 2000, whereas total sales were only 30,000,000 pounds. This leaves an additional 135,000,000 pounds of Fair Trade coffee produced by cooperatives that are not receiving a Fair Trade price.

Source: © 2004 Global Exchange. Used with permission. www.globalexchange.org/economy/coffee/starbucks, accessed 10/6/02.

---

[6]Starbucks reported that buyers paid $1.26/lb for non-organic green and $1.41/lb for organic green in 2001, when New York C prices were hovering at roughly $0.50/pound. Although production costs varied significantly across countries and regions, coffee growers associations estimated average production costs to be $0.80/pound.

[7]Starbucks gave $120,000 to CARE in fiscal 2001, bringing its cumulative contributions over time to more than $1.8 million. Starbucks' work with CARE began in 1991.

## Summary of Learning Objectives

*Define and classify foreign political risks*

- Political risks can be defined by classifying them on three levels: *firm-specific*, *country-specific*, and *global-specific*.

- *Firm-specific risks*, also known as *micro risks*, are those that affect the MNE at the project or corporate level.

- *Country-specific risks*, also known as *macro risks*, are those that affect the MNE at the project or corporate level but that originate at the country level.

- *Global-specific risks* are those that affect the MNE at the project or corporate level but that originate at the global level.

*Analyze firm-specific risks*

- The main firm-specific risk is *governance risk*, which is the ability to exercise control over the MNE as a whole, globally, and within a specific country's legal and political environment on the individual subsidiary level.

- The most important type of governance risk arises from a goal conflict between bona fide objectives of governments and private firms.

- The main tools used to manage goal conflict are to negotiate an investment agreement; to purchase investment insurance and guarantees; and to modify operating strategies in production, logistics, marketing, finance, organization, and personnel.

*Examine country-specific risks*

- The main *country-specific risks* are *transfer risk*, known as *blocked funds*, and certain cultural and institutional risks.

- Blocked funds can be managed by any of five strategies: (1) management should consider including blocked funds in their original capital budgeting analysis; (2) fronting loans; (3) creating unrelated exports; (4) obtaining special dispensation; and (5) planning for forced reinvestment.

- Cultural and institutional risks emanate from host country policies with respect to ownership structure, human resource norms, religious heritage, nepotism and corruption, intellectual property rights, and protectionism.

- Managing cultural and institutional risks requires the MNE to understand the differences, take legal actions in host country courts, support worldwide treaties to protect intellectual property rights, and support government efforts to create regional markets.

*Identify global-specific risks*

- The main global-specific risks are currently caused by terrorism and war, the anti-globalization movement, environmental concerns, poverty, and cyberattacks.

- In order to manage global-specific risks, an MNE should adopt a crisis plan to protect its employees and property and to secure its supply chain integrity. However, the MNE largely relies on government to protect its citizens and firms from global-specific threats.

## QUESTIONS

1. **Political risk definition.** In order for an MNE to identify, measure, and manage its political risks, it needs to define and classify these risks. Define the following political risks:

   **a.** Firm-specific risks

   **b.** Country-specific risks

   **c.** Transfer risk

   **d.** Cultural and institutional risk

   **e.** Global-specific risk

2. **Country risk ratings.** Exhibit 17.2 shows country risk ratings for selected countries. Using Moody's, S&P, and Euromoney rating services, prepare a country risk rating for Argentina.

3. **Governance risk.**

   **a.** Define what is meant by the term *governance risk*.

   **b.** What is the most important type of governance risk?

4. **Investment agreement.** An investment agreement spells out the specific rights and responsibilities of a foreign firm and its host government. What are the main financial policies that should be included in an investment agreement?

5. **Investment insurance and guarantees (OPIC).**

   **a.** What is OPIC?

   **b.** What types of political risks can OPIC insure against?

6. **Operating strategies after the FDI decision.** The following operating strategies, among others, are expected to reduce damage from political risk. Explain each one and how it reduces damage.

   a. Local sourcing

   b. Facility location

   c. Control of technology

   d. Thin equity base

   e. Multiple-source borrowing

7. **Country-specific risk.** Define the following terms

   a. Transfer risk

   b. Blocked funds

   c. Sovereign credit risk

8. **Blocked funds.** Explain the strategies that an MNE can use to counter blocked funds.

9. **Cultural and institutional risks.** Identify and explain the main types of cultural and institutional risks, except protectionism.

10. **Strategies to manage cultural and institutional risks.** Explain the strategies that an MNE can use to manage each of the cultural and institutional risks that you identified in Question 9, except protectionism.

11. **Protectionism defined.**

    a. Define protectionism and identify the industries that are typically protected.

    b. Explain the "infant industry" argument for protectionism.

12. **Managing protectionism.**

    a. What are the traditional methods for countries to implement protectionism?

    b. What are some typical nontariff barriers to trade?

    c. How can MNEs overcome host-country protectionism?

13. **Global-specific risks.** What are the main types of political risks that are global in origin?

14. **Managing global-specific risks.** What are the main strategies MNEs can use to manage the global-specific risks you identified in Question 13?

15. **U.S. anti-bribery law.** The United States has a law prohibiting U.S. firms from bribing foreign officials and business persons, even in countries where bribery is a normal practice. Some U.S. firms claim this places them at a disadvantage compared to host-country firms and other foreign firms that are not hampered by such a law. Discuss the ethics and practicality of the U.S. anti-bribery law.

16. **Fair Trade movement.** How does the Fair Trade movement differ from the traditional income redistribution plans used by many countries?

17. **Starbucks' coffee procurement.** Do you think Starbucks should pay a higher-than-market price to its growers, even if there is no significant difference in the quality of the coffee or reliability of production?

18. **Corporate social responsibility.** What is Starbucks' strategy for corporate social responsibility? Is it consistent with shareholder wealth maximization?

19. **Cool Cola Company.** Cool Cola Company, one of the world's major manufacturers of cola soft drinks, is considering the establishment of a very large cola bottling plant in India. Cool Cola expects to sell half its product within India and to export the other half to southeast Asian countries. If the Kashmir conflict could be resolved, Pakistan and even Afghanistan might become important markets.

    a. Prepare an analysis of all the potential areas of goal conflict between Cool Cola and India.

    b. Considering your answers to part a, prepare a political risk forecast for Cool Cola's bottling plant in India. Consider the potential for political unrest in India or for war with Pakistan, as well as whether a foreign-owned soft drink plant would be affected by such unrest. Use current periodicals and newspapers to gather your data.

    c. Assume Cool Cola Company decides to build a large bottling plant in India. Recommend operating strategies for Cool Cola Company that would reduce its political risk. Include strategies for marketing, production, finance, and organization.

    d. Prepare a crisis plan for Cool Cola in India in case political conditions deteriorate.

20. **Divestment: China.** Assume that Cool Cola Company also has a network of soft drink bottling plants throughout China, but political stresses between the United States and China increase to the degree that Cool Cola would like to divest. What should Cool Cola consider in developing a plan that will enable it to divest its investment in bottling plants and distributions systems in China with minimum loss?

## Internet Exercises

1.  **The World Bank.** The World Bank provides a growing set of informational and analytical resources to aid in the assessment and management of cross-border risk. The Risk Management Support Group has a variety of political risk assessment tools, which are under constant development. Visit the following site and compose an executive briefing (one page or less) of what the political risk insurance provided by the World Bank will and will not cover.

    World Bank Risk Management
    http://www.worldbank.org/business/
    01risk_manage.html

2.  **Global corruption report.** Transparency International (TI) is considered by many to be the leading nongovernmental anti-corruption organization in the world today. It has recently introduced its own annual survey analyzing recent developments, identifying ongoing challenges, and offering potential solutions to individuals or organizations. One dimension of this analysis is the Bribe Payers Index. Visit TI's Web site to view the latest edition of the Bribe Payers Index.

    Transparency International
    http://www.transparency.org/surveys/
    index.html#bpi

3.  **Sovereign credit ratings criteria.** The evaluation of credit risk and all other relevant risks associated with the multitude of borrowers on world debt markets requires a structured approach to international risk assessment. Use Standard & Poor's criteria, described in depth on their Web site, to differentiate the various risks (local currency risk, default risk, currency risk, transfer risk, etc.) contained in major sovereign ratings worldwide. Use any of the major Internet search engines to find recent evaluations on sovereign ratings and individual country rating changes.

4.  **Milken Capital Access Index.** The Milken Institute's Capital Access Index (CAI) is one of the newest informational indices that evaluates how accessible world capital markets are to MNEs and governments of many emerging market countries. According to the CAI, which countries have seen the largest deterioration in their access to capital in the last two years?

    Milken Institute
    http://www.milkeninstitute.org/

5.  **Overseas Private Investment Corporation.** The Overseas Private Investment Corporation (OPIC) provides long-term political risk insurance and limited recourse project financing aid to U.S.–based firms investing abroad. Using the organization's Web site, answer the following questions.

    a.  Exactly what types of risk will OPIC insure against?

    b.  What financial limits and restrictions are there on this insurance protection?

    c.  How should a project be structured to aid in its approval for OPIC coverage?

    Overseas Private Investment Corp
    http://www.opic.gov/

# Multinational
# Capital Budgeting

## LEARNING OBJECTIVES

Extend the domestic capital budgeting analysis to evaluate
a greenfield foreign project

Distinguish between the project viewpoint and the parent
viewpoint when analyzing a potential foreign investment

Adjust the capital budgeting analysis of a foreign project
for risk

Introduce the use of real option analysis as a complement
to discounted cash flow analysis in the evaluation of
potential international investments

This chapter describes in detail the issues and principles related to the investment in real productive assets in foreign countries, generally referred to as *multinational capital budgeting*.

Although the original decision to undertake an investment in a particular foreign country may be determined by a mix of strategic, behavioral, and economic decisions, the specific project, as well as all reinvestment decisions, should be justified by traditional financial analysis. For example, a production efficiency opportunity may exist for a U.S. firm to invest abroad, but the type of plant, mix of labor and capital, kinds of equipment, method of financing, and other project variables must be analyzed within the traditional financial framework of discounted cash flows. It must also consider the impact of the proposed foreign project on consolidated net earnings, cash flows from subsidiaries in other countries, and on the market value of the parent firm.

Multinational capital budgeting, like traditional domestic capital budgeting, focuses on the cash inflows and outflows associated with prospective long-term investment projects. Multinational capital budgeting techniques are used in traditional FDI analysis, such as the construction of a manufacturing plant in another country, as well as in the growing field of international mergers and acquisitions.

Capital budgeting for a foreign project uses the same theoretical framework as domestic capital budgeting — with a few very important differences. The basic steps are

1. Identify the initial capital invested or put at risk.
2. Estimate cash flows to be derived from the project over time, including an estimate of the terminal or salvage value of the investment.
3. Identify the appropriate discount rate for determining the present value of the expected cash flows.
4. Apply traditional capital budgeting decision criteria such as net present value (NPV) and internal rate of return (IRR) to determine the acceptability of or priority ranking of potential projects.

This chapter will first describe the complexities of budgeting for a foreign project. Second, we describe the insights gained by valuing a project from both the project's viewpoint and the parent's viewpoint. We then use a hypothetical investment by Cemex of Mexico in Indonesia to detail the process of multinational capital budgeting in practice. We conclude the chapter with an introduction to the concept of real options analysis, an alternative method for evaluating the potential returns to a project or investment.

## Complexities of Budgeting for a Foreign Project

Capital budgeting for a foreign project is considerably more complex than the domestic case. Several factors contribute to this greater complexity:

- Parent cash flows must be distinguished from project cash flows. Each of these two types of flows contributes to a different view of value.
- Parent cash flows often depend on the form of financing. Thus we cannot clearly separate cash flows from financing decisions, as we can in domestic capital budgeting.
- Additional cash flows generated by a new investment in one foreign subsidiary may be in part or in whole taken away from another subsidiary, with the net result

that the project is favorable from a single subsidiary's point of view but contributes nothing to worldwide cash flows.

- The parent must explicitly recognize remittance of funds because of differing tax systems, legal and political constraints on the movement of funds, local business norms, and differences in the way financial markets and institutions function.

- An array of nonfinancial payments can generate cash flows from subsidiaries to the parent, including payment of license fees and payments for imports from the parent.

- Managers must anticipate differing rates of national inflation because of their potential to cause changes in competitive position, and thus changes in cash flows over a period of time.

- Managers must keep the possibility of unanticipated foreign exchange rate changes in mind because of possible direct effects on the value of local cash flows, as well as indirect effects on the competitive position of the foreign subsidiary.

- Use of segmented national capital markets may create an opportunity for financial gains or may lead to additional financial costs.

- Use of host-government subsidized loans complicates both capital structure and the parent's ability to determine an appropriate weighted average cost of capital for discounting purposes.

- Managers must evaluate political risk because political events can drastically reduce the value or availability of expected cash flows.

- Terminal value is more difficult to estimate because potential purchasers from the host, parent, or third countries, or from the private or public sector, may have widely divergent perspectives on the value to them of acquiring the project.

Since the same theoretical capital budgeting framework is used to choose among competing foreign and domestic projects, it is critical that we have a common standard. Thus all foreign complexities must be quantified as modifications to either expected cash flow or the rate of discount. Although in practice many firms make such modifications arbitrarily, readily available information, theoretical deduction, or just plain common sense can be used to make less arbitrary and more reasonable choices.

## Project Versus Parent Valuation

A strong theoretical argument exists in favor of analyzing any foreign project from the viewpoint of the parent. Cash flows to the parent are ultimately the basis for dividends to stockholders, reinvestment elsewhere in the world, repayment of corporate-wide debt, and other purposes that affect the firm's many interest groups. However, since most of a project's cash flows to its parent, or to sister subsidiaries, are financial cash flows rather than operating cash flows, the parent viewpoint usually violates a cardinal concept of capital budgeting, namely, that financial cash flows should not be mixed with operating cash flows. Often the difference is not important because the two are almost identical, but in some instances a sharp divergence in these cash flows will exist. For example, funds that are permanently blocked from repatriation, or "forcibly reinvested," are not available for dividends to the stockholders or for repayment of parent corporate debt. Therefore shareholders will not perceive the blocked earnings as contributing to the value of the firm, and creditors will not count on them in calculating interest coverage ratios and other evidence of ability to service debt.

Evaluation of a project from the local viewpoint serves some useful purposes, but it should be subordinated to evaluation from the parent's viewpoint. In evaluating a foreign project's performance relative to the potential of a competing project in the same host country, we must pay attention to the project's local return. Almost any project should at least be able to earn a cash return equal to the yield available on host government bonds with a maturity the same as the project's economic life, if a free market exists for such bonds. Host government bonds ordinarily reflect the local risk-free rate of return, including a premium equal to the expected rate of inflation. If a project cannot earn more than such a bond yield, the parent firm should buy host government bonds rather than invest in a riskier project — or, better yet, invest somewhere else!

Multinational firms should invest only if they can earn a risk-adjusted return greater than locally based competitors can earn on the same project. If they are unable to earn superior returns on foreign projects, their stockholders would be better off buying shares in local firms, where possible, and letting those companies carry out the local projects. Apart from these theoretical arguments, surveys over the past 35 years show that in practice multinational firms continue to evaluate foreign investments from both the parent and project viewpoint.

The attention paid to project returns in various surveys probably reflects emphasis on maximizing reported consolidated net earnings per share as a corporate financial goal. As long as foreign earnings are not blocked, they can be consolidated with the earnings of both the remaining subsidiaries and the parent. As mentioned previously, U.S. firms must consolidate foreign *subsidiaries* that are over 50% owned. If a firm is owned between 20% and 49% by a parent, it is called an *affiliate*. Affiliates are consolidated with the parent owner on a pro rata basis. Subsidiaries less than 20% owned are normally carried as unconsolidated investments. Even in the case of temporarily blocked funds, some of the most mature MNEs do not necessarily eliminate a project from financial consideration. They take a very long-run view of world business opportunities.

If reinvestment opportunities in the country where funds are blocked are at least equal to the parent firm's required rate of return (after adjusting for anticipated exchange rate changes), temporary blockage of transfer may have little practical effect on the capital budgeting outcome, because future project cash flows will be increased by the returns on forced reinvestment. Since large multinationals hold a portfolio of domestic and foreign projects, corporate liquidity is not impaired if a few projects have blocked funds; alternate sources of funds are available to meet all planned uses of funds. Furthermore, a long-run historical perspective on blocked funds does indeed lend support to the belief that funds are almost never permanently blocked. However, waiting for the release of such funds can be frustrating, and sometimes the blocked funds lose value while blocked because of inflation or unexpected exchange rate deterioration, even though they have been reinvested in the host country to protect at least part of their value in real terms.

In conclusion, most firms appear to evaluate foreign projects from both parent and project viewpoints. The parent's viewpoint gives results closer to the traditional meaning of net present value in capital budgeting. Project valuation provides a closer approximation of the effect on consolidated earnings per share, which all surveys indicate is of major concern to practicing managers. To illustrate the foreign complexities of multinational capital budgeting, we analyze a hypothetical market-seeking foreign direct investment by Cemex in Indonesia.

## Illustrative Case: Cemex Enters Indonesia[1]

It is early in 1998. Cementos Mexicanos, Cemex, is considering the construction of a cement manufacturing facility on the Indonesian island of Sumatra. The project, Semen Indonesia (the Indonesian word for "cement" is *semen*), would be a wholly-owned greenfield investment with a total installed capacity of 20 million metric tons per year (mmt/y). Although that is large by Asian production standards, Cemex believes that its latest cement manufacturing technology would be most efficiently utilized with a production facility of this scale.

Cemex has three driving reasons for the project: (1) the firm wishes to initiate a productive presence of its own in Southeast Asia, a relatively new market for Cemex; (2) the long-term prospects for Asian infrastructure development and growth appear very good over the longer term; and (3) there are positive prospects for Indonesia to act as a produce-for-export site as a result of the depreciation of the Indonesian rupiah (Rp) in 1997.

Cemex, the world's third-largest cement manufacturer, is an MNE headquartered in an emerging market but competing in a global arena. The firm competes in the global marketplace for both market share and capital. The international cement market, like markets in other commodities such as oil, is a dollar-based market. For this reason, and for comparisons against its major competitors in both Germany and Switzerland, Cemex considers the U.S. dollar its functional currency.

Cemex's shares are listed in both Mexico City and New York (OTC: CMXSY). The firm has successfully raised capital — both debt and equity — outside Mexico in U.S. dollars. Its investor base is increasingly global, with the U.S. share turnover rising rapidly as a percentage of total trading. As a result, its cost and availability of capital are internationalized and dominated by U.S. dollar investors. Ultimately, the Semen Indonesia project will be evaluated — in both cash flows and capital cost — in U.S. dollars.

### OVERVIEW

A roadmap of the complete multinational capital budgeting analysis for Cemex in Indonesia is illustrated in Exhibit 18.1. The basic principle is that, starting at the top left, the parent company invests U.S. dollar-denominated capital, which flows clockwise through the creation and operation of an Indonesian subsidiary, which then generates cash flows that are eventually returned in a variety of forms to the parent company — in U.S. dollars. The first step is to construct a set of *pro forma* financial statements for Semen Indonesia, all in Indonesian rupiah (Rp). The next step is to create two capital budgets, the *project viewpoint* and the *parent viewpoint*.

Semen Indonesia will take only one year to build the plant, with actual operations commencing in year 1. The Indonesian government has only recently deregulated the heavier industries to allow foreign ownership. The following analysis is conducted assuming that purchasing power parity (PPP) holds for the Rp/US$ exchange rate for the life of the Indonesian project. This is a standard financial assumption made by Cemex for its foreign investments. The projected inflation rates for Indonesia and the United States are 30% per annum and 3% per annum, respectively.

If we assume an initial spot rate of Rp10,000/US$, and Indonesian and U.S. inflation rates of 30% and 3% per annum, respectively, for the life of the project, forecasted

[1]Cemex is a real company; the greenfield investment described here is hypothetical.

**EXHIBIT 18.1**

A Roadmap to the
Construction of
Semen
Indonesia's
Capital Budget

spot exchange rates follow the usual PPP calculation. For example, the forecasted exchange rate for year 1 of the project would be

$$\text{Spot rate (year 1)} = \text{Rp}10,000 / \text{US}\$ \times \frac{1+.30}{1+.03} = \text{Rp}12,621 / \text{US}\$$$

## FINANCIAL ASSUMPTIONS

The following series of financial statements are based on these assumptions.

**CAPITAL INVESTMENT.**    Although the cost of building new cement manufacturing capacity anywhere in the industrial countries was estimated at roughly $150/ton of installed capacity, Cemex believed that it could build a state-of-the-art production and shipment facility in Sumatra at roughly $110/ton (see Exhibit 18.2). Assuming a 20 million metric tons per year capacity and a year 0 average exchange rate of Rp10,000/$, this cost will constitute an investment of Rp22 trillion ($2.2 billion). This figure includes an investment of Rp17.6 trillion in plant and equipment, giving rise to an annual depreciation charge of Rp1.76 trillion if we assume a 10-year straight-line depreciation schedule. The relatively short depreciation schedule is one of the policies of the Indonesian tax authorities meant to attract foreign investment.

**FINANCING.**    This massive investment would be financed with 50% equity, all from Cemex, and 50% debt, 75% from Cemex and 25% from a bank consortium arranged by the Indonesian government. Cemex's own U.S. dollar-based weighted average cost of capital (WACC) was estimated at 11.98%. The WACC on a local Indonesian level in rupiah terms, for the project itself, was estimated at 33.257%. The details of this calculation are discussed later in this chapter.

The explicit debt structures, including repayment schedules, are presented in Exhibit 18.3. The loan arranged by the Indonesian government, part of the government's economic development incentive program, is an eight-year loan, in rupiah, at

## EXHIBIT 18.2

Investment and Financing of the Semen Indonesia Project (all values in 000s unless otherwise noted)

| INVESTMENT | | FINANCING | |
|---|---|---|---|
| Average exchange rate, Rp/$ | 10,000 | Equity | Rp 11,000,000,000 |
| Cost of installed capacity, $/tonne | $110 | Debt | |
| Installed capacity | 20,000 | Rupiah debt | 2,750,000,000 |
| Investment in US$ | $2,200,000 | US$ debt, Rp | 8,250,000,000 |
| Investment in rupiah | 22,000,000,000 | Total | Rp 22,000,000,000 |
| Plant and equipment, Rp | 17,600,000,000 | | |
| Annual depreciation, Rp | 1,760,000,000 | | |

### COSTS OF CAPITAL: CEMEX

| | | | |
|---|---|---|---|
| Risk-free rate | 6.000% | Cemex beta | 1.500 |
| Credit premium | 2.000% | Equity risk premium | 7.000% |
| Cost of debt | 8.000% | Cost of equity | 16.500% |
| Cost of debt, after tax | 5.200% | Percent equity | 60% |
| Percent debt | 40% | WACC | 11.980% |

### COSTS OF CAPITAL: SEMEN INDONESIA

| | | | |
|---|---|---|---|
| Risk-free rate | 33.000% | Semen Indonesia beta | 1.000 |
| Credit premium | 2.000% | Equity risk premium | 6.000% |
| Cost of rupiah debt | 35.000% | Cost of equity | 40.000% |
| Cost of US$ debt, after tax | 5.200% | Percent equity | 50% |
| Cost of US$ debt (rupiah equivalent) | 38.835% | | |
| Cost of US$ debt, after tax (rup. equiv.) | 27.184% | | |
| Percent debt | 50% | WACC | 33.257% |

Assumes corporate income tax rates of 35% and 30% in Mexico and Indonesia, respectively. The cost of the US$ loan is stated in rupiah terms assuming purchasing power parity and U.S. dollar and Indonesian rupiah inflation rates of 3% and 30%, respectively, throughout the subject period.

35% annual interest, fully amortizing. The interest payments are fully deductible against corporate tax liabilities.

The majority of the debt, however, is being provided by the parent company, Cemex. After raising the capital from its financing subsidiary, Cemex will relend the capital to Semen Indonesia. The loan is denominated in U.S. dollars, five years maturity, with an annual interest rate of 10%. Because the debt will have to be repaid from the rupiah earnings of the Indonesian enterprise, the pro forma financial statements are constructed so that the expected costs of servicing the dollar debt are included in the firm's pro forma income statement. The dollar loan, if the rupiah follows the purchasing power parity forecast, will have an effective interest expense in rupiah terms of 38.835%. We find this rate by determining the internal rate of return of repaying the dollar loan in full in rupiah (see Exhibit 18.3).

**REVENUES.**    Given that the existing cement manufacturing in Indonesia is depressed, all sales are based on export. The 20 mmt/y facility is expected to operate at only 40% capacity (producing 8 million metric tons). Cement produced will be sold in the export

## EXHIBIT 18.3

Semen Indonesia's Debt Service Schedules and Foreign Exchange Gains/Losses

| Spot rate (Rp/$) | 10,000 | 12,621 | 15,930 | 20,106 | 25,376 | 32,028 |
|---|---|---|---|---|---|---|
| *Project year* | *0* | *1* | *2* | *3* | *4* | *5* |

### *Indonesian loan @ 35% for 8 years (millions of Rp)*

| | | | | | | |
|---|---|---|---|---|---|---|
| Loan principal | 2,750,000 | | | | | |
| Interest payment | | (962,500) | (928,921) | (883,590) | (822,393) | (739,777) |
| Principal payment | | (95,939) | (129,518) | (174,849) | (236,046) | (318,662) |
| Total payment | | (1,058,439) | (1,058,439) | (1,058,439) | (1,058,439) | (1,058,439) |

### *Cemex loan @ 10% for 5 years (millions of US$)*

| | | | | | | |
|---|---|---|---|---|---|---|
| Principal | 825 | | | | | |
| Interest payment | | (82.5) | (69.0) | (54.1) | (37.8) | (19.8) |
| Principal payment | | (135.1) | (148.6) | (163.5) | (179.9) | (197.8) |
| Total payment | | (217.6) | (217.6) | (217.6) | (217.6) | (217.6) |

### Cemex loan converted to Rp at scheduled and current spot rates (millions of Rp):

*Scheduled at Rp10,000/$:*

| | | | | | | |
|---|---|---|---|---|---|---|
| Interest payment | | (825,000) | (689,867) | (541,221) | (377,710) | (197,848) |
| Principal payment | | (1,351,329) | (1,486,462) | (1,635,108) | (1,798,619) | (1,978,481) |
| Total payment | | (2,176,329) | (2,176,329) | (2,176,329) | (2,176,329) | (2,176,329) |

*Actual (at current spot rate):*

| | | | | | | |
|---|---|---|---|---|---|---|
| Interest payment | | (1,041,262) | (1,098,949) | (1,088,160) | (958,480) | (633,669) |
| Principal payment | | (1,705,561) | (2,367,915) | (3,287,494) | (4,564,190) | (6,336,691) |
| Total payment | | (2,746,823) | (3,466,864) | (4,375,654) | (5,522,670) | (6,970,360) |

### Cash flows in Rp on Cemex loan (millions of Rp):

| | | | | | | |
|---|---|---|---|---|---|---|
| Total actual cash flows | 8,250,000 | (2,746,823) | (3,466,864) | (4,375,654) | (5,522,670) | (6,970,360) |
| IRR of cash flows | 38.835% | | | | | |

### Foreign exchange losses on Cemex loan (millions of Rp):

| | | | | | | |
|---|---|---|---|---|---|---|
| Foreign exchange losses on interest | | (216,262) | (409,082) | (546,940) | (580,770) | (435,821) |
| Foreign exchange losses on principal | | (354,232) | (881,453) | (1,652,385) | (2,765,571) | (4,358,210) |
| Total foreign exchange losses on debt | | (570,494) | (1,290,535) | (2,199,325) | (3,346,341) | (4,794,031) |

The loan by Cemex to the Indonesian subsidiary is denominated in U.S. dollars. The loan will therefore have to be repaid in U.S. dollars, not rupiah. At the time of the loan agreement, the spot exchange rate is Rp10,000/$. This is the assumption used in calculating the "scheduled" repaying of principal and interest in rupiah. The rupiah, however, is expected to depreciate in line with purchasing power parity. As it is repaid, the "actual" exchange rate will therefore give rise to a foreign exchange loss as it takes more and more rupiah to acquire U.S. dollars for debt service, both principal and interest. The foreign exchange losses on this debt service will be recognized on the Indonesian income statement.

market at $58/ton (delivered). Note also that, at least for the conservative baseline analysis, we assume no increase in the price received over time.

COSTS.     The cash costs of cement manufacturing (labor, materials, power, etc.) are estimated at Rp115,000 per ton for 1999, rising at about the rate of inflation, 30% per year. Additional production costs of Rp20,000 per ton for year 1 are also assumed to rise at the rate of inflation. As a result of all production being exported, loading costs of $2.00/ton and shipping of $10.00/ton must also be included. Note that these costs are originally stated in U.S. dollars, and for the purposes of Semen Indonesia's income statement, they must be converted to rupiah terms. This is the case because both ship-loading and shipping costs are international services governed by contracts denominated in dollars. As a result, they are expected to rise over time only at the U.S. dollar rate of inflation (3%).

Semen Indonesia's *pro forma* income statement is illustrated in Exhibit 18.4. This is the typical financial statement measurement of the profitability of any business, whether domestic or international. The baseline analysis assumes a capacity utilization

## EXHIBIT 18.4

Semen Indonesia's *Pro Forma* Income Statement (Millions of Rupiah)

| Exchange Rate (Rp/$) | 10,000 | 12,621 | 15,930 | 20,106 | 25,376 | 32,038 |
|---|---|---|---|---|---|---|
| *Project year* | *0* | *1* | *2* | *3* | *4* | *5* |
| Sales volume | | 8,000 | 10,000 | 12,000 | 12,000 | 12,000 |
| Sales price (US$) | | 58.00 | 58.00 | 58.00 | 58.00 | 58.00 |
| Sales price (Rp) | | 732,039 | 923,933 | 1,166,128 | 1,471,808 | 1,857,627 |
| Total revenue | | 5,856,311 | 9,239,325 | 13,993,541 | 17,661,751 | 22,291,530 |
| Less cash costs | | (920,000) | (1,495,000) | (2,332,200) | (3,031,860) | (3,941,418) |
| Less other production costs | | (160,000) | (260,000) | (405,600) | (527,280) | (685,464) |
| Less loading costs | | (201,942) | (328,155) | (511,922) | (665,499) | (865,149) |
| Less shipping costs | | (1,009,709) | (1,640,777) | (2,559,612) | (3,327,495) | (4,325,744) |
| Total production costs | | (2,291,650) | (3,723,932) | (5,809,334) | (7,552,134) | (9,817,774) |
| Gross profit | | 3,564,660 | 5,515,393 | 8,184,207 | 10,109,617 | 12,473,756 |
| Gross margin | | 61% | 60% | 58% | 57% | 56% |
| Less license fees | | (117,126) | (184,787) | (279,871) | (353,235) | (445,831) |
| Less general and administrative | | (468,505) | (831,539) | (1,399,354) | (1,942,792) | (2,674,984) |
| EBITDA | | 2,979,029 | 4,499,067 | 6,504,982 | 7,813,589 | 9,352,941 |
| Less depreciation and amortization | | (1,760,000) | (1,760,000) | (1,760,000) | (1,760,000) | (1,760,000) |
| EBIT | | 1,219,029 | 2,739,067 | 4,744,982 | 6,053,589 | 7,592,941 |
| Less interest on Cemex debt | | (825,000) | (689,867) | (541,221) | (377,710) | (197,848) |
| Foreign exchange losses on debt | | (570,494) | (1,290,535) | (2,199,325) | (3,346,341) | (4,794,031) |
| Less interest on local debt | | (962,500) | (928,921) | (883,590) | (822,393) | (739,777) |
| EBT | | (1,138,965) | (170,256) | 1,120,846 | 1,507,145 | 1,861,285 |
| Less income taxes (30%) | | — | — | — | (395,631) | (558,386) |
| Net income | | (1,138,965) | (170,256) | 1,120,846 | 1,111,514 | 1,302,900 |
| Net income (millions of US$) | | (90) | (11) | 56 | 44 | 41 |
| Return on sales | | −19% | −2% | 8% | 6% | 6% |

EBITDA = earnings before interest, taxes, depreciation, and amortization; EBIT = earnings before interest and taxes; EBT = earnings before taxes. Tax credits resulting from current period losses are carried forward toward next year's tax liabilities. Dividends are not distributed in the first year of operations as a result of losses, and are distributed at a 50% rate in years 2000–2003. All calculations are exact, but may appear not to add due to reported decimal places and rounding. The tax payment for year 3 is zero, and year 4 is less than 30%, as a result of tax loss carry-forwards from previous years.

rate of only 40% (year 1), 50% (year 2), and 60% in the following years. Management believes this is necessary since existing in-country cement manufacturers are averaging only 40% of capacity at this time.

Additional expenses in the pro forma financial analysis include license fees paid by the subsidiary to the parent company of 2.0% of sales, and general and administrative expenses for Indonesian operations of 8.0% per year (and growing an additional 1% per year). Foreign exchange gains and losses are those related to the servicing of the U.S. dollar-denominated debt provided by the parent and are drawn from the bottom of Exhibit 18.3. In summary, the subsidiary operation is expected to begin turning an accounting profit in its fourth year of operations (2000), with profits rising as capacity utilization increases over time.

## PROJECT VIEWPOINT CAPITAL BUDGET

The capital budget for the Semen Indonesia manufacturing project from a project viewpoint is shown in Exhibit 18.5. We find the net cash flow, or *free cash flow* (FCF) as it is often called, by summing EBITDA (earnings before interest, taxes, depreciation, and amortization), recalculated taxes, and changes in net working capital (the sum of the net additions to receivables, inventories, and payables necessary to support sales growth).

Note that EBITDA, not EBT, is used in the capital budget, which contains both depreciation and interest expense. Depreciation and amortization are noncash expenses of the firm and therefore contribute positive cash flow. Because the capital budget creates cash flows that will be discounted to present value with a discount rate, and the discount rate includes the cost of debt — interest — we do not wish to subtract interest twice. Therefore, taxes are recalculated on the basis of EBITDA. (This highlights the distinction between an income statement and a capital budget. The project's income statement shows losses the first two years of operations as a result of interest

## EXHIBIT 18.5

Semen Indonesia's Capital Budget: Project Viewpoint (Millions of Rupiah)

| | | | | | | |
|---|---|---|---|---|---|---|
| Exchange Rate (Rp/$) | 10,000 | 12,621 | 15,930 | 20,106 | 25,376 | 32,038 |
| *Project year* | *0* | *1* | *2* | *3* | *4* | *5* |
| EBITDA | | 2,979,029 | 4,499,067 | 6,504,982 | 7,813,589 | 9,352,941 |
| Less recalculated taxes | | (893,709) | (1,349,720) | (1,951,495) | (2,344,077) | (2,805,882) |
| Net operating cash flow | | 2,085,320 | 3,149,347 | 4,553,487 | 5,469,512 | 6,547,059 |
| Less additions to NWC | | (240,670) | (139,028) | (436,049) | (289,776) | (626,314) |
| Initial investment | (22,000,000) | | | | | |
| Terminal value | | | | | | 19,686,451 |
| Free cash flow (FCF) | (22,000,000) | 1,844,650 | 3,010,319 | 4,117,438 | 5,179,736 | 25,607,196 |
| NPV @ 33.257% | (9,443,538) | | | | | |
| IRR | 15.4 % | | | | | |

NWC = net working capital. NPV = net present value. Discount rate is Semen Indonesia's WACC of 33.257%. IRR = internal rate of return, the rate of discount yielding an NPV of exactly zero. Values in exhibit are exact and are rounded to the nearest million.

expenses and forecast foreign exchange losses, so it is not expected to pay taxes. But the capital budget, constructed on the basis of EBITDA, before these financing and foreign exchange expenses, calculates a positive tax payment.) The firm's cost of capital used in discounting also includes the deductibility of debt interest in its calculation.

The initial investment of Rp22 trillion is the total capital invested to support these earnings. Although receivables average 50 to 55 days sales outstanding (DSO) and inventories 65 to 70 DSO, payables and trade credit are also relatively long at 114 DSO in the Indonesian cement industry. Semen Indonesia expects to add approximately 15 net DSO to its investment with sales growth. The remaining elements to complete the project viewpoint's capital budget are the terminal value (discussed below) and the discount rate of 33.257% (the firm's WACC).

**TERMINAL VALUE.**    The terminal value (TV) of the project represents the continuing value of the cement manufacturing facility in the years after year 5, the last year of the detailed *pro forma* financial analysis shown here. This value, like all asset values according to financial theory, is the present value of all future free cash flows that the asset is expected to yield. We calculate the TV as the present value of a perpetual net operating cash flow (NOCF) generated in the fifth year by Semen Indonesia, the growth rate assumed for that net operating cash flow (g), and the firm's weighted average cost of capital ($k_{WACC}$):

$$\text{Terminal value} = \frac{NOCF_5(1+g)}{k_{WACC} - g} = \frac{6,547,059(1+0)}{.33257 - 0} = Rp19,686,457$$

or Rp19.686 trillion (Rp19,686,450,933,000). The assumption that g = 0, that is, that NOCFs will not grow past year 5, is probably not true, but it is a prudent assumption for Cemex to use when estimating future cash flows so far into the future.

The results of the capital budget from the project viewpoint indicate a negative net present value (NPV) of Rp9,443,538 million (or about Rp9.4 trillion) and an internal rate of return (IRR) of only 15.4% compared to the 33.257% cost of capital. These are the returns the project would yield to a local or Indonesian investor in Indonesian rupiah. The project, from this viewpoint, is not acceptable.

## REPATRIATING CASH FLOWS TO CEMEX

Exhibit 18.6 now collects all incremental earnings to Cemex from the prospective investment project in Indonesia. As described in the section preceding the case, a foreign investor's assessment of a project's returns depends on the actual cash flows that are returned to it, in its own currency. For Cemex, this means that the investment must be analyzed in terms of U.S. dollar cash inflows and outflows associated with the investment over the life of the project, after-tax, discounted at its appropriate cost of capital.

We build this *parent viewpoint capital budget* in two steps.

First, we isolate the individual cash flows, adjusted for any withholding taxes imposed by the Indonesian government and converted to U.S. dollars. (Statutory withholding taxes on international transfers are set by bilateral tax treaties, but individual firms may negotiate lower rates with governmental tax authorities. In the case of

## EXHIBIT 18.6

Semen Indonesia's Remittance and Capital Budget: Parent Viewpoint (Millions of Rp and US$)

| Exchange Rate (Rp/$) | 10,000 | 12,621 | 15,930 | 20,106 | 25,376 | 32,038 |
|---|---|---|---|---|---|---|
| **Project year** | **0** | **1** | **2** | **3** | **4** | **5** |
| **Dividend Remittance** | | | | | | |
| Dividends paid (Rp) | | — | — | 560,423 | 555,757 | 651,450 |
| Less withholding tax | | | | (84,063) | (83,364) | (97,717) |
| Net dividend remitted (Rp) | | — | — | 476,360 | 472,393 | 553,732 |
| Net dividend remitted (US$) | | — | — | 23.7 | 18.6 | 17.3 |
| **License Fees Remittance** | | | | | | |
| License fees remitted (Rp) | | 117,126 | 184,787 | 279,871 | 353,235 | 445,831 |
| Less withholding tax | | (5,856) | (9,239) | (13,994) | (17,662) | (22,292) |
| Net dividend remitted (Rp) | | 111,270 | 175,547 | 265,877 | 335,573 | 423,539 |
| Net license fees remitted (US$) | | 8.8 | 11.0 | 13.2 | 13.2 | 13.2 |
| **Debt Service Remittance** | | | | | | |
| Promised interest paid (US$) | | 82.5 | 69.0 | 54.1 | 37.8 | 19.8 |
| Less withholding tax @ 10% | | (8.25) | (6.90) | (5.41) | (3.78) | (1.98) |
| Net interest remitted (US$) | | 74.25 | 62.09 | 48.71 | 33.99 | 17.81 |
| Principal payments remitted (US$) | | 135.1 | 148.6 | 163.5 | 179.9 | 197.8 |
| **Capital Budget: Parent Viewpoint (Millions of US$)** | | | | | | |
| Dividends | | — | — | 23.7 | 18.6 | 17.3 |
| License fees | | 8.8 | 11.0 | 13.2 | 13.2 | 13.2 |
| Debt service | | 209.4 | 210.7 | 212.2 | 213.9 | 215.7 |
| Total earnings | | 218.2 | 221.8 | 249.1 | 245.7 | 246.2 |
| Initial investment | (1,925.0) | | | | | |
| Terminal value | | | | | | 614.7 |
| Free cash flow (FCF) | (1,925.0) | 218.2 | 221.8 | 249.1 | 245.7 | 860.8 |
| NPV @ 17.98% | (925.6) | | | | | |
| IRR | −1.84 % | | | | | |

NPV calculated using a company-determined discount rate of WACC + foreign investment premium, or 11.98% + 6.00% = 17.98%.

Semen Indonesia, dividends will be charged a 15% withholding tax, 10% interest payments, and 5% license fees.) Mexico does not tax repatriated earnings since they have already been taxed in Indonesia. (The United States does levy a contingent tax on repatriated earnings of foreign source income. This is a complex calculation and is covered in Chapter 20.)

The second step, the actual parent viewpoint capital budget, combines these U.S. dollar after-tax cash flows with the initial investment to determine the net present value of the proposed Semen Indonesia subsidiary in the eyes (and pocketbook) of Cemex. This is illustrated in Exhibit 18.6, which shows all incremental earnings to Cemex from the prospective investment project. A specific peculiarity of this parent viewpoint capital budget is that only the capital invested into the project by Cemex itself, $1,925 million, is included in the initial investment (the $1,100 million in equity and the $825 million loan). The Indonesian debt of Rp2.75 billion ($275 million) is not included in the Cemex parent viewpoint capital budget.

## PARENT VIEWPOINT CAPITAL BUDGET

Finally, all cash flow estimates are now constructed to form the parent viewpoint's capital budget, detailed in Exhibit 18.6. The cash flows generated by Semen Indonesia from its Indonesian operations, dividends, license fees, debt service payments, and terminal value are now valued in U.S. dollar terms after-tax.

In order to evaluate the project's cash flows that are returned to the parent company, Cemex must discount these at the corporate cost of capital. Remembering that Cemex considers its functional currency to be the U.S. dollar, it calculates its cost of capital in U.S. dollars. As described in Chapter 11, the customary weighted average cost of capital formula is as follows:

$$k_{WACC} = k_e \frac{E}{V} + k_d(1-t)\frac{D}{V}$$

$k_e$ = risk-adjusted cost of equity
$k_d$ = before-tax cost of debt
t = marginal tax rate
E = market value of the firm's equity
D = market value of the firm's debt
V = total market value of the firm's securities (E + D)

Cemex's cost of equity is calculated using the capital asset pricing model (CAPM):

$$k_e = k_{rf} + (k_m - k_{rf})\beta_{Cemex} = 6.00\% + (13.00\% - 6.00\%)1.5 = 16.50\%$$

$k_e$ = risk-adjusted cost of equity
$k_{rf}$ = risk-free rate of interest (U.S. Treasury intermediate bond yield)
$k_m$ = expected rate of return in U.S. equity markets (large stock)
$\beta_{Cemex}$ = measure of Cemex's individual risk relative to the market

The calculation assumes the current risk-free rate is 6.00%, the expected return on U.S. equities is 13.00%, and Cemex's beta is 1.5. The result is a cost of equity — required rate of return on equity investment in Cemex — of 16.50%.

The investment will be funded internally by the parent company, roughly in the same debt/equity proportions as the consolidated firm, 40% debt (D/V) and 60% equity (E/V). The current cost of debt for Cemex is 8.00%, and the effective tax rate is 35%. The cost of equity, when combined with the other components, results in a weighted average cost of capital for Cemex of

$$k_{WACC} = k_e \frac{E}{V} + k_d(1-t)\frac{D}{V} = (16.50\%)(.60) + (8.00\%)(1-.35)(.40) = 11.98\%$$

Cemex customarily uses this weighted average cost of capital of 11.98% to discount prospective investment cash flows for project ranking purposes. The Indonesian investment poses a variety of risks, however, which the typical domestic investment does not.

If Cemex were undertaking an investment of the same relative degree of risk as the firm itself, a simple discount rate of 11.980% might be adequate. Cemex, however, generally requires new investments to yield an additional 3% over the cost of capital for domestic investments, and 6% more for international projects. The discount rate for Semen Indonesia's cash flows repatriated to Cemex will therefore be discounted at 11.98% + 6.00%, or 17.98%. The project's baseline analysis indicates a negative NPV of US$925.6 million (IRR of −1.84%), which means that it is an unacceptable investment from the parent's viewpoint.

Most corporations require that new investments more than cover the cost of the capital employed in their undertaking. It is therefore not unusual for the firm to require a hurdle rate of 3% to 6% above its cost of capital in order to identify potential investments that will literally add value to stockholder wealth. A NPV of zero means the investment is "acceptable," but NPV values that exceed zero are literally the present value of wealth that is expected to be added to that of the firm and its shareholders. For foreign projects, as discussed previously, we must adjust for agency costs and foreign exchange risks and costs.

## SENSITIVITY ANALYSIS: PROJECT VIEWPOINT MEASUREMENT

So far the project investigation team has used a set of "most likely" assumptions to forecast rates of return. It is now time to subject the most likely outcome to sensitivity analyses. The same probabilistic techniques are available to test the sensitivity of results to political and foreign exchange risks as are used to test sensitivity to business and financial risks. Many decision makers feel more uncomfortable about the necessity to guess probabilities for unfamiliar political and foreign exchange events than they do about guessing their own more familiar business or financial risks. Therefore it is more common to test sensitivity to political and foreign exchange risk by simulating what would happen to net present value and earnings under a variety of "what if" scenarios.

**POLITICAL RISK.**    What if Indonesia should impose controls on the payment of dividends or license fees to Cemex? The impact of blocked funds on the rate of return from Cemex's perspective would depend on when the blockage occurs, what reinvestment opportunities exist for the blocked funds in Indonesia, and when the blocked funds would eventually be released to Cemex. We could simulate various scenarios for blocked funds and rerun the cash flow analysis in Exhibit 18.6 to estimate the effect on Cemex's rate of return.

What if Indonesia should expropriate Semen Indonesia? The effect of expropriation would depend on the following five factors.

1. When the expropriation occurs, in terms of number of years after the business began operation.

2. How much compensation the Indonesian government will pay, and how long after expropriation the payment will be made.

3. How much debt is still outstanding to Indonesian lenders, and whether the parent, Cemex, will have to pay this debt because of its parental guarantee.

4. The tax consequences of the expropriation.

5. Whether the future cash flows are forgone.

Many expropriations eventually result in some form of compensation to the former owners. This compensation can come from a negotiated settlement with the host government or from payment of political risk insurance by the parent government. Negotiating a settlement takes time, and the eventual compensation is sometimes paid in installments over a further period of time. Thus the present value of the compensation is often much lower than its nominal value. Furthermore, most settlements are based on book value of the firm at the time of expropriation rather than the firm's market value.

Repayment of parent guaranteed local debt would usually receive first claim on any compensation funds paid. If Cemex had guaranteed Semen Indonesia's debt to Indonesian lenders, they would be paid before Cemex could receive any settlement funds. In fact, the settlement agreement would probably provide for this. Alternatively, Cemex might have refused to guarantee Semen Indonesia's debt, protecting itself in the case of an expropriation but probably causing Semen Indonesia to pay a higher rate of interest and making the subsidiary less profitable to its parent.

If no compensation agreement is negotiated, Semen Indonesia, as an independently incorporated subsidiary of Cemex, might default on its debt. Cemex would not be obligated for Semen Indonesia's own debt, lacking a parent guarantee. As a practical matter, this is likely to occur only when the subsidiary's debt is borrowed locally, as in the case of Semen Indonesia. If Semen Indonesia had borrowed from, say, banks in Singapore, parent Cemex would feel an obligation to repay the debt even if it was not technically obligated.

The tax consequences of expropriation would depend on the timing and amount of capital loss recognized by Mexico. This loss would usually be based on the uncompensated book value of the Indonesian investment. The problem is that there is often some doubt as to when a write-off is appropriate for tax purposes, particularly if negotiations for a settlement drag on. In some ways a nice clear expropriation without hope of compensation, such as occurred in Cuba in the early 1960s, is preferred to a slow "bleeding death" in protracted negotiations. The former leads to an earlier use of the tax shield and a one-shot write-off against earnings, whereas the latter tends to depress earnings for years, as legal and other costs continue and no tax shelter is achieved.

**FOREIGN EXCHANGE RISK.**    The project team assumed that the Indonesian rupiah would depreciate versus the U.S. dollar at the purchasing power parity "rate" (approximately 20.767% per year in the baseline analysis). What if the rate of rupiah depreciation were greater? Although this event would make the assumed cash flows to Cemex worth less in dollars, operating exposure analysis would be necessary to determine whether the cheaper rupiah made Semen Indonesia more competitive. For example, since Semen Indonesia's exports to Taiwan are denominated in U.S. dollars, a weakening of the rupiah versus the dollar could result in greater rupiah earnings from those export sales. This serves to somewhat offset the imported components that Semen Indonesia purchases from the parent company that are also denominated in U.S. dollars. Semen Indonesia is representative of firms today which have both cash inflows and outflows denominated in foreign currencies, providing a partial natural hedge against currency movements.

What if the rupiah should *appreciate* against the dollar? The same kind of economic exposure analysis is needed. In this particular case we might guess that the effect would be positive on both local sales in Indonesia and the value in dollars of dividends and license fees paid to Cemex by Semen Indonesia. Note, however, that an appreciation of the rupiah might lead to more competition within Indonesia from firms in other countries with now-lower cost structures, lessening Semen Indonesia's sales.

**OTHER PROJECT SENSITIVITY VARIABLES.** The project rate of return to Cemex would also be sensitive to a change in the assumed terminal value, the capacity utilization rate, the size of the license fee paid by Semen Indonesia, the size of the initial project cost, the amount of working capital financed locally, and the tax rates in Indonesia and Mexico. Since some of these variables are within control of Cemex it is still possible that the Semen Indonesia project could be improved in its value to the firm and become acceptable.

## SENSITIVITY ANALYSIS: PARENT VIEWPOINT MEASUREMENT

When a foreign project is analyzed from the parent's point of view, the additional risk that stems from its "foreign" location can be measured in at least two ways: *adjusting the discount rates* or *adjusting the cash flows*.

**ADJUSTING DISCOUNT RATES.** The first method is to treat all foreign risk as a single problem, by adjusting the discount rate applicable to foreign projects relative to the rate used for domestic projects to reflect the greater foreign exchange risk, political risk, agency costs, asymmetric information, and other uncertainties perceived in foreign operations. However, adjusting the discount rate applied to a foreign project's cash flow to reflect these uncertainties does not penalize net present value in proportion either to the actual amount at risk or to possible variations in the nature of that risk over time. Combining all risks into a single discount rate may thus cause us to discard much information about the uncertainties of the future.

In the case of foreign exchange risk, changes in exchange rates have a potential effect on future cash flows because of operating exposure. The direction of the effect, however, can either decrease or increase net cash inflows, depending on where the products are sold and where inputs are sourced. To increase the discount rate applicable to a foreign project, on the assumption that the foreign currency might depreciate more than expected, ignores the possible favorable effect of a foreign currency depreciation on the project's competitive position. Increased sales volume might more than offset a lower value of the local currency. Such an increase in the discount rate also ignores the possibility that the foreign currency may appreciate (two-sided risk).

**ADJUSTING CASH FLOWS.** In the second method, we incorporate foreign risks in adjustments to forecasted cash flows of the project. The discount rate for the foreign project is risk-adjusted only for overall business and financial risk, in the same manner as for domestic projects. Simulation-based assessment utilizes scenario development to estimate cash flows to the parent arising from the project over time under different alternative economic futures.

Certainty regarding the quantity and timing of cash flows in a prospective foreign investment is, to quote from *The Maltese Falcon*, the stuff that dreams are made of. Due to the complexity of economic forces at work in major investment projects, it is paramount that the analyst realize the subjectivity of the forecast cash flows. Humility in analysis is a valuable trait.

**SHORTCOMINGS OF EACH.**    In many cases, however, neither adjusting the discount rate nor adjusting cash flows is optimal. For example, political uncertainties are a threat to the entire investment, not just the annual cash flows. Potential loss depends partly on the terminal value of the unrecovered parent investment, which will vary depending on how the project was financed, whether political risk insurance was obtained, and what investment horizon is contemplated. Furthermore, if the political climate were expected to be unfavorable in the near future, any investment would probably be unacceptable. Political uncertainty usually relates to possible adverse events that might occur in the more distant future, but that cannot be foreseen at the present. Adjusting the discount rate for political risk thus penalizes early cash flows too heavily while not penalizing distant cash flows enough.

**REPERCUSSIONS TO THE INVESTOR.**    Apart from anticipated political and foreign exchange risks, MNEs sometimes worry that taking on foreign projects may increase the firm's overall cost of capital because of investors' perceptions of foreign risk. This worry seemed reasonable if a firm had significant investments in Iraq, Iran, Russia, Serbia, or Afghanistan in the 1990s. However, the argument loses persuasiveness when applied to diversified foreign investments with a heavy balance in the industrial countries of Canada, Western Europe, Australia, Latin America, and Asia where, in fact, the bulk of FDI is located. These countries have a reputation for treating foreign investments by consistent standards, and empirical evidence confirms that a foreign presence in these countries may not increase the cost of capital. In fact, some studies indicate that required returns on foreign projects may even be lower than those for domestic projects.

**MNE PRACTICES.**    Surveys of MNEs over the past 35 years have shown that about half of them adjust the discount rate and half adjust the cash flows. One recent survey indicated a rising use of adjusting discount rates over adjusting cash flows. However, the survey also indicated an increasing use of multifactor methods — discount rate adjustment, cash flow adjustment, real options analysis, and qualitative criteria — in evaluating foreign investments.[2]

## PORTFOLIO RISK MEASUREMENT

As we discussed in Chapter 15, the field of finance has distinguished two definitions of risk: (1) the risk of the individual security (standard deviation of expected return) and (2) the risk of the individual security as a component of a portfolio (*beta*). A foreign investment undertaken in order to enter a local or regional market — market seeking — will have returns that are more or less correlated with those of the local market. A portfolio-based assessment of the investment's prospects would then seem appropriate. A foreign investment undertaken for *resource-seeking* or *production-seeking* purposes may have returns related to those of the parent company or units located somewhere else in the world and have little to do with local markets. Cemex's proposed investment in Semen Indonesia is both *market seeking* and *production seeking*

[2]Keck,Tom, Eric Levengood, and Al Longield, "Using Discounted Cash Flow Analysis in an International Setting: A Survey of Issues in Modeling the Cost of Capital," *Journal of Applied Corporate Finance*, vol. 11, no. 3, Fall 1998, pp. 82–99.

(for export). The decision about which approach is to be used by the MNE in evaluating prospective foreign investments may be the single most important analytical decision it makes. An investment's acceptability may change dramatically from one criteria to the other.

For comparisons within the local host country, we should overlook a project's actual financing or parent-influenced debt capacity, since these would probably be different for local investors than they are for a multinational owner. In addition, the risks of the project to local investors might differ from those perceived by a foreign multinational owner because of the opportunities an MNE has to take advantage of market imperfections. Moreover, the local project may be only one out of an internationally diversified portfolio of projects for the multinational owner; if undertaken by local investors it might have to stand alone without international diversification. Since diversification reduces risk, the MNE can require a lower rate of return than is required by local investors.

Thus the discount rate used locally must be a hypothetical rate based on a judgment as to what independent local investors would probably demand were they to own the business. Consequently, application of the local discount rate to local cash flows provides only a rough measure of the value of the project as a stand-alone local venture, rather than an absolute valuation.

## Real Option Analysis

The discounted cash flow (DCF) approach used in the valuation of Semen Indonesia — and capital budgeting and valuation in general — has long had its critics. Investments that have long lives, cash flow returns in later years, or higher levels of risk than those typical of the firm's current business activities are often rejected by traditional DCF financial analysis. More importantly, when MNEs evaluate competitive projects, traditional discounted cash flow analysis is typically unable to capture the *strategic options* that an individual investment option may offer. This has led to the development of *real option analysis*. Real option analysis is the application of option theory to capital budgeting decisions.

Real options is a different way of thinking about investment values. At its core, it is a cross between decision-tree analysis and pure option-based valuation. It is particularly useful for analyzing investment projects that will follow very different value paths at decision points in time where management decisions are made regarding project pursuit. This wide range of potential outcomes is at the heart of real option theory. These wide ranges of value are *volatilities*, the basic element of option pricing theory described previously in Chapter 7.

Real option valuation also allows us to analyze a number of managerial decisions which in practice characterize many major capital investment projects:

1. The option to defer
2. The option to abandon
3. The option to alter capacity
4. The option to start up or shut down (switching)

Real option analysis treats cash flows in terms of future value in a positive sense, whereas DCF treats future cash flows negatively (on a discounted basis). Real option analysis is a particularly powerful device when addressing potential investment projects with extremely long life spans, or investments that do not commence until future dates. Real option analysis acknowledges the way information is gathered over time to support decision making. Management learns from both active (searching it out) and passive (observing market conditions) knowledge gathering and then uses this knowledge to make better decisions. The mini-case that follows illustrates an application of real option analysis.

## MINI-CASE

# Trident's Chinese Market Entry — An Application of Real Option Analysis

Trident is evaluating the possibility of entering the Chinese market. The senior management team, headed by CEO Charles Darwin, has concluded from a number of preliminary studies (code named *Beagle*) performed by a consultant that within three to five years this market could well determine who the major players are to be in Trident's telecommunications industry. The corporate finance team, headed by the CFO Maria Gonzalez, has concluded a preliminary financial analysis of its own on the basis of the numbers presented by the consultants.

The results of the corporate finance team's expected value analysis were not, however, encouraging. As illustrated in Exhibit 1, the expected gross profits of the venture were estimated to be only $10 million.

- Revenues were expected to follow one of two paths — either *high* (approximately $130 million at a 50% probability) or *low* ($50 million at a 50% probability). Therefore, using expected value analysis, revenues were estimated at $90 million.
- Costs were expected to be either high ($120 million), medium ($80 million), or low ($40 million), all with an

equal 33.3% expected probability of occurrence. The expected value of costs were $80 million.

What made this $10 million gross profit all the more unattractive was that the market development group was requesting an additional $15 million for upfront research and development (R&D). This capital expense could not be justified. The expected total return on the project would then be a negative $5 million: ($15) + $ 10 = ($5). The corporate finance team concluded that the project was not an acceptable investment in its present form.

Charles was clearly frustrated with the corporate finance team during the presentation of their results. After some heated debate over individual values, Charles asked what specifically would be learned if the added $15 million in market research and development were actually spent. Would it improve the expected profitability of the project?

After some additional analysis, the corporate finance team concluded that nothing significant would be learned about the market which would change either the probabilities or expected values of revenues. However, after the

## EXHIBIT 1

Trident's Analysis of Chinese Market Entry

| Revenues | Value (in millions) | Probability | Expected Value (in millions) |
|---|---|---|---|
| High | $130 | 0.50 | $65.00 |
| Low | 50 | 0.50 | 25.00 |
| Expected value | | | $90.00 |

| Costs | | | |
|---|---|---|---|
| High | $120 | 0.33 | $40.00 |
| Medium | 80 | 0.33 | 26.67 |
| Low | 40 | 0.33 | 13.33 |
| Expected value | | | $80.00 |

Expected project gross profit = revenues − costs = $90 − $80 = $10.

additional R&D expenditure, the team felt certain that the cost of operations would be better known.

Charles then asked the corporate finance team about an alternative approach to viewing the project.

*"What if the expenditure of $15 million were looked upon as the purchase of a call option on the project? What I mean is, if we spend the $15 million, we would then have the ability to identify the actual cost associated with undertaking the project. Even though we still would not really know the revenues — we still have business risk — we would be able to decide more intelligently whether to stop or proceed with the project at that point in time."*

As illustrated in Exhibit 2, after the investment (or expenditure) of the $15 million in market research and development, the firm would know which of the three cost paths it would be on — high, medium, or low. Regardless of the expected revenue, still assumed to be $90 million, the firm could make an intelligent choice to either stop or proceed at that point. This was, in Charles' opinion, a much more logical way to pursue the analysis.

Maria Gonzalez and her finance team, however, were still not convinced. Maria said, "But we would still be spending the $15 million up front and still be looking at the same expected outcomes. I don't see how your approach changes anything."

Charles continued, "It changes a lot. After spending the $15 million we would know — with added certainty — what the likely outcome would be. If it is either the medium- or low-cost path, we would proceed and end up with a gross operating profit of either $10 or $50 million, depending on revenues. If it is the high-cost path, we would stop all work immediately, before incurring additional operating costs. The expected value, at least according to my calculations, is a positive $20 million."

$$\text{Expected Value} = (\$15) + [(0.333 \times \$0) + (0.333 \times \$10) + (0.333 \times \$50)] = \$20$$

It then dawned upon Maria what Charles was saying. The purchase of the call option, the expenditure of the $15 million, would allow Trident to avoid the loss-making option (the high-cost path with an expected outcome of negative $30 million), so the high-cost path would enter the calculation of expected value as zero. The purchase of the call option would indeed allow Trident to undertake the investment, if it wished, only after gaining additional time and knowledge.

Charles and the senior management team then concluded that they had won the argument (as senior management always does) and approved the project.

## The Potential of Real Option Analysis

Real options analysis, like DCF and other investment analysis techniques, is nothing other than a tool. The two techniques are complementary. Management should employ both methods in the analysis of potential investments and gather information from both.

Unlike our example, real option analysis is not ordinarily a simple technique. There is an enormous amount of technical "comfort" required on the part of the analyst

**EXHIBIT 2**

Trident's Option Analysis of Chinese Market Entry

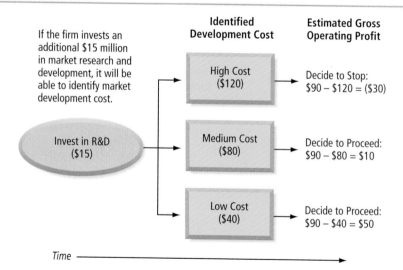

Investing in the market R&D is equivalent to buying a call option. Amounts are in millions.

in order to implement the technique correctly. Like most techniques derived from financial theory, it is easily abused. Those who will utilize the information provided by real option analysis must be trained in the proper interpretation of its results.

But real option analysis is gaining in use and popularity. Consistent with the example of Trident, it is often favored first by senior management because it has two characteristics they like. Its structure acknowledges the time sequence of a project, describing cash inflows and outflows at different points in time. This is more consistent with the way management frequently sees a project unfold. Real option analysis also seems to value "management" by its very nature; it credits the ability of man-

agement to gain new information and make good business decisions at the points in time when those decisions must be made.

## Case Questions

1. How does real option analysis differ from traditional expected value analysis?
2. How does real option analysis use information gathering differently from discounted cash flow analysis?
3. Recalculate both the expected return analysis and the real option analysis for the Chinese market entry assuming that the revenue probabilities were 25% high and 75% low. Is the project acceptable under either of the decision-making methodologies?

## Summary of Learning Objectives

*Extend the domestic capital budgeting analysis to evaluate a greenfield foreign project*

- The proposed greenfield investment in Indonesia by Cemex was analyzed within the traditional capital budgeting framework (base case).

- Foreign complications, including foreign exchange and political risks, were introduced to the analysis.

*Distinguish between the project viewpoint and the parent viewpoint when analyzing a potential foreign investment*

- Parent cash flows must be distinguished from project cash flows. Each of these two types of flows contributes to a different view of value.

- Parent cash flows often depend on the form of financing. Thus cash flows cannot be clearly separated from financing decisions, as is done in domestic capital budgeting.

- Additional cash flows generated by a new investment in one foreign subsidiary may be in part or wholly taken away from another subsidiary, with the net result that the project is favorable from a single subsidiary point of view but contributes nothing to worldwide cash flows.

- Remittance of funds to the parent must be explicitly recognized because of differing tax systems, legal and political constraints on the movement of funds, local business norms, and differences in how financial markets and institutions function.

- Cash flows from subsidiaries to parent can be generated by an array of nonfinancial payments, including payment of license fees and payments for imports from the parent.

- Differing rates of national inflation must be anticipated because of their importance in causing changes in competitive position and thus cash flows over a period of time.

*Adjust the capital budgeting analysis of a foreign project for risk*

- A foreign project's capital budgeting analysis should be adjusted for potential foreign exchange and/or political risks associated with the investment.

- A number of alternative methods are used for adjusting for risk, including adding an additional risk premium to the discount factor used, decreasing expected cash flows, and conducting detailed sensitivity and scenario analysis on expected project outcomes.

*Introduce the use of real option analysis as a complement to discounted cash flow analysis in the evaluation of potential international investments*

- Real option is a different way of thinking about investment values. At its core, it is a cross between decision-tree analysis and pure option-based valuation.

- Real option valuation also allows us to evaluate the option to defer, the option to abandon, the option to alter capacity, and the option to start up or shut down a project.

## QUESTIONS

1. **Capital budgeting theoretical framework.** Capital budgeting for a foreign project uses the same theoretical framework as domestic capital budgeting. What are the basic steps in domestic capital budgeting?

2. **Foreign complexities.** Capital budgeting for a foreign project is considerably more complex than for a domestic project. What are the factors that add complexity?

3. **Project versus parent valuation.**

   a. Why should a foreign project be evaluated from both a project and a parent viewpoint?

   b. Which viewpoint, project or parent, gives results closer to the traditional meaning of net present value in capital budgeting?

   c. Which viewpoint gives results closer to the effect on consolidated earnings per share?

4. **Cash flow.** Capital projects provide both operating cash flows and financial cash flows. Why are operating cash flows preferred for domestic capital budgeting but financial cash flows given major consideration in international projects?

5. **Risk-adjusted return.** Should the anticipated internal rate of return (IRR) for a proposed foreign project be compared to (a) alternative home country proposals, (b) returns earned by local companies in the same industry and/or risk class, or (c) both of the above? Justify your answer.

6. **Blocked cash flows.** In the context of evaluating foreign investment proposals, how should a multinational firm evaluate cash flows in the host foreign country that are blocked from being repatriated to the firm's home country?

7. **Host country inflation.** How should an MNE factor host country inflation into its evaluation of an investment proposal?

8. **Cost of equity.** A foreign subsidiary does not have an independent cost of capital. However, in order to estimate the discount rate for a comparable host country firm, the analyst should try to calculate a hypothetical cost of capital. As part of this process, the analyst can estimate the subsidiary's proxy cost of equity by using the traditional equation: $k_e = k_{rf} + \beta(k_m - k_{rf})$. Define each variable in this equation and explain how the variable might be different for a proxy host country firm compared to the parent MNE.

9. **Viewpoints.** What are the differences in the cash flows used in a project point of view analysis and a parent point of view analysis?

10. **Foreign exchange risk.** How is foreign exchange risk sensitivity factored into the capital budgeting analysis of a foreign project?

11. **Expropriation risk.** How is expropriation risk factored into the capital budgeting analysis of a foreign project?

12. **Real option analysis.** What is real option analysis? How is it a better method of making investment decisions than traditional capital budgeting analysis?

## PROBLEMS

1. **Sarasota Corporation.** Sarasota Corporation (USA) expects to receive cash dividends from a French joint venture over the coming three years. The first dividend, to be paid December 31, 2004, is expected to be €720,000. The dividend is then expected to grow 10.0% per year over the following two years. The current exchange rate (December 30, 2003) is $1.25/€. Sarasota's weighted average cost of capital is 12%.

   a. What is the present value of the expected euro dividend stream if the euro is expected to appreciate 4.00% per annum against the dollar?

   b. What is the present value of the expected dividend stream if the euro were to depreciate 3.00% per annum against the dollar?

2. **Trefica de Honduras.** Texas Pacific, a U.S.-based private equity firm, is trying to determine what it should pay for a tool manufacturing firm in Honduras named Trefica. Texas Pacific estimates that Trefica will generate a free cash flow of 13 million Honduran lempiras (Lp) next year, and

that this free cash flow will continue to grow at a constant rate of 8.0% per annum indefinitely.

A private equity firm like Texas Pacific, however, is not interested in owning a company for long, and plans to sell Trefica at the end of three years for approximately 10 times Trefica's free cash flow in that year. The current spot exchange rate is Lp14.80/$, but the Honduran inflation rate is expected to remain at a relatively high rate of 16.0% per annum compared to the U.S. dollar inflation rate of only 2.0% per annum. Texas Pacific expects to earn at least a 20% annual rate of return on international investments like Trefica.

a. What would Trefica be worth if the Honduran lempira were to remain fixed over the three-year investment period?

b. What would Trefica be worth if the Honduran lempira were to change in value over time according to purchasing power parity?

3. **Baltimore Tile Company.** Baltimore Tile Company (U.S.) is considering investing Rs50,000,000 in India to create a wholly-owned tile manufacturing plant to export to the European market. After five years the subsidiary would be sold to Indian investors for Rs100,000,000. A *pro forma* income statement for the Indian operation predicts the generation of Rs7,000,000 of annual cash flow, as follows:

| | |
|---|---|
| Annual sales revenue | Rs 30,000,000 |
| Less cash operating expenses | − 17,000,000 |
| Less depreciation | − 1,000,000 |
| Income before interest and taxes | Rs 12,000,000 |
| Less Indian taxes at 50% | − 6,000,000 |
| Net income | Rs 6,000,000 |
| Add back depreciation | + 1,000,000 |
| Annual cash flow | Rs 7,000,000 |

The initial investment will be made on December 31, 2002, and cash flows will occur on December 31 of each succeeding year. Annual cash dividends to Baltimore Tile from India will equal 75% of accounting income.

The U.S. corporate tax rate is 40% and the Indian corporate tax rate is 50%. Because the Indian tax rate is greater than the U.S. tax rate, annual dividends paid to Baltimore Tile will not be subject to additional taxes in the United States. There are no capital gains taxes on the final sale. Baltimore Tile uses a weighted average cost of capital of 14% on domestic investments, but will add six percentage points for the Indian investment because of perceived greater risk. Baltimore Tile forecasts the rupee/dollar exchange rate for December 31 on the next six years to be

| Year | Exchange Rate | Year | Exchange Rate |
|---|---|---|---|
| 2002 | Rs50.00/$ | 2005 | Rs62.00/$ |
| 2003 | Rs54.00/$ | 2006 | Rs66.00/$ |
| 2004 | Rs58.00/$ | 2007 | Rs70.00/$ |

What is the net present value and internal rate of return on this investment?

4. **Berkeley Devices.** Berkeley Devices, Inc., manufactures design components for personal computers. Until now, manufacturing has been subcontracted to other companies, but for reasons of quality control Berkeley Devices has decided to manufacture the components itself in Asia. Analysis has narrowed the choice to two possibilities, Penang in Malaysia and Manila in the Philippines. At the moment only the following summary of expected, after-tax, cash flows is available. Although most operating outflows would be in Malaysian ringgit or Philippine pesos, some additional U.S. dollar cash outflows would be necessary, as shown.

| Berkeley in Penang | 2002 | 2003 | 2004 | 2005 | 2006 | 2007 |
|---|---|---|---|---|---|---|
| Net ringgit cash flows | (26,000) | 8,000 | 6,800 | 7,400 | 9,200 | 10,000 |
| Net dollar cash flows | — | (100) | (120) | (150) | (150) | — |

| Berkeley in Manila | 2002 | 2003 | 2004 | 2005 | 2006 | 2007 |
|---|---|---|---|---|---|---|
| Net peso cash flows | (560,000) | 190,000 | 180,000 | 200,000 | 210,000 | 200,000 |
| Dollar cash outflows | — | (100) | (200) | (300) | (400) | — |

The Malaysia ringgit currently trades at RM3.80/$ and the Philippine peso trades at Ps50.00/$. Berkeley expects the Malaysian ringgit to appreciate 2.0% per year against the dollar and the

Philippine peso to depreciate 5.0% per year against the dollar. If the weighted average cost of capital for Berkeley Devices is 14.0%, which project looks most promising?

5. **Superior Machine Oil Company.** Privately owned Superior Machine Oil Company is considering investing in the Czech Republic so as to have a refinery source closer to its European customers. The original investment in Czech korunas would amount to K250 million, or $5,000,000 at the current spot rate of K32.50/$, all in fixed assets, which will be depreciated over 10 years by the straight-line method. An additional K100,000,000 will be needed for working capital.

For capital budgeting purposes, Superior assumes sale as a going concern at the end of the third year, at a price (after all taxes) equal to the net book value of fixed assets alone (not including working capital). All free cash flow will be repatriated to the United States as soon as possible. In evaluating the venture, Superior uses the following U.S. dollar forecasts:

| End of Year | Unit Demand | Unit Sales Price | Exchange Rate (Korunas/$) | Fixed Cash Operating Expenses | Depreciation |
|---|---|---|---|---|---|
| 0 | | | 32.5 | | |
| 1 | 700,000 | $10.00 | 30.0 | $1,000,000 | $500,000 |
| 2 | 900,000 | 10.30 | 27.5 | 1,030,000 | 500,000 |
| 3 | 1,000,000 | 10.60 | 25.0 | 1,060,000 | 500,000 |

Variable manufacturing costs are expected to be 50% of sales. No additional funds need be invested in the U.S. subsidiary during the period under consideration. The Czech Republic imposes no restrictions on repatriation of any funds of any sort. The Czech corporate tax rate is 25% and the U.S. rate is 40%. Both countries allow a tax credit for taxes paid in other countries. Superior uses 18% as its weighted average cost of capital, and its objective is to maximize present value. Is the investment attractive to Superior?

6. **Tostadas de Baja, S.A.** Tostadas de Baja, S.A., located in the state of Baja California, Mexico, manufactures frozen Mexican food which enjoys a large following in the U.S. states of California and Arizona to the north. In order to be closer to its U.S. market, Tostadas de Baja is considering moving some of its manufacturing operations to southern California. Operations in California would begin in 2003 and have the following attributes:

a. The 2003 sales price in the United States would average $5.00 per package, and prices would increase 3.0% per annum.

b. 2003 production and sales would be 1 million packets. Unit sales would grow at 10.0% per annum through 2004 and then stabilize forever.

c. Production costs are estimated at $4.00 per packet in 2003, and would increase by 4.0% per year.

d. General and administration expenses would be $100,000 per year, and depreciation expenses were estimated at a constant $80,000 per year.

e. Tostadas de Baja has assigned a weighted average cost of capital of 16.0% to the project.

f. Tostadas de Baja will assign an after-tax value to its California plant at the end of 2005 equal to an infinite stream of 2005 dividends, discounted at 20% per annum. The higher discount rate is because the company is concerned about the political risk of a Mexican firm manufacturing in California.

g. All production is for sale (production volume equals sales volume), and all sales are for cash.

h. Combined federal and state tax rate in the United States is 30%; Mexico's is 25%.

i. Actual and expected exchange rates, by year, are

2002: Ps8.00/$      2004: Ps10.00/$

2003: Ps9.00/$      2005: Ps11.00/$

j. Tostadas de Baja will remit 80.0% of its reported profits each period back to the parent company as an annual cash dividend.

What is the maximum U.S. dollar cost Tostadas de Baja can afford in 2002 for the investment?

## SANTA CLARA ELECTRONICS. *USE THE FOLLOWING PROBLEM AND ASSUMPTIONS TO ANSWER QUESTIONS 7 THROUGH 10.*

Santa Clara Electronics, Inc., of California exports 24,000 sets of low-density lightbulbs per year to Argentina under an import license that expires in five years. In Argentina the lightbulbs are sold for the Argentine peso equivalent of $60 per set. Direct manufacturing costs in the United States and shipping together amount to $40 per set. The market for this type of bulb in Argentina is stable, neither growing nor shrinking, and Santa Clara holds the major portion of the market.

The Argentine government has invited Santa Clara to open a manufacturing plant so imported bulbs can be replaced by locally produced bulbs. If Santa Clara makes the investment, it will operate the plant for five years and then sell the building and equipment to Argentine investors at net book value at the time of sale plus the value of any net working capital. (Net working capital is the amount of current assets less any portion financed by local debt.) Santa Clara will be allowed to repatriate all net income and depreciation funds to the United States each year. Santa Clara traditionally evaluates all foreign investments in U.S. dollar terms.

- **Investment.** Santa Clara's anticipated cash outlay in U.S. dollars in 2003 would be

  | | |
  |---|---|
  | Building and equipment | $1,000,000 |
  | Net working capital | 1,000,000 |
  | Total investment | $2,000,000 |

  All investment outlays will be made in 2003, and all operating cash flows will occur at the end of years 2004 through 2008.

- **Depreciation and investment recovery.** Building and equipment will be depreciated over five years on a straight-line basis. At the end of the fifth year, the $1,000,000 of net working capital may also be repatriated to the United States, as may the remaining net book value of the plant.

- **Sale price of bulbs.** Locally manufactured bulbs will be sold for the Argentine peso equivalent of $60 per set.

- **Operating expenses per set of bulbs.** Material purchases are as follows:

  | | |
  |---|---|
  | Materials purchased in Argentina (U.S. dollar equivalent) | $20 per set |
  | Materials imported from Santa Clara | +$10 per set |
  | Total variable costs | $30 per set |

- **Transfer prices.** The $10 transfer price per set for raw material sold by the parent consists of $5 of direct and indirect costs incurred in the United States on their manufacture, creating $5 of pretax profit to Santa Clara.

- **Taxes.** The corporate income tax rate is 40% in Argentina and in the United States (combined federal and state/province). There are no capital gains taxes on the future sale of the Argentine subsidiary, either in Argentina or in the United States.

- **Discount rate.** Santa Clara Electronics uses a 15% discount rate to evaluate all domestic and foreign projects.

7. **Santa Clara Electronics: Baseline analysis.** Evaluate the proposed investment in Argentina by Santa Clara Electronics (US). Santa Clara's management wishes the baseline analysis to be performed in U.S. dollars (and implicitly also assumes the exchange rate remains fixed throughout the life of the project). Create a project viewpoint capital budget and a parent viewpoint capital budget. What do you conclude from your analysis?

8. **Santa Clara Electronics: Revenue growth scenario.** As a result of their analysis in the previous question, Santa Clara wishes to explore the implications of being able to grow sales volume by 4% per year. Argentine inflation is expected to average 5% per year, so sales price and material cost increases of 7% and 6% per year, respectively, are thought reasonable. Although material costs in Argentina are expected to rise, U.S.-based costs are not expected to change over the five-year period. Evaluate this scenario for both the project and parent viewpoints. Under this revenue growth scenario is the project acceptable?

9. **Santa Clara Electronics: Revenue growth and sales price scenario.** In addition to the assumptions employed in Problem 8, Santa Clara now wishes to evaluate the prospect of being able to sell the Argentine subsidiary at the end of year 5 at a multiple of the business's earnings in that year. Santa Clara believes that a multiple of 6 is a conservative estimate of the market value of the firm at that time. Evaluate the project and parent viewpoint capital budgets.

10. **Santa Clara Electronics: Revenue growth, sales price, and currency risk scenario.** One of the new analysts at Santa Clara, a recent business school graduate, believes that it is a fundamental error to evaluate the Argentine project's prospective earnings and cash flows in dollars, rather than first estimating their Argentine peso (Ps) value and then converting cash flow returns to the U.S. in dollars. She believes the correct method is to use the end-of-year spot rate in 2003 of Ps3.50/$ and assume it will change in relation to purchasing power. (She is assuming U.S. inflation to be 1% per annum and Argentine inflation to be 5% per annum). She also believes that Santa Clara should use a risk-adjusted discount rate in Argentina that reflects Argentine capital costs (20% is her estimate) and a risk-adjusted discount rate for the parent viewpoint capital budget (18%) on the assumption that international projects in a risky currency environment should require a higher expected return than other, lower-risk projects. How do these assumptions and changes alter Santa Clara's perspective on the proposed investment?

 ## Internet Exercises

1. **Capital projects and the EBRD.** The European Bank for Reconstruction and Development (EBRD) was established to "foster the transition towards open market-oriented economies and to promote private and entrepreneurial initiative in the countries of central and eastern Europe and the Commonwealth of Independent States (CIS) committed to and applying the principles of multiparty democracy, pluralism and market economics." Use the EBRD Web site to determine which projects and companies EBRD is currently undertaking.

    European Bank for Reconstruction and Development
    http://www.ebrd.org

2. **Emerging markets: China.** Long-term investment projects abroad such as electrical power generation require a thorough understanding of all attributes of doing business in that country. These include import/export restrictions, and labor relations, supplier financing, tax rules, depreciation schedules, currency properties and restrictions, and sources of short-term and long-term debt, to name a few. China is currently the focus of investment and market penetration strategies of multinational firms worldwide. Using the Web (you might start with the Web sites listed below), build a database on doing business in China, and prepare an update of many of the factors, such as average receivables outstanding and currency convertibility, discussed in this chapter.

    Ministry of Foreign Trade and Economic Cooperation, PRC
    http://www.chinamarket.com.cn/E
    China Investment Trust & Investment Corporation
    http://www.citic.com/english/index.asp
    ChinaNet Investment Pages
    http://www.business-china.com/invest

# Managing Multinational Operations

In Part 6 you learn the intricacies of managing an MNE's ongoing global operations, a task that requires the most attention of financial managers. Daily attention to the details of everyday operations determines how much value can be added to the shareholders that have approved an MNE's global reach through foreign direct investment as described in Part 5.

**CHAPTER 19** describes all the elements of traditional export and import trade financing. You will learn how an MNE, or any exporter-importer, can reduce the risk of nonpayment on a trade transaction. We describe all the key documents that are needed to accomplish this task. In particular, you will learn about the use and details of letters of credit, drafts, bankers' acceptances, and bills of lading. These documents not only reduce the danger of nonpayment but also provide a documentary basis for collateralizing short-term trade financing by commercial banks. We document a typical trade transaction so that you can understand how the individual documents are linked. We describe various government programs available to help finance exports. The chapter concludes with an analysis of various trade financing alternatives, including bankers' acceptances, trade acceptances, factoring, securitization, bank credit line, commercial paper, and forfaiting.

**CHAPTER 20** describes the global tax environment. You learn about tax morality and the importance of tax neutrality to governments as they design how their tax laws would affect an MNE's business decisions. You will also learn how tax treaties between countries attempt to provide a level playing field for competing MNEs. Furthermore, different types of taxes, such as the value-added tax, complicate the MNE's goal of minimizing its worldwide tax burden. The chapter continues with a detailed description of how the United States taxes the foreign-source income of its MNEs. The chapter then analyzes how Trident should manage its foreign-source income in order to minimize its worldwide taxes. We conclude with a description of tax haven subsidiaries and offshore financial centers.

**CHAPTER 21** analyzes how an MNE can reposition funds across borders while overcoming political, foreign exchange, tax, and transaction cost constraints. You will learn about the importance of unbundling fund transfers. Unbundling means that rather than depending on dividends alone to transfer funds internally, an MNE should utilize other conduits, such as license fees, royalties, and contributions to overhead by foreign subsidiaries. We analyze how an MNE can manage its working capital efficiently. We use the case of Trident Brazil to illustrate an MNE's operating cycle. You will learn how an MNE can minimize the amount of funds it has tied up in working capital, a goal that is important for maximizing the after-tax return on its invested capital. In addition to managing accounts receivable you will learn about how to manage inventory and cash balances. MNEs manage cash balances through international payments netting systems in order to minimize the funds tied up in cash and the transactions costs incurred every time cash is moved through the banking system. The chapter concludes by showing you how an MNE can utilize the banking system to finance short-term working capital needs. You will learn how an MNE can use its own in-house bank, as well as tapping the commercial banking services offered by both multinational and local host country banks.

# International Trade Finance

## LEARNING OBJECTIVES

Learn how international trade alters both the supply chain and the general value chain of the domestic firm, thereby beginning the globalization process in the trade phase

Consider what the key elements of an import or export transaction are in business

Discover how the three key documents in import-export — the letter of credit, the draft, and the bill of lading — combine to finance the transaction and to manage its risks

Identify what the documentation sequence is for a typical international trade transaction

Learn how the various stages and their costs affect the ability of an exporter to enter a foreign market and potentially compete in both credit terms and pricing

See what organizations and resources are available for exporters to aid in managing trade risk and financing

Examine the various trade financing alternatives

The purpose of this chapter is to explain how international trade — exports and imports — is financed. The contents are of direct practical relevance to both domestic firms that just import and export and to multinational firms that trade with related and unrelated entities.

The chapter begins by explaining the types of trade relationships that exist. Next we explain the trade dilemma: exporters want to be paid before they export and importers do not want to pay until they receive the goods. The next section explains the benefits of the current international trade protocols. This is followed by a section describing the elements of a trade transaction and the various documents that are used to facilitate the trade's completion and financing. The next section identifies international trade risks, namely, currency risk and noncompletion risk. The following sections describe the key trade documents, including letter of credit, draft, and bill of lading. The next section summarizes the documentation of a typical trade transaction. This is followed by a description of government programs to help finance exports, including export credit insurance and specialized banks such as the Export-Import Bank of the United States. Next, we compare the various types of short-term receivables financing and then the use of forfaiting for longer term receivables. The mini-case at the end of the chapter, "Crosswell International's Precious Ultra-Thin Diapers," illustrates how an export requires the integration of management, marketing, and finance.

## The Trade Relationship

As we saw in Chapter 1, the first significant global activity by a domestic firm is the importing and exporting of goods and services. The purpose of this chapter is to analyze the *international trade phase* for a domestic firm that begins to import goods and services from foreign suppliers and to export to foreign buyers. In the case of Trident, this trade phase began with suppliers from Mexico and buyers from Canada.

Trade financing shares a number of common characteristics with the traditional value chain activities conducted by all firms. All companies must search out suppliers for the many goods and services required as inputs to their own goods production or service provision processes. Trident's Purchasing and Procurement Department must determine whether each potential supplier is capable of producing the product to required quality specifications, producing and delivering in a timely and reliable manner, and continuing to work with Trident in the ongoing process of product and process improvement for continued competitiveness. All must be at an acceptable price and payment terms. As illustrated in Exhibit 19.1, these issues apply to potential customers as well, because their continued business is equally as critical to Trident's operations and success.

Understanding the nature of the relationship between the exporter and the importer is critical to understanding the methods for import-export financing utilized in industry. Exhibit 19.2 provides an overview of the three categories of relationships: *unaffiliated unknown*, *unaffiliated known*, and *affiliated*.

- A foreign importer with which Trident has not previously conducted business would be considered *unaffiliated unknown*. In this case the two parties would need to enter into a detailed sales contract, outlining the specific responsibilities and expectations of the business agreement. Trident would also need to seek out protection against the possibility that the importer would not make payment in full in a timely fashion.

**EXHIBIT 19.1**

Financing Trade:
The Flow of
Goods and Funds

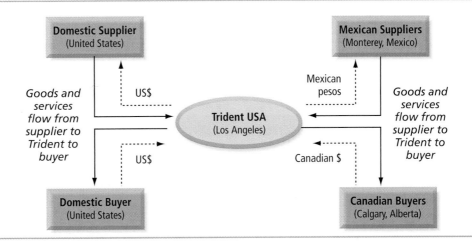

- A foreign importer with which Trident has previously conducted business success-fully would be considered *unaffiliated known*. In this case the two parties may still enter into a detailed sales contract, but specific terms and shipments or provisions of services may be significantly looser in definition. Depending on the depth of the relationship, Trident may seek some third-party protection against noncompletion or conduct the business on an open-account basis.

- A foreign importer which is a subsidiary business unit of Trident, such as Trident Brazil, would be an *affiliated party* (sometimes referred to as *intrafirm trade*).

**EXHIBIT 19.2**

Alternative
International
Trade
Relationships

Because both businesses are part of the same MNE, the most common practice would be to conduct the trade transaction without a contract or protection against nonpayment. This is not, however, always the case. In a variety of international business situations it may still be in Trident's best interest to detail the conditions for the business transaction, and to possibly protect against any political or country-based interruption to the completion of the trade transaction.

## The Trade Dilemma

International trade must work around a fundamental dilemma. Imagine an importer and an exporter who would like to do business with one another. Because of the distance between the two, it is not possible to simultaneously hand over goods with one hand and accept payment with the other. The importer would prefer the arrangement at the top of Exhibit 19.3, while the exporter would prefer the arrangement shown at the bottom.

The fundamental dilemma of being unwilling to trust a stranger in a foreign land is solved by using a highly respected bank as intermediary. A greatly simplified view is described in Exhibit 19.4. In this simplified view, the importer obtains the bank's promise to pay on its behalf, knowing that the exporter will trust the bank. The bank's promise to pay is called a *letter of credit*.

The exporter ships the merchandise to the importer's country. Title to the merchandise is given to the bank on a document called an *order bill of lading*. The exporter asks the bank to pay for the goods, and the bank does so. The document to request payment is a *sight draft*. The bank, having paid for the goods, now passes title to the importer, whom the bank trusts. At that time or later, depending on their agreement, the importer reimburses the bank.

Financial managers of MNEs must understand these three basic documents. Their firms will often trade with unaffiliated parties, and the system of documentation provides a source of short-term capital that can be drawn upon even when shipments are to sister subsidiaries.

**EXHIBIT 19.3**

The Mechanics of
Import and
Export

**EXHIBIT 19.4**

The Bank as the
Import-Export
Intermediary

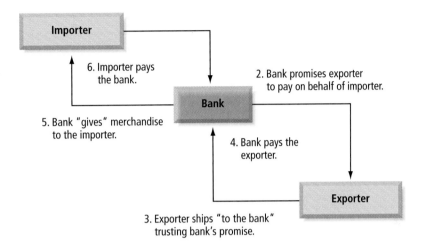

1. Importer obtains bank's promise
to pay on importer's behalf.

**Importer**

6. Importer pays
the bank.

2. Bank promises exporter
to pay on behalf of importer.

**Bank**

5. Bank "gives" merchandise
to the importer.

4. Bank pays the
exporter.

**Exporter**

3. Exporter ships "to the bank"
trusting bank's promise.

## Benefits of the System

The three key documents and their interaction are described later in this chapter. They constitute a system developed and modified over centuries to protect both importer and exporter from the risk of noncompletion and foreign exchange risk, as well as to provide a means of financing.

### PROTECTION AGAINST RISK OF NONCOMPLETION

As stated above, once importer and exporter agree on terms, the seller usually prefers to maintain legal title to the goods until paid, or at least until assured of payment. The buyer, however, will be reluctant to pay before receiving the goods, or at least before receiving title to them. Each wants assurance that the other party will complete its portion of the transaction. The letter of credit, sight draft, and bill of lading are part of a system carefully constructed to determine who suffers the financial loss if one of the parties defaults at any time.

### PROTECTION AGAINST FOREIGN EXCHANGE RISK

In international trade, foreign exchange risk arises from *transaction exposure*. If the transaction requires payment in the exporter's currency, the importer carries the foreign exchange risk. If the transaction calls for payment in the importer's currency, the exporter has the foreign exchange risk.

Transaction exposure can be hedged by the techniques described in Chapter 8, but in order to hedge, the exposed party must be certain that payment of a specified amount will be made on or near a particular date. The three key documents described in this chapter ensure both amount and time of payment and thus lay the groundwork for effective hedging.

The risk of noncompletion and foreign exchange risk are most important when the international trade is episodic, with no outstanding agreement for recurring shipments and no sustained relationship between buyer and seller. When the import-export relationship is of a recurring nature, as in the case of manufactured goods shipped weekly or monthly to a final assembly or retail outlet in another country, and when it is between countries whose currencies are considered strong, the exporter may well bill the importer on open account after a normal credit check. Banks provide credit information and collection services outside of the system of processing drafts drawn against letters of credit.

## FINANCING THE TRADE

Most international trade involves a time lag during which funds are tied up while the merchandise is in transit. Once the risks of noncompletion and of exchange rate changes are disposed of, banks are willing to finance goods in transit. A bank can finance goods in transit, as well as goods held for sale, based on the key documents, without exposing itself to questions about the quality of the merchandise or other physical aspects of the shipment.

## INTERNATIONAL TRADE: TIME LINE AND STRUCTURE

In order to understand the risks associated with international trade transactions, it is helpful to understand the sequence of events in any such transaction. Exhibit 19.5 illustrates, in principle, the series of events associated with a single export transaction.

From a financial management perspective, the two primary risks associated with an international trade transaction are *currency risk* and *risk of noncompletion*. Exhibit 19.5 illustrates the traditional business problem of credit management: the exporter quotes a price, finalizes a contract, and ships the goods, losing physical control over the

**EXHIBIT 19.5**

The Trade Transaction Time Line and Structure

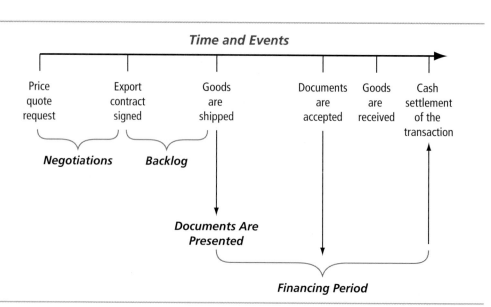

goods based on trust of the buyer or the promise of a bank to pay based on documents presented. The risk of default on the part of the importer is present as soon as the financing period begins, as depicted in Exhibit 19.5.

In many cases the initial task of analyzing the credit worth of foreign customers is similar to procedures for analyzing domestic customers. If Trident has had no experience with a foreign customer but that customer is a large, well-known firm in its home country, Trident may simply ask for a bank credit report on that firm. Trident may also talk to other firms that have had dealings with the foreign customer. If these investigations show the foreign customer (and country) to be completely trustworthy, Trident would likely ship to them on open account, with a credit limit, just as they would for a domestic customer. This is the least costly method of handling exports because there are no heavy documentation or bank charges. However, before a regular trading relationship has been established with a new or unknown firm, Trident must face the possibility of nonpayment for its exports or noncompletion of its imports. The risk of nonpayment can be eliminated through the use of a letter of credit issued by a creditworthy bank.

## Key Documents

The three key documents described in the following pages — the *letter of credit*, *draft*, and *bill of lading* — constitute a system developed and modified over centuries to protect both importer and exporter from the risk of noncompletion of the trade transaction as well as to provide a means of financing. The three key trade documents are part of a carefully constructed system to determine who bears the financial loss if one of the parties defaults at any time.

## Letter of Credit (L/C)

A *letter of credit* (L/C) is a bank's promise to pay issued by a bank at the request of an importer (the applicant/buyer), in which the bank promises to pay an exporter (the beneficiary of the letter) upon presentation of documents specified in the L/C. An L/C reduces the risk of noncompletion, because the bank agrees to pay against documents rather than actual merchandise. The relationship between the three parties is illustrated in Exhibit 19.6.

An importer (buyer) and exporter (seller) agree on a transaction, and the importer then applies to its local bank for the issuance of an L/C. The importer's bank issues an L/C and cuts a sales contract based on its assessment of the importer's creditworthiness, or the bank might require a cash deposit or other collateral from the importer in advance. The importer's bank will want to know the type of transaction, the amount of money involved, and what documents must accompany the draft that will be drawn against the L/C.

If the importer's bank is satisfied with the credit standing of the applicant, it will issue an L/C guaranteeing to pay for the merchandise if shipped in accordance with the instructions and conditions contained in the L/C.

The essence of an L/C is the promise of the issuing bank to pay *against specified documents*, which must accompany any draft drawn against the credit. The L/C is not a guarantee of the underlying commercial transaction. Indeed, the L/C is a separate transaction from any sales or other contracts on which it might be based. To constitute

**EXHIBIT 19.6**

Parties to a Letter
of Credit (L/C)

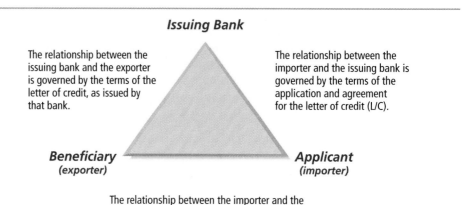

**Issuing Bank**

The relationship between the
issuing bank and the exporter
is governed by the terms of the
letter of credit, as issued by
that bank.

The relationship between the
importer and the issuing bank is
governed by the terms of the
application and agreement
for the letter of credit (L/C).

**Beneficiary**
*(exporter)*

**Applicant**
*(importer)*

The relationship between the importer and the
exporter is governed by the sales contract.

a true L/C transaction, all of the following five elements must be present with respect to the issuing bank:

1. The issuing bank must receive a fee or other valid business consideration for issuing the L/C.
2. The bank's L/C must contain a specified expiration date or a definite maturity.
3. The bank's commitment must have a stated maximum amount of money.
4. The bank's obligation to pay must arise only on the presentation of specific documents, and the bank must not be called on to determine disputed questions of fact or law.
5. The bank's customer must have an unqualified obligation to reimburse the bank on the same condition as the bank has paid.

Commercial letters of credit are also classified as follows.

**IRREVOCABLE VERSUS REVOCABLE.**     An irrevocable L/C obligates the issuing bank to honor drafts drawn in compliance with the credit and can be neither canceled nor modified without the consent of all parties, including in particular the beneficiary (exporter). A revocable L/C can be canceled or amended at any time before payment; it is intended to serve as a means of arranging payment but not as a guarantee of payment.

**CONFIRMED VERSUS UNCONFIRMED.**     An L/C issued by one bank can be confirmed by another, in which case the confirming bank undertakes to honor drafts drawn in compliance with the credit. An unconfirmed L/C is the obligation only of the issuing bank. An exporter is likely to want a foreign bank's L/C confirmed by a domestic bank when the exporter has doubts about the foreign bank's ability to pay. Such doubts can arise when the exporter is unsure of the financial standing of the foreign bank, or if political or economic conditions in the foreign country are unstable. The essence of an L/C is shown in Exhibit 19.7.

Most commercial letters of credit are *documentary*, meaning that certain documents must be included with any drafts drawn under their terms. Required documents usually include an order bill of lading (discussed in more detail later in the chapter), a

**EXHIBIT 19.7**

Essence of a
Letter of Credit
(L/C)

> **Bank of the East, Ltd.**
> *[Name of Issuing Bank]*
>
> Date: September 18, 2004
> L/C Number 123456
>
> Bank of the East, Ltd. hereby issues this irrevocable documentary Letter of Credit to Jones Company *[name of exporter]* for US$500,000, payable 90 days after sight by a draft drawn against Bank of the East, Ltd., in accordance with Letter of Credit number 123456.
>
> The draft is to be accompanied by the following documents:
> **1.** Commercial invoice in triplicate
> **2.** Packing list
> **3.** Clean on board order bill of lading
> **4.** Insurance documents, paid for by buyer
>
> At maturity Bank of the East, Ltd. will pay the face amount of the draft to the bearer of that draft.
>
> *Authorized Signature*

commercial invoice, and any of the following: consular invoice, insurance certificate or policy, and packing list.

## ADVANTAGES AND DISADVANTAGES OF LETTERS OF CREDIT

The primary advantage of an L/C is that it reduces risk — the exporter can sell against a bank's promise to pay rather than against the promise of a commercial firm. The exporter is also in a more secure position as to the availability of foreign exchange to pay for the sale, since banks are more likely to be aware of foreign exchange conditions and rules than is the importing firm itself. If the importing country should change its foreign exchange rules during the course of a transaction, the government is likely to allow already outstanding bank letters of credit to be honored for fear of throwing its own domestic banks into international disrepute. Of course, if the L/C is confirmed by a bank in the exporter's country, the exporter avoids any problem of blocked foreign exchange.

An exporter may find that an order backed by an irrevocable L/C will facilitate obtaining pre-export financing in the home country. If the exporter's reputation for delivery is good, a local bank may lend funds to process and prepare the merchandise for shipment. Once the merchandise is shipped in compliance with the terms and conditions of the credit, payment for the business transaction is made and funds will be generated to repay the pre-export loan.

The major advantage of an L/C to the importer is that the importer need not pay out funds until the documents have arrived at a local port or airfield and unless all conditions stated in the credit have been fulfilled. The main disadvantages are the fee charged by the importer's bank for issuing its L/C and the possibility that the L/C reduces the importer's borrowing line of credit with its bank. It may, in fact, be a competitive disadvantage for the exporter to demand automatically an L/C from an importer, especially if the importer has a good credit record and there is no concern regarding the economic or political conditions of the importer's country.

## Draft

A *draft*, sometimes called a *bill of exchange* (B/E), is the instrument normally used in international commerce to effect payment. A draft is simply an order written by an exporter (seller) instructing an importer (buyer) or its agent to pay a specified amount of money at a specified time. Thus it is the exporter's formal demand for payment from the importer.

The person or business initiating the draft is known as the *maker, drawer,* or *originator*. Normally this is the exporter who sells and ships the merchandise. The party to whom the draft is addressed is the *drawee*. The drawee is asked to *honor* the draft, that is, to pay the amount requested according to the stated terms. In commercial transactions the drawee is either the buyer, in which case the draft is called a *trade draft*, or the buyer's bank, in which case the draft is called a *bank draft*. Bank drafts are usually drawn according to the terms of an L/C. A draft may be drawn as a bearer instrument, or it may designate a person to whom payment is to be made. This person, known as the *payee*, may be the drawer itself or it may be some other party such as the drawer's bank.

### NEGOTIABLE INSTRUMENTS

If properly drawn, drafts can become *negotiable instruments*. As such, they provide a convenient instrument for financing the international movement of the merchandise. To become a negotiable instrument, a draft must conform to the following four requirements (Uniform Commercial Code, Section 3104(1)):

1. It must be in writing and signed by the maker or drawer.
2. It must contain an unconditional promise or order to pay a definite sum of money.
3. It must be payable on demand or at a fixed or determinable future date.
4. It must be payable to order or to bearer.

If a draft is drawn in conformity with the above requirements, a person receiving it with proper endorsements becomes a "holder in due course." This is a privileged legal status that enables the holder to receive payment despite any personal disagreements between drawee and maker because of controversy over the underlying transaction. If the drawee dishonors the draft, payment must be made to any holder in due course by any prior endorser or by the maker. This clear definition of the rights of parties who hold a negotiable instrument as a holder in due course has contributed significantly to the widespread acceptance of various forms of drafts, including personal checks.

### TYPES OF DRAFTS

Drafts are of two types: *sight drafts* and *time drafts*. A sight draft is payable on presentation to the drawee; the drawee must pay at once or dishonor the draft. A time draft, also called a *usance draft*, allows a delay in payment. It is presented to the drawee, who accepts it by writing or stamping a notice of acceptance on its face. Once accepted, the time draft becomes a promise to pay by the accepting party (the buyer). When a time draft is drawn on and accepted by a bank, it becomes a *banker's acceptance*; when drawn on and accepted by a business firm, it becomes a *trade acceptance*.

The time period of a draft is referred to as its *tenor*. To qualify as a negotiable instrument, and so be attractive to a holder in due course, a draft must be payable on a fixed or determinable future date. For example, "60 days after sight" is a fixed date, which is established precisely at the time the draft is accepted. However, payment "on arrival of goods" is not determinable since the date of arrival cannot be known in advance. Indeed, there is no assurance that the goods will arrive at all.

## BANKERS' ACCEPTANCES

When a draft is accepted by a bank, it becomes a bankers' acceptance. As such it is the unconditional promise of that bank to make payment on the draft when it matures. In quality the bankers' acceptance is practically identical to a marketable bank certificate of deposit (CD). The holder of a bankers' acceptance need not wait until maturity to liquidate the investment, but may sell the acceptance in the money market, where constant trading in such instruments occurs. The amount of the discount depends entirely on the credit rating of the bank that signs the acceptance, or another bank that reconfirmed the bankers' acceptance, for a fee. The all-in-cost of using a bankers' acceptance compared to other short-term financing instruments is analyzed later in this chapter.

## Bill of Lading (B/L)

The third key document for financing international trade is the *bill of lading* (B/L). The bill of lading is issued to the exporter by a common carrier transporting the merchandise. It serves three purposes: as a receipt, as a contract, and as a document of title.

As a receipt, the bill of lading indicates that the carrier has received the merchandise described on the face of the document. The carrier is not responsible for ascertaining that the containers hold what is alleged to be their contents, so descriptions of merchandise on bills of lading are usually short and simple. If shipping charges are paid in advance, the bill of lading will usually be stamped "freight paid" or "freight prepaid." If merchandise is shipped collect — a less common procedure internationally than domestically — the carrier maintains a lien on the goods until freight is paid.

As a contract, the bill of lading indicates the obligation of the carrier to provide certain transportation in return for certain charges. Common carriers cannot disclaim responsibility for their negligence through inserting special clauses in a bill of lading. The bill of lading may specify alternative ports in the event that delivery cannot be made to the designated port, or it may specify that the goods will be returned to the exporter at the exporter's expense.

As a document of title, the bill of lading is used to obtain payment or a written promise of payment before the merchandise is released to the importer. The bill of lading can also function as collateral against which funds may be advanced to the exporter by its local bank prior to or during shipment and before final payment by the importer.

### CHARACTERISTICS OF THE BILL OF LADING

The bill of lading is typically made payable to the order of the exporter, who thus retains title to the goods after they have been handed to the carrier. Title to the merchandise remains with the exporter until payment is received, at which time the exporter endorses the order bill of lading (which is negotiable) in blank or to the party making the payment, usually a bank. The most common procedure would be for payment to be advanced against a documentary draft accompanied by the endorsed order bill of lading. After paying the draft, the exporter's bank forwards the documents through bank clearing channels to the bank of the importer. The importer's bank, in turn, releases the documents to the importer after payment (sight drafts); after acceptance (time drafts addressed to the importer and marked D/A); or after payment terms have been agreed upon (drafts drawn on the importer's bank under provisions of a L/C).

## Example: Documentation in a Typical Trade Transaction

Although a trade transaction could conceivably be handled in many ways, we shall now turn to a hypothetical example which illustrates the interaction of the various documents. Assume that Trident USA receives an order from a Canadian buyer. For Trident, this will be an export financed under a L/C requiring a bill of lading, with the exporter collecting via a time draft accepted by the Canadian buyer's bank. Such a transaction is illustrated in Exhibit 19.8.

1. The Canadian buyer places an order with Trident, asking if Trident is willing to ship under an L/C.

2. Trident agrees to ship under an L/C and specifies relevant information such as prices and terms.

3. The Canadian buyer applies to its bank, Northland Bank (Bank I), for an L/C to be issued in favor of Trident for the merchandise it wishes to buy.

**EXHIBIT 19.8**

Steps in a Typical
Trade Transaction

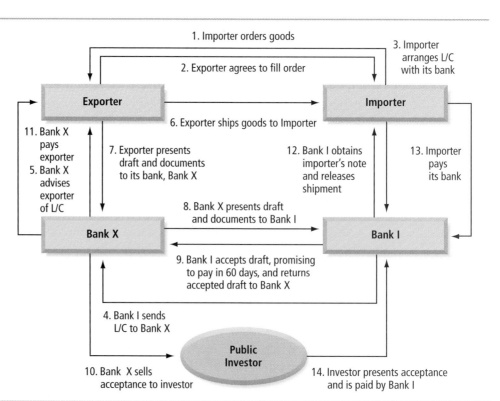

4. Northland Bank issues the L/C in favor of Trident and sends it to the Southland Bank (Bank X–Trident's bank).

5. Southland Bank advises Trident of the opening of an L/C in Trident's favor. Southland Bank may or may not confirm the L/C to add its own guarantee to the document.

6. Trident ships the goods to the Canadian buyer.

7. Trident prepares a time draft and presents it to Southland Bank. The draft is drawn (i.e., addressed to) Northland Bank in accordance with Northland Bank's L/C and accompanied by other documents as required, including the bill of lading. Trident endorses the bill of lading in blank (making it a bearer instrument) so that title to the goods goes with the holder of the documents —Southland Bank at this point in the transaction.

8. Southland Bank presents the draft and documents to Northland Bank for acceptance. Northland Bank accepts the draft by stamping and signing it making it a bankers' acceptance, takes possession of the documents, and promises to pay the now-accepted draft at maturity — say, 60 days.

9. Northland Bank returns the accepted draft to Southland Bank. Alternatively, Southland Bank might ask Northland Bank to accept and discount the draft. Should this occur, Northland Bank would remit the cash less a discount fee rather than return the accepted draft to Southland Bank.

10. Southland Bank, having received back the accepted draft, now a *bankers' acceptance*, may choose between several alternatives. Southland Bank may sell the acceptance in the open market at a discount to a portfolio investor. The investor will typically be a corporation or financial institution with excess cash it wants to invest for a short period of time. Southland Bank may also hold the acceptance in its own portfolio.

11. If Southland Bank discounted the acceptance with Northland Bank (mentioned in step 9 above) or discounted it in the local money market, Southland Bank will transfer the proceeds less any fees and discount to Trident. Another possibility would be for Trident itself to take possession of the acceptance, hold it for 60 days, and present it for collection. Normally, however, exporters prefer to receive the discounted cash value of the acceptance at once rather than wait for the acceptance to mature and receive a slightly greater amount of cash at a later date.

12. Northland Bank notifies the Canadian buyer of the arrival of the documents. The Canadian buyer signs a note or makes some other agreed-upon plan to pay Northland Bank for the merchandise in 60 days, Northland Bank releases the underlying documents so that the Canadian buyer can obtain physical possession of the shipment at once.

13. After 60 days, Northland Bank receives from the Canadian buyer funds to pay the maturing acceptance.

14. On the same day, the sixtieth day after acceptance, the holder of the matured acceptance presents it for payment and receives its face value. The holder may present it directly to Northland Bank, as in the diagram, or return it to Southland Bank and have Southland Bank collect it through normal banking channels.

Although this is a typical transaction involving an L/C, few international trade transactions are ever truly typical. Business, and more specifically international business, requires flexibility and creativity by management at all times as illustrated by

## Real World Example 19.1
### THE LETTER OF CREDIT GOES ONLINE

The landscape of trade finance in Asia is changing, and fast. Given the proliferation of electronic and online facilities, traditional trade finance resources such as the letter of credit (L/C) stand to be replaced, perhaps totally, in a very short time. More importantly, banks and companies need to change their business mindset in order to accommodate the different type of financing arrangements required by the e-commerce business model. Tai Kah Chye, vice president and Asia Head, e-commerce trade and supply chain at JP Morgan, sums up the shift of balance: "The emergence of e-commerce technologies continues to capture the headlines in trade financing. Whilst it is true that e-commerce is not a substitute for financing, it is nonetheless fundamentally changing the way that trade financing has been conducted in the past."

Although the L/C is the most conventional trade finance tool, and one that still has a function in the region, its level of usage has declined in some Asian countries. Notes Wenyir Lu, senior vice president and general manager at Bank SinoPac in Taiwan: "In Taiwan, the use of the L/C has declined from 50% to 60% of total trade transactions three years ago to below 30% today." The main reason for the drop in L/C usage in countries like Taiwan, Hong Kong, and Singapore is the long processing time: negotiating an L/C (from the time of shipment to the time of presentation by the issuing bank) can take over 20 days.

It's easy to pick electronic and online application service providers in the market. One is Bolero, a service launched in late 1999 and jointly owned by SWIFT and the Through Transport Club. By standardizing the architecture through which electronic documents are exchanged, Bolero acts as a third-party authenticator of messages, allowing trading parties and banks to exchange documents with confidence. This means the entire L/C cycle can be processed electronically, with greater speed and with less fraud.

Source: Adapted from "The LC Goes On-Line," *Asiamoney*, February 2001, pp. 72–76.

*Real World Example 19.1.* The mini-case at the end of this chapter presents an application of the mechanics of a real business situation. The result is a classic challenge to management: when and on what basis do you compromise typical procedure in order to accomplish strategic goals?

## Government Programs to Help Finance Exports

Governments of most export-oriented industrialized countries have special financial institutions that provide some form of subsidized credit to their own national exporters. These export finance institutions offer terms that are better than those generally available from the competitive private sector. Thus domestic taxpayers are subsidizing lower financial costs for foreign buyers in order to create employment and maintain a technological edge. The most important institutions usually offer export credit insurance and a government supported bank for export financing.

### EXPORT CREDIT INSURANCE

The exporter who insists on cash or an L/C payment for foreign shipments is likely to lose orders to competitors from other countries that provide more favorable credit terms. Better credit terms are often made possible by means of export credit insurance, which provides assurance to the exporter or the exporter's bank that, should the foreign customer default on payment, the insurance company will pay for a major portion of the loss. Because of the availability of export credit insurance, commercial banks are willing to provide medium- to long-term financing (five to seven years) for exports. Importers prefer that the exporter purchase export credit insurance to pay for non-performance risk by the importer. In this way the importer does not need to pay to have an L/C issued and does not reduce its credit line.

Competition between nations to increase exports by lengthening the period for which credit transactions can be insured may lead to a credit war and to unsound credit decisions. To prevent such an unhealthy development, a number of leading trading nations joined together in 1934 to create the Berne Union (officially, the Union d'Assureurs des Credits Internationaux) for the purpose of establishing a voluntary international understanding on export credit terms. The Berne Union recommends maximum credit terms for many items, including heavy capital goods (five years), light capital goods (three years), and consumer durable goods (one year).

## EXPORT CREDIT INSURANCE IN THE UNITED STATES

In the United States, export credit insurance is provided by the Foreign Credit Insurance Association (FCIA). This is an unincorporated association of private commercial insurance companies operating in cooperation with the Export-Import Bank (see below).

The FCIA provides policies protecting U.S. exporters against the risk of nonpayment by foreign debtors as a result of commercial and political risks. Losses due to commercial risk are those that result from the insolvency or protracted payment default of the buyer. Political losses arise from actions of governments beyond the control of buyer or seller.

## EXPORT-IMPORT BANK AND EXPORT FINANCING

The Export-Import Bank of the United States (Ex-Im Bank) is another independent agency of the U.S. government, established in 1934 to stimulate and facilitate the foreign trade of the United States. Interestingly, the Ex-Im Bank was originally created primarily to facilitate exports to the Soviet Union. In 1945 the Ex-Im Bank was rechartered "to aid in financing and to facilitate exports and imports and the exchange of commodities between the United States and any foreign country or the agencies or nationals thereof."

The Ex-Im Bank facilitates the financing of U.S. exports through various loan guarantee and insurance programs. The Ex-Im Bank guarantees repayment of medium-term (181 days to five years) and long-term (five years to ten years) export loans extended by U.S. banks to foreign borrowers. The Ex-Im Bank's medium- and long-term, direct-lending operation is based on participation with private sources of funds. Essentially, the Ex-Im Bank lends dollars to borrowers outside the United States for the purchase of U.S. goods and services. Proceeds of such loans are paid to U.S. suppliers. The loans themselves are repaid with interest in dollars to the Ex-Im Bank. The Ex-Im Bank requires private participation in these direct loans in order to (1) ensure that it complements rather than competes with private sources of export financing; (2) spread its resources more broadly; and (3) ensure that private financial institutions will continue to provide export credit.

The Ex-Im Bank also guarantees lease transactions; finances the costs involved in the preparation by U.S. firms of engineering, planning, and feasibility studies for non-U.S. clients on large capital projects; and supplies counseling for exporters, banks, or others needing help in finding financing for U.S. goods.

# Trade Financing Alternatives

In order to finance international trade receivables, firms use the same financing instruments as they use for domestic trade receivables, plus a few specialized instruments that are only available for financing international trade. Exhibit 19.9 identifies the main short-term financing instruments and their approximate costs as of March 11, 2003. The last section describes a longer term instrument called *forfaiting*.

## BANKERS' ACCEPTANCES

Bankers' acceptances, described earlier in this chapter, can be used to finance both domestic and international trade receivables. Exhibit 19.9 shows that bankers' acceptances earn a yield comparable to other money market instruments, especially marketable bank certificates of deposit. However, the all-in-cost to a firm of creating and discounting a bankers' acceptance also depends upon the commission charged by the bank that accepts the firm's draft.

The first owner of the bankers' acceptance created from an international trade transaction will be the exporter, who receives the accepted draft back after the bank has stamped it "accepted." The exporter may hold the acceptance until maturity and then collect. On an acceptance of, say, $100,000 for three months, the exporter would receive the face amount less the bank's acceptance commission of 1.5% per annum:

| | | |
|---|---|---|
| Face amount of the acceptance | $100,000 | |
| Less 1.5% per annum commission for three months | −375 | (.015 × 3/12 × $100,000) |
| Amount received by exporter in three months | $99,625 | |

Alternatively, the exporter may "discount" — that is, sell at a reduced price — the acceptance to its bank in order to receive funds at once. The exporter will then receive the face amount of the acceptance less both the acceptance fee and the going market rate of discount for bankers' acceptances. If the discount rate were 1.14% per annum as shown in Exhibit 19.9, the exporter would receive the following:

| | | |
|---|---|---|
| Face amount of the acceptance | $100,000 | |
| Less 1.5% per annum commission for three months | −375 | (.015 × 3/12 × $100,000) |
| Less 1.14% per annum discount rate for three months | −285 | (.0114 × 3/12 × $100,000) |
| Amount received by exporter at once | $99,340 | |

**EXHIBIT 19.9**

Instruments for Financing Short-Term Domestic and International Trade Receivables

| Instrument | Cost or Yield on March 11, 2003 for three-month maturity |
|---|---|
| Bankers' acceptances* | 1.14% yield annualized |
| Trade acceptances* | 1.17% yield annualized |
| Factoring | Variable rate but much higher cost than bank credit lines |
| Securitization | Variable rate but competitive with bank credit lines |
| Bank credit lines (covered by export credit insurance) | 4.25% plus points (fewer points if covered by export credit insurance) |
| Commercial paper* | 1.15% yield annualized |

* These instruments compete with three-month marketable bank time certificates of deposit that yielded 1.17% on March 11, 2003.

Therefore, the annualized all-in-cost of financing this bankers' acceptance is

$$\frac{\text{Commission} + \text{discount}}{\text{Proceeds}} \times \frac{360}{90} = \frac{\$375 + \$285}{\$99,340} \times \frac{360}{90} = .0266 \text{ or } 2.66\%$$

The discounting bank may hold the acceptance in its own portfolio, earning for itself the 1.14% per annum discount rate, or the acceptance may be resold in the acceptance market to portfolio investors. Investors buying bankers' acceptances provide the funds that finance the transaction.

## TRADE ACCEPTANCES

*Trade acceptances* are similar to bankers' acceptances except that the accepting entity is a commercial firm, like General Motors Acceptance Corporation (GMAC), rather than a bank. The cost of a trade acceptance depends on the credit rating of the accepting firm plus the commission it charges. Like bankers' acceptances, trade acceptances are sold at a discount to banks and other investors at a rate that is competitive with other money market instruments (see Exhibit 19.9).

## FACTORING

Specialized firms, known as *factors*, purchase receivables at a discount on either a *nonrecourse* or *recourse* basis. Nonrecourse means that the factor assumes the credit, political, and foreign exchange risk of the receivables it purchases. Recourse means that the factor can give back receivables that are not collectable. Since the factor must bear the cost and risk of assessing the credit worth of each receivable, the cost of factoring is usually quite high. It is more than borrowing at the prime rate plus points.

The all-in-cost of factoring nonrecourse receivables is similar in structure to acceptances. The factor charges a commission to cover the nonrecourse risk, typically 1.5% to 2.5%, plus interest deducted as a discount from the initial proceeds. On the other hand, the firm selling the nonrecourse receivables avoids the cost of determining credit worth of its customers. It also does not have to show debt borrowed to finance these receivables on its balance sheet. Furthermore, the firm avoids both foreign exchange and political risk on these nonrecourse receivables.

## SECURITIZATION

The *securitization* of export receivables for financing trade is an attractive supplement to bankers' acceptance financing and factoring. A firm can *securitize* its export receivables by selling them to a legal entity established to create marketable securities based on a package of individual export receivables. An advantage of this technique is to remove the export receivables from the exporter's balance sheet because they have been sold without recourse.

The receivables are normally sold at a discount. The size of the discount depends on four factors:

1. The historic collection risk of the exporter
2. The cost of credit insurance
3. The cost of securing the desirable cash flow stream to the investors
4. The size of the financing and services fees

Securitization is more cost effective if there is a large volume of transactions with a known credit history and default probability. A large exporter could establish its own securitization entity. While the initial setup cost is high, the entity can be used on an ongoing basis. As an alternative, smaller exporters could use a common securitization entity provided by a financial institution, thereby saving the expensive setup costs.

### BANK CREDIT LINE COVERED BY EXPORT CREDIT INSURANCE

A firm's bank credit line can typically be used to finance up to a fixed upper limit, say 80%, of accounts receivable. Export receivables can be eligible for inclusion in bank credit line financing. However, credit information on foreign customers may be more difficult to collect and assess. If a firm covers its export receivables with export credit insurance, it can greatly reduce the credit risk of those receivables. This insurance enables the bank credit line to cover more export receivables and lower the interest rate for that coverage. Of course, any foreign exchange risk must be handled by the transaction exposure techniques described in Chapter 8.

The cost of using a bank credit line is usually the prime rate of interest plus *points* to reflect a particular firm's credit risk. As usual, 100 points is equal to one percent. In the United States, borrowers are also expected to maintain a compensating deposit balance at the lending institution. In Europe and many other places lending is done on an *overdraft* basis. An overdraft agreement allows a firm to overdraw its bank account up to the limit of its credit line. Interest at prime plus points is based only on the amount of overdraft borrowed. In either case, the all-in-cost of bank borrowing using a credit line is higher than acceptance financing as shown in Exhibit 19.9.

### COMMERCIAL PAPER

A firm can issue *commercial paper* — unsecured promissory notes — to fund its short-term financing needs, including both domestic and export receivables. However, only the large, well-known firms with favorable credit ratings have access to the domestic or euro commercial paper market. As shown in Exhibit 19.9, commercial paper interest rates lie at the low end of the yield curve and compete directly with marketable bank time certificates of deposit.

## Forfaiting: Medium and Long-Term Financing

*Forfaiting* is a specialized technique to eliminate the risk of nonpayment by importers in instances where the importing firm and/or its government is perceived by the exporter to be too risky for open account credit. The name of the technique comes from the French *à forfait*, a term that implies "to forfeit or surrender a right."

### ROLE OF THE FORFAITER

The essence of forfaiting is the nonrecourse sale by an exporter of bank-guaranteed promissory notes, bills of exchange, or similar documents received from an importer in another country. The exporter receives cash at the time of the transaction by selling the notes or bills at a discount from their face value to a specialized finance firm called a *forfaiter*. The forfaiter arranges the entire operation prior to the actual transaction taking place. Although the exporting firm is responsible for the quality of delivered goods, it receives a clear and unconditional cash payment at the time of the transaction. All political and commercial risk of nonpayment by the importer is carried by the guaranteeing bank. Small exporters who trust their clients to pay find the forfaiting technique invaluable because it eases cash flow problems.

During the Soviet era expertise in the technique was centered in German and Austrian banks, which used forfaiting to finance sales of capital equipment to eastern Europe, the Soviet bloc countries. British, Scandinavian, Italian, Spanish, and French exporters have now adopted the technique, but U.S. and Canadian exporters are reported to be slow to use forfaiting, possibly because they are suspicious of its simplicity and lack of complex documentation.[1] Nevertheless, some American firms now specialize in the technique, and the Association of Forfaiters in the Americas (AFIA) has over twenty members. Major export destinations financed via the forfaiting technique are Asia, Eastern Europe, the Middle East, and Latin America.[2]

## A TYPICAL FORFAITING TRANSACTION

A typical forfaiting transaction involves five parties, as shown in Exhibit 19.10. The steps in the process are as follows.

**STEP 1: AGREEMENT.**    Importer and exporter agree between themselves on a series of imports to be paid for over a period of time, typically three to five years. However, periods up to ten years or as short as 180 days have been financed by the technique. The normal minimum size for a transaction is $100,000. The importer agrees to make periodic payments, often against progress on delivery or completion of a project.

**STEP 2: COMMITMENT.**   The forfaiter promises to finance the transaction at a fixed discount rate, with payment to be made when the exporter delivers to the forfaiter the appropriate promissory notes or other specified paper. The agreed-upon discount rate is based on the cost of funds in the Euromarket, usually on LIBOR for the average life of the transaction, plus a margin over LIBOR to reflect the perceived risk in the deal. This risk premium is influenced by the size and tenor of the deal, country risk, and the

**EXHIBIT 19.10**

Typical Forfaiting
Transaction

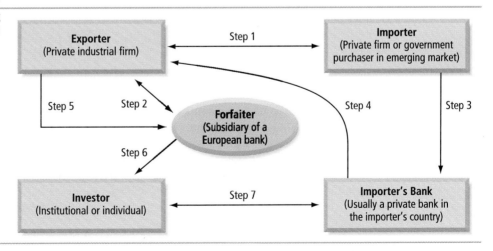

[1]*User's Guide — Forfaiting: What Is It, Who Uses It and Why?* British-American Forfaiting Company, P.O. Box 16872, St. Louis, Missouri 63105. www.tradecompass.com.

[2]Association of Forfaiters in the Americas (AFIA). 2 Park Avenue, Suite 1522. New York, NY, 10016.

quality of the guarantor institution. On a five-year deal, for example, with ten semi-annual payments, the rate used would be based on the $2^{1}/_{4}$-year LIBOR rate. This discount rate is normally added to the invoice value of the transaction so that the cost of financing is ultimately borne by the importer. The forfaiter charges an additional commitment fee of from 0.5% per annum to as high as 6.0% per annum from the date of its commitment to finance until receipt of the actual discount paper issued in accordance with the finance contract. This fee is also normally added to the invoice cost and passed on to the importer.

**STEP 3: *AVAL* OR GUARANTEE.**   The importer obligates itself to pay for its purchases by issuing a series of promissory notes, usually maturing every six or twelve months, against progress on delivery or completion of the project. These promissory notes are first delivered to the importer's bank where they are endorsed (that is, guaranteed) by that bank. In Europe this unconditional guarantee is referred to as an *aval*, which translates into English as "backing." At this point the importer's bank becomes the primary obligor in the eyes of all subsequent holders of the notes. The bank's aval or guarantee must be irrevocable, unconditional, divisible, and assignable. Because U.S. banks do not issue avals, U.S. transactions are guaranteed by a standby letter of credit (L/C), which is functionally similar to an aval but more cumbersome. For example, L/Cs can normally be transferred only once.

**STEP 4: DELIVERY OF NOTES.**   The now-endorsed promissory notes are delivered to the exporter.

**STEP 5: DISCOUNTING.**   The exporter endorses the notes "without recourse" and discounts them with the forfaiter, receiving the agreed-upon proceeds. Proceeds are usually received two days after the documents are presented. By endorsing the notes "without recourse," the exporter frees itself from any liability for future payment on the notes and thus receives the discounted proceeds without having to worry about any further payment difficulties.

**STEP 6: INVESTMENT.**   The forfaiting bank either holds the notes until full maturity as an investment or endorses and rediscounts them in the international money market. Such subsequent sale by the forfaiter is usually without recourse. The major rediscount markets are in London and Switzerland, plus New York for notes issued in conjunction with Latin American business.

**STEP 7: MATURITY.**   At maturity the investor holding the notes presents them for collection to the importer or to the importer's bank. The promise of the importer's bank is what gives the documents their value.

In effect, the forfaiter functions both as a money market firm and a specialist in packaging financial deals involving country risk. As a money market firm, the forfaiter divides the discounted notes into appropriately sized packages and resells them to various investors having different maturity preferences. As a country risk specialist, the forfaiter assesses the risk that the notes will eventually be paid by the importer or the importer's bank and puts together a deal that satisfies the needs of both exporter and importer.

Success of the forfaiting technique springs from the belief that the aval or guarantee of a commercial bank can be depended on. Although commercial banks are the normal and preferred guarantors, guarantees by government banks or government ministries of finance are accepted in some cases. On occasion large commercial enterprises have been accepted as debtors without a bank guarantee. An additional aspect of the technique is that the endorsing bank's aval is perceived to be an "off balance sheet" obligation, the debt is presumably not considered by others in assessing the financial structure of the commercial banks.

# Crosswell International's Precious Ultra-Thin Diapers

Crosswell International is a U.S.–based manufacturer and distributor of health care products, including children's diapers. Crosswell has been approached by Leonardo Sousa, the president of Material Hospitalar, a distributor of health care products throughout Brazil. Sousa is interested in distributing Crosswell's major diaper product, Precious, but only if an acceptable arrangement regarding pricing and payment terms can be reached.

## Exporting to Brazil

Crosswell's manager for export operations, Geoff Mathieux, followed up the preliminary discussions by putting together an estimate of export costs and pricing for discussion purposes with Sousa. Crosswell needs to know all of the costs and pricing assumptions for the entire supply and value chain as it reaches the consumer. Mathieux believes it critical that any arrangement that Crosswell enters into results in a price to consumers in the Brazilian marketplace that is both fair to all parties involved and competitive, given the market niche Crosswell hopes to penetrate. This first cut on pricing Precious diapers into Brazil is presented in Exhibit 1.

Crosswell proposes to sell the basic diaper line to the Brazilian distributor for $34.00 per case, FAS (free alongside ship) Miami docks. This means that the seller, Crosswell, agrees to cover all costs associated with getting the diapers to the Miami docks. The cost of loading the diapers aboard ship, the actual cost of shipping (freight), and associated documents is $4.32 per case. The running subtotal, $38.32 per case, is termed CFR (cost and freight). Finally, the insurance expenses related to the potential loss of the goods while in transit to final port of destination, export insurance, are $0.86 per case. The total CIF (cost, insurance, and freight) is $39.18 per case, or 97.95 Brazilian real per case, assuming an exchange rate of 2.50 Brazilian real (R$) per U.S. dollar ($). In summary, the CIF cost of R$97.95 is the price charged by the exporter to the importer on arrival in Brazil, and is calculated as follows:

$$CIF = FAS + freight + export\ insurance =$$
$$(\$34.00 + \$4.32 + \$0.86) \times R\$2.50/\$ = R\$97.95.$$

The actual cost to the distributor of getting the diapers through the port and customs warehouses must also be calculated in terms of what Leonardo Sousa's costs are in reality. The various fees and taxes detailed in Exhibit 1 raise the fully landed cost of the Precious diapers to R$107.63 per case. The distributor would now bear storage and inventory costs totaling R$8.33 per case, which would bring the costs to R$115.96. The distributor then adds a margin for distribution services of 20% (R$23.19), raising the price as sold to the final retailer to R$139.15 per case.

Finally, the retailer (a supermarket or other retailer of consumer health care products) would include its expenses, taxes, and markup to reach the final shelf price of R$245.48 per case. This final retail price estimate now allows both Crosswell and Material Hospitalar to evaluate the price competitiveness of the Precious Ultra-Thin Diaper in the Brazilian marketplace, and provides a basis for further negotiations between the two parties.

Mathieux provides the above export price quotation, an outline of a potential representation agreement (for Sousa to represent Crosswell's product lines in the Brazilian marketplace), and payment and credit terms to Leonardo Sousa. Crosswell's payment and credit terms are that Sousa either pay in full in cash in advance, or with a confirmed irrevocable documentary L/C with a time draft specifying a tenor of 60 days.

Crosswell also requests from Sousa financial statements, banking references, foreign commercial references, descriptions of regional sales forces, and sales forecasts for the Precious diaper line. These last requests by Crosswell are very important for Crosswell to be able to assess Material Hospitalar's ability to be a dependable, creditworthy, and capable long-term partner and representative of the firm in the Brazilian marketplace. The discussions that follow focus on finding acceptable common ground between the two parties and working to increase the competitiveness of the Precious diaper in the Brazilian marketplace.

## Crosswell's Proposal

The proposed sale by Crosswell to Material Hospitalar, at least in the initial shipment, is for 10 containers of 968 cases of diapers at $39.18 per case, CIF Brazil, payable in U.S. dollars. This is a total invoice amount of $379,262.40. Payment terms are that a confirmed L/C will be required of Material Hospitalar on a U.S. bank. The payment will be based on a time draft of 60 days, presentation to the bank for acceptance with other documents on the date of shipment. Both the exporter and the exporter's bank will expect payment from the importer or importer's bank 60 days from this date of shipment.

## EXHIBIT 1

Export Pricing for the Precious Diaper Line to Brazil

The Precious Ultra-Thin Diaper will be shipped via container. Each container will hold 968 cases of diapers. The costs and prices below are calculated on a per-case basis, although some costs and fees are assessed by container.

| Exports Costs and Pricing to Brazil | Per Case | Rates and Calculation |
|---|---|---|
| FAS price per case, Miami | $34.00 | |
| Freight, loading, and documentation | 4.32 | $4,180 per container/968 = $4.32 |
| CFR price per case, Brazilian port (Santos) | $38.32 | |
| Export insurance | 0.86 | 2.25% of CIF |
|    CIF to Brazilian port | $39.18 | |
|    CIF to Brazilian port, in Brazilian real | R$97.95 | 2.50 Real/US$ × $39.18 |
| **Brazilian Importation Costs** | | |
| Import duties | 1.96 | 2.00% of CIF |
| Merchant marine renovation fee | 2.70 | 25.00% of freight |
| Port storage fees | 1.27 | 1.30% of CIF |
| Port handling fees | 0.01 | R$12 per container |
| Additional handling fees | 0.26 | 20.00% of storage and handling |
| Customs brokerage fees | 1.96 | 2.00% of CIF |
| Import license fee | 0.05 | R$50 per container |
| Local transportation charges | 1.47 | 1.50% of CIF |
|    Total cost to distributor in real | R$107.63 | |
| **Distributor's Costs and Pricing** | | |
| Storage cost | 1.47 | 1.50% of CIF × months |
| Cost of financing diaper inventory | 6.86 | 7.00% of CIF × months |
| Distributor's margin | 23.19 | 20.00% of price + storage + financing |
|    Price to retailer in real | R$139.15 | |
| **Brazilian Retailer Costs and Pricing** | | |
| Industrial product tax (IPT) | 20.87 | 15.00% of price to retailer |
| Mercantile circulation services tax (MCS) | 28.80 | 18.00% of price + IPT |
| Retailer costs and markup | 56.65 | 30.00% of price + IPT + MCS |
|    Price to consumer in real | R$245.48 | |

| Diaper Prices to Consumers | Diapers per Case | Price per Diaper |
|---|---|---|
| Small size | 352 | R$0.70 |
| Medium size | 256 | R$0.96 |
| Large size | 192 | R$1.28 |

**What should Crosswell expect?** Assuming Material Hospitalar acquires the L/C and it is confirmed by Crosswell's bank in the United States, Crosswell will ship the goods after the initial agreement, say 15 days, as illustrated in Exhibit 2.

Simultaneous with the shipment, in which Crosswell has lost physical control over the goods, Crosswell will present the bill of lading acquired at the time of shipment with the other needed documents to its bank requesting payment. Because the export is under a confirmed L/C,

assuming all documents are in order, Crosswell's bank will give Crosswell two choices:

1. Wait the full period of the time draft (60 days) and receive the entire payment in full ($379,262.40)

2. Receive the discounted value of this amount today. The discounted amount, assuming U.S. dollar interest rate of 6.00% per annum (1.00% per 60 days), is

$$\frac{\$379,262.40}{(1+0.01)} = \frac{\$379,262.40}{1.01} = \$375,507.33$$

**EXHIBIT 2**

Export Payment
Terms on
Crosswell's
Export to Brazil

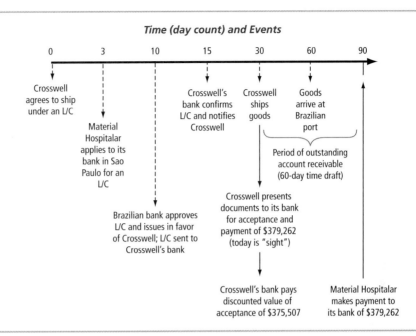

Because the invoice is denominated in U.S. dollars, Crosswell need not worry about currency value changes (currency risk). And, because its bank has confirmed the L/C, it is protected against changes or deteriorations in Material Hospitalar's ability to pay on the future date.

**What should Material Hospitalar expect?** Material Hospitalar will receive the goods on or before day 60. It will then move the goods through its distribution system to retailers. Depending on the payment terms between Material Hospitalar and its buyers (retailers), it could receive either cash or terms for payment for the goods. Because Material Hospitalar purchased the goods via the 60-day time draft and an L/C from its Brazilian bank, total payment of $379,262.40 is due on day 90 (shipment and presentation of documents was on day 30 + 60 day time draft) to the Brazilian bank. Material Hospitalar, because it is a Brazilian-based company and has agreed to make payment in U.S. dollars (foreign currency), carries the currency risk of the transaction.

## Crosswell/Material Hospitalar's Concern

The concern the two companies have, however, is that the total price to the consumer in Brazil, R$245.48 per case, or R$0.70/diaper (small size), is too high. The major competitors in the Brazilian market for premium quality diapers, Kenko do Brasil (Japan), Johnson & Johnson (USA), and Procter & Gamble (USA), are cheaper (see Exhibit 3).

The competitors all manufacture in-country, thus avoiding the series of import duties and tariffs, which have added significantly to Crosswell's landed prices in the Brazilian marketplace.

**EXHIBIT 3**

Competitive Diaper Prices in the Brazilian Market (in Brazilian real)

| Company (Country) | Brand | Price per Diaper by Size | | |
| | | Small | Medium | Large |
|---|---|---|---|---|
| Kenko (Japan) | Monica Plus | 0.68 | 0.85 | 1.18 |
| Procter & Gamble (USA) | Pampers Uni | 0.65 | 0.80 | 1.08 |
| Johnson & Johnson (USA) | Sempre Seca Plus | 0.65 | 0.80 | 1.08 |
| Crosswell (USA) | Precious | 0.70 | 0.96 | 1.40 |

## Case Questions

1. How are pricing, currency of denomination, and financing interrelated in the value chain for Crosswell's penetration of the Brazilian market? Can you summarize them using Exhibit 2?
2. How important is Sousa to the value chain of Crosswell? What worries might Crosswell have regarding Sosa's ability to fulfill his obligations?
3. If Crosswell is to penetrate the market, some way of reducing its prices will be required. What do you suggest?

## Summary of Learning Objectives

*Learn how international trade alters both the supply chain and the general value chain of the domestic firm, thereby beginning the globalization process in the trade phase*

- International trade takes place between three categories of relationships: unaffiliated unknown parties, unaffiliated known parties, and affiliated parties.

- International trade transactions between affiliated parties typically do not require contractual arrangements or external financing. Trade transactions between unaffiliated parties typically require contracts and some type of external financing, such as that available through letters of credit.

*Consider what the key elements of an import or export transaction are in business*

- Over many years, established procedures have arisen to finance international trade. The basic procedure rests on the interrelationship between three key documents: the letter of credit, the draft, and the bill of lading.

- Variations in each of the three key documents — the letter of credit, the draft, and the bill of lading — provide a variety of ways to accommodate any type of transaction.

*Discover how the three key documents in import-export — the letter of credit, the draft, and the bill of lading — combine to finance the transaction and to manage its risks*

- In the simplest transaction, in which all three documents are used and in which financing is desirable, an importer applies for and receives an L/C from its bank.

- In the L/C, the bank substitutes its credit for that of the importer and promises to pay if certain documents are submitted to the bank. The exporter may now rely on the promise of the bank rather than on the promise of the importer.

*Identify what the documentation sequence is for a typical international trade transaction*

- The exporter typically ships on an order bill of lading, attaches the order bill of lading to a draft ordering payment from the importer's bank, and presents these documents, plus any of a number of additional documents, through its own bank to the importer's bank.

- If the documents are in order, the importer's bank either pays the draft (a sight draft) or accepts the draft (a time draft). In the latter case the bank promises to pay in the future. At this step the importer's bank acquires title to the merchandise through the bill of lading; it then releases the merchandise to the importer against payment or promise of future payment.

- If a sight draft is used, the exporter is paid at once. If a time draft is used, the exporter receives the accepted draft, now a bankers' acceptance, back from the bank. The exporter may hold the bankers' acceptance until maturity or sell it at a discount in the money market.

*Learn how the various stages and their costs affect the ability of an exporter to enter a foreign market and potentially compete in both credit terms and pricing*

- The total costs of an exporter entering a foreign market include the transaction costs of the trade financing, the import and export duties and tariffs applied by exporting and importing nations, and the costs of foreign market penetration, which include distribution expenses, inventory costs, and transportation expenses.

*See what organizations and resources are available for exporters to aid in managing trade risk and financing*

- Export credit insurance provides assurance to exporters (or exporters' banks) that should the foreign customer default on payment, the insurance company will pay for a major portion of the loss.

- In the United States, export credit insurance is provided by the Foreign Credit Insurance Association (FCIA), an unincorporated association of private commercial insurance companies operating in cooperation with the Export-Import Bank of the United States.

- The Export-Import Bank (Ex-Im Bank) is an independent agency established to stimulate and facilitate the foreign trade of the United States.

*Examine the various trade financing alternatives*

- Trade financing uses the same financing instruments as domestic receivables financing, plus some specialized instruments that are only available for financing international trade.

- A popular instrument for short-term financing is a bankers' acceptance. Its all-in-cost is comparable to other money market instruments, such as marketable bank certificates of deposit.

- Other short-term financing instruments with a domestic counterpart are trade acceptances, factoring, securitization, bank credit lines (usually covered by export credit insurance), and commercial paper.

- Forfaiting is an international trade technique that can provide medium and long-term financing.

## QUESTIONS

1. **Unaffiliated buyers.** Why might different documentation be used for an export to a nonaffiliated foreign buyer who is a new customer, as compared with an export to a nonaffiliated foreign buyer to whom the exporter has been selling for many years?

2. **Affiliated buyers.** For what reason might an exporter use standard international trade documentation (letter of credit, draft, order bill of lading) on an intrafirm export to its parent or sister subsidiary?

3. **Related party trade.** What reasons can you give for the observation that intrafirm trade is now greater than trade between nonaffiliated exporters and importers?

4. **Documents.** Explain the difference between a letter of credit (L/C) and a draft. How are they linked?

5. **Risks.** What is the major difference between currency risk and risk of noncompletion? How are these risks handled in a typical international trade transaction?

6. **Letter of credit.** Identify each party to a letter of credit (L/C) and indicate its responsibility.

7. **Confirming a letter of credit.** Why would an exporter insist on a confirmed letter of credit?

8. **Documenting an export of hard drives.** List the steps involved in the export of computer hard disk drives from Penang, Malaysia, to San Jose, California, using an unconfirmed letter of credit authorizing payment on sight.

9. **Documenting an export of lumber from Portland to Yokohama.** List the steps involved in the export of lumber from Portland, Oregon, to Yokohama, Japan, using a confirmed letter of credit, payment to be made in 120 days.

10. **Inca Breweries of Peru.** Inca Breweries of Lima, Peru, has received an order for 10,000 cartons of beer from Alicante Importers of Alicante, Spain. The beer will be exported to Spain under the terms of a letter of credit issued by a Madrid bank on behalf of Alicante Importers. The letter of credit specifies that the face value of the shipment, $720,000 U.S. dollars, will be paid 90 days after the Madrid bank accepts a draft drawn by Inca Breweries in accordance with the terms of the letter of credit.

    The current discount rate on three-month banker's acceptances is 8% per annum, and Inca Breweries estimates its weighted average cost of capital to be 20% per annum. The commission for selling a banker's acceptance in the discount market is 1.2% of the face amount.

    How much cash will Inca Breweries receive from the sale if it holds the acceptance until maturity? Do you recommend that Inca Breweries hold the acceptance until maturity or discount it at once in the U.S. banker's acceptance market?

11. **Swishing Shoe Company.** Swishing Shoe Company of Durham, North Carolina, has received an order for 50,000 cartons of athletic shoes from Southampton Footware, Ltd., of Great Britain, payment to be in British pounds sterling. The shoes will be shipped to Southampton Footware under the terms of a letter of credit issued by a London bank on behalf of Southampton Footware. The letter of credit specifies that the face value of the shipment, £400,000, will be paid 120 days after the London bank accepts a draft drawn by Southampton Footware in accordance with the terms of the letter of credit.

    The current discount rate in London on 120-day banker's acceptances is 12% per annum, and Southampton Footware estimates its weighted average cost of capital to be 18% per annum. The commission for selling a banker's acceptance in the discount market is 2.0% of the face amount.

a. Would Swishing Shoe Company gain by holding the acceptance to maturity, as compared to discounting the banker's acceptance at once?

b. Does Swishing Shoe Company incur any other risks in this transaction?

12. **Going abroad.** Assume that Great Britain charges a duty of 10% on shoes imported into the United Kingdom. Swishing Shoe Company, in the previous question, discovers that it can manufacture shoes in Ireland and import them into Great Britain free of any import duty.

What factors should Swishing consider in deciding to continue to export shoes from North Carolina versus manufacture them in Ireland?

13. **Governmentally supplied credit.** Various governments have established agencies to insure against nonpayment for exports and/or to provide export credit. This shifts credit risk away from private banks and to the citizen taxpayers of the country whose government created and backs the agency. Why would such an arrangement be of benefit to the citizens of that country?

## PROBLEMS

1. **Bankers' acceptance: Wisconsin Distillers (A).** Wisconsin Distillers exports beer to Australia and invoices its customers in U.S. dollars. Sydney Wholesale Imports has purchased $1,000,000 of beer from Wisconsin Distillers, with payment due in six months. The payment will be made with a bankers' acceptance issued by Charter Bank of Sydney at a fee of 1.75% per annum. Wisconsin Distillers has a weighted average cost of capital of 10%. If Wisconsin Distillers holds this acceptance to maturity, what is its annualized percentage all-in-cost?

2. **Bankers' acceptance: Wisconsin Distillers (B).** Assuming the facts in Problem 1, Bank of America is now willing to buy Wisconsin Distiller's bankers' acceptance for a discount of 6% per annum. What would be Wisconsin Distiller's annualized percentage all-in-cost of financing its $1,000,000 Australian receivable?

3. **Trade acceptance: Cutler Toyota.** Cutler Toyota buys its cars from Toyota Motors-USA, and sells them to U.S. customers. One of its customers is Green Transport, a car rental firm that buys cars from Cutler Toyota at a wholesale price. Final payment is due to Cutler Toyota in six months. Green Transport has bought $200,000 worth of cars from Cutler, with a cash down payment of $40,000 and the balance due in six months without any interest charged as a sales incentive. Cutler Toyota will have the Green Transport receivable accepted by Alliance Acceptance for a 2% fee, and then sell it at a 3% per annum discount to Wells Fargo Bank.

a. What is the annualized percentage all-in-cost to Cutler Toyota?

b. What are Cutler Transport's net cash proceeds, including the cash down payment?

4. **Trade acceptance: Sun Microsystems (A).** Assume Sun Microsystems has sold Internet servers to Telecom Italia for €700,000. Payment is due in three months and will be made with a trade acceptance from Telecom Italia Acceptance. The acceptance fee is 1.0% per annum of the face amount of the note. This acceptance will be sold at a 4% per annum discount. What is the annualized percentage all-in-cost in euros of this method of trade financing?

5. **Foreign exchange acceptance: Sun Microsystems (B).** Assume that Sun Microsystems prefers to receive U.S. dollars rather than euros for the trade transaction described in Problem 4. It is considering two alternatives: 1) It can sell the acceptance for euros at once and convert the euros immediately to U.S. dollars at the spot rate of exchange of $1.00/€; or 2) it can hold the euro acceptance until maturity but at the start sell the expected euro proceeds forward for dollars at the three-month forward rate of $1.02/€.

a. What are the U.S. dollar net proceeds received at once from the discounted trade acceptance in alternative 1?

b. What are the U.S. dollar net proceeds received in three months in alternative 2?

c. What is the breakeven investment rate that would equalize the net U.S. dollar proceeds from both alternatives?

d. Which alternative should Sun Microsystems choose?

6. **Bank credit line with export credit insurance: Hollywood Entertainment (A).** Hollywood Entertainment has sold a combination of films and DVDs to Hong Kong Media Incorporated for US$100,000, with payment due in six months. Hollywood Entertainment has the following alternatives for financing this receivable: (1) Use its bank credit line. Interest would be at the prime rate of 5% plus 150 basis points per annum. Hollywood Enterprises would need to maintain a compensating balance of 20% of the loan's face amount. No interest will be paid on the compensating balance by the bank. (2) Use its bank credit line but purchase export credit insurance for a 1% fee. Because of the reduced risk, the bank interest rate would be reduced to 5% per annum without any points.

   **a.** What are the annualized percentage all-in-costs of each alternative?

   **b.** What are the advantages and disadvantages of each alternative?

   **c.** Which alternative would you recommend?

7. **Hollywood Entertainment (B): Factoring.** Hollywood Entertainment has been approached by a factor that offers to purchase the Hong Kong Media Imports receivable in Problem 6 at a 16% per annum discount plus a 2% charge for a nonrecourse clause.

   **a.** What is the annualized percentage all-in-cost of this factoring alternative?

   **b.** What are the advantages and disadvantages of the factoring alternative compared to the alternatives in Hollywood Entertainment (A)?

8. **Forfaiting at Kaduna Oil (Nigeria).** Kaduna Oil of Nigeria has purchased $1,000,000 of oil drilling equipment from Unicorn Drilling of Houston, Texas. Kaduna Oil must pay for this purchase over the next five years at a rate of $200,000 per year due on March 1 of each year.

   Bank of Zurich, a Swiss forfaiter, has agreed to buy the five notes of $200,000 each at a discount. The discount rate would be approximately 8% per annum based on the expected three-year LIBOR rate plus 200 basis points, paid by Kaduna Oil. Bank of Zurich also would charge Kaduna

Oil an additional commitment fee of 2% per annum from the date of its commitment to finance until receipt of the actual discounted notes issued in accordance with the financing contract. The $200,000 promissory notes will come due on March 1 in successive years.

   The promissory notes issued by Kaduna Oil will be endorsed by their bank, Lagos City Bank, for a 1% fee and delivered to Unicorn Drilling. At this point Unicorn Drilling will endorse the notes *without recourse* and discount them with the forfaiter, Bank of Zurich, receiving the full $200,000 principal amount. Bank of Zurich will sell the notes by rediscounting them to investors in the international money market without recourse. At maturity the investors holding the notes will present them for collection at Lagos City Bank. If Lagos City Bank defaults on payment, the investors will collect on the notes from Bank of Zurich.

   **a.** What is the annualized percentage all-in-cost to Kaduna Oil of financing the first $200,000 note due March 1, 2004?

   **b.** What might motivate Kaduna Oil to use this relatively expensive alternative for financing?

9. **Letter of credit: Andersen Sports (A).** Andersen Sports (Andersen) is considering bidding to sell $100,000 of ski equipment to Kim Family Enterprises of Seoul, Korea. Payment would be due in six months. Since Andersen cannot find good credit information on Kim, Andersen wants to protect its credit risk. It is considering the following financing solution.

   Kim's bank issues a letter of credit on behalf of Kim and agrees to accept Andersen's draft for $100,000 due in six months. The acceptance fee would cost Kim $500, plus reduce Kim's available credit line by $100,000. The bankers' acceptance note of $100,000 would be sold at a 2% per annum discount in the money market. What is the annualized percentage all-in-cost to Andersen of this bankers' acceptance financing?

10. **Andersen Sports (B): Bank credit line with export credit insurance.** Andersen could also buy export credit insurance from FCIA for a 1.5% premium. It finances the $100,000 receivable from Kim from its credit line at 6% per annum interest. No compensating bank balance would be required.

**a.** What is Andersen's annualized percentage all-in-cost of financing?

**b.** What are Kim's costs?

**c.** What are the advantages and disadvantages of this alternative compared to the bankers' acceptance financing in Andersen (A)? Which alternative would you recommend?

## Internet Exercises

**1. Letter of credit services.** Commercial banks worldwide provide a variety of services to aid in the financing of foreign trade. Contact any of the many major multinational banks (a few are listed below) to determine what types of letter of credit services and other trade financing services they are able to provide.

Bank of America
   http://www. bankamerica.com
Citibank
   http://www.citibank.com
Barclays
   http://www.barclays.com
Deutsche Bank
   http://www.deutschebank.com
Union Bank of Switzerland
   http://www.ubs.com

**2. Export-Import Bank of the United States.** The Ex-Im Bank of the United States provides financing for U.S.–based exporters. Like most major industrial country trade-financing organizations, it is intended to aid in the export sale of products in which the buyer needs attractive financing terms. Use the Ex-Im Bank's Web site to determine the current country limits, fees, and other restrictions which currently apply. (Note: the Ex-Im Bank's Web site provides excellent links in international business and statistics.)

Export-Import Bank of the United States
   http://www.exim.gov

# *Multinational Tax Management*

## LEARNING OBJECTIVES

Identify the differences between tax systems employed by governments around the globe

Compare corporate income and withholding tax rates used across countries and the way tax treaties affect MNEs

Understand how value-added taxes are levied by some countries today

Explain the use of transfer pricing to manage corporate tax burdens

Compare tax liabilities of domestic and foreign source income for U.S.-based firms

Demonstrate how U.S.-based multinationals manage their excess foreign tax credits and deficits to minimize their global tax liabilities

Examine the use of tax-haven subsidiaries and international offshore financial centers

Tax planning for multinational operations is an extremely complex but vitally important aspect of international business. To plan effectively, MNEs must understand not only the intricacies of their own operations worldwide, but also the different structures and interpretations of tax liabilities across countries. *The primary objective of multinational tax planning is the minimization of the firm's worldwide tax burden.* This objective, however, must not be pursued without full recognition that decision-making within the firm must always be based on the economic fundamentals of the firm's line of business, and not on convoluted policies undertaken purely for the reduction of tax liability. As evident from previous chapters, taxes have a major impact on corporate net income and cash flow through their influence on foreign investment decisions, financial structure, determination of the cost of capital, foreign exchange management, working capital management, and financial control.

The purpose of this chapter is to provide an overview of the way taxes are applied to MNEs globally, how the United States taxes the global earnings of U.S.–based MNEs, and how U.S.–based multinationals manage their global tax liabilities. We do this in four parts. The first section acquaints you with the overall international tax environment. This includes a brief overview of the tax environments which an MNE is likely to encounter globally and the basics of most intercountry tax treaties. The second part examines transfer pricing. The third part of the chapter describes how the United States government taxes income generated abroad by U.S.–based multinationals, highlighting the tax management dilemma faced by Trident Corporation. Although we use U.S. taxes as illustrations, our intention is not to make this chapter or this book U.S.-centric. Most of the U.S. practices that we describe have close parallels in other countries, albeit modified to fit their specific national overall tax system. The fourth and final part of the chapter examines the use of tax-haven subsidiaries and international offshore financial centers.

## Tax Principles

The sections that follow explain the most important aspects of the international tax environments and specific features that affect MNEs. Before we explain the specifics of multinational taxation in practice, however, it is necessary to introduce two areas of fundamental importance: *tax morality* and *tax neutrality*.

### TAX MORALITY

The MNE faces not only a morass of foreign taxes but also an ethical question. In many countries taxpayers, corporate or individual, do not voluntarily comply with the tax laws. Smaller domestic firms and individuals are the chief violators. The MNE must decide whether to follow a practice of full disclosure to tax authorities or adopt the philosophy of "when in Rome, do as the Romans do." Given the local prominence of most foreign subsidiaries and the political sensitivity of their position, most MNEs follow the full disclosure practice. Some firms, however, believe that their competitive position would be eroded if they did not avoid taxes to the same extent as their domestic competitors. There is obviously no prescriptive answer to the problem, since business ethics are partly a function of cultural heritage and historical development.

Some countries have imposed what seem to be arbitrary punitive tax penalties on MNEs for presumed violations of local tax laws. Property or wealth tax assessments are sometimes perceived by the foreign firm to be excessively large when compared with those levied on locally owned firms. The problem is then how to respond to tax penalties that are punitive or discriminatory.

## TAX NEUTRALITY

When a government decides to levy a tax, it must consider not only the potential revenue from the tax, or how efficiently it can be collected, but also the effect the proposed tax can have on private economic behavior. For example, the U.S. government's policy on taxation of foreign source income does not have as its sole objective the raising of revenue but has multiple objectives. These include the following:

- Neutralizing tax incentives that might favor (or disfavor) U.S. private investment in developed countries
- Providing an incentive for U.S. private investment in developing countries
- Improving the U.S. balance of payments by removing the advantages of artificial tax havens and encouraging repatriation of funds
- Raising revenue

The ideal tax should not only raise revenue efficiently but also have as few negative effects on economic behavior as possible. Some theorists argue that the ideal tax should be completely *neutral* in its effect on private decisions and completely *equitable* among taxpayers. However, other theorists claim that national policy objectives such as balance of payments or investment in developing countries should be encouraged through an active *tax incentive policy*. Most tax systems compromise between these two viewpoints.

One way to view neutrality is to require that the burden of taxation on each dollar, euro, pound, or yen of profit earned in home country operations by an MNE be equal to the burden of taxation on each currency-equivalent of profit earned by the same firm in its foreign operations. This is called *domestic neutrality*. A second way to view neutrality is to require that the tax burden on each foreign subsidiary of the firm be equal to the tax burden on its competitors in the same country. This is called *foreign neutrality*. The latter interpretation is often supported by MNEs because it focuses more on the competitiveness of the individual firm in individual country markets.

The issue of *tax equity* is also difficult to define and measure. In theory, an equitable tax is one that imposes the same total tax burden on all taxpayers who are similarly situated and located in the same tax jurisdiction. In the case of foreign investment income, the U.S. Treasury argues that since the United States uses the nationality principle to claim tax jurisdiction, U.S.-owned foreign subsidiaries are in the same tax jurisdiction as U.S. domestic subsidiaries. Therefore a dollar earned in foreign operations should be taxed at the same rate and paid at the same time as a dollar earned in domestic operations.

## NATIONAL TAX ENVIRONMENTS

Despite the fundamental objectives of national tax authorities, it is widely agreed that taxes do affect economic decisions made by MNEs. Tax treaties between nations, and differential tax structures, rates, and practices all result in a less than level playing field for the MNEs competing on world markets.

Exhibit 20.1 provides an overview of corporate tax rates as applicable to Japan, Germany, and the United States. The categorizations of income (e.g., distributed versus undistributed profits), the differences in tax rates, and the discrimination in tax rates applicable to income earned in specific countries serve to introduce the critical dimensions of tax planning for the MNE.

Nations typically structure their tax systems along one of two basic approaches: the *worldwide approach* or the *territorial approach*. Both approaches are attempts to determine which firms, foreign or domestic by incorporation, or which incomes, foreign or domestic in origin, are subject to the taxation of host country tax authorities.

**WORLDWIDE APPROACH.**   The *worldwide approach*, also referred to as the *residential* or *national approach*, levies taxes on the income earned by firms that are incorporated in the host country, regardless of where the income was earned (domestically or abroad). An MNE earning income both at home and abroad would therefore find its worldwide income taxed by its home country tax authorities. For example, a country like the United States taxes the income earned by firms based in the United States regardless of whether the income earned by the firm is domestically or foreign

**EXHIBIT 20.1**

Comparison of Corporate Tax Rates for Japan, Germany and the United States

| Taxable income category | Japan | Germany | United States |
|---|---|---|---|
| Corporate income tax rates: | | | |
|    Profits distributed to stockholders | 30.0% | 30.5% | 35.0% |
|    Undistributed profits | 30.0% | 30.5% | 35.0% |
|    Branches of foreign corporations | 30.0% | 30.5% | 35.0% |
| Withholding taxes on dividends (portfolio): | | | |
|    with Japan | — | 20.0% | 10.0% |
|    with Germany | 10.0% | — | 5.0% |
|    with United States | 10.0% | 15.0% | — |
| Withholding taxes on dividends (substantial holdings): | | | |
|    with Japan | — | 15.0% | 15.0% |
|    with Germany | 15.0% | — | 15.0% |
|    with United States* | 15.0% | 5.0% | — |
| Withholding taxes on interest: | | | |
|    with Japan | — | 10.0% | 10.0% |
|    with Germany | 10.0% | — | 0.0% |
|    with United States | 10.0% | 0% to 25% | — |
| Withholding taxes on royalties: | | | |
|    with Japan | — | 10.0% | 10.0% |
|    with Germany | 10.0% | — | 0.0% |
|    with United States | 10.0% | 0.0% | — |

Source: PricewaterhouseCoopers, *Corporate Taxes 2003–2004, Worldwide Summaries*, 2004.

*"Substantial holdings" for the United States applies only to intercorporate dividend payments. In Germany and Japan, "substantial holdings" applies to corporate shareholders of greater than 25% interest in the enterprise. The German corporate tax rate of 30.5% is the sum of a 25.0% basic income tax rate plus a 5.5% solidarity levy.

sourced. In the case of the United States, ordinary foreign sourced income is taxed only as remitted to the parent firm. As with all questions of tax, however, numerous conditions and exceptions exist. The primary problem is that this does not address the income earned by foreign firms operating within the United States. Countries like the United States then apply the principle of *territorial taxation* to foreign firms within their legal jurisdiction, taxing all income earned by foreign firms within their borders as well.

**TERRITORIAL APPROACH.**   The *territorial approach,* also termed the *source approach,* focuses on the income earned by firms within the legal jurisdiction of the host country, not on the country of firm incorporation. Countries like Germany that follow the territorial approach apply taxes equally to foreign and domestic firms on income earned within the country but in principle not on income earned outside the country. The territorial approach, like the worldwide approach, results in a major gap in coverage if resident firms earn income outside the country but are not taxed by the country in which the profits are earned. In this case, tax authorities extend tax coverage to income earned abroad if it is not covered by foreign tax jurisdictions. Once again, a mix of the two tax approaches is necessary for full coverage of income.

**TAX DEFERRAL.**   If the worldwide approach to international taxation is followed to the letter, it would end the *tax-deferral* privilege for many MNEs. Foreign subsidiaries of MNEs pay host country corporate income taxes, but many parent countries defer claiming additional income taxes on that foreign source income *until it is remitted to the parent firm.* For example, U.S. corporate income taxes on some types of foreign source income of U.S.-owned subsidiaries incorporated abroad are deferred until the earnings are remitted to the U.S. parent. However, in October 2004 the U.S. tax laws were modified to encourage foreign source tax-deferred income earned before 2003 to be repatriated to the United States at a low 5.25% tax rate. This money has to be repatriated before the end of 2005 and be used to stimulate job creation in the United States to qualify for the low rate. It has been estimated that as much as $300 billion will be returned depending on the final U.S. Treasury tax guidelines that will determine exactly how the repatriated funds can be used.[1]

## TAX TREATIES

A network of bilateral tax treaties, many of which are modeled after one proposed by the Organisation for Economic Cooperation and Development (OECD), provides a means of reducing double taxation. Tax treaties normally define whether taxes are to be imposed on income earned in one country by the nationals of another, and if so, how. Tax treaties are bilateral, with the two signatories specifying what rates are applicable to which types of income between themselves alone. Exhibit 20.1's specification of withholding taxes on dividends, interest, and royalty payments between resident corporations of Japan, Germany, and the United States, is a classic example of the structure of tax treaties. Note that Germany, for example, imposes a 10% withholding tax on royalty payments to Japanese investors, while royalty payments to U.S. investors are withheld at a 0% rate.

---

[1]*Business Week,* December 27, 2004, pp. 42–44.

The individual bilateral tax jurisdictions as specified through tax treaties are particularly important for firms that are primarily exporting to another country rather than doing business there through a "permanent establishment." The latter would be the case for manufacturing operations. A firm that only exports would not want any of its other worldwide income taxed by the importing country. Tax treaties define what is a "permanent establishment" and what constitutes a limited presence for tax purposes.

Tax treaties also typically result in reduced withholding tax rates between the two signatory countries, the negotiation of the treaty itself serving as a forum for opening and expanding business relationships between the two countries. This practice is important to both MNEs operating through foreign subsidiaries, earning *active income*, and individual portfolio investors simply receiving *passive income* in the form of dividends, interest, or royalties.

## TAX TYPES

Taxes are classified on the basis of whether they are applied directly to income, called *direct taxes*, or on the basis of some other measurable performance characteristic of the firm, called *indirect taxes*. Exhibit 20.2 illustrates the wide range of corporate income taxes in the world today.

**INCOME TAX.**    Many governments rely on personal and corporate income taxes for their primary revenue source. Corporate income taxes are widely used today. Some countries impose different corporate tax rates on distributed income versus undistributed income. Corporate income tax rates vary over a relatively wide range, rising as high as 45% in Guyana and falling as low as 16% in Hong Kong, 15% in the British Virgin Islands, 10% in Cyprus, and effectively 0% in a number of offshore tax havens (discussed later in this chapter).

**WITHHOLDING TAX.**    Passive income (dividends, interest, royalties) earned by a resident of one country within the tax jurisdiction of a second country are normally subject to a withholding tax in the second country. The reason for the institution of withholding taxes is actually quite simple: governments recognize that most international investors will not file a tax return in each country in which they invest, and the government therefore wishes to assure that a minimum tax payment is received. As the term *withholding* implies, the taxes are withheld by the corporation from the payment made to the investor, and the withheld taxes are then turned over to government authorities. Withholding taxes are a major subject of bilateral tax treaties, and generally range between 0% and 25%.

**VALUE-ADDED TAX.**    One type of tax that has achieved great prominence is the *value-added tax*. The value-added tax is a type of national sales tax collected at each stage of production or sale of consumption goods in proportion to the value added during that stage. In general, production goods such as plant and equipment have not been subject to the value-added tax. Certain basic necessities such as medicines and other health-related expenses, education and religious activities, and the postal service are usually exempt or taxed at lower rates. The value-added tax has been adopted as the main source of revenue from indirect taxation by all members of the European Union, most other countries in Western Europe, a number of Latin American countries, Canada, and scattered other countries. A numerical example of a value-added tax computation is shown in Exhibit 20.3.

## EXHIBIT 20.2

Corporate Tax Rates for Selected Countries (percentage of taxable income)

| Country | Tax rate | Country | Tax rate | Country | Tax rate |
|---|---|---|---|---|---|
| Antigua & Barbuda | 40 | Greece | 35 | Peru | 27 |
| Argentina | 25 | Guatemala | 31 | Philippines | 32 |
| Australia | 30 | Guyana | 45 | Poland | 27 |
| Austria | 34 | Hong Kong | 16 | Portugal | 33 |
| Azerbaijan | 25 | Hungary | 18 | Puerto Rico | 20 |
| Bahamas | 0 | India | 36.75 | Qatar | 35 |
| Bahrain | 0 | Indonesia | 30 | Romania | 25 |
| Barbados | 36 | Iran | 25 | Russian Federation | 24 |
| Belgium | 34 | Ireland | 12.5/25 | St. Lucia | 33.33 |
| Bermuda | 0 | Isle of Man | 18 | Saudi Arabia | 30 |
| Bolivia | 25 | Israel | 36 | Singapore | 22 |
| Botswana | 5/15 | Italy | 34 | Slovak Republic | 25 |
| Brazil | 15 | Ivory Coast (Cote d'Ivore) | 35 | Slovenia | 25 |
| British Virgin Islands | 15/1 | Jamaica | 33.3 | Solomon Islands | 30 |
| Brunei Darussalam | 30 | Japan | 30 | South Africa | 30 |
| Bulgaria | 23.5 | Kazakhstan | 30 | Spain | 35 |
| Cambodia | 20 | Kenya | 30 | Sri Lanka | 30 |
| Canada | 33/38 | Korea | 27 | Swaziland | 30 |
| Cayman Islands | 0 | Latvia | 15 | Sweden | 28 |
| Channel Islands, Guernsey | 20 | Liechtenstein | 15 | Switzerland | 17–30 |
| Channel Islands, Jersey | 20 | Lithuania | 15 | Tahiti | 35 |
| Chile | 17 | Luxembourg | 22 | Taiwan | 25 |
| China | 30 | Macau | 15 | Tanzania | 30 |
| Colombia | 36.7 | Malaysia | 28 | Thailand | 30 |
| Congo | 40 | Malta | 35 | Trinidad & Tobago | 30 |
| Costa Rica | 30 | Mauritius | 25 | Turkey | 30 |
| Croatia | 20 | Mexico | 35 | Ukraine | 30 |
| Cyprus | 10 | Morocco | 35 | United Kingdom | 33 |
| Czech Republic | 31 | Mozambique | 32 | United States | 35 |
| Denmark | 30 | Namibia | 35 | Uruguay | 35 |
| Dominican Republic | 25 | Netherlands | 34.5 | Uzbekistan | 20 |
| Ecuador | 25 | Netherlands Antilles | 34.5 | Venezuela | 34 |
| Egypt | 40 | New Caledonia | 30 | Vietnam | 25 |
| Estonia | 35 | New Zealand | 33 | Zambia | 35 |
| Faroe Islands | 20 | Norway | 28 | Zimbabwe | 30.9 |
| Fiji | 32 | Oman | 30 | | |
| Finland | 29 | Pakistan | 35p/45np | | |
| France | 33.33 | Panama | 30 | | |
| Germany | 26.5 | Papua New Guinea | 25 | | |
| Ghana | 32.5 | Paraguay | 30 | | |

Notes: Botswana rates differ between manufacturing (5%) and nonmanufacturing (15%); the British Virgin Islands impose a 1% tax on foreign-source income; Canada imposes a 33% rate on manufacturing and processing industries, 38% on all others; Chile imposes a 35% withholding tax on income remitted to foreign residents from domestic operations; Ireland imposes a 12.5% rate on trading companies, 25% on nontrading companies; Pakistan rates differ between publicly owned (p, 35%) and nonpublic ownership (np, 45%); Switzerland's effective rate depends greatly on the canton of residence. These rates are representative rates, and often vary by industry and activities within each country. For actual tax liability calculations, see original source.

Source: PricewaterhouseCoopers, *Corporate Taxes 2003–2004, Worldwide Summaries*, 2004.

**EXHIBIT 20.3**

Value-Added Tax Applied to the Sale of a Wooden Fence Post

This is an example of how a wooden fence post would be assessed for value-added taxes in the course of its production and subsequent sale. A value-added tax of 10% is assumed.

**Step 1.** The original tree owner sells to the lumber mill, for $0.20, that part of a tree that ultimately becomes the fence post. The grower has added $0.20 in value up to this point by planting and raising the tree. While collecting $0.20 from the lumber mill, the grower must set aside $0.02 to pay the value-added tax to the government.

**Step 2.** The lumber mill processes the tree into fence posts and sells each post for $0.40 to the lumber wholesaler. The lumber mill has added $0.20 in value ($0.40 less $0.20) through its processing activities. Therefore the lumber mill owner must set aside $0.02 to pay the mill's value-added tax to the government. In practice, the owner would probably calculate the mill's tax liability as 10% of $0.40, or $0.04, with a tax credit of $0.02 for the value-added tax already paid by the tree owner.

**Steps 3 and 4.** The lumber wholesaler and retailer also add value to the fence post through their selling and distribution activities. They are assessed $0.01 and $0.03 respectively, making the cumulative value-added tax collected by the government $0.08, or 10% of the final sales price.

| Stage of production | Sales price | Value added | Value-added tax at 10% | Cumulative value-added tax |
|---|---|---|---|---|
| Tree owner | $0.20 | $0.20 | $0.02 | $0.02 |
| Lumber mill | $0.40 | $0.20 | $0.02 | $0.04 |
| Lumber wholesaler | $0.50 | $0.10 | $0.01 | $0.05 |
| Lumber retailer | $0.80 | $0.30 | $0.03 | $0.08 |

**OTHER NATIONAL TAXES.**    There are a variety of other national taxes, which vary in importance from country to country. The *turnover tax* (tax on the purchase or sale of securities in some country stock markets) and the *tax on undistributed profits* were mentioned before. *Property* and *inheritance taxes,* also termed *transfer taxes,* are imposed in a variety of ways to achieve intended social redistribution of income and wealth as much as to raise revenue. There are a number of red-tape charges for public services that are in reality user taxes. Sometimes foreign exchange purchases or sales are in effect hidden taxes, in as much as the government earns revenue rather than just regulates imports and exports for balance of payments reasons.

## FOREIGN TAX CREDITS

To prevent double taxation of the same income, most countries grant a *foreign tax credit* for income taxes paid to the host country. Countries differ on how they calculate the foreign tax credit and what kinds of limitations they place on the total amount claimed. Normally foreign tax credits are also available for withholding taxes paid to other countries on dividends, royalties, interest, and other income remitted to the parent. The value-added tax and other sales taxes are not eligible for a foreign tax credit but are typically deductible from pretax income as an expense.

A *tax credit* is a direct reduction of taxes that would otherwise be due and payable. It differs from a *deductible expense,* which is an expense used to reduce taxable income before the tax rate is applied. A $100 tax credit reduces taxes payable by the full $100, whereas a $100 deductible expense reduces taxable income by $100 and taxes payable by

$100 \times t$, where t is the tax rate. Tax credits are more valuable on a dollar-for-dollar basis than are deductible expenses.

If there were no credits for foreign taxes paid, sequential taxation by the host government and then by the home government would result in a very high cumulative tax rate. To illustrate, assume the wholly-owned foreign subsidiary of an MNE earns $10,000 before local income taxes and pays a dividend equal to all of its after-tax income. The host country income tax rate is 30%, and the home country of the parent tax rate is 35%. For simplicity we will assume no withholding taxes. Total taxation with and without allowances for tax credits is shown in Exhibit 20.4.

If tax credits are not allowed, sequential levying of a 30% host country tax and then a 35% home country tax on the income that remains results in an effective 54.5% tax, a cumulative rate that would render many MNEs uncompetitive with single-country local firms. The effect of allowing tax credits is to limit total taxation on the *original* before-tax income to no more than the highest single rate among jurisdictions. In the case depicted in Exhibit 20.4, the effective overall tax rate of 35% with foreign tax credits is equivalent to the higher tax rate of the home country (and is the tax rate payable if the income had been earned at home).

The $500 of additional home country tax under the tax credit system in Exhibit 20.4 is the amount needed to bring total taxation ($3,000 already paid plus the additional $500) up to but not beyond 35% of the original $10,000 of before-tax foreign income.

## EXHIBIT 20.4

Foreign Tax Credits

| | Without foreign tax credits | With foreign tax credits |
|---|---|---|
| Before-tax foreign income | $10,000 | $10,000 |
| Less foreign tax at 30% | −3,000 | −3,000 |
| Available to parent and paid as dividend | $ 7,000 | $ 7,000 |
| Less additional parent-country tax at 35% | −2,450 | |
| Less incremental tax (after credits) | | −500 |
| Profit after all taxes | $ 4,550 | $ 6,500 |
| | | |
| Total taxes, both jurisdictions | $ 5,450 | $ 3,500 |
| Effective overall tax rate (total taxes paid ÷ foreign income) | 54.5% | 35.0% |

## Transfer Pricing

The pricing of goods, services, and technology transferred to a foreign subsidiary from an affiliated company, called *transfer pricing*, is the first and foremost method of transferring funds out of a foreign subsidiary. These costs enter directly into the cost-of-goods-sold component of the subsidiary's income statement. This is a particularly sensitive problem for MNEs. Even purely domestic firms find it difficult to reach agreement on the best method for setting prices on transactions between related units. In the case of MNEs managers must balance conflicting considerations such as fund positioning and income taxes.

## FUND POSITIONING EFFECT

A parent company wishing to transfer funds out of a particular country can charge higher prices on goods sold to its subsidiary in that country, to the degree that government regulations allow. A foreign subsidiary can be financed by the reverse technique, a lowering of transfer prices. Payment by the subsidiary for imports from its parent or sister subsidiary transfers funds out of the subsidiary. A higher transfer price permits funds to be accumulated in the selling country. Transfer pricing may also be used to transfer funds between sister subsidiaries. Multiple sourcing of component parts on a worldwide basis allows switching between suppliers from within the corporate family to function as a device to transfer funds.

## INCOME TAX EFFECT

A major consideration in setting a transfer price is the *income tax effect*. Worldwide corporate profits may be influenced by setting transfer prices to minimize taxable income in a country with a high income tax rate and maximize income in a country with a low income tax rate. A parent company wishing to reduce the taxable profits of a subsidiary in a high-tax environment may set transfer prices at a higher rate to increase the costs of the subsidiary thereby reducing taxable income. *Real World Example 20.1* illustrates some apparent distortions to transfer prices by U.S. MNEs.

## Real World Example 20.1
### OVER- AND UNDER-INVOICING

A recent study raises questions over the legitimacy of the invoicing practices of many importers and exporters operating in the United States. Import transactions were examined for *over-invoicing*, the use of a transfer price to pay more than is typical for that product or service. Over-invoicing is one method of moving funds out of the United States. Export transactions were examined for *under-invoicing*, the use of a lower-than-normal export price to reposition profits outside the United States.

The study examined approximately 15,000 import commodity code categories and 8,000 export commodity codes to determine the average selling prices — import and export — to determine implied prices. The study first calculated the medium price, lower export quartile price, and upper import quartile price by bilateral transfers (between the United States and nearly 230 individual countries). The following is a sample of some of the more suspicious results.

| Over-Priced Imports | | | Under-Priced Exports | | |
|---|---|---|---|---|---|
| **Item** | **From** | **Unit price** | **Item** | **To** | **Unit price** |
| Sunflower seeds | France | $5,519/kg | Truck caps | Mexico | $4.09/unit |
| Toothbrushes | U.K. | $5,655/unit | Turbojet engines | Romania | $10,000/unit |
| Hacksaw blades | Germany | $5,485/unit | Cameras (SLRs) | Mexico | $3.30/unit |
| Razor blades | India | $461/unit | Soybeans | Netherlands | $1.58/ton |
| Vinegar | Canada | $5,430/ltr | ATM machines | Salvador | $35.93/unit |
| Flashlights | Japan | $5,000/unit | Bulldozers | Mexico | $527.94/unit |
| Sawdust | U.K. | $642/kg | Rocket launchers | Bolivia | $40.00/unit |
| Iron/steel ladders | Slovenia | $15,852/unit | Toilets, porcelian | Hong Kong | $1.08/unit |
| Inkjet printers | Colombia | $179,000/unit | Prefabricated bldgs | St. Lucia | $0.82/unit |
| Lard | Canada | $484/kg | Video projectors | Malta | $28.71/unit |
| Hypodermic syringes | Switzerland | $2,306/unit | Radial bus tires | U.K. | $8.46/unit |

Source: "U.S. Trade with the World: An Estimate of 2000 Lost U.S. Federal Income Tax Revenues Due to Over-Invoiced Imports and Under-Invoiced Exports," Simon Pak and John Zdanowicz, Florida International University, November 1, 2001, unpublished.

The income tax effect is illustrated in Exhibit 20.5. Trident Europe is operating in a relatively high-tax environment (German corporate income taxes are 45%). Trident USA is in a significantly lower tax environment (U.S. corporate income tax rates are 35%), motivating Trident to charge Trident Europe a higher transfer price on goods produced in the United States and sold to Trident Europe.

If Trident Corporation adopts a high-markup policy by "selling" its merchandise at an intracompany sales price of $1,700,000, the same $800,000 of pretax consolidated income is allocated more heavily to low-tax Trident USA and less heavily to high-tax Trident Europe. (Note that it is Trident Corporation, the corporate parent, which must adopt a transfer pricing policy which directly alters the profitability of each of the individual subsidiaries.) As a consequence, total taxes drop by $30,000 and consolidated net income increases by $30,000 to $500,000 — all while total sales remain constant.

Trident would naturally prefer the high-markup policy for sales from the United States to Europe (Germany in this case). Needless to say, government tax authorities are aware of the potential income distortion from transfer price manipulation. There are a variety of regulations and court cases on the reasonableness of transfer prices, including fees and royalties as well as prices set for merchandise. If a government taxing authority does not accept a transfer price, taxable income will be deemed larger than was calculated by the firm and taxes will be increased.

Section 482 of the U.S. Internal Revenue Code is typical of laws circumscribing freedom to set transfer prices. Under this authority, the Internal Revenue Service (IRS) can reallocate gross income, deductions, credits, or allowances between related corporations in order to prevent tax evasion or to reflect more clearly a proper allocation of income. Under the IRS guidelines and subsequent judicial interpretation, the burden of proof is on the taxpaying firm to show that the IRS has been arbitrary or unreasonable in reallocating income. This "guilty until proven innocent" approach

## EXHIBIT 20.5

Effect of Low versus High Transfer Price on Trident Europe's Net Income (thousands of U.S. dollars)

| Low-markup policy | Trident USA (subsidiary) | Trident Europe (subsidiary) | Trident (combined) |
|---|---|---|---|
| Sales | $1,400 | $2,000 | $2,000 |
| Less cost of goods sold* | (1,000) | (1,400) | (1,000) |
| Gross profit | $ 400 | $ 600 | $1,000 |
| Less operating expenses | (100) | (100) | (200) |
| Taxable income | $ 300 | $ 500 | $ 800 |
| Less income taxes | 35% (105) | 45% (225) | (330) |
| Net income | $ 195 | $ 275 | $ 470 |
| **High-markup policy** | | | |
| Sales | $1,700 | $2,000 | $2,000 |
| Less cost of goods sold* | (1,000) | (1,700) | (1,000) |
| Gross profit | $ 700 | $ 300 | $ 1,000 |
| Less operating expenses | (100) | (100) | (200) |
| Taxable income | $ 600 | $ 200 | $ 800 |
| Less income taxes | 35% (210) | 45% (90) | (300) |
| Net income | $ 390 | $ 110 | $ 500 |

* Trident USA's sales price becomes cost of goods sold for Trident Europe.

means that MNEs must keep good documentation of the logic and costs behind their transfer prices. The "correct price" according to the guidelines is the one that reflects an *arm's length price,* that is, a sale of the same goods or service to a comparable unrelated customer.

## METHODS OF DETERMINING TRANSFER PRICES

IRS regulations provide three methods to establish arm's length prices: comparable uncontrolled prices, resale prices, and cost-plus calculations. All three of these methods are recommended for use in member countries by the OECD Committee on Fiscal Affairs. In some cases combinations of these three methods are used.

**COMPARABLE UNCONTROLLED PRICE METHOD.**   A comparable, uncontrolled price is regarded as the best evidence of arm's length pricing. The transfer price is the same as prices of bona fide sales of the same items between the MNE and unrelated customers, or between two unrelated firms. Although such a market-determined price is ideal, in practice it is difficult to apply because of variations in quality, quantity, timing of sale, and proprietary trademarks. Perhaps even more important is the fact that sales between subsidiaries are often of custom-designed items — a generator sold by Ford USA for a European model is unlikely to be sold to, or even usable by, say, General Motors in Europe.

**RESALE PRICE METHOD.**   The resale price method, a second-best approach to arm's length pricing, starts with the final selling price to an independent purchaser and subtracts an appropriate markup for the distribution subsidiary. The allowed markup is to cover the distribution subsidiary's costs and profits. This price is then used as the intracompany transfer price for similar, but not necessarily identical, items. Nevertheless, determination of an appropriate markup is difficult, especially if the distribution subsidiary adds value to the item through subsequent processing or packaging.

**COST-PLUS METHOD.**   The cost-plus method sets the allowable transfer price by adding an appropriate profit markup to the seller's full cost, where *full cost* is the accounting definition of direct costs plus overhead allocation. This method is often used where semifinished products are sold between subsidiaries. Allocation of overhead in determining full cost is always a very subjective matter, especially when joint products are involved, so the method allows room for negotiation.

## OTHER TRANSFER PRICING CONSIDERATIONS

Many tax authorities allow lower transfer prices when a new market is being established. For example, a manufacturing subsidiary may cut its price to the distribution subsidiary so that the latter can get market penetration. However, the price cut must be passed on to the final customer — it cannot be used to accumulate more profits in the distribution subsidiary. Another approach is to negotiate an advance pricing agreement (APA) with both home country and host country tax authorities. APAs involve time and expense to negotiate, but they do provide the firm with advanced assurance that its transfer pricing policies are acceptable. Without them, a firm may try to follow tax guidelines on transfer prices and still find itself in expensive tax appeals after the fact, defending a decision process it thought conformed to the letter of the tax rule.

## MANAGERIAL INCENTIVES AND EVALUATION

When a firm is organized with decentralized profit centers, transfer pricing between centers can disrupt evaluation of managerial performance. This problem is not unique to MNEs but is also a controversial issue in the "centralization versus decentralization" debate in domestic circles. In the domestic case, however, a modicum of coordination at the corporate level can alleviate some of the distortion that occurs when any profit center suboptimizes its profit for the corporate good. Also in most domestic cases the company can file a single (for that country) consolidated tax return, so the issue of cost allocation between related companies is not critical from a tax-payment point of view.

In the multinational case, coordination is often hindered by longer and less-efficient channels of communication, the need to consider the unique variables that influence international pricing, and separate taxation. Even with the best intentions, a manager in one country may find it difficult to know what is best for the firm as a whole when buying at a negotiated price from related companies in another country. Yet, if corporate headquarters establishes transfer prices and sourcing alternatives, one of the main advantages of a decentralized profit center system disappears: local management loses the incentive to act for its own benefit.

To illustrate, refer back to Exhibit 20.5, where an increase in the transfer price led to a worldwide income gain: Trident Corporation's income rose by $195,000 (from $195,000 to $390,000) while Trident Europe's income fell by only $165,000 (from $275,000 to $110,000), for a net gain of $30,000. Should the managers of the European subsidiary lose their bonuses (or even their jobs) because of their "sub-par" performance? Bonuses are usually determined by a companywide formula based in part on the profitability of individual subsidiaries, but in this case Trident Europe "sacrificed" for the greater good of the whole. Arbitrarily changing transfer prices can create measurement problems.

Specifically, transferring profit from high-tax Trident Europe to low-tax Trident USA changes the following for one or both companies:

- Import tariffs paid (importer only) and hence profit levels
- Measurements of foreign exchange exposure, such as the amount of net exposed assets, because of changes in amounts of cash and receivables
- Liquidity tests, such as the current ratio, receivables turnover, and inventory turnover
- Operating efficiency, as measured by the ratio of gross profit to either sales or to total assets
- Income tax payments
- Profitability, as measured by the ratio of net income to either sales or capital invested
- Dividend payout ratio, in that a constant dividend will show a varied payout ratio as net income changes. Alternatively, if the payout ratio is kept constant, the amount of dividend is changed by a change in transfer price.
- Internal growth rate, as measured by the ratio of retained earnings to existing ownership equity

## EFFECT ON JOINT-VENTURE PARTNERS

Joint ventures pose a special problem in transfer pricing, because serving the interest of local stockholders by maximizing local profit may be suboptimal from the overall viewpoint of the MNE. Often the conflicting interests are irreconcilable. Indeed the local joint venture partner could be viewed as a potential Trojan horse if they complain to local authorities about the MNE's transfer pricing policy.

## FLEXIBILITY IN TRANSFER PRICING

Although all governments have an interest in monitoring transfer pricing by MNEs, not all governments use these powers to the detriment of MNEs. In particular, transfer pricing has some political advantages over other techniques of transferring funds. Although the recorded transfer price is known to the governments of both the exporting and importing countries, the underlying cost data are not available to the importing country. Thus the importing country finds it difficult to judge the reasonableness of the transfer price, especially for nonstandard items such as specialized components.

Additionally, even if cost data could be obtained, some of the more sophisticated governments might continue to ignore the transfer pricing leak. They recognize that foreign investors must be able to repatriate a reasonable profit by their own standards, even if this profit seems unreasonable locally. An unknown or unproved transfer price leak makes it more difficult for local critics to blame their government for allowing the country to be "exploited" by foreign investors. Thus within the potential and actual constraints established by governments, opportunities may exist for MNEs to alter transfer prices away from an arm's length market price. On the other hand, if a host government sours on foreign investment, past transfer price leaks may be exploited to penalize the foreigners.

# U.S. Taxation of Foreign Source Income

As we noted previously, the United States employs the *worldwide approach* to international taxation to U.S. multinationals operating globally, but the *territorial approach* to foreign firms operating within its borders. This part of the chapter focuses on how U.S. tax authorities tax the foreign sourced income of U.S.–based multinationals.

## U.S. CALCULATION OF FOREIGN TAX CREDITS

Dividends received from U.S. corporate subsidiaries are fully taxable in the United States at U.S. tax rates but with credit allowed for direct taxes paid on income in a foreign country. The amount of foreign tax allowed as a credit depends on five tax parameters:

1. Foreign corporate income tax rate
2. U.S. corporate income tax rate
3. Foreign corporate dividend withholding tax rate for nonresidents (per the applicable bilateral tax treaty between the specific country and the United States)
4. Proportion of ownership held by the U.S. corporation in the foreign firm
5. Proportion of net income distributed, the dividend payout rate

The five cases depicted in Exhibit 20.6 are based on a foreign subsidiary of a U.S. corporation that earns $10,000 before local taxes. The U.S. corporate income tax rate is 35%. The foreign tax rate is 30% in Cases 1 through 4 and 40% in Case 5.

**EXHIBIT 20.6**

U.S. Taxation of Foreign Source Income

| | A | B | C | D | E | F |
|---|---|---|---|---|---|---|
| 1 | Exhibit 20.6 U.S. Taxation of Foreign Source Income | | | | | |
| 2 | **Baseline Values** | **Case 1** | **Case 2** | **Case 3** | **Case 4** | **Case 5** |
| 3 | Foreign corporate income tax rate | 30% | 30% | 30% | 30% | 40% |
| 4 | U.S. corporate income tax rate | 35% | 35% | 35% | 35% | 35% |
| 5 | Foreign dividend witholding tax rate | 0% | 10% | 10% | 10% | 10% |
| 6 | U.S. ownership in foreign firm | 100% | 100% | 100% | 40% | 40% |
| 7 | Dividend payout rate of foreign firm | 100% | 100% | 50% | 50% | 50% |
| 8 | **Foreign Subsidiary Tax Computation** | | | | | |
| 9 | Taxable income of foreign subsidiary | $ 10,000 | $ 10,000 | $ 10,000 | $ 10,000 | $ 10,000 |
| 10 | Less foreign corporate income tax | 3,000 | 3,000 | 3,000 | 3,000 | 4,000 |
| 11 | Net income available for distribution | $ 7,000 | $ 7,000 | $ 7,000 | $ 7,000 | $ 6,000 |
| 12 | Retained earnings | - | - | 3,500 | 3,500 | 3,000 |
| 13 | Distributed earnings | 7,000 | 7,000 | 3,500 | 3,500 | 3,000 |
| 14 | Distribution to U.S. parent company | $ 7,000 | $ 7,000 | $ 3,500 | $ 1,400 | $ 1,200 |
| 15 | Withholding taxes on dividends | - | 700 | 350 | 140 | 120 |
| 16 | Net remittance to U.S. parent | $ 7,000 | $ 6,300 | $ 3,150 | $ 1,260 | $ 1,080 |
| 17 | **U.S. Corporate Tax Computation on Foreign Source Income** | | | | | |
| 18 | Dividend received (before withholding) | $ 7,000 | $ 7,000 | $ 3,500 | $ 1,400 | $ 1,200 |
| 19 | Add-back foreign deemed-paid tax | 3,000 | 3,000 | 1,500 | 600 | 800 |
| 20 | Grossed-up foreign dividend | $ 10,000 | $ 10,000 | $ 5,000 | $ 2,000 | $ 2,000 |
| 21 | Tentative U.S. tax liability | 3,500 | 3,500 | 1,750 | 700 | 700 |
| 22 | Less credit for foreign taxes | | | | | |
| 23 | Foreign income taxes paid | $ 3,000 | $ 3,000 | $ 1,500 | $ 600 | $ 800 |
| 24 | Foreign withholding taxes paid | - | 700 | 350 | 140 | 120 |
| 25 | Total | $ 3,000 | $ 3,700 | $ 1,850 | $ 740 | $ 920 |
| 26 | Additional U.S. taxes due | 500 | - | - | - | - |
| 27 | Excess foreign tax credits | - | 200 | 100 | 40 | 220 |
| 28 | After-tax income from foreign subsidiary | $ 6,500 | $ 6,300 | $ 3,150 | $ 1,260 | $ 1,080 |
| 29 | **Tax Burden Measurement** | | | | | |
| 30 | Total taxes paid on remitted income | $ 3,500 | $ 3,700 | $ 1,850 | $ 740 | $ 920 |
| 31 | Effective tax rate on foreign income | 35% | 37% | 37% | 37% | 46% |
| 32 | Key Cell Entries | | | | | |
| 33 | Entries in Column B are to be copied across to Columns C, D, E, and F. | | | | | |
| 34 | B10: =B9*B3               B21: =B20*B4 | | | | | |
| 35 | B11: =B9 – B10             B23: =B19 | | | | | |
| 36 | B12: =B11*(1 – B7)          B24: =B15 | | | | | |
| 37 | B13: =B11*B7             B25: =SUM(B23:B24) | | | | | |
| 38 | B14: =B13*B6             B26: =IF(B21>B25,B21 – B25,0) | | | | | |
| 39 | B15: =B14*B5             B27: =IF(B21<B25,B25 – B21,0) | | | | | |
| 40 | B16: =B14 – B15            B28: =B20 – B25 – B26 | | | | | |
| 41 | B18: =B14               B30: =B21+B27 | | | | | |
| 42 | B19: =(B14/B11)*B10         B31: =B30/B20 | | | | | |
| 43 | B20: =SUM(B18:B19) | | | | | |
| 44 | | | | | | |

**CASE 1: FOREIGN SUBSIDIARY WITH 100% PAYOUT (NO WITHHOLDING TAX).**
Assuming the foreign subsidiary earns $10,000 before local taxes in its overall tax basket, it pays $3,000 in foreign taxes (30% foreign tax rate) and distributes all $7,000 in net income to its U.S. parent (100% payout rate). Because there are no withholding taxes, the U.S. parent receives a net remittance of the full $7,000.

The U.S. parent corporation takes the *full* before-tax foreign income of the foreign corporation — apportioned by its proportional ownership in the foreign corporation (in this case 100%) — into its taxable income. This is called *grossing-up*.

The U.S. parent then calculates a tentative U.S. tax against the grossed-up foreign income. Assuming a 35% U.S. tax rate, the tentative U.S. tax on a grossed-up income of $10,000 is $3,500. The U.S. parent is then entitled under U.S. tax law to reduce this U.S. tax liability by a *deemed-paid foreign tax credit* for taxes already paid on the same income in the foreign country. The deemed-paid tax credit is calculated as follows:

$$\text{Deemed–paid credit} = \frac{\substack{\text{Dividends received} \\ \text{(including withholding tax)} \times \text{Creditable foreign taxes}}}{\text{After–tax net profits of the foreign corporation}}$$

*Creditable taxes* are foreign income taxes paid on earnings by a foreign corporation that has paid a dividend to a qualifying U.S. corporation. In order to qualify, a U.S. corporation must own at least 10% of the voting power of the distributing foreign corporation.

The deemed-paid credit in Case 1 is calculated as follows:

$$\text{Deemed–paid credit} = \frac{\$7,000 \times \$3,000}{\$7,000} = \$3,000$$

The U.S. parent owes an additional $500 in U.S. taxes ($3,500 tentative U.S. tax less the deemed-paid credit of $3,000). The after-tax income earned by the U.S. parent corporation is $6,500, and the overall tax rate on the foreign income is 35% (total taxes of $3,500 on total income of $10,000). Note that although the foreign corporate tax rate was lower (30% to the U.S. 35% rate), the U.S. corporation ends up paying the higher effective rate.

**CASE 2: FOREIGN SUBSIDIARY WITH 100% PAYOUT (10% WITHHOLDING TAX).**
Assume that the same foreign corporation earns the same income, but now all dividends paid to the U.S. parent corporation are subject to a 10% withholding tax. All other values remain the same as in Case 1. Although the actual net remittance to the U.S. parent is now lower, $6,300 instead of $7,000, the U.S. parent calculates the tentative U.S. tax on a grossed-up dividend of $7,000.

The tentative U.S. tax liability is again $3,500. The U.S. corporation can then deduct the amount of the deemed-paid credit ($3,000) and the full amount of withholding tax ($700) from its U.S. tax liability. Because the total foreign tax credits of $3,700 are greater than the tentative U.S. tax of $3,500, the U.S. parent owes no additional U.S. taxes. The U.S. parent has, in fact, an *excess foreign tax credit* of $200 ($3,700 – $3,500) which it can carry back two years or carry forward five years. The effective foreign tax rate is now 37% as a result of paying higher taxes abroad than it would have theoretically paid at home, including the withholding tax.

**CASE 3: FOREIGN SUBSIDIARY WITH 50% PAYOUT (10% WITHHOLDING TAX).** In this case it is assumed that all tax rates remain the same, but the foreign subsidiary chooses to pay out only 50% of net income rather than 100%. As a result, all dividends, withholding taxes, deemed-paid credits, tentative U.S. tax liabilities, foreign tax credits, after-tax income from the foreign subsidiary, and, finally, total taxes paid, are cut in half. The overall effective tax rate is again 37%, higher than what would have theoretically been paid if the income had been earned inside rather than outside the United States.

**CASE 4: FOREIGN SUBSIDIARY WITH 50% PAYOUT (10% WITHHOLDING TAX).** Case 4 illustrates to what degree these cash flows change when the U.S. parent corporation owns only 40% of the foreign corporation. As illustrated in Exhibit 20.5, the 40% ownership acts only as a "scale factor" in apportioning dividends paid, withholding tax withheld, and tax liabilities and credits resulting. Once again the U.S. parent corporation has excess foreign tax credits as a result of paying more taxes abroad than it is liable for at home. The overall effective tax rate on the reduced after-tax net income for the foreign subsidiary of $1,400 is 37%.

**CASE 5: FOREIGN SUBSIDIARY WITH 50% PAYOUT (40% FOREIGN CORPORATE TAX, 10% WITHHOLDING TAX).** This fifth and final case illustrates the increasing tax burden on the U.S. parent corporation when the corporate income tax in the foreign country is higher than that in the United States. The combined impact of a 40% foreign income tax and a 10% withholding tax, even after calculation of deemed-paid foreign tax credits, results in a rising excess foreign tax credit and a substantially higher effective tax rate of 46%. Clearly, when the implications of Case 5 are combined with the number of countries with corporate tax rates higher than that of the United States (see Exhibit 20.2), the tax burden borne by U.S.–based MNEs is a significant competitive concern.

## EXCESS FOREIGN TAX CREDITS

If a U.S.–based MNE receives income from a foreign country that imposes higher corporate income taxes than the United States (or combined income and withholding tax), total creditable taxes will exceed U.S. taxes on that foreign income. The result is *excess foreign tax credits*. All firms wish to manage their tax liabilities globally, however, so that they do not end up paying more on foreign sourced income than they do on domestically sourced income. The proper management of global taxes is not simple, however, and combines three different components: (1) *foreign tax credit limitations*; (2) *tax credit carry-forward/carry-back*; and (3) *foreign tax averaging*.

**FOREIGN TAX CREDIT LIMITATION.** The amount of credit a taxpayer can use in any year is limited to the U.S. tax on that foreign income. Foreign tax credits *cannot* be used to reduce taxes levied on domestic income. The total foreign tax creditable in any one year is limited according to the following formula:

$$\text{Creditable tax limit} = \frac{\text{total foreign taxable income}}{\text{total taxable income}} \times \text{U.S. tax on total income}$$

This requires the consideration of not only foreign source income, but the U.S. tax liabilities associated with the firm's domestic income.

**TAX CREDIT CARRY-FORWARD/CARRY-BACK.**    Excess foreign tax credits, like domestic tax credits, may be carried forward five years and carried back two years against similar tax liabilities. Unfortunately, since excess foreign tax credits arise from tax differentials, and tax rates typically change slowly, a firm experiencing an excess foreign tax credit one year may experience it year after year.

**TAX AVERAGING.**    The good news is that under U.S. tax law it is possible to offset foreign tax credits derived from one source against foreign tax liabilities from another source, assuming they are derived from the same type of income. This is termed *tax averaging*. In principle this means that if income is derived from a high-tax country, creating excess foreign tax credits, these credits can in turn be used against a deficit foreign tax credit position formed from repatriating income from a low-tax country.

The primary obstacle to tax averaging is the inability to average across different categories or "baskets" of income. The U.S. tax code specifies a *general limitation income basket*. This is the basket that includes the majority of income derived by U.S. corporations abroad, such as manufacturing, services, and sales income. The U.S. tax code specifies eight other baskets of income into which foreign sourced income may fall. For example, a U.S.–based firm cannot average deficit foreign tax credits on active income from a low-tax country against excess foreign tax credits on passive income from a high-tax country. This basket limitation provides fewer incentives for MNEs to position certain types of profits in low tax countries. Many countries, however, do not restrict the use of foreign tax credits by income category, or they may choose to ignore foreign sourced income altogether.

## CONTROLLED FOREIGN CORPORATIONS AND SUBPART F INCOME

The rule that U.S. shareholders do not pay U.S. taxes on foreign sourced income until that income is remitted to the United States was amended in 1962 by the creation of special *Subpart F income*. The revision was designed to prevent the use of arrangements between operating companies and base companies located in tax havens as a means of deferring U.S. taxes and to encourage greater repatriation of foreign incomes. A *controlled foreign corporation* (CFC) is any foreign corporation in which U.S. shareholders, including corporate parents, own more than 50% of the combined voting power or total value.

*Subpart F income* is subject to immediate U.S. taxation *even when not remitted*. It is income of a type otherwise easily shifted offshore to avoid current taxation. It includes (1) passive income received by the foreign corporation such as dividends, interest, rents, royalties, net foreign currency gains, net commodities gains, and income from the sale of nonincome-producing property; (2) income from the insurance of U.S. risks; (3) financial service income; (4) shipping income; (5) oil-related income; and (6) certain related-party sales and service income.

## BRANCH VERSUS LOCALLY INCORPORATED SUBSIDIARY

An MNE normally has a choice whether to organize a foreign subsidiary as a branch of the parent or as a local corporation. Both tax and nontax consequences must be considered. Nontax factors include the locus of legal liability, public image in the host country, managerial incentive considerations, and local legal and political requirements.

One major tax consideration is whether the foreign subsidiary is expected to run at a loss for several years after start-up. If so, it might be preferable to organize originally as a branch operation to permit these anticipated losses to be consolidated in the parent's income statement for tax purposes. For example, tax laws in the United States and many other countries do not permit a foreign corporation to be consolidated for tax purposes, even though it is consolidated for reporting purposes, but do permit consolidation of foreign branches for tax purposes.

A second tax consideration is the net tax burden after paying withholding taxes on dividends. An MNE must weigh the benefit of potential tax deferral of home country taxes on foreign source income from a fully incorporated foreign subsidiary, versus the total tax burden of paying foreign corporate income taxes and withholding taxes once the income is distributed to the parent corporation. A foreign branch's income would typically only bear the burden of home-country taxation because its income is concurrently consolidated with that of the parent, with no foreign corporate income taxes or withholding taxes applied.

## FOREIGN SALES CORPORATIONS

Over the years the United States has introduced into U.S. tax laws special incentives dealing with international operations. To benefit from these incentives, a firm may have to form separate corporations for qualifying and nonqualifying activities. The most important U.S. special corporation is a foreign sales corporation (FSC). FSCs were introduced in the Tax Reform Act of 1984 as a device to provide tax-exempt income for U.S. persons or corporations having export-oriented activities.

"Exempt foreign trade income" of an FSC is not subject to U.S. income taxes. Exempt foreign trade income is income from foreign sources that is not effectively connected with the conduct of a trade or business within the United States. Exempt income is limited to 34% of the FSC's total trade income.

An FSC's total foreign trade income is derived from gross receipts from the sale of export property, lease or rental of export property, incidental services provided with the sale or lease of export property, and fees for engineering, architectural, or managerial services. The exempt portion of the FSC's total foreign trade income depends on the pricing rules used. "Export property" is manufactured, produced, grown, or extracted from the United States by an entity other than the FSC and is sold, leased, or rented outside the United States.

In 1999, however, the World Trade Organization (WTO) ruled that FSCs were an illegal subsidy worth billions of dollars to thousands of U.S. exporters. Although it is unlikely that FSCs will be discontinued, their role in aiding U.S.-based exporters is increasingly controversial. The European Union threatened to impose penalty tariffs in 2004 or later.

## U.S. TAXATION: SUMMARY POINTS

Exhibit 20.7 provides an overview of the primary tax issues facing a U.S.-based MNE.

- *Domestic-source income* and *foreign source income* are separated. Tax credits or deficits in one category cannot be applied to net positions in the other category.
- foreign source income is separated into *active* and *passive* categories. Active income is taxed by U.S. tax authorities only as it is remitted to the U.S. parent. Passive income is taxed as it is earned, regardless of whether it is remitted to the U.S. parent or not.

**EXHIBIT 20.7**

U.S. Taxation of a
U.S.–Based
Multinational
Enterprise

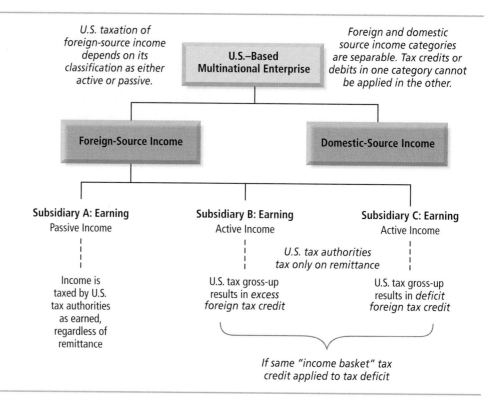

- If the remittance of active income from one subsidiary results in an excess foreign tax credit, and the remittance from a second subsidiary results in a foreign tax deficit, the credit may be applied to the deficit if the incomes are of the same "basket" under U.S. tax law.

Although multinational taxation is complex, the global management of tax liabilities is one of the most important financial management tasks facing any MNE. A multinational enterprise that effectively manages its global tax liabilities by reducing its global tax payments creates shareholder value.

## TAX MANAGEMENT AT TRIDENT

Exhibit 20.8 summarizes the key tax management issue for Trident when remitting dividend income back to the United States from Trident Europe and Trident Brazil.

- Because corporate income tax rates in Germany (40%) are higher than those in the United States (35%), dividends remitted to the U.S. parent result in *excess* foreign tax credits. Any applicable withholding taxes on dividends between Germany and the United States only increase the amount of the excess foreign tax credit.
- Because corporate income tax rates in Brazil (25%) are lower than those in the United States (35%), dividends remitted to the U.S. parent result in *deficit* foreign tax credits. If there are withholding taxes applied to the dividends by Brazil on remittances to the United States, this will reduce the size of the deficit, but not eliminate it.

**EXHIBIT 20.8**

Trident's Tax
Management of
Foreign-Source
Income

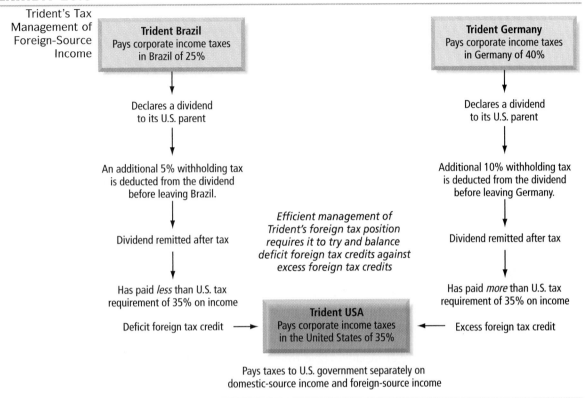

Trident's management would like to manage the two dividend remittances in order to match the deficits with the credits. The most straightforward method of doing this is to adjust the amount of dividend distributed from each foreign subsidiary so that, after all applicable income and withholding taxes have been applied, Trident's excess foreign tax credits from Trident Europe (Germany) exactly match the excess foreign tax deficits from Trident Brazil. There are a number of other methods of managing the global tax liabilities of Trident, so-called *repositioning of funds*, which are examined in detail in the following chapter.

## Tax-Haven Subsidiaries and International Offshore Financial Centers

Many MNEs have foreign subsidiaries that act as tax havens for corporate funds awaiting reinvestment or repatriation. Tax-haven subsidiaries, categorically referred to as *international offshore financial centers*, are partially a result of tax-deferral features on earned foreign income allowed by some of the parent countries. Tax-haven subsidiaries are typically established in a country that can meet the following requirements:

- A low tax on foreign investment or sales income earned by resident corporations and a low dividend withholding tax on dividends paid to the parent firm
- A stable currency to permit easy conversion of funds into and out of the local currency. This requirement can be met by permitting and facilitating the use of Eurocurrencies.

- The facilities to support financial services such as good communications, professional qualified office workers, and reputable banking services
- A stable government that encourages the establishment of foreign-owned financial and service facilities within its borders

Exhibit 20.9 provides a map of most of the world's major offshore financial centers. The typical tax-haven subsidiary owns the common stock of its related operating foreign subsidiaries. There might be several tax-haven subsidiaries scattered around the world. The tax-haven subsidiary's equity is typically 100% owned by the parent firm. All transfers of funds might go through the tax-haven subsidiaries, including dividends and equity financing. Thus the parent country's tax on foreign source income, which might normally be paid when a dividend is declared by a foreign subsidiary, could continue to be deferred until the tax-haven subsidiary itself pays a dividend to the parent firm. This event can be postponed indefinitely if foreign operations continue to grow and require new internal financing from the tax-haven subsidiary. Thus MNEs are able to operate a corporate pool of funds for foreign operations without having to repatriate foreign earnings through the parent country's tax machine.

For U.S. MNEs the tax deferral privilege operating through a foreign subsidiary was not originally a tax loophole. On the contrary, it was granted by the U.S. government to allow U.S. firms to expand overseas and place them on a par with foreign competitors, which also enjoy similar types of tax deferral and export subsidies of one type or another.

Unfortunately, some U.S. firms distorted the original intent of tax deferral into tax avoidance. Transfer prices on goods and services bought from or sold to related subsidiaries were artificially rigged to leave all the income from the transaction in the tax-haven subsidiary. This manipulation could be done by routing the legal title to the goods or services through the tax-haven subsidiary, even though physically the goods or services never entered the tax-haven country. This maneuver left no residual tax base for either exporting or importing subsidiaries located outside the tax-haven country. Needless to say, tax authorities of both exporting and importing countries were dismayed by the lack of taxable income in such transactions.

**EXHIBIT 20.9**

International Offshore Financial Centers

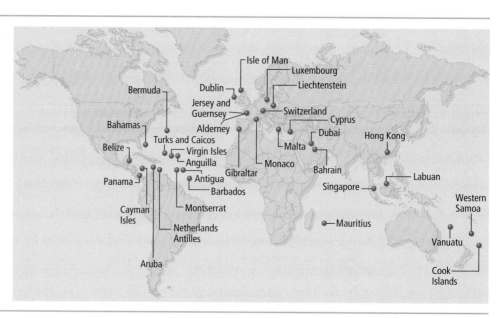

One purpose of the U.S. Internal Revenue Act of 1962 was to eliminate the tax advantages of these "paper" foreign corporations without destroying the tax-deferral privilege for those foreign manufacturing and sales subsidiaries that were established for business and economic motives rather than tax motives. Although the tax motive has been removed, some firms have found these subsidiaries useful as finance control centers for foreign operations. *Real World Example 20.2* provides a categorization of the primary activities of offshore financial centers.

## Real World Example 20.2
### THE ACTIVITIES OF OFFSHORE FINANCIAL CENTERS

Offshore financial centers provide financial management services to foreign users in exchange for foreign exchange earnings. The comparative advantage for clients? Several, including very low tax rates, minimal administrative formalities, and confidentiality and discretion. This environment allows wealthy international clients to minimize potential tax liability while protecting income and assets from political, fiscal, and legal risks. There are many vehicles through which offshore financial services can be provided. These include the following:

- Offshore banking, which can handle foreign exchange operations for corporations or banks. These operations are not subject to either capital, corporate, capital gains, dividend, or interest taxes or to exchange controls.
- International business corporations, which are often tax-exempt, limited-liability companies used to operate businesses or raise capital through issuing shares, bonds, or other instruments.

- Offshore insurance companies, which are established to minimize taxes and manage risk
- Asset management and protection allows individuals and corporations in countries with fragile banking systems or unstable political regimes to keep assets offshore to protect against the collapse of domestic currencies and banks.
- Tax planning: multinationals may route transactions through offshore centers to minimize taxes through transfer pricing. Individuals can make use of favorable tax regimes offered by offshore centers through trust and foundations.

The tax concessions and secrecy offered by offshore financial centers can be used for many legitimate purposes, but they have also been used for illegitimate ends, including money laundering and tax evasion.

Source: "Caribbean Centers: Stricter Rules Change Climate for Offshore Financial Centers," *IMF Survey*, International Monetary Fund, August 5, 2002, p. 252.

## MINI-CASE

# Stanley Works and Corporate Inversion*

*This strategic initiative will strengthen our company over the long-term. An important portion of our revenues and earnings are derived from outside the United States, where nearly 50% of our people reside. Moreover, an increasing proportion of our materials are being purchased from global sources. This change will create greater operational flexibility, better position us to manage international cash flows and help us to deal with our complex international tax structure. As a* result, our competitiveness, one of the three legs of our vision to become a Great Brand, will be enhanced. The business, regulatory and tax environments in Bermuda are expected to create considerable value for share owners. In addition to operational flexibility, improved worldwide cash management and competitive advantages, the new corporate structure will enhance our ability to access international capital markets, which is favorable for organic growth, future strategic

*This mini-case was derived from *Stanley Works and Corporate Inversion*, Thunderbird Case Series, Copyright ©2003 Thunderbird, The American Graduate School of International Management, prepared by Professors Dale Davison and Michael H. Moffett. Reprinted with permission.

*alliances and acquisitions, Finally, enhanced flexibility to manage worldwide tax liabilities should reduce our global effective tax rate from its current 32% to within the range of 23%–25%.*

Stanley Works, Form 14A, Securities and Exchange Commission, 8 February 2002

*Over and over again courts have said that there is nothing sinister in so arranging one's affairs as to keep taxes as low as possible. Everybody does so, rich and poor, and all do right, for nobody owes any public duty to pay more than the law demands: taxes are enforced extractions, not voluntary contributions. To demand more in the name of morals is mere cant.*

Judge Learned Hand, Commissioner v. Newman, 159 F.2d 848 (CA-2, 1947)

On February 8, 2002, Stanley Works (USA) announced that it would enter into a *corporate inversion*, whereby the company would reincorporate itself as a Bermuda-based corporation. This was termed an *outbound inversion*, as the reincorporation was to move the company's incorporation out of the United States to a foreign country. Currently a U.S.–based corporation with head offices in New Britain, Connecticut, Stanley would make all U.S. operations a wholly-owned subsidiary of a new parent company based in Bermuda — Stanley Tools, Ltd. Corporate headquarters, in fact all company offices and operational centers, would remain in Connecticut. The reasoning was simple: Stanley expected to save close to $30 million annually in corporate income taxes by changing its citizenship. On the date of the announcement the market value of Stanley increased by $199 million.

But the announcement was met with heated opposition from employees, stockholders, and local, state, and federal authorities. The change required a two-thirds approval by its stockholders. Stanley suffered through a controversial vote on the move in May 2002. Due to confusing corporate communiques to shareholders, a second vote had to be scheduled. In August 2002 Stanley found itself a lightning rod for public debate on the responsibilities of a corporate citizen and the ethics of tax reduction and patriotism. Many regulators were now accusing the company of treaty shopping. The senior management team now wished to reevaluate their inversion decision.

## Corporate Inversion

The purpose of a *corporate inversion* was — for all intents and purposes — to reduce tax liability. The United States taxed U.S.–based multinational companies on their worldwide income. As a U.S.–based company, Stanley paid corporate income taxes on all income generated in the United States (*domestic-source income*) and income

earned abroad and repatriated or deemed repatriated to the parent company in the United States (*foreign source income*). It was this latter tax on foreign source income which was at the heart of the dilemma for companies like Stanley.

Other countries, for example Germany, taxed only income deemed earned *within* the country, termed *territorial taxation*. Multinational companies with their parent company located in countries like Germany had lower effective tax burdens imposed by their home country tax structures. Offshore tax havens — countries such as Bermuda, the Cayman Islands, and British Virgin Islands — imposed no taxes on foreign source income and few or negligible taxes on domestic income of multinational companies incorporated there. This provided a literal tax haven for a multinational company incorporated in that country although it had little or no operational or structural presence there.

## History of Inversions

Corporate inversions were not a new tax strategy. The first outbound inversion of note was that undertaken by the McDermott Company in 1983. McDermott exchanged the shares held by its U.S. stockholders for shares in McDermott International, a Panamanian subsidiary of the company prior to the restructuring. The IRS had ruled the exchange of shares a taxable event, taxing all of the U.S. shareholders on the sale of their shares as capital gains. This unexpected consequence was thought to be a significant deterrent to future inversions, and the U.S. Congress soon followed with new tax legislation, Section 1248(i) of the IRS Code, which made it easier for the IRS to construe some inversions as taxable events for U.S. shareholders.

The next major corporate inversion of note was that undertaken by Helen of Troy, a beauty supply company located in Texas, in 1993. This was the first so-called *pure inversion* in that the company set up a completely new company offshore as its corporate headquarters (instead of selling the company's shares to an existing company or subsidiary). Management hoped that this strategy would be ruled a *reorganization*, rather than a taxable sale. The IRS once again, however, ruled the transaction a taxable event: "if US transferors owned, in the aggregate, 50% or more in the vote of value of the transferee foreign corporation immediately after the exchange." Although the McDermott and Helen of Troy tax rulings were thought to constitute significant deterrents to outbound corporate inversions, more and more companies have considered and, in some cases, completed the reorganization to offshore incorporation. The pace quickened in the late 1990s, with companies like Tyco and Ingersoll-Rand moving offshore to reduce tax liabilities.

An additional consideration was the equity market's response to inversions. On average the market rewarded the announcement of an outbound inversion with a 1.7% appreciation in the company's share price.[1] This share price reaction was thought to represent the present value of cash flow savings resulting from both reduction in taxes due on foreign source income and the reduction of domestic (U.S.) tax savings on domestic income as a result of the restructuring of operations postinversion.

## Tax Strategy

Stanley, like many other U.S.–based multinational companies, felt increasingly burdened by the U.S. corporate income tax structure. Stanley's U.S. earnings were taxed at the U.S. corporate income tax rate of 35%. This U.S. corporate rate, which had only varied up or down by about 1% over 15 years, had become increasingly high relative to corporate tax rates globally, as many countries reduced corporate tax rates consistently and significantly throughout the 1990s.

The problem faced by Stanley and other multinationals was that more and more of their earnings were being generated outside of the United States, and U.S. tax authorities taxed those profits when remitted back to the parent company in the United States. As illustrated in Exhibit 1, if Stanley's European operations generated a profit, they would first pay local taxes to the host government in, say, France or Germany, and then additional taxes on those profits when the earnings were remitted back to the U.S. parent company.

However, under Subpart F of the U.S. Internal Revenue Service Tax Code, Sections 951–964, a U.S. parent company is subject to current U.S. tax on certain income earned by a foreign subsidiary, without regard to whether the income is remitted to the U.S. corporation or not.[2] This income, typically referred to as Subpart F income, was income generated by a controlled foreign corporation and earned primarily through ownership of assets, not through the active production of goods or services. The U.S. tax authorities taxed this income as earned, rather than waiting to tax it when (or if) it was remitted to the U.S. parent company. This Subpart F provision had been specifically constructed to prevent foreign source income from being permanently parked in offshore tax havens, such as Bermuda, which assessed no corporate income taxes.

## EXHIBIT 1

Stanley Works
U.S. Tax
Liabilities Before
the Outbound
Corporate
Inversion

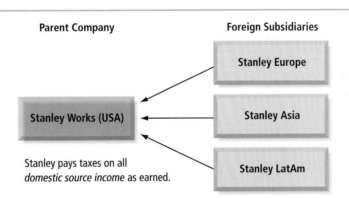

**Parent Company**

**Foreign Subsidiaries**

Stanley Europe

Stanley Works (USA)

Stanley Asia

Stanley LatAm

Stanley pays taxes on all *domestic source income* as earned.

Stanley pays taxes on *foreign source income* as follows:
1. Active earnings of foreign subsidiaries only when those earnings are remitted to the parent
2. Passive earnings of foreign subsidiaries (controlled foreign corporations) as the income is earned, regardless of remittance

[1]Mihir A. Desai and James R. Hines, Jr., "Expectations and Expatriations: Tracing the Causes and Consequence of Corporate Inversions," *NBER Working Paper 9057*, July 2002, www.nber.org/papers/w9057.

[2]This specifically applied to *controlled foreign corporations* or *CFCs*. A *CFC* was defined as any foreign corporation with more than 50% of its voting stock owned directly or indirectly by U.S. shareholders. Thus, most foreign subsidiaries of U.S–based multinationals were classified as CFCs.

The U.S. tax code did have a number of features to eliminate the potential for double taxation (taxes paid in both Europe and the U.S., for example) or at least to lessen the burden. Many of the corporate taxes paid to host governments were credited against potential U.S. tax liabilities. This had proven quite effective when corporate tax rates abroad were higher than in the United States, but as many countries lowered their rates below those in the U.S., profits returned to the United States now resulted in additional taxes due.

The specific tax goals of the outbound corporate inversion were (see Exhibit 2):[3]

- First, Bermuda, as is typical of most offshore financial centers, does not tax foreign source income. (In fact, Bermuda does not have a corporate income tax.) Stanley's profits generated throughout the world could be freely redistributed throughout the global business, including the parent, without creating additional tax liabilities in the country of the parent company (now Bermuda instead of the United States).
- Second, the U.S. operations of Stanley would now be conducted as the U.S. subsidiary of a foreign corporation. This would most likely pose restructuring possibilities whereby the U.S. subsidiary would have increasing obligations to the Bermuda parent such as royalties,

debt service, and licensing fees, which were legitimate deductible expenses in the U.S. but income to the parent company in Bermuda. The result would be a net reduction in U.S. tax liabilities from Stanley's business conducted in the United States.

This second dimension of the tax benefits of corporate inversion is often termed *earnings stripping*. The term refers to the practice of structuring operations within the United States to position as many corporate costs as legally possible to reduce taxable profits within the higher tax environment of the United States.

There was, however, considerable debate as to the actual tax benefits to be gained versus the growing public relations costs of inversion. The earnings per share (EPS) benefits had been touted by Stanley as a simple reduction in the effective tax rate for the overall organization. For example, using the pro forma earnings estimates for 2003, Stanley was expected to pay $134 million in taxes in 2003 on $420 million in earnings before tax, as shown in Exhibit 3. This assumed an effective tax rate of 32%. If Stanley were to reincorporate in Bermuda, Stanley estimated the effective tax rate would fall to 24%, yielding a $33 million savings for Stanley and its stockholders.[4]

## EXHIBIT 2

Stanley Works U.S. Tax Liabilities After the Outbound Corporate Inversion

[3]"Special Report: Outbound Inversion Transactions." *Tax Notes*, New York State Bar Association Tax Section, July 1, 2002, pp. 127–149.

[4]Stanley had consistently followed a conservative estimate in its public discussions of a $30 million tax savings, as opposed to the $33 million calculation here.

**EXHIBIT 3**

Prospective Changes in Stanley Works' Earnings After Inversion

| | Pro forma 2003 earnings | | |
|---|---|---|---|
| | **Before** | **After** | **Savings** |
| Earnings before tax | $420 | $420 | |
| Tax liability (32%/24%) | (134) | (101) | |
| Earnings after tax | $286 | $319 | + $33 |
| | | | |
| Shares outstanding (millions) | 88.0 | 88.0 | |
| Earnings per share (EPS) | $3.250 | $3.625 | + $0.375 or 11.5% |

## Patriotism and Inversion

*How would you like to keep living in your current home, but tell the Internal Revenue Service to go pound sand in Bermuda, because you're a legal resident of that lovely island? You can't, but tool-maker Stanley Works plans to save $30 million a year by moving. So what if our country is at war against terrorism and is spending billions extra for defense and homeland security? That's our problem, not the tax dodgers. Their problem is raising profits to get their stock price higher. What could possibly be more important, since a good stock market is good for America, right?*

Allan Sloan, "The Tax-Free Bermuda Getaway,"
*Newsweek,* April 15, 2002

John Trani's other worries surrounded the image of Stanley. The move to reincorporate offshore was portrayed by many as unpatriotic — unsupportive of the United States during a time of recession and continuing terrorist threats in the post-September 11th world. In addition to the growing debate in Congress over the increasing use of corporate inversions, there was strong opposition to the move by Stanley workers and their unions. Although Stanley was not doing anything illegal, and was paying its taxes in accordance with current law, the company was portrayed as "working too hard" to avoid future income tax obligations.

John Trani and his senior management team returned to the conference room. Time was running out. Stanley needed to reschedule the stockholder vote now if it was to continue to pursue corporate inversion. The question remained as to whether the benefits exceeded the costs of *moving* offshore.

## Case Questions

1. If Stanley did indeed reincorporate offshore, how do you think the company would restructure its operations, both inside and outside the United States?
2. Do you believe that the U.S. government should allow a company like Stanley to reincorporate outside the country in order to pay lower taxes?
3. If you were John Trani, would you continue to pursue the outbound inversion or choose to stay put?

## Summary of Learning Objectives

*Identify the differences between tax systems employed by governments around the globe*

- Nations typically structure their tax systems along one of two basic approaches: the *worldwide approach* or the *territorial approach*.

- Both approaches are attempts to determine which firms, foreign or domestic by incorporation, or which incomes, foreign or domestic in origin, are subject to the taxation of host country tax authorities.

- The *worldwide approach*, also referred to as the *residential* or *national approach*, levies taxes on the income earned by firms that are incorporated in the host country, regardless of where the income was earned (domestically or abroad).

- The *territorial approach*, also termed the *source approach*, focuses on the income earned by firms within the legal jurisdiction of the host country, not on the country of firm incorporation.

*Compare corporate income and withholding tax rates used across countries and the way tax treaties affect MNEs*

- A network of bilateral tax treaties, many of which are modeled after one proposed by the OECD, provides a means of reducing double taxation.

- Tax treaties normally define whether taxes are to be imposed on income earned in one country by the nationals of another, and if so, how. Tax treaties are bilateral, with the two signatories specifying what rates are applicable to which types of income between themselves alone.

*Understand how value-added taxes are levied by some countries today*

- The *value-added tax* is a type of national sales tax collected at each stage of production or sale of consumption goods in proportion to the value added during that stage.

*Explain the use of transfer pricing to manage corporate tax burdens*

- Transfer pricing is the pricing of goods, services, and technology between related companies

- High or low transfer prices have an effect on income taxes, fund positioning, managerial incentives and evaluation, and joint venture partners

- To establish an arm's length price three methods are typically used: (1) comparable uncontrolled price, (2) resale prices, and (3) cost plus.

*Compare tax liabilities of domestic and foreign-source income of U.S.–based firms*

- The United States differentiates foreign-source income from domestic-source income. Each is taxed separately, and tax deficits/credits in one category may not be used against deficits/credits in the other category.

*Demonstrate how U.S.–based multinationals manage their excess foreign tax credits and deficits to minimize their global tax liabilities*

- If a U.S.–based MNE receives income from a foreign country that imposes higher corporate income taxes than the United States (or combined income and withholding tax), total creditable taxes will exceed U.S. taxes on that foreign income. The result is *excess foreign tax credits*.

- All firms wish to manage their tax liabilities globally so that they do not end up paying more on foreign-source income than they do on domestic-source income.

*Examine the use of tax-haven subsidiaries and international offshore financial centers*

- MNEs have foreign subsidiaries that act as tax havens for corporate funds awaiting reinvestment or repatriation.

- Tax-havens are typically located in countries that have a low corporate tax rate, a stable currency, facilities to support financial services, and a stable government.

## QUESTIONS

1. **Tax morality.**
   a. What is meant by the term *tax morality*?
   b. Your company has a subsidiary in Russia, where tax evasion is a fine art. Discuss whether you should comply fully with Russian tax laws or should violate the laws, as do your local competitors.

2. **Tax neutrality.**
   a. Define the term *tax neutrality*.
   b. What is the difference between *domestic neutrality* and *foreign neutrality*?
   c. What are a country's objectives when determining tax policy on foreign-source income?

3. **Worldwide versus territorial approach.** Nations typically structure their tax systems along one of two basic approaches: the *worldwide approach* or the *territorial approach*. Explain these two approaches and how they differ from each other.

4. **Tax deferral.**
   a. What is meant by the term *tax deferral*?
   b. Why do countries allow tax deferral on foreign-source income?

5. **Tax treaties.**
   a. What is a bilateral tax treaty?
   b. What is the purpose of a bilateral tax treaty?
   c. What policies do most tax treaties cover?

6. **Tax types.** Taxes are classified on the basis of whether they are applied directly to income, called *direct taxes*, or to some other measurable performance characteristic of the firm, called *indirect taxes*. Classify each of the following types of taxes as being direct or indirect or something else.

   a. Corporate income tax paid by a Japanese subsidiary on its operating income

   b. Royalties paid to Saudi Arabia for oil extracted and shipped to world markets

   c. Interest received by a U.S. parent on bank deposits held in London

   d. Interest received by a U.S. parent on a loan to a subsidiary in Mexico

   e. Principal repayment received by a U.S. parent from Belgium on a loan to a wholly-owned subsidiary in Belgium

   f. Excise tax paid on cigarettes manufactured and sold within the United States

   g. Property taxes paid on the corporate headquarters building in Seattle

   h. A direct contribution to the International Committee of the Red Cross for refugee relief

   i. Deferred income tax, shown as a deduction on the U.S. parent's consolidated income tax

   j. Withholding taxes withheld by Germany on dividends paid to a U.K. parent corporation

7. **Foreign tax credit.** What is a foreign tax credit? Why do countries give credit for taxes paid on foreign-source income?

8. **Tax averaging.** How does tax averaging help or hinder a U.S.–based MNE in managing its global tax liabilities?

9. **Passive versus active income.** What is the difference between passive and active income?

10. **Value-added tax.**

    a. What is a value-added tax?

    b. What are the advantages and disadvantages of a value-added tax?

    c. Although the value-added tax has been proposed numerous times, the Unites States has never adopted one. Why do you think the attitude toward value-added tax is so negative in the United States when the value-added tax is widely used in the rest of the world?

11. **Subpart F income.** The rule that U.S. shareholders do not pay taxes on foreign-source income until that income is remitted to the United States (tax deferral) was amended in 1962 by the creation of special Subpart F income.

    a. Why was this revision adopted?

    b. What is defined as being Subpart F income?

    c. When is Subpart F income taxed?

12. **Transfer pricing motivation.** What is a transfer price and can a government regulate it? What difficulties and motives does a parent multinational firm face in setting transfer prices?

13. **Sister subsidiaries.** Subsidiary Alpha in Country Able faces a 40% income tax rate. Subsidiary Beta in Country Baker faces only a 20% income tax rate. At present each subsidiary imports from the other an amount of goods and services exactly equal in monetary value to what each exports to the other. This method of balancing intracompany trade was imposed by a management keen to reduce all costs, including the costs (spread between bid and ask) of foreign exchange transactions. Both subsidiaries are profitable, and both could purchase all components domestically at approximately the same prices as they are paying to their foreign sister subsidiary. Does this seem like an optimal situation to you?

14. **Correct pricing.** Section 482 of the U.S. Internal Revenue Code specifies use of a "correct" transfer price, and the burden of proof that the transfer price is "correct" lies with the company. What guidelines exist for determining the proper transfer price?

15. **Branch income.** Branches are often used as the organizational structure for foreign operations that are expected to lose substantial amounts of money in their first years of operation. Why would branches be preferable to wholly-owned subsidiaries?

16. **Foreign sales corporation (FSC).** What is a foreign sales corporation? Why are many other countries arguing that the U.S. FSCs are illegal under the World Trade Organization's current rules for the conduct of international trade?

17. **Tax haven subsidiary.**

    a. What is meant by the term *tax haven*?

**b.** What are the desired characteristics for a country if it expects to be used as a tax haven?

**c.** Identify five tax havens.

**d.** What are the advantages leading an MNE to use a tax haven subsidiary?

**e.** What are the potential distortions of an MNE's taxable income that are opposed by tax authorities in nontax haven countries?

**18. Tax treaties.** What do most bilateral tax treaties cover? How do they affect the operations and structure of MNEs?

**19. Passive.** Why do the U.S. authorities tax passive income generated offshore differently from active income?

## PROBLEMS

 **1. U.S. taxation of foreign-source income.** Using the structure for calculating U.S. taxes for foreign-source income from Exhibit 20.6, assume a foreign subsidiary has $3,400,000 in gross earnings, U.S. and foreign corporate income taxes are 35% and 28%, respectively, and foreign withholding taxes are 15%.

**a.** What is the total tax payment, foreign and domestic combined, for this income?

**b.** What is the effective tax rate paid on this income by the U.S.–based parent company?

**c.** What would be the total tax payment and effective tax rate if the foreign corporate tax rate were 45% and there were no withholding taxes on dividends?

**d.** What would be the total tax payment and effective tax rate if the income were earned by a branch of the U.S. corporation?

**2. Discovery Bay Airlines (Hong Kong).** Discovery Bay Airlines is a U.S.–based air freight firm with a wholly-owned subsidiary in Hong Kong. The subsidiary, DBay-Hong Kong, has just completed a long-term planning report for the parent company in San Francisco, in which it has estimated the following expected earnings and payout rates for the years 2004 to 2007.

The current Hong Kong corporate tax rate on this category of income is 16.5%. Hong Kong imposes no withholding taxes on dividends remitted to U.S. investors (per the Hong Kong–United States bilateral tax treaty). The U.S. corporate income tax rate is 35%. The parent company wants to repatriate 75% of net income as dividends annually.

**a.** Calculate the net income available for distribution by the Hong Kong subsidiary for the years 2004 to 2007.

**b.** What is the amount of the dividend expected to be remitted to the U.S. parent each year?

**c.** After gross-up for U.S. tax liability purposes, what is the total dividend after tax (all Hong Kong and U.S. taxes) expected each year?

**d.** What is the effective tax rate on this foreign-sourced income per year?

| Discovery Bay–Hong Kong (millions of U.S. dollars) | 2004 | 2005 | 2006 | 2007 |
|---|---|---|---|---|
| Earnings before interest and taxes (EBIT) | 8,000 | 10,000 | 12,000 | 14,000 |
| Less interest expenses | (800) | (1,000) | (1,200) | (1,400) |
| Earnings before taxes (EBT) | 7,200 | 9,000 | 10,800 | 12,600 |

**3. Jurgen-Strut of Germany.** Jurgen-Strut (JS) is a German-based company that manufactures electronic fuel-injection carburetor assemblies for several large automobile companies in Germany, including Mercedes, BMW, and Opel. The firm, like many firms in Germany today, is revising its financial policies in line with the increasing degree of disclosure required by firms if they wish to list their shares publicly in or out of Germany.

JS's primary problem is that the German corporate income tax code applies a different rate to income depending on whether it is retained (45%) or distributed to stockholders (30%).

| | |
|---|---|
| Earnings before interest and taxes (EBIT) | €580,000,000 |
| Less interest expenses | (96,500,000) |
| Earnings before taxes (EBT) | €483,500,000 |
| Less corporate income taxes | _____ |
| Net income | €_____ |
| Retained earnings | _____ |
| Distributed earnings | _____ |

**a.** If Jurgen-Strut planned to distribute 50% of its net income, what would be its total net income and total corporate tax bills?

**b.** If Jurgen-Strut were attempting to choose between a 40% and 60% payout rate to stockholders, what arguments and values would management use to convince stockholders which of the two payouts is in everyone's best interest?

***Kowloon Blade Company.*** Use the following company case to answer Questions 4 through 6. Kowloon Blade Company (Hong Kong) exports razor blades to its wholly-owned parent company, Cranfield Eversharp (Great Britain). Hong Kong tax rates are 16% and British tax rates are 30%. Kowloon calculates its profit per container as follows (all values in British pounds):

| Constructing price | Kowloon Blade | Cranfield Eversharp |
|---|---|---|
| Direct costs | £10,000 | £16,100 |
| Overhead | 4,000 | 1,000 |
| Total costs | £14,000 | £17,100 |
| Desired markup (15%) | 2,100 | 2,565 |
| Transfer price (sales price) | £16,100 | £19,665 |

*Income statements (assumes a volume of 1,000 units)*

| | Kowloon Blade | Cranfield Eversharp |
|---|---|---|
| Sales revenue | £16,100,000 | £19,665,000 |
| Less total costs | (14,000,000) | (17,100,000) |
| Taxable income | £2,100,000 | £2,565,000 |
| Less taxes (16%) | (336,000) | (30%) (769,500) |
| Post-tax profit | £1,764,000 | £1,795,500 |
| Consolidated profit | | £3,559,50 |

4. **Kowloon Blade (A).** Corporate management of Cranfield Eversharp is considering repositioning profits within the multinational company. What happens to the profits of Kowloon Blade and Cranfield Eversharp, and the consolidated results of both if the markup at Kowloon were increased to 20% and the markup at Cranfield were reduced to 10%? What is the impact of this repositioning on consolidated tax payments?

5. **Kowloon Blade (B).** Encouraged by the results from the previous problem's analysis, corporate management of Cranfield Eversharp wishes to continue to reposition profit in Hong Kong. It is, however, facing two constraints. First, the final sales price in Great Britain must be £20,000 or less to remain competitive. Secondly, the British tax authorities — in working with Cranfield Eversharp's cost accounting staff — has established a maximum transfer price allowed (from Hong Kong) of £17,800. What combination of markups do you recommend for Cranfield Eversharp to institute? What is the impact of this repositioning on consolidated profits after tax and total tax payments?

6. **Kowloon Blade (C).** Not to leave any potential tax repositioning opportunities unexplored, Cranfield Eversharp wants to combine the components of Question 4 with a redistribution of overhead costs. If overhead costs could be reallocated between the two units, but still total £5,000 per unit, and maintain a minimum of £1,750 per unit in Hong Kong, what is the impact of this repositioning on consolidated profits after tax and total tax payments?

7. **Gamboa's tax averaging.** Gamboa Incorporated is a relatively new U.S.-based retailer of specialty fruits and vegetables. The firm is vertically integrated with fruit- and vegetable-sourcing subsidiaries in Central America and distribution outlets throughout the southeastern and northeastern regions of the United States. Gamboa's two Central American subsidiaries are in Belize and Costa Rica.

Emilia Gamboa, the daughter of the firm's founder, is being groomed to take over the firm's financial management in the near future. Like many firms of similar size, Gamboa has not possessed a very high degree of sophistication in financial management because of time and cost considerations. Emilia, however, has recently finished her MBA and is now attempting to put some specialized knowledge of U.S. taxation practices to work to save Gamboa money. Her first concern is tax averaging for foreign tax liabilities arising from the two Central American subsidiaries.

Costa Rican operations are slightly more profitable than Belize operations, because Costa Rica is a relatively low-tax country. Costa Rican corporate taxes are a flat 30%, and no withholding taxes are imposed on dividends paid by foreign firms with operations there. Belize has a higher corporate income tax rate, 40%, and imposes a 10% withholding tax on all dividends distributed to foreign investors. The current U.S. corporate income tax rate is 35%.

|  | Belize | Costa Rica |
|---|---|---|
| Earnings before taxes | $1,000,000 | $1,500,000 |
| Corporate income tax rate | 40% | 30% |
| Dividend withholding tax rate | 10% | 0% |

**a.** If Maria Gamboa assumes a 50% payout rate from each subsidiary, what are the additional taxes due on foreign-source income from Belize and Costa Rica individually? How much in additional U.S. taxes would be due if Maria averaged the tax credits/liabilities of the two units?

**b.** Keeping the payout rate from the Belize subsidiary at 50%, how should Maria change the payout rate of the Costa Rican subsidiary in order to most efficiently manage her total foreign tax bill?

**c.** What is the minimum effective tax rate Maria can achieve on her foreign-source income?

8. **Hazelnut, Incorporated.** Jerry Filbert is the Vice President of Tax Planning for the U.S.-based firm, Hazelnut, Inc. Mr. Filbert is attempting to determine what the actual tax liabilities of Hazelnut will be for 2005, given solid forecasts of all expected values (it is now December 15, 2004). Hazelnut (USA) has a wholly-owned manufacturing subsidiary in Cádiz, Spain.

The Spanish subsidiary, Hazelnut Cádiz, had earnings before tax (EBT) in 2004 of €40 million. The earnings were of two types: manufacturing and sales of chocolate-covered hazelnut candy bars (80% of the total) and dividend income from a wholly-owned subsidiary in Switzerland (20% of the total). The average exchange rate for the year was $1.20/€. Corporate tax rates in Spain and the United States are both 35%. Dividends distributed from Spain to the United States are subject to a 15% withholding tax. Mr. Filbert was recently told that the Spanish subsidiary will declare an end-of-year dividend of 50% of net income available for distribution.

**a.** What will be the amount in U.S. dollars of the net dividend remitted?

**b.** What will be the U.S. tax liability associated with the Hazelnut Cádiz 2005 operations?

9. **Ballantyne Brand Services (A).** Ballantyne Brand Services is a U.S.-based brand development and management services consultancy. It is privately held and although now incorporated was originally a small consulting firm started by Sara Ballantyne. The company signs contracts for services well into the future and has estimated its income before tax for the 2005–2007 period as follows (note that it has a very large contract already committed for the 2004 year in Australia). All values have been converted to U.S. dollars for tax planning purposes.

| Assumptions | 2005 | 2006 | 2007 |
|---|---|---|---|
| U.S. domestic income for tax purposes | $2,500,000 | $3,500,000 | $2,500,000 |
| Australian earnings before tax | $200,000 | $2,000,000 | $250,000 |

The U.S. and Australian corporate income tax rates are 35% and 36%, respectively, in 2005. But the corporate income tax in Australia is scheduled to be reduced to 32% in 2006 and years after that. The reduction in tax rates will also apply to dividend withholding taxes on income remitted outside of Australia, currently 10%, to be reduced to 0% beginning in 2006. Ballantyne intends to remit 75% of all Australian earnings to its parent company each year.

**a.** What is the net dividend Ballantyne expects to remit to the U.S. parent from its Australian subsidiary in each of the three years?

**b.** What are the additional U.S. taxes due, or foreign tax credits arising from, the expected dividend remittance to the U.S. parent from Australia?

**c.** Assuming excess foreign tax credits can be carried forward five years, what is the actual additional tax payment due on the Australian foreign-source income in each year?

**d.** Assuming carry-forward, what is the cumulative excess foreign tax credits balance at the end of 2007?

**e.** What is the creditable tax limit on Ballantyne's foreign-source income in each year?

10. **Ballantyne Brand Services (B).** Ballantyne Brand Services, the same firm and situation as described in the previous problem, has just been informed by its Australian law firm that the Australian tax revision will not take place as previously expected. The Australian corporate tax rate will

stay at 36% for the foreseeable future, and there will be no reduction in the 10% withholding tax on dividend distributions.

**a.** What is the net dividend Ballantyne can now expect to remit to the U.S. parent from its Australian subsidiary in each of the three years?

**b.** What are the additional U.S. taxes due, or foreign tax credits arising from, the expected dividend remittance to the U.S. parent from Australia?

**c.** Assuming excess foreign tax credits can be carried forward five years, what is the actual additional tax payment due on the Australian foreign-source income in each year?

**d.** Assuming carry-forward, what is the cumulative excess foreign tax credits balance at the end of 2007?

 ## Internet Exercises

**1.** **Official government tax authorities.** Tax laws are constantly changing, and an MNE's tax-planning and management processes must therefore include a continual updating of tax practices by country. Use the following government tax sites to address specific issues related to those countries.

Hong Kong's ownership change to China:
  http://www.info.gov.hk/eindex.htm
Ireland's international financial services centre:
  http://www.revenue.ie/
Czech Republic's tax incentives for investment:
  http://www.czech.cz/index.php?section-2&menu-22

**2.** **Tax practices for international business.** Many of the major accounting firms provide online information and advisory services for international business activities as related to tax and accounting practices. Use the following Web sites to gain up-to-date information on tax law changes or practices.

Ernst & Young
  http://www.ey.com/tax/
Deloitte & Touche
  http://www.dttus.com/
KPMG
  http://www.kpmg.com/
PricewaterhouseCoopers
  http://www.pwcglobal.com/

# *Working Capital Management*

## LEARNING OBJECTIVES

Demonstrate the operation of working capital management
in a multinational enterprise and its various foreign subsidiaries

Analyze how multinational companies reposition their
profits, cash flows, and capital within their multinational
structures to maximize profitability, minimize global tax
liability, and optimize their use of capital

Describe the role that royalties and license fees play in
the repositioning strategies employed by MNEs

Learn how international dividend remittances are determined

Apply management guidelines to minimize the costs of
funding working capital requirements

Identify devices used to manage cross-border cash
settlement processes

Describe the different internal and external banking
and financial services that may be used by MNEs in the
conduct of global business

*Working capital management* in an MNE requires repositioning cash flows, as well as managing current assets and liabilities, when faced with political, foreign exchange, tax, and liquidity constraints. The overall goal is to reduce funds tied up in working capital while simultaneously providing sufficient funding and liquidity for the conduct of global business. This should enhance return on assets and return on equity. It also should improve efficiency ratios and other evaluation of performance parameters.

The first section of this chapter describes Trident's operating cycle. The second section analyzes Trident's fund repositioning decisions. The third section examines the constraints that affect the repositioning of Trident's funds. The fourth section identifies alternative conduits for moving funds. The fifth section introduces the management of net working capital, including accounts receivable, inventory, and cash. The sixth and final section examines how working capital is financed, including the various types of banking services available.

## Trident Brazil's Operating Cycle

The *operating* and *cash conversion cycles* for Trident Brazil are illustrated in Exhibit 21.1. The operating cycle can be decomposed into five periods, each with business, accounting, and potential cash flow implications.

### QUOTATION PERIOD

First noted in Chapter 8 when we introduced transaction exposure, the quotation period extends from the time of price quotation, $t_0$, to the point when the customer places an order, $t_1$. If the customer is requesting a price quote in foreign currency terms, say Chilean pesos, Trident Brazil would have a potential but uncertain foreign

**EXHIBIT 21.1**

Operating and Cash Cycles for Trident Brazil

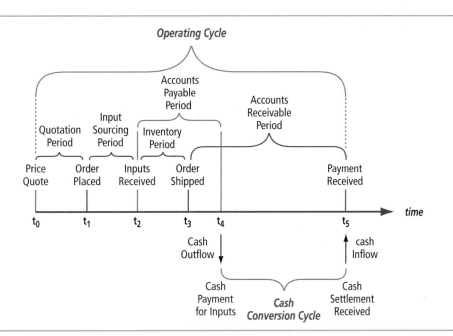

exchange transaction exposure. The quotation itself is not listed on any of the traditional financial statements of the firm, although a firm like Trident Brazil would keep a worksheet of quotations extended and their time periods.

## INPUT SOURCING PERIOD

Once a customer has accepted a quotation, the order is placed at time $t_1$. The buyer and seller sign a contract describing the product to be delivered, likely timing of delivery, conditions of delivery, and price and financing terms. At this time Trident Brazil would order the material inputs that it requires to manufacture the product that it does not currently hold in inventory. Depending on the individual sale, the buyer may make a cash deposit or down payment. This would constitute the first actual cash flow associated with the order, a cash inflow to Trident Brazil, and that would initiate the cash conversion cycle for this transaction.

## INVENTORY PERIOD

As it receives inputs, Trident Brazil assembles and manufactures the goods. The length of this inventory-manufacturing period, from $t_1$ to $t_2$, depends on the type of product (off-the-shelf versus custom built-to-specification), the supply-chain integration of Trident Brazil with its various internal and external suppliers, and the technology employed by Trident.

## ACCOUNTS PAYABLE PERIOD

As inputs arrive Trident lists them as material and component inventories on the left-hand side of Trident Brazil's balance sheet, with corresponding accounts payable entries on the right-hand side of the balance sheet. If the inputs are invoiced in foreign currencies, whether from Trident USA, a sister subsidiary, or external suppliers, they constitute foreign currency transaction exposures to Trident Brazil.

Note that the accounts payable period shown in Exhibit 21.1 begins at the same time as the inventory period, $t_2$, but may extend in time to $t_4$, after the inventory period ends. If Trident Brazil's suppliers extend trade credit, Trident Brazil would be able to postpone paying for the inventory for an extended period. Of course, if Trident Brazil chooses not to accept trade credit, it may pay for the inputs as delivered. In this case the accounts payable period would end before the inventory period — the manufacturing period — ends at time $t_3$. At whatever point in time Trident Brazil chooses to settle its outstanding accounts payable, it incurs a cash outflow.

## ACCOUNTS RECEIVABLE PERIOD

When the goods are finished and shipped, Trident Brazil records the transaction as a sale on its income statement and as an account receivable on its balance sheet. If it is a foreign currency-denominated invoice, the spot exchange rate on that date, $t_4$, is used to record the sale value in local currency. The exchange rate in effect on the date of cash settlement, $t_5$, would then be used in the calculation of any foreign exchange gains and losses associated with the transaction — the transaction exposure.

The length of the accounts receivable period depends on the credit terms offered by Trident Brazil, the choice made by the buyer to either accept trade credit or pay in cash, and country-specific and industry-specific payment practices. At cash settlement Trident Brazil receives a cash inflow (finally) in payment for goods delivered. At time

$t_5$ the transaction is concluded and all accounting entries — inventory items, accounts payable, accounts receivable — are eliminated.

## Trident's Repositioning Decisions

Next we describe the variety of goals and constraints on the repositioning of funds within Trident Corporation. Exhibit 21.2 depicts Trident, its wholly-owned subsidiaries, the currency and tax rates applicable to each unit, and management's present conclusions regarding each subsidiary's growth prospects. Trident's three foreign subsidiaries each present a unique set of concerns.

- **Trident Europe,** the oldest of the three, is operating in a relatively high-tax environment (compared in principle to the tax rate in the parent country, the United States). It is operating in a relatively stable currency — the euro — and is free to move capital in and out of the country with few restrictions. The business itself is mature, with few significant growth prospects in the near future.
- **Trident Brazil,** the result of a recent acquisition, is operating in a low-tax environment, but historically a volatile currency environment. It is subject to only a few current capital restrictions. Trident believes the business has very good growth prospects in the short to medium term if it is able to inject additional capital and managerial expertise into the business.

**EXHIBIT 21.2**

Trident's Foreign
Subsidiaries

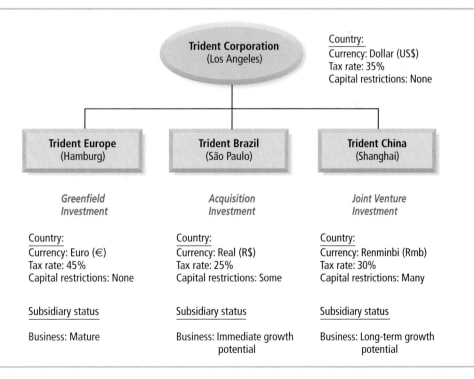

- **Trident China,** a new joint venture with an in-country partner that is a former unit of the Chinese government, is operating in a relatively low-tax environment, with a fixed exchange rate (the renminbi is managed within a very narrow band relative to the U.S. dollar). It is subject to a number of restrictions on capital. The business is believed to have the greatest potential — in the long run.

In practice, Trident's senior management in the parent company (*corporate*) will first determine its strategic objectives regarding the business developments in each subsidiary, and then design a financial management plan for the repositioning of profits, cash flows, and capital for each subsidiary. As a result of this process, Trident will now attempt to pursue the following repositioning objectives by subsidiary:

- **Trident Europe:** Reposition profits from Germany to the United States while maintaining the value of the European market's maturity to Trident Corporation.
- **Trident Brazil:** Reposition or in some way manage the capital at risk in Brazil subject to foreign exchange rate risk while providing adequate capital for immediate growth prospects.
- **Trident China:** Reposition the quantity of funds in and out of China to protect against blocked funds (transfer risk), while balancing the needs of the joint venture partner.

## Constraints on Repositioning Funds

Fund flows between units of a domestic business are generally unimpeded, but that is not the case in a multinational business. A firm operating globally faces a variety of political, tax, foreign exchange, and liquidity considerations which limit its ability to move funds easily and without cost from one country or currency to another. These constraints are why multinational financial managers must plan ahead for repositioning funds within an MNE. Advance planning is essential even when constraints do not exist, for at some future date political events may lead to unexpected restrictions.

### POLITICAL CONSTRAINTS

Political constraints can block the transfer of funds either overtly or covertly. Overt blockage occurs when a currency becomes inconvertible or is subject to government exchange controls that prevent its transfer at reasonable exchange rates. Covert blockage occurs when dividends or other forms of fund remittances are severely limited, heavily taxed, or excessively delayed by a bureaucratic approval process.

### TAX CONSTRAINTS

Tax constraints arise because of the complex and possibly contradictory tax structures of various national governments through whose jurisdictions funds might pass. A firm does not want funds in transit eroded by a sequence of nibbling tax collectors in every jurisdiction through which such funds might flow.

### TRANSACTION COSTS

Foreign exchange transaction costs are incurred when one currency is exchanged for another. These costs, in the form of fees and/or the difference between bid and offer quotations, are revenue for the commercial banks and dealers that operate the foreign exchange market. Although usually a small percentage of the amount of money exchanged, such costs become significant for large or frequent transfers. Transaction costs are sufficiently large enough to warrant planning to avoid unnecessary back-and-forth transfers such as would occur if a subsidiary remitted a cash dividend to its parent at approximately the same time as the parent paid the subsidiary for goods purchased. Sending foreign exchange simultaneously in two directions is obviously a sheer waste of corporate resources, but it sometimes occurs when one part of a firm is not coordinated with another.

## LIQUIDITY NEEDS

Despite the overall advantage of worldwide cash handling, liquidity needs in each individual location must be satisfied and good local banking relationships maintained. The size of appropriate balances is in part a judgmental decision not easily measurable. Nevertheless such needs constrain a pure optimization approach to worldwide cash positioning.

## Conduits for Moving Funds by Unbundling Them

Multinational firms often *unbundle* their transfer of funds into separate flows for specific purposes. Host countries are then more likely to perceive that a portion of what might otherwise be called *remittance of profits* constitutes an essential purchase of specific benefits that command worldwide values and benefit the host country. Unbundling allows a multinational firm to recover funds from subsidiaries without piquing host country sensitivities over large dividend drains. For example, Trident might transfer funds from its foreign subsidiaries to the parent, Trident Corporation, by any of the conduits shown in Exhibit 21.3.

**EXHIBIT 21.3**

Potential Conduits for Moving Funds from Subsidiary to Parent

The conduits are separable into those that are *before-tax* and *after-tax* in the host country. Although not always the focus of intraunit fund movement, tax goals frequently make this a critical distinction for foreign subsidiary financial structures. An increase in the funds flow (charges) in any of the before-tax categories reduces the taxable profits of the foreign subsidiary *if* the host country tax authorities acknowledge the charge as a legitimate expense. The before-tax/after-tax distinction is also quite significant to a parent company attempting to repatriate funds in the most tax-efficient method if it is attempting to manage its own foreign tax credit/deficits between foreign units.

An item-by-item matching of remittance to input, such as royalties for intellectual property with fees for patents and advice, is equitable to host country and foreign investor alike. It allows each party to see the reason for each remittance and to judge its acceptance independently. If all investment inputs are *unbundled*, part of what might have been classified as residual profits may turn out to be tax-deductible expenses related to a specific purchased benefit. Unbundling also facilitates allocation of overhead from a parent's international division, so-called *shared services*, to each operating subsidiary in accordance with a predetermined formula. Predetermination of the allocation method means a host country is less likely to view a given remittance as capricious and thus inappropriate. Finally, unbundling facilitates the entry of local capital into joint-venture projects, because total remuneration to different owners can be in proportion to the value of the varied contributions of each, rather than only in proportion to the amount of monetary capital they have invested.

## International Dividend Remittances

Payment of dividends is the classic method by which firms transfer profit back to owners, be those owners individual shareholders or parent corporations. International dividend policy now incorporates tax considerations, political risk, and foreign exchange risk, as well as a return for business guidance and technology.

### TAX IMPLICATIONS

Host country tax laws influence the dividend decision. Countries such as Germany tax retained earnings at one rate and distributed earnings at a lower rate. Most countries levy withholding taxes on dividends paid to foreign parent firms and investors. Again, most (but not all) parent countries levy a tax on foreign dividends received, but allow a *tax credit* for foreign taxes already paid on that income stream. That said, dividends remain the most tax inefficient method for repatriating funds because they are distributed on an after-tax basis. This means that the parent company will frequently be faced with the generation of excess foreign tax credits on a dividend. Remittance of license or royalty fees is on a pretax basis in the foreign subsidiary; the only tax typically applied is that of withholding, a rate considerably below that of corporate income taxes.

### POLITICAL RISK

Political risk may motivate parent firms to require foreign subsidiaries to remit all locally generated funds above that required to internally finance growth in sales (working capital requirements) and planned capital expansions (*capex* or capital expenditures). Such policies, however, are not universal.

One strategy employed by MNEs in response to potential government restrictions may be to maintain a constant dividend payout ratio so as to demonstrate that an established policy is being consistently carried out. This establishes a precedent for remittance of dividends and removes the perception of some host country governments that dividend distributions are by managerial election. (Note that even the terminology, *declare a dividend*, implies managerial discretion.)

## FOREIGN EXCHANGE RISK

If it anticipates a foreign exchange loss, an MNE may speed up the transfer of funds out of the country via dividends. This "lead" is usually part of a larger strategy of moving from weak currencies to strong currencies, and can include speeding up intrafirm payments on accounts receivable and payable. However, decisions to accelerate dividend payments ahead of what might be normal must take into account interest rate differences and the negative impact on host country relations.

## DISTRIBUTIONS AND CASH FLOWS

Dividends are a cash payment to owners equal to all or a portion of earnings of a prior period. To pay dividends, a subsidiary needs both past earnings and available cash. Subsidiaries sometimes have earnings without cash because earnings are measured at the time of a sale but cash is received later, when the receivable is collected (a typical distinction between accounting profits and cash flow). Profits of rapidly growing subsidiaries are often tied up in ever-increasing receivables and inventory (working capital). Hence rapidly growing foreign subsidiaries may lack the cash to remit a dividend equal to even a portion of earnings.

The reverse may also be true; firms may be receiving cash from the collection of old receivables even when profits are down because current sales have fallen off or current expenses have risen relative to current sales prices. Such firms might want to declare a dividend in order to remove a bountiful supply of cash from a country, but lack the earnings against which to charge such payments. For either of these reasons a firm must look at both measured earnings and available cash before settling on a cash dividend policy.

## JOINT VENTURE FACTORS

Existence of joint-venture partners or local stockholders also influences dividend policy. Optimal positioning of funds internationally cannot dominate the valid claims of independent partners or local stockholders for dividends. The latter do not benefit from the worldwide success of the MNE parent, but only from the success of the particular joint venture in which they own a share. Firms might hesitate to reduce dividends when earnings falter. They also might hesitate to increase dividends following a spurt in earnings because of possible adverse reaction to reducing dividends later should earnings decline. Many MNEs insist on 100% ownership of subsidiaries in order to avoid possible conflicts of interest with outside shareholders.

## Net Working Capital

If Trident Brazil's business continues to expand, it will continually add to inventories and accounts payable (A/P) in order to fill increased sales in the form of accounts receivable (A/R). These three components make up *net working capital* (NWC). The combination is "net" as a result of the spontaneous funding capability of accounts payable; accounts payable provide part of the funding for increased levels of inventory and accounts receivable.

$$\text{Net Working Capital (NWC)} = (\text{A/R} + \text{Inventory}) - (\text{A/P})$$

Because both A/R and inventory are components of current assets on the left-hand side of the balance sheet, as they grow they must be financed by additional liabilities of some form on the right-hand side of the balance sheet. A/P may provide a part of the funding. Exhibit 21.4 illustrates Trident Brazil's net working capital. Note that we do not include cash or short-term debt as part of net working capital. Although they are part of current assets and current liabilities, respectively, they are the result of management discretion, and do not spontaneously change with operations. Their determinates are discussed later in this chapter.

In principle, Trident attempts to minimize its net working capital balance. It reduces A/R if collections are accelerated. It reduces inventories by carrying lower levels of unfinished and finished goods, and by speeding the rate at which goods are manufactured — reducing so-called *cycle time*. All of these measures must be balanced with their customer costs. Sales could be reduced if inventories are not on hand, or if credit sales are reduced. On the other side of the balance sheet, NWC can be reduced by stretching A/P out. Again, if not done carefully, this could potentially damage the company's relationship with its key suppliers, thereby reducing reliability and supply-chain partnerships.

**EXHIBIT 21.4**

Trident Brazil's
Net Working
Capital
Requirements

*Net working capital (NWC) is the net investment required of the firm to support ongoing sales. NWC components typically grow as the firm buys inputs, produces products, and sells finished goods.*

Trident's Balance Sheet

Note that NWC is *not* the same as current assets and current liabilities.

## A/P VERSUS SHORT-TERM DEBT

Exhibit 21.4 also illustrates one of the key managerial decisions for any subsidiary: Should A/P be paid off early, taking discounts if offered by suppliers? The alternative financing for NWC balances is short-term debt.

For example, payment terms in Brazil are quite long by global standards, often extending 60 to 90 days. Paraña Electronics is one of Trident Brazil's key suppliers. It delivers a shipment of electronic components and invoices Trident Brazil R\$180,000. Paraña Electronics offers credit terms of 5/10 net 60. This means that the entire amount of the A/P, R\$180,000, is due in 60 days. Alternatively, if Trident Brazil wishes to pay within the first 10 days, a 5% discount is given:

$$R\$180,000 \times (1 - 0.05) = R\$171,000$$

Trident Brazil's financial manager, Maria Gonzalez, must decide which is the lower-cost method of financing the NWC. Short-term debt in Brazilian real, because of the relatively higher inflationary conditions common in Brazil, costs 24% per year.

What is the annual cost of the discount offered by Paraña Electronics? Trident Brazil is effectively paid 5% for giving up 50 days of financing (60 days less the 10-day period for discounts). Assuming a 365-day count for interest calculation,

$$\frac{365 \, \text{days}}{50 \, \text{days}} = 7.30$$

To calculate the effective annual interest cost of supplier financing, we must compound the 5% discount for 50 days 7.30 times, yielding a *cost of carry* provided by Paraña Electronics of

$$(1 + 0.05)^{7.3} = 1.428, \text{ or } 42.8\% \text{ per year}$$

Paraña Electronics is therefore charging Trident Brazil 42.8% per year for financing. Alternatively, Trident Brazil could borrow real from local banks in São Paulo for 24% per year, use the funds to pay Paraña Electronics early, and take the discounts offered. The latter is the obvious choice in this case.

The choice between taking supplier-provided financing and short-term debt is not always purely a matter of comparing interest costs. In many countries the foreign subsidiaries of foreign MNEs have limited access to local currency debt. In other cases, the subsidiary may be offered funds from the parent company at competitive rates. We will return to this topic, *internal banking*, in the last section of this chapter.

## DAYS WORKING CAPITAL

A common method of benchmarking working capital management practice is to calculate the NWC of the firm on a "days sales" basis. If the value of A/R, inventories, and A/P on the balance sheet are divided by the annual daily sales (annual sales/365 days), we can summarize the firm's NWC in the number of days of sales NWC constitutes. Exhibit 21.5 provides the results of a survey by *CFO Magazine* in both the United States and Europe in 2001 for the technology hardware and equipment industry segment.

**EXHIBIT 21.5**

Days Working Capital for Selected U.S. and European Technology Hardware and Equipment Firms, 2001

| Company | Country | Days working capital | Days receivables | Days inventory | Days payables |
|---|---|---|---|---|---|
| Intel Corporation | US | 48 | 47 | 21 | 20 |
| Cisco Systems | US | 54 | 46 | 20 | 12 |
| Dell Computer | US | (2) | 41 | 6 | 49 |
| Texas Instruments | US | 34 | 65 | 32 | 63 |
| Applied Materials | US | 41 | 82 | 52 | 93 |
| Apple Computer | US | 2 | 48 | 2 | 48 |
| Sun Microsystems | US | 58 | 67 | 12 | 21 |
| Gateway Inc. | US | 0 | 25 | 8 | 33 |
| Average | US | 29 | 53 | 19 | 42 |
| ST Microelectronics | France-Italy | 58 | 65 | 52 | 59 |
| Nokia | Finland | 66 | 72 | 31 | 37 |
| Philips Electronics | Netherlands | 71 | 59 | 51 | 39 |
| GN Store Nord | Denmark | 100 | 92 | 40 | 32 |
| Spirent | United Kingdom | 107 | 66 | 63 | 22 |
| Getronics | Netherlands | 51 | 80 | 20 | 49 |
| Infinecon Tech | Germany | 75 | 57 | 69 | 51 |
| Average | Europe | 75 | 70 | 47 | 41 |

Source: *CFO Magazine*, "2001 Working Capital Survey," July 2, 2001, and *CFO Europe Magazine*, "2001 Working Capital Survey," July/August 2001. Days working capital = days receivables + days inventory − days payables.

We must use care in viewing the survey results. First, the days sales values are for the consolidated companies, not specific country-level subsidiaries. Therefore the averages could reflect very different working capital structures for individual subsidiaries of the firms listed. Secondly, without knowing the specific business and country areas included, we have difficulty evaluating the short-term financing decisions discussed in the previous section as made by management of the listed firms.

Despite these reservations, there are some clear differences between the U.S. and European averages, as well as between individual firms. The days working capital average for the selected U.S. firms of 29 days is less than half the 75 days for the European sample. A closer look at the subcategories indicates a radically sparse attitude toward inventory among the U.S. firms, averaging 19 days sales. Days sales held in accounts receivable at 53 days on average is nearly 20 days less than the European average of 70. Payables are essentially identical between the two groups. Clearly, European-based technology hardware firms are carrying a significantly higher level of net working capital in their financial structures than comparable U.S.–based firms to support the same level of sales.

Among individual firms, Dell lives up to its billing as one of the most aggressive working capital managers across all industries. Dell's net working capital level of negative two days indicates exactly what it says — a level of A/P which surpasses the sum of receivables and inventory. Even with that accomplishment, its inventory days of six is still three times that of Apple Computer's two days in inventory.

## INTRAFIRM WORKING CAPITAL

The MNE itself poses some unique challenges in the management of working capital. Many multinationals manufacture goods in a few specific countries and then ship the intermediate products to other facilities globally for completion and distribution. The payables, receivables, and inventory levels of the various units are a combination of intrafirm and interfirm. The varying business practices observed globally regarding payment terms — both days and discounts — create severe mismatches in some cases.

For example, Exhibit 21.6 illustrates the challenges in working capital management faced by Trident Brazil. Because Trident Brazil purchases inputs from Trident USA and then uses additional local material input to finish the products for local distribution, it must manage two different sets of payables. Trident USA sells intrafirm on common U.S. payment terms, net 30 days. Local suppliers in Brazil, however, use payment terms closer to Brazilian norms of 60 days net (although this is in many cases still quite short for Brazilian practices, which have been known to extend to as long as 180 days). Similarly, since the customers of Trident Brazil are Brazilian, they expect the same common payment terms of 60 days. Trident Brazil is then "squeezed," having to pay Trident USA much faster than it pays other local suppliers and long before it receives cash settlement from its customers.

In addition to Trident's need to determine intrafirm payment practices that do not put undue burdens on their foreign subsidiaries, the question of currency of invoice will also be extremely important. If Trident Brazil sells only domestically, it does not have natural inflows of U.S. dollars or other hard currencies — it earns only Brazilian real. If Trident USA then invoices it for inputs in U.S. dollars, Trident Brazil will be constantly short dollars and will incur continuing currency management costs. Trident USA should invoice in Brazilian real and manage the currency exposure centrally (possibly through a reinvoicing center, as discussed in Chapter 8).

**EXHIBIT 21.6**

Trident's Multinational Working Capital Sequence

Cash inflows to Trident Brazil arise from local market sales. These cash flows are used to repay both intrafirm payables (to Trident USA) and local suppliers.

**Brazilian Business Practices**
Payment terms in Brazil are longer than those typical of North America. Trident Brazil must offer 60-day terms to local customers to be competitive with other firms in the local market.

**U.S. Business Practices**
Payment terms used by Trident USA are typical of North America, 30 days. Trident USA's local customers will expect to be paid in 30 days. Trident USA may consider extending longer terms to Brazil to reduce the squeeze.

**Result:** Trident Brazil is squeezed in terms of cash flow. It receives inflows in 60 days but must pay Trident USA in 30 days.

## MANAGING RECEIVABLES

A firm's operating cash inflow is derived primarily from collecting its accounts receivable. Multinational accounts receivable are created by two separate types of transactions: sales to related subsidiaries and sales to independent or unrelated buyers.

**INDEPENDENT CUSTOMERS.**    Management of accounts receivable from independent customers involves two types of decisions: In what currency should the transaction be denominated, and what should be the terms of payment? Domestic sales are almost always denominated in the local currency. At issue is whether export sales should be denominated in the currency of the exporter, the currency of the buyer, or a third-country currency. Competition or custom will often dictate the answer, but if negotiating room exists, the seller prefers to price and to invoice in the strongest currency, while an informed buyer prefers to pay in the weakest currency.

**PAYMENT TERMS.**    Terms of payment are another bargaining factor. Considered by themselves, receivables from sales in weak currencies should be collected as soon as possible to minimize loss of exchange value between sales date and collection date. Accounts receivable resulting from sales in hard currencies may be allowed to remain outstanding longer. In fact, if the seller is expecting an imminent devaluation of its home currency, it might want to encourage slow payment of its hard currency receivables, especially if the home government requires immediate exchange of foreign currency receipts into the home currency. An alternative, if legal, would be for the seller to accept the proceeds abroad and keep them on deposit abroad rather than return them to the home country.

In inflationary economies, the demand for credit usually exceeds the supply. Often, however, a large business (be it multinational or a large local concern) has better access to the limited, cheaper credit that is available locally than do smaller domestic businesses, such as local distributors, retail merchants, or smaller manufacturers.

**SELF-LIQUIDATING BILLS.**    Some banking systems, often for reasons of tradition, have a predilection toward self-liquidating, discountable bills. In many European countries it is easier to borrow from a bank on the security of bills (receivables in negotiable form) generated from sales than on the security of physical inventory. Napoleon is alleged to have had a philosophy that no good French merchant should be required to wait for funds if good merchandise has been sold to good people, provided a document exists showing sales of the items. The document must have the signature of the buyer and the endorsement of the seller and the rediscounting bank. Thus in France it is often possible to reduce net investment in receivables to zero by selling entirely on trade acceptances that can be discounted at the bank

The European use of discountable bills has a very real rationale behind it. According to European commercial law, based on the Code Napoleon, the claim certified by the signature of the buyer on the bill is separated from the claim based on the underlying transaction. For example, a bill is easily negotiable because objections about the quality of the merchandise by the buyer do not affect the claim of the bill holder. In addition, defaulted bills can be collected through a particularly speedy judicial process that is much faster than the collection of normal receivables.

**OTHER TERMS.**    In many countries government bodies facilitate inventory financing in the guise of receivable financing by extending export credit or by guaranteeing export credit from banks at advantageous interest rates. When the term of the special export financing can be extended to match the payment of the foreign purchaser, the foreign purchaser is in effect able to finance its inventory through the courtesy of the exporter's government.

In some environments credit terms extended by manufacturers to retailers are of such long maturities as to constitute "purchase" of the retailer, such "purchase" being necessary to build an operational distribution system between manufacturer and ultimate customer. In Japan, for example, customer payment terms of 120 days are fairly common, and a manufacturer's sales effort is not competitive unless sufficient financial aid is provided to retailers to make it possible or beneficial for them to buy the manufacturer's product. Financial aid is reported to take the form of outright purchase of the retailer's capital stock, working capital loans, equipment purchase, subsidy or loan, and consideration of payment terms. Such manufacturer-supplied financing is a normal way of doing business in Japan — and contributes to the lack of domestic competition prevalent in that country.

## INVENTORY MANAGEMENT

Operations in inflationary, devaluation-prone economies sometimes force management to modify its normal approach to inventory management. In some cases management may choose to maintain inventory and reorder levels far in excess of what would be called for in an economic order-quantity model.

Under conditions where local currency devaluation is likely, management must decide whether to build up inventory of imported items in anticipation of the expected devaluation. After the devaluation, imported inventory will cost more in local currency terms. One tradeoff is a higher holding cost because of the bloated level of inventory and high local interest rates that normally reflect the expected devaluation. A less obvious tradeoff is the possibility that local government will enforce a price freeze following devaluation. This freeze would prevent the imported inventory from being sold for an appropriate markup above its now-higher replacement value. Still worse, the devaluation may not occur as anticipated, leaving management holding an excessive level of inventory until it can be worked down. Disposing of excessive inventory will be particularly painful if competitors have followed the same strategy of speculating on imported inventory.

## FREE-TRADE ZONES AND FREE INDUSTRIAL ZONES

A *free-trade zone* combines the old idea of duty-free ports with legislation that reduces or eliminates customs duties to retailers or manufacturers who structure their operations to benefit from the technique. Income taxes may also be reduced for operations in a free-trade zone. The old duty-free ports, typically located in the dock area of major seaports, were where goods were held, duty free, until the owner was ready to deliver them within the country. Modern free-trade zones, by comparison, are often located away from a port area. For example, the Italian firm of Olivetti has such a zone in Harrisburg, Pennsylvania.

Free-trade zones function in several ways. As mentioned, they may be a place to off-load merchandise for subsequent sale within the country where the zone is located. An example of such a zone would be a storage area for imported Toyota automobiles in the Port of Los Angeles. A large quantity of differentiated models can be held until sold by a dealer, at which time the cars are "imported" into the United States from the free-trade zone. The advantage of such an arrangement is that a variety of models can be kept near the point of sale for quick delivery, but import duties need be paid only when the merchandise passes from the zone into California.

A second type of zone involves the assembly of components for subsequent sale within the country where the zone is located. An example would be the Mercedes assembly line in Alabama. Components are imported into the free-trade zone where assembly work is finished. The import duty is paid only when the finished car is removed from the zone. Furthermore the duty is lower than it would be for a finished car because the charges on components are less than the charge on a finished vehicle.

A third type of zone is a full-fledged manufacturing center with a major portion of its output reexported out of the country. Two examples are Penang, Malaysia, and Madagascar, where such zones are officially designated "free industrial zones." In Penang, companies as diverse as Dell, National Semiconductor, Sony, Bosch, and Trane Air Conditioning manufacture final products. A major portion of production is reexported, avoiding Malaysian customs altogether but providing jobs for Malaysian workers and engineers. The portion of production sold in Malaysia is assessed duties only on the components originally imported. However, the variety of firms permits one to buy from another; Dell buys Pentium chips from Intel and disk drives from Seagate, both of which are located less than a mile from the Dell plant.

## International Cash Management

*International cash management* is the set of activities determining the levels of cash balances held throughout the MNE, and the facilitation of its movement cross-border. These activities are typically handled by the international treasury of the MNE.

### MOTIVES FOR HOLDING CASH

The level of cash maintained by an individual subsidiary is determined independently of the working capital management decisions discussed previously. Cash balances, including marketable securities, are held partly to enable normal day-to-day cash disbursements and partly to protect against unanticipated variations from budgeted cash flows. These two motives are called the *transaction motive* and the *precautionary motive*.

Cash disbursed for operations is replenished from two sources: (1) internal working capital turnover, and (2) external sourcing, traditionally short-term borrowing. Short-term borrowing can also be "negative," as when excess cash is used to repay outstanding short-term loans. In general, individual subsidiaries of MNEs typically maintain only minimal cash balances necessary to meet the transaction purposes. Efficient cash management aims to reduce cash tied up unnecessarily in the system, without diminishing profit or increasing risk, so as to increase the rate of return on invested assets.

### INTERNATIONAL CASH SETTLEMENTS AND PROCESSING

Multinational business increases the complexity of making payments and settling cash flows between related and unrelated firms. Over time a number of techniques and services have evolved that simplify and reduce the costs of making these cross-border payments. We focus here on four such techniques: wire transfers, cash pooling, payment netting, and electronic fund transfers.

## WIRE TRANSFERS

Although there are a variety of computer-based networks used for effecting international transactions and settlements, two have come to dominate the international financial sector, CHIPS and SWIFT. The primary distinction among systems is whether they are for secure communications alone, or for actual transfer and settlement.

**CHIPS.** CHIPS, the Clearing House Interbank Payment System, is a computerized network that connects major banks globally. CHIPS is owned and operated by its member banks, making it the single largest privately operated and final-payments system in the world. Developed in 1970 when international currency transactions were dominated by the U.S. dollar, CHIPS has continued to dominate the transfer and settlement of U.S. dollar transactions for more than 34 years.

CHIPS is actually a subsidiary of the New York Clearing House, the oldest and largest payments processor of bank transactions. The New York Clearing House was first established in 1853 to provide a central place — a clearinghouse — where all banks in New York City could daily settle transactions, such as the many personal checks written by private individuals and corporations, among themselves. CHIPS itself is simply a computer-based evolutionary result of this need. Because banks are still the primary financial service provider for MNEs, businesses transferring payments both interfirm and intrafirm globally use banks for effecting the payments and the banks in turn utilize CHIPS.

**SWIFT.** The Society for Worldwide Interbank Financial Telecommunications, SWIFT, also facilitates the wire transfer settlement process globally. Whereas CHIPS actually clears financial transactions, SWIFT is purely a communications system. By providing a secure and standardized transfer process, SWIFT has greatly reduced the errors and associated costs of effecting international cash transfers.

In recent years SWIFT has expanded its messaging services beyond banks to broker-dealers and investment managers. In the mid-1990s its services gained wider breadth as SWIFT expanded market infrastructure to payments in treasury, derivatives, and securities and trade services. It is now in the forefront of the evolution of Internet-based products and services for e-payments, expanding beyond banks to non-financial sector customers conducting business-to-business electronic commerce.

## CASH POOLING AND CENTRALIZED DEPOSITORIES

Any business with widely dispersed operating subsidiaries can gain operational benefits by centralizing cash management. Internationally the procedure calls for each subsidiary to hold minimum cash for its own transactions and no cash for precautionary purposes. However, the central pool has authority to override this general rule. All excess funds are remitted to a central cash depository, where a single authority invests the funds in such currencies and money market instruments as best serve the worldwide firm.

A central depository provides an MNE with at least four advantages:

1. Obtaining information
2. Holding precautionary cash balances

3. Reducing interest rate costs

4. Locating cost in desirable financial centers

**INFORMATION ADVANTAGE.**     A central depository's size gives it an advantage in obtaining information. It should be located in one of the world's major financial centers so information needed for opinions about the relative strengths and weaknesses of various currencies can easily be obtained. Rate of return and risk information on alternative investments in each currency and facilities for executing orders must also be available. The information logic of centralization is that an office that specializes and operates with larger sums of money can get better information from banks, brokers, and other financial institutions, as well as better service in executing orders.

**PRECAUTIONARY BALANCE ADVANTAGE.**     A second reason for holding all precautionary balances in a central pool is that the total pool, if centralized, can be reduced in size without any loss in the level of protection. Trident USA, for example, has subsidiaries in Europe, Brazil, and China. Assume each of these subsidiaries maintains its own precautionary cash balance equal to its expected cash needs plus a safety margin of three standard deviations of historical variability of actual cash demands. Cash needs are assumed to be normally distributed in each country, and the needs are independent from one country to another. Three standard deviations means there exists a 99.87% chance that actual cash needs will be met; that is, only a 0.13% chance that any European subsidiary will run out of cash.

Cash needs of the individual subsidiaries, and the total precautionary cash balances held, are shown in Exhibit 21.7. Total precautionary cash balances held by Trident Europe, Brazil, and China, add up to $46,000,000, consisting of $28,000,000 in expected cash needs, and $18,000,000 in idle cash balances (the sum of three standard deviations of individual expected cash balances) held as a safety margin.

What would happen if the three Trident subsidiaries maintained all precautionary balances in a single account with Trident USA? Because variances are additive when probability distributions are independent (see footnote b to Exhibit 21.7), cash needed would drop from $46,000,000 to $39,224,972, calculated as follows:

| Centralized cash balance | = | Sum of expected cash needs | + | Three standard deviations of expected sum |
|---|---|---|---|---|
| | = | $28,000,000 | + | $(3 \times \$3,741,657)$ |
| | = | $28,000,000 | + | $11,224,972 |
| | = | $39,224,972 | | |

A budgeted cash balance three standard deviations above the aggregate expected cash need requires only $11,224,972 in potentially idle cash, as opposed to the previous cash balance of $18,000,000. Trident saves $6,755,028 in cash balances without reducing its safety.

**INTEREST RATE ADVANTAGE.**     A third advantage of centralized cash management is that one subsidiary will not borrow at high rates at the same that another holds surplus funds idle or invests them at low rates. Managers of the central pool can locate the least expensive locations to borrow and the most advantageous returns to be earned

## EXHIBIT 21.7

Decentralized versus Centralized Cash Depositories

### DECENTRALIZED CASH DEPOSITORIES

| Subsidiary | Expected cash need (A) | One standard deviation (B) | Cash balance budgeted for adequate protection[a] (A + 3B) |
|---|---|---|---|
| Trident Europe | $10,000,000 | $1,000,000 | $13,000,000 |
| Trident Brazil | 6,000,000 | 2,000,000 | 12,000,000 |
| Trident China | 12,000,000 | 3,000,000 | 21,000,000 |
| Total | $28,000,000 | $ 6,000,000 | $46,000,000 |

### CENTRALIZED CASH DEPOSITORY

| Subsidiary | Expected cash need (A) | One standard deviation (B) | Cash balance budgeted for adequate protection[a] (A + 3B) |
|---|---|---|---|
| Trident Europe | $10,000,000 | | |
| Trident Brazil | 6,000,000 | | |
| Trident China | 12,000,000 | | |
| Total | $28,000,000 | $ 3,741,657[b] | $39,224,972 |

[a] Adequate protection is defined as the expected cash balance plus three standard deviations, assuming that the cash flows of all three individual units are normally distributed.

[b] The standard deviation of the expected cash balance of the centralized depository is calculated as follows:

$$\text{Standard deviation} = \sqrt{(1,000,000)^2 + (2,000,000)^2 + (3,000,000)^2} = \$3,741,657$$

on excess funds. When additional cash is needed, the central pool manager determines the location of such borrowing. A local subsidiary manager can avoid borrowing at a rate above the minimum available to the pool manager. If the firm has a worldwide cash surplus, the central pool manager can evaluate comparative rates of return in various markets, transaction costs, exchange risks, and tax effects.

**LOCATION.**    Central money pools are usually maintained in major money centers such as London, New York, Zurich, Singapore, and Tokyo. Additional popular locations for money pools include Liechtenstein, Luxembourg, the Bahamas, and Bermuda. Although these countries do not have strong diversified economies, they offer most of the other prerequisites for a corporate financial center: freely convertible currency, political and economic stability, access to international communications, and clearly defined legal procedures. Their additional advantage as a so-called tax haven is desirable.

The need for a centralized depository system means that multinational banks have an advantage over single-country banks in designing and offering competitive services. However single-country banks can be incorporated into the system if the desired results can still be achieved, for the essence of the operation is centralized information and decisions. MNEs can place actual funds in as many banks as they desire.

## MULTILATERAL NETTING

*Multilateral netting* is defined as the process that cancels, via offset, all or part of the debt owed by one entity to another related entity. Multilateral netting of payments is useful primarily when a large number of separate foreign exchange transactions occur between subsidiaries in the normal course of business. Netting reduces the settlement cost of what would otherwise be a large number of crossing spot transactions.

Multilateral netting is an extension of bilateral netting. Assume Trident Brazil owes Trident China $5,000,000, and Trident China simultaneously owes Trident Brazil $3,000,000. A bilateral settlement calls for a single payment of $2,000,000 from Brazil to China and the cancellation, via offset, of the remainder of the debt.

A multilateral system is an expanded version of this simple bilateral concept. Assume that payments are due between Trident's operations at the end of each month. Each obligation reflects the accumulated transactions of the prior month. These obligations for a particular month might be as shown in Exhibit 21.8.

Without netting, Trident Brazil makes three separate payments and receives three separate receipts at the end of the month. If Trident Brazil paid its intracompany obligations daily, or even weekly, rather than accumulating a balance to settle at the end of the month, it would generate a multitude of costly small bank transactions. The daily totals would add up to the monthly accumulated balances shown in the diagram.

In order to reduce bank transaction costs, such as the spread between foreign exchange bid and ask quotations and transfer fees, MNEs like Trident establish in-house multilateral netting centers. Other firms contract with banks to manage their netting system. Assume that Trident's net intracompany obligations for a given month can be summarized as in Exhibit 21.9.

**EXHIBIT 21.8**

Multilateral Matrix Before Netting (Thousands of U.S. Dollars)

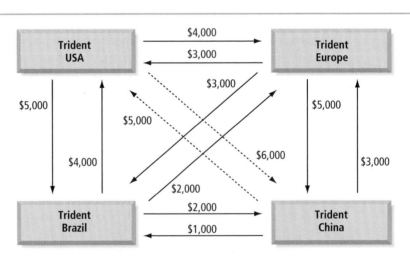

Prior to netting, the four sister Trident companies have numerous intrafirm payments between them. Each payment results in transfer charges.

**EXHIBIT 21.9**

Calculation of Trident Intrasubsidiary Net Obligations (Thousands of U.S. Dollars)

| Receiving Subsidiary | Paying Subsidiary | | | | Total receipts | Net receipts (payments) |
|---|---|---|---|---|---|---|
| | USA | Brazil | Europe | China | | |
| USA | — | $4,000 | $3,000 | $5,000 | $12,000 | ($3,000) |
| Brazil | 5,000 | — | 3,000 | 1,000 | 9,000 | $1,000 |
| Europe | 4,000 | 2,000 | — | 3,000 | 9,000 | ($2,000) |
| China | 6,000 | 2,000 | 5,000 | | 13,000 | $4,000 |
| Total payments | $15,000 | $8,000 | $11,000 | $9,000 | $43,000 | — |

Note that payment obligations and expected receipts add up to $43,000,000 because one subsidiary's debts are another's receivables. If the cost of foreign exchange transactions and transfer fees were 0.5%, the total cost of settlement would be $205,000. Using information from the netting matrix in Exhibit 21.9, the netting center at Trident USA can order three payments to settle the entire set of obligations. Trident USA will itself remit $3,000,000 to China, and Europe will be instructed to send $1,000,000 each to Brazil and China. Total foreign exchange transfers are reduced to $5,000,000, and transaction costs at 0.5% are reduced to $25,000. This is shown in Exhibit 21.10.

Some countries limit or prohibit netting, while others permit netting on a "gross payment" basis only. For a single settlement period all payments may be combined into a single payment, and all receipts will be received as a single transfer. However, these two may not be netted and thus must pass through the local banking system.

**EXHIBIT 21.10**

Multilateral Matrix After Netting (Thousands of U.S. Dollars)

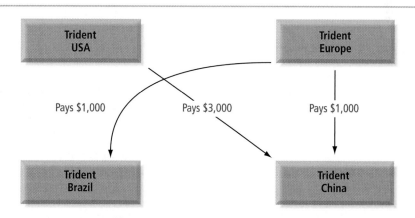

After netting, the four sister Trident companies have only three net payments to make among themselves to settle all intrafirm obligations.

## Financing Working Capital

The MNE enjoys a much greater choice of banking sources to fund its working capital needs than do domestic firms. Banking sources available to MNEs include in-house banks funded by unrepatriated capital, international banks, and local banks where subsidiaries are located. In-house banks and the various types of external commercial banking offices are described in the remainder of this chapter.

### IN-HOUSE BANKS

Some MNEs have found that their financial resources and needs are either too large or too sophisticated for the financial services available in many locations where they operate. One solution to this has been the establishment of an *in-house* or *internal bank* within the firm. An in-house bank is not a separate corporation; rather, it is a set of functions performed by the existing treasury department. Acting as an independent entity, the central treasury of the firm transacts with the various business units of the firm on an arm's length basis. The purpose of the in-house bank is to provide bank-like services to the various units of the firm. The in-house bank may be able to provide services not available in many countries, and do so at lower cost when they are available. In addition to traditional banking activities, the in-house bank may be able to offer services to units of the firm which aid in the management of ongoing transaction exposures. Lastly, because it is in-house, credit analysis is not a part of the bank's decision making.

For example, the in-house bank of Trident Corporation could work with Trident Europe and Trident Brazil. Trident Brazil sells all its receivables to the in-house bank as they arise, reducing some of its domestic working capital needs. Additional working capital needs are supplied by the in-house bank directly to Trident Brazil. Because the in-house bank is part of the same company, interest rates it charges may be significantly lower than what Trident Brazil could obtain on its own. The source of funds for the in-house bank may arise from the deposits of excess cash balances from Trident Europe. If the in-house bank can pay Trident Europe a higher deposit rate than it could obtain on its own, and if the in-house bank can lend these funds to Trident Brazil at an interest rate lower than it could obtain on its own in Brazil, then both operating units benefit. Assuming the loan rate is greater than the deposit rate, the in-house bank profits by the margin between the two, but this margin or spread must be smaller than would be available from a commercial bank.

How can the in-house bank operate with a smaller spread than a regular commercial bank? First, its costs are lower because it does not have to conform to the stringent capital requirements imposed on commercial banks worldwide. Second, in-house banks do not have the overhead costs of supporting large dealing rooms, branch networks, retail "store fronts," and other services required for commercial bank competitiveness. Third, they need not assess the creditworthiness of the corporate units with which they deal, since the units are all in the same family. Nor need they provide for credit losses.

In addition to providing financing benefits, in-house banks allow for more effective currency risk management. In the case of Trident Brazil, the sale of foreign currency receivables to the in-house bank shifts transaction exposure to the bank. The in-house bank is better equipped to deal with currency exposures and has a greater volume of international cash flows allowing Trident USA overall to gain from more effective use of netting and matching. This frees the units of the firm from struggling to manage transaction exposures and allows them to focus on their primary business activities.

## COMMERCIAL BANKING OFFICES

MNEs depend on their commercial banks to handle most of their trade financing needs, such as letters of credit, but also to provide advice on government support, country risk assessment, introductions to foreign firms and banks, and general financing availability. MNEs interface with their banks through a variety of types of banking offices, many of which perform specialized functions. Therefore it is important for financial managers to understand which bank offices provide which kinds of activities. The main points of bank contact are with correspondent banks, representative offices, branch banks, and subsidiaries. In the United States, a more specialized banking facility is available: the Edge Act Corporation.

**CORRESPONDENT BANKS.** Most major banks of the world maintain correspondent banking relationships with local banks in each of the major foreign cities of the world. The two-way link between banks is essentially one of correspondence via fax, cable, and mail, and a mutual deposit relationship. For example, a U.S. bank may have a correspondent bank in Kuala Lumpur, Malaysia, and the U.S. bank will in turn be the correspondent bank for the Malaysian bank. Each will maintain a deposit in the other in local currency.

Correspondent services include accepting drafts, honoring letters of credit, and furnishing credit information. Services are centered around collecting or paying foreign funds, often because of import or export transactions. However, a visiting business person can use the home bank's introduction to meet local bankers. Under a correspondent banking relationship neither of the correspondent banks maintains its own personnel in the other country. Direct contact between the banks is usually limited to periodic visits between members of the banks' management.

For the business person the main advantage of banking at home with a bank having a large number of foreign correspondent relationships is having the ability to handle financial matters in a large number of foreign countries through local bankers whose knowledge of local customs should be extensive. The disadvantages are the lack of ability to deposit in, borrow from, or disburse from a branch of one's own home bank. There is a possibility that correspondents will put a lower priority on serving the foreign banks' customer than on serving their own permanent customers.

**REPRESENTATIVE OFFICES.** A bank establishes a representative office in a foreign country primarily to help parent bank clients when they are doing business in that country or in neighboring countries. It also functions as a geographically convenient location from which to visit correspondent banks in its region rather than sending bankers from the parent bank at greater financial and physical cost. A representative office is not a bank office. It cannot accept deposits, make loans, commit the parent bank to a loan, or deal in drafts, letters of credit, or the Eurocurrency market. Indeed, a tourist cannot even cash a traveler's check from the parent bank in the representative office.

If the parent bank eventually decides to open a local general banking office, the existence of a representative office for some prior period usually provides a valuable base of contacts and expertise to facilitate the change. However, representative offices are not necessarily a prelude to a general banking office, nor need an eventual general banking office be the major reason for opening a representative office.

**BRANCH BANKS.** A foreign branch bank is a legal and operational part of the parent bank, with the full resources of that parent behind the local office. A branch bank does not have its own corporate charter, its own board of directors, or any shares of stock outstanding. Although for managerial and regulatory purposes it will maintain its own set of books, its assets and liabilities are in fact those of the parent bank. However, branch deposits are not subject to reserve requirements or FDIC insurance, in the case of U.S. banks, unless the deposits are reloaned to the U.S. parent bank.

Branch banks are subject to two sets of banking regulations. As part of the parent, they are subject to home-country regulations. However, they are also subject to regulations of the host country, which may provide any of a variety of restrictions on their operations.

The major advantage to a business of using a branch bank is that the branch will conduct a full range of banking services under the name and legal obligation of the parent. A deposit in a branch is a legal obligation of the parent. Services to customers are based on the worldwide value of the client relationship rather than just on the relationship to the local office. Legal loan limits are a function of the size of the parent, not of the branch.

From the point of view of a banker, the profits of a foreign branch are subject to immediate taxation at home, and losses of a foreign branch are deductible against taxable income at home. A new office expected to have losses in its early years creates a tax advantage if it is initially organized as a branch, even if eventually the intent is to change it to a separately incorporated subsidiary. From an organizational point of view a foreign branch is usually simpler to create and staff than is a separately incorporated subsidiary.

The major disadvantage of a branch bank is one that accrues to the bank rather than to its customers. The parent bank (not just the branch) may be sued at the local level for debts or other activities of the branch.

**BANKING SUBSIDIARIES.**   A subsidiary bank is a separately incorporated bank, owned entirely or in major part by a foreign parent, that conducts a general banking business. As a separate corporation, the banking subsidiary must comply with all the laws of the host country. Its lending limit is based on its own equity capital rather than that of the parent bank. This limits its ability to service large borrowers, but local incorporation also limits the liability of the parent bank to its equity investment in the subsidiary.

A foreign banking subsidiary often appears as a local bank in the eyes of potential customers in host countries and is thus often able to attract additional local deposits. This will especially be true if the bank was independent prior to being purchased by the foreign parent. Management may well be local, giving the bank greater access to the local business community. A foreign-owned bank subsidiary is more likely to be involved in both domestic and international business than is a foreign branch, which is more likely to appeal to the foreign business community but may well encounter difficulty in attracting banking business from local firms.

**EDGE ACT CORPORATIONS.**   Edge Act corporations are subsidiaries of U.S. banks, incorporated in the United States under Section 25 of the Federal Reserve Act as amended, to engage in international banking and financing operations. Not only may such subsidiaries engage in general international banking, they may also finance commercial, industrial, or financial projects in foreign countries through long-term loans or equity participation. Such participation, however, is subject to the day-to-day practices and policies of the Federal Reserve System.

Edge Act corporations generally engage in two types of activities: direct international banking, including acting as a holding company for the stock of one or more foreign banking subsidiaries, and financing development activities not closely related to traditional banking operations.

## MINI-CASE

# Honeywell and Pakistan International Airways

The Space and Avionics Control Group (SAC) of Honeywell, Incorporated (USA) was quite frustrated in June of 1997. The cockpit retrofit proposal with Pakistan International Airlines had been under negotiation for seven months, and over the past weekend a new request had been thrown in — to accept payment in Pakistan rupee. This was against corporate policy at Honeywell, but if an exception was not made, the deal — worth $23.7 million — was most likely dead.

## Pakistan International Airlines (PIA)

Pakistan International Airlines Corporation (PIA) was the national carrier of the Islamic Republic of Pakistan. Founded in 1954, PIA operated scheduled passenger and cargo services. The firm was 57% state owned, with the remaining 43% held by private investors internal to Pakistan.

PIA's fleet was aging. Although the airline had planned a significant modernization program, recent restrictions placed on government spending by the International Monetary Fund (IMF) had killed the program. With the cancellation of the fleet modernization program, PIA now had to move fast to ensure compliance with U.S. Federal Aviation Administration (FAA) safety mandates. If it did not comply with the FAA mandates for quieter engines and upgraded avionics by June 30, 1998, PIA would be locked out of its very profitable U.S. gates. PIA would first retrofit the aircraft utilized on the long-haul flights to the United States, primarily the Boeing 747 classics. Due to SAC's extensive experience with a variety of control systems for Boeing and its recent work on cockpit retrofit for McDonnell Douglas aircraft, SAC felt it was the preferred supplier for PIA. However, SAC had not undertaken Boeing cockpit retrofits to date (no one had), and looked to the PIA deal as an opportunity to build a new competitive base. PIA's insistence on payment in local currency terms was now thought to be a tactic to extract better concessions from SAC and their agent, Makran.

## Ibrahim Makran Pvt. Ltd

In countries like Pakistan, the use of an agent is often considered a necessary evil. The agent can often help to bridge two business cultures and provide invaluable information, but at some cost. Honeywell's agent, Ibrahim Makran Pvt. Ltd., based in Hyderabad, was considered one of the most reliable and well connected in Pakistan. Makran traced its roots back to a long association with the Sperry Aerospace and Marine Group, the precursor to Honeywell's SAC unit (Sperry was acquired in 1986). Makran was also one of the largest import/export trading houses in Pakistan. It was 100% family-owned and managed.

Standard practice in the avionics business was to provide the agent with a 10% commission, although this was negotiable. The 10% was based on the final sales and was paid after all payments were received. Typically it was the agent who spotted the business opportunity and submitted a proposal to SAC Marketing.

When PIA contacted Makran regarding their latest demand, Makran knew that SAC would want to maintain the deal in U.S. dollars. Makran had therefore inquired as to the availability of dollar funds for a deal of this size from its own finance department. The finance department confirmed that they had the necessary U.S. dollar funds to pay SAC, but warned that policy was to charge 5% for services rendered and currency risks.

Makran advised SAC that it would be willing to purchase the receivable for an additional 5% (in addition to the 10% commission). Makran's U.S. subsidiary in Los Angeles would credit SAC within 30 days of SAC invoicing Makran. PIA advised Makran that if SAC accepted payment in Pakistan rupees, then local (Pakistan) payment terms would apply. This meant 180 days in principle, but often was much longer in practice. The agent also advised SAC that the Pakistan rupee was due for another devaluation. When pressed for more information, Makran simply replied that the company president, the elder Ibrahim Makran, had "good connections."

## Pakistan Rupee

A central part of the IMF's austerity program was a devaluation of the Pakistan rupee by 7.86% against the U.S. dollar on October 22, 1996. Now, roughly six months later, there was renewed speculation that another devaluation was imminent in order to limit imports and help the export sector earn badly needed hard currency. Another recent economic setback had been the ruling by the European Union that Pakistan was guilty of dumping cotton, and had imposed anti-dumping fines on Pakistani cotton. This was a painful blow to the export sector. The current exchange rate of 40.4795 Pakistan rupee (Rp) per dollar was maintained by the Pakistani Central Bank. The parallel market rate — *the black market rate* — was approaching Rp50/US$. At present, there was no forward market for the Pakistan rupee.

## Honeywell's Working Capital

Honeywell's finance department was attempting to reduce net working capital and had just concluded a thorough review of existing payment terms and worldwide days sales receivable (DSR) rates. The department's goal was to reduce worldwide DSR rates from 55 to 45 days in the current fiscal year. The *pay for performance* target for the current year (the annual performance bonus system at Honeywell) included net working capital goals. There was concern in the organization that the net working capital goal could prove the obstacle to achieving a bonus despite excellent sales growth. The latest DSR report is shown below.

### SAC Control Systems' Average Days Sales Receivables by Region

| Region | Actual | Target | Amount |
|---|---|---|---|
| North America | 44 | 40 | $31.0 million |
| South America | 129 | 70 | $2.1 million |
| Europe | 55 | 45 | $5.7 million |
| Middle East | 93 | 60 | $3.2 million |
| Asia | 75 | 55 | $11.0 million |
| PIA | 264 | 180 | $0.7 million |
| Boeing | 39 | 30 | $41.0 million |
| McDonnell Douglas | 35 | 30 | $18.0 million |
| Airbus Industries | 70 | 45 | $13.0 million |

**Notes**

1. U.S.–based airline trading companies distort the actual local payment terms.
2. The spread between individual customers within regions can be extremely large.
3. Some collection activity is assumed. Specific customers are periodically targeted.
4. Disputed invoices are included. Amount is for all products, services, and exchanges.
5. One of the criteria for granting "preferred" pricing is a 30-day DSR. The 10% reduction can be substantial but typically only motivates the larger customers.

Honeywell payment terms were net 30 from date of invoice. However, payment terms and practices varied dramatically across country and region. Payment terms were generally not published, with the exception of some private reports by credit rating agencies. Honeywell had not in the past enforced stringent credit terms on many customers. For example, neither contracts nor invoices stated any penalties for late payment. Many airlines did pay on time, but others availed themselves of Honeywell's cheap financing.

A review of PIA's account receivable history indicated that they consistently paid their invoices late. The current average DSR was 264 days. PIA had been repeatedly put on hold by the collections department, forcing marketing staff representatives to press the agent who in turn pressed PIA for payment. Honeywell was very concerned about this deal. It had in fact asked for guarantees that PIA would pay promptly. Honeywell's concern was also reflected in the 20% advance payment clause in the contract. Although marketing took the high DSR rate up with PIA and the agent, the current proposed deal was expected to be the same if not worse.

One positive attribute of the proposed contract was that delivery would not occur until one year after the contract was signed. The invoice for the full amount outstanding would be issued at that time. If the expected improvements to the DSR were made in the meantime, maybe the high DSR rate on the PIA deal could be averaged with the rest of Asia. The 20% advance payment would be used to fund the front-end engineering work.

Global treasury at Honeywell was headquartered along with corporate in Minneapolis, Minnesota. Corporate treasury was a profit center and charged 1% commission on all sales. Treasury, however, passed on the currency risk to the business unit. If a local subsidiary required local currency, treasury would try to match those requirements by accepting the A/R in the local currency. They had advised SAC that for many developing countries where Honeywell had little or no activities, such as Pakistan, this was done only on an exception basis. Global treasury also evaluated all deals in present value terms given the extended payment periods, and the corporate cost of capital was set at 12%.

## Negotiations

Honeywell now speculated that the local currency request was a result of the 20% advance payment clause. The project was considered one of the riskiest SAC had undertaken, and the 20% advance payment would help reach the group's DSR goals. The DSR was being watched on a daily basis by division management. This project had already been forced to secure group-level approval because it fell below the minimum return-on-sales target. SAC's management had counted on the deal to make its annual sales targets, and that now seemed in jeopardy. It would need to act soon if it was to reach its targets.

## Case Questions

1. Estimate what cash flows in which currencies the proposal would probably yield. What is the expected U.S. dollar value that would, in the end, be received?

2. Do you think the services that Makran is offering are worth the costs?

3. What would you do if you were heading the Honeywell SAC group negotiating the deal?

## Summary of Learning Objectives

*Demonstrate the operation of working capital management in a multinational enterprise and its various foreign subsidiaries*

- The *operating cycle* of a business generates funding needs, cash inflows and outflows — the cash conversion cycle — and potential foreign exchange rate and credit risks.

- The funding needs generated by the *operating cycle* of the firm constitute *working capital*. The operating cycle of a business extends along a time line from the point at which a customer requests a price quote to the time at which payment is received from the customer for goods delivered.

- The *cash conversion cycle*, a subcomponent of the operating cycle, is that period of time extending between cash outflows for purchased inputs and materials and when cash inflow is received from cash settlement.

*Analyze how multinational companies reposition their profits, cash flows, and capital within their multinational structures to maximize profitability, minimize global tax liability, and optimize their use of capital*

- The MNE is constantly striving to create shareholder value by maximizing the after-tax profitability of the firm. One dimension of this task is to *reposition the profits* of the firm, as legally and practically possible, in low-tax environments.

- Repositioning profits allows the firm to increase its after-tax profits by lowering its tax liabilities with the same amount of sales.

- In addition to tax management, repositioning is useful when an MNE wishes to move cash flows or funds in general from where they are not needed to where they may be redeployed in more value-creating activities, or to minimize exposure to a potential currency collapse or potential political or economic crisis.

*Describe the role that royalties and license fees play in the repositioning strategies employed by MNEs*

- *Royalty fees* are compensation for the use of intellectual property belonging to some other party. Royalty fees are usually a stated percentage of sales revenue (price times volume) so that the owner is compensated in proportion to the volume of sales.

- *License fees* are remuneration paid to the owners of technology, patents, trade names, and copyrighted material (including moving pictures, video tapes, compact disks, software, and books).

- License fees are usually based on a percentage of the value of the product or on the volume of production. As such they are calculated independently of the amount of sales.

*Learn how international dividend remittances are determined*

- International dividend policy now incorporates tax considerations, political risk, and foreign exchange risk, as well as a return for business guidance and technology.

- Dividends are the most tax-inefficient method for repatriating funds because they are distributed on an after-tax basis. This means that the parent company will frequently be faced with the generation of excess foreign tax credits on a dividend.

- Remittance of license or royalty fees is on a pretax basis in the foreign subsidiary, the only tax that is typically applied is withholding, at a rate considerably below that of corporate income taxes.

*Apply management guidelines to minimize the costs of funding working capital requirements*

- In principle, firms attempt to minimize their net working capital balance. A/R is reduced if collections are accelerated. Inventories held by the firm are reduced by carrying lower levels of both unfinished and finished goods, and by speeding the rate at which goods are manufactured, reducing so-called *cycle time*.

- All firms must determine whether A/P should be paid off early, taking discounts if offered by suppliers, and whether to finance these payments with short-term debt. Note that short-term debt is not included within NWC because it does not spontaneously increase with operations, but must be acquired as part of management's financing choices.

*Identify devices used to manage cross-border cash settlement processes*

- Over time a number of techniques and services have evolved which simplify and reduce the costs of making cross-border payments. This includes wire transfers, cash pooling, payment netting, and electronic fund transfers.

*Describe the different internal and external banking and financial services that may be used by MNEs in the conduct of global business*

- MNEs can finance working capital needs through in-house banks, international banks, and local banks where subsidiaries are located.

- International banks finance MNEs and service these accounts through representative offices, correspondent banking relationships, branch banks, banking subsidiaries, affiliates, and Edge Act corporations (United States only).

## QUESTIONS

1.  **Constraints on positioning funds.** Each of the following factors is sometimes a constraint on the free movement of funds internationally. Why would a government impose such a constraint? How might the management of a multinational argue that such a constraint is not in the best interests of the government that has imposed it?

    a. Government-mandated restrictions on moving funds out of the country

    b. Withholding taxes on dividend distributions to foreign owners

    c. Dual-currency regimes, with one rate for imports and another rate for exports

    d. Refusal to allow foreign firms in the country to net cash inflows and outflows into a single payment

2.  **Unbundling.** What does this term mean? Why would unbundling be needed for international cash flows from foreign subsidiaries, but not for domestic cash flows between related domestic subsidiaries and their parent?

3.  **Conduits.** In the context of unbundling cash flows from subsidiary to parent, explain how each of the following creates a conduit. What are the tax consequences of each?

    a. Imports of components from the parent

    b. Payment to cover overhead expenses of parent managers temporarily assigned to the subsidiary

    c. Payment of royalties for the use of proprietary technology

    d. Subsidiary borrowing of funds on an intermediate or long-term maturity from the parent

    e. Payment of dividends to the parent

4.  **Sister subsidiaries.** Subsidiary Alpha in Country Able faces a 40% income tax rate. Subsidiary Beta in Country Baker faces only a 20% income tax rate. At present each subsidiary imports from the other an amount of goods and services exactly equal in monetary value to what each exports to the other. This method of balancing intracompany trade was imposed by a management keen to reduce all costs, including the costs (spread between bid and ask) of foreign exchange transactions. Both subsidiaries are profitable, and both could purchase all components domestically at approximately the same prices as they are paying to their foreign sister subsidiary. Does this seem like an optimal situation to you?

5.  **Allocated fees — 1.** What is the difference between a license fee and a royalty fee? Do you think license and royalty fees should be covered by the tax rules that regulate transfer pricing? Why?

6.  **Allocated fees — 2.** What are the differences between a management fee, a technical assistance fee, and a license fee for patent usage? Should they be treated differently for income tax purposes?

7. **Distributed overhead.** What methods might the U.S. Internal Revenue Service use to determine whether allocations of distributed overhead are being fairly allocated to foreign subsidiaries?

8. **Fee treatment.** In the context of unbundling cash flows from subsidiary to parent, why might a host government be more lenient in its treatment of fees than in its treatment of dividends? What difference does it make to the subsidiary and to the parent?

9. **The cycle.** The operating cycle of a firm, domestic or multinational, consists of the following four time periods:
   a. Quotation period
   b. Input sourcing period
   c. Inventory period
   d. Accounts receivable period

   For each of these periods, explain whether a cash outflow or a cash inflow is associated with the beginning and the end of the period.

10. **Accounts payable period.** Exhibit 21.1 shows the accounts payable period to be longer than the inventory period. Could this be otherwise, and what would be the cash implications?

11. **Payables and receivables.** As a financial manager, would you prefer that the accounts payable period end before, at the same time, or after the beginning of the accounts receivable period? Explain.

12. **Transaction exposure.** Assuming the flow illustrated in Exhibit 21.1, where does transaction exposure begin and end if inputs are purchased with one currency at $t_1$ and proceeds from the sale are received at $t_5$? Is there more than one interval of transaction exposure?

13. **Operating exposure.** Is any operating exposure created during the course of a firm's operating cycle?

14. **Accounting exposure.** Is any accounting exposure created during the course of a firm's operating cycle?

15. **Reducing NWC.** Assume a firm purchases inventory with one foreign currency and sells it for another foreign currency, neither currency being the home currency of the parent or subsidiary where the manufacturing process takes place. What can the firm do to reduce the amount of net working capital?

16. **Trade terms.** Roberts and Sons, Inc., of Great Britain has just purchased inventory items costing Kronor 1,000,000 from a Swedish supplier. The supplier has quoted terms 3/15, net 45. Under what conditions might Roberts and Sons reasonably take the discount, and when might it be a reasonable idea to wait the full 45 days to pay?

17. **Inventory turnover.** Japanese industry is often praised for its just-in-time inventory practice between industrial buyers and industrial sellers. In the context of the "Days Receivables" turnover in Exhibit 21.5, what is the comparative impact of the just-in-time system in Japan? Are there any risks associated with this system? Do you think this applies equally to Japanese manufacturing firms sourcing raw material and components in Japan and those sourcing similar items from Thailand and Malaysia?

18. **Receivables turnover.** Why might the time lag for multinational intrafirm accounts receivable and payable (i.e., all received or paid to a parent or sister subsidiary) differ substantially from the time lags reported for transactions with nonaffiliated companies?

19. **Devaluation risk.** Merlin Corporation of the United States imports raw material from Indonesia on terms of 2/10, net 30. Merlin expects a 36% devaluation of the Indonesian rupiah at any moment. Should Merlin take the discount? Discuss aspects of the problem.

20. **Free-trade zones.** What are the advantages of a free-trade zone? Are there any disadvantages?

21. **Motives.** Explain the difference between the transaction motive and the precautionary motive for holding cash.

22. **Cash cycle.** The operating cash cycle of a multinational firm goes from cash collection from customers, cash holding for anticipated transaction needs (the transaction motive for holding cash), possible cash repositioning into another currency, and eventual cash disbursements to pay operating expenses. Assuming the initial cash collection is in one currency and the eventual cash disbursement is in another currency, what can a multinational firm do to shorten its cash cycle and what risks are involved?

23. **Electro-Beam Company.** Electro-Beam Company generates and disburses cash in the currencies of four countries: Singapore, Malaysia, Thailand, and Vietnam. What would be the characteristics you might consider if charged with designing a centralized cash depository system for Electro-Beam Company's Southeast Asian subsidiaries?

24. **France.** During the era of the French franc, France imposed a rule on its banks and subsidiaries of international companies operating in France that precluded those subsidiaries from netting cash flow obligations between France and non-French entities. Why do you suppose the French government imposed such a rule, and what if anything could subsidiaries in France have done about it?

25. **Foreign bank office.** What is the difference between a foreign branch and a foreign subsidiary of a home-country bank?

## PROBLEMS

1. **Quinlan Company.** The following events take place.

   March 1: Quinlan Company seeks a sale at a price of €10,000,000 for items to be sold to a long-standing client in Poland. To achieve the order, Quinlan offered to denominate the order in zlotys (Z), Poland's currency, for Z20,000,000. This price was arrived at by multiplying the euro price by Z2.00/€, the exchange rate on the day of the quote. The zloty is expected to fall in value by 0.5% per month versus the euro.

   April 1: Quinlan receives an order worth Z20,000,000 from that customer. On the same day, Quinlan places orders with its vendors for €4,000,000 of components needed to complete the sale.

   May 1: Quinlan receives the components and is billed €4,000,000 by the vendor on terms of 2/20, net 60. During the next two months Quinlan assigns direct labor to work on the project. The expense of direct labor was €5,000,000.

   July 1: Quinlan ships the order to the customer and bills the customer Z20,000,000. On its corporate books Quinlan debits accounts receivable and credits sales.

   Sept 1: Quinlan's customer pays Z20,000,000 to Quinlan.

   a. Draw a cash flow diagram for this transaction in the style of Exhibit 21.1 and explain the steps involved.

   b. What working capital management techniques might Quinlan use to better its position vis-à-vis this particular customer?

2. **Super-Do, K.K.** Super-Do, K.K., the Japanese subsidiary of a U.S. company, has ¥100,000,000 in accounts receivable for sales billed to customers on terms of 2/30 net 60. Customers usually pay in 30 days. Super-Do also has ¥60,000,000 of accounts payable billed to it on terms of 3/10 net 60. Super-Do delays payment until the last minute because it is normally short of cash. Super-Do, K.K. normally carries an average cash balance for transactions of ¥30,000,000. How much cash could Super-Do, K.K. save by taking the discount?

3. **Alpine Ski Company.** Alpine Ski Company of Grenoble, France, manufactures and sells in France, Switzerland, and Italy, and also maintains a corporate account in Frankfurt, Germany. Alpine has been setting a separate operating cash balance in each country at a level equal to expected cash needs plus two standard deviations above those needs, based on a statistical analysis of cash flow volatility. Expected operating cash needs and one standard deviation of those needs are

   | | Expected cash need | One standard deviation |
   |---|---|---|
   | Switzerland | €5,000,000 | €1,000,000 |
   | Italy | 3,000,000 | 400,000 |
   | France | 2,000,000 | 300,000 |
   | Germany | 800,000 | 40,000 |
   | | €10,800,000 | €1,740,000 |

   Alpine's Frankfurt bank suggests that the same level of safety could be maintained if all precautionary balances were combined in a central account at the Frankfurt headquarters.

   a. How much lower would Alpine Ski Company's total cash balances be if all precautionary balances were combined? Assume cash needs in each country are normally distributed and are independent of each other.

   b. What other advantages might accrue to Alpine Ski Company from centralizing its cash holdings? Are these advantages realistic?

4. **Futebal do Brasil, S.A.** Futebal do Brazil, S.A. purchases newly sewn soccer balls from Pakistani manufacturers and distributes them in Argentina, Brazil, and Chile. All operations are through wholly-owned subsidiaries. The three subsidiaries have submitted the following daily cash reports (all amounts in thousands of U.S. dollars), which the Brazilian company uses for cash management purposes. Each of the two foreign subsidiaries is allowed to carry a $1,000,000 cash balance overnight, with the remainder remitted to a U.S. dollar account maintained in Sao Paulo, unless instructed otherwise by the Brazilian financial staff. As a general matter, the cost of moving funds is such that funds should not be moved for one day and then returned the next, but a movement for two days which is then reversed is financially advantageous. The Brazilian headquarters invests surplus cash balance over US$5,000,000 in U.S. money market instruments purchased through the Miami correspondent bank of the firm's Brazilian bank. Anticipated cash flows, in thousands of U.S. dollars, are shown below:

| | Companhia Futebal do Brasil | Compañía Fútbal de Argentina | Compañía Fútbal de Chile |
|---|---|---|---|
| Day-end cash balance | $6,000 | $5,000 | $5,000 |
| Minimum operating balance required: | $5,000 | $1,000 | $1,000 |
| Expected receipts (+) or disbursements (−): | | | |
| +1 day | +3,000 | −2,000 | +5,000 |
| +2 days | -0- | +1,000 | −3,000 |
| +3 days | −5,000 | −3,000 | +2,000 |

Design an advantageous cash movement plan that complies with Futebal do Brasil general policies.

5. **Earth Technology, Inc.** Earth Technology, Inc., manufactures basic farm equipment in China, Spain, and Iowa. Each subsidiary has monthly unsettled balances due to or from other subsidiaries. At the end of December, unsettled intra-company debts in U.S. dollars were as follows:

Earth Technology China:
  Owes $8 million to Spanish subsidiary
  Owes $9 million to Iowa parent

Earth Technology Spain:
  Owes $5 million to Chinese subsidiary
  Owes $6 million to Iowa parent

Earth Technology Iowa:
  Owes $4 million to Chinese subsidiary
  Owes $10 million to Spanish subsidiary

Foreign exchange transaction spreads average 0.4% of funds transferred.

a. How could Earth Technology net these intra-company debts? How much would be saved in transaction expenses over the no-netting alternative?

b. Before settling the above accounts, Earth Technology decides to invest $6,000,000 of parent funds in a new farm equipment manufacturing plant in the new free industrial zone at Subic Bay, Philippines. How can this decision be incorporated into the settlement process? What would the total bank charges be? Explain.

6. **Crystal Publishing Company.** Crystal Publishing Company publishes books in Europe through separate subsidiaries in several countries. On a Europe-wide basis Crystal Publishing experiences uneven cash flows. Any given book creates a cash outflow during the period of writing and publishing, followed by a cash inflow in subsequent months and years as the book is sold. To handle these imbalances, Crystal decided to create an in-house bank.

At the beginning of April Crystal's in-house bank held deposits, on which it paid 4.8% interest, as follows:

| | |
|---|---|
| From Crystal Germany | €20,000,000 |
| From Crystal Spain | €5,000,000 |
| From Crystal Britain | £12,000,000 |

At the beginning of April, Crystal's in-house bank advanced funds at an annual rate of 5.4% as follows:

| | |
|---|---|
| To Crystal France | €12,000,000 |
| To Crystal Italy | €8,000,000 |
| To Crystal Greece | €6,000,000 |

The exchange rate between pounds sterling and the euro is €1.6000/£.

a. What would be the net interest earnings (i.e., interest earned less interest paid, before administrative expenses), of Crystal's in-house bank for the month of April?

**b.** If parent Crystal Publishing subsidized the in-house bank for all of its operating expenses, how much more could the in-house bank loan at the beginning of April?

7. **Balanced Tire Company (A).** Balanced Tire Company manufactures automobile tires for sale to retail outlets in the United States and, through a wholly-owned distribution subsidiary, in neighboring Canada. Annual capacity of the U.S. factory is 700,000 tires per year, but present production is only 450,000, of which 300,000 are sold in the United States and 150,000 are exported to Canada. Federal and state income tax rates in both countries add up to 40%.

   Within the United States Balanced Tire sells to retail outlets for the U.S. dollar equivalent of C$80 per tire. After-tax profit is equivalent to C$10.80 per tire calculated as follows, with all prices expressed in the Canadian dollar equivalent of U.S. dollars.

*Balanced Tire's U.S. profit calculation, expressed in Canadian dollars*

| | |
|---|---|
| Balanced Tire's U.S. sales price per tire | C$80.00 |
| less direct labor in U.S. | −20.00 |
| less direct material in U.S. | −20.00 |
| less U.S. manufacturing overhead | −12.00 |
| Total manufacturing costs | 52.00 |
| U.S. factory margin | 28.00 |
| less selling and administrative costs | −10.00 |
| Pretax profit per set | 18.00 |
| less 40% U.S. income taxes | −7.20 |
| After-tax profit per tire in the United States | C$10.80 |

   Direct labor consists of hourly payroll costs for factory workers, and direct material is for raw material purchased in the United States. Manufacturing overhead is a fixed cost that includes supervision and depreciation. Selling and administrative costs are fixed expenses for management salaries, office expenses, and rent.

   For its exports to Canada, Balanced Tire sells sets to its Canadian subsidiary at a U.S. dollar transfer price equal to C$56 per tire, this being U.S. manufacturing cost of C$52 plus a C$4.00 profit. Transportation and distribution costs add an additional C$2.00 per tire, and the tires are resold to Canadian retail outlets for C$80, the equivalent of the U.S. price. This price was arrived at independently, based on the following analysis of elasticity of demand in Canada.

*Accounts in Canadian dollars*

| | | | | | |
|---|---|---|---|---|---|
| Unit sales price in Canada | $85.00 | $80.00 | $75.00 | $70.00 | $65.00 |
| less import | −56.00 | −56.00 | −56.00 | −56.00 | −56.00 |
| less shipping | −2.00 | −2.00 | −2.00 | −2.00 | −2.00 |
| Unit profit before tax | 27.00 | 22.00 | 17.00 | 12.00 | 7.00 |
| less 40% Canadian tax | −10.80 | −8.80 | −6.80 | −4.80 | −5.40 |
| Unit profit after tax | 16.20 | 13.20 | 10.20 | 7.20 | 4.20 |
| expected unit volume | ×110,000 | ×150,000 | ×180,000 | ×250,000 | ×400,000 |
| Total profit (000) | 1,782 | 1,980 | 1,836 | 1,800 | 1,680 |

Maximum profit is at a sales price of C$80.00.

   In making this calculation, Balanced Tire determined that unit demand in Canada was a function only of the sales price. Hence it seemed self-evident to Balanced Tire's management that a transfer price to Canada of C$80.00 per tire maximized Canada's contribution to profits at a total figure of C$1,980,000. Is Balanced Tire's present pricing strategy for Canada correct?

8. **Balanced Tire Company (B).** Assume Balanced Tire (previous problem) wants to divide profits on export sales evenly between Canada and the United States so as to avoid difficulties with either tax authority.

   **a.** What final transfer price and unit price in Canada should the firm adopt?

   **b.** If Canada's income tax rate remains 40%, but the United States lowers its tax rate to 25%, should a new transfer price be adopted? What policy issues are involved?

9. **Surgical Tools, Inc.** Surgical Tools, Inc. of Illinois wants to set up a regular procedure for transferring funds from its newly opened manufacturing subsidiary in Korea to the United States. The precedent set by the transfer method or methods is likely to prevail over any government objections that might otherwise arise in future years. The Korean subsidiary manufactures surgical tools for export to all Asian countries. The following *pro forma* financial information portrays the results expected in the first full year of operations.

| Sales | Won 2,684,000,000 |
|---|---|
| Cash manufacturing expenses | 1,342,000,000 |
| Depreciation | 335,500,000 |
| Pretax profit | 1,006,500,000 |
| Korean taxes at 28% | 281,820,000 |
| Profit after taxes | Won 724,680,000 |
| Exchange rate | Won 1342/$ |
| Korean income tax rate | 28% |
| U.S. income tax rate | 34% |

Compare the tax and income impacts of the following two alternatives:

**a.** Declare a dividend of Won 362,340,000, equal to 50% of profit after taxes. The dividend would be taxable in the United States after a gross up for Korean taxes already paid.

**b.** Add a license fee of Won 362,340,000 to the above expenses, and remit that amount annually. The license fee would be fully taxable in the United States.

10. **Adams Corporation (A).** Adams Corporation (USA), a recently divested unit of Pfizer and the owner of a series of valuable consumer brands such as Listerine and Halls, owns 100% of Adams Brazil, S.A. This year Adams Brazil, S.A. earned R$52,000,000, equal to $20,000,000 at the current exchange rate of R$2.60/$. The exchange rate is not expected to change.

Adams Corporation wants to transfer half of its Brazilian earnings to the United States and wonders whether this sum should be remitted (1) by a cash dividend of $10,000,000 or (2) by a cash dividend of $5,000,000 and a royalty of $5,000,000. Brazilian income taxes are 15% and U.S. income taxes are 30%. Which do you recommend and why?

11. **Adams Corporation (B).** The Brazilian government under President Lula has instituted a new tax policy aimed at encouraging foreign MNEs to come to Brazil and reinvest their profits in the country, rather than pulling them out. Assume that all of the same conditions exist as in the previous problem, but now assume Brazil has instituted the following withholding taxes on dividends, royalties, and licensing fee remittances.

| Type of remittance | Withholding tax rate |
|---|---|
| Dividends | 30% |
| Royalty payments | 5% |
| License fees | 5% |

Which of the alternatives do you recommend Adams use in remitting the $10 million to Adams (USA)?

# Internet Exercises

1. **Working capital management.** Many major multinational banks provide a variety of working capital and multinational cash management services described in this chapter. Using the Web sites of a variety of these cross-border banks, research which banks offer multinational cash management services that would combine banking with foreign exchange management. Which banks provide specific services through regional or geographic service centers?

   Bank of America
   http://www.bankamerica.com/corporate/
   Bank of Montreal
   http://www.bmo.com/cebssite/

2. **Clearinghouse associations.** Associations like the New York Clearinghouse Association have played major roles in the international financial system for centuries. Use the following Web sites to prepare a two-page executive briefing on the role of clearinghouses in history and in contemporary finance. Use the Web site for the Clearing House Interbank Payments System (CHIPS) to estimate the volume of international financial transactions.

   New York Clearinghouse Association
   http://www.theclearinghouse.org/
   Clearing House Interbank Payments System
   http://www.chips.org/

**Accounting exposure.** Another name for translation exposure. *See* Translation exposure.

**ADB.** Asian Development Bank.

**Adjusted present value.** A type of present value analysis in capital budgeting in which operating cash flows are discounted separately from (1) the various tax shields provided by the deductibility of interest and other financial charges, and (2) the benefits of project-specific concessional financing. Each component cash flow is discounted at a rate appropriate for the risk involved.

**ADR.** *See* American Depositary Receipt.

**Ad valorem duty.** A customs duty levied as a percentage of the assessed value of goods entering a country.

**AfDB.** African Development Bank.

**Affiliate.** A foreign enterprise in which the parent company owns a minority interest.

**Agency for International Development (AID).** A unit of the U.S. government dealing with foreign aid.

**All-equity discount rate.** A discount rate in capital budgeting that would be appropriate for discounting operating cash flows if the project were financed entirely with owners' equity.

**American Depositary Receipt (ADR).** A certificate of ownership, issued by a U.S. bank, representing a claim on underlying foreign securities. ADRs may be traded in lieu of trading in the actual underlying shares.

**American option.** An option that can be exercised at any time up to and including the expiration date.

**American selling price (ASP).** For customs purposes, the use of the domestic price of competing merchandise in the United States as a tax base for determining import duties. The ASP is generally higher than the actual foreign price, so its use is a protectionist technique.

**American terms.** Foreign exchange quotations for the U.S. dollar, expressed as the number of U.S. dollars per unit of non-U.S. currency.

**A/P.** In international trade documentation, abbreviation for authority to purchase or authority to pay. In accounting, abbreviation for accounts payable.

**Appreciation.** In the context of exchange rate changes, a rise in the foreign exchange value of a currency that is pegged to other currencies or to gold. Also called revaluation.

**Arbitrage.** A trading strategy based on the purchase of a commodity, including foreign exchange, in one market at one price while simultaneously selling it in another market at a more advantageous price, in order to obtain a risk-free profit on the price differential.

**Arbitrageur.** An individual or company that practices arbitrage.

**Arithmetic return.** The mean is simply the average of the annual percentage changes in capital appreciation plus dividend distributions.

**Arm's-length price.** The price at which a willing buyer and a willing unrelated seller freely agree to carry out a transaction. In effect, a free market price. Applied by tax authorities in judging the appropriateness of transfer prices between related companies.

**Asian currency unit.** A trading department within a Singaporean bank that deals in foreign (non-Singaporean) currency deposits and loans.

**Ask price.** The price at which a dealer is willing to sell foreign exchange, securities or commodities. Also called offer price.

**Asset market approach.** Whether foreigners are willing to hold claims in monetary form depends on an extensive set of investment considerations or drivers.

**At-the-money.** An option whose exercise price is the same as the spot price of the underlying currency.

**Back-to-back loan.** A loan in which two companies in separate countries borrow each other's currency for a specific period of time and repay the other's currency at an agreed maturity. Sometimes the two loans are channeled through an intermediate bank. Back-to-back financing is also called link financing.

**Balance of payments.** A financial statement summarizing the flow of goods, services, and investment funds between residents of a given country and residents of the rest of the world.

**Balance of trade.** An entry in the balance of payments measuring the difference between the monetary value of merchandise exports and merchandise imports.

**Balance sheet hedge.** Requires an equal amount of exposed foreign currency assets and liabilities on a firm's consolidated balance sheet.

**Bank for International Settlements.** (BIS) A bank in Basle, Switzerland, that functions as a bank for European central banks.

**Bank rate.** The interest rate at which central banks for various countries lend to their own monetary institutions.

**Bankers' acceptance.** An unconditional promise of a bank to make payment on a draft when it matures. The acceptance is in the form of the bank's endorsement (acceptance) of a draft drawn against that bank in accordance with the terms of a letter of credit issued by the bank.

**Barter.** International trade conducted by the direct exchange of physical goods, rather than by separate purchases and sales at prices and exchange rates set by a free market.

**Basic Balance.** In a country's balance of payments, the net of exports and imports of goods and services, unilateral transfers, and long-term capital flows.

**Basis point.** One one-hundredth of one percentage point, often used in quotations of spreads between interest rates or to describe changes in yields in securities.

**Basis risk.** That type of interest rate risk in which the interest rate base is mismatched.

**Bearer bond.** Corporate or governmental debt in bond form that is not registered to any owner. Possession of the bond implies ownership, and interest is obtained by clipping a coupon attached to the bond. The advantage of the bearer form is easy transfer at the time of a sale, easy use as collateral for a debt, and what some cynics call taxpayer anonymity, meaning that governments find it hard to trace interest payments in order to collect income taxes. Bearer bonds are common in Europe, but are seldom issued any more in the United States. The alternate form to a bearer bond is a registered bond.

**Beta.** Second letter of Greek alphabet, used as a statistical measure of risk in the Capital Asset Pricing Model. Beta is the covariance between returns on a given asset and returns on the market portfolio, divided by the variance of returns on the market portfolio.

**Bid.** The price which a dealer is willing to pay for (i.e., buy) foreign exchange or a security.

**Bid-ask spread.** The difference between a bid and an ask quotation.

**Big Bang.** The October 1986 liberalization of the London capital markets.

**Bill of exchange (B/E).** A written order requesting one party (such as an importer) to pay a specified amount of money at a specified time to the order of the writer of the bill of exchange. Also called a draft. *See* Sight draft.

**Bill of lading (B/L).** A contract between a common carrier and a shipper to transport goods to a named destination. The bill of lading is also a receipt for the goods. Bills of lading are usually negotiable, meaning they are made to the order of a particular party and can be endorsed to transfer title to another party.

**Black market.** An illegal foreign exchange market.

**Blocked funds.** Funds in one country's currency that may not be exchanged freely for foreign currencies because of exchange controls.

**Border tax adjustments.** The fiscal practice, under the General Agreement on Tariffs and Trade, by which imported goods are subject to some or all of the tax charged in the importing country and re-exported goods are exempt from some or all of the tax charged in the exporting country.

**Branch.** A foreign operation not incorporated in the host country, in contradistinction to a subsidiary.

**Bretton Woods Conference.** An international conference in 1944 that established the international monetary system in effect from 1945 to 1971. The conference was held in Bretton Woods, New Hampshire, USA.

**Bridge financing.** Short-term financing from a bank, used while a borrower obtains medium- or long-term fixed-rate financing from capital markets.

**Bulldogs.** British pound-denominated bonds issued within the United Kingdom by a foreign borrower.

**Cable.** The U.S. dollar per British pound cross rate.

**CAD.** Cash against documents. International trade term.

**Call option.** The right, but not the obligation, to buy foreign exchange or some other financial contract at a specified price within a specified time. *See* Option.

**Capital account.** A section of the balance of payments accounts. Under the revised format of the International Monetary Fund, the capital account measures capital transfers and the acquisition and disposal of nonproduced, nonfinancial assets. Under traditional definitions, still used by many countries, the capital account measures public and private international lending and investment. Most of the traditional definition of the capital account is now incorporated in IMF statements as the financial account.

**Capital Asset Pricing Model (CAPM).** A theoretical model that relates the return on an asset to its risk, where risk is the contribution of the asset to the volatility of a portfolio. Risk and return are presumed determined in competitive and efficient financial markets.

**Capital budgeting.** The analytical approach used to determine whether investment in long-lived assets or projects is viable.

**Capital flight.** Movement of funds out of a country because of political risk.

**Capital markets.** The financial markets in various countries in which various types of long-term debt and/or ownership securities, or claims on those securities, are purchased and sold.

**Capital mobility.** The degree to which private capital moves freely from country to country seeking the most promising investment opportunities.

**Cash budgeting.** The planning for future receipts and disbursements of cash.

**Cash flow return on investment (CFROI).** A measure of corporate performance in which the numerator is profit from continuing operations less cash taxes and depreciation. This is divided by cash investment which is taken to mean the replacement cost of capital employed.

**Certificate of Deposit (CD).** A negotiable receipt issued by a bank for funds deposited for a certain period of time. CDs can be purchased or sold prior to their maturity in a secondary market, making them an interest-earning marketable security.

**CIF.** *See* Cost, insurance, and freight.

**CKD.** Completely knocked down. International trade term for components shipped into a country for assembly there. Often used in the automobile industry.

**Clearing house.** An institution through which financial obligations are cleared by the process of netting obligations of various members.

**Clearinghouse Interbank Payments System (CHIPS).** A New York-based computerized clearing system used by banks to settle interbank foreign exchange obligations (mostly U.S. dollars) between members.

**Collar option.** The simultaneous purchase of a put option and sale of a call option, or vice versa. Thus a form of hybrid option.

**COMECON.** Acronym for Council for Mutual Economic Assistance. An association of the former Soviet Union and Eastern European governments formed to facilitate international trade among European Communist countries. COMECON ceased to exist after the breakup of the Soviet Union.

**Commercial risk.** In banking, the likelihood that a foreign debtor will be unable to repay its debts because of business (as distinct from political) events.

**Common market.** An association through treaty of two or more countries that agree to remove all trade barriers between themselves. The best known is the European Common Market, now called the European Union.

**Comparative advantage.** A theory that everyone gains if each nation specializes in the production of those goods that it produces relatively most efficiently and imports those goods that other countries produce relatively most efficiently. The theory supports free trade arguments.

**Competitive exposure.** *See* Operating exposure.

**Concession agreement.** An understanding or contract between a foreign corporation and a host government defining the rules under which the corporation may operate in that country.

**Consolidated financial statement.** A corporate financial statement in which accounts of subsidiaries and the parent are added together to produce a statement which reports the status of the worldwide enterprise as if it were a single corporation. Internal obligations are eliminated in consolidated statements.

**Consolidation.** In the context of accounting for multinational corporations, the process of preparing a single reporting currency financial statement that combines financial statements of subsidiaries that are in fact measured in different currencies.

**Contagion.** The spread of a crisis in one country to its neighboring countries and other countries that have similar characteristics – at least in the eyes of cross-border investors.

**Controlled foreign corporation (CFC).** A foreign corporation in which U.S. shareholders own more than 50% of the combined voting power or total value. Under U.S. tax law, U.S. shareholders may be liable for taxes on undistributed earnings of the controlled foreign corporation.

**Convertible bond.** A bond or other fixed-income security that may be exchanged for a number of shares of common stock.

**Convertible currency.** A currency that can be exchanged freely for any other currency without government restrictions.

**Corporate governance.** The relationship among stakeholders used to determine and control the strategic direction and performance of an organization.

**Corporate wealth maximization.** The corporate goal of maximizing the total wealth of the corporation itself rather than just the shareholders' wealth. Wealth is defined to include not just financial wealth but also the technical, marketing and human resources of the corporation.

**Correspondent bank.** A bank that holds deposits for and provides services to another bank, located in another geographic area, on a reciprocal basis.

**Cost and freight (C&F).** Price, quoted by an exporter, that includes the cost of transportation to the named port of destination.

**Cost, insurance, and freight (CIF).** Exporter's quoted price including the cost of packaging, freight or carriage, insurance premium, and other charges paid in respect of the goods from the time of loading in the country of export to their arrival at the named port of destination or place of transshipment.

**Counterparty.** The opposite party to a double transaction; that is, to a transaction involving an exchange of financial instruments or obligations now and a reversal of that same transaction at some agreed-upon later date.

**Counterparty risk.** The potential exposure any individual firm bears that the second party to any financial contract is unable to fulfill its obligations under the contract's specifications.

**Countertrade.** A type of international trade in which parties exchange goods directly rather than for money. Hence a type of barter.

**Countervailing duty.** An import duty charged to offset an export subsidy by another country.

**Country risk.** In banking, the likelihood that unexpected events within a host country will influence a client's or a government's ability to repay a loan. Country risk is often divided into sovereign (political) risk and foreign exchange (currency) risk.

**Country-specific risk.** Political risks that affect the MNE at the country level, such as transfer risk (blocked funds) and cultural and institutional risks.

**Covered interest arbitrage.** The process whereby an investor earns a risk-free profit by (1) borrowing funds in one currency, (2) exchanging those funds in the spot market for a foreign currency, (3) investing the foreign currency at interest rates in a foreign country, (4) selling forward, at the time of original investment, the investment proceeds to be received at maturity, (5) using the proceeds of the forward sale to repay the original loan, and (6) having a remaining profit balance.

**Covering.** A transaction in the forward foreign exchange market or money market that protects the value of future cash flows. Covering is another term for hedging. *See* Hedge.

**Crawling peg.** A foreign exchange rate system in which the exchange rate is adjusted very frequently to reflect prevailing rate of inflation.

**Credit risk.** The possibility that a borrower's credit worth, at the time of renewing a credit, is reclassified by the lender.

**Crisis planning.** Educating management and other employees about how to react to various scenarios of violence.

**Cross-border acquisition.** A firm acquires through purchase another firm located in another country.

**Cross-currency swap.** *See* Currency swap.

**Cross-listing.** The listing of shares of common stock on two or more stock exchanges.

**Cross rate.** An exchange rate between two currencies derived by dividing each currency's exchange rate with a third currency. For example, if ¥/$ is 108 and DKr/$ is 6.80, the cross rate between ¥ and DKr is ¥108 ÷ DKr 6.80 = ¥15.88/DKr.

**Cumulative translation adjustment (CTA) account.** An entry in a translated balance sheet in which gains and/or losses from translation have been accumulated over a period of years.

**Currency basket.** The value of a portfolio of specific amounts of individual currencies, used as the basis for setting the market value of another currency. Also called currency cocktail.

**Currency Board.** A currency board exists when a country's central bank commits to back its money supply entirely with foreign reserves at all times.

**Currency swap.** A transaction in which two counterparties exchange specific amounts of two different currencies at the outset and then repay over time according to an agreed upon contract that reflects interest payments and possibly amortization of principal. In a currency swap, the cash flows are similar to those in a spot and forward foreign exchange transaction. *Also see* Swaps.

**Current account.** In the balance of payments, the net flow of goods, services, and unilateral transfers (such as gifts) between a country and all foreign countries.

**Current rate method.** A method of translating the financial statements of foreign subsidiaries into the parent's reporting currency. All assets and liabilities are translated at the current exchange rate.

**Current/noncurrent method.** A method of translating the financial statements of foreign subsidiaries into the parent's reporting currency. All current assets and current liabilities are translated at the current rate, and all noncurrent accounts at their historical rates.

**D/A.** Documents against acceptance. International trade term.

**Deemed-paid tax.** That portion of taxes paid to a foreign government that is allowed as a credit (reduction) in taxes due to a home government.

**Delta.** The change in an option's price divided by the change in the price of the underlying instrument. Hedging strategies are based on delta ratios.

**Demand deposit.** A bank deposit that can be withdrawn or transferred at any time without notice, in contradistinction to a time deposit where (theoretically) the bank may require a waiting period before the deposit can be withdrawn. Demand deposits may or may not earn interest. A time deposit is the opposite of a demand deposit.

**Depositary receipts.** *See* American depositary receipts.

**Depreciate.** In the context of foreign exchange rates, a drop in the spot foreign exchange value of a floating currency; i.e., a currency the value of which is determined by open market transactions. *See* Devaluation. In the context of accounting, a periodic charge (expense) that represents the allocation of the cost of a fixed asset to various time periods.

**Devaluation.** A drop in the spot foreign exchange value of a currency that is pegged to other currencies or to gold. *See* Depreciate.

**Direct quote.** The price of a unit of foreign exchange expressed in the home country's currency. The term has meaning only when the home country is specified.

**Directed public share issue.** An issue that is targeted at investors in a single country and underwritten in whole or in part by investment institutions from that country.

**Dirty float.** A system of floating (i.e., market-determined) exchange rates in which the government intervenes from time to time to influence the foreign exchange value of its currency.

**Discount (in foreign exchange market).** The amount by which a currency is cheaper for future delivery than for spot (immediate) delivery. The opposite of discount is premium.

**Dollarization.** Dollarization is the use of the U.S. dollar as the official currency of the country.

**Domestic International Sales Corporation (DISC).** Under the U.S. tax code, a type of subsidiary formed to reduce taxes on exported U.S.-produced goods. It has been ruled illegal by the World Trade Organization.

**D/P.** Documents against payment. International trade term.

**Draft.** An unconditional written order requesting one party (such as an importer) to pay a specified amount of money at a specified time to the order of the writer of the draft. Also called a bill of exchange. Personal checks are one type of draft.

**Dragon bond.** A U.S. dollar denominated bond sold in the so-called Dragon economies of Asia, such as Hong Kong, Taiwan, and Singapore.

**D/S.** Days after sight. International trade term.

**Dumping.** The practice of offering goods for sale in a foreign market at a price that is lower than that of the same product in the home market or a third country. As used in GATT, a special case of differential pricing.

**Economic exposure.** Another name for operating exposure. *See* Operating exposure.

**Economic Value Added (EVA).** A widely used measure of corporate financial performance. It is calculated as the difference between net operating profits after-tax of the business less the cost of capital invested (both debt and equity). EVA is a registered trademark of Stern Stewart & Company.

**Edge Act and Agreement Corporation.** Subsidiary of a U.S. bank incorporated under federal law to engage in various international banking and financing operations, including equity participations that are not allowed to regular domestic banks. The Edge Act subsidiary may be located in a state other than that of the parent bank.

**Effective exchange rate.** An index measuring the change in value of a foreign currency determined by calculating a weighted average of bilateral exchange rates. The weighting reflects the importance of each foreign country's trade with the home country.

**Efficient market.** A market in which all relevant information is already reflected in market prices. The term is most frequently applied to foreign exchange markets and securities markets.

**EOM.** End of month. International trade term.

**Equity risk premium.** The average annual return of the market expected by investors over and above riskless debt.

**Euro.** A new currency unit that replaced the individual currencies of 12 European countries that belong to the European Union.

**Euro equity public issue.** A new equity issue that is underwritten and distributed in multiple foreign equity markets, sometimes simultaneously with distribution in the domestic market.

**Eurobank.** A bank, or bank department, which bids for time deposits and makes loans in currencies other than that of the country where the bank is located.

**Eurobond.** A bond originally offered outside the country in whose currency it is denominated. For example, a dollar-denominated bond originally offered for sale to investors outside the United States.

**Eurocredit.** Bank loans to MNEs, sovereign governments, international institutions, and banks denominated in Eurocurrencies and extended by banks in countries other than the country in whose currency the loan is denominated.

**Euro-Commercial Paper.** Short-term notes (30, 60, 90, 120, 180, 270, and 360 days) sold in international money markets.

**Eurocurrency.** A currency deposited in a bank located in a country other than the country issuing the currency.

**Eurodollar.** A U.S. dollar deposited in a bank outside the United States. A Eurodollar is one type of Eurocurrency.

**Euronote.** Short- to medium-term debt instruments sold in the Eurocurrency market.

**European Central Bank (ECB).** Conducts monetary policy of the European Monetary Union. Its goal is to safeguard the stability of the euro and minimize inflation.

**European Currency Unit (ECU).** Composite currency created by the European Monetary System prior to the euro to function as a reserve currency numeraire. The ECU was used as the numeraire for denominating a number of financial instruments and obligations.

**European Economic Community (EEC).** The European common market composed of Austria, Belgium, Denmark, Finland, France, Germany, Greece, Ireland, Italy, Luxembourg, the Netherlands, Portugal, Spain, and the United Kingdom. Officially renamed the European Union (EU) January 1, 1994.

**European Free Trade Association (EFTA).** European countries not part of the European Union but having no internal tariffs.

**European Monetary System (EMS).** A monetary alliance of fifteen European countries (same members as the European Union).

**European option.** An option that can be exercised only on the day on which it expires.

**European terms.** Foreign exchange quotations for the U.S. dollar, expressed as the number of non-U.S. currency units per U.S. dollar.

**European Union (EU).** The official name of the former European Economic Community (EEC) as of January 1, 1994.

**Exchange rate.** The price of a unit of one country's currency expressed in terms of the currency of some other country.

**Exchange Rate Mechanism (ERM).** The means by which members of the EMS formerly maintained their currency exchange rates within an agreed upon range with respect to the other member currencies.

**Exchange rate pass-through.** The degree to which the prices of imported and exported goods change as a result of exchange rate changes.

**Ex dock.** Followed by the name of a port of import. International trade term in which seller agrees to pay for the costs (shipping, insurance, customs duties, etc.) of placing the goods on the dock at the named port.

**Export credit insurance.** Provides assurance to the exporter or the exporter's bank that, should the foreign customer default on payment, the insurance company will pay for a major portion of the loss. *See also* Foreign Credit Insurance Association (FCIA).

**Export-Import Bank (Eximbank).** A U.S. government agency created to finance and otherwise facilitate imports and exports.

**Expropriation.** Official government seizure of private property, recognized by international law as the right of any sovereign state provided expropriated owners are given prompt compensation and fair market value in convertible currencies.

**FAF.** Fly away free. International trade term.

**FAQ.** Free at quay. International trade term.

**FASB 8.** A regulation of the Financial Accounting Standards Board requiring U.S. companies to translate foreign affiliate financial statements by the temporal method. FASB 8 was in effect from 1976 to 1981. It is still used under specific circumstances.

**FASB 52.** A regulation of the Financial Accounting Standards Board requiring U.S. companies to translate foreign subsidiary financial statements by the current rate (closing rate) method. FASB 52 became effective in 1981.

**FI.** Free in. International trade term meaning that all expenses for loading into the hold of a vessel are for the account of the consignee.

**FIFO.** First in, first out. An inventory valuation approach in which the cost of the earliest inventory purchases is charged against current sales. The opposite is LIFO, or last in, first out.

**Factoring.** Specialized firms, known as factors, purchase receivables at a discount on either a non-recourse or recourse basis.

**Financial account.** A section of the balance of payments accounts. Under the revised format of the International Monetary Fund, the financial account measures long-term financial flows including direct foreign investment, portfolio investments, and other long-term movements. Under the traditional definition, still used by many countries, items in the financial account were included in the capital account.

**Financial derivative.** A financial instrument, such as a futures contract or option, whose value is derived from an underlying asset like a stock or currency.

**Financial engineering.** Those basic building blocks, such as spot positions, forwards, and options, used to construct positions that provide the user with desired risk and return characteristics.

**Firm-specific risks.** Political risks that affect the MNE at the project or corporate level. Governance risk due to goal conflict between an MNE and its host government is the main political firm-specific risk.

**Fisher Effect.** A theory that nominal interest rates in two or more countries should be equal to the required real rate of return to investors plus compensation for the expected amount of inflation in each country.

**Fixed exchange rates.** Foreign exchange rates tied to the currency of a major country (such as the United States), to gold, or to a basket of currencies such as Special Drawing Rights.

**Flexible exchange rates.** The opposite of fixed exchange rates. The foreign exchange rate is adjusted periodically by the country's monetary authorities in accordance with their judgment and/or an external set of economic indicators.

**Floating exchange rates.** Foreign exchange rates determined by demand and supply in an open market that is presumably free of government interference.

**Floating rate note (FRN).** Medium-term securities with interest rates pegged to LIBOR and adjusted quarterly or semiannually.

**FOB.** Free on board. International trade term in which exporter's quoted price includes the cost of loading goods into transport vessels at a named point.

**Foreign affiliate.** A foreign business unit that is less than 50% owned by the parent company.

**Foreign bond.** A bond issued by a foreign corporation or government for sale in the domestic capital market of another country, and denominated in the currency of that country.

**Foreign Corrupt Practices Act of 1977.** A U.S. law that punishes companies and their executives if they pay bribes or make other improper payments to foreigners.

**Foreign Credit Insurance Association (FCIA).** An unincorporated association of private commercial insurances companies, in cooperation with the Export-Import Bank of the United States, that provides export credit insurance to U.S. firms.

**Foreign currency translation.** The process of restating foreign currency accounts of subsidiaries into the reporting currency of the parent company in order to prepare a consolidated financial statement.

**Foreign direct investment (FDI).** Purchase of physical assets, such as plant and equipment, in a foreign country, to be managed by the parent corporation. FDI is in contradistinction to foreign portfolio investment.

**Foreign exchange broker.** An individual or firm which arranges foreign exchange transactions between two parties, but is not itself a principal in the trade. Foreign exchange brokers earn a commission for their efforts.

**Foreign exchange risk.** The likelihood that an unexpected change in exchange rates will alter the home currency value of foreign currency cash payments expected from a foreign source. Also, the likelihood that an unexpected change in exchange rates will alter the amount of home currency needed to repay a debt denominated in a foreign currency.

**Foreign exchange dealer (or trader).** An individual or firm that buys foreign exchange from one party (at a bid price), and then sells it (at an ask price) to another party. The dealer is a principal in two transactions and makes a profit on the spread between its buying and selling prices.

**Foreign exchange rate.** The price of one country's currency in terms of another currency, or in terms of a commodity such as gold or silver. *See also* Exchange rates and Foreign exchange.

**Foreign sales corporation (FSC).** Under U.S. tax code, a type of foreign corporation that provides tax-exempt or tax-deferred income for U.S. persons or corporations having export-oriented activities.

**Foreign tax credit.** The amount by which a domestic firm may reduce (credit) domestic income taxes for income tax payments to a foreign government.

**Forfaiting.** A technique for arranging nonrecourse medium-term export financing, used most frequently to finance imports into Eastern Europe. A third party, usually a specialized financial institution, guarantees the financing.

**Forward contract.** An agreement to exchange currencies of different countries at a specified future date and at a specified forward rate.

**Forward differential.** The difference between spot and forward rates, expressed as an annual percentage.

**Forward discount or premium.** The same as forward differential.

**Forward rate.** An exchange rate quoted today for settlement at some future date. The rate used in a forward transaction.

**Forward rate agreement.** An interbank-traded contract to buy or sell interest rate payments on a notional principal.

**Forward transaction.** A foreign exchange transaction agreed upon today but to be settled at some specified future date, often one, two, or three months after the transaction date.

**Free alongside (FAS).** An international trade term in which the seller's quoted price for goods includes all costs of delivery of the goods alongside a vessel at the port of embarkation.

**Freely floating exchange rates.** Exchange rates determined in a free market without government interference, in contradistinction to dirty float.

**Free trade zone.** An area within a country into which foreign goods may be brought duty free, often for purposes of additional manufacture, inventory storage, or packaging. Such goods are subject to duty only when they leave the duty-free zone to enter other parts of the country.

**Fronting loan.** A parent-to-subsidiary loan channeled through a financial intermediary such as a large international bank in order to reduce political risk. Presumably government authorities are less likely to prevent a foreign subsidiary repaying an established bank than repaying the subsidiary's corporate parent.

**Functional currency.** In the context of translating financial statements, the currency of the primary economic environment in which a foreign subsidiary operates and in which it generates cash flows.

**Futures, or futures contracts.** Exchange-traded agreements calling for future delivery of a standard amount of any good, e.g., foreign exchange, at a fixed time, place, and price.

**Gamma.** A measure of the sensitivity of an option's delta ratio to small unit changes in the price of the underlying security.

**Gap risk.** That type of interest rate risk in which the timing of maturities is mismatched.

**General Agreement on Tariffs and Trade (GATT).** A framework of rules for nations to manage their trade policies, negotiate lower international tariff barriers, and settle trade disputes.

**Generally Accepted Accounting Principles (GAAP).** The Financial Accounting Standards Board (FASB) defines approved accounting principles for U.S. firms.

**Geometric return.** The mean uses the beginning and ending returns to calculate the annual average rate of compounded growth, similar to an internal rate of return.

**Global registered shares.** Similar to ordinary shares, global registered shares have the added benefit of being able to be traded on equity exchanges around the globe in a variety of currencies.

**Global-specific risks.** Political risks that originate at the global level, such as terrorism, the anti-globalization movement, environmental concerns, poverty, and cyber attacks.

**Gold standard.** A monetary system in which currencies are defined in terms of their gold content, and payment imbalances between countries are settled in gold.

**Greenfield investment.** An initial investment in a new foreign subsidiary being created from a brand new start with no predecessor operation in that location. This is in contrast to a new subsidiary created by the purchase of an already existing operation. Thus, a Greenfield investment is one that starts, conceptually if not literally, with the bare ground (presumably covered in green grass) and builds from that point forward.

**Gross up.** *See* Deemed-paid tax.

**Hard currency.** A freely convertible currency that is not expected to depreciate in value in the foreseeable future.

**Hedge.** The purchase of a contract (including forward foreign exchange) or tangible good that will rise in value and offset a drop in value of another contract or tangible good. Hedges are undertaken to reduce risk by protecting an owner from loss.

**Hedge accounting.** An accounting procedure specifying that gains and losses on hedging instruments be recognized in earnings at the same time as the effects of changes in the value of the items being hedged are recognized.

**Historical exchange rate.** In accounting, the exchange rate in effect when an asset or liability was acquired.

**Hot money.** Money which moves internationally from one currency and/or country to another in response to interest rate differences, and moves away immediately when the interest advantage disappears.

**Hybrid foreign currency options.** Purchase of a put option and the simultaneous sale of a call (or vice versa) so that the overall cost is less than the cost of a straight option.

**Hyperinflation countries.** Countries with a very high rate of inflation. Under United States FASB 52, these are defined as countries where the cumulative three-year inflation amounts to 100% or more.

**IMM.** International Monetary Market. A division of the Chicago Mercantile Exchange.

**Impossible Trinity.** An ideal currency would have exchange rate stability, full financial integration, and monetary independence.

**Indirect quote.** The price of a unit of a home country's currency expressed in terms of a foreign country's currency.

**In-house bank.** If an MNE's needs are either too large or too sophisticated for local banks, it can establish an in-house or internal bank within this firm. The in-house bank is not a separate corporation but is performing a set of functions by the existing treasury department. Acting as an independent entity, the in-house bank transacts with the various internal business units of the firm on an arm's length basis.

**In-the-money.** An option that would be profitable, excluding the cost of the premium, if exercised immediately.

**Integrated foreign entity.** One that operates as an extension of the parent company, with cash flows and general business lines that are highly interrelated with those of the parent.

**Intellectual property rights.** Grant the exclusive use of patented technology and copyrighted creative materials. A worldwide treaty to protect intellectual property rights has been ratified by most major countries, including most recently by China.

**International Capital Asset Pricing Model.** The primary distinction in the estimation of the cost of equity for an individual firm using an internationalized version of the domestic capital asset pricing model is the definition of the "market" and a recalculation of the firm's beta for that market.

**Interest rate futures.** *See* Futures, or futures contracts.

**Interest rate parity.** A theory that the differences in national interest rates for securities of similar risk and maturity should be equal to but opposite in sign to the forward exchange rate discount or premium for the foreign currency.

**Interest rate swap.** A transaction in which two counterparties exchange interest payment streams of different character (such as floating vs. fixed), based on an underlying notional principal amount.

**Interest rate swaps.** Contractual agreements to exchange or swap a series of interest cash flows.

**Internal rate of return (IRR).** A capital budgeting approach in which the discount rate is found that matches the present value of expected future cash inflows with the present value of outflows.

**Internalization.** A theory that the key ingredient for maintaining a firm-specific competitive advantage in international competition is the possession of proprietary information and control of human capital that can generate new information through expertise in research, management, marketing, or technology.

**International Bank for Reconstruction and Development (IBRD, or World Bank).** International development bank owned by member nations that makes development loans to member countries.

**International Banking Facility (IBF).** A department within a U.S. bank that may accept foreign deposits and make loans to foreign borrowers as if it were a foreign subsidiary. IBFs are free of U.S. reserve requirements, deposit insurance, and interest rate regulations.

**International Fisher Effect.** A theory that the spot exchange rate should change by an amount equal to the difference in interest rates between two countries.

**International Monetary Fund (IMF).** An international organization created in 1944 to promote exchange rate stability and provide temporary financing for countries experiencing balance of payments difficulties.

**International Monetary Market (IMM).** A branch of the Chicago Mercantile Exchange which specializes in trading currency and financial futures contracts.

**International monetary system.** The structure within which foreign exchange rates are determined, international trade and capital flows are accommodated, and balance of payments adjustments made.

**Intrinsic value.** The financial gain if an option is exercised immediately.

**Investment agreement.** Spells out specific rights and responsibilities of both the investing foreign firm and the host government.

**Joint venture.** A business venture that is owned by two or more other business ventures. Often the several business owners are from different countries.

**Jumbo loans.** Loans of $1 billion or more.

**Kangaroo bonds.** Australian dollar-denominated bonds issued within Australia by a foreign borrower.

**Lag.** In the context of leads and lags, payment of a financial obligation later than is expected or required.

**Lambda.** A measure of the sensitivity of an option premium to a unit change in volatility.

**Law of one price.** If the identical product or service can be sold in two different markets, and no restrictions exist on the sale or transportation costs of moving the product between markets, the product's price should be the same in both markets.

**Lead.** In the context of leads and lags, payment of a financial obligation earlier than is expected or required.

**Letter of credit (L/C).** An instrument issued by a bank, in which the bank promises to pay a benefi-ciary upon presentation of documents specified in the letter of credit.

**LIFO.** Last in, first out. An inventory valuation approach in which the cost of the latest inventory purchases is charged against current sales. The opposite is FIFO, or first in, first out.

**Link financing.** *See* Back-to-back loan or Fronting loan.

**Location-specific advantage.** Market imperfections or genuine comparative advantages that attract foreign direct investment to particular locations.

**London Interbank Offered Rate (LIBOR).** The deposit rate applicable to interbank loans in London. LIBOR is used as the reference rate for many international interest rate transactions.

**Long position.** A position in which foreign currency assets exceed foreign currency liabilities. The opposite of a long position is a short position.

**Maastricht Treaty.** A treaty among the 12 European Union countries that specified a plan and timetable for the introduction of a single European currency, to be called the euro.

**Macro risk.** *See* country-specific risks.

**Macroeconomic uncertainty.** Operating exposure's sensitivity to key macroeconomic variables, such as exchange rates, interest rates, and inflation rates.

**Managed float.** A country allows its currency to trade within a given band of exchange rates.

**Margin.** A deposit made as security for a financial transaction otherwise financed on credit.

**Marked to market.** The value of a futures contract is marked to market daily, and all changes in value are paid in cash daily. The value of the contract is revalued using the closing price for the day. The amount to be paid is called the variation margin.

**Market liquidity.** The degree to which a firm can issue a new security without depressing the existing market price, as well as the degree to which a change in price of its securities elicits a substantial order flow.

**Market segmentation.** If all capital markets are fully integrated, securities of comparable expected return and risk should have the same required rate of return in each national market after adjusting for foreign exchange risk and political risk. If the required rates of return diverge from full integration, that market is segmented.

**Matching currency cash flows.** One way to offset an anticipated continuous long exposure to a particular currency is to acquire debt denominated in that currency.

**Merchant bank.** A bank that specializes in helping corporations and governments finance by any of a variety of market and/or traditional techniques. European merchant banks are sometimes differentiated from clearing banks, which tend to focus on bank deposits and clearing balances for the majority of the population.

**Micro risk.** *See* firm-specific risks.

**Monetary/nonmonetary method.** A method of translating the financial statements of foreign subsidiaries into the parent's reporting currency. All monetary accounts are translated at the current rate, and all nonmonetary accounts are translated at their historical rates. Sometimes called temporal method in the United States.

**Money market hedge.** Use of foreign currency borrowing to reduce transaction or accounting foreign exchange exposure.

**Money Markets.** The financial markets in various countries in which various types of short-term debt instruments, including bank loans, are purchased and sold.

**Monetary assets or liabilities.** Assets in the form of cash or claims to cash (such as accounts receivable), or liabilities payable in cash. Monetary assets minus monetary liabilities are called net monetary assets.

**Most-favored-nation (MFN) treatment.** Application by a country of import duties on the same, or most favored, basis to all countries accorded such treatment. Any tariff reduction granted in a bilateral negotiation will be extended to all other nations that have been granted most-favored-nation status. Hence in fact most-favored-nation status means normal treatment rather than being discriminated against.

**Multinational enterprise (MNE).** A firm that has operating subsidiaries, branches, or affiliates located in foreign countries.

**Negotiable instrument.** A draft or promissory note that is in writing, signed by the maker or drawer, contains an unconditional promise or order to pay a definite sum of money on demand or at a determinable future date, and is payable to order or to bearer. A holder in due course of a negotiable instrument is entitled to payment despite any personal disagreements between drawee and maker.

**Nepotism.** The practice of showing favor to relatives in preference to other qualified persons in conferring such benefits as the awarding of contracts, granting of special prices, promotions to various ranks, etc.

**Net present value.** A capital budgeting approach in which the present value of expected future cash inflows is subtracted from the present value of outflows to determine the net present value.

**Netting.** The mutual offsetting of sums due between two or more business entities.

**Nominal exchange rate.** The actual foreign exchange quotation, in contradistinction to real exchange rate, which is adjusted for changes in purchasing power.

**Nontariff barrier.** Trade restrictive practices other than custom tariffs. Examples are import quotas, voluntary restrictions, variable levies, and special health regulations.

**North American Free Trade Agreement (NAFTA).** A treaty allowing free trade and investment between Canada, the United States, and Mexico.

**Note issuance facility (NIF).** An agreement by which a syndicate of banks indicates a willingness to accept short-term notes from borrowers and resell those notes in the Eurocurrency markets. The discount rate is often tied to LIBOR.

**Notional principal.** The size of a derivative contract, in total currency value, as used in futures contracts, forward contracts, option contracts, or swap agreements..

**NPV.** *See* Net present value.

**n.s.f.** Not sufficient funds. Term used by a bank when a draft or check is drawn on an account not having sufficient credit balance.

**O/A.** Open account. Arrangement in which the importer (or other buyer) pays for the goods only after the goods are received and inspected. The importer is billed directly after shipment, and payment is not tied to any promissory notes or similar documents.

**OLI paradigm.** An attempt to create an overall framework to explain why MNEs choose foreign direct investment rather than serve foreign markets through alternative modes such as licensing, joint ventures, strategic alliances, management contracts, and exporting.

**Offer.** The price at which a trader is willing to sell foreign exchange, securities, or commodities. Also called ask.

**Official Reserves Account.** Total reserves held by official monetary authorities within the country, such as gold, SDRs, and major currencies.

**Offshore finance subsidiary.** A foreign financial subsidiary owned by a corporation in another country. Offshore finance subsidiaries are usually located in tax-free or low-tax jurisdictions to enable the parent multinational firm to finance international operations without being subject to home country taxes or regulations.

**Operating exposure.** The potential for a change in expected cash flows, and thus in value, of a foreign subsidiary as a result of an unexpected change in exchange rates. Also called economic exposure.

**Option.** In foreign exchange, a contract giving the purchaser the right, but not the obligation, to buy or sell a given amount of foreign exchange at a fixed price per unit for a specified time period. Options to buy are calls and options to sell are puts.

**Order bill of lading.** A shipping document through which possession and title to the shipment reside with the owner of the order bill of lading.

**Organization of Petroleum Exporting Countries (OPEC).** An alliance of most major crude oil producing countries, formed for the purpose of allocating and controlling production quotas so as to influence the price of crude oil in world markets.

**Out-of-the-money.** An option that would not be profitable, excluding the cost of the premium, if exercised immediately.

**Outright quotation.** The full price, in one currency, of a unit of another currency. *See* Points quotation.

**Outsourcing.** *See* Supply chain management.

**Overseas Private Investment Corporation (OPIC).** A U.S. government-owned insurance company that insures U.S. corporations against various political risks.

**Overvalued currency.** A currency with a current foreign exchange value (i.e., current price in the foreign exchange market) greater than the worth of that currency. Because "worth" is a subjective concept, overvaluation is a matter of opinion. If the euro has a current market value of $1.20 (i.e., the current exchange rate is $1.20/€) at a time when its "true" value as derived from purchasing power parity or some other method is deemed to be $1.10, the euro is overvalued. The opposite of overvalued is undervalued.

**Over-the-counter market.** A market for share of stock, options (including foreign currency options), or other financial contracts conducted via electronic connections between dealers. The over-the-counter market has no physical location or address, and is thus differentiated from organized exchanges which have a physical location where trading takes place.

**Owner-specific advantage.** A firm must have competitive advantages in its home market. These must be firm-specific, not easily copied, and in a form that allows them to be transferred to foreign subsidiaries.

**Parallel loan.** Another name for a back-to-back loan, in which two companies in separate countries borrow each other's currency for a specific period of time, and repay the other's currency at an agreed maturity.

**Parallel market.** An unofficial foreign exchange market tolerated by a government but not officially sanctioned. The exact boundary between a parallel market and a black market is not very clear, but official tolerance of what would otherwise be a black market leads to use of the term parallel market.

**Parity conditions.** In the context of international finance, a set of basic economic relationships that provide for equilibrium between spot and forward foreign exchange rates, interest rates, and inflation rates.

**Participating forward.** A complex option position which combines a bought put and a sold call option at the same strike price to create a net zero position. Also called zero-cost option and forward participation agreement.

**Phi.** The expected change in an option premium caused by a small change in the foreign interest rate (interest rate for the foreign currency).

**Points.** A point is the smallest unit of price change quoted, given a conventional number of digits in which a quotation is stated.

**Points quotation.** A forward quotation expressed only as the number of decimal points (usually four decimal points) by which it differs from the spot quotation.

**Political risk.** The possibility that political events in a particular country will have an influence on the economic well-being of firms in that country. *Also see* Sovereign risk.

**Portfolio investment.** Purchase of foreign stocks and bonds, in contradistinction to foreign direct investment.

**Possessions Corporation.** A U.S. corporation, the subsidiary of another U.S. corporation located in a U.S. possession such as Puerto Rico, which for tax purposes is treated as if it were a foreign corporation.

**Premium (in foreign exchange market).** The amount by which a currency is more expensive for future delivery than for spot (immediate) delivery. The opposite of premium is discount.

**Private placement.** The sale of a security issue to a small set of qualified institutional buyers.

**Project finance.** Arrangement of financing for long-term capital projects, large in scale, long in life, and generally high in risk.

**Protectionism.** A political attitude or policy intended to inhibit or prohibit the import of foreign goods and services. The opposite of free trade policies.

**Psychic distance.** Firms tend to invest first in countries with a similar cultural, legal, and institutional environment.

**Purchasing power parity.** A theory that the price of internationally traded commodities should be the same in every country, and hence the exchange rate between the two currencies should be the ratio of prices in the two countries.

**Put.** An option to sell foreign exchange or financial contracts. *See* Option.

**Qualified institutional buyer.** An entity (except a bank or a savings and loan) that owns and invests on a discretionary basis $100 million in securities of nonaffiliates.

**Quota.** A limit, mandatory or voluntary, set on the import of a product.

**Quotation.** In foreign exchange trading, the pair of prices (bid and ask) at which a dealer is willing to buy or sell foreign exchange.

**Range forward.** A complex option position that combines the purchase of a put option and the sale of a call option with strike prices equidistant from the forward rate. Also called flexible forward, cylinder option, option fence, mini-max, and zero-cost tunnel.

**Real exchange rate.** An index of foreign exchange adjusted for relative price level changes since a base period. Sometimes referred to as real effective exchange rate, it is used to measure purchasing-power-adjusted changes in exchange rates.

**Real option analysis.** The application of option theory to capital budgeting decisions.

**Reference rate.** The rate of interest used in a standardized quotation, loan agreement, or financial derivative valuation.

**Registered bond.** Corporate or governmental debt in a bond form in which the owner's name appears on the bond and in the issuer's records, and interest payments are made to the owner.

**Reinvoicing center.** A central financial subsidiary used by a multinational firm to reduce transaction exposure by having all home country exports billed in the home currency and then reinvoiced to each operating subsidiary in that subsidiary's local currency.

**Relative purchasing power parity.** If the spot exchange rate between two countries starts in equilibrium, any change in the differential rate of inflation between them tends to be offset over the long run by an equal but opposite change in the spot exchange rate.

**Reporting currency.** In the context of translating financial statements, the currency in which a parent firm prepares its own financial statements. Usually this is the parent's home currency.

**Repositioning funds.** An MNE faces a variety of political, tax, foreign exchange, and liquidity constraints that limit its ability to move funds easily and without cost from one currency or country to another.

**Representative office.** A bank establishes a representative office in a foreign country to help bank clients doing business in that country. It also functions as a geographically convenient location from which to visit correspondent banks in its region rather than sending bankers from the parent bank at greater financial and physical cost.

**Repricing risk.** The risk of changes in interest rates charged or earned at the time a financial contract's rate is reset.

**Revaluation.** A rise in the foreign exchange value of a currency that is pegged to other currencies or to gold. Also called appreciation.

**Rho.** The expected change in an option premium caused by a small change in the domestic interest rate (interest rate for the home currency).

**Risk.** The likelihood that an actual outcome will differ from an expected outcome. The actual outcome could be better or worse than expected (two-sided risk), although in common practice risk is more often used only in the context of an adverse outcome (one-sided risk). Risk can exist for any number of uncertain future situations, including future spot rates or the results of political events.

**Risk-sharing agreement.** A contractual arrangement in which the buyer and seller agree to share or split currency movement impacts on payments between them.

**Rules of the Game.** The basis of exchange rate determination under the international gold standard during most of the 19th and early 20th centuries. All countries agreed informally to follow the rule of buying and selling their currency at a fixed and predetermined price against gold.

**Samurai bonds.** Yen-denominated bonds issued within Japan by a foreign borrower.

**Sarbanes-Oxley Act.** An act passed in 2002 to regulate corporate governance in the United States.

**SEC Rule 144A.** Permits qualified institutional buyers to trade privately-placed securities without requiring SEC registration.

**Section 482.** The set of U.S. Treasury regulations governing transfer prices.

**Securitization.** The replacement of nonmarketable loans (such as direct bank loans) with negotiable securities (such as publicly traded marketable notes and bonds), so that the risk can be spread widely among many investors, each of whom can add or subtract the amount of risk carried by buying or selling the marketable security.

**Self-sustaining foreign entity.** One that operates in the local economic environment independent of the parent company.

**Shared services.** A charge to compensate the parent for costs incurred in the general management of international operations and for other corporate services provided to foreign subsidiaries that must be recovered by the parent firm.

**Shareholder wealth maximization.** The corporate goal of maximizing the total value of the shareholders' investment in the company.

**Sharpe measure.** Calculates the average return over and above the risk free rate of return per unit of portfolio risk. It uses the standard deviation of a portfolio's total return as the measure of risk.

**Shogun bonds.** Foreign currency-denominated bonds issued within Japan by Japanese corporations.

**Short position.** *See* Long position.

**SIBOR.** Singapore interbank offered rate.

**Sight draft.** A bill of exchange (B/E) that is due on demand; i.e., when presented to the bank. *Also see* Bill of exchange.

**SIMEX.** Singapore International Monetary Exchange.

**Society for Worldwide Interbank Financial Telecommunications (SWIFT).** A dedicated computer network providing funds transfer messages between member banks around the world.

**Soft currency.** A currency expected to drop in value relative to other currencies. Free trading in a currency deemed soft is often restricted by the monetary authorities of the issuing country.

**Sovereign risk.** The risk that a host government may unilaterally repudiate its foreign obligations or may prevent local firms from honoring their foreign obligations. Sovereign risk is often regarded as a subset of political risk.

**Special Drawing Right (SDR).** An international reserve asset, defined by the International Monetary Fund as the value of a weighted basket of five currencies.

**Speculation.** An attempt to make a profit by trading on expectations about future prices.

**Spot rate.** The price at which foreign exchange can be purchased (its bid) or sold (its ask) in a spot transaction. *See* Spot transaction.

**Spot transaction.** A foreign exchange transaction to be settled (paid for) on the second following business day.

**Spread.** The difference between the bid (buying) quote and the ask (selling) quote.

**Stakeholder capitalism.** Another name for corporate wealth maximization.

**Strategic alliance.** A formal relationship, short of a merger or acquisition, between two companies, formed for the purpose of gaining synergies because in some aspect the two companies complement each other.

**Stripped bonds.** Bonds issued by investment bankers against coupons or the maturity (corpus) portion of original bearer bonds, where the original bonds are held in trust by the investment banker. Whereas the original bonds will have coupons promising interest at each interest date (say June and December for each of the next twenty years), a given stripped bond will represent a claim against all interest payments from the entire original issue due on a particular interest date. A stripped bond is in effect a zero coupon bond manufactured by the investment banker.

**Subpart F.** A type of foreign income, as defined in the U.S. tax code, which under certain conditions is taxed immediately in the United States even though it has not been repatriated to the United States. It is income of a type that is otherwise easily shifted offshore to avoid current taxation.

**Subsidiary.** A foreign operation incorporated in the host country and owned 50% or more by a parent corporation. Foreign operations that are not incorporated are called branches.

**Supply chain management.** Focuses on cost reduction through imports from less costly (lower wages) foreign locations.

**Sushi bonds.** Eurodollar or other non-yen denominated bonds issued by a Japanese corporation for sale to Japanese investors.

**Swap.** This term is used in many contexts. In general it is the simultaneous purchase and sale of foreign exchange or securities, with the purchase being effected at once and the sale back to the same party to be carried out at a price agreed upon today but to be completed at a specified future date. Swaps include interest rate swaps, currency swaps, and credit swaps. A swap rate is a forward foreign exchange quotation expressed in terms of the number of points by which the forward rate differs from the spot rate.

**SWIFT.** *See* Society for Worldwide Interbank Financial Telecommunications.

**Syndicated loan.** A large loan made by a group of banks to a large multinational firm or government. Syndicated loans allow the participating banks to maintain diversification by not lending too much to a single borrower.

**Synthetic forward.** A complex option position which combines the purchase of a put option and the sale of a call option, or vice versa, both at the forward rate.

**Systematic risk.** In portfolio theory, the risk of the market itself, i.e., risk that cannot be diversified away.

**T/A.** Trade acceptance. International trade term.

**Tariff.** A duty or tax on imports that can be levied as a percentage of cost or as a specific amount per unit of import.

**Tax deferral.** Foreign subsidiaries of MNEs pay host country corporate income taxes, but many parent countries, including the United States, defer claiming additional taxes on that foreign source income until it is remitted to the parent firm.

**Tax exposure.** The potential for tax liability on a given income stream or on the value of an asset. "Tax exposure" is usually used in the context of a multinational firm being able to minimize its tax liabilities by locating some portion of operations in a country where the tax liability is minimized.

**Tax haven.** A country with either no or very low tax rates that uses its tax structure to attract foreign investment or international financial dealings.

**Tax morality.** The MNE must decide whether to follow a practice of full disclosure to local tax authorities or adopt the philosophy, "When in Rome, do as the Romans do."

**Tax neutrality.** *Domestic tax neutrality* requires that the burden of taxation on earnings in home country operations by an MNE be equal to the burden of taxation on each currency equivalent of profit earned by the same firm in its foreign operations. *Foreign tax neutrality* requires that the tax burden on each foreign subsidiary of the firm be equal to the tax burden on its competitors in the same country.

**Tax treaties.** A network of bilateral tax treaties provides a means of reducing double taxation.

**Technical analysis.** Technical analysts focus on price and volume data to determine past trends that are expected to continue into the future. They believe that future exchange rates are based on the current exchange rate.

**Temporal method.** In the United States, term for a codification of a translation method essentially similar to the monetary/nonmonetary method.

**Tequila effect.** Term used to describe how the Mexican peso crisis of December 1994 quickly spread to other Latin American currency and equity markets through the contagion effect.

**Terms of trade.** The weighted average exchange ratio between a nation's export prices and its import prices, used to measure gains from trade. Gains from trade refers to increases in total consumption resulting from production specialization and international trade.

**Territorial approach to taxes.** Taxes income earned by firms within the legal jurisdiction of the host country, not on the country of the firm's incorporation.

**Theta.** The expected change in an option premium caused by a small change in the time to expiration.

**Time draft.** Allows a delay in payment. It is presented to the drawee, who accepts it by writing a notice of acceptance on its face. Once accepted, the time draft becomes a promise to pay by the accepting party. *See also* Bankers' acceptance.

**Total Shareholder Return (TSR).** A measure of corporate performance based on the sum of share price appreciation and current dividends.

**Tranche.** An allocation of shares, typically to underwriters that are expected to sell to investors in their designated geographic markets.

**Transaction exposure.** The potential for a change in the value of outstanding financial obligations entered into prior to a change in exchange rates but not due to be settled until after the exchange rates change.

**Transfer pricing.** The setting of prices to be charged by one unit (such as a foreign subsidiary) of a multiunit corporation to another unit (such as the parent corporation) for goods or services sold between such related units.

**Translation exposure.** The potential for an accounting-derived change in owners' equity resulting from exchange rate changes and the need to restate financial statements of foreign subsidiaries in the single currency of the parent corporation. Also called Accounting exposure.

**Transnational firm.** One that is owned by a coalition of investors located in different countries.

**Transparency.** Describes the degree to which an investor can discern the true activities and value drivers of a company from the disclosures and financial results reported.

**Treynor measure.** Calculates the average return over and above the risk free rate of return per unit of portfolio risk. It uses the portfolio's beta as the measure of risk.

**Unbiased predictor.** A theory that spot prices at some future date will be equal to today's forward rates.

**Unbundling.** Dividing cash flows from a subsidiary to a parent into their many separate components, such as royalties, lease payments, dividends, etc., so as to increase the likelihood that some fund flows will be allowed during economically difficult times.

**Uncovered interest arbitrage.** Investors borrow in countries and currencies exhibiting relatively low interest rates and convert the proceeds into currencies that offer much higher interest rates. The transaction is "uncovered" because the investor does not sell the higher yielding currency proceeds forward.

**Undervalued.** A currency with a current foreign exchange value (i.e., current price in the foreign exchange market) below the worth of that currency. Because "worth" is a subjective concept, undervaluation is a matter of opinion. If the euro has a current market value of $1.20 (i.e., the current exchange rate is $1.20/€) at a time when its "true" value as derived from purchasing power parity or some other method is deemed to be $1.30, the euro is undervalued. The opposite of undervalued is overvalued.

**Unsystematic risk.** In a portfolio, the amount of risk that can be eliminated by diversification.

**Value-added tax.** A type of national sales tax collected at each stage of production or sale of consumption goods, and levied in proportion to the value added during that stage.

**Value date.** The date when value is given (i.e., funds are deposited) for foreign exchange transactions between banks.

**Value today.** A spot foreign exchange transaction in which delivery and payment are made on the same day as the contract. Normal delivery is two business days after the contract.

**Value tomorrow.** A spot foreign exchange transaction in which delivery and payment are made on the next business day after the contract. Normal delivery is two business days after the contract.

**Volatility.** In connection with options, the standard deviation of daily spot price movement.

**Weighted average cost of capital (WACC).** The sum of the proportionally weighted costs of different sources of capital, used as the minimum acceptable target return on new investments.

**World Bank.** *See* International Bank for Reconstruction and Development.

**Worldwide approach to taxes.** Levies taxes on the income earned by firms that are incorporated in the host country, regardless of where the income was earned.

**Yankee bonds.** Dollar-denominated bonds issued within the United States by a foreign borrower.

**Yield to maturity.** The rate of interest (discount) which equates future cash flows of a bond, both interest and principal, with the present market price. Yield to maturity is thus the time-adjusted rate of return earned by a bond investor.

**Zero coupon bond.** A bond which pays no periodic interest, but simply returns a given amount of principal at a stated maturity date. Zero coupon bonds are sold at a discount from the maturity amount to provide the holder a compound rate of return for the holding period.

# INDEX

# Currencies of the World

| Country | Currency | Symbol | Subdivision | ISO-4217 Code |
|---|---|---|---|---|
| Afghanistan | afghani | Af | 100 puls | AFN 971 |
| Albania | lek | L | 100 qindarka (qintars) | ALL 008 |
| Algeria | dinar | DA | 100 centimes | DZD 012 |
| American Samoa | see United States | | | |
| Andorra | Uses the European euro. | | | |
| Angola | kwanza (new kwanza, 2001–) | Kz | 100 lwei | AOA 024 |
| Anguilla | dollar | EC$ | 100 cents | XCD 951 |
| Antarctica | Each Antarctic base uses the currency of its home country. | | | |
| Antigua and Barbuda | dollar | EC$ | 100 cents | XCD 951 |
| Argentina | austral (–1991) | double-dashed A | | ARA — |
| Argentina | peso (1991–) | $ | 100 centavos | ARS 032 |
| Armenia | dram | | 100 luma | AMD 051 |
| Aruba | guilder (a.k.a. florin or gulden) | Afl. | 100 cents | AWG 533 |
| Australia | dollar | A$ | 100 cents | AUD 036 |
| Austria | euro (1999–) | € | 100 cents | EUR 978 |
| Azerbaijan | manat | | 100 gopik | AZM 031 |
| Bahamas | dollar | B$ | 100 cents | BSD 044 |
| Bahrain | dinar | BD | 1,000 fils | BHD 048 |
| Bangladesh | taka | Tk | 100 paisa (poisha) | BDT 050 |
| Barbados | dollar | Bds$ | 100 cents | BBD 052 |
| Belarus | ruble (2000–) | BR | | BYR 112 |
| Belgium | euro (1999–) | € | 100 cents | EUR 978 |
| Belize | dollar | BZ$ | 100 cents | BZD 084 |
| Belorussia | old name of Belarus | | | |
| Benin | franc | CFAF | 100 centimes | XOF 952 |
| Bermuda | dollar | Bd$ | 100 cents | BMD 060 |
| Bhutan | ngultrum | Nu | 100 chetrum | BTN 064 |
| Bolivia | boliviano | Bs | 100 centavos | BOB 068 |
| Bosnia–Herzegovina | convertible mark (1999–) | KM | 100 fennig | BAM 977 |
| Botswana | pula | P | 100 thebe | BWP 072 |
| Brazil | real (1994–) | R$ | 100 centavos | BRL 986 |
| British Indian Ocean Territory | Legal currency is GBP, but mostly USD is used. | | | |
| British Virgin Islands | see United States | | | |
| Brunei | ringgit (a.k.a. Bruneian dollar) | B$ | 100 sen (a.k.a. 100 cents) | BND 096 |
| Bulgaria | new lev (1999–) | Lv | 100 stotinki | BGN 975 |
| Burkina Faso | franc | CFAF | 100 centimes | XOF 952 |
| Burma | now Myanmar | | | |
| Burundi | franc | FBu | 100 centimes [*] | BIF 108 |
| Cambodia | new riel | CR | 100 sen | KHR 116 |
| Cameroon | franc | CFAF | 100 centimes | XAF 950 |
| Canada | dollar | Can$ | 100 cents | CAD 124 |
| Canton and Enderbury Islands | see Kiribati | | | |
| Cape Verde Islands | escudo | C.V.Esc. | 100 centavos | CVE 132 |
| Cayman Islands | dollar | CI$ | 100 cents | KYD 136 |
| Central African Republic | franc | CFAF | 100 centimes | XAF 950 |
| Chad | franc | CFAF | 100 centimes | XAF 950 |
| Chile | peso | Ch$ | 100 centavos | CLP 152 |
| China | yuan renminbi | Y | 10 jiao = 100 fen | CNY 156 |
| Christmas Island | see Australia | | | |
| Cocos (Keeling) Islands | see Australia | | | |
| Colombia | peso | Col$ | 100 centavos | COP 170 |
| Comoros | franc | CF | | KMF 174 |
| Congo | franc | CFAF | 100 centimes [*] | XAF 950 |
| Congo, Dem. Rep. (former Zaïre) | franc | | 100 centimes | CDF 180 |
| Congo, Dem. Rep. | franc (2001–) | | 100 centimes | CDF 976 |
| Cook Islands | see New Zealand | | | |
| Costa Rica | colon | slashed C | 100 centimos | CRC 188 |
| Côte d'Ivoire | franc | CFAF | 100 centimes | XOF 952 |
| Croatia | kuna | HRK | 100 lipas | HRK 191 |
| Cuba | peso | Cu$ | 100 centavos | CUP 192 |
| Cyprus | pound | £C | 100 cents | CYP 196 |
| Cyprus (Northern) | see Turkey | | | |
| Czechoslovakia | Split into Czech Republic and Slovak Republic on January 1, 1993. | | | |
| Czech Republic | koruna | Kč | 100 haleru | CZK 203 |
| Denmark | krone (pl. kroner) | Dkr | 100 øre | DKK 208 |
| Djibouti | franc | DF | 100 centimes | DJF 262 |
| Dominica | dollar | EC$ | 100 cents | XCD 951 |
| Dominican Rep. | peso | RD$ | 100 centavos | DOP 214 |
| Dronning Maud Land | see Norway | | | |
| East Timor | see Indonesia | | | |
| Ecuador | sucre | S/ | 100 centavos | ECS 218 |
| Ecuador | Country adopted the USD on September 15, 2000. | | | |
| Egypt | pound | £E | 100 piasters or 1,000 milliemes | EGP 818 |
| El Salvador | colon | ¢ | 100 centavos | SVC 222 |
| Equatorial Guinea | franc | CFAF | 100 centimos | GQE 226 |
| Eritrea | nakfa | Nfa | 100 cents | ERN 232 |
| Estonia | kroon (pl. krooni) | KR | 100 senti | EEK 233 |
| Ethiopia | birr | Br | 100 cents | ETB 230 |
| European Union | European currency unit (–1998) | ecu | | XEU 954 |
| European Union | euro[1] (1999–) | € | 100 cents | EUR 978 |
| Faeroe Islands (Føroyar) | see Denmark | | | |
| Falkland Islands | pound | £F | 100 pence | FKP 238 |
| Fiji | dollar | F$ | 100 cents | FJD 242 |
| Finland | euro (1999–) | € | 100 cents | EUR 978 |
| France | euro (1999–) | € | 100 cents | EUR 978 |
| French Guiana | see France | | | |
| French Polynesia | franc | CFPF (Comptoirs Français du Pacifique Francs) | 100 centimes | XPF 953 |
| Gabon | franc | CFAF | 100 centimes [*] | XAF 950 |
| Gambia | dalasi | D | 100 butut | GMD 270 |
| Gaza | see Israel and Jordan | | | |
| Georgia | lari | | 100 tetri | GEL 981 |
| Germany | euro (1999–) | € | 100 cents | EUR 978 |
| Ghana | new cedi | ¢ | 100 psewas | GHC 288 |
| Gibraltar | pound | £G | 100 pence | GIP 292 |
| Great Britain | see United Kingdom | | | |
| Greece | euro (2001–) | € | 100 cents | EUR 978 |

[*] Indicates that the subdivision is no longer in use.

[1] The euro is only used in Austria, Belgium, Finland, France, Germany, Greece, Ireland, Italy, Luxembourg, Netherlands, Spain, and Portugal; it is not used in other E.U. countries.

# Currencies of the World (continued)

| Country | Currency | Symbol | Subdivision | ISO-4217 Code |
|---|---|---|---|---|
| Greenland | see Denmark | | | |
| Grenada | dollar | EC$ | 100 cents | XCD 951 |
| Guadeloupe | see France | | | |
| Guam | see United States | | | |
| Guatemala | quetzal | Q | 100 centavos | GTQ 320 |
| Guernsey | see United Kingdom | | | |
| Guinea-Bissau | peso (–April 1997) | PG | 100 centavos | GWP 624 |
| Guinea-Bissau | franc (May 1997–) | CFAF | 100 centimes [*] | XOF 952 |
| Guinea | syli | FG | 10 francs, 1 franc = 100 centimes | GNS 324 |
| Guinea | franc | FG | 100 centimes | GNF 324 |
| Guyana | dollar | G$ | 100 cents | GYD 328 |
| Haiti | gourde | G | 100 centimes | HTG 332 |
| Heard and McDonald Islands | see Australia | | | |
| Honduras | lempira | L | 100 centavos | HNL 340 |
| Hong Kong | dollar | HK$ | 100 cents | HKD 344 |
| Hungary | forint | Ft | –none– | HUF 348 |
| Iceland | króna | Ikr | 100 aurar (sg. aur) | ISK 352 |
| India | rupee | Rs | 100 paise | INR 356 |
| Indonesia | rupiah | Rp | 100 sen (no longer used) | IDR 360 |
| International Monetary Fund | Special Drawing Right | SDR | | XDR 960 |
| Iran | rial | Rls | 10 rials = 1 toman | IRR 364 |
| Iraq | dinar | ID | 1,000 fils | IQD 368 |
| Ireland | euro (1999–) | € | 100 cents | EUR 978 |
| Isle of Man | see United Kingdom | | | |
| Israel | new shekel | NIS | 100 new agorot | ILS 376 |
| Italy | lira (pl. lire) (–1998) | Lit | no subdivision in use | ITL 380 |
| Italy | euro (1999–) | € | 100 cents | EUR 978 |
| Ivory Coast | see Côte d'Ivoire | | | |
| Jamaica | dollar | J$ | 100 cents | JMD 388 |
| Japan | yen | ¥ | 100 sen (not used) | JPY 392 |
| Jersey | see United Kingdom | | | |
| Johnston Island | see United States | | | |
| Jordan | dinar | JD | 1,000 fils | JOD 400 |
| Kampuchea | see Cambodia | | | |
| Kazakhstan | tenge | | 100 tiyn | KZT 398 |
| Kenya | shilling | K Sh | 100 cents | KES 404 |
| Kiribati | see Australia | | | |
| Korea, North | won | Wn | 100 chon | KPW 408 |
| Korea, South | won | W | 100 chon [*] | KRW 410 |
| Kuwait | dinar | KD | 1,000 fils | KWD 414 |
| Kyrgyzstan | som | | 100 tyyn | KGS 417 |
| Laos | new kip | KN | 100 at [*] | LAK 418 |
| Latvia | lat | Ls | 100 santims | LVL 428 |
| Lebanon | pound (livre) | L.L. | 100 piastres | LBP 422 |
| Lesotho | loti, pl., maloti | L, pl., M | 100 lisente | LSL 426 |
| Liberia | dollar | $ | 100 cents | LRD 430 |
| Libya | dinar | LD | 1,000 dirhams | LYD 434 |
| Liechtenstein | see Switzerland | | | |
| Lithuania | litas, pl., litai | | 100 centu | LTL 440 |
| Luxembourg | franc (–1998) | LuxF | 100 centimes | LUF 442 |
| Luxembourg | euro (1999–) | € | 100 cents | EUR 978 |
| Macao (Macau) | pataca | P | 100 avos | MOP 446 |
| Macedonia (Former Yug. Rep.) | denar | MKD | 100 deni | MKD 807 |
| Madagascar | ariary = 5 francs | FMG | 1 franc = 100 centimes [*] | MGF 450 |
| Malawi | kwacha | MK | 100 tambala | MWK 454 |
| Malaysia | ringgit | RM | 100 sen | MYR 458 |
| Maldives | rufiyaa | Rf | 100 lari | MVR 462 |
| Mali | franc | CFAF | 100 centimes | XOF 952 |
| Malta | lira, pl., liri | Lm | 100 cents | MTL 470 |
| Martinique | see France | | | |
| Mauritania | ouguiya | UM | 5 khoums | MRO 478 |
| Mauritius | rupee | Mau Rs | 100 cents | MUR 480 |
| Micronesia | see United States | | | |
| Midway Islands | see United States | | | |
| Mexico | peso | Mex$ | 100 centavos | MXN 484 |
| Moldova | leu, pl., lei | | | MDL 498 |
| Monaco | see France | | | |
| Mongolia | tugrik | Tug | 100 mongos | MNT 496 |
| Montserrat | dollar | EC$ | 100 cents | XCD 951 |
| Morocco | dirham | DH | 100 centimes | MAD 504 |
| Mozambique | metical | Mt | 100 centavos | MZM 508 |
| Myanmar | kyat | K | 100 pyas | MMK 104 |
| Nauru | see Australia | | | |
| Namibia | dollar | N$ | 100 cents | NAD 516 |
| Nepal | rupee | NRs | 100 paise | NPR 524 |
| Netherlands Antilles | guilder (a.k.a. florin or gulden) | Ant.f or NAf. | 100 cents | ANG 532 |
| Netherlands | guilder (a.k.a. florin or gulden) (–1998) | f. | 100 cents | NLG 528 |
| Netherlands | euro (1999–) | € | 100 cents | EUR 978 |
| New Caledonia | franc | CFPF (Comptoirs Français du Pacifique Francs) | 100 centimes | XPF 953 |
| New Zealand | dollar | NZ$ | 100 cents | NZD 554 |
| Nicaragua | gold cordoba | C$ | 100 centavos | NIO 558 |
| Niger | franc | CFAF | 100 centimes | XOF 952 |
| Nigeria | naira | double-dashed N | 100 kobo | NGN 566 |
| Niue | see New Zealand | | | |
| Norfolk Island | see Australia | | | |
| Norway | krone (pl. kroner) | NKr | 100 øre | NOK 578 |
| Oman | rial | RO | 1,000 baizas | OMR 512 |
| Pakistan | rupee | Rs | 100 paisa | PKR 586 |
| Palau | see United States | | | |
| Panama | balboa | B | 100 centesimos | PAB 590 |
| Panama Canal Zone | see United States | | | |
| Papua New Guinea | kina | K | 100 toeas | PGK 598 |
| Paraguay | guarani | slashed G | 100 centimos [*] | PYG 600 |
| Peru | inti | | 100 centimos | PEI — |
| Peru | new sol | S/. | 100 centimos | PEN 604 |
| Philippines | peso | dashed P | 100 centavos | PHP 608 |
| Pitcairn Island | see New Zealand | | | |